Mercury Villager & Nissan Quest Automotive Repair Manual

by Jeff Kibler
and John H Haynes
Member of the Guild of Motoring Writers

Models covered:
All Mercury Villager and Nissan Quest models
1993 through 2001

(4E5 - 64200)

ABCDE
FGHIJ
KLMNO

Haynes Publishing Group
Sparkford Nr Yeovil
Somerset BA22 7JJ England

Haynes North America, Inc
861 Lawrence Drive
Newbury Park
California 91320 USA

About this manual

Its purpose

The purpose of this manual is to help you get the best value from your vehicle. It can do so in several ways. It can help you decide what work must be done, even if you choose to have it done by a dealer service department or a repair shop; it provides information and procedures for routine maintenance and servicing; and it offers diagnostic and repair procedures to follow when trouble occurs.

We hope you use the manual to tackle the work yourself. For many simpler jobs, doing it yourself may be quicker than arranging an appointment to get the vehicle into a shop and making the trips to leave it and pick it up. More importantly, a lot of money can be saved by avoiding the expense the shop must pass on to you to cover its labor and overhead costs. An added benefit is the sense of satisfaction and accomplishment that you feel after doing the job yourself.

Using the manual

The manual is divided into Chapters. Each Chapter is divided into numbered Sections, which are headed in bold type between horizontal lines. Each Section consists of consecutively numbered paragraphs.

At the beginning of each numbered Section you will be referred to any illustrations which apply to the procedures in that Section. The reference numbers used in illustration captions pinpoint the pertinent Section and the Step within that Section. That is, illustration 3.2 means the illustration refers to Section 3 and Step (or paragraph) 2 within that Section.

Procedures, once described in the text, are not normally repeated. When it's necessary to refer to another Chapter, the reference will be given as Chapter and Section number. Cross references given without use of the word "Chapter" apply to Sections and/or paragraphs in the same Chapter. For example, "see Section 8" means in the same Chapter.

References to the left or right side of the vehicle assume you are sitting in the driver's seat, facing forward.

Even though we have prepared this manual with extreme care, neither the publisher nor the author can accept responsibility for any errors in, or omissions from, the information given.

NOTE

A **Note** provides information necessary to properly complete a procedure or information which will make the procedure easier to understand.

CAUTION

A **Caution** provides a special procedure or special steps which must be taken while completing the procedure where the Caution is found. Not heeding a Caution can result in damage to the assembly being worked on.

WARNING

A **Warning** provides a special procedure or special steps which must be taken while completing the procedure where the Warning is found. Not heeding a Warning can result in personal injury.

Acknowledgements

We are grateful for the help and cooperation of Nissan Motor Company, Ltd., for assistance with technical information and certain illustrations. Wiring diagrams were originated exclusively for Haynes North America, Inc. by Valley Forge Technical Information Services. Technical writers who contributed to this project include Rob Maddox, Jay Storer and Larry Warren.

© Haynes North America, Inc. 1999, 2001

With permission from J.H. Haynes & Co. Ltd.

A book in the Haynes Automotive Repair Manual Series

Printed in the U.S.A.

ISBN 1 56392 448 X

Library of Congress Control Number: 2001095959

Contents

1

2A

2B

3

4

5

6

7

8

9

10

11

12

IND

Haynes mechanic, author and photographer with 1996 Mercury Villager

Introduction to the Mercury Villager and Nissan Quest

The Mercury Villager and Nissan Quest are available in a Mini-van body style only.

All models are equipped with a 3.0L V6 engine. The engines are equipped with a multi-port fuel injection system and an electronic ignition system.

All models are equipped with a trans-versely mounted four-speed automatic transaxle, driving the front wheels via independent driveaxles.

Independent suspension, featuring coil spring/strut damper units, is used on the front wheels, while a beam-type rear axle with leaf springs and shock absorbers is used at the rear. The rack-and-pinion steering unit is mounted behind the engine, with power-assist as standard equipment.

The brakes are disc on the front and drum on the rear wheels, with an Anti-Lock Brake System (ABS) standard on most models.

Vehicle identification numbers

Modifications are a continuing and unpublicized process in vehicle manufacturing. Since spare parts lists and manuals are compiled on a numerical basis, the individual vehicle numbers are necessary to correctly identify the component required.

Vehicle Identification Number (VIN)

This very important identification number is stamped on a plate attached to the dashboard inside the windshield on the driver's side of the vehicle (see illustration). The VIN also appears on the Vehicle Certificate of Title and Registration. It contains information such as where and when the vehicle was manufactured, the model year and the body style.

VIN engine and model year codes

Two particularly important pieces of information found in the VIN are the engine code and the model year code. Counting from the left, the engine code letter designation is the 8th digit and the model year code letter designation is the 10th digit.

On the models covered by this manual the engine code is:

1 .... 3.0L V6 (1993 through 1998)

On the models covered by this manual the model year codes are:

P....................................1993
R....................................1994
S....................................1995
T....................................1996
V....................................1997
W...................................1998
X....................................1999
Y....................................2000
1....................................2001

Vehicle Certification Label

The Vehicle Certification Label is attached to the driver's side door pillar (see illustration). Information on this label includes the name of the manufacturer, the month and year of production, as well as information on the options with which it is equipped. This label is especially useful for matching the color and type of paint for repair work.

Engine identification number

Where used, the engine identification number can be found on the left side, on the exhaust crossover pipe heat shield, which is beneath the power brake booster.

Transaxle identification number

Where used, the automatic transaxle ID number is affixed to a label on the transaxle bellhousing on earlier models and on the left-end transaxle cover on later models.

Vehicle Emissions Control Information label

This label is found in the engine compartment. See Chapter 6 for more information on this label.

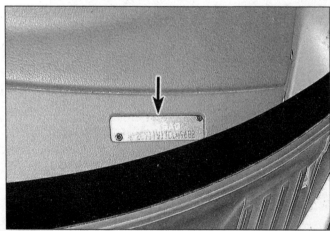

The Vehicle Identification Number (VIN) is stamped into a metal plate fastened to the dashboard on the driver's side (arrow) - it is visible through the windshield

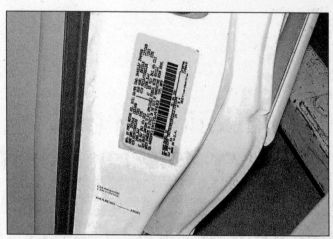

The Vehicle Safety Certification label is affixed to the driver's door pillar

Buying parts

Replacement parts are available from many sources, which generally fall into one of two categories - authorized dealer parts departments and independent retail auto parts stores. Our advice concerning these parts is as follows:

Retail auto parts stores: Good auto parts stores will stock frequently needed components which wear out relatively fast, such as clutch components, exhaust systems, brake parts, tune-up parts, etc. These stores often supply new or reconditioned parts on an exchange basis, which can save a considerable amount of money. Discount auto parts stores are often very good places to buy materials and parts needed for general vehicle maintenance such as oil, grease, filters, spark plugs, belts, touch-up paint, bulbs, etc. They also usually sell tools and general accessories, have convenient hours, charge lower prices and can often be found not far from home.

Authorized dealer parts department: This is the best source for parts which are unique to the vehicle and not generally available elsewhere (such as major engine parts, transmission parts, trim pieces, etc.).

Warranty information: If the vehicle is still covered under warranty, be sure that any replacement parts purchased - regardless of the source - do not invalidate the warranty!

To be sure of obtaining the correct parts, have engine and chassis numbers available and, if possible, take the old parts along for positive identification.

Maintenance techniques, tools and working facilities

Maintenance techniques

There are a number of techniques involved in maintenance and repair that will be referred to throughout this manual. Application of these techniques will enable the home mechanic to be more efficient, better organized and capable of performing the various tasks properly, which will ensure that the repair job is thorough and complete.

Fasteners

Fasteners are nuts, bolts, studs and screws used to hold two or more parts together. There are a few things to keep in mind when working with fasteners. Almost all of them use a locking device of some type, either a lockwasher, locknut, locking tab or thread adhesive. All threaded fasteners should be clean and straight, with undamaged threads and undamaged corners on the hex head where the wrench fits. Develop the habit of replacing all damaged nuts and bolts with new ones. Special locknuts with nylon or fiber inserts can only be used once. If they are removed, they lose their locking ability and must be replaced with new ones.

Rusted nuts and bolts should be treated with a penetrating fluid to ease removal and prevent breakage. Some mechanics use turpentine in a spout-type oil can, which works quite well. After applying the rust penetrant, let it work for a few minutes before trying to loosen the nut or bolt. Badly rusted fasteners may have to be chiseled or sawed off or removed with a special nut breaker, available at tool stores.

If a bolt or stud breaks off in an assembly, it can be drilled and removed with a special tool commonly available for this purpose. Most automotive machine shops can perform this task, as well as other repair procedures, such as the repair of threaded holes that have been stripped out.

Flat washers and lockwashers, when removed from an assembly, should always be replaced exactly as removed. Replace any damaged washers with new ones. Never use a lockwasher on any soft metal surface (such as aluminum), thin sheet metal or plastic.

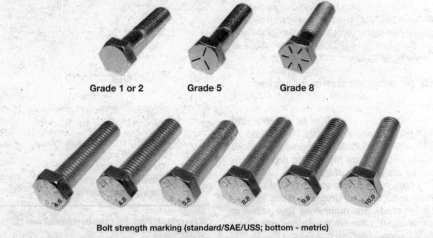

Grade 1 or 2   Grade 5   Grade 8

Bolt strength marking (standard/SAE/USS; bottom - metric)

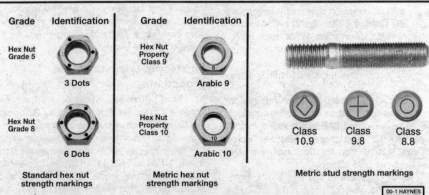

Grade	Identification	Grade	Identification
Hex Nut Grade 5	3 Dots	Hex Nut Property Class 9	Arabic 9
Hex Nut Grade 8	6 Dots	Hex Nut Property Class 10	Arabic 10

Standard hex nut strength markings

Metric hex nut strength markings

Class 10.9   Class 9.8   Class 8.8

Metric stud strength markings

00-1 HAYNES

Fastener sizes

For a number of reasons, automobile manufacturers are making wider and wider use of metric fasteners. Therefore, it is important to be able to tell the difference between standard (sometimes called U.S. or SAE) and metric hardware, since they cannot be interchanged.

All bolts, whether standard or metric, are sized according to diameter, thread pitch and length. For example, a standard 1/2 - 13 x 1 bolt is 1/2 inch in diameter, has 13 threads per inch and is 1 inch long. An M12 - 1.75 x 25 metric bolt is 12 mm in diameter, has a thread pitch of 1.75 mm (the distance between threads) and is 25 mm long. The two bolts are nearly identical, and easily confused, but they are not interchangeable.

In addition to the differences in diameter, thread pitch and length, metric and standard bolts can also be distinguished by examining the bolt heads. To begin with, the distance across the flats on a standard bolt head is measured in inches, while the same dimension on a metric bolt is sized in millimeters (the same is true for nuts). As a result, a standard wrench should not be used on a metric bolt and a metric wrench should not be used on a standard bolt. Also, most standard bolts have slashes radiating out from the center of the head to denote the grade or strength of the bolt, which is an indication of the amount of torque that can be applied to it. The greater the number of slashes, the greater the strength of the bolt. Grades 0 through 5 are commonly used on automobiles. Metric bolts have a property class (grade) number, rather than a slash, molded into their heads to indicate bolt strength. In this case, the higher the number, the stronger the bolt. Property class numbers 8.8, 9.8 and 10.9 are commonly used on automobiles.

Strength markings can also be used to distinguish standard hex nuts from metric hex nuts. Many standard nuts have dots stamped into one side, while metric nuts are marked with a number. The greater the number of dots, or the higher the number, the greater the strength of the nut.

Metric studs are also marked on their ends according to property class (grade). Larger studs are numbered (the same as metric bolts), while smaller studs carry a geometric code to denote grade.

It should be noted that many fasteners, especially Grades 0 through 2, have no distinguishing marks on them. When such is the case, the only way to determine whether it is standard or metric is to measure the thread pitch or compare it to a known fastener of the same size.

Standard fasteners are often referred to as SAE, as opposed to metric. However, it should be noted that SAE technically refers to a non-metric fine thread fastener only. Coarse thread non-metric fasteners are referred to as USS sizes.

Since fasteners of the same size (both standard and metric) may have different

Metric thread sizes	Ft-lbs	Nm
M-6	6 to 9	9 to 12
M-8	14 to 21	19 to 28
M-10	28 to 40	38 to 54
M-12	50 to 71	68 to 96
M-14	80 to 140	109 to 154

Pipe thread sizes		
1/8	5 to 8	7 to 10
1/4	12 to 18	17 to 24
3/8	22 to 33	30 to 44
1/2	25 to 35	34 to 47

U.S. thread sizes		
1/4 - 20	6 to 9	9 to 12
5/16 - 18	12 to 18	17 to 24
5/16 - 24	14 to 20	19 to 27
3/8 - 16	22 to 32	30 to 43
3/8 - 24	27 to 38	37 to 51
7/16 - 14	40 to 55	55 to 74
7/16 - 20	40 to 60	55 to 81
1/2 - 13	55 to 80	75 to 108

Standard (SAE and USS) bolt dimensions/grade marks

- G   Grade marks (bolt strength)
- L   Length (in inches)
- T   Thread pitch (number of threads per inch)
- D   Nominal diameter (in inches)

Metric bolt dimensions/grade marks

- P   Property class (bolt strength)
- L   Length (in millimeters)
- T   Thread pitch (distance between threads in millimeters)
- D   Diameter

strength ratings, be sure to reinstall any bolts, studs or nuts removed from your vehicle in their original locations. Also, when replacing a fastener with a new one, make sure that the new one has a strength rating equal to or greater than the original.

Tightening sequences and procedures

Most threaded fasteners should be tightened to a specific torque value (torque is the twisting force applied to a threaded component such as a nut or bolt). Overtightening the fastener can weaken it and cause it to break, while undertightening can cause it to eventually come loose. Bolts, screws and studs, depending on the material they are made of and their thread diameters, have

specific torque values, many of which are noted in the Specifications at the beginning of each Chapter. Be sure to follow the torque recommendations closely. For fasteners not assigned a specific torque, a general torque value chart is presented here as a guide. These torque values are for dry (unlubricated) fasteners threaded into steel or cast iron (not aluminum). As was previously mentioned, the size and grade of a fastener determine the amount of torque that can safely be applied to it. The figures listed here are approximate for Grade 2 and Grade 3 fasteners. Higher grades can tolerate higher torque values.

Fasteners laid out in a pattern, such as cylinder head bolts, oil pan bolts, differential cover bolts, etc., must be loosened or tightened in sequence to avoid warping the com-

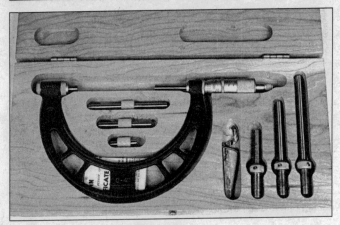

Micrometer set

Dial indicator set

ponent. This sequence will normally be shown in the appropriate Chapter. If a specific pattern is not given, the following procedures can be used to prevent warping.

Initially, the bolts or nuts should be assembled finger-tight only. Next, they should be tightened one full turn each, in a criss-cross or diagonal pattern. After each one has been tightened one full turn, return to the first one and tighten them all one-half turn, following the same pattern. Finally, tighten each of them one-quarter turn at a time until each fastener has been tightened to the proper torque. To loosen and remove the fasteners, the procedure would be reversed.

Component disassembly

Component disassembly should be done with care and purpose to help ensure that the parts go back together properly. Always keep track of the sequence in which parts are removed. Make note of special characteristics or marks on parts that can be installed more than one way, such as a grooved thrust washer on a shaft. It is a good idea to lay the disassembled parts out on a clean surface in the order that they were removed. It may also be helpful to make sketches or take instant photos of components before removal.

When removing fasteners from a component, keep track of their locations. Sometimes threading a bolt back in a part, or putting the washers and nut back on a stud, can prevent mix-ups later. If nuts and bolts cannot be returned to their original locations, they should be kept in a compartmented box or a series of small boxes. A cupcake or muffin tin is ideal for this purpose, since each cavity can hold the bolts and nuts from a particular area (i.e. oil pan bolts, valve cover bolts, engine mount bolts, etc.). A pan of this type is especially helpful when working on assemblies with very small parts, such as the carburetor, alternator, valve train or interior dash and trim pieces. The cavities can be marked with paint or tape to identify the contents.

Whenever wiring looms, harnesses or connectors are separated, it is a good idea to identify the two halves with numbered pieces of masking tape so they can be easily reconnected.

Gasket sealing surfaces

Throughout any vehicle, gaskets are used to seal the mating surfaces between two parts and keep lubricants, fluids, vacuum or pressure contained in an assembly.

Many times these gaskets are coated with a liquid or paste-type gasket sealing compound before assembly. Age, heat and pressure can sometimes cause the two parts to stick together so tightly that they are very difficult to separate. Often, the assembly can be loosened by striking it with a soft-face hammer near the mating surfaces. A regular hammer can be used if a block of wood is placed between the hammer and the part. Do not hammer on cast parts or parts that could be easily damaged. With any particularly stubborn part, always recheck to make sure that every fastener has been removed.

Avoid using a screwdriver or bar to pry apart an assembly, as they can easily mar the gasket sealing surfaces of the parts, which must remain smooth. If prying is absolutely necessary, use an old broom handle, but keep in mind that extra clean up will be necessary if the wood splinters.

After the parts are separated, the old gasket must be carefully scraped off and the gasket surfaces cleaned. Stubborn gasket material can be soaked with rust penetrant or treated with a special chemical to soften it so it can be easily scraped off. A scraper can be fashioned from a piece of copper tubing by flattening and sharpening one end. Copper is recommended because it is usually softer than the surfaces to be scraped, which reduces the chance of gouging the part. Some gaskets can be removed with a wire brush, but regardless of the method used, the mating surfaces must be left clean and smooth. If for some reason the gasket surface is gouged, then a gasket sealer thick enough to fill scratches will have to be used during reassembly of the components. For most applications, a non-drying (or semi-drying) gasket sealer should be used.

Hose removal tips

Warning: *If the vehicle is equipped with air conditioning, do not disconnect any of the A/C hoses without first having the system depressurized by a dealer service department or a service station.*

Hose removal precautions closely parallel gasket removal precautions. Avoid scratching or gouging the surface that the hose mates against or the connection may leak. This is especially true for radiator hoses. Because of various chemical reactions, the rubber in hoses can bond itself to the metal spigot that the hose fits over. To remove a hose, first loosen the hose clamps that secure it to the spigot. Then, with slip-joint pliers, grab the hose at the clamp and rotate it around the spigot. Work it back and forth until it is completely free, then pull it off. Silicone or other lubricants will ease removal if they can be applied between the hose and the outside of the spigot. Apply the same lubricant to the inside of the hose and the outside of the spigot to simplify installation.

As a last resort (and if the hose is to be replaced with a new one anyway), the rubber can be slit with a knife and the hose peeled from the spigot. If this must be done, be careful that the metal connection is not damaged.

If a hose clamp is broken or damaged, do not reuse it. Wire-type clamps usually weaken with age, so it is a good idea to replace them with screw-type clamps whenever a hose is removed.

Tools

A selection of good tools is a basic requirement for anyone who plans to maintain and repair his or her own vehicle. For the owner who has few tools, the initial investment might seem high, but when compared to the spiraling costs of professional auto maintenance and repair, it is a wise one.

To help the owner decide which tools are needed to perform the tasks detailed in this manual, the following tool lists are offered: *Maintenance and minor repair, Repair/overhaul* and *Special*.

The newcomer to practical mechanics

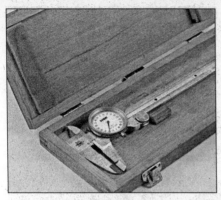

Dial caliper

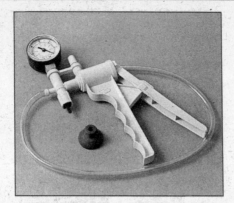

Hand-operated vacuum pump

Timing light

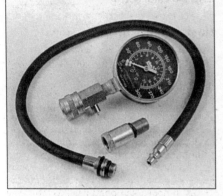

Compression gauge with spark plug hole adapter

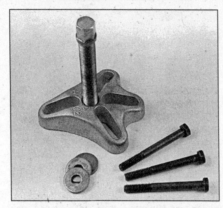

Damper/steering wheel puller

General purpose puller

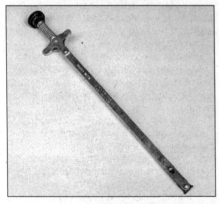

Hydraulic lifter removal tool

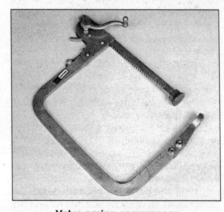

Valve spring compressor

Valve spring compressor

Ridge reamer

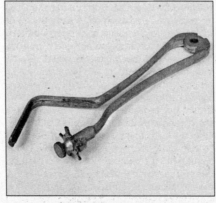

Piston ring groove cleaning tool

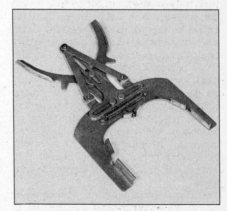

Ring removal/installation tool

Ring compressor

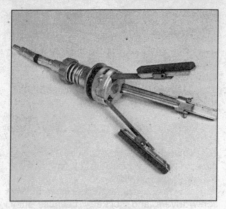

Cylinder hone

Brake hold-down spring tool

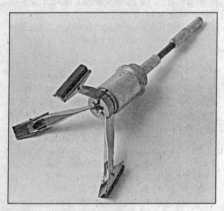

Brake cylinder hone

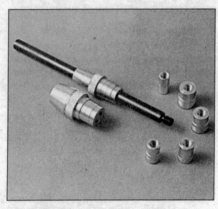

Clutch plate alignment tool

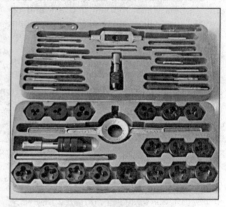

Tap and die set

should start off with the *maintenance and minor repair* tool kit, which is adequate for the simpler jobs performed on a vehicle. Then, as confidence and experience grow, the owner can tackle more difficult tasks, buying additional tools as they are needed. Eventually the basic kit will be expanded into the *repair and overhaul* tool set. Over a period of time, the experienced do-it-yourselfer will assemble a tool set complete enough for most repair and overhaul procedures and will add tools from the special category when it is felt that the expense is justified by the frequency of use.

Maintenance and minor repair tool kit

The tools in this list should be considered the minimum required for performance of routine maintenance, servicing and minor repair work. We recommend the purchase of combination wrenches (box-end and open-end combined in one wrench). While more expensive than open end wrenches, they offer the advantages of both types of wrench.

Combination wrench set (1/4-inch to 1 inch or 6 mm to 19 mm)
Adjustable wrench, 8 inch
Spark plug wrench with rubber insert
Spark plug gap adjusting tool
Feeler gauge set
Brake bleeder wrench

Standard screwdriver (5/16-inch x 6 inch)
Phillips screwdriver (No. 2 x 6 inch)
Combination pliers - 6 inch
Hacksaw and assortment of blades
Tire pressure gauge
Grease gun
Oil can
Fine emery cloth
Wire brush
Battery post and cable cleaning tool
Oil filter wrench
Funnel (medium size)
Safety goggles
Jackstands (2)
Drain pan

Note: *If basic tune-ups are going to be part of routine maintenance, it will be necessary to purchase a good quality stroboscopic timing light and combination tachometer/dwell meter. Although they are included in the list of special tools, it is mentioned here because they are absolutely necessary for tuning most vehicles properly.*

Repair and overhaul tool set

These tools are essential for anyone who plans to perform major repairs and are in addition to those in the maintenance and minor repair tool kit. Included is a comprehensive set of sockets which, though expensive, are invaluable because of their versatil-

ity, especially when various extensions and drives are available. We recommend the 1/2-inch drive over the 3/8-inch drive. Although the larger drive is bulky and more expensive, it has the capacity of accepting a very wide range of large sockets. Ideally, however, the mechanic should have a 3/8-inch drive set and a 1/2-inch drive set.

Socket set(s)
Reversible ratchet
Extension - 10 inch
Universal joint
Torque wrench (same size drive as sockets)
Ball peen hammer - 8 ounce
Soft-face hammer (plastic/rubber)
Standard screwdriver (1/4-inch x 6 inch)
Standard screwdriver (stubby - 5/16-inch)
Phillips screwdriver (No. 3 x 8 inch)
Phillips screwdriver (stubby - No. 2)
Pliers - vise grip
Pliers - lineman's
Pliers - needle nose
Pliers - snap-ring (internal and external)
Cold chisel - 1/2-inch
Scribe
Scraper (made from flattened copper tubing)
Centerpunch
Pin punches (1/16, 1/8, 3/16-inch)
Steel rule/straightedge - 12 inch

Allen wrench set (1/8 to 3/8-inch or
   4 mm to 10 mm)
A selection of files
Wire brush (large)
Jackstands (second set)
Jack (scissor or hydraulic type)

Note: Another tool which is often useful is an electric drill with a chuck capacity of 3/8-inch and a set of good quality drill bits.

Special tools

The tools in this list include those which are not used regularly, are expensive to buy, or which need to be used in accordance with their manufacturer's instructions. Unless these tools will be used frequently, it is not very economical to purchase many of them. A consideration would be to split the cost and use between yourself and a friend or friends. In addition, most of these tools can be obtained from a tool rental shop on a temporary basis.

This list primarily contains only those tools and instruments widely available to the public, and not those special tools produced by the vehicle manufacturer for distribution to dealer service departments. Occasionally, references to the manufacturer's special tools are included in the text of this manual. Generally, an alternative method of doing the job without the special tool is offered. However, sometimes there is no alternative to their use. Where this is the case, and the tool cannot be purchased or borrowed, the work should be turned over to the dealer service department or an automotive repair shop.

Valve spring compressor
Piston ring groove cleaning tool
Piston ring compressor
Piston ring installation tool
Cylinder compression gauge
Cylinder ridge reamer
Cylinder surfacing hone
Cylinder bore gauge
Micrometers and/or dial calipers
Hydraulic lifter removal tool
Balljoint separator
Universal-type puller
Impact screwdriver
Dial indicator set
Stroboscopic timing light (inductive
   pick-up)
Hand operated vacuum/pressure pump
Tachometer/dwell meter
Universal electrical multimeter
Cable hoist
Brake spring removal and installation
   tools
Floor jack

Buying tools

For the do-it-yourselfer who is just starting to get involved in vehicle maintenance and repair, there are a number of options available when purchasing tools. If maintenance and minor repair is the extent of the work to be done, the purchase of individual tools is satisfactory. If, on the other hand, extensive work is planned, it would be a good idea to purchase a modest tool set from one

of the large retail chain stores. A set can usually be bought at a substantial savings over the individual tool prices, and they often come with a tool box. As additional tools are needed, add-on sets, individual tools and a larger tool box can be purchased to expand the tool selection. Building a tool set gradually allows the cost of the tools to be spread over a longer period of time and gives the mechanic the freedom to choose only those tools that will actually be used.

Tool stores will often be the only source of some of the special tools that are needed, but regardless of where tools are bought, try to avoid cheap ones, especially when buying screwdrivers and sockets, because they won't last very long. The expense involved in replacing cheap tools will eventually be greater than the initial cost of quality tools.

Care and maintenance of tools

Good tools are expensive, so it makes sense to treat them with respect. Keep them clean and in usable condition and store them properly when not in use. Always wipe off any dirt, grease or metal chips before putting them away. Never leave tools lying around in the work area. Upon completion of a job, always check closely under the hood for tools that may have been left there so they won't get lost during a test drive.

Some tools, such as screwdrivers, pliers, wrenches and sockets, can be hung on a panel mounted on the garage or workshop wall, while others should be kept in a tool box or tray. Measuring instruments, gauges, meters, etc. must be carefully stored where they cannot be damaged by weather or impact from other tools.

When tools are used with care and stored properly, they will last a very long time. Even with the best of care, though, tools will wear out if used frequently. When a tool is damaged or worn out, replace it. Subsequent jobs will be safer and more enjoyable if you do.

How to repair damaged threads

Sometimes, the internal threads of a nut or bolt hole can become stripped, usually from overtightening. Stripping threads is an all-too-common occurrence, especially when working with aluminum parts, because aluminum is so soft that it easily strips out.

Usually, external or internal threads are only partially stripped. After they've been cleaned up with a tap or die, they'll still work. Sometimes, however, threads are badly damaged. When this happens, you've got three choices:

1) *Drill and tap the hole to the next suitable oversize and install a larger diameter bolt, screw or stud.*
2) *Drill and tap the hole to accept a threaded plug, then drill and tap the plug to the original screw size. You can also buy a plug already threaded to the original size. Then you simply drill a hole to*

the specified size, then run the threaded plug into the hole with a bolt and jam nut. Once the plug is fully seated, remove the jam nut and bolt.
3) *The third method uses a patented thread repair kit like Heli-Coil or Slimsert. These easy-to-use kits are designed to repair damaged threads in straight-through holes and blind holes. Both are available as kits which can handle a variety of sizes and thread patterns. Drill the hole, then tap it with the special included tap. Install the Heli-Coil and the hole is back to its original diameter and thread pitch.*

Regardless of which method you use, be sure to proceed calmly and carefully. A little impatience or carelessness during one of these relatively simple procedures can ruin your whole day's work and cost you a bundle if you wreck an expensive part.

Working facilities

Not to be overlooked when discussing tools is the workshop. If anything more than routine maintenance is to be carried out, some sort of suitable work area is essential.

It is understood, and appreciated, that many home mechanics do not have a good workshop or garage available, and end up removing an engine or doing major repairs outside. It is recommended, however, that the overhaul or repair be completed under the cover of a roof.

A clean, flat workbench or table of comfortable working height is an absolute necessity. The workbench should be equipped with a vise that has a jaw opening of at least four inches.

As mentioned previously, some clean, dry storage space is also required for tools, as well as the lubricants, fluids, cleaning solvents, etc. which soon become necessary.

Sometimes waste oil and fluids, drained from the engine or cooling system during normal maintenance or repairs, present a disposal problem. To avoid pouring them on the ground or into a sewage system, pour the used fluids into large containers, seal them with caps and take them to an authorized disposal site or recycling center. Plastic jugs, such as old antifreeze containers, are ideal for this purpose.

Always keep a supply of old newspapers and clean rags available. Old towels are excellent for mopping up spills. Many mechanics use rolls of paper towels for most work because they are readily available and disposable. To help keep the area under the vehicle clean, a large cardboard box can be cut open and flattened to protect the garage or shop floor.

Whenever working over a painted surface, such as when leaning over a fender to service something under the hood, always cover it with an old blanket or bedspread to protect the finish. Vinyl covered pads, made especially for this purpose, are available at auto parts stores.

Jacking and towing

Jacking

Warning: *The jack supplied with the vehicle should only be used for changing a tire or placing jackstands under the frame. Never work under the vehicle or start the engine while this jack is being used as the only means of support.*

The vehicle should be on level ground. Place the shift lever in Park. Block the wheel diagonally opposite the wheel being changed. Set the parking brake.

Remove the spare tire and jack from stowage. Remove the wheel cover and trim ring (if so equipped) with the tapered end of the lug nut wrench by inserting and twisting the handle and then prying against the back of the wheel cover. Loosen the wheel lug nuts about 1/4-to-1/2 turn each.

Place the scissors-type jack under the side of the vehicle and adjust the jack height until it fits in the notch in the vertical rocker panel flange nearest the wheel to be changed. There is a front and rear jacking point on each side of the vehicle **(see illustration)**.

Turn the jack handle clockwise until the tire clears the ground. Remove the lug nuts and pull the wheel off. Replace it with the spare.

Install the lug nuts with the beveled edges facing in. Tighten them snugly. Don't attempt to tighten them completely until the vehicle is lowered or it could slip off the jack. Turn the jack handle counterclockwise to lower the vehicle. Remove the jack and

The jack fits under the rocker panel (there are two jacking points on each side of the vehicle, indicated by a notch in the rocker panel flange)

tighten the lug nuts in a diagonal pattern.

Install the cover (and trim ring, if used) and be sure it's snapped into place all the way around.

Stow the tire, jack and wrench. Unblock the wheels.

Towing

As a general rule, the vehicle should be towed from the front with the front (drive) wheels off the ground. If the vehicle must be towed from the rear, place the front wheels on a towing dolly. **Caution:** *Never tow a front-wheel drive vehicle from the rear with the front wheels on the ground.*

Equipment specifically designed for

towing should be used. It should be attached to the main structural members of the vehicle, not the bumpers or brackets. Do not use the tie-down hooks at the front or the rear of the vehicle for towing. These hooks are designed for securing the vehicle during transport; if used for towing, damage to the front or rear bumper may occur.

The ignition key must be in the ACC position, since the steering lock mechanism isn't strong enough to hold the front wheels straight while towing. Pace the shift lever in neutral and release the parking brake.

Safety is a major consideration when towing and all applicable state and local laws must be obeyed. A safety chain system must be used at all times.

Booster battery (jump) starting

Observe these precautions when using a booster battery to start a vehicle:

a) *Before connecting the booster battery, make sure the ignition switch is in the Off position.*
b) *Turn off the lights, heater and other electrical loads.*
c) *Your eyes should be shielded. Safety goggles are a good idea.*
d) *Make sure the booster battery is the same voltage as the dead one in the vehicle.*
e) *The two vehicles MUST NOT TOUCH each other!*
f) *Make sure the transaxle is in Neutral (manual) or Park (automatic).*
g) *If the booster battery is not a maintenance-free type, remove the vent caps and lay a cloth over the vent holes.*

Connect the red jumper cable to the positive (+) terminals of each battery **(see illustration)**.

Connect one end of the black jumper cable to the negative (-) terminal of the booster battery. The other end of this cable should be connected to a good ground on the vehicle to be started, such as a bolt or bracket on the body.

Start the engine using the booster battery, then, with the engine running at idle speed, disconnect the jumper cables in the reverse order of connection.

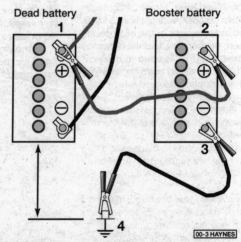

Make the booster battery cable connections in the numerical order shown (note that the negative cable of the booster battery is NOT attached to the negative terminal of the dead battery)

Automotive chemicals and lubricants

A number of automotive chemicals and lubricants are available for use during vehicle maintenance and repair. They include a wide variety of products ranging from cleaning solvents and degreasers to lubricants and protective sprays for rubber, plastic and vinyl.

Cleaners

Carburetor cleaner and choke cleaner is a strong solvent for gum, varnish and carbon. Most carburetor cleaners leave a dry-type lubricant film which will not harden or gum up. Because of this film it is not recommended for use on electrical components.

Brake system cleaner is used to remove grease and brake fluid from the brake system, where clean surfaces are absolutely necessary. It leaves no residue and often eliminates brake squeal caused by contaminants.

Electrical cleaner removes oxidation, corrosion and carbon deposits from electrical contacts, restoring full current flow. It can also be used to clean spark plugs, carburetor jets, voltage regulators and other parts where an oil-free surface is desired.

Demoisturants remove water and moisture from electrical components such as alternators, voltage regulators, electrical connectors and fuse blocks. They are non-conductive, non-corrosive and non-flammable.

Degreasers are heavy-duty solvents used to remove grease from the outside of the engine and from chassis components. They can be sprayed or brushed on and, depending on the type, are rinsed off either with water or solvent.

Lubricants

Motor oil is the lubricant formulated for use in engines. It normally contains a wide variety of additives to prevent corrosion and reduce foaming and wear. Motor oil comes in various weights (viscosity ratings) from 5 to 80. The recommended weight of the oil depends on the season, temperature and the demands on the engine. Light oil is used in cold climates and under light load conditions. Heavy oil is used in hot climates and where high loads are encountered. Multi-viscosity oils are designed to have characteristics of both light and heavy oils and are available in a number of weights from 5W-20 to 20W-50.

Gear oil is designed to be used in differentials, manual transmissions and other areas where high-temperature lubrication is required.

Chassis and wheel bearing grease is a heavy grease used where increased loads and friction are encountered, such as for wheel bearings, balljoints, tie-rod ends and universal joints.

High-temperature wheel bearing grease is designed to withstand the extreme temperatures encountered by wheel bearings in disc brake equipped vehicles. It usually contains molybdenum disulfide (moly), which is a dry-type lubricant.

White grease is a heavy grease for metal-to-metal applications where water is a problem. White grease stays soft under both low and high temperatures (usually from -100 to +190-degrees F), and will not wash off or dilute in the presence of water.

Assembly lube is a special extreme pressure lubricant, usually containing moly, used to lubricate high-load parts (such as main and rod bearings and cam lobes) for initial start-up of a new engine. The assembly lube lubricates the parts without being squeezed out or washed away until the engine oiling system begins to function.

Silicone lubricants are used to protect rubber, plastic, vinyl and nylon parts.

Graphite lubricants are used where oils cannot be used due to contamination problems, such as in locks. The dry graphite will lubricate metal parts while remaining uncontaminated by dirt, water, oil or acids. It is electrically conductive and will not foul electrical contacts in locks such as the ignition switch.

Moly penetrants loosen and lubricate frozen, rusted and corroded fasteners and prevent future rusting or freezing.

Heat-sink grease is a special electrically non-conductive grease that is used for mounting electronic ignition modules where it is essential that heat is transferred away from the module.

Sealants

RTV sealant is one of the most widely used gasket compounds. Made from silicone, RTV is air curing, it seals, bonds, waterproofs, fills surface irregularities, remains flexible, doesn't shrink, is relatively easy to remove, and is used as a supplementary sealer with almost all low and medium temperature gaskets.

Anaerobic sealant is much like RTV in that it can be used either to seal gaskets or to form gaskets by itself. It remains flexible, is solvent resistant and fills surface imperfections. The difference between an anaerobic sealant and an RTV-type sealant is in the curing. RTV cures when exposed to air, while an anaerobic sealant cures only in the absence of air. This means that an anaerobic sealant cures only after the assembly of parts, sealing them together.

Thread and pipe sealant is used for sealing hydraulic and pneumatic fittings and vacuum lines. It is usually made from a Teflon compound, and comes in a spray, a paint-on liquid and as a wrap-around tape.

Chemicals

Anti-seize compound prevents seizing, galling, cold welding, rust and corrosion in fasteners. High-temperature anti-seize, usually made with copper and graphite lubricants, is used for exhaust system and exhaust manifold bolts.

Anaerobic locking compounds are used to keep fasteners from vibrating or working loose and cure only after installation, in the absence of air. Medium strength locking compound is used for small nuts, bolts and screws that may be removed later. High-strength locking compound is for large nuts, bolts and studs which aren't removed on a regular basis.

Oil additives range from viscosity index improvers to chemical treatments that claim to reduce internal engine friction. It should be noted that most oil manufacturers caution against using additives with their oils.

Gas additives perform several functions, depending on their chemical makeup. They usually contain solvents that help dissolve gum and varnish that build up on carburetor, fuel injection and intake parts. They also serve to break down carbon deposits that form on the inside surfaces of the combustion chambers. Some additives contain upper cylinder lubricants for valves and piston rings, and others contain chemicals to remove condensation from the gas tank.

Miscellaneous

Brake fluid is specially formulated hydraulic fluid that can withstand the heat and pressure encountered in brake systems. Care must be taken so this fluid does not come in contact with painted surfaces or plastics. An opened container should always be resealed to prevent contamination by water or dirt.

Weatherstrip adhesive is used to bond weatherstripping around doors, windows and trunk lids. It is sometimes used to attach trim pieces.

Undercoating is a petroleum-based, tar-like substance that is designed to protect metal surfaces on the underside of the vehicle from corrosion. It also acts as a sound-deadening agent by insulating the bottom of the vehicle.

Waxes and polishes are used to help protect painted and plated surfaces from the weather. Different types of paint may require the use of different types of wax and polish. Some polishes utilize a chemical or abrasive cleaner to help remove the top layer of oxidized (dull) paint on older vehicles. In recent years many non-wax polishes that contain a wide variety of chemicals such as polymers and silicones have been introduced. These non-wax polishes are usually easier to apply and last longer than conventional waxes and polishes.

Conversion factors

Length (distance)

Inches (in)	X	25.4	= Millimetres (mm)	X 0.0394	= Inches (in)
Feet (ft)	X	0.305	= Metres (m)	X 3.281	= Feet (ft)
Miles	X	1.609	= Kilometres (km)	X 0.621	= Miles

Volume (capacity)

Cubic inches (cu in; in³)	X	16.387	= Cubic centimetres (cc; cm³)	X 0.061	= Cubic inches (cu in; in³)
Imperial pints (Imp pt)	X	0.568	= Litres (l)	X 1.76	= Imperial pints (Imp pt)
Imperial quarts (Imp qt)	X	1.137	= Litres (l)	X 0.88	= Imperial quarts (Imp qt)
Imperial quarts (Imp qt)	X	1.201	= US quarts (US qt)	X 0.833	= Imperial quarts (Imp qt)
US quarts (US qt)	X	0.946	= Litres (l)	X 1.057	= US quarts (US qt)
Imperial gallons (Imp gal)	X	4.546	= Litres (l)	X 0.22	= Imperial gallons (Imp gal)
Imperial gallons (Imp gal)	X	1.201	= US gallons (US gal)	X 0.833	= Imperial gallons (Imp gal)
US gallons (US gal)	X	3.785	= Litres (l)	X 0.264	= US gallons (US gal)

Mass (weight)

Ounces (oz)	X	28.35	= Grams (g)	X 0.035	= Ounces (oz)
Pounds (lb)	X	0.454	= Kilograms (kg)	X 2.205	= Pounds (lb)

Force

Ounces-force (ozf; oz)	X	0.278	= Newtons (N)	X 3.6	= Ounces-force (ozf; oz)
Pounds-force (lbf; lb)	X	4.448	= Newtons (N)	X 0.225	= Pounds-force (lbf; lb)
Newtons (N)	X	0.1	= Kilograms-force (kgf; kg)	X 9.81	= Newtons (N)

Pressure

Pounds-force per square inch (psi; lbf/in²; lb/in²)	X	0.070	= Kilograms-force per square centimetre (kgf/cm²; kg/cm²)	X 14.223	= Pounds-force per square inch (psi; lbf/in²; lb/in²)
Pounds-force per square inch (psi; lbf/in²; lb/in²)	X	0.068	= Atmospheres (atm)	X 14.696	= Pounds-force per square inch (psi; lbf/in²; lb/in²)
Pounds-force per square inch (psi; lbf/in²; lb/in²)	X	0.069	= Bars	X 14.5	= Pounds-force per square inch (psi; lbf/in²; lb/in²)
Pounds-force per square inch (psi; lbf/in²; lb/in²)	X	6.895	= Kilopascals (kPa)	X 0.145	= Pounds-force per square inch (psi; lbf/in²; lb/in²)
Kilopascals (kPa)	X	0.01	= Kilograms-force per square centimetre (kgf/cm²; kg/cm²)	X 98.1	= Kilopascals (kPa)

Torque (moment of force)

Pounds-force inches (lbf in; lb in)	X	1.152	= Kilograms-force centimetre (kgf cm; kg cm)	X 0.868	= Pounds-force inches (lbf in; lb in)
Pounds-force inches (lbf in; lb in)	X	0.113	= Newton metres (Nm)	X 8.85	= Pounds-force inches (lbf in; lb in)
Pounds-force inches (lbf in; lb in)	X	0.083	= Pounds-force feet (lbf ft; lb ft)	X 12	= Pounds-force inches (lbf in; lb in)
Pounds-force feet (lbf ft; lb ft)	X	0.138	= Kilograms-force metres (kgf m; kg m)	X 7.233	= Pounds-force feet (lbf ft; lb ft)
Pounds-force feet (lbf ft; lb ft)	X	1.356	= Newton metres (Nm)	X 0.738	= Pounds-force feet (lbf ft; lb ft)
Newton metres (Nm)	X	0.102	= Kilograms-force metres (kgf m; kg m)	X 9.804	= Newton metres (Nm)

Vacuum

Inches mercury (in. Hg)	X	3.377	= Kilopascals (kPa)	X 0.2961	= Inches mercury
Inches mercury (in. Hg)	X	25.4	= Millimeters mercury (mm Hg)	X 0.0394	= Inches mercury

Power

Horsepower (hp)	X	745.7	= Watts (W)	X 0.0013	= Horsepower (hp)

Velocity (speed)

Miles per hour (miles/hr; mph)	X	1.609	= Kilometres per hour (km/hr; kph)	X 0.621	= Miles per hour (miles/hr; mph)

Fuel consumption*

Miles per gallon, Imperial (mpg)	X	0.354	= Kilometres per litre (km/l)	X 2.825	= Miles per gallon, Imperial (mpg)
Miles per gallon, US (mpg)	X	0.425	= Kilometres per litre (km/l)	X 2.352	= Miles per gallon, US (mpg)

Temperature

Degrees Fahrenheit = (°C x 1.8) + 32   Degrees Celsius (Degrees Centigrade; °C) = (°F - 32) x 0.56

*It is common practice to convert from miles per gallon (mpg) to litres/100 kilometres (l/100km),
where mpg (Imperial) x l/100 km = 282 and mpg (US) x l/100 km = 235*

Safety first!

Regardless of how enthusiastic you may be about getting on with the job at hand, take the time to ensure that your safety is not jeopardized. A moment's lack of attention can result in an accident, as can failure to observe certain simple safety precautions. The possibility of an accident will always exist, and the following points should not be considered a comprehensive list of all dangers. Rather, they are intended to make you aware of the risks and to encourage a safety conscious approach to all work you carry out on your vehicle.

Essential DOs and DON'Ts

DON'T rely on a jack when working under the vehicle. Always use approved jackstands to support the weight of the vehicle and place them under the recommended lift or support points.

DON'T attempt to loosen extremely tight fasteners (i.e. wheel lug nuts) while the vehicle is on a jack - it may fall.

DON'T start the engine without first making sure that the transmission is in Neutral (or Park where applicable) and the parking brake is set.

DON'T remove the radiator cap from a hot cooling system - let it cool or cover it with a cloth and release the pressure gradually.

DON'T attempt to drain the engine oil until you are sure it has cooled to the point that it will not burn you.

DON'T touch any part of the engine or exhaust system until it has cooled sufficiently to avoid burns.

DON'T siphon toxic liquids such as gasoline, antifreeze and brake fluid by mouth, or allow them to remain on your skin.

DON'T inhale brake lining dust - it is potentially hazardous (see *Asbestos* below).

DON'T allow spilled oil or grease to remain on the floor - wipe it up before someone slips on it.

DON'T use loose fitting wrenches or other tools which may slip and cause injury.

DON'T push on wrenches when loosening or tightening nuts or bolts. Always try to pull the wrench toward you. If the situation calls for pushing the wrench away, push with an open hand to avoid scraped knuckles if the wrench should slip.

DON'T attempt to lift a heavy component alone - get someone to help you.

DON'T rush or take unsafe shortcuts to finish a job.

DON'T allow children or animals in or around the vehicle while you are working on it.

DO wear eye protection when using power tools such as a drill, sander, bench grinder, etc. and when working under a vehicle.

DO keep loose clothing and long hair well out of the way of moving parts.

DO make sure that any hoist used has a safe working load rating adequate for the job.

DO get someone to check on you periodically when working alone on a vehicle.

DO carry out work in a logical sequence and make sure that everything is correctly assembled and tightened.

DO keep chemicals and fluids tightly capped and out of the reach of children and pets.

DO remember that your vehicle's safety affects that of yourself and others. If in doubt on any point, get professional advice.

Asbestos

Certain friction, insulating, sealing, and other products - such as brake linings, brake bands, clutch linings, torque converters, gaskets, etc. - may contain asbestos. Extreme care must be taken to avoid inhalation of dust from such products, since it is hazardous to health. If in doubt, assume that they do contain asbestos.

Fire

Remember at all times that gasoline is highly flammable. Never smoke or have any kind of open flame around when working on a vehicle. But the risk does not end there. A spark caused by an electrical short circuit, by two metal surfaces contacting each other, or even by static electricity built up in your body under certain conditions, can ignite gasoline vapors, which in a confined space are highly explosive. Do not, under any circumstances, use gasoline for cleaning parts. Use an approved safety solvent.

Always disconnect the battery ground (-) cable at the battery before working on any part of the fuel system or electrical system. Never risk spilling fuel on a hot engine or exhaust component. It is strongly recommended that a fire extinguisher suitable for use on fuel and electrical fires be kept handy in the garage or workshop at all times. Never try to extinguish a fuel or electrical fire with water.

Fumes

Certain fumes are highly toxic and can quickly cause unconsciousness and even death if inhaled to any extent. Gasoline vapor falls into this category, as do the vapors from some cleaning solvents. Any draining or pouring of such volatile fluids should be done in a well ventilated area.

When using cleaning fluids and solvents, read the instructions on the container carefully. Never use materials from unmarked containers.

Never run the engine in an enclosed space, such as a garage. Exhaust fumes contain carbon monoxide, which is extremely poisonous. If you need to run the engine, always do so in the open air, or at least have the rear of the vehicle outside the work area.

If you are fortunate enough to have the use of an inspection pit, never drain or pour gasoline and never run the engine while the vehicle is over the pit. The fumes, being heavier than air, will concentrate in the pit with possibly lethal results.

The battery

Never create a spark or allow a bare light bulb near a battery. They normally give off a certain amount of hydrogen gas, which is highly explosive.

Always disconnect the battery ground (-) cable at the battery before working on the fuel or electrical systems.

If possible, loosen the filler caps or cover when charging the battery from an external source (this does not apply to sealed or maintenance-free batteries). Do not charge at an excessive rate or the battery may burst.

Take care when adding water to a non maintenance-free battery and when carrying a battery. The electrolyte, even when diluted, is very corrosive and should not be allowed to contact clothing or skin.

Always wear eye protection when cleaning the battery to prevent the caustic deposits from entering your eyes.

Household current

When using an electric power tool, inspection light, etc., which operates on household current, always make sure that the tool is correctly connected to its plug and that, where necessary, it is properly grounded. Do not use such items in damp conditions and, again, do not create a spark or apply excessive heat in the vicinity of fuel or fuel vapor.

Secondary ignition system voltage

A severe electric shock can result from touching certain parts of the ignition system (such as the spark plug wires) when the engine is running or being cranked, particularly if components are damp or the insulation is defective. In the case of an electronic ignition system, the secondary system voltage is much higher and could prove fatal.

Troubleshooting

Contents

Engine

1 Engine will not rotate when attempting to start

1 Battery terminal connections loose or corroded. Check the cable terminals at the battery; tighten cable clamp and/or clean off corrosion as necessary (see Chapter 1).
2 Battery discharged or faulty. If the cable ends are clean and tight on the battery posts, turn the key to the On position and switch on the headlights or windshield wipers. If they won't run, the battery is discharged.
3 Automatic transmission not engaged in park (P) or Neutral (N).
4 Broken, loose or disconnected wires in the starting circuit. Inspect all wires and connectors at the battery, starter solenoid and ignition switch (on steering column).
5 Starter motor pinion jammed in driveplate ring gear. Remove starter (Chapter 5) and inspect pinion and driveplate (Chapter 2).
6 Starter solenoid faulty (Chapter 5).
7 Starter motor faulty (Chapter 5).
8 Ignition switch faulty (Chapter 12).
9 Engine seized. Try to turn the crankshaft with a large socket and breaker bar on the pulley bolt.
10 Starter relay faulty (Chapter 5).
11 Transmission Range (TR) sensor out of adjustment or defective (Chapter 6).

2 Engine rotates but will not start

1 Fuel tank empty.
2 Battery discharged (engine rotates slowly).
3 Battery terminal connections loose or corroded.
4 Fuel not reaching fuel injectors. Check for clogged fuel filter or lines and defective fuel pump. Also make sure the tank vent lines aren't clogged (Chapter 4).
5 Low cylinder compression. Check as described in Chapter 2.
6 Water in fuel. Drain tank and fill with new fuel.
7 Defective ignition coil (Chapter 5).
8 Dirty or clogged fuel injector(s) (Chapter 4).
9 Wet or damaged ignition components (Chapters 1 and 5).
10 Worn, faulty or incorrectly gapped spark plugs (Chapter 1).
11 Broken, loose or disconnected wires in the starting circuit (see previous Section).
12 Broken, loose or disconnected wires at the ignition coil or faulty coil (Chapter 5).
13 Timing belt failure or wear affecting valve timing (Chapter 2).
14 Fuel injection or engine control systems failure (Chapters 4 and 6).
15 Defective MAF sensor (Chapter 6).

3 Starter motor operates without turning engine

1 Starter pinion sticking. Remove the starter (Chapter 5) and inspect.
2 Starter pinion or driveplate teeth worn or broken. Remove the inspection cover and inspect.

4 Engine hard to start when cold

1 Battery discharged or low. Check as described in Chapter 1.
2 Fuel not reaching the fuel injectors. Check the fuel filter, lines and fuel pump (Chapters 1 and 4).
3 Defective spark plugs (Chapter 1).
4 Defective engine coolant temperature sensor (Chapter 6).
5 Fuel injection or engine control systems malfunction (Chapters 4 and 6).

5 Engine hard to start when hot

1 Air filter dirty (Chapter 1).
2 Bad engine ground connection.
3 Fuel injection or engine control systems malfunction (Chapters 4 and 6).

6 Starter motor noisy or engages roughly

1 Pinion or driveplate teeth worn or broken. Remove the inspection cover on the left side of the engine and inspect.
2 Starter motor mounting bolts loose or missing.

7 Engine starts but stops immediately

1 Loose or damaged wire harness connections at distributor, coil or alternator.
2 Intake manifold vacuum leaks. Make sure all mounting bolts/nuts are tight and all vacuum hoses connected to the manifold are attached properly and in good condition.
3 Insufficient fuel pressure (see Chapter 4).
4 Fuel injection or engine control systems malfunction (Chapters 4 and 6).

8 Engine 'lopes' while idling or idles erratically

1 Vacuum leaks. Check mounting bolts at the intake manifold for tightness. Make sure that all vacuum hoses are connected and in good condition. Use a stethoscope or a length of fuel hose held against your ear to listen for vacuum leaks while the engine is running. A hissing sound will be heard. A soapy water solution will also detect leaks. Check the intake manifold gasket surfaces.
2 Leaking EGR valve or plugged PCV valve (see Chapters 1 and 6).
3 Air filter clogged (Chapter 1).
4 Fuel pump not delivering sufficient fuel (Chapter 4).
5 Leaking head gasket. Perform a cylinder compression check (Chapter 2).
6 Timing belt worn (Chapter 2).
7 Camshaft lobes worn (Chapter 2).
8 Valves burned or otherwise leaking (Chapter 2).
9 Ignition timing out of adjustment (Chapter 1).
10 Ignition system not operating properly (Chapters 1 and 5).
11 Fuel injection or engine control systems malfunction (Chapters 4 and 6).

9 Engine misses at idle speed

1 Spark plugs faulty or not gapped properly (Chapter 1).
2 Faulty spark plug wires (Chapter 1).
3 Wet or damaged ignition components (Chapter 5).
4 Short circuits in ignition, coil or spark plug wires.
5 Sticking or faulty emissions systems (see Chapter 6).
6 Clogged fuel filter and/or foreign matter in fuel. Remove the fuel filter (Chapter 1) and inspect.
7 Vacuum leaks at intake manifold or hose connections. Check as described in Section 8.
8 Low or uneven cylinder compression. Check as described in Chapter 2.
9 Fuel injection or engine control systems malfunction (Chapters 4 and 6).

10 Excessively high idle speed

1 Sticking throttle linkage (Chapter 4).
2 Vacuum leaks at intake manifold or hose connections. Check as described in Section 8.
3 Fuel injection or engine control systems malfunction (Chapters 4 and 6).

11 Battery will not hold a charge

1 Alternator drivebelt defective or not adjusted properly (Chapter 1).
2 Battery cables loose or corroded (Chapter 1).
3 Alternator not charging properly (Chapter 5).
4 Loose, broken or faulty wires in the charging circuit (Chapter 5).
5 Short circuit causing a continuous drain on the battery.
6 Battery defective internally.

12 Alternator light stays on (or gauge registers a low charge)

1   Fault in alternator or charging circuit (Chapter 5).
2   Alternator drivebelt defective or not properly adjusted (Chapter 1).

13 Alternator light fails to come on when key is turned on

1   Faulty bulb (Chapter 12).
2   Defective alternator (Chapter 5).
3   Fault in the printed circuit, dash wiring or bulb holder (Chapter 12).

14 Engine misses throughout driving speed range

1   Fuel filter clogged and/or impurities in the fuel system. Check fuel filter (Chapter 1) or clean system (Chapter 4).
2   Faulty or incorrectly gapped spark plugs (Chapter 1).
3   Incorrect ignition timing (Chapters 1 and 5).
4   Defective spark plug wires (Chapter 1).
5   Emissions system components faulty (Chapter 6).
6   Low or uneven cylinder compression pressures. Check as described in Chapter 2.
7   Weak or faulty ignition coil(s) (Chapter 5).
8   Weak or faulty ignition system (Chapter 5).
9   Vacuum leaks at intake manifold or vacuum hoses (see Section 8).
10 Dirty or clogged fuel injector(s) (Chapter 4).
11 Leaky EGR valve (Chapter 6).
12 Fuel injection or engine control systems malfunction (Chapters 4 and 6).

15 Hesitation or stumble during acceleration

1   Ignition system not operating properly (Chapter 5).
2   Dirty or clogged fuel injector(s) (Chapter 4).
3   Low fuel pressure. Check for proper operation of the fuel pump and for restrictions in the fuel filter and lines (Chapter 4).
4   Fuel injection or engine control systems malfunction (Chapters 4 and 6).

16 Engine stalls

1   Idle speed incorrect (Chapters 1 and 5).
2   Fuel filter clogged and/or water and impurities in the fuel system (Chapter 1).
3   Damaged or wet distributor cap and wires.

4   Emissions system components faulty (Chapter 6).
5   Faulty or incorrectly gapped spark plugs (Chapter 1). Also check the spark plug wires (Chapter 1).
6   Vacuum leak at the intake manifold or vacuum hoses. Check as described in Section 8.
7   Fuel injection or engine control systems malfunction (Chapters 4 and 6).

17 Engine lacks power

1   Incorrect ignition timing (Chapter 5).
2   Faulty or incorrectly gapped spark plugs (Chapter 1).
3   Air filter dirty (Chapter 1).
4   Faulty ignition coil (Chapter 5).
5   Brakes binding (Chapters 1 and 9).
6   Automatic transmission fluid level incorrect, causing slippage (Chapter 1).
7   Fuel filter clogged and/or impurities in the fuel system (Chapters 1 and 4).
8   EGR system not functioning properly (Chapter 6).
9   Use of sub-standard fuel. Fill tank with proper octane fuel.
10 Low or uneven cylinder compression pressures. Check as described in Chapter 2.
11 Vacuum leak at intake manifold or vacuum hoses (check as described in Section 8).
12 Dirty or clogged fuel injector(s) (Chapters 1 and 4).
13 Fuel injection or engine control systems malfunction (Chapters 4 and 6).
14 Restricted exhaust system (Chapter 4).

18 Engine backfires

1   EGR system not functioning properly (Chapter 6).
2   Ignition timing incorrect (Chapter 5).
3   Damaged valve springs or sticking valves (Chapter 2).
4   Vacuum leak at the intake manifold or vacuum hoses (see Section 8).

19 Engine surges while holding accelerator steady

1   Vacuum leak at the intake manifold or vacuum hoses (see Section 8).
2   Restricted air filter (Chapter 1).
3   Fuel pump or pressure regulator defective (Chapter 4).
4   Fuel injection or engine control systems malfunction (Chapters 4 and 6).

20 Pinging or knocking engine sounds when engine is under load

1   Incorrect grade of fuel. Fill tank with fuel of the proper octane rating.

2   Ignition timing incorrect (Chapters 1 and 5).
3   Carbon build-up in combustion chambers. Remove cylinder head(s) and clean combustion chambers (Chapter 2).
4   Incorrect spark plugs (Chapter 1).
5   Fuel injection or engine control systems malfunction (Chapters 4 and 6).
6   Restricted exhaust system (Chapter 4).

21 Engine diesels (continues to run) after being turned off

Leaking fuel injectors or other fuel-injection system malfunction causing fuel injectors to continue spraying fuel after the key is turned off.

22 Low oil pressure

1   Improper grade of oil.
2   Oil pump worn or damaged (Chapter 2).
3   Engine overheating (refer to Section 27).
4   Clogged oil filter (Chapter 1).
5   Clogged oil strainer (Chapter 2).
6   Oil pressure gauge not working properly (Chapter 2).

23 Excessive oil consumption

1   Loose oil drain plug.
2   Loose bolts or damaged oil pan gasket (Chapter 2).
3   Loose bolts or damaged front cover gasket (Chapter 2).
4   Front or rear crankshaft oil seal leaking (Chapter 2).
5   Loose bolts or damaged valve cover gasket (Chapter 2).
6   Loose oil filter (Chapter 1).
7   Loose or damaged oil pressure switch (Chapter 2).
8   Pistons and cylinders excessively worn (Chapter 2).
9   Piston rings not installed correctly on pistons (Chapter 2).
10 Worn or damaged piston rings (Chapter 2).
11 Intake and/or exhaust valve oil seals worn or damaged (Chapter 2).
12 Worn or damaged valves/guides (Chapter 2).
13 Faulty or incorrect PCV valve allowing too much crankcase airflow.

24 Excessive fuel consumption

1   Dirty or clogged air filter element (Chapter 1).
2   Incorrect ignition timing (Chapters 1 and 4).
3   Low tire pressure or incorrect tire size (Chapter 10).
4   Inspect for binding brakes.

5   Fuel leakage. Check all connections, lines and components in the fuel system (Chapter 4).
6   Dirty or clogged fuel injectors (Chapter 4).
7   Fuel injection or engine control systems malfunction (Chapters 4 and 6).
8   Thermostat stuck open or not installed.
9   Improperly operating transmission.

25   Fuel odor

1   Fuel leakage. Check all connections, lines and components in the fuel system (Chapter 4).
2   Fuel tank overfilled. Fill only to automatic shut-off.
3   Charcoal canister filter in Evaporative Emissions Control system clogged (Chapter 1).
4   Vapor leaks from Evaporative Emissions Control system lines (Chapter 6).

26   Miscellaneous engine noises

1   A strong dull noise that becomes more rapid as the engine accelerates indicates worn or damaged crankshaft bearings or an unevenly worn crankshaft. To pinpoint the trouble spot, remove the spark plug wire from one plug at a time and crank the engine over. If the noise stops, the cylinder with the removed plug wire indicates the problem area. Replace the bearing and/or service or replace the crankshaft (Chapter 2).
2   A similar (yet slightly higher pitched) noise to the crankshaft knocking described in the previous paragraph, that becomes more rapid as the engine accelerates, indicates worn or damaged connecting rod bearings (Chapter 2). The procedure for locating the problem cylinder is the same as described in Paragraph 1.
3   An overlapping metallic noise that increases in intensity as the engine speed increases, yet diminishes as the engine warms up indicates abnormal piston and cylinder wear (Chapter 2). To locate the problem cylinder, use the procedure described in Paragraph 1.
4   A rapid clicking noise that becomes faster as the engine accelerates indicates a worn piston pin or piston pin hole. This sound will happen each time the piston hits the highest and lowest points in the stroke (Chapter 2). The procedure for locating the problem piston is described in Paragraph 1.
5   A metallic clicking noise coming from the water pump indicates worn or damaged water pump bearings or pump. Replace the water pump with a new one (Chapter 3).
6   A rapid tapping sound or clicking sound that becomes faster as the engine speed increases indicates "valve tapping." This can be identified by holding one end of a section of hose to your ear and placing the other end at different spots along the valve cover. The

point where the sound is loudest indicates the problem valve. If the camshaft and rocker arm components are in good shape, you likely have a collapsed valve lifter. Changing the engine oil and adding a high viscosity oil treatment will sometimes cure a stuck lifter problem. If the problem persists, the lifters and rocker arms must be removed for inspection (see Chapter 2).

Cooling system

27   Overheating

1   Insufficient coolant in system (Chapter 1).
2   Water pump drivebelt defective or out of adjustment (Chapter 1).
3   Radiator core blocked or grille restricted (Chapter 3).
4   Thermostat faulty (Chapter 3).
5   Electric cooling fan blades broken or cracked (Chapter 3).
6   Cooling fan electrical problem (Chapter 3).
7   Radiator cap not maintaining proper pressure (Chapter 3).

28   Overcooling

Faulty thermostat (Chapter 3).

29   External coolant leakage

1   Deteriorated/damaged hoses or loose clamps (Chapters 1 and 3).
2   Water pump seal defective (Chapters 1 and 3).
3   Leakage from radiator core or header tank (Chapter 3).
4   Engine drain or water jacket core plugs leaking (Chapter 2).

30   Internal coolant leakage

1   Leaking cylinder head gasket (Chapter 2).
2   Cracked cylinder bore or cylinder head (Chapter 2).

31   Coolant loss

1   Too much coolant in system (Chapter 1).
2   Coolant boiling away because of overheating (Chapter 3).
3   Internal or external leakage (Chapter 3).
4   Faulty radiator cap (Chapter 3).

32   Poor coolant circulation

1   Inoperative water pump (Chapter 3).
2   Restriction in cooling system (Chapters 1 and 3).
3   Water pump drivebelt defective or out of adjustment (Chapter 1).
4   Thermostat sticking (Chapter 3).

Automatic transaxle

Note: *Due to the complexity of the automatic transaxle, it's difficult for the home mechanic to properly diagnose and service this component. For problems other than the following, the vehicle should be taken to a dealer service department or a transmission shop.*

33   Fluid leakage

1   Automatic transmission fluid is a deep red color. Fluid leaks should not be confused with engine oil, which can easily be blown by air flow to the transaxle.
2   To pinpoint a leak, first remove all built-up dirt and grime from the transaxle housing with degreasing agents and/or steam cleaning. Drive the vehicle at low speeds so air flow will not blow the leak far from its source. Raise the vehicle and determine where the leak is coming from. Common areas of leakage are:

a) *Pan (Chapters 1 and 7).*
b) *Filler pipe (Chapter 7).*
c) *Transaxle oil lines (Chapter 7).*
d) *Speedometer gear or sensor (Chapter 7).*

34   Transaxle fluid brown or has a burned smell

Transaxle overheated. Change the fluid (Chapter 1).

35   General shift mechanism problems

1   Chapter 7 deals with checking and adjusting the shift linkage on automatic transaxles. Common problems which may be attributed to poorly adjusted linkage are:

a) *Engine starting in gears other than Park or Neutral.*
b) *Indicator on shifter pointing to a gear other than the one actually being used.*
c) *Vehicle moves when in Park.*

2   Refer to Chapter 7 for the shift linkage adjustment procedure.

36 Transaxle will not downshift with accelerator pedal pressed to the floor

Transmission Range Sensor problem (Chapter 7).

37 Engine will start in gears other than Park or Neutral

Park/Neutral switch malfunctioning (Chapter 7).

38 Transaxle slips, shifts roughly, is noisy or has no drive in forward or reverse gears

There are many probable causes for the above problems, but the home mechanic should be concerned with only one possibility - fluid level. Before taking the vehicle to a repair shop, check the level and condition of the fluid as described in Chapter 1.

Correct the fluid level as necessary or change the fluid and filter if needed. If the problem persists, have a professional diagnose the probable cause with a factory scan tool.

Driveaxles

39 Clicking noise in turns

Worn or damaged outer CV joint. Check for cut or damaged boots (Chapter 1). Repair as necessary (Chapter 8).

40 Knock or clunk when accelerating after coasting

Worn or damaged CV joint. Check for cut or damaged boots (Chapter 1). Repair as necessary (Chapter 8).

41 Shudder or vibration during acceleration

1   Excessive inner CV joint angle. Check and correct as necessary (Chapter 8).
2   Worn or damaged CV joints. Repair or replace as necessary (Chapter 8).
3   Sticking inboard joint assembly. Correct or replace as necessary (Chapter 8).

Brakes

Note: *Before assuming that a brake problem exists, make sure the tires are in good condition and properly inflated (Chapter 1), the front end alignment is correct (Chapter 10),* *and the vehicle isn't loaded with weight in an unequal manner. All service procedures for the brakes are included in Chapter 9, unless otherwise noted.*

42 Vehicle pulls to one side during braking

1   Incorrect tire pressures (Chapter 1).
2   Front end out of alignment (have the front end aligned).
3   Unmatched tires on same axle.
4   Restricted brake lines or hoses (Chapter 9).
5   Malfunctioning brake assembly (Chapter 9).
6   Loose suspension parts (Chapter 10).
7   Loose brake calipers (Chapter 9).
8   Contaminated brake linings (Chapters 1 and 9).

43 Noise (high-pitched squeal when the brakes are applied)

Front disc brake pads worn out. The noise comes from the wear sensor rubbing against the disc. Replace pads with new ones immediately (Chapter 9).

44 Brake roughness or chatter (pedal pulsates)

Note: *Some brake pedal pulsation during operation of the Anti-Lock Brake System (ABS) is normal.*
1   Excessive front brake disc lateral runout (Chapter 9).
2   Uneven pad wear caused by caliper not sliding due to improper clearance or dirt (Chapter 9).
3   Defective brake disc (Chapter 9).

45 Excessive pedal effort required to stop vehicle

1   Malfunctioning power brake booster (Chapter 9).
2   Partial system failure (Chapter 9).
3   Excessively worn pads (Chapter 9).
4   One or more caliper pistons or wheel cylinders seized or sticking (Chapter 9).
5   Brake pads contaminated with oil or grease (Chapter 9).
6   New pads installed and not yet seated. It will take a while for the new material to seat.

46 Excessive brake pedal travel

1   Partial brake system failure (Chapter 9).
2   Insufficient fluid in master cylinder (Chapters 1 and 9).
3   Air trapped in system (Chapters 1 and 9).
4   Excessively worn rear shoes (Chapter 9).

47 Dragging brakes

1   Master cylinder pistons not returning correctly (Chapter 9).
2   Negative clearance between the brake booster pushrod and the master cylinder (Chapter 9).
3   Restricted brakes lines or hoses (Chapters 1 and 9).
4   Incorrect parking brake adjustment (Chapter 9).
5   Sticking pistons in calipers (Chapter 9).

48 Grabbing or uneven braking action

1   Malfunction of brake pressure control valve (Chapter 9).
2   Malfunction of power brake booster unit (Chapter 9).
3   Binding brake pedal mechanism (Chapter 9).
4   Sticking pistons in calipers (Chapter 9).

49 Brake pedal feels spongy when depressed

1   Air in hydraulic lines (Chapter 9).
2   Master cylinder mounting bolts loose (Chapter 9).
3   Master cylinder defective (Chapter 9).

50 Brake pedal travels to the floor with little resistance

Little or no fluid in the master cylinder reservoir caused by leaking caliper or wheel cylinder pistons, loose, damaged or disconnected brake lines (Chapter 9).

51 Parking brake does not hold

Check the parking brake (Chapter 9).

Suspension and steering systems

Note: *Before attempting to diagnose the suspension and steering systems, perform the following preliminary checks:*
a) *Check the tire pressures and look for uneven wear.*
b) *Check the steering universal joints or coupling from the column to the steering gear for loose fasteners and wear.*
c) *Check the front and rear suspension and the steering gear assembly for loose and damaged parts.*
d) *Look for out-of-round or out-of-balance tires, bent rims and loose and/or rough wheel bearings.*

52 Vehicle pulls to one side

1 Mismatched or uneven tires (Chapter 10).
2 Broken or sagging springs (Chapter 10).
3 Front wheel alignment incorrect (Chapter 10).
4 Front brakes dragging (Chapter 9).

53 Abnormal or excessive tire wear

1 Front wheel alignment incorrect (Chapter 10).
2 Sagging or broken springs (Chapter 10).
3 Tire out-of-balance (Chapter 10).
4 Worn shock absorber or strut (Chapter 10).
5 Overloaded vehicle.
6 Tires not rotated regularly.

54 Wheel makes a "thumping" noise

1 Blister or bump on tire (Chapter 1).
2 Improper strut or shock absorber action (Chapter 10).

55 Shimmy, shake or vibration

1 Tire or wheel out-of-balance or out-of-round (Chapter 10).
2 Loose or worn wheel bearings (Chapter 10).
3 Worn tie-rod ends (Chapter 10).
4 Worn balljoints (Chapter 10).
5 Excessive wheel runout (Chapter 10).
6 Blister or bump on tire (Chapter 1).

56 Hard steering

1 Lack of lubrication at balljoints, tie-rod ends and steering gear assembly (Chapter 10).
2 Front wheel alignment incorrect (Chapter 10).
3 Low tire pressure (Chapter 1).

57 Steering wheel does not return to center position correctly

1 Lack of lubrication at balljoints and tie-rod ends (Chapter 10).
2 Binding in steering column (Chapter 10).
3 Defective rack-and-pinion assembly (Chapter 10).
4 Front wheel alignment problem (Chapter 10).

58 Abnormal noise at the front end

1 Lack of lubrication at balljoints and tie-rod ends (Chapter 1).
2 Loose upper strut mount (Chapter 10).
3 Worn tie-rod ends (Chapter 10).
4 Loose stabilizer bar (Chapter 10).
5 Loose wheel lug nuts (Chapter 1).
6 Loose suspension bolts (Chapter 10).

59 Wander or poor steering stability

1 Mismatched or uneven tires (Chapter 10).
2 Worn balljoints or tie-rod ends (Chapters 1 and 10).
3 Worn struts or shock absorbers (Chapter 10).
4 Loose stabilizer bar (Chapter 10).
5 Broken or sagging springs (Chapter 10).
6 Front wheel alignment incorrect (Chapter 10).
7 Worn steering gear clamp bushings (Chapter 10).

60 Erratic steering when braking

1 Wheel bearings worn (Chapters 8 and 10).
2 Broken or sagging springs (Chapter 10).
3 Leaking wheel cylinder or caliper (Chapter 9).
4 Warped brake discs (Chapter 9).
5 Worn steering gear clamp bushings (Chapter 10).

61 Excessive pitching and/or rolling around corners or during braking

1 Loose stabilizer bar (Chapter 10).
2 Worn shock absorbers or mounts (Chapter 10).
3 Broken or sagging springs (Chapter 10).
4 Overloaded vehicle.
5 Malfunction in the air suspension system (if equipped) (Chapter 10).

62 Suspension bottoms

1 Overloaded vehicle.
2 Worn struts or shock absorbers (Chapter 10).
3 Incorrect, broken or sagging springs (Chapter 10).
4 Malfunction in the air-suspension system (if equipped) (Chapter 10).

63 Cupped tires

1 Front wheel alignment incorrect (Chapter 10).
2 Worn struts or shock absorbers (Chapter 10).
3 Wheel bearings worn (Chapters 8 and 10).
4 Excessive tire or wheel runout (Chapter 10).
5 Worn balljoints (Chapter 10).

64 Excessive tire wear on outside edge

1 Inflation pressures incorrect (Chapter 1).
2 Excessive speed in turns.
3 Front end alignment incorrect (excessive toe-in or positive camber). Have professionally aligned.
4 Suspension arm bent or twisted (Chapter 10).

65 Excessive tire wear on inside edge

1 Inflation pressures incorrect (Chapter 1).
2 Front end alignment incorrect (toe-out or excessive negative camber). Have professionally aligned.
3 Loose or damaged steering components (Chapter 10).

66 Tire tread worn in one place

1 Tires out-of-balance.
2 Damaged or buckled wheel. Inspect and replace if necessary.
3 Defective tire (Chapter 1).

67 Excessive play or looseness in steering system

1 Wheel bearings worn (Chapter 10).
2 Tie-rod end loose or worn (Chapter 10).
3 Steering gear loose (Chapter 10).

68 Rattling or clicking noise in rack and pinion

Steering gear clamps loose (Chapter 10).

Chapter 1
Tune-up and routine maintenance

Contents

Specifications

Recommended lubricants and fluids

Note: *Listed here are manufacturer recommendations at the time this manual was written. Manufacturers occasionally upgrade their fluid and lubricant specifications, so check with your local auto parts store for current recommendations.*

Engine oil
    Type.. API grade SH or SH/CC multigrade and fuel efficient oil
    Viscosity .... See accompanying chart

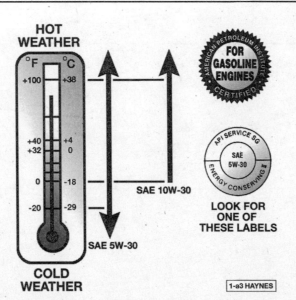

Recommended engine oil viscosity

1-a3 HAYNES

Recommended lubricants and fluids (continued)

Fuel	Unleaded gasoline, 87 octane or higher
Engine coolant	50/50 mixture of ethylene glycol based antifreeze and water
Brake fluid	DOT 3 heavy duty brake fluid

Power steering fluid

Villager	Ford Premium Power Steering fluid or equivalent
Quest	Type F automatic transmission fluid or equivalent
Automatic transaxle fluid	Dexron III or Mercon automatic transmission fluid or equivalent

Capacities*

Engine oil (with filter change)	4.2 quarts
Fuel tank	20 gallons

Cooling system

Standard heater	12.0 quarts
Auxiliary rear heater	13.0 quarts

Automatic transaxle

Drain and refill	4.0 quarts
Dry	8.8 to 10.0 quarts

All capacities approximate. Add as necessary to bring to appropriate level.

General

Radiator cap pressure rating	16 psi
Disc brake pad thickness (minimum)	1/8 inch

Drum brake shoe thickness (minimum)

Bonded	1/8 inch
Riveted	1/16 inch

Ignition system

Spark plug type and gap

Villager	Motorcraft AGSP-32C or equivalent @ 0.035 inch
Quest	NGK BKR5EY or equivalent @ 0.035 inch
Firing order	1-2-3-4-5-6
Ignition timing	13 to 17-degrees BTDC

Idle speed adjustment

Transaxle in Park or Neutral	750 rpm

Torque specifications

	Ft-lbs (unless otherwise noted)
Wheel lug nuts	72 to 87
Spark plugs	14 to 22
Oil pan drain plug	22 to 29

Automatic transaxle

Drain plug	22 to 29
Pan bolts	62 to 79 in-lbs

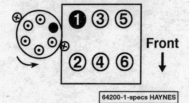

Front

Cylinder location and distributor rotation

The blackened terminal shown on the distributor cap indicates the Number One spark plug wire position

64200-1-specs HAYNES

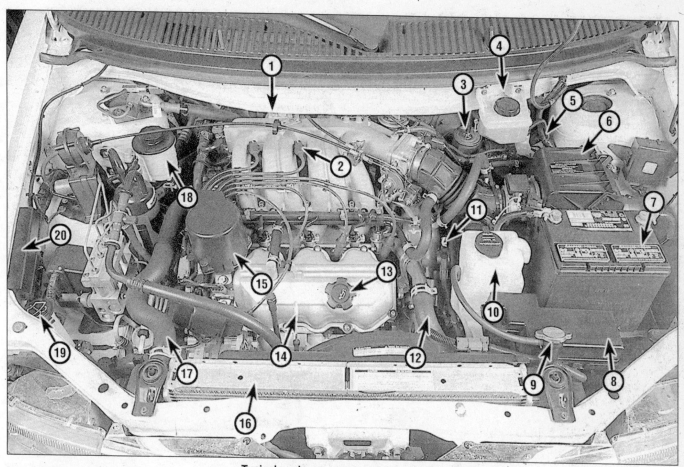

Typical engine compartment components

1   Idle speed adjustment screw
2   Rear bank spark plugs (not visible)
3   Fuel filter
4   Brake master cylinder fluid reservoir
5   Charcoal canister
6   Air filter housing
7   Battery

8   Engine compartment relay box
9   Radiator cap
10 Engine coolant reservoir
11 Automatic transaxle fluid dipstick
12 Radiator hose
13 Engine oil filler cap
14 Engine oil dipstick

15 Distributor
16 Radiator
17 Radiator hose
18 Power steering fluid reservoir
19 Windshield washer fluid reservoir
20 Engine compartment fuse box

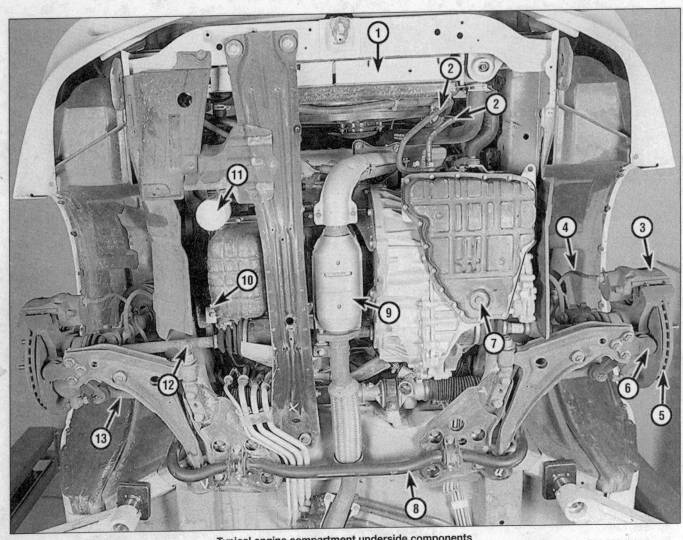

Typical engine compartment underside components

1 Radiator	*6 Balljoint*
2 Transaxle cooler lines	*7 Automatic transaxle drain plug*
3 Brake caliper	*8 Stabilizer bar*
4 Brake hose	*9 Exhaust system*
5 Brake disc	

10   Engine oil drain plug
11   Oil filter
12   Driveaxle
13   Tie-rod end

Typical rear underside components

1	Fuel tank	4	Axle beam	7	Parking brake cable
2	Stabilizer bar	5	Leaf spring	8	Exhaust pipe
3	Brake drum	6	Shock absorber		

1 Mercury Villager/Nissan Quest Maintenance schedule

The following maintenance intervals are based on the assumption that the vehicle owner will be doing the maintenance or service work, as opposed to having a dealer service department or other repair shop do the work. Although the time/mileage intervals are loosely based on factory recommendations, most have been shortened to ensure, for example, that such items as lubricants and fluids are checked/changed at intervals that promote maximum engine/driveline service life. Also, subject to the preference of the individual owner interested in keeping his or her vehicle in peak condition at all times, and with the vehicle's ultimate resale in mind, many of the maintenance procedures may be performed more often than recommended in the following schedule. We encourage such owner initiative.

When the vehicle is new it should be serviced initially by a factory authorized dealer service department to protect the factory warranty. In many cases the initial maintenance check is done at no cost to the owner (check with your dealer service department for more information).

Every 250 miles or weekly, whichever comes first

Check the engine oil level (Section 4)
Check the engine coolant level (Section 4)
Check the windshield washer fluid level (Section 4)
Check the brake level (Section 4)
Check the tires and tire pressures (Section 5)

Every 3000 miles or 3 months, whichever comes first

All items listed above, plus:

Check the power steering fluid level (Section 6)
Check the automatic transaxle fluid level (Section 7)
Change the engine oil and oil filter (Section 8)

Every 6000 miles or 6 months, whichever comes first

All items listed above, plus:

Check and service the battery (Section 9)
Inspect and replace, if necessary, the windshield wiper blades (Section 10)
Rotate the tires (Section 11)
Inspect the exhaust system (Section 12)
Check the seat belt operation (Section 13)
Check and, if necessary, adjust the engine drivebelts (Section 14)

Every 15,000 miles or 12 months, whichever comes first

All items listed above, plus:

Inspect and replace, if necessary, all underhood hoses (Section 15)
Inspect the cooling system (Section 16)
Check the fuel system (Section 17)
Inspect the steering and suspension components (Section 18)
Inspect the brakes (Section 19)

Every 30,000 miles or 24 months, whichever comes first

Replace the air filter (Section 20)*
Replace the fuel filter (Section 21)
Check and adjust if necessary, the idle speed (Section 22)
Check and adjust if necessary, the ignition timing (Section 23)
Service the cooling system (drain, flush and refill) (Section 24)
Change the automatic transaxle fluid and filter (Section 25)**
Change the brake fluid (Section 26)
Check the PCV valve (Section 27)
Replace the spark plugs (Section 28)
Inspect the spark plug wires, distributor cap and wires (Section 29)

Every 60,000 miles or 48 months, whichever comes first

Replace the timing belt (1993 models) (see Chapter 2A)

Every 105,000 miles or 5 years, whichever comes first

Replace the timing belt (1994 and later models) (see Chapter 2A)

    * *Replace more often if is the vehicle is driven in dusty areas.*
   ** *If the vehicle is operated in continuous stop-and-go driving or in mountainous areas, change at 15,000 miles.*

2   Introduction

This Chapter is designed to help the home mechanic maintain the Mercury Villager and Nissan Quest with the goals of maximum performance, economy, safety and reliability in mind.

Included is a master maintenance schedule followed by procedures dealing specifically with each item on the schedule. Visual checks, adjustments, component replacement and other helpful items are included. Refer to the **accompanying illustrations** of the engine compartment and the underside of the vehicle for the locations of various components.

Servicing the vehicle, in accordance with the mileage/time maintenance schedule and the step-by-step procedures will result in a planned maintenance program that should produce a long and reliable service life. Keep in mind that it is a comprehensive plan, so maintaining some items but not others at the specified intervals will not produce the same results.

As you service the vehicle, you will discover that many of the procedures can - and should - be grouped together because of the nature of the particular procedure you're performing or because of the close proximity of two otherwise unrelated components to one another.

For example, if the vehicle is raised for chassis lubrication, you should inspect the exhaust, suspension, steering and fuel systems while you're under the vehicle. When you're rotating the tires, it makes good sense to check the brakes since the wheels are already removed. Finally, let's suppose you have to borrow or rent a torque wrench. Even if you only need it to tighten the spark plugs, you might as well check the torque of as many critical fasteners as time allows.

The first step in this maintenance program is to prepare yourself before the actual work begins. Read through all the procedures you're planning to do, then gather up all the parts and tools needed. If it looks like you might run into problems during a particular job, seek advice from a mechanic or an experienced do-it-yourselfer.

3   Tune-up general information

The term tune-up is used in this manual to represent a combination of individual operations rather than one specific procedure.

If, from the time the vehicle is new, the routine maintenance schedule is followed closely and frequent checks are made of fluid levels and high wear items, as suggested throughout this manual, the engine will be kept in relatively good running condition and the need for additional work will be minimized.

More likely than not, however, there will be times when the engine is running poorly due to lack of regular maintenance. This is

4.2 The engine oil dipstick (arrow) is located on the front side of the engine on all models

even more likely if a used vehicle, which has not received regular and frequent maintenance checks, is purchased. In such cases, an engine tune-up will be needed outside of the regular routine maintenance intervals.

The first step in any tune-up or diagnostic procedure to help correct a poor running engine is a cylinder compression check. A compression check (see Chapter 2B) will help determine the condition of internal engine components and should be used as a guide for tune-up and repair procedures. If, for instance, a compression check indicates serious internal engine wear, a conventional tune-up will not improve the performance of the engine and would be a waste of time and money. Because of its importance, the compression check should be done by someone with the right equipment and the knowledge to use it properly.

The following procedures are those most often needed to bring a generally poor running engine back into a proper state of tune.

Minor tune-up

Check all engine related fluids (Section 4)
Clean, inspect and test the battery (Section 9)
Check the drivebelts (Section 14)
Check all underhood hoses (Section 15)
Check the cooling system (Section 16)
Check the fuel system (Section 17)
Check the air filter (Section 20)

Major tune-up

All items listed under Minor tune-up, plus . . .
Replace the fuel filter (Section 21)
Replace the air filter (Section 20)
Replace the PCV valve (Section 27)
Replace the spark plugs (Section 28)

Replace the spark plug wires (Section 29)
Replace the distributor cap and rotor (Section 29)
Check the charging system (Chapter 5)

4   Fluid level checks (every 250 miles or weekly)

1   Fluids are an essential part of the lubrication, cooling, brake and windshield washer systems. Because the fluids gradually become depleted and/or contaminated during normal operation of the vehicle, they must be periodically replenished. See *Recommended lubricants and fluids* at the beginning of this Chapter before adding fluid to any of the following components. **Note:** *The vehicle must be on level ground when fluid levels are checked.*

Engine oil

Refer to illustrations 4.2, 4.4 and 4.6

2   The engine oil level is checked with a dipstick, which is located on the front side of the engine **(see illustration)**. The dipstick extends through a metal tube down into the oil pan.

3   The oil level should be checked before the vehicle has been driven, or about 15 minutes after the engine has been shut off. If the oil is checked immediately after driving the vehicle, some of the oil will remain in the upper part of the engine, resulting in an inaccurate reading on the dipstick.

4   Pull the dipstick out of the tube and wipe all the oil from the end with a clean rag or paper towel. Insert the clean dipstick all the way back into the tube and pull it out again. Note the oil at the end of the dipstick. At its highest point, the level should be above the ADD mark and within the crosshatched

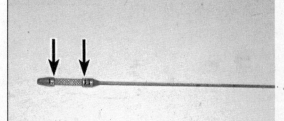

4.4 The oil level must be maintained between the marks (arrows) at all times - it takes one quart of oil to raise the level from the lower mark to the upper mark

4.6 The engine oil filler cap is clearly marked and is located on the valve cover which faces the front of the engine compartment on all models - turn the oil filler cap counterclockwise to remove it

4.8 The coolant reservoir is located on the left side (driver's side) of the engine compartment - the coolant level can be checked by observing it through the translucent reservoir

4.15 The brake fluid reservoir is located on the left side (driver's side) of the engine compartment - the fluid level should be kept at or near the MAX line on the side of the translucent plastic reservoir

section of the dipstick **(see illustration)**.

5   It takes one quart of oil to raise the level from the lower (ADD) mark to the upper (FULL) mark on the dipstick. Do not allow the level to drop below the ADD mark or oil starvation may cause engine damage. Conversely, overfilling the engine (adding oil above the FULL mark) may cause oil-fouled spark plugs, oil leaks or oil seal failures.

6   To add oil, remove the filler cap from the valve cover **(see illustration)**. After adding oil, wait a few minutes to allow the level to stabilize, then pull out the dipstick and check the level again. Add more oil if required. Install the filler cap and tighten it by hand only.

7   Checking the oil level is an important preventive maintenance step. A consistently low oil level indicates oil leakage through damaged seals, defective gaskets or past worn rings or valve guides. If the oil looks milky in color or has water droplets in it, the cylinder head gasket(s) may be blown or the head(s) or block may be cracked. The engine should be checked immediately. The condition of the oil should also be checked. Whenever you check the oil level, slide your thumb and index finger up the dipstick before wiping off the oil. If you see small dirt or metal particles clinging to the dipstick, the oil should be changed (see Section 8).

Engine coolant

Refer to illustration 4.8

Warning: *Do not allow antifreeze to come in contact with your skin or painted surfaces of the vehicle. Flush contaminated areas immediately with plenty of water. Don't store new coolant or leave old coolant lying around where it's accessible to children or pets - they're attracted by its sweet smell and may drink it. Ingestion of even a small amount of coolant can be fatal! Wipe up garage floor and drip pan spills immediately. Keep antifreeze containers covered and repair cooling system leaks as soon as they're noticed.*

8   All vehicles covered by this manual are equipped with a coolant recovery system. A white plastic coolant reservoir located in the engine compartment is connected by a hose to the radiator filler neck **(see illustration)**. If the engine overheats, coolant escapes through a valve in the radiator cap and travels through the hose into the reservoir. As the engine cools, the coolant is automatically drawn back into the cooling system to maintain the correct level.

9   The coolant level in the reservoir should be checked regularly. **Warning:** *Do not remove the radiator cap to check the coolant level when the engine is warm.* The level in the reservoir varies with the temperature of the engine. When the engine is cold, the coolant level should be at or slightly above the MAX mark on the reservoir. If it isn't, allow the engine to cool, then remove the cap from the reservoir and add a 50/50 mixture of ethylene glycol-based antifreeze and water.

10   If the coolant level drops within a short time after replenishment, there may be a leak in the system. Inspect the radiator, hoses, engine coolant filler cap, drain plugs, air bleeder plugs and water pump. If no leak is evident, have the radiator cap pressure tested by your dealer. **Warning:** *Never remove the radiator cap or the coolant recovery reservoir cap when the engine is running or has just been shut down, because the cooling system is hot. Escaping steam and scalding liquid could cause serious injury.*

11   If it is necessary to open the radiator cap, wait until the system has cooled completely, then wrap a thick cloth around the cap and turn it to the first stop. If any steam escapes, wait until the system has cooled further, then remove the cap.

12   When checking the coolant level, always note its condition. It should be relatively clear. If it is brown or rust colored, the system should be drained, flushed and refilled. Even if the coolant appears to be normal, the corrosion inhibitors wear out with use, so it must

be replaced at the specified intervals.

13   Do not allow antifreeze to come in contact with your skin or painted surfaces of the vehicle. Flush contacted areas immediately with plenty of water.

Brake fluid

Refer to illustration 4.15

14   The brake fluid level is checked by looking through the plastic reservoir mounted on the firewall in the left (driver's side) rear corner of the engine compartment and connected by a hose to the master cylinder.

15   The fluid level should be at or near the MAX line on the side of the reservoir **(see illustration)**. Add fluid if the level is at the MAX line.

16   If the fluid level is low, wipe the top of the reservoir and the cap with a clean rag to prevent contamination of the system as the cap is unscrewed.

17   Add only the specified brake fluid to the reservoir (refer to *Recommended lubricants and fluids* at the front of this Chapter or your owner's manual). Mixing different types of brake fluid can damage the system. Fill the reservoir to the MAX line. **Warning:** *Brake fluid can harm your eyes and damage painted surfaces, so use extreme caution when handling or pouring it. Do not use brake fluid that has been standing open or is more than one year old. Brake fluid absorbs moisture from the air, which can cause a dangerous loss of braking effectiveness.*

18   While the reservoir cap is off, check the master cylinder reservoir for contamination. If rust deposits, dirt particles or water droplets are present, the system should be drained and refilled by a dealer service department or repair shop.

19   After filling the reservoir to the proper level, make sure the cap is seated to prevent fluid leakage and/or contamination.

20   The fluid level in the master cylinder will drop slightly as the brake shoes or pads at each wheel wear down during normal opera-

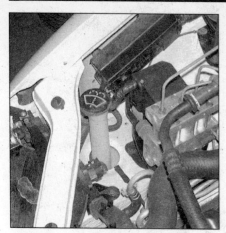

4.22 The windshield washer reservoir is located at the right front corner of the engine compartment

Windshield washer fluid

Refer to illustration 4.22

22   Fluid for the windshield washer system is stored in a plastic reservoir located at the right (passenger) side of the engine compartment **(see illustration)**.

23   In milder climates, plain water can be used in the reservoir, but it should be kept no more than 2/3 full to allow for expansion if the water freezes. In colder climates, use windshield washer system antifreeze, available at any auto parts store, to lower the freezing point of the fluid. Mix the antifreeze with water in accordance with the manufacturer's directions on the container. **Caution:** *Do not use cooling system antifreeze - it will damage the vehicle's paint.*

---

5   Tire and tire pressure checks (every 250 miles or weekly)

Refer to illustrations 5.2, 5.3, 5.4a, 5.4b and 5.8

1   Periodic inspection of the tires may spare you the inconvenience of being stranded with a flat tire. It can also provide you with vital information regarding possible problems in the steering and suspension systems before major damage occurs.

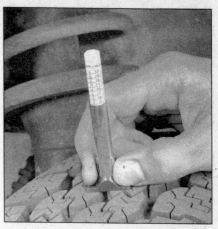

5.2 Use a tire tread depth indicator to monitor tire wear - they are available at auto parts stores and service stations and cost very little

2   The original tires on this vehicle are equipped with 1/2-inch wide bands that will appear when tread depth reaches 1/16-inch, at which point they can be considered worn out. Tread wear can be monitored with a simple, inexpensive device known as a tread depth indicator **(see illustration)**.

3   Note any abnormal tread wear **(see illustration)**. Tread pattern irregularities such

tion. If the brake fluid level drops consistently, check the entire system for leaks immediately. Examine all brake lines, hoses and connections, along with the calipers, wheel cylinders and master cylinder (see Section 19).

21   When checking the fluid level, if you discover that the reservoir is empty, the brake system should be bled and the system inspected thoroughly (see Chapter 9).

1

UNDERINFLATION

CUPPING

Cupping may be caused by:
- Underinflation and/or mechanical irregularities such as out-of-balance condition of wheel and/or tire, and bent or damaged wheel.
- Loose or worn steering tie-rod or steering idler arm.
- Loose, damaged or worn front suspension parts.

OVERINFLATION

INCORRECT TOE-IN OR EXTREME CAMBER

FEATHERING DUE TO MISALIGNMENT

5.3 This chart will help you determine the condition of the tires, the probable cause(s) of abnormal wear and the corrective action necessary

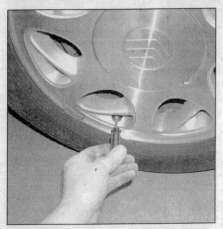

5.4a If a tire loses air on a steady basis, check the valve stem core first to make sure it's snug (special inexpensive wrenches are commonly available at auto parts stores)

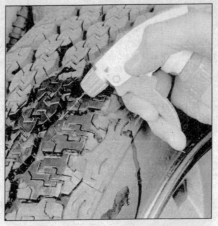

5.4b If the valve stem core is tight, raise the corner of the vehicle with the low tire and spray a soapy water solution onto the tread as the tire is turned slowly - leaks will cause small bubbles to appear

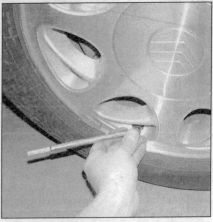

5.8 To extend the life of the tires, check the air pressure at least once a week with an accurate gauge (don't forget the spare!)

as cupping, flat spots and more wear on one side than the other are indications of front end alignment and/or balance problems. If any of these conditions are noted, take the vehicle to a tire shop or service station to correct the problem.

4   Look closely for cuts, punctures and embedded nails or tacks. Sometimes a tire will hold air pressure for a short time or leak down very slowly after a nail has embedded itself in the tread. If a slow leak persists, check the valve stem core to make sure it is tight **(see illustration)**. Examine the tread for an object that may have embedded itself in the tire or for a "plug" that may have begun to leak (radial tire punctures are repaired with a plug that is installed in a puncture). If a puncture is suspected, it can be easily verified by spraying a solution of soapy water onto the puncture area **(see illustration)**. The soapy solution will bubble if there is a leak. Unless the puncture is unusually large, a tire shop or service station can usually repair the tire.

5   Carefully inspect the inner sidewall of each tire for evidence of brake fluid leakage. If you see any, inspect the brakes immediately.

6   Correct air pressure adds miles to the life span of the tires, improves mileage and enhances overall ride quality. Tire pressure cannot be accurately estimated by looking at a tire, especially if it's a radial. A tire pressure gauge is essential. Keep an accurate gauge in the glove compartment. The pressure gauges attached to the nozzles of air hoses at gas stations are often inaccurate.

7   Always check tire pressure when the tires are cold. Cold, in this case, means the vehicle has not been driven over a mile in the three hours preceding a tire pressure check. A pressure rise of four to eight pounds is not uncommon once the tires are warm.

8   Unscrew the valve cap protruding from the wheel or hubcap and push the gauge firmly onto the valve stem **(see illustration)**. Note the reading on the gauge and compare

the figure to the recommended tire pressure shown on the tire placard on the driver's side door. Be sure to reinstall the valve cap to keep dirt and moisture out of the valve stem mechanism. Check all four tires and, if necessary, add enough air to bring them up to the recommended pressure.

9   Don't forget to keep the spare tire inflated to the specified pressure (refer to your owner's manual or the decal attached to the right door pillar). Note that the pressure recommended for the temporary (mini) spare is higher than for the tires on the vehicle.

6   Power steering fluid level check (every 3000 miles or 3 months)

Refer to illustration 6.2

1   Check the power steering fluid level periodically to avoid steering system problems, such as damage to the pump. **Caution:** *DO NOT hold the steering wheel against either stop (extreme left or right turn) for more than five seconds. If you do, the power steering pump could be damaged.*

2   The power steering fluid reservoir is located at the right rear corner of the engine compartment and is connected by a hose to the power steering pump **(see illustration)**.

3   Park the vehicle on level ground and apply the parking brake.

4   Run the engine until it has reached normal operating temperature. With the engine at idle, turn the steering wheel back-and-forth several times to get any air out of the steering system.

5   Check the level of the fluid in the reservoir. It must be at or near the MAX line on the translucent plastic reservoir.

6   If additional fluid is required, remove the cap and pour the specified type directly into the reservoir, using a funnel to prevent spills. Add small amounts of fluid until the level is correct. **Caution:** *Do not overfill the reservoir.*

6.2 The translucent plastic power steering fluid reservoir makes it easy to check the fluid level

If too much fluid is added, remove the excess with a clean syringe or suction pump.

7   Automatic transaxle fluid level check (every 3000 miles or 3 months)

Refer to illustrations 7.4, 7.6a and 7.6b

1   The automatic transaxle fluid level should be carefully maintained. Low fluid level can lead to slipping or loss of drive, while overfilling can cause foaming and loss of fluid. Either condition can cause transaxle damage.

2   Since transaxle fluid expands as it heats up, the fluid level should only be checked when the transaxle is warm (at normal operating temperature). If the vehicle has just been driven over 20 miles, the transaxle can be considered warm. **Caution:** *If the vehicle has just been driven for a long time at high speed or in city traffic in hot weather, or if it has just been pulling a trailer, an accurate fluid level reading cannot be obtained. Allow the*

7.4 The automatic transaxle dipstick (arrow) is located on the driver's side of the vehicle just behind the coolant reservoir

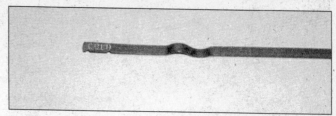

7.6a If the fluid is cold the level should be between the two notches on the back side of the dipstick

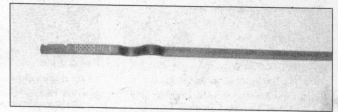

7.6b When the fluid with the transaxle at normal operating temperature - the level should be kept in the HOT range in the cross-hatched area (don't add fluid if the level is anywhere in the cross-hatched area)

transaxle to cool down for about 30 minutes. You can also check the transaxle fluid level when the transaxle is cold. If the vehicle has not been driven for over five hours and the fluid is about room temperature (70 to 95-degrees F), the transaxle is cold. However, the fluid level is normally checked with the transaxle warm to ensure accurate results.

3   Immediately after driving the vehicle, park it on a level surface, set the parking brake and start the engine. While the engine is idling, depress the brake pedal and move the selector lever through all the gear ranges, beginning and ending in Park.

4   Locate the automatic transaxle dipstick tube in the engine compartment **(see illustration)**.

5   With the engine still idling, pull the dipstick from the tube, wipe it off with a clean rag, push it all the way back into the tube and withdraw it again, then note the fluid level.

6   If the transaxle is cold, the level should be in the cold temperature range on one side of the dipstick (between the two notches); if it's warm, the fluid level should be in the operating temperature range (in the cross-hatched area) on the other side **(see illustration)**. If the level is low, add the specified automatic transmission fluid through the dipstick tube - use a funnel to prevent spills.

7   Add just enough of the recommended fluid to fill the transaxle to the proper level. It takes about one pint to raise the level from the low mark to the high mark when the fluid is hot, so add the fluid a little at a time and keep checking the level until it's correct.

8   The condition of the fluid should also be checked along with the level. If the fluid is black or a dark reddish-brown color, or if it smells burned, it should be changed (see Section 25). If you are in doubt about its condition, purchase some new fluid and compare the two for color and smell.

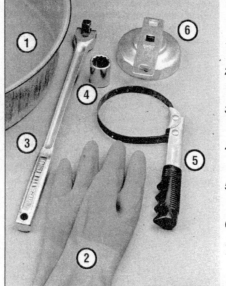

8   Engine oil and filter change (every 3000 miles or 3 months)

Refer to illustrations 8.2, 8.7, 8.12 and 8.15

1   Frequent oil changes are the most important preventive maintenance procedures that can be done by the home mechanic. As engine oil ages, in becomes diluted and contaminated, which leads to premature engine wear.

2   Make sure that you have all the necessary tools before you begin this procedure **(see illustration)**. You should also have plenty of rags or newspapers handy for mopping up oil spills.

3   Access to the oil drain plug and filter will be improved if the vehicle can be lifted on a hoist, driven onto ramps or supported by jackstands. **Warning:** Do not work under a

8.2 These tools are required when changing the engine oil and filter

1   **Drain pan** - It should be fairly shallow in depth, but wide to prevent spills

2   **Rubber gloves** - When removing the drain plug and filter, you will get oil on your hands (the gloves will prevent burns)

3   **Breaker bar** - Sometimes the oil drain plug is tight, and a long breaker bar is needed to loosen it

4   **Socket** – To be used with the breaker bar or a ratchet (must be the correct size to fit the drain plug - six-point preferred)

5   **Filter wrench** - This is a metal band-type wrench, which requires clearance around the filter to be effective

6   **Filter wrench** - This type fits on the bottom of the filter and can be turned with a ratchet or breaker bar (different-size wrenches are available for different types of filters)

vehicle supported only by a jack - always use jackstands!

4   If you haven't changed the oil on this vehicle before, get under it and locate the oil drain plug and the oil filter. The exhaust components will be warm as you work, so note how they are routed to avoid touching them when you are under the vehicle.

5   Start the engine and allow it to reach normal operating temperature - oil and sludge will flow out more easily when warm. If new oil, a filter or tools are needed, use the vehicle to go get them and warm up the engine/oil at the same time. Park on a level surface and shut off the engine when it's warmed up. Remove the oil filler cap from the valve cover.

6   Raise the vehicle and support it on jackstands. Make sure it is safely supported!

7   Being careful not to touch the hot

8.7 Use a proper size box-end wrench or socket to remove the oil drain plug and avoid rounding it off

8.12 The oil filter is usually on very tight and will require a special oil filter wrench to remove it - DO NOT use the wrench to tighten the new filter

8.15 Lubricate the oil filter gasket with clean engine oil before installing the filter on the engine

exhaust components, position a drain pan under the plug in the bottom of the engine, then remove the plug **(see illustration)**. It's a good idea to wear a rubber glove while unscrewing the plug the final few turns to avoid being scalded by hot oil.

8   It may be necessary to move the drain pan slightly as oil flow slows to a trickle. Inspect the old oil for the presence of metal particles.

9   After all the oil has drained, wipe off the drain plug with a clean rag. Any small metal particles clinging to the plug would immediately contaminate the new oil.

10   Clean the area around the drain plug opening, reinstall the plug and tighten it securely, but don't strip the threads.

11   Move the drain pan into position under the oil filter.

12   Loosen the oil filter by turning it counterclockwise with a filter wrench **(see illustration)**. Any standard filter wrench will work.

13   Once the filter is loose, use your hands to unscrew it from the block. Just as the filter is detached from the block, immediately tilt the open end up to prevent the oil inside the filter from spilling out.

14   Using a clean rag, wipe off the mounting surface on the block. Also, make sure that none of the old gasket remains stuck to the mounting surface. It can be removed with a scraper if necessary.

15   Compare the old filter with the new one to make sure they are the same type. Smear some engine oil on the rubber gasket of the new filter and screw it into place **(see illustration)**. Overtightening the filter will damage

the gasket, so don't use a filter wrench. Most filter manufacturers recommend tightening the filter by hand only. Normally they should be tightened 3/4-turn after the gasket contacts the block, but be sure to follow the directions on the filter or container.

16   Remove all tools and materials from under the vehicle, being careful not to spill the oil in the drain pan, then lower the vehicle.

17   Add new oil to the engine through the oil filler cap. Use a funnel to prevent oil from spilling onto the top of the engine. Pour four quarts of fresh oil into the engine. Wait a few minutes to allow the oil to drain into the pan, then check the level on the dipstick (see Section 4 if necessary). If the oil level is in the OK range (hatched area), install the filler cap.

18   Start the engine and run it for about a minute. While the engine is running, look

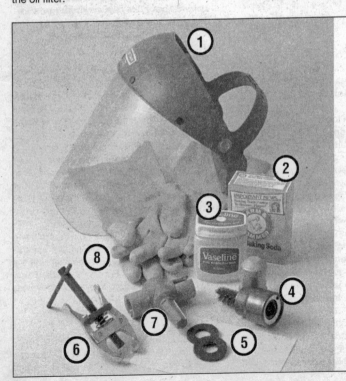

9.1 Tools and materials required for battery maintenance

1   *Face shield/safety goggles* - When removing corrosion with a brush, the acidic particles can easily fly up into your eyes

2   *Baking soda* - A solution of baking soda and water can be used to neutralize corrosion

3   *Petroleum jelly* - A layer of this on the battery posts will help prevent corrosion

4   *Battery post/cable cleaner* - This wire brush cleaning tool will remove all traces of corrosion from the battery posts and cable clamps

5   *Treated felt washers* - Placing one of these on each post, directly under the cable clamps, will help prevent corrosion

6   *Puller* - Sometimes the cable clamps are very difficult to pull off the posts, even after the nut/bolt has been completely loosened. This tool pulls the clamp straight up and off the post without damage

7   *Battery post/cable cleaner* - Here is another cleaning tool which is a slightly different version of Number 4 above, but it does the same thing

8   *Rubber gloves* - Another safety item to consider when servicing the battery; remember that's acid inside the battery!

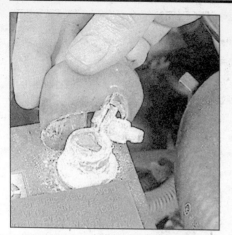

9.6a Battery terminal corrosion usually appears as light, fluffy powder

9.6b Removing the cable from a battery post with a wrench - sometimes special battery pliers are required for this procedure if corrosion has caused deterioration of the nut hex (always remove the ground cable first and hook it up last!)

9.7a When cleaning the cable clamps, all corrosion must be removed

9.7b Regardless of the type of tool used on the battery posts, a clean, shiny surface should be the result (the post is tapered to match the clamp, so don't remove too much material)

under the vehicle and check for leaks at the oil pan drain plug and around the oil filter. If either one is leaking, stop the engine and tighten the plug or filter slightly.

19 Wait a few minutes, then recheck the level on the dipstick. Add oil as necessary to bring the level into the OK range.

20 During the first few trips after an oil change, make it a point to check frequently for leaks and proper oil level.

21 The old oil drained from the engine cannot be reused in its present state and should be discarded. Oil reclamation centers, auto repair shops and gas stations will normally accept the oil, which can be recycled. After the oil has cooled, it can be drained into a container (plastic jugs, bottles, milk cartons, etc.) for transport to a disposal site.

9 Battery check, maintenance and charging (every 6000 miles or 6 months)

Refer to illustrations 9.1, 9.6a, 9.6b, 9.7a and 9.7b

Warning: *Certain precautions must be followed when checking and servicing the battery. Hydrogen gas, which is highly flammable, is always present in the battery cells, so keep lighted tobacco and all other open flames and sparks away from the battery. The electrolyte inside the battery is actually dilute sulfuric acid, which will cause injury if splashed on your skin or in your eyes. It will also ruin clothes and painted surfaces. When removing the battery cables, always detach the negative cable first and hook it up last!*

1 A routine preventive maintenance program for the battery in your vehicle is the only way to ensure quick and reliable starts. But before performing any battery maintenance, make sure that you have the proper equipment necessary to work safely around the battery **(see illustration)**.

2 There are also several precautions that should be taken whenever battery maintenance is performed. Before servicing the bat-

tery, always turn the engine and all accessories off and disconnect the cable from the negative terminal of the battery.

3 The battery produces hydrogen gas, which is both flammable and explosive. Never create a spark, smoke or light a match around the battery. Always charge the battery in a ventilated area.

4 Electrolyte contains poisonous and corrosive sulfuric acid. Do not allow it to get in your eyes, on your skin on your clothes. Never ingest it. Wear protective safety glasses when working near the battery. Keep children away from the battery.

5 Note the external condition of the battery. If the positive terminal and cable clamp on your vehicle's battery is equipped with a rubber protector, make sure that it's not torn or damaged. It should completely cover the terminal. Look for any corroded or loose connections, cracks in the case or cover or loose hold-down clamps. Also check the entire length of each cable for cracks and frayed conductors.

6 If corrosion, which looks like white, fluffy deposits **(see illustration)** is evident, particularly around the terminals, the battery should be removed for cleaning. Loosen the cable clamp bolts with a wrench, being careful to remove the ground cable first, and slide them off the terminals **(see illustration)**. Then disconnect the hold-down clamp bolt and nut, remove the clamp and lift the battery from the engine compartment.

7 Clean the cable clamps thoroughly with a battery brush or a terminal cleaner and a solution of warm water and baking soda **(see illustration)**. Wash the terminals and the top of the battery case with the same solution but make sure that the solution doesn't get into the battery. When cleaning the cables, terminals and battery top, wear safety goggles and rubber gloves to prevent any solution from coming in contact with your eyes or hands.

Wear old clothes too - even diluted, sulfuric acid splashed onto clothes will burn holes in them. If the terminals have been extensively corroded, clean them up with a terminal cleaner **(see illustration)**. Thoroughly wash all cleaned areas with plain water.

8 Make sure that the battery tray is in good condition and the hold-down clamp bolts are tight. If the battery is removed from the tray, make sure no parts remain in the bottom of the tray when the battery is reinstalled. When reinstalling the hold-down clamp bolts, do not overtighten them.

9 Information on removing and installing the battery can be found in Chapter 5. Information on jump starting can be found at the front of this manual. For more detailed battery checking procedures, refer to the *Haynes Automotive Electrical Manual.*

Cleaning

10 Corrosion on the hold-down components, battery case and surrounding areas can be removed with a solution of water and

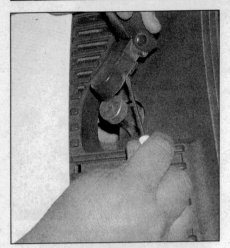

10.3 Lift the release lever with a small screwdriver and remove the wiper arm from the wiper shaft splines, then check them for corrosion

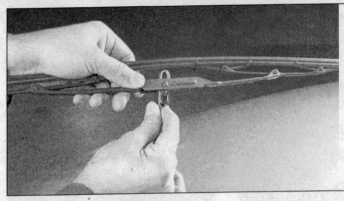

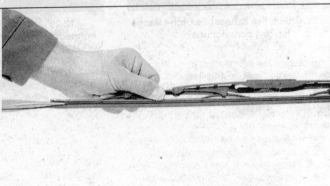

10.5 Press on the release tab and push the blade assembly down and away from the hook in the arm

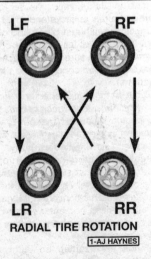

10.6 Use needle-nose pliers to compress the rubber element, then slide the element out - slide the new element in and lock the blade assembly fingers into the notches of the wiper element

baking soda. Thoroughly rinse all cleaned areas with plain water.

11   Any metal parts of the vehicle damaged by corrosion should be covered with a zinc-based primer, then painted.

Charging

Warning: *When batteries are being charged, hydrogen gas, which is very explosive and flammable, is produced. Do not smoke or allow open flames near a charging or a recently charged battery. Wear eye protection when near the battery during charging. Also, make sure the charger is unplugged before connecting or disconnecting the battery from the charger.*

12   Slow-rate charging is the best way to restore a battery that's discharged to the point where it will not start the engine. It's also a good way to maintain the battery charge in a vehicle that's only driven a few miles between starts. Maintaining the battery charge is particularly important in the winter when the battery must work harder to start the engine and electrical accessories that drain the battery are in greater use.

13   It's best to use a one or two-amp battery charger (sometimes called a "trickle" charger). They are the safest and put the least strain on the battery. They are also the least expensive. For a faster charge, you can use a higher amperage charger, but don't use one rated more than 1/10th the amp/hour rating of the battery. Rapid boost charges that claim to restore the power of the battery in one to two hours are hardest on the battery and can damage batteries not in good condition. This type of charging should only be used in emergency situations.

14   The average time necessary to charge a battery should be listed in the instructions that come with the charger. As a general rule, a trickle charger will charge a battery in 12 to 16 hours.

10   Windshield wiper blade inspection and replacement (every 6000 miles or 6 months)

Refer to illustrations 10.3, 10.5 and 10.6

1   The windshield wiper and blade assembly should be inspected periodically for damage, loose components and cracked or worn blade elements.

2   Road film can build up on the wiper blades and affect their efficiency, so they should be washed regularly with a mild detergent solution.

3   The action of the wiping mechanism can loosen bolts, nuts and fasteners, so they should be checked and tightened, as necessary, at the same time the wiper blades are checked. Use a small screwdriver to lift the release lever, detach the wiper arm and inspect the wiper shaft splines for corrosion **(see illustration)**. Clean the splines with a wire brush if necessary and press the wiper arm back into place until it locks.

4   If the wiper blade elements are cracked, worn or warped, or no longer clean adequately, they should be replaced with new ones.

5   Lift the arm assembly away from the glass for clearance, press on the release lever, then slide the wiper blade assembly out of the hook in the end of the arm **(see illustration)**.

6   Use needle-nose pliers to compress the blade element, then slide the element out of the frame and discard it **(see illustration)**.

7   Installation is the reverse of removal.

11   Tire rotation (every 6000 miles or 6 months)

Refer to illustration 11.2

1   The tires should be rotated at the specified intervals and whenever uneven wear is noticed. Since the vehicle will be raised and the tires removed anyway, check the brakes also (see Section 19).

2   Radial tires must be rotated in a specific pattern **(see illustration)**. If your vehicle has a compact spare tire, don't include it in the rotation pattern.

11.2 The recommended tire rotation pattern for these vehicles

12.2a Check the exhaust flex tube flange (arrow) connections . . .

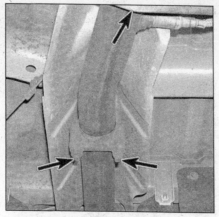

12.2b . . . and the exhaust pipe connections (arrow) for exhaust leaks - also check that the retaining nuts (arrows) or bolts are securely tightened

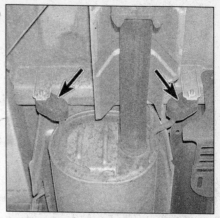

12.2c Check the exhaust system hangers (arrows) for damage and cracks

3   Refer to the information in *Jacking and towing* at the front of this manual for the proper procedure to follow when raising the vehicle and changing a tire. If the brakes must be checked, don't apply the parking brake as stated.

4   The vehicle must be raised on a hoist or supported on jackstands to get all four wheels off the ground. Make sure the vehicle is safely supported!

5   After the rotation procedure is finished, check and adjust the tire pressures as necessary and be sure to check the lug nut tightness.

12 Exhaust system check (every 6000 miles or 6 months)

Refer to illustrations 12.2a, 12.2b and 12.2c

1   With the engine cold (at least three hours after the vehicle has been driven), check the complete exhaust system from the engine to the end of the tailpipe. Ideally, the inspection should be done with the vehicle on a hoist to permit unrestricted access. If a hoist isn't available, raise the vehicle and support it securely on jackstands.

2   Check the exhaust pipes and connections for evidence of leaks, severe corrosion and damage. Make sure that all brackets and hangers are in good condition and tight **(see illustrations)**.

3   At the same time, inspect the underside of the body for holes, corrosion, open seams, etc. which may allow exhaust gases to enter the passenger compartment. Seal all body openings with silicone or body putty.

4   Rattles and other noises can often be traced to the exhaust system, especially the mounts and hangers. Try to move the pipes, muffler and catalytic converter. If the components can come in contact with the body or suspension parts, secure the exhaust system with new mounts.

5   Check the running condition of the engine by inspecting inside the end of the tailpipe. The exhaust deposits here are an indication of engine state-of-tune. If the pipe

is black and sooty or coated with white deposits, the engine may need a tune-up, including a thorough fuel system inspection and adjustment.

13 Seat belt check (every 6000 miles or 6 months)

1   Check seat belts, buckles, latch plates and guide loops for obvious damage and signs of wear.

2   See if the seat belt reminder light comes on when the key is turned to the Run or Start position. A chime should also sound. On passive restraint systems, the shoulder belt should move into position in the A-pillar.

3   The seat belts are designed to lock up during a sudden stop or impact, yet allow free movement during normal driving. Make sure the retractors return the belt against your chest while driving and rewind the belt fully when the buckle is unlatched.

4   If any of the above checks reveal problems with the seat belt system, replace parts as necessary.

14 Drivebelt check, adjustment and replacement (every 6000 miles or 6 months)

Refer to illustrations 14.3, 14.4, 14.5a, 14.5b and 14.5c

Check

1   The alternator, power steering pump and air conditioning compressor drivebelts are located at the right end of the engine. The good condition and proper adjustment of the alternator belt is critical to the operation of the engine. Because of their composition and the high stresses to which they are subjected, drivebelts stretch and deteriorate as they get older. They must therefore be periodically inspected.

2   The number of belts used on a particular vehicle depends on the accessories installed. The main belt transmits power from the crankshaft to the water pump and the power steering pump. The second belt transmits power from the crankshaft to the alternator and the third belt drives the air conditioning compressor.

3   With the engine off, open the hood and locate the drivebelts. With a flashlight, check

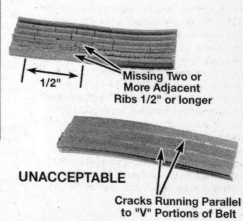

14.3 Here are some of the more common problems associated with drivebelts (check the belts very carefully to prevent an untimely breakdown)

Cracks Running Across "V" Portions of Belt
ACCEPTABLE

1/2"
Missing Two or More Adjacent Ribs 1/2" or longer

UNACCEPTABLE

Cracks Running Parallel to "V" Portions of Belt

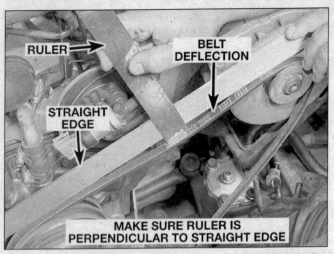

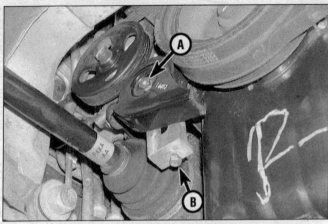

14.4 Measuring drivebelt deflection with a straightedge and ruler

14.5a To adjust the power steering/water pump drivebelt, loosen the tensioner pulley lock nut (A) then turn the adjusting bolt (B) counterclockwise to loosen or clockwise to tighten the belt

each belt for separation of the adhesive rubber on both sides of the core, core separation from the belt side, a severed core, separation of the ribs from the adhesive rubber, cracking or separation of the ribs, and torn or worn ribs or cracks in the inner ridges of the ribs **(see illustration)**. Also check for fraying and glazing, which gives the belt a shiny appearance. Both sides of the belt should be inspected, which means you will have to twist the belt to check the underside. Use your fingers to feel the belt where you can't see it. If any of the above conditions are evident, replace the belt (go to Step 6).

4   Check the belt tension by pushing firmly on the belt with your thumb at a distance halfway between the pulleys and note how far the belt can be pushed (deflected). Measure this deflection with a ruler **(see illustration)**. The belt should deflect 1/4-inch if the distance from pulley center to pulley center is between 7 and 11 inches; the belt should deflect 1/2-inch if the distance from pulley center to pulley center is between 12 and 16 inches.

Adjustment

5   Belt tension of the power steering pump and water pump is adjusted by moving the tensioner pulley **(see illustration)**. To adjust the air conditioning compressor belt, loosen the tensioner pulley bolt and turn the tensioner adjusting bolt **(see illustration)**. The alternator drivebelt is adjusted by loosening the adjuster lock bolt, then turning the adjusting bolt **(see illustration)**. Measure the belt tension in accordance with the above method. Repeat this Step until the drivebelt is adjusted properly.

Replacement

6   To replace a belt, loosen the drivebelt adjustment bolt, slip the belt off the crankshaft pulley and remove it. If you are replacing the alternator/power steering pump/water pump belts, you'll have to remove the air conditioning compressor belt

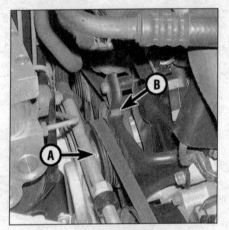

14.5b To adjust the air conditioning compressor drivebelt, loosen the tensioner pulley bolt (A) and turn the adjusting bolt (B)

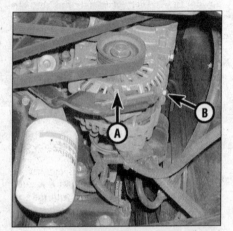

14.5c To adjust the alternator drivebelt, loosen the adjuster lock bolt (A) and turn the adjusting bolt (B)

first because of the way they are arranged on the crankshaft pulley. Because of this and because belts tend to wear out more or less together, it is a good idea to replace all of the belts at the same time. Mark each belt and its appropriate pulley groove so the replacement belts can be installed in their proper positions.
7   Take the old belts to the parts store in order to make a direct comparison for length, width and design.
8   After replacing ribbed drivebelts, make sure that it fits properly in the ribbed grooves in the pulleys. It is essential that the belt be properly centered.
9   Adjust the belt(s) in accordance with the procedure outlined above.

15   Underhood hose check and replacement (every 15,000 miles or 12 months)

Warning: *Replacement of air conditioning hoses must be left to a dealer service depart-*

ment or air conditioning shop that has the equipment to depressurize the system safely. Never remove air conditioning components or hoses until the system has been depressurized.

General

1   High temperatures under the hood can cause deterioration of the rubber and plastic hoses used for engine, accessory and emission systems operation. Periodic inspection should be made for cracks, loose clamps, material hardening and leaks.
2   Information specific to the cooling system hoses can be found in Section 16.
3   Most (but not all) hoses are secured to the fittings with clamps. Where clamps are used, check to be sure they haven't lost their tension, allowing the hose to leak. If clamps aren't used, make sure the hose has not expanded and/or hardened where it slips over the fitting, allowing it to leak.

PCV system hose

4   To reduce hydrocarbon emissions, crankcase blow-by gas is vented through the

PCV valve in the rocker arm cover to the intake manifold via a rubber hose on most models. The blow-by gases mix with incoming air in the intake manifold before being burned in the combustion chambers.

5 Check the PCV hose for cracks, leaks and other damage. Disconnect it from the valve cover and the intake manifold and check the inside for obstructions. If it's clogged, clean it out with solvent.

Vacuum hoses

6 It's quite common for vacuum hoses, especially those in the emissions system, to be color coded or identified by colored stripes molded into them. Various systems require hoses with different wall thickness, collapse resistance and temperature resistance. When replacing hoses, be sure the new ones are made of the same material.

7 Often the only effective way to check a hose is to remove it completely from the vehicle. If more than one hose is removed, be sure to label the hoses and fittings to ensure correct installation.

8 When checking vacuum hoses, be sure to include any plastic T-fittings in the check. Inspect the fittings for cracks and the hose where it fits over each fitting for distortion, which could cause leakage.

9 A small piece of vacuum hose (1/4-inch inside diameter) can be used as a stethoscope to detect vacuum leaks. Hold one end of the hose to your ear and probe around vacuum hoses and fittings, listening for the "hissing" sound characteristic of a vacuum leak. **Warning:** *When probing with the vacuum hose stethoscope, be careful not to come into contact with moving engine components such as drivebelts, the cooling fan, etc.*

Fuel hose

Warning: *Gasoline is extremely flammable, so take extra precautions when you work on any part of the fuel system. Don't smoke or allow open flames or bare light bulbs near the work area, and don't work in a garage where a natural gas-type appliance (such as a water heater or clothes dryer) with a pilot light is present. Since gasoline is carcinogenic, wear latex gloves when there's a possibility of being exposed to fuel, and, if you spill any fuel on your skin, rinse it off immediately with soap and water. Mop up any spills immediately and do not store fuel-soaked rags where they could ignite. The fuel system is under constant pressure, so, if any fuel lines are to be disconnected, the fuel pressure in the system must be relieved first (see Chapter 4 for more information). When you perform any kind of work on the fuel system, wear safety glasses and have a Class B type fire extinguisher on hand.*

10 The fuel lines are usually under pressure, so if any fuel lines are to be disconnected be prepared to catch spilled fuel. **Warning:** *Your vehicle is equipped with fuel injection and you must relieve the fuel system*

pressure before servicing the fuel lines. Refer to Chapter 4 for the fuel system pressure relief procedure.

11 Check all flexible fuel lines for deterioration and chafing. Check especially for cracks in areas where the hose bends and just before fittings, such as where a hose attaches to the fuel pump, fuel filter and fuel injection unit.

12 When replacing a hose, use only hose that is specifically designed for high-pressure fuel injection systems.

13 Spring-type clamps are sometimes used on fuel return or vapor lines. These clamps often lose their tension over a period of time, and can be "sprung" during removal. Replace all spring-type clamps with screw clamps whenever a hose is replaced. Some fuel lines use spring-lock type couplings, which require a special tool to disconnect. See Chapter 4 for more information on these type of couplings.

Metal lines

14 Sections of metal line are often used for fuel line between the fuel pump and the fuel injection unit. Check carefully to make sure the line isn't bent, crimped or cracked.

15 If a section of metal fuel line must be replaced, use seamless steel tubing only, since copper and aluminum tubing do not have the strength necessary to withstand vibration caused by the engine.

16 Check the metal brake lines where they enter the master cylinder and brake proportioning unit (if used) for cracks in the lines and loose fittings. Any sign of brake fluid leakage calls for an immediate thorough inspection of the brake system.

---

16 Cooling system check (every 15,000 miles or 12 months)

Refer to illustration 16.4

1 Many major engine failures can be attributed to a faulty cooling system. If the vehicle is equipped with an automatic transaxle, the cooling system also cools the transaxle fluid and thus plays an important role in prolonging transaxle life.

2 The cooling system should be checked with the engine cold. Do this before the vehicle is driven for the day or after the engine has been shut off for at least three hours.

3 Remove the radiator cap by turning it to the left until it reaches a stop. If you hear a hissing sound (indicating there is still pressure in the system), wait until it stops. Now press down on the cap with the palm of your hand and continue turning to the left until the cap can be removed. Thoroughly clean the cap, inside and out, with clean water. Also clean the filler neck on the radiator. All traces of corrosion should be removed. The coolant inside the radiator should be relatively transparent. If it's rust colored, the system should be drained and refilled (see Section 24). If the coolant level isn't up to the top, add addi-

Check for a chafed area that could fail prematurely.

Check for a soft area indicating the hose has deteriorated inside.

Overtightening the clamp on a hardened hose will damage the hose and cause a leak.

Check each hose for swelling and oil-soaked ends. Cracks and breaks can be located by squeezing the hose.

16.4 Hoses, like drivebelts, have a habit of failing at the worst possible time - to prevent the inconvenience of a blown radiator or heater hose, inspect them carefully as shown here

---

tional antifreeze/coolant mixture (see Section 4).

4 Carefully check the large upper and lower radiator hoses along with the smaller diameter heater hoses which run from the engine to the firewall. Inspect each hose along its entire length, replacing any hose which is cracked, swollen or shows signs of deterioration. Cracks may become more apparent if the hose is squeezed **(see illustration).** Regardless of condition, it's a good idea to replace hoses with new ones every two years.

5 Make sure that all hose connections are tight. A leak in the cooling system will usually show up as white or rust colored deposits on the areas adjoining the leak. If spring-type clamps are used at the ends of the hoses, it is a good idea to replace them with more secure screw-type clamps.

6   Use compressed air or a soft brush to remove bugs, leaves, etc. from the front of the radiator or air conditioning condenser. Be careful not to damage the delicate cooling fins or cut yourself on them.

7   Every other inspection, or at the first indication of cooling system problems, have the cap and system pressure tested. If you don't have a pressure tester, most gas stations and repair shops will do this for a minimal charge.

17   Fuel system check (every 15,000 miles or 12 months)

Refer to illustrations 17.5 and 17.6
Warning: *Gasoline is extremely flammable, so take extra precautions when you work on any part of the fuel system. Don't smoke or allow open flames or bare light bulbs near the work area, and don't work in a garage where a natural gas-type appliance (such as a water heater or clothes dryer) with a pilot light is present. Since gasoline is carcinogenic, wear latex gloves when there's a possibility of being exposed to fuel, and, if you spill any fuel on your skin, rinse it off immediately with soap and water. Mop up any spills immediately and do not store fuel-soaked rags where they could ignite. When you perform any kind of work on the fuel system, wear safety glasses and have a Class B type fire extinguisher on hand. The fuel system is under constant pressure, so, before any lines are disconnected, the fuel system pressure must be relieved. See Chapter 4.*

1   If you smell gasoline while driving or after the vehicle has been sitting in the sun, inspect the fuel system immediately.

2   Remove the gas filler cap and inspect it for damage and corrosion. The gasket should have an unbroken sealing imprint. If the gasket is damaged or corroded, install a new cap.

3   Inspect the fuel feed and return lines for cracks. Make sure that the connections between the fuel lines and the fuel injection system and between the fuel lines and the in-line fuel filter are tight. **Warning:** *Your vehicle is fuel injected, so you must relieve the fuel system pressure before servicing fuel system components. The fuel system pressure relief procedure is outlined in Chapter 4.*

4   Since some components of the fuel system - the fuel tank and part of the fuel feed and return lines, for example - are underneath the vehicle, they can be inspected more easily with the vehicle raised on a hoist. If that's not possible, raise the vehicle and support it on jackstands.

5   With the vehicle raised and safely supported, inspect the gas tank and filler neck for punctures, cracks and other damage. The connection between the filler neck and the tank is particularly critical. Sometimes a rubber filler neck will leak because of loose clamps or deteriorated rubber **(see illustration)**. Inspect all fuel tank mounting brackets

17.5 Inspect fuel filler hoses for cracks and make sure the clamps (arrows) are tight

and straps to be sure that the tank is securely attached to the vehicle. **Warning:** *Do not, under any circumstances, try to repair a fuel tank (except rubber components). A welding torch or any open flame can easily cause fuel vapors inside the tank to explode.*

6   Carefully check all rubber hoses and metal lines leading away from the fuel tank **(see illustration)**. Check for loose connections, deteriorated hoses, crimped lines and other damage. Repair or replace damaged sections as necessary (see Chapter 4).

18   Suspension, steering and driveaxle boot check (every 15,000 miles or 12 months)

Note: *The steering linkage and suspension components should be checked periodically. Worn or damaged suspension and steering linkage components can result in excessive and abnormal tire wear, poor ride quality and vehicle handling, and reduced fuel economy. For detailed illustrations of the steering and suspension components, refer to Chapter 10.*

Shock absorber check

Refer to illustration 18.6
1   Park the vehicle on level ground, turn the engine off and set the parking brake. Check the tire pressures.

2   Push down at one corner of the vehicle, then release it while noting the movement of the body. It should stop moving and come to rest in a level position within one or two bounces.

3   If the vehicle continues to move up-and-down or if it fails to return to its original position, a worn or weak shock absorber is probably the reason.

4   Repeat the above check at each of the three remaining corners of the vehicle.

5   Raise the vehicle and support it securely on jackstands.

6   Check the front struts and rear shock absorbers for evidence of fluid leakage **(see**

17.6 Carefully inspect fuel line couplings for damage

illustration). A light film of fluid is no cause for concern. Make sure that any fluid noted is from the shocks and not from some other source. If leakage is noted, replace the shocks as a set.

7   Check the shocks to be sure that they are securely mounted and undamaged. Check the upper mounts for damage and wear. If damage or wear is noted, replace the shocks as a set (front or rear).

8   If the shocks must be replaced, refer to Chapter 10 for the procedure.

Steering and suspension check

Refer to illustrations 18.9a, 18.9b and 18.11
9   Visually inspect the steering and suspension components for damage and distortion. Look for damaged seals, boots and bushings and leaks of any kind **(see illustrations)**.

10   Clean the lower end of the steering knuckle. Have an assistant grasp the lower edge of the tire and move the wheel in-and-out while you look for movement at the steering knuckle-to-control arm balljoint. If there is any movement the suspension balljoint(s) must be replaced.

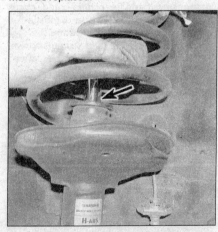

18.6 Check the front struts for leakage at the indicated area

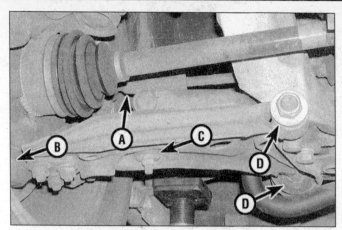

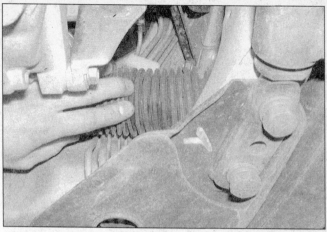

18.9a Inspect the tie-rod ends and lower balljoints for torn grease seals (A and B); check the stabilizer bar link bushings and control arm bushings (C and D) for cracking and general deterioration

18.9b Check the steering gear boots for cracks and leaking steering fluid

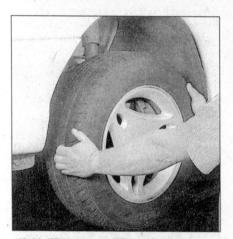

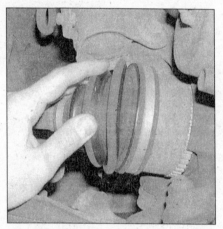

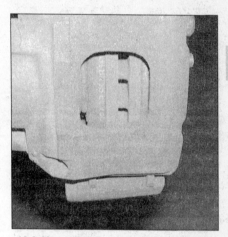

18.11 With the steering wheel in the lock position and the vehicle raised, grasp the front tire as shown and try to move it back-and-forth - if any play is noted, check the steering gear mounts and tie rod ends for looseness

18.14 Flex the inner and outer driveaxle boots by hand to check for cracks and/or leaking grease

19.6 You will find an inspection hole like this in each caliper - placing a ruler across the hole should enable you to determine the thickness of remaining pad material on the inner pad

11   Grasp each front tire at the front and rear edges, push in at the front, pull out at the rear and feel for play in the steering system components If any freeplay is noted, check the steering gear mounts and the tie-rod ends for looseness **(see illustration).**

12   Additional steering and suspension system information and illustrations can be found in Chapter 10.

Driveaxle boot check)

Refer to illustration 18.14

13   The driveaxle boots are very important because they prevent dirt, water and foreign material from entering and damaging the constant velocity (CV) joints. Oil and grease can cause the boot material to deteriorate prematurely, so it's a good idea to wash the boots with soap and water. Because it constantly pivots back and forth following the steering action of the front hub, the outer CV boot wears out sooner and should be inspected regularly.

14   Inspect the boots for tears and cracks as well as loose clamps **(see illustration).** If there is any evidence of cracks or leaking lubricant, they must be replaced as described in Chapter 8.

19   Brake check (every 15,000 miles or 12 months)

Warning: *The dust created by the brake system may contain asbestos, which is harmful to your health. Never blow it out with compressed air and don't inhale any of it. An approved filtering mask should be worn when working on the brakes. Do not, under any circumstances, use petroleum-based solvents to clean brake parts. Use brake system cleaner only! Try to use non-asbestos replacement parts whenever possible.*

Note: *For detailed photographs of the brake system, refer to Chapter 9.*

1   In addition to the specified intervals, the brakes should be inspected every time the wheels are removed or whenever a defect is suspected.

2   Any of the following symptoms could indicate a potential brake system defect: The vehicle pulls to one side when the brake pedal is depressed; the brakes make squealing or dragging noises when applied; brake pedal travel is excessive; the pedal pulsates; brake fluid leaks, usually onto the inside of the tire or wheel.

3   Loosen the wheel lug nuts.

4   Raise the vehicle and place it securely on jackstands.

5   Remove the wheels (see *Jacking and towing* at the front of this manual, or your owner's manual, if necessary).

Disc brakes

Refer to illustrations 19.6, 19.9 and 19.11

6   There are two pads (an outer and an inner) in each caliper. The pads are visible through inspection holes in each caliper **(see illustration).**

7   Check the pad thickness by looking at each end of the caliper and through the inspection hole in the caliper body. If the lin-

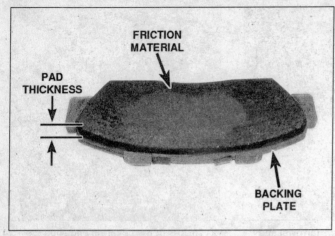

19.9 Measure the pad thickness to determine how much friction material remains on the brake backing plate

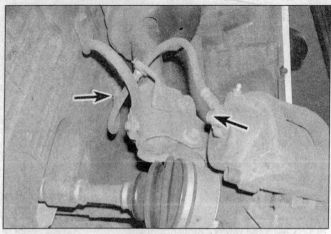

19.11 Check along the brake hoses and at each fitting (arrows) for deterioration and cracks

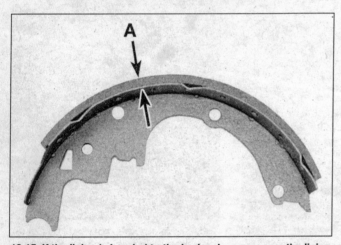

19.15 If the lining is bonded to the brake shoe, measure the lining thickness from the outer surface to the metal shoe, as shown here. If the lining is riveted to the shoe, measure from the lining outer surface to the rivet head

19.16 Typical assembled view of a rear drum brake (left side shown, right side is the exact opposite)

ing material is less than the thickness listed in this Chapter's Specifications, replace the pads. **Note:** *Keep in mind that the lining material is riveted or bonded to a metal backing plate and the metal portion is not included in this measurement.*

8   If it is difficult to determine the exact thickness of the remaining pad material by the above method, or if you are at all concerned about the condition of the pads, remove the caliper(s), then remove the pads from the calipers for further inspection (refer to Chapter 9).

9   Once the pads are removed from the calipers, clean them with brake cleaner and re-measure them with a ruler or a vernier caliper **(see illustration)**.

10   Measure the disc thickness with a micrometer to make sure that it still has service life remaining. If any disc is thinner than the specified minimum thickness, replace it (refer to Chapter 9). Even if the disc has service life remaining, check its condition. Look for scoring, gouging and burned spots. If these conditions exist, remove the disc and

have it resurfaced (see Chapter 9).

11   Before installing the wheels, check all brake lines and hoses for damage, wear, deformation, cracks, corrosion, leakage, bends and twists, particularly in the vicinity of the rubber hoses at the calipers **(see illustration)**. Check the clamps for tightness and the connections for leakage. Make sure that all hoses and lines are clear of sharp edges, moving parts and the exhaust system. If any of the above conditions are noted, repair, reroute or replace the lines and/or fittings as necessary (see Chapter 9).

Drum brakes

Refer to illustrations 19.15, 19.16 and 19.17

12   On rear drum brakes, make sure the parking brake is off then proceed to tap on the outside of the drum with a rubber mallet to loosen it.

13   Remove the brake drums.

14   With the drums removed, carefully clean the brake assembly with brake system cleaner. **Warning:** *Don't blow the dust out with compressed air and don't inhale any of it*

(it may contain asbestos, which is harmful to your health).

15   Note the thickness of the lining material on both front and rear brake shoes. If the material has worn away to within 1/16-inch of the recessed rivets or 1/8-inch of the metal backing on bonded type shoes, the shoes should be replaced **(see illustration)**. The shoes should also be replaced if they're cracked, glazed (shiny areas), or covered with brake fluid.

16   Make sure all the brake assembly springs are connected and in good condition **(see illustration)**.

17   Check the brake components for signs of fluid leakage. With your finger or a small screwdriver, carefully pry back the rubber cups on the wheel cylinder located at the top of the brake shoes **(see illustration)**. Any leakage here is an indication that the wheel cylinders should be overhauled immediately (see Chapter 9). Also, check all hoses and connections for signs of leakage.

18   Wipe the inside of the drum with a clean rag and rubbing alcohol or brake system

19.17 Check the wheel cylinder boots for leaking fluid indicating that the cylinder must be replaced or rebuilt

20.2a Detach the clips (arrows) and separate the cover from the air cleaner housing

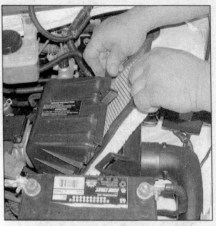

20.2b Lift the cover up and slide the element out of the housing

21.3 The fuel filter is mounted in a clip on the firewall on most models - detach it from the clip for access to the fuel lines

cleaner. Again, be careful not to breathe the dangerous asbestos dust.

19   Check the inside of the drum for cracks, score marks, deep scratches and "hard spots" which will appear as small discolored areas. If imperfections cannot be removed with fine emery cloth, the drum must be taken to an automotive machine shop for resurfacing.

20   Repeat the procedure for the remaining wheel. If the inspection reveals that all parts are in good condition, reinstall the brake drums, install the wheels and lower the vehicle to the ground.

Brake booster check

21   Sit in the driver's seat and perform the following sequence of tests.

22   With the brake fully depressed, start the engine - the pedal should move down a little when the engine starts.

23   With the engine running, depress the brake pedal several times - the travel distance should not change.

24   Depress the brake, stop the engine and hold the pedal in for about 30 seconds - the pedal should neither sink nor rise.

25   Restart the engine, run it for about a minute and turn it off. Then firmly depress the brake several times - the pedal travel should decrease with each application.

26   If your brakes do not operate as described, the brake booster has failed. Refer to Chapter 9 for the replacement procedure.

Parking brake

27   Rear drum brakes utilize a self-adjusting parking brake mechanism and do not require regular scheduled maintenance or routine adjustment. For more detailed information on the parking brake assembly see Chapter 9.

20   Air filter check and replacement (every 30,000 miles or 24 months)

Refer to illustrations 20.2a and 20.2b

1   The air filter is located inside a housing at the left (driver's) side of the engine compartment.

2   To remove the air filter, release the spring clips that secure the two halves of the air cleaner housing together, then lift the cover up and remove the air filter element **(see illustrations)**.

3   Inspect the outer surface of the filter element. If it is dirty, replace it. If it is only moderately dusty, it can be reused by blowing it clean from the back to the front surface with compressed air. Because it is a pleated paper type filter, it cannot be washed or oiled. If it cannot be cleaned satisfactorily with compressed air, discard and replace it. While the cover is off, be careful not to drop anything down into the housing. **Caution:** *Never drive the vehicle with the air cleaner removed. Excessive engine wear could result and backfiring could even cause a fire under the hood.*

4   Wipe out the inside of the air cleaner housing.

5   Place the new filter into the air cleaner housing, making sure it seats properly.

6   Installation of the housing is the reverse of removal.

21   Fuel filter replacement (every 30,000 miles or 24 months)

Refer to illustration 21.3

Warning: *Gasoline is extremely flammable, so take extra precautions when you work on any part of the fuel system. Don't smoke or allow open flames or bare light bulbs near the work area, and don't work in a garage where a natural gas-type appliance (such as a water heater or clothes dryer) with a pilot light is present. Since gasoline is carcinogenic, wear latex gloves when there's a possibility of being exposed to fuel, and, if you spill any fuel on your skin, rinse it off immediately with soap and water. Mop up any spills immediately and do not store fuel-soaked rags where they could ignite. When you perform any kind of work on the fuel system, wear safety glasses and have a Class B type fire extin-*

guisher on hand.

1   The canister-type filter is mounted in a clip on the firewall below the brake fluid reservoir on most models. On some models it is located below the vehicle and is held in place by a clamp.

2   Depressurize the fuel system (see Chapter 4), then disconnect the cable from the negative terminal of the battery.

3   On firewall-mounted filters, detach the filter from the bracket, loosen the screw clamps, then detach the hoses from the top and bottom of the fuel filter and remove it **(see illustration)**. On filters located under the vehicle, detach the hoses from the filter, then loosen the nuts and remove the filter from the bracket, noting the direction of installation.

4   Note that the inlet and outlet pipes are clearly labeled on their respective ends of the filter. Make sure the new filter is installed so that it's facing the proper direction as noted above. When correctly installed, the filter should be installed so the outlet pipe faces up and the inlet pipe faces down on firewall-mounted filters. On filters mounted under the vehicle, the outlet pipe should face forward and the inlet pipe toward the rear of the vehicle.

22.8 The idle adjustment screw is located at the top of the upper intake manifold (plenum)

5   Installation is the reverse of removal.
6   Install the inlet and outlet fittings and tighten the screw clamps securely. Reconnect the battery cable, start the engine and check for leaks.

22   Idle speed check and adjustment (every 30,000 miles or 24 months)

Refer to illustration 22.8
1   Engine idle speed is the speed at which the engine operates when no accelerator pedal pressure is applied, as when stopped at a traffic light. This speed is critical to the performance of the engine itself, as well as many subsystems.

Check

2   Connect a hand-held tachometer in accordance with the tool manufacturer's instructions.
3   Set the parking brake firmly and block the wheels to prevent the vehicle from rolling. Place the transaxle in Park or Neutral.
4   Start the engine and allow it to warm up to normal operating temperature. Run the engine at around 2000 rpm for two minutes, increasing the speed to over 3000 rpm three times, then allow the engine to idle for one minute.
5   Stop the engine and disconnect the electrical connector from the Idle Air Control (IAC) valve (see Chapter 4).
6   Start the engine, increase its speed to over 3000 rpm three times and let the engine idle.
7   Note the idle speed rpm on the tachometer and compare it to that listed on the VECI label or in this Chapter's Specifications. **Note:** *If the idle speed listed on the VECI label is different than that listed in this Chapter's Specifications, use the specification shown on the VECI label.*

Adjustment

8   If the idle speed is too low or too high, turn the idle speed adjustment screw to obtain the specified idle speed **(see illustration)**.

9   Shut the engine off and connect the IAC valve electrical connector.
10   Start the engine and make sure the idle speed is still correct with the IAC valve connected. If the idle speed is incorrect or cannot be adjusted, check the IAC assembly and verify that there are no defective components or intake leaks that will cause the idle to fluctuate abnormally (see Chapter 4).
11   Turn off the engine and disconnect the tachometer.

23   Ignition timing check and adjustment (every 30,000 miles or 24 months)

Note: *It is imperative that the procedures included on the tune-up or Vehicle Emissions Control Information (VECI) label be followed when adjusting the ignition timing. The label will include all information concerning preliminary steps to be performed before adjusting the timing, as well as the timing specifications.*

Check

Refer to illustration 23.1
1   With the ignition switch off, connect a timing light in accordance with the tool manufacturer's instructions **(see illustration)**. Install the inductive pick-up onto the number one cylinder spark plug wire.
2   Set the parking brake firmly and block the wheels to prevent the vehicle from rolling. Place the transaxle in Park or Neutral.
3   Locate the timing notches on the crankshaft pulley and the pointer on the timing cover. The notches on the pulley are spaced 5 degrees apart and the yellow mark indicates Top Dead Center (TDC). Count to the right of the yellow TDC mark to find the specified notch (three notches indicates 15-degrees BTDC, for instance). Mark the notch with white paint or chalk so it will be easy to see.
4   Start the engine, allow it to warm up to normal operating temperature and verify that the idle speed is correct (see Section 22). Rev up the engine to approximately 3000 rpm a few times, then let the engine idle. Stop the engine and disconnect the electrical connector from the Idle Air Control (IAC) valve (see Chapter 4).
5   Start the engine, aim the timing light at the timing marks on the front of the engine and check the ignition timing. The specified notch on the pulley will appear stationary and be aligned with the pointer if the timing is correct. **Note:** *If the ignition timing listed on the VECI label is different than that listed in this Chapter's Specifications, use the specification shown on the VECI label.*

Adjustment

6   If an adjustment is required, loosen the adjusting bolt and rotate the distributor slightly until the timing is correct.
7   Tighten the adjusting bolt and recheck

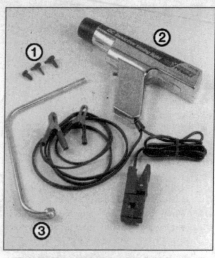

23.1 Tools needed to check and adjust the ignition timing

1   Vacuum plugs - *Vacuum plugs will, in most cases, have to be disconnected and plugged. Molded plugs in various shapes and sizes are available for this*
2   Inductive pick-up timing light - *flashes a bright, concentrated beam of light when the number one spark plug fires. Connect the leads according to the instructions supplied with the light*
3   Distributor wrench - *On some models, the hold-down bolt for the distributor is difficult to reach and turn with conventional wrenches or sockets. A special wrench like this must be used*

the timing.
8   Shut the engine off, connect the IAC valve electrical connector and disconnect the timing light.

24   Cooling system servicing (draining, flushing and refilling) (every 30,000 miles or 24 months)

Refer to illustrations 24.5, 24.6, 24.13, 24.18, 24.19 and 24.22
Warning: *Do not allow antifreeze to come in contact with your skin or painted surfaces of the vehicle. Rinse off spills immediately with plenty of water. Antifreeze is highly toxic if ingested. Never leave antifreeze lying around in an open container or in puddles on the floor; children and pets are attracted by it's sweet smell and may drink it. Check with local authorities about disposing of used antifreeze. Many communities have collection centers which will see that antifreeze is disposed of safely.*
1   Periodically, the cooling system should be drained, flushed and refilled to replenish the antifreeze mixture and prevent formation of rust and corrosion, which can impair the performance of the cooling system and cause engine damage.

24.5 Push the radiator cap downward and rotate it counterclockwise - never remove it when the engine is hot!

2   At the same time the cooling system is serviced, all hoses and the radiator cap should be inspected and replaced if defective (see Section 16).

3   Since antifreeze is poisonous, be careful not to spill any of the coolant mixture on your skin. Also, antifreeze will damage paint. If antifreeze contacts your skin or the vehicle's paint, rinse it off immediately with plenty of clean water. Consult local authorities about the dumping of antifreeze before draining the cooling system. In many areas, reclamation centers have been set up to collect automobile oil and drained antifreeze/water mixtures, rather than allowing them to be added to the sewage system.

Draining

Warning: *Wait until the engine is completely cool before beginning this procedure.*

4   Apply the parking brake and block the wheels. If the vehicle has just been driven, wait several hours to allow the engine to cool down before beginning this procedure.

5   Once the engine is completely cool, remove the radiator cap and the reservoir cap

24.6 The radiator drain fitting (arrow) is located at the lower corner of the radiator - connect a hose to the port on the fitting and direct the hose into a drain pan

(see illustration).

6   Drain the radiator by opening the drain plug at the bottom of the radiator **(see illustration)**. If the drain plug is corroded and can't be turned easily, or if the radiator isn't equipped with a plug, disconnect the lower radiator hose to allow the coolant to drain. Be careful not to get antifreeze on your skin or in your eyes.

7   After the coolant stops flowing out of the radiator, remove the lower radiator hose and allow the remaining coolant in the engine block to drain. If the vehicle is equipped with an auxiliary (rear) heater, disconnect the heater hoses and drain the coolant into a container, then reconnect the hoses.

8   While the coolant is draining from the engine block, disconnect the hose from the coolant reservoir and remove the reservoir (see Chapter 3 if necessary). Flush the reservoir out with water until it's clean, and if necessary, wash the inside with soapy water and a brush to make reading the fluid level easier.

9   While the coolant is draining, check the condition of the radiator hoses, heater hoses

and clamps (refer to Section 16 if necessary).

10   Replace any damaged clamps or hoses.

Flushing

11   Once the system is completely drained, remove the thermostat from the engine (see Chapter 3). Then reinstall the thermostat housing without the thermostat. This will allow the system to be flushed.

12   Reinstall the radiator hoses and tighten the radiator drain plug.

13   Disconnect the upper radiator hose from the radiator, then place a garden hose in the upper radiator inlet and flush the system until the water runs clear out of the upper radiator hose **(see illustration)**.

14   In severe cases of contamination or clogging of the radiator, remove the radiator (see Chapter 3) and have a radiator repair facility clean and repair it if necessary.

15   Many deposits can be removed by the chemical action of a cleaner available at auto parts stores. Follow the procedure outlined in the manufacturer's instructions. **Note:** *When the coolant is regularly drained and the system refilled with the correct antifreeze/water mixture, there should be no need to use chemical cleaners or descalers.*

Refilling

Caution: *During refilling it is necessary to bleed the cooling system of air. If this is not done, overheating (and subsequent engine damage) may result.*

16   To refill the system, install the thermostat, reconnect any radiator hoses and install the reservoir and the overflow hose.

17   Place the heater temperature control in the maximum heat position. If equipped with a rear heater, set the rear heater control to the maximum heat position also.

18   Loosen the air relief plug on the passenger's side of the radiator three turns **(see illustration)**.

19   Locate the engine air relief plug near the back of the upper intake manifold (plenum)

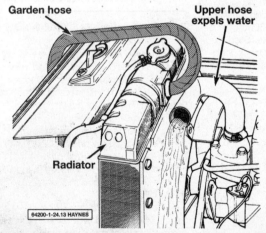

24.13 With the thermostat removed, disconnect the upper radiator hose and flush the radiator and engine block with a garden hose

Garden hose

Upper hose expels water

Radiator

64200-1-24.13 HAYNES

24.18 The radiator air relief plug is located on the right side of the radiator, near the upper radiator hose fitting (arrow)

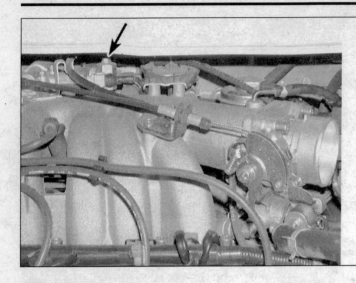

24.19 Location of the engine air relief plug (arrow)

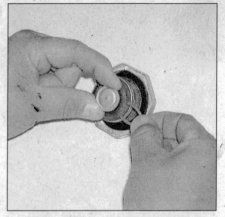

24.22 Insert a piece of bent wire under the relief valve of the radiator cap to prevent vacuum or pressure from forming in the cooling system during the bleeding procedure

(see illustration). Remove the plug.

20   Find the air relief cap for the heater pipe. It's located behind the throttle body. Attach a length of clear, 1/4-inch I.D. hose (approximately 3-1/2 feet in length) to the air relief fitting and insert the other end of the hose into the coolant reservoir. Fill the coolant reservoir with a 50/50 mixture of antifreeze and water up to the MAX level. Make sure the end of the hose is submerged in coolant.

21   Fill the cooling system with a 50/50 mixture of antifreeze and water through the radiator filler neck. Pour the coolant in slowly, allowing the air in the system to escape through the bleed ports. When coolant starts to flow from the radiator air relief plug, tighten the plug securely. Add more coolant and occasionally squeeze the upper radiator hose to expel any trapped air. Do this until no more coolant can be added. **Note:** *You may have to wait a few minutes between each addition of coolant to let the air escape.*

22   Before proceeding to the next Step, the radiator cap will have to be temporarily modified. Cut a 1-1/2 inch length of heavy-gauge wire (approximately 2 mm [5/64-inch] in diameter) and bend it into a "U" shape. Insert this wire under the negative pressure valve of the radiator cap (this will prevent a vacuum from forming in the cooling system) **(see illustration).** Set the cap aside for now - don't install it.

23   Start the engine and run it at approximately 2500 rpm until the engine cooling fan comes on, then goes off. If, during this step, the coolant begins to flow from the engine air relief plug hole, install the air relief plug and tighten it securely. If the coolant begins to overflow at the radiator filler neck, install the radiator cap. If the coolant level drops, add more of the coolant mixture to the system.

24   Stop the engine and install and tighten the engine air relief plug securely (if not installed in the previous Step). Allow the engine to cool completely.

25   Add coolant to the radiator filler neck if the level has dropped. Also add coolant to the reservoir, if necessary.

26   Install the modified radiator cap and

start the engine, allowing it to reach normal operating temperature (until the cooling fan comes on, then goes off). As the engine warms up, keep an eye on the temperature gauge. If the gauge begins to register above normal, stop the engine and let it cool completely, then repeat Step 25.

Models without a rear heater

27   Set the temperature control knob in the full WARM setting. Start the engine and run it at 3000 rpm for approximately five minutes. Check to make sure the air coming from the heater outlets is hot. Repeat his procedure two more times.

Models with a rear heater

28   Set the front temperature control knob in the full COOL setting and set the rear temperature control knob in the full WARM setting. Turn both blower switches (front and rear) On (to any blower speed). Start the engine and run it at 3000 rpm for approximately five minutes. Check to make sure the air coming from the rear heater outlet is hot. Shut the engine off and add coolant to the reservoir as necessary.

29   Turn the rear blower switch Off, then set the front temperature control knob to the full WARM setting. Run the engine at approximately 3000 rpm for five minutes. Check to make sure the air coming from the front heater outlets is hot.

All models

30   Turn the engine off and add coolant to the reservoir, if necessary up to the MAX level. Allow the engine too cool down, then remove the radiator cap and take out the piece of wire that was installed in Step 22. Add coolant to the radiator filler neck, if necessary, then reinstall the radiator cap.

31   Detach the hose connected to the heater pipe air relief port and install the cap as quickly as possible. Tighten the clamp securely.

32   Clean up any spills, then check for leaks.

25   Automatic transaxle fluid and filter change (every 30,000 miles or 24 months)

Refer to illustrations 25.5, 25.8a, 25.8b and 25.10

1   At the specified time intervals, the transaxle fluid should be drained and replaced. Since the fluid will remain hot long after driving, perform this procedure only after everything has cooled down completely.

2   Before beginning work, purchase the specified transaxle fluid (see *Recommended lubricants and fluids* at the front of this Chapter) and a new filter.

3   Other tools necessary for this job include jackstands to support the vehicle in a raised position, a drain pan capable of holding several quarts, newspapers and clean rags.

4   Raise the vehicle and support it securely on jackstands.

5   With a drain pan in place, remove the drain plug **(see illustration)**, allow the fluid to drain and remove the transaxle pan mounting bolts. **Note:** *Measure the amount of fluid drained and record it; when refilling the transaxle, start with that amount.*

6   Carefully pry the transaxle pan loose with a screwdriver and detach the pan and gasket. Carefully clean the gasket surface of the transaxle to remove all traces of the old gasket and sealant.

7   Drain the remaining fluid from the transaxle pan, clean the pan with solvent and dry it with compressed air or a clean rag. Be careful not to lose the magnets.

8   Remove the bolts and detach the filter **(see illustrations)**.

9   Install the new filter.

10   Make sure the gasket surface on the transaxle pan is clean, then install the magnet and a new gasket **(see illustration)**. Put the pan in place against the transaxle and install the bolts. Working around the pan, tighten

25.5 Remove the drain plug (arrow), allow the fluid to drain fully, then remove the pan bolts

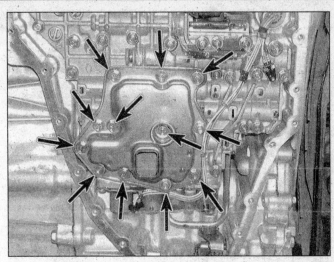

25.8a Remove the filter retaining bolts (arrows)

25.8b Detach the filter and lower it from the transaxle

25.10 After cleaning the pan, place the magnets in position and install the new gasket

each bolt a little at a time until the final torque figure listed in this Chapter's Specifications is reached. Don't overtighten the bolts!

11 Lower the vehicle and add the same amount of new automatic transmission fluid that was measured in Step 5 through the filler tube (see Section 7).

12 With the shift lever in Park and the parking brake set, run the engine at a fast idle, but don't race it.

13 Move the shift lever through each gear and back to Park. Check the fluid level and add some, as necessary, to bring it to the appropriate level. **Caution:** *Add fluid a little at a time to avoid overfilling.*

14 Check under the vehicle for leaks during the first few trips.

26 Brake fluid change (every 30,000 miles or 24 months)

Warning: *Brake fluid can harm your eyes and damage painted surfaces, so use extreme caution when handling or pouring it. Do not use brake fluid that has been standing open or is more than one year old. Brake fluid absorbs moisture from the air. Excess moisture can cause a dangerous loss of braking effectiveness.*

1 At the specified intervals, the brake fluid should be drained and replaced. Since the brake fluid may drip or splash when pouring it, place plenty of rags around the master cylinder to protect any surrounding painted surfaces.

2 Before beginning work, purchase the specified brake fluid (see *Recommended lubricants and fluids* at the beginning of this Chapter).

3 Remove the cap from the master cylinder reservoir.

4 Using a hand suction pump or similar device, withdraw the fluid from the master cylinder reservoir.

5 Add new fluid to the master cylinder until it rises to the base of the filler neck.

6 Bleed the brake system as described in Chapter 9 at all four brakes until new and uncontaminated fluid is expelled from the bleeder screw. Be sure to maintain the fluid level in the master cylinder as you perform the bleeding process. If you allow the master cylinder to run dry, air will enter the system.

7 Refill the master cylinder with fluid and check the operation of the brakes. The pedal should feel solid when depressed, with no sponginess. **Warning:** *Do not operate the vehicle if you are in doubt about the effectiveness of the brake system.*

27 Positive Crankcase Ventilation (PCV) valve check (every 30,000 miles or 24 months)

Refer to illustration 27.1

Note: *To maintain efficient operation of the PCV system, clean the hoses and check the PCV valve at the intervals recommended in the maintenance schedule. For additional information on the PCV system, refer to Chapter 6.*

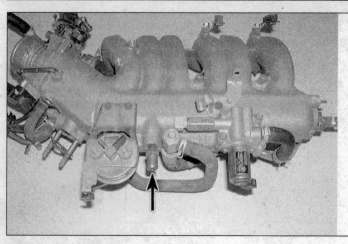

27.1 The PCV valve (arrow) is located on the back side of the intake plenum under the cowl (plenum removed for clarity)

1   The PCV valve threads into the rear side of the intake plenum (see illustration).
2   Start the engine and allow it to idle, then disconnect the hose from the PCV valve. You should be able to hear a hissing noise from the valve. Place your finger over the valve and feel for vacuum. If vacuum is felt, the PCV valve is working properly.
3   If no vacuum is felt, replace the PCV valve.
4   Check the PCV hose for cracks or obstructions, cleaning or replacing the hose as necessary.

28   Spark plug check and replacement (every 30,000 miles or 24 months)

Refer to illustrations 28.2, 28.5a, 28.5b, 28.8, 28.9 and 28.10
All spark plugs located in the right hand cylinder head (adjacent to the firewall) must be removed from below the vehicle.

1   All vehicles covered by this manual are equipped with transversely mounted V6 engines which locate the spark plugs on the side of the engine at the front and the rear of the engine compartment. The left side (front) spark plugs can be reached from the front of the vehicle while the right side (rear) spark plugs are located between the engine and the firewall which requires removal from beneath the vehicle.
2   In most cases, the tools necessary for spark plug replacement include a spark plug socket which fits onto a ratchet (spark plug sockets are padded inside to prevent damage to the porcelain insulators on the new plugs), various extensions and a gap gauge to check and adjust the gap on the new plugs (see illustration). A special plug wire removal tool is available for separating the wire boots from the spark plugs, and is a good idea on these models because the boots fit very tightly. A torque wrench should be used to tighten the new plugs. It is a good idea to allow the engine to cool before removing or installing the spark plugs.
3   The best approach when replacing the spark plugs is to purchase the new ones in advance, adjust them to the proper gap and replace the plugs one at a time. When buying the new spark plugs, be sure to obtain the correct plug type for your particular engine. The plug type can be found in the Specifications at the front of this Chapter and on the Emission Control Information label located under the hood. If these two sources list different plug types, consider the emission control label correct.
4   Allow the engine to cool completely before attempting to remove any of the plugs. While you are waiting for the engine to cool, check the new plugs for defects and adjust the gap.
5   Check the gap by inserting the proper thickness gauge between the electrodes at the tip of the plug (see illustration). The gap between the electrodes should be the same as the one specified on the Emissions Control Information label or in Chapter 5. The wire should slide between the electrodes with a slight amount of drag. If the gap is incorrect, use the adjuster on the gauge body to bend the curved side electrode slightly until the proper gap is obtained (see illustration). If the side electrode is not exactly over the center electrode, bend it with the adjuster until it is. Check for cracks in the porcelain insulator (if any are found, the plug should not be used).
6   With the engine cool, remove the spark plug wire as described in Section 29 from one spark plug. Pull only on the boot at the end of the wire - do not pull on the wire. A plug wire removal tool should be used if available.
7   If compressed air is available, use it to blow any dirt or foreign material away from the spark plug hole. The idea here is to eliminate the possibility of debris falling into the cylinder as the spark plug is removed.
8   The spark plugs on these models are, for the most part, difficult to reach so a spark plug socket incorporating a universal joint may be necessary. Place the spark plug socket over the plug and remove it from the engine by turning it in a counterclockwise direction (see illustration).
9   Compare the spark plug with the chart shown on the inside back cover of this manual to get an indication of the general running condition of the engine. Before installing the new plugs, it is a good idea to apply a thin coat of anti-seize compound to the threads (see illustration).
10   Thread one of the new plugs into the hole until you can no longer turn it with your fingers, then tighten it with a torque wrench (if available) or the ratchet. It's a good idea to slip a short length of rubber hose over the end of the plug to use as a tool to thread it into place (see illustration). The hose will grip the plug well enough to turn it, but will start to slip if the plug begins to cross-thread in the hole - this will prevent damaged threads and the accompanying repair costs.
11   Before pushing the spark plug wire onto the end of the plug, inspect it following the

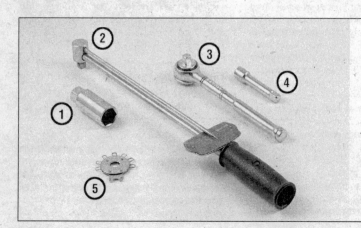

28.2 Tools required for changing spark plugs

1   **Spark plug socket** - This will have special padding inside to protect the spark plug's porcelain insulator
2   **Torque wrench** - Although not mandatory, using this tool is the best way to ensure the plugs are tightened properly
3   **Ratchet** - Standard hand tool to fit the spark plug socket
4   **Extension** - Depending on model and accessories, you may need special extensions and universal joints to reach one or more of the plugs
5   **Spark plug gap gauge** - This gauge for checking the gap comes in a variety of styles. Make sure the gap for your engine is included

28.5a Spark plug manufacturers recommend using a wire-type gauge when checking the gap - if the wire does not slide between the electrodes with a slight drag, adjustment is required

28.5b To change the gap, bend the side electrode only, as indicated by the arrows, and be very careful not to crack or chip the porcelain insulator surrounding the center electrode

28.8 Use a spark plug socket wrench and extension to unscrew the spark plug

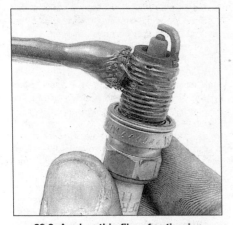

28.9 Apply a thin film of anti-seize compound to the spark plug threads to prevent damage to the cylinder head

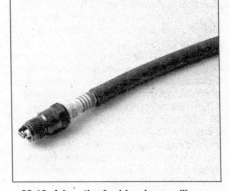

28.10 A length of rubber hose will save time and prevent damaged threads when installing the spark plugs

29.4 When removing the spark plug wires from the spark plug, pull only on the boot and use a twisting/pulling motion

procedures outlined in Section 29.

12   Attach the plug wire to the new spark plug, again using a twisting motion on the boot until it's seated on the spark plug.

13   Repeat the procedure for the remaining spark plugs, replacing them one at a time to prevent mixing up the spark plug wires.

29 Spark plug wire, distributor cap and rotor check and replacement (every 30,000 miles or 24 months)

Refer to illustrations 29.4, 29.8, 29.11 and 29.12

1   The spark plug wires should be checked whenever new spark plugs are installed.

2   Begin this procedure by making a visual check of the spark plug wires while the engine is running. In a darkened garage (make sure there is adequate ventilation) start the engine and observe each plug wire. Be careful not to come into contact with any moving engine parts. If there is a break in the wire, you will see arcing or a small spark at the damaged

area. If arcing is noticed, make a note to obtain new wires, then allow the engine to cool and check the distributor cap and rotor.

3   The spark plug wires should be inspected one at a time to prevent mixing up the order, which is essential for proper engine operation. Each original plug wire should be numbered to help identify its location. If the number is illegible, a piece of tape can be marked with the correct number and wrapped around the plug wire.

4   Disconnect the plug wire from the spark plug. A removal tool can be used for this purpose or you can grasp the rubber boot, twist the boot half a turn and pull the boot free. Do not pull on the wire itself **(see illustration)**.

5   Check inside the boot for corrosion, which will look like a white crusty powder.

6   Push the wire and boot back onto the end of the spark plug. It should fit tightly onto the end of the plug. If it doesn't, remove the wire and use pliers to carefully crimp the metal connector inside the wire boot until the fit is snug.

7   Using a clean rag, wipe the entire length of the wire to remove built-up dirt and grease. Once the wire is clean, check for burns,

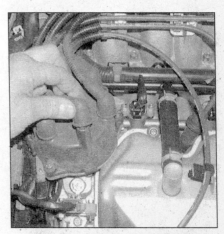

29.8 Remove the wires from the distributor by pulling only on the boots as well

cracks and other damage. Do not bend the wire sharply, because the conductor might break.

8   Disconnect the wire from the distributor **(see illustration)**. Again, pull only on the rubber boot. Check for corrosion and a tight fit.

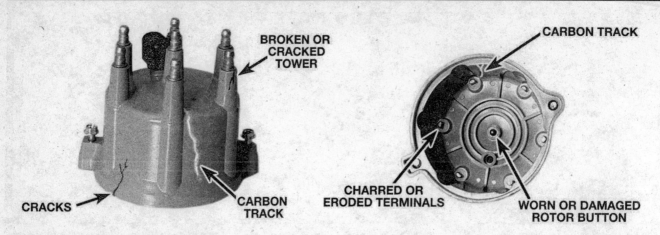

29.11 Shown here are some of the common defects to look for when inspecting the distributor cap (if in doubt about its condition, install a new one)

Replace the wire in the distributor.

9   Inspect the remaining spark plug wires, making sure that each one is securely fastened at the distributor and spark plug when the check is complete.

10   If new spark plug wires are required, purchase a set for your specific engine model. Remove and replace the wires one at a time to avoid mix-ups in the firing order.

11   Detach the distributor cap by loosening the three cap retaining screws. Look inside it for cracks, carbon tracks and worn, burned or loose contacts **(see illustration).**

12   Loosen the retaining screw and pull the rotor off the distributor shaft and examine it for cracks and carbon tracks **(see illustra-**tion). Replace the cap and rotor if any damage or defects are noted.

13   It is common practice to install a new cap and rotor whenever new spark plug wires are installed, but if you wish to continue using the old cap, check the resistance between the spark plug wires and the cap first. If the indicated resistance is more than the maximum value listed in this Chapter's Specifications, replace the cap and/or wires.

14   When installing a new cap, remove the wires from the old cap one at a time and attach them to the new cap in the exact same location **Note:** *If an accidental mix-up occurs, refer to the firing order Specifications at the beginning of this Chapter.*

29.12 The ignition rotor should be checked for wear, corrosion at the points shown as well as cracks and carbon tracks (if in doubt about its condition, buy a new one)

Chapter 2 Part A Engine

Contents

2A

Specifications

General

Cylinder numbers (timing belt end-to-transaxle end)	
Rear (firewall) side	1-3-5
Front (radiator) side	2-4-6
Firing order	1-2-3-4-5-6
Bore	3.43 inches
Stroke	3.27 inches
Displacement	181 cubic inches (3.0 liters)

64200-2A-00 HAYNES

**Cylinder location and
distributor rotation**

*The blackened terminal shown on the
distributor cap indicates the Number
One spark plug wire position*

Camshaft and rocker arms

Camshaft endplay	0.0012 to 0.0024 inch
Rocker arm shaft diameter	0.7078 to 0.7087 inch
Rocker arm bore diameter	0.7089 to 0.7098 inch
Rocker arm-to-shaft oil clearance	0.0003 to 0.0019 inch

Oil pump

Outer rotor-to-body clearance	0.0045 to 0.0079 inch
Outer rotor-to-inner rotor tip clearance	0.0071 inch maximum
Cover-to-rotor clearance	
Inner rotor	0.0018 to 0.0036 inch
Outer rotor	0.0020 to 0.0043 inch
Inner rotor ridge-to-body clearance	0.0018 to 0.0036 inch

Torque specifications

	Ft-lbs (unless otherwise indicated)
Camshaft thrust plate bolt	58 to 65
Camshaft sprocket bolt	58 to 65
Crankshaft pulley bolt	
1995 and earlier	90 to 98
1996 and later	141 to 156
Cylinder head bolts (in sequence - **see illustration 11.22**)	
Step one	22
Step two	43
Step three	Loosen all bolts (in reverse of tightening sequence)
Step four	22
Step five	40 to 47
Valve cover bolts	9 to 26 in-lbs
Driveplate bolts	
1997 and earlier	61 to 69
1998 and later	33 to 43
Exhaust manifold nuts	13 to 16
Intake manifold	
Upper intake manifold bolts	13 to 16
Lower intake manifold bolts/nuts	
Step one (all)	26 to 43 in-lbs
Step two	
Nuts	17 to 20
Bolts	144 to 168 in-lbs
Step three	Repeat step 2
Oil pan bolts/nuts	62 to 70 in-lbs
Oil pan drain plug	22 to 29
Oil pick-up screen mounting bolts	12 to 15
Oil pump mounting bolts	
Long	108 to 144 in-lbs
Short	53 to 62 in-lbs
Oil pump cover screws	36 to 44 in-lbs
Rocker arm shaft bolts	13 to 16
Timing belt tensioner nut	32 to 43
Timing belt cover bolts	27 to 44 in-lbs
Transaxle-to-engine brace bolts	22 to 30
Rear main oil seal retainer bolts	27 to 44 in-lbs
Right front engine mount through-bolts	58 to 65
Right rear engine mount through-bolts	58 to 65
Left front engine mount through-bolt	47 to 54
Left front engine mount bracket bolts	30 to 38
Left rear engine mount through-bolt	32 to 41
Left rear engine mount lower nuts	32 to 41

1   General information

This Part of Chapter 2 is devoted to in-vehicle repair procedures for the 3.0L V6 engine. All information concerning engine removal and installation and engine block and cylinder head overhaul can be found in Chapter 2, Part B.

The following repair procedures are based on the assumption that the engine is installed in the vehicle. If the engine has been removed from the vehicle and mounted on a stand, many of the steps outlined in this Part of Chapter 2 will not apply.

The Specifications included in this Part of Chapter 2 apply only to the procedures contained in this Part. Part B of Chapter 2 contains the Specifications necessary for cylinder head and engine block rebuilding.

2   Repair operations possible with the engine in the vehicle

Many major repair operations can be accomplished without removing the engine from the vehicle.

Clean the engine compartment and the exterior of the engine with some type of degreaser before any work is done. It will make the job easier and help keep dirt out of the internal areas of the engine.

Depending on the components involved, it may be helpful to remove the hood to improve access to the engine as repairs are performed (refer to Chapter 11 if necessary). Cover the fenders to prevent damage to the paint. Special pads are available, but an old bedspread or blanket will also work.

If vacuum, exhaust, oil or coolant leaks develop, indicating a need for gasket or seal replacement, the repairs can generally be made with the engine in the vehicle. The intake and exhaust manifold gaskets, oil pan gasket, crankshaft oil seals and cylinder head gaskets are all accessible with the engine in place.

Exterior engine components, such as the intake and exhaust manifolds, the oil pan, the oil pump, the water pump (see Chapter 3), the starter motor, the alternator, the distributor (see Chapter 5) and the fuel system components (see Chapter 4) can be removed for repair with the engine in place.

Since the cylinder heads can be removed without pulling the engine, valve component servicing can also be accomplished with the engine in the vehicle. Replacement of the camshafts, timing belt and sprockets is also possible with the

3.6 Mark the distributor housing (arrow) below the number one spark plug wire terminal

3.8 Align the yellow notch on pulley with the pointer on the timing belt cover (arrow)

engine in the vehicle, although the cylinder heads must be removed from the engine to replace the camshafts.

In extreme cases caused by a lack of necessary equipment, repair or replacement of piston rings, pistons, connecting rods and rod bearings is possible with the engine in the vehicle. However, this practice is not recommended because of the cleaning and preparation work that must be done to the components involved.

---

3 Top Dead Center (TDC) for number one piston - locating

Refer to illustrations 3.6 and 3.8

Note: *The following procedure is based on the assumption that the distributor is correctly installed. If you are trying to locate TDC to install the distributor correctly, piston position must be determined by feeling for compression at the number one spark plug hole, then aligning the ignition timing marks as described in Step 8.*

1   Top Dead Center (TDC) is the highest point in the cylinder that each piston reaches as it travels up-and-down when the crankshaft turns. Each piston reaches TDC on the compression stroke and again on the exhaust stroke, but TDC generally refers to piston position on the compression stroke.

2   Positioning the piston(s) at TDC is an essential part of several procedures such as camshaft and timing belt/sprocket removal and distributor removal.

3   Before beginning this procedure, be sure to place the transaxle in Neutral and apply the parking brake or block the rear wheels. Also, disable the ignition system by detaching the coil wire from its terminal on the distributor cap and grounding it on the engine block with a jumper wire. Remove the spark plugs (see Chapter 1).

4   In order to bring any piston to TDC, the crankshaft must be turned using one of the methods outlined below. When looking at the timing belt end of the engine, normal crankshaft rotation is clockwise.

a)   *The preferred method is to remove the lower splash shield on the passenger side and turn the crankshaft with a socket and ratchet attached to the bolt threaded into the front of the crankshaft.*

b)   *A remote starter switch, which may save some time, can also be used. Follow the instructions included with the switch. Once the piston is close to TDC, use a socket and ratchet as described in the previous paragraph.*

c)   *If an assistant is available to turn the ignition switch to the Start position in short bursts, you can get the piston close to TDC without a remote starter switch. Make sure your assistant is out of the vehicle, away from the ignition switch, then use a socket and ratchet as described in Paragraph a) to complete the procedure.*

5   Note the position of the terminal for the number one spark plug wire on the distributor cap. If the plug wire isn't marked, follow the plug wire from the number one cylinder spark plug to the cap.

6   Use a felt-tip pen or chalk to make a mark on the distributor body directly under the number 1 terminal **(see illustration)**.

7   Detach the cap from the distributor and set it aside (see Chapter 1 if necessary).

8   Turn the crankshaft (see Step 4) until the TDC mark in the crankshaft pulley is aligned with the pointer on the timing belt cover **(see illustration)**. **Note:** *There are several marks on the pulley; the TDC mark is the yellow mark.*

9   Look at the distributor rotor - it should be pointing directly at the mark you made on the distributor body.

10   If the rotor is 180-degrees off, the number one piston is at TDC on the exhaust stroke.

11   To get the piston to TDC on the compression stroke if the rotor is 180-degrees off, turn the crankshaft one complete turn (360-

degrees) clockwise. The rotor should now be pointing at the mark on the distributor. When the rotor is pointing at the number one spark plug wire terminal in the distributor cap and the ignition timing marks are aligned, the number one piston is at TDC on the compression stroke.

12   After the number one piston has been positioned at TDC on the compression stroke, TDC for any of the remaining pistons can be located by turning the crankshaft and following the firing order. Mark the remaining spark plug wire terminal locations on the distributor body just like you did for the number one terminal, then number the marks to correspond with the cylinder numbers. As you turn the crankshaft, the rotor will also turn. The crankshaft must be turned 120-degrees to move from one cylinder to the next one in the firing order. When it's pointing directly at one of the marks on the distributor, the piston for that particular cylinder is at TDC on the compression stroke.

---

4 Valve covers - removal and installation

Refer to illustrations 4.6 and 4.11

1   Relieve the fuel system pressure (see Chapter 4).

2   Disconnect the negative cable from the battery.

Removal

Front (radiator side) cover

3   Remove the distributor (see Chapter 5).

4   Remove the number 2, 4 and 6 spark plug wires from the spark plugs. Mark them clearly with pieces of masking tape to prevent confusion during installation.

5   Remove the breather hose by sliding the hose clamp back and pulling the hose off the fitting on the valve cover.

6   Remove the valve cover bolts and washers **(see illustration)**.

4.6 Detach the breather hose (A) and remove the bolts (arrows)

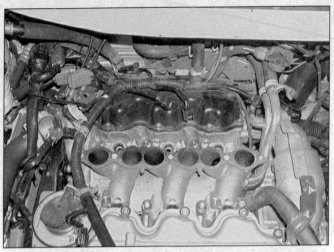

4.11 The rear valve cover may be slipped out from under the electrical harness if care is taken

7   Detach the valve cover. **Caution:** *If the cover is stuck to the cylinder head, bump one end with a block of wood and a hammer to jar it loose. If that doesn't work, try to slip a flexible putty knife between the cylinder head and cover to break the gasket seal. Don't pry at the cover-to-cylinder head joint or damage to the sealing surfaces may occur (leading to oil leaks in the future).*

Rear (firewall side) cover

8   Remove the upper intake plenum (see Section 9).
9   Label and detach the spark plug wires.
10   Release the wiring retainers. Label and move the wiring and hoses aside.
11   Remove the valve cover bolts and washers and lift off the valve cover **(see illustration)**. Refer to the **Caution** in Step 7.

Installation

12   The mating surfaces of each cylinder head and valve cover must be perfectly clean when the covers are installed. Use a gasket scraper to remove all traces of sealant and old gasket material, then clean the mating surfaces with lacquer thinner or acetone. If there's sealant or oil on the mating surfaces when the cover is installed, oil leaks may develop.
13   If necessary, clean the mounting bolt threads with a die to remove any corrosion and restore damaged threads. Make sure the threaded holes in the cylinder head are clean - run a tap into them to remove corrosion and restore damaged threads.
14   The gaskets should be mated to the covers before the covers are installed. Apply a thin coat of RTV sealant to the cover groove, then position the gasket inside the cover and allow the sealant to set up so the gasket adheres to the cover. If the sealant isn't allowed to set, the gasket may fall out of the cover as it's installed on the engine.
15   Carefully position the cover on the cylinder head and install the bolts.
16   Tighten the bolts in three or four steps to the torque listed in this Chapter's Specifications.
17   The remaining installation steps are the reverse of removal.
18   Start the engine and check carefully for oil leaks.

5   Rocker arm assembly - removal, inspection and installation

Removal

Refer to illustrations 5.2, 5.3 and 5.4
1   Remove the valve covers (see Section 4).
2   Loosen the rocker arm shaft retaining bolts **(see illustration)** in two or three stages, working from the ends toward the middle of the shafts. **Caution:** *Some of the valves will be open when you loosen the rocker arm shaft bolts and the rocker arm shafts will be under a certain amount of valve spring pressure. Therefore, the bolts must be loosened gradually. Loosening a bolt all at once near a rocker arm under spring pressure could distort the rocker arm shaft.*
3   Prior to removal, scribe or paint identifying marks on the rockers to ensure they will be installed in their original locations **(see illustration)**.
4   Remove the bolts and lift off the rocker arm shaft assemblies one at a time. Lay them down on a nearby workbench in the same

5.2 Loosen the rocker arm shaft bolts (arrows) a little at a time to avoid bending the shaft

5.3 Mark the rockers to identify their locations - these are marked FI for Front Intake and FE for Front Exhaust

5.4 The rocker arm shaft assemblies are installed with the large notches (arrows) on the intake manifold side - the small notches on the other shaft must face the exhaust manifold

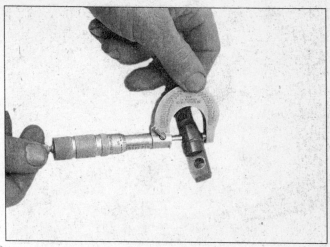

5.6 Measure the rocker arm shaft diameter at each journal where a rocker arm rides on the shaft

relationship to each other that they're in when installed. They must be reinstalled on the same cylinder head. Note that the shafts with the larger notches go on the intake manifold side **(see illustration)**.

Inspection

Refer to illustrations 5.6 and 5.7

5   Check the rocker arms and shafts for abnormal wear, pits, galling, score marks and rough spots. Don't attempt to restore rocker arms by grinding the pad surfaces.

6   Measure the outside diameter of the rocker arm shaft at each rocker arm journal **(see illustration)**. Compare the measurements to the rocker arm shaft outside diameter specified in this Chapter.

7   Measure the inside diameter of each rocker arm with either an inside micrometer or a dial caliper **(see illustration)**. Compare the measurements to the rocker arm bore diameter specified in this Chapter.

8   Subtract the outside diameter of each rocker arm shaft journal from the correspond-

ing rocker arm bore diameter to compute the clearance between the rocker arm shaft and the rocker arm. Compare the measurements to the clearance specified in this Chapter. If any of them fall outside the specified limits, replace either the rocker arms or the shaft, or both.

Installation

9   Installation is the reverse of the removal procedure. Tighten the rocker arm shaft retaining bolts, in several steps, to the torque listed in this Chapter's Specifications. Work from the ends of the shafts toward the middle.

6   Valve springs, retainers and seals - replacement

Refer to illustrations 6.5, 6.7, 6.13a, 6.13b and 6.15

Note: *Broken valve springs and defective valve stem seals can be replaced without*

removing the cylinder heads. Two special tools and a compressed air source are normally required to perform this operation, so read through this Section carefully. The universal shaft-type valve spring compressor required for the tight valve spring pockets of this vehicle may not be available at all tool rental yards, so check on the availability before beginning the job.

1   Remove the valve cover(s) (see Section 4).

2   Refer to Section 5 and remove the rocker arm assembly, then refer to Section 8 and remove the lifter assembly.

3   Remove the spark plug from the cylinder that has the defective component. If all of the valve stem seals are being replaced, all of the spark plugs should be removed.

4   Turn the crankshaft until the piston in the affected cylinder is at Top Dead Center on the compression stroke (refer to Section 3). If you're replacing all of the valve stem seals, begin with cylinder number one and work on the valves for one cylinder at a time. Move from cylinder-to-cylinder following the firing order sequence (see this Chapter's Specifications).

5   Thread a long adapter into the spark plug hole and connect an air hose from a compressed air source to it **(see illustration)**. Most auto parts stores can supply the air hose adapter. **Note:** *Because of the length of the spark plug tubes, it will be necessary to use a long spark plug adapter with a length of hose attached (as used on many cylinder compression gauges) utilizing a quick-disconnect fitting to hook to your air source.*

6   Apply compressed air to the cylinder. **Warning:** *The piston may be forced down by the compressed air, causing the crankshaft to turn suddenly. If the wrench used when positioning the number one piston at TDC is still attached to the bolt in the crankshaft nose, it could cause damage or injury when the crankshaft moves.*

7   Stuff shop rags into the cylinder head holes around the valves to prevent parts and

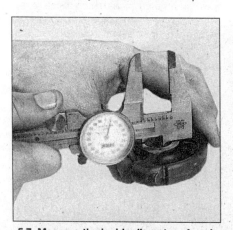

5.7 Measure the inside diameter of each rocker arm bore, subtract the corresponding rocker arm shaft diameter to obtain the clearance and compare the results to Specifications

6.5 The air hose adapter threads into the spark plug hole - they're commonly available from auto parts stores

2A

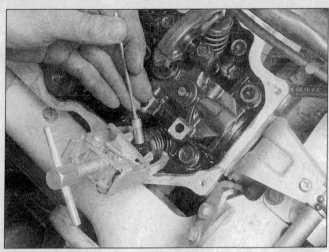

6.7 Compress the valve spring enough to release the valve stem locks and lift them out with a magnet or needle-nose pliers

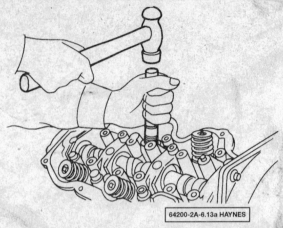

6.13a Intake valve seals can be installed with a special tool, or a deep socket and hammer - tap the seal only until seated

tools from falling into the engine, then use a valve spring compressor to compress the spring **(see illustration)**. Remove the valve stem locks with small needle-nose pliers or a magnet. **Note:** *The valves should be held in place by the air pressure. If the valve faces or seats are in poor condition, leaks may prevent air pressure from retaining the valves. If the valves cannot hold air, the cylinder head should be removed for a valve job at a machine shop.*

8   Remove the spring retainer, shield and valve spring, then remove the valve stem seal.

9   Wrap a rubber band or tape around the top of the valve stem so the valve won't fall into the combustion chamber, then release the air pressure.

10 Inspect the valve stem for damage. Rotate the valve in the guide and check the end for eccentric movement, which would indicate that the valve is bent.

11 Move the valve up-and-down in the guide and make sure it doesn't bind. If the valve stem binds, either the valve is bent or the guide is damaged. In either case, the cylinder head will have to be removed for repair.

12 Reapply air pressure to the cylinder to retain the valve in the closed position, then remove the tape or rubber band from the valve stem.

13 Lubricate the valve stem with engine oil and install a new valve stem seal **(see illustrations)**. **Caution:** *Intake and exhaust seals are different, do not mix them up.*

14 Install the inner and outer springs in position over the valve, with the more closely-wound spring coils toward the cylinder head.

15 Install the valve spring retainer. Compress the valve springs and carefully position the valve stem locks in the groove. Apply a small dab of grease to the inside of each valve stem lock to hold it in place **(see illustration)**.

16 Remove the pressure from the spring tool and make sure the valve stem locks are seated.

17 Disconnect the air hose and remove the adapter from the spark plug hole.

18 Refer to Section 8 and install the lifter assembly, then refer to Section 5 and install the rocker arm assembly.

19 Refer to Section 4 and install the valve cover.

20 Install the spark plug(s) and hook up the wire(s).

21 Start and run the engine, then check for oil leaks and unusual sounds coming from the valve cover area.

7   Timing belt and sprockets - removal and installation

Removal

Refer to illustrations 7.9, 7.11, 7.12, 7.13a, 7.13b, 7.14, 7.15a, 7.15b, 7.17 and 7.18

1   Disconnect the cable from the negative terminal of the battery and drain the cooling system (see Chapter 1).

2   Remove all of the drivebelts (see Chapter 1).

3   Loosen the lug nuts on the right front wheel.

4   Raise the front of the vehicle and support it securely on jackstands. Apply the parking brake.

5   Remove the right front wheel and detach the splash shield from the inner fenderwell (see Chapter 11).

6   Remove the splash pan and drain the cooling system (see Chapter 1).

7   Position the number one piston at TDC on the compression stroke (see Section 3). Remove the spark plugs (see Chapter 1).

8   Disconnect the radiator hose and bypass hose from the thermostat housing. Remove the water pump pulley.

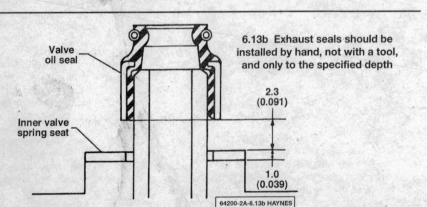

Valve oil seal

Inner valve spring seat

6.13b Exhaust seals should be installed by hand, not with a tool, and only to the specified depth

2.3 (0.091)

1.0 (0.039)

6.15 Apply a small dab of grease to each valve stem lock as shown here before installation - it will hold them in place on the valve stem as the spring is released

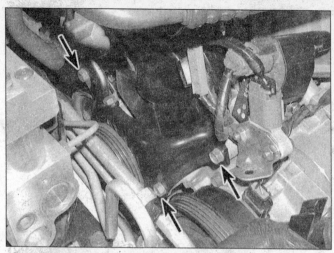

7.9 Remove the three bolts (arrows) and remove the air-
conditioning belt idler pulley and bracket

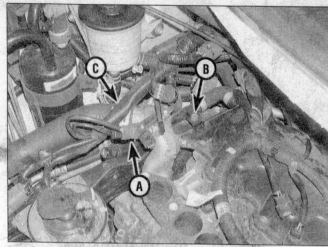

7.11 Disconnect the electrical connectors at the front of the
intake manifold (A), remove the bolt (B) holding the wiring harness
and move it aside, then disconnect the upper radiator hose (C)

9   Remove the air conditioning compressor idler pulley and bracket **(see illustration)**.
10   Remove the crankshaft pulley (see Section 12). **Note:** *Don't allow the crankshaft to rotate during removal of the pulley. If the crankshaft moves, the number one piston will no longer be at TDC.*

11   Disconnect the hoses and wiring harness at the top of the upper timing belt cover **(see illustration)**.
12   Remove the bolts securing the timing belt upper and lower covers **(see illustration)**. Note that various types and sizes of bolts are used. They must be reinstalled in

their original locations. Mark each bolt or make a sketch to help remember where they go.
13   Confirm that the number one piston is still at TDC on the compression stroke by verifying that the timing marks on the camshaft and crankshaft sprockets are aligned with

2A

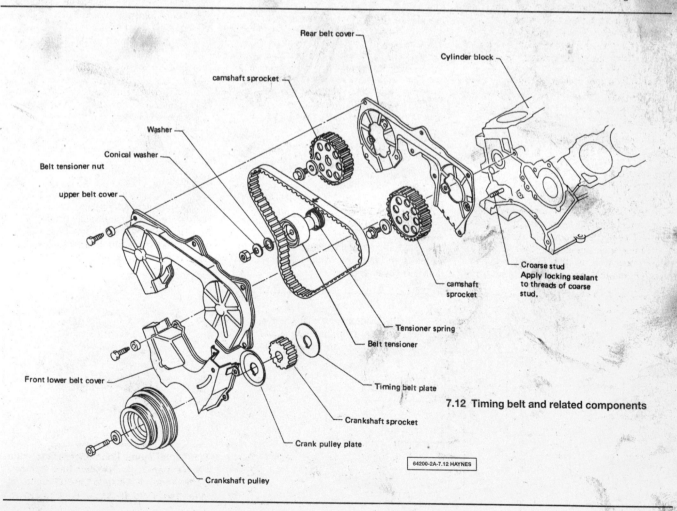

7.12 Timing belt and related components

Rear belt cover

camshaft sprocket

Cylinder block

Washer

Conical washer

Belt tensioner nut

upper belt cover

Croarse stud
Apply locking sealant
to threads of coarse
stud.

camshaft
sprocket

Tensioner spring

Belt tensioner

Front lower belt cover

Timing belt plate

Crankshaft sprocket

Crank pulley plate

Crankshaft pulley

64200-2A-7.12 HAYNES

7.13a Make sure the marks on the camshaft sprockets align with the marks on the timing belt cover (arrows)

7.13b The mark on the crankshaft sprocket aligns with the mark on the oil pump housing (arrows)

7.14 Loosen the locking nut (arrow) in the middle of the timing belt tensioner

7.15a The timing belt should be marked (arrow) to indicate which side faces out - if not, use chalk to make an arrow on the belt before removal

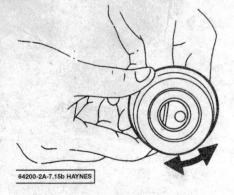

64200-2A-7.15b HAYNES

7.15b Check the belt tensioner and spring for wear and damage - the pulley should rotate smoothly

their respective stationary alignment marks **(see illustrations)**.

14   Relieve tension on the timing belt by loosening the nut in the middle of the timing belt tensioner **(see illustration)**.

15   Check to see if the timing belt is marked with an arrow indicating which side faces out **(see illustration)**. If there isn't a mark, paint one on (only if the same belt will be reinstalled). Slide the timing belt off the sprock-

ets. If the belt is cracked, worn or contaminated with oil or coolant, replace it with a new one. Check the condition of the tensioner **(see illustration)**.

16   Make sure the camshaft and crankshaft sprockets are in good condition - if they're worn or damaged, replace them.

17   Insert a screwdriver through a hole in the

camshaft sprocket to lock it in place while loosening the mounting bolt **(see illustration)**.

18   Once the bolt is out, the sprocket can be removed by hand. **Note:** *Each sprocket is marked with either an R or L (see illustration). If you're removing both camshaft sprockets, don't mix them up. They must be installed on the same cam they were removed from.*

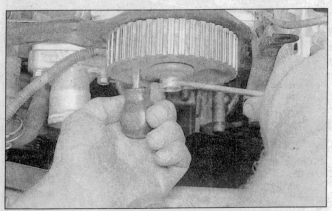

7.17 Insert a screwdriver through the camshaft sprocket to hold it while loosening the bolt

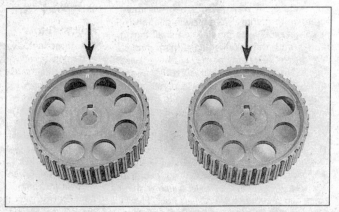

7.18 When installing the camshaft timing belt sprockets, note the R and L marks (arrows) which designate the right (rear cylinder bank) and left (front cylinder bank) camshaft sprockets - don't mix them up!

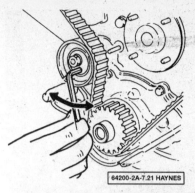

7.21 To adjust timing belt tension, loosen the tensioner nut, move the tensioner with an Allen wrench inserted into the hex hole, then tighten the nut

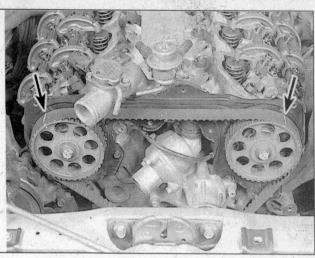

7.23a Align the white marks on the belt (arrows) with the punch marks on the camshaft sprockets and the rear timing belt cover to ensure correct valve timing - this is extremely important - don't continue with belt installation until you're sure it's correct!

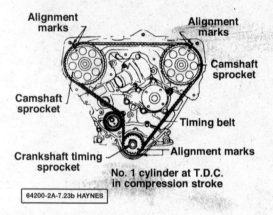

7.23b Make sure all the marks are aligned

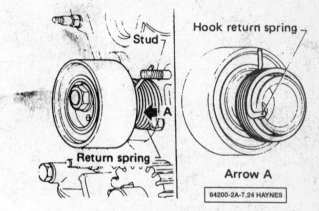

7.24 Belt tensioner spring mounting details (if the stud is removed, use a thread locking compound on the threads during installation)

2A

19 To replace the crankshaft sprocket, refer to Section 12.

Installation

Refer to illustrations 7.21, 7.23a, 7.23b, 7.24, 7.25, 7.27 and 7.28

20 Verify that you have the correct belt for your vehicle. A new factory belt will have three white marks that ease installation by aligning exactly with the two camshaft timing marks and the crankshaft timing marks. Aftermarket belts may or may not have these marks. **Note:** *If your vehicle is a 1993 model, check the tooth design on the camshaft or crankshaft sprockets. The teeth have a SQUARE edge at the bottom of the groove on 1993 engines, while later models are ROUNDED. The replacement belts are available as either straight-tooth or rounded, and they are NOT interchangeable. Use only a belt that matches the tooth design of your sprockets. Use of the wrong belt will cause whining noise and premature failure.*

21 Prepare to install the timing belt by turning the tensioner clockwise with an Allen wrench and temporarily tightening the locking nut **(see illustration)**.

22 Install the timing belt with the directional arrow pointing away from the engine.

23 Align the factory white lines on the timing belt with the punch mark on each of the camshaft sprockets **(see illustration)** and the crankshaft sprocket. Make sure all three sets of timing marks are properly aligned **(see illustration)**.

Adjustment

24 If the tensioner was removed, reinstall it and make sure the spring is positioned properly **(see illustration)**. Push on the belt with a force of approximately 22 lbs. between the tensioner and the rear camshaft sprocket (push the belt towards the water outlet). Keep the tensioner steady with the Allen wrench and loosen the locking nut.

25 Using the Allen wrench, swing the tensioner 70 to 80-degrees in a clockwise direction and temporarily tighten the locking nut **(see illustration)**.

26 Slowly turn the crankshaft clockwise two full revolutions, returning the number one piston to TDC on the compression stroke. **Caution:** *If excessive resistance is felt while turning the crankshaft, it's an indication that*

the pistons are coming into contact with the valves. Go back over the procedure to correct the situation before proceeding.

27 Midway between the front and rear camshaft sprockets, push downward on the

7.25 Use an Allen wrench to turn the tensioner pulley 70 to 80-degrees in a CLOCKWISE direction

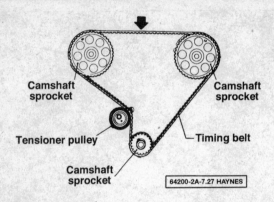

7.27 The deflection of the timing belt is checked exactly half-way between the front and rear camshaft sprockets

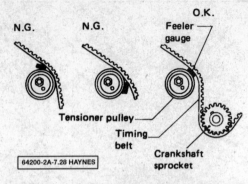

7.28 Position the feeler gauge between the tensioner pulley and the belt, then turn the crankshaft to move the feeler gauge to the point shown here (it must be exact, so work carefully)

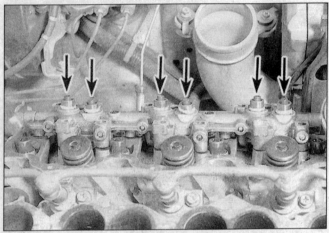

8.2 Wrap each lifter with a rubber band so it can't fall out of the lifter guide

8.3 With the lifters retained by rubber bands, the lifter guide assembly can be removed from the cylinder head

belt with 22 lbs. of force and measure the belt deflection, which should be 0.51 to 0.59 inch **(see illustration)**. If the deflection is as specified, the belt tension is adjusted properly. If not, loosen the tensioner locking nut while keeping the tensioner steady with the Allen wrench. **Note:** *Another person to help with the following procedure will be helpful.*

28   Place a 0.014-inch thick feeler gauge (or a combination of gauges to obtain this thickness) adjacent to the tensioner pulley and slowly turn the crankshaft clockwise until the feeler gauge is between the belt and the tensioner pulley **(see illustration)**.

29   Keeping the tensioner steady against the belt and feeler gauges with the Allen wrench, tighten the tensioner locking nut.

30   Turn the crankshaft to remove the feeler gauge and continue turning for two revolutions and return the number one piston to TDC.

31   Recheck the belt tension as in Step 27, and readjust the belt if necessary. **Note:** *If proper tension can't be achieved, install a new belt.*

32   Install the various components removed during disassembly, referring to the appropriate Sections as necessary.

8   Camshafts, lifters and seals - removal and installation

Removal

Lifters

Refer to illustrations 8.2, 8.3 and 8.5

1   Remove the valve cover (see Section 4) and the rocker arm shaft assemblies (see Section 5).

2   Secure the lifters by raising them slightly and wrapping a rubber band around each one to prevent them from falling out of the guides **(see illustration)**. **Note:** *If a lifter should fall out of the guide, immediately put it back in its original location.*

3   Remove the lifter guide assembly **(see illustration)**.

4   Remove the lifters from the bores one at a time. Keep them in order. Each lifter must be reinstalled in its original bore. **Caution:** *Do not lay the lifters on their side or upside down, or air can become trapped inside and the lifter will have to be bled as follows. The lifters can be laid on their side only if they are submerged in a pan of clean engine oil until reassembly.*

5   With the lifter in its bore, push down on it **(see illustration)**. If it moves more than

8.5 Depress the valve lifter by hand and note the movement

8.12 Remove the cover plate bolts (arrows) and gently pry off the cover (front cylinder head shown, rear cylinder head similar)

8.13a Hold the camshaft lug (arrow) . . .

8.13b . . . with pliers or a wrench to prevent the camshaft from moving while loosening the bolt

0.040-inch (1 mm), air may be trapped inside the lifter.

6   If you think air is trapped inside a valve lifter, reinstall the rocker arm shaft assemblies and valve cover.

7   Bleed air from the lifters by running the engine at 1,000 rpm under no load for about 10 minutes.

8   Remove the valve cover and rocker arm shaft assemblies again. Repeat the procedure in Step 5 once more. If there's still air in the lifter, replace it with a new one.

9   While the lifters are out of the engine, inspect them for wear. Refer to Chapter 2, Part B for inspection procedures.

10   Installation is the reverse of removal. Be sure to lubricate each lifter with liberal amounts of clean engine oil prior to installation.

Camshafts

Refer to illustrations 8.12, 8.13a, 8.13b, 8.14 and 8.15

11   Remove the cylinder heads from the engine (see Section 11).

12   Remove the bolts **(see illustration)** and gently pry off the camshaft cover plate at the transaxle end of the cylinder head.

13   Use the holding lugs **(see illustration)** to secure the camshaft while loosening the

retaining bolt **(see illustration)**. Remove the bolt and the thrust plate.

14   Carefully pry the camshaft oil seal out of the cylinder head with a small screwdriver **(see illustration)**. Don't scratch or nick the camshaft in the process!

15   Carefully pull the camshaft out the front of the cylinder head using a twisting motion **(see illustration)**. **Caution:** *Don't scratch the bearing surfaces with the cam lobes.* Refer to Chapter 2, Part B for camshaft and bearing inspection procedures.

Installation

Refer to illustrations 8.18 and 8.21

16   Lubricate the camshaft bearing journals and lobes with moly-based engine assembly lube, then install it carefully in the cylinder head. Don't scratch the bearing surfaces with the camshaft lobes!

17   Install the camshaft thrust plate and retaining bolt at the rear of the camshaft and tighten it to the torque listed in this Chapter's Specifications. **Note:** *You can temporarily install the camshaft sprocket and use a two-pin spanner to hold the sprocket and camshaft*

while the thrust plate bolt is tightened.

18   With the camshaft installed in the cylinder head, mount a dial indicator to check the end play **(see illustration)**.

19   Move the camshaft as far as possible to the rear of the cylinder head.

20   Zero the dial indicator. Move the cam forward as far as possible. Compare the results to the Specifications in this Chapter.

2A

8.14 Carefully pry the camshaft oil seal out with a small screwdriver

8.15 Withdraw the camshaft from the cylinder head, using both hands to support it to avoid damage to the bearing surfaces in the cylinder head

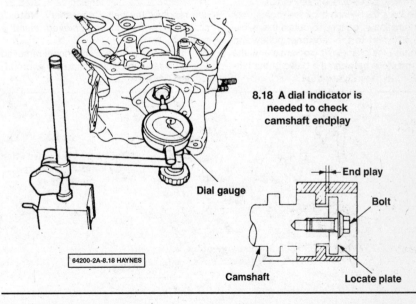

8.18 A dial indicator is needed to check camshaft endplay

Dial gauge

End play

Bolt

Camshaft

Locate plate

64200-2A-8.18 HAYNES

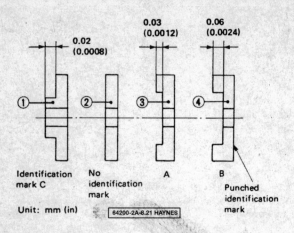

8.21 If the camshaft endplay exceeds the specified limit, select a different thrust plate to bring the endplay within specification

8.24 Use a seal driver to press the new camshaft seal squarely into place

21   Endplay outside the specified range requires thrust plate replacement. Measure the old plate **(see illustration)** and obtain a new one that will produce endplay as close to the specification as possible.

22   The remainder of the cylinder head assembly is the reverse of the disassembly procedure. Refer to Section 11 for cylinder head installation.

Camshaft seals

Refer to illustration 8.24

23   In the course of replacing a camshaft, the old seal is removed **(see illustration 8.14)**. If you are replacing the seals only (the camshaft has not been replaced) the procedure is the same.

24   After the camshaft has been installed, use a seal installation tool, deep socket or piece of pipe of the appropriate diameter (see Section 12, Step 12). to press the new seal squarely into the cylinder head **(see illustration)**. Press the seal in only until the seal bottoms.

9   Intake manifold - removal and installation

Upper intake manifold (plenum)

Refer to illustrations 9.4, 9.5a, 9.5b and 9.6

1   Relieve the fuel pressure (see Chapter 4) and then disconnect the negative cable from the battery.

2   Drain the coolant into a clean container (see Chapter 1).

3   Refer to Chapter 4 and remove the air intake duct, then disconnect the throttle linkage, hoses and electrical connectors from the throttle body.

4   Detach the spark plug wires from the rear cylinder bank spark plugs and remove the spark plug wires from the retainers on the plenum. Remove the distributor cap from the distributor and position the distributor cap and spark plug wires aside. Label and disconnect the hoses and electrical connectors

attached to the plenum **(see illustration)**. **Note:** *The are a number of hoses at the firewall side of the plenum, including the fast idle control solenoid, heater vacuum connection, and PCV hose. Make sure you have labeled and disconnected every hose or wire before attempting to remove the plenum. Space and visibility limitations behind the plenum make this difficult.*

5   Remove the two ground straps attached to the plenum, then unbolt the breather tube brackets from the plenum **(see illustrations)**.

6   Remove the upper intake manifold bolts and remove the manifold with the throttle body attached **(see illustration)**.

7   To install the upper manifold, clean the mounting surfaces of the lower manifold with lacquer thinner and remove all traces of the old gasket material or sealant.

8   Install the new gasket over the lower manifold studs, then install the upper intake manifold. Tighten the bolts to the torque listed in this Chapter's Specifications, working from the center out to the ends.

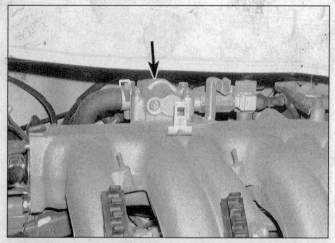

9.4 At the top/rear of the plenum, disconnect the hoses and electrical connector from the fast idle control valve (arrow), then unbolt the fast idle control valve to allow more clearance between the plenum and the cowl

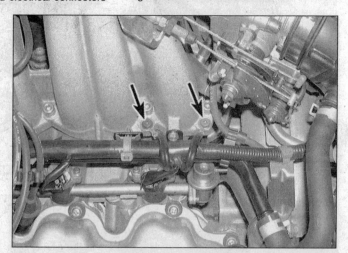

9.5a Remove the bolts and detach the two ground straps (arrows) on the plenum

9.5b Remove the bolts (arrows) retaining the breather tube to the plenum

9.6 Remove the five Allen-head bolts (arrows) and remove the intake manifold plenum

Lower intake manifold

Refer to illustrations 9.10, 9.13 and 9.14

9   Remove the upper intake manifold (see Steps 1 through 8). Refer to Chapter 4 and disconnect the electrical connectors at the fuel injectors (label all connectors first) and remove the fuel rails from the lower intake manifold.

10   Remove the bolts and disconnect the coolant pipes at the transaxle end of the intake manifold **(see illustration)**.

11   Remove the mounting nuts and bolts, then detach the lower intake manifold from the cylinder heads. If the manifold is stuck, don't pry between the gasket mating surfaces or damage may result.

12   Carefully use a scraper to remove all traces of old gasket material and sealant from the manifold and cylinder heads, then clean the mating surfaces with lacquer thinner or acetone.

13   Inspect the coolant pipes below the intake before installing the new gaskets and

9.10 Remove the bolts and disconnect the coolant pipes (arrow) from the rear of the lower intake manifold

lower intake manifold **(see illustration)**. Install new gaskets, then position the lower manifolds on the engine. Make sure the gaskets and manifolds are aligned over the dowels in the cylinder heads and install the nuts.

14   Following the recommended tightening sequence, tighten the nuts/bolts, in three equal steps, to the torque listed in this Chap-

ter's Specifications **(see illustration)**. **Note:** *The torque specifications for the nuts are different than the bolts.*

15   The remainder of the installation is the reverse of the removal procedure. Refill the cooling system and change the engine oil (see Chapter 1). Run the engine and check for fuel, vacuum and coolant leaks.

9.13 Check the condition of the coolant pipes and the gasket (arrow) between the pipes and the thermostat housing - they are only accessible when the lower intake manifold is off

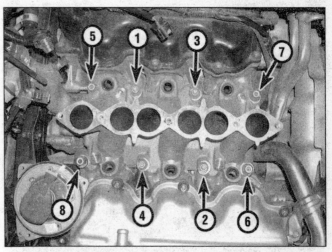

9.14 Lower intake manifold fastener TIGHTENING sequence

2A

10.4 On 1994 and later models, remove the bolts (arrows) and remove the heat shield from the exhaust manifold crossover pipe

10.5 On 1994 and later models, unbolt the crossover flange fasteners (arrows indicate two of the three) at the front exhaust manifold

10 Exhaust manifolds - removal and installation

Note: *The engine must be completely cool before beginning this procedure.*

Removal

Refer to illustrations 10.4, 10.5, 10.6, 10.8 and 10.11

1   Disconnect the negative cable from the battery and support the vehicle on jackstands.
2   Spray penetrating oil on the exhaust manifold fasteners and allow it to soak in.
3   Remove the air inlet and air cleaner housing from the throttle body (see Chapter 4).
4   On 1994 and later models, remove the bolts and the heat shield from the crossover pipe at the transaxle end of the engine **(see illustration)**.
5   On 1994 and later models, unbolt the flange connections between the crossover pipe and the front manifold **(see illustration)**. **Note:** *On 1993 models, no crossover pipe is used; each exhaust manifold is connected directly to the exhaust pipe. On 1994 and later models the crossover pipe connects the rear manifold to the front manifold.*

Front (radiator side) manifold

6   Remove the bracket holding the engine oil dipstick to provide access to the manifold fasteners, and remove the upper row of manifold nuts **(see illustration)**. Work from the ends toward the middle when removing the manifold fasteners.
7   Disconnect the electrical connector from the oxygen sensor. Detach the exhaust pipe from the exhaust manifold. **Note 1:** *On some 1999 and later models, the catalytic converter is an integral part of the front exhaust manifold.* **Note 2:** *Some models may have a separate heat shield over the pipe-to-manifold flange. This shield must be removed to access the flange fasteners.*
8   Working from below, remove the lower row of manifold fasteners and remove the manifold **(see illustration)**.

Rear (firewall side) manifold

9   On 1994 and later models, refer to Chapter 3 and set aside the coolant recovery tank for clearance. Refer to Chapter 4 and disconnect the electrical connectors in the area of the throttle body, including the EGR solenoid connector, TPS, EVAP canister

solenoid and MAP/BARO sensor. Label all the connectors before separating them.
10   On 1993 models, support the engine and remove the front and rear engine mounts and crossmember (see Section 17). Remove the rear engine mount bracket from the engine block.
11   Unbolt the EGR pipe from the rear manifold. On 1993 models, detach the exhaust pipe from the exhaust manifold. Remove the rear manifold nuts and remove the manifold **(see illustration)**.

Installation

12   Carefully inspect the manifolds and fasteners for cracks and damage.
13   Use a scraper to remove all traces of old gasket material and carbon deposits from the manifold and cylinder head mating surfaces. If the gasket was leaking, have the manifold checked for warpage at an automotive machine shop and resurfaced if necessary.
14   Position new gaskets over the cylinder head studs.
15   Install the manifold and thread the mounting nuts into place. The rear manifold and crossover pipe should be installed first.

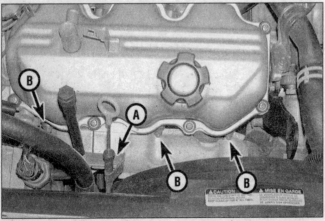

10.6 Unbolt the dipstick bracket (A) and remove the upper row of exhaust manifold nuts (B)

10.8 Remove the lower row of manifold nuts (arrows) from below

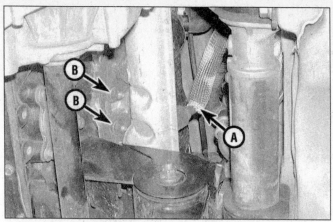

10.11 Disconnect the EGR pipe (A) from the rear manifold, then remove the manifold mounting nuts (B indicates two of the three lower nuts, upper nuts similar to front manifold)

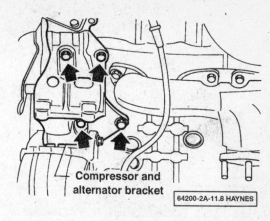

Compressor and alternator bracket

64200-2A-11.8 HAYNES

11.8 Remove the bolts (arrows) and detach the compressor and alternator bracket

16 Working from the center out, tighten the nuts to the torque listed in this Chapter's Specifications in three or four equal steps.

17 Reinstall the remaining parts in the reverse order of removal. Use new gaskets when connecting the exhaust pipe to the front manifold.

18 Run the engine and check for exhaust leaks.

11 Cylinder heads - removal and installation

Note 1: *Allow the engine to cool completely before beginning this procedure.*
Note 2: *The cylinder head bolts must not be reused, obtain new bolts before beginning installation.*

Removal

1 Refer to Chapter 1 and drain the cooling system. Remove the timing belt, camshaft sprocket(s) and rear timing cover (see Section 7). Also remove the bolts holding the coolant pipes to the rear (transaxle end) of each cylinder head at the camshaft end plates.

2 Remove the intake manifold (see Section 9), and set aside the fuel injectors and

their harnesses.

3 Remove the rocker arm components (see Section 5) and lifters (see Section 8).

4 Remove the exhaust manifold(s) (see Section 10).

5 Label and disconnect the hoses and electrical harness connectors at the timing belt end of the engine.

Front (radiator side) cylinder head

Refer to illustration 11.8

6 Remove the spark plug wires, distributor and coil (see Chapter 5).

7 Remove the air conditioning compressor from the bracket without disconnecting the refrigerant hoses (see Chapter 3) and set it aside. Secure the compressor to the vehicle with rope or wire to make sure it doesn't hang by its hoses. **Note:** *There isn't room to fully remove the upper compressor bolts until the compressor is moved aside.*

8 Remove the compressor and alternator bracket **(see illustration).**

9 Remove the bracket holding the engine oil dipstick tube to the cylinder head **(see illustration 10.6).**

10 Remove the coolant pipe mounting bolts in the valley between the heads (refer to Section 9).

Rear (firewall side) cylinder head

11 Detach the heater hoses and brackets from the transaxle end of the cylinder head.

Both cylinder heads

Refer to illustration 11.12

12 Loosen the cylinder head bolts with a hex drive tool in 1/4-turn increments until they can be removed by hand. Be sure to follow the proper numerical sequence, removing the small bolt, located outside of the cylinder head first **(see illustration).**

13 Remove the washers from the cylinder head bolts and discard the bolts (except the small bolt on the outside of the cylinder head). NEW cylinder head bolts must be used on reassembly **Note:** *The cylinder head bolt washers can be reused.*

14 Lift the cylinder head off the engine block. If resistance is felt, dislodge the cylinder head by striking it with a wood block and hammer. If prying is required, be very careful not to damage the cylinder head or engine block!

Installation

Refer to illustrations 11.15, 11.19, 11.21 and 11.22

15 Remove the old cylinder head gaskets **(see illustration).** The mating surfaces of the

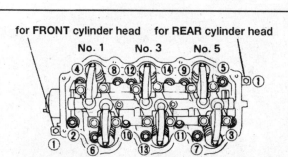

for FRONT cylinder head   for REAR cylinder head

No. 1   No. 3   No. 5

Loosen in numerical order.

64200-2A-11.12 HAYNES

11.12 Cylinder head bolt LOOSENING sequence (remove bolt no.1, then loosen the rest of the bolts 1/4-turn at a time until they can be removed by hand)

11.15 Remove the old gaskets and clean the engine block and cylinder head mating surfaces thoroughly

2A

11.19 Position the gasket over the dowel pins (arrows) so that all the holes line up

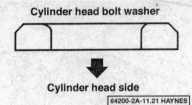

Cylinder head bolt washer

Cylinder head side

64200-2A-11.21 HAYNES

11.21 The cylinder head bolt washers must be installed with the chamfered side against the bolt head and the flat side against the cylinder head

cylinder heads and engine block must be perfectly clean when the heads are installed.

16   Use a gasket scraper to remove all traces of carbon and old gasket material, then clean the mating surfaces with lacquer thinner or acetone. If there's oil on the mating surfaces when the heads are installed, the gaskets may not seal correctly and leaks may develop. Use a vacuum cleaner to remove any debris that falls into the cylinders.

17   Check the engine block and cylinder head mating surfaces for nicks, deep scratches and other damage. If damage is slight, it can be removed with a file - if it's excessive, machining may be the only alternative.

18   Use a tap of the correct size to chase the threads in the cylinder head bolt holes. Dirt, corrosion, sealant and damaged threads will affect torque readings. Ensure that the threaded holes in the engine block are clean and dry.

19   Position the new gaskets over the dowel pins in the engine block **(see illustration)**.

20   Carefully position the heads on the engine block without disturbing the gaskets.

21   Lightly oil the threads of the NEW cylinder head bolts and install in the proper locations **(see illustration 11.22)**. Tighten them finger tight. Make sure the washers are in place on the bolts - the chamfered side of the washer must be against the bolt head, which means the flat side must be against the cylin-

der head surface **(see illustration)**.

22 Follow the recommended sequence and tighten the bolts (except the small bolt on the outside of the cylinder head) in five steps to the torque specified in this Chapter **(see illustration)**. **Caution:** *Bolts 4, 5, 12 and 13 in the sequence are longer than the others - be sure all bolts are in their proper locations!*

23   Tighten the small bolt on the outside of the cylinder head to 80 to 104 in-lbs.

24   The remaining installation steps are the reverse of removal.

25   Add coolant and change the engine oil and filter (see Chapter 1), then start the engine and check carefully for oil and coolant leaks.

12   Crankshaft front oil seal - replacement

Refer to illustrations 12.4, 12.5, 12.10, 12.11, 12.12a and 12.12b

1   Disconnect the negative cable from the battery. Raise the front of the vehicle, remove the right front wheel, and secure the vehicle on jackstands.

2   Remove the drivebelts (see Chapter 1).

3   Remove the inner splash shield from the right fenderwell.

4   Use a strap wrench around the crankshaft pulley to hold it while using a

breaker bar and socket to remove the crankshaft pulley center bolt **(see illustration)**.

5   Wedge a prybar or two screwdrivers behind the crankshaft pulley and carefully pry it off the crankshaft **(see illustration)**. If the pulley is difficult to remove, use a bolt-type puller and pull it off.

6   Refer to Section 7 and remove the timing belt covers and timing belt.

7   Carefully remove the crankshaft sprocket with a prybar or two screwdrivers, be very careful not to damage the oil pump body.

8   If the sprocket cannot be pried off, drill and tap two holes into the face of the sprocket and use a bolt-type puller to pull it off the crankshaft. **Caution:** *Do not reuse a drilled sprocket - replace it.*

9   Remove the timing belt guide, noting the side facing out (mark it if necessary).

10   Carefully pry the oil seal out with a screwdriver **(see illustration)**. Don't scratch or nick the crankshaft in the process!

11   Before installation, apply a thin coat of multi-purpose grease to the inside of the seal **(see illustration)**.

12   Fabricate a seal installation tool with a short length of pipe of equal or slightly smaller outside diameter than the seal itself. File the end of the pipe that will bear down on the seal until it's free of sharp edges. You'll also need a long bolt of the same thread pitch as the crankshaft pulley bolt and a large washer, slightly larger in diameter than the pipe, on which the bolt head can seat **(see**

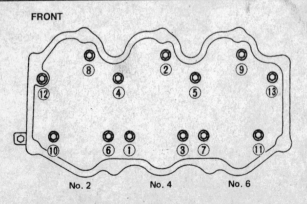

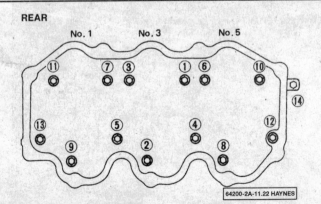

FRONT   REAR

64200-2A-11.22 HAYNES

11.22 Cylinder head bolt TIGHTENING sequence - note that bolts 4, 5, 12 and 13 in the sequence are 5.0 inches long, the rest (except no. 14) are 4.17 inches in length; make sure the bolts are installed in the correct locations

12.4 Use strap wrench to hold the crankshaft pulley while removing the center bolt (a chain-type wrench may be used if you wrap a section of old drivebelt around the crankshaft pulley first)

12.5 Use two screwdrivers or a pry bar to carefully pry the crankshaft pulley off

12.10 Pry the seal out very carefully with a seal removal tool or screwdriver - if the crankshaft is nicked or otherwise damaged, the new seal will leak!

illustration). Install the oil seal by pressing it into position with the seal installation tool (see illustration). When the seal is bottomed in the housing, don't turn the bolt any more or you'll damage the seal.

13   Install the inner timing belt guide onto the nose of the crankshaft.

14   Make sure the Woodruff key is in place in the crankshaft.

15   Apply a thin coat of assembly lube to the inside of the timing belt sprocket and slide it onto the crankshaft.

16   Installation of the remaining components is the reverse of removal. Refer to Section 7 for the timing belt installation and adjustment procedure. Tighten all bolts to the torque listed in this Chapter's Specifications.

13   Oil pan - removal and installation

Removal

Refer to illustrations 13.6a, 13.6b, 13.9 and 13.14

1   Disconnect the negative cable from the battery.

12.11 Apply multi-purpose grease or clean engine oil to the lips of the new seal before installing it (if you apply a small amount of grease to the outer edge, it will be easier to press into the bore)

2   Raise the vehicle and support it securely on jackstands.

3   Remove the under-vehicle splash pan.

4   Drain the engine oil and remove the oil filter (see Chapter 1).

5   Unbolt the exhaust pipe from the front

12.12a Fabricate a seal installation tool from a piece of pipe, a long bolt and a large washer - the outside diameter of the pipe must be the same size or slightly smaller than the outer diameter of the seal (the pipe must bear against the outer edge of the seal)

manifold and lower the pipe (see Section 10).

6   Remove the braces joining the engine to the transaxle (see illustration) and detach the bellhousing cover (see illustration).

12.12b Install the seal installation tool and press the seal into the bore by tightening the bolt

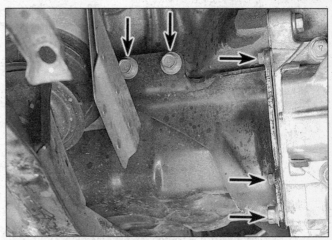

13.6a Remove the bolts (arrows) and detach the engine-to-transaxle brace on each side

13.6b Once the braces are removed, the bellhousing cover can be removed

13.9 Remove the bolt retaining the rear heater/air conditioning lines (A), then remove the crossmember bolts (B)

7   Support the engine/transaxle securely with a hoist from above or with two hydraulic jacks, one placed under the crankshaft pulley and the other under the transaxle bellhousing. Protect the pulley and bellhousing by placing a wood block on the jack head. **Warning:** *Be absolutely certain the engine/transaxle is securely supported! DO NOT place any part of your body under the engine/transaxle - it could crush you if the jack or hoist fails!*

8   Unbolt the two passenger-side engine mounts from the crossmember (see Section 17).

9   Remove the engine-mount crossmember from beneath the oil pan **(see illustration)**.

10   Remove the alternator (see Chapter 5).

11   Remove the oil pan bolts, following the reverse of the tightening sequence **(see illustration 13.19)**.

12   Detach the oil pan. Don't pry between the pan and engine block or damage to the sealing surfaces may result and oil leaks could develop. If the pan is stuck, dislodge it with a soft-face hammer.

13   Use a gasket scraper to remove all traces of old gasket material and sealant from the engine block and pan. Clean the mating surfaces with lacquer thinner or acetone.

14   Unbolt the oil pick-up tube and screen assembly **(see illustration)**.

Installation

Refer to illustrations 13.15, 13.17, 13.18 and 13.19

15   Replace the O-ring on the flange of the oil pick-up tube **(see illustration)** and reinstall the tube. Tighten the pick-up tube bolts to the torque listed in this Chapter's Specifications.

16   Ensure that the threaded holes in the engine block are clean (use a tap to remove any sealant or corrosion from the threads).

17   Apply RTV sealant to the ends of the seals **(see illustration)** and position them on the oil pump and rear seal housings.

18   Apply a continuous 5/32-inch (3.5 mm) bead of RTV sealant to the inner sealing surface of the oil pan **(see illustration)**. **Note:** *Install the oil pan within five minutes of sealant application.*

19   Install the oil pan and tighten the bolts in

three or four steps following the sequence shown **(see illustration)** to the torque listed in this Chapter's Specifications.

20   The remaining installation steps are the reverse of removal.

21   Allow at least 30 minutes for the sealant to dry, add oil and a new oil filter, start the engine and check for oil pressure and leaks.

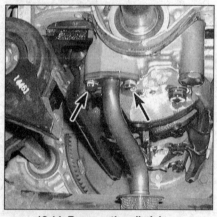

13.14 Remove the oil pick-up tube bolts (arrows)

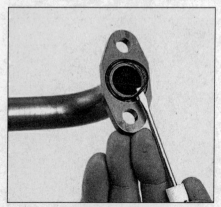

13.15 Before installing the oil pick-up tube, replace the rubber O-ring

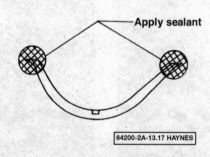

13.17 Apply sealant to the points shown here on the rubber end seals

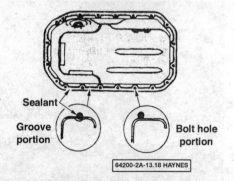

13.18 Apply RTV sealant in the groove and to the inside of the bolt holes, around the pan mounting surface

13.19 Oil pan bolt TIGHTENING sequence

14.3 Remove the power steering pump bracket bolts (arrows)

14 Oil pump - removal, inspection and installation

Removal

Refer to illustrations 14.3 and 14.4

1   Remove the timing belt and the crankshaft sprocket (see Section 7). Remove the oil pan and pick-up tube (Section 13).

2   Refer to Chapter 5 and remove the alternator adjusting bar and the bar-to-oil pump bolt.
3   Unbolt the power steering pump (see Chapter 10) and without disconnecting the hoses, position it aside. Remove the power steering pump bracket **(see illustration)**.
4   Remove the oil pump-to-engine block bolts from the front of the engine **(see illustration)**. **Note:** *The pickup tube and oil*

filter adapter can remain attached to the pump at this time if desired. One of the two long oil pump mounting bolts is the bolt removed in Step 2 that held the alternator adjusting bar.
5   Use a block of wood and a hammer to break the oil pump gasket seal.
6   Pull out on the oil pump to remove it from the engine block.
7   Use a scraper to remove old gasket material and sealant from the oil pump and engine block mating surfaces. Clean the mating surfaces with lacquer thinner or acetone.

Inspection

Refer to illustrations 14.8, 14.10a, 14.10b, 14.11a, 14.11b, 14.11c and 14.11d

8   Use a large Phillips screwdriver to remove the screws holding the rear cover on the oil pump **(see illustration)**.
9   Clean all components with solvent, then inspect them for wear and damage.
10   Remove the oil pressure regulator cap, washer, spring and valve **(see illustrations)**. Check the oil pressure regulator valve sliding surface and valve spring. If either the spring or the valve is damaged, they must be replaced as a set.

2A

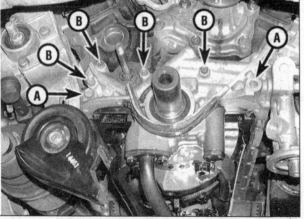

14.4 Remove the oil pump mounting bolts (A indicates the two long bolts, B the shorter bolts) and detach the pump from the engine

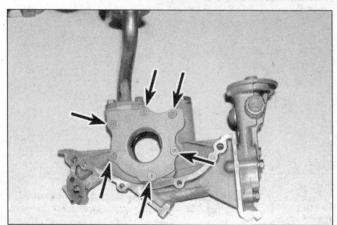

14.8 Remove the screws and lift the cover off

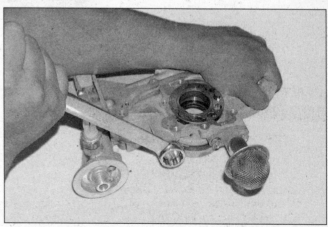

14.10a Remove the oil pressure relief valve plug

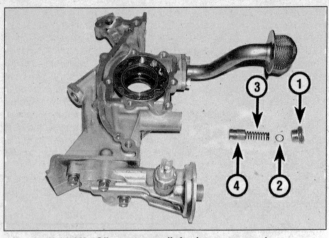

14.10b Oil pressure relief valve components

1 Plug   3 Spring
2 Washer   4 Relief valve

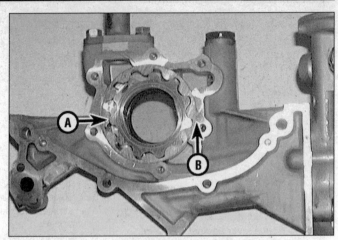

14.11a Use feeler gauges to measure the rotor tooth tip clearance (A) and the outer rotor-to-body clearance (B)

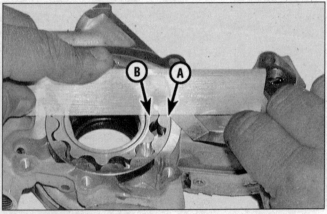

14.11b Measure the cover-to-rotor end clearance with a straightedge and feeler gauge - measure (A) above the outer rotor and (B) above the inner rotor

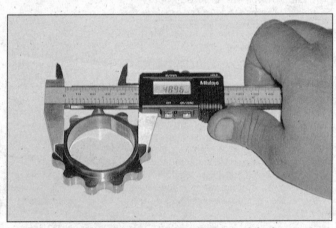

14.11c Use calipers to measure the diameter of the inner rotor ridge (the part of the inner rotor that rides in the pump body) . . .

11   Check the clearance following oil pump components with a feeler gauge **(see illustrations)** and compare the measurements to the clearance listed in this Chapter's Specifications:

a) *Rotor tooth tip clearance*

b) *Outer rotor-to-body clearance*
c) *Cover-to-inner rotor clearance*
d) *Cover-to-outer rotor clearance*
e) *Inner rotor ridge clearance*

    If any clearance is excessive, replace the entire oil pump assembly.

12   **Note:** *Pack the pump with petroleum jelly to prime it.* Assemble the oil pump and tighten the screws securely. Install the oil pressure regulator valve, spring and washer, then tighten the oil pressure regulator valve cap.

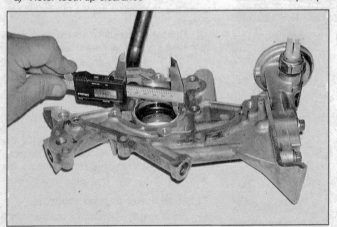

14.11d . . . and subtract the inner rotor ridge diameter from the opening in the pump body where the inner rotor rides to obtain the inner rotor ridge-to-body clearance

14.14 There is a flat surface (arrow) on each side of the crankshaft - align them with the flats on the gear

15.2 Hold a lever against a casting protrusion on the engine block or place a screwdriver through a hole in the driveplate to hold the driveplate while the mounting bolts are removed - note the painted marks made at the crank and driveplate for alignment

Installation

Refer to illustration 14.14

13 Apply RTV sealant to the oil pump mounting surface.

14 Use new gaskets on all disassembled parts and reverse the removal procedure for installation. Align the flats on the crankshaft **(see illustration)** with the flats on the oil pump gear. Tighten all fasteners to the torque listed in this Chapter's Specifications. **Note:** *Before installing the oil pump pick-up, replace the rubber O-ring* **(see illustration 13.15).**

---

15 Driveplate - removal and installation

Refer to illustration 15.2

1 Remove the transaxle (see Chapter 7). If it's leaking, now would be a very good time to replace the front pump seal/O-ring. **Warning:** *The engine must be supported from*

above with an engine hoist or three-bar support fixture before working underneath the vehicle with the transaxle removed.

2 Remove the bolts that secure the driveplate to the crankshaft **(see illustration)**. **Note:** *If a reinforcing ring is used between the bolts and the driveplate, mark it so that you know which side should face the driveplate on reassembly.*

3 Remove the driveplate. **Warning:** *The ring gear teeth can be sharp, so wear gloves or handle the driveplate with rags.*

4 Clean the driveplate and inspect the surface for cracks. Check for worn, cracked or broken ring-gear teeth. Lay the driveplate on a flat surface and use a straightedge to check for warpage.

5 Clean and inspect the mating surfaces of the driveplate and the crankshaft. If the crankshaft oil seal is leaking, replace it before reinstalling the driveplate (see Section 16).

6 Position the driveplate against the crankshaft, aligning the marks made during removal. Install the reinforcement plate. Apply threadlocking compound to the threads and install the bolts.

7 Hold the crankshaft from turning **(see illustration 15.2)**. Working in several stages and following a criss-cross pattern, tighten the bolts to the torque listed in this Chapter's Specifications.

8 The remainder of installation is the reverse of the removal procedure.

---

16 Rear main oil seal - replacement

Refer to illustrations 16.2 and 16.3

1 The transaxle must be removed from the vehicle for this procedure (see Chapter 7). **Warning:** *The engine must be supported from above with an engine hoist or three-bar support fixture before working underneath the vehicle with the transaxle removed.* Remove the driveplate (see Section 15).

2 Carefully pry out the old seal out of the retainer with a seal removal tool or screwdriver **(see illustration)**.

3 Apply multi-purpose grease to the crankshaft seal journal and the lip of the new seal. Preferably, use a seal installation tool to press the new seal into place. If the proper seal installation tool is unavailable, use a large socket, section of pipe or a blunt tool and carefully drive the new seal into place **(see illustration)**. The lip is stiff so carefully work it onto the seal journal of the crankshaft. Don't rush it or you may damage the seal. **Note:** *Install the seal squarely and only until flush with the back of the seal plate, no further.*

4 The remaining steps are the reverse of removal.

---

17 Engine mounts - check and replacement

---

1 There are four engine mounts; front and rear mounts on the right side of the vehicle attached to the crossmember, and front and rear mounts on the left side attached to the transaxle.

Check

2 During the check, the engine must be raised slightly to remove the weight from the mounts.

3 Raise the vehicle and support it securely on jackstands. Position two jacks, one under the crankshaft pulley and the other under the transaxle bellhousing. Place a block of wood between the jack head and the crankshaft pulley or bellhousing, then carefully raise the engine/transaxle just enough to take the weight off the mounts. **Warning:** *DO NOT place any part of your body under the engine when it's supported only by a jack!*

4 Check the mounts to see if the rubber is cracked, hardened or separated from the metal plates. Sometimes the rubber will split right down the center.

5 Check for relative movement between the mount plates and the engine or frame (use a large screwdriver or prybar to attempt to move the mounts). If movement is noted, lower the engine and tighten the mount fasteners.

6 Rubber preservative should be applied to the mounts to slow deterioration.

Replacement

Refer to illustrations 17.9, 17.14, 17.16 and 17.17

7 Disconnect the negative battery cable from the battery, then set the parking brake, block the rear wheels, raise the front of the vehicle and support it securely on jackstands. Remove the splash shields from under the vehicle.

Front and rear engine mounts

8 Position a floorjack under the crankshaft pulley. Place a wood block between the jack head and the pulley and raise the jack just enough to support the weight of the engine.

16.2 Pry the seal out very carefully with a seal removal tool or screwdriver - if the crankshaft is damaged the new seal will leak!

16.3 If you don't have a seal installer tool, use a blunt tool (such as a brass punch) to carefully work the edge of the seal evenly into the bore and around the crankshaft

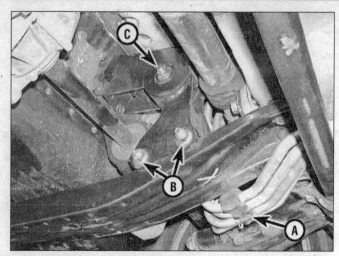

17.9 Remove the auxiliary heating/air conditioning pipe bracket bolt (A), then remove the mount-to-crossmember through-bolts (B indicates right-rear mount, right-front similar) - (C) indicates the mount-to-engine through-bolt

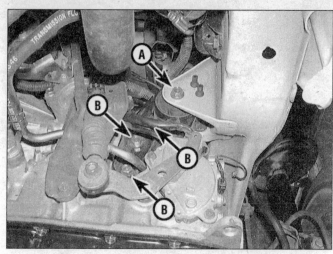

17.14 To remove the left-front transaxle mount, remove the through-bolt (A), then the three bolts (B) retaining the mount to the transaxle

9   Remove the through-bolts from the right-front and right rear mounts where they attach to the crossmember, then remove the bolt retaining the bracket over the auxiliary heating/air conditioning pipes **(see illustration)**.

10   When the lower bolts of both engine mounts have been removed, remove the crossmember-to-chassis bolts **(see illustration 13.9)**.

11   Remove the crossmember, remove the mount-to-engine bracket through-bolts and remove the mounts **(see illustration 17.9)**.

12   Installation is the reverse of removal. **Note:** *Tighten the bolts to Specifications only after the engine weight is back onto the mounts and the jack is removed. If more than one mount has been replaced, see Final tightening below.*

Front and rear transaxle mounts

13   There are two transaxle mounts, one at the radiator side of the transaxle (left-front

mount) and one at the top of the transaxle (left-rear mount).

Left-front mount

14   Support the transaxle with a jack placed under the transaxle bellhousing. Remove the through-bolt at the chassis, then the bolts holding the mount to the transaxle and remove the mount **(see illustration)**.

15   Installation is the reverse of removal. **Note:** *Tighten the bolts to Specifications only after the powertrain weight is back onto the mounts and the jack is removed. If more than one mount has been replaced, see Final tightening below.*

Left-rear mount

16   From below, remove the nuts at the mount bracket on the transaxle **(see illustration)**.

17   From above, remove the through-bolt at the chassis bracket **(see illustration)**.

18   Lower the transaxle enough for the

studs to clear the transaxle bracket and remove the mount.

19   Installation is the reverse of removal. **Note:** *Tighten the bolts to Specifications only after the powertrain weight is back onto the mounts and the jack is removed. If more than one mount has been replaced, see Final tightening below.*

Final tightening

20   To ensure maximum bushing life and prevent excessive noise and vibration, the vehicle should be level and the engine weight should be on the mounts during the final tightening stage. **Note:** *Use thread-locking compound on the nuts/bolts. Ensure that the bushings are not twisted or offset. If you have replaced more than one mount, or when you are installing the engine, tighten the mounts in the following order: crossmember bolts, right-rear mount, left-front mount, right-front mount, and left-rear mount.*

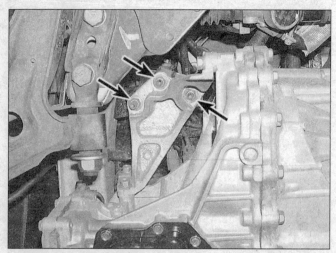

17.16 Remove the three nuts (arrows) at the rear transaxle bracket from below (driveaxle removed for clarity)

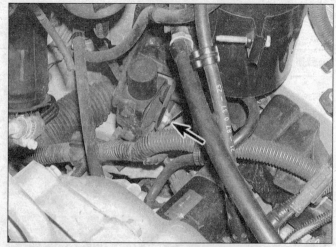

17.17 With the air cleaner and air inlet removed, there is access at the top to remove the left-rear mount through-bolt (arrow)

Chapter 2 Part B
General engine overhaul procedures

Contents

Specifications

General

Bore	3.43 inches
Stroke	3.27 inches
Displacement	181 cubic inches (3.0 liters)
Oil pressure	
At idle	More than 17 psi
At 3200 rpm	57 to 70 psi
Cylinder compression pressure (at 300 rpm)	
Standard	175 psi
Minimum	130 psi
Maximum difference between cylinders	14 psi

Cylinder head

Warpage limit	0.004 inch
Cylinder head height	4.205 to 4.220 inches

Valves and related components

Rocker arm-to-shaft oil clearance	0.0003 to 0.0019 inch
Valve stem diameter	
Intake	0.2742 to 0.2748 inch
Exhaust	0.3136 to 0.3138 inch
Valve margin	
Intake	0.0453 to 0.0571 inch
Exhaust	0.0531 to 0.0650 inch
Service limit	0.020 inch minimum
Valve spring free length	
Outer	2.016 inches
Inner	1.736 inches
Valve spring out of square limit	
Outer	0.087 inch
Inner	0.075 inch
Valve stem to guide clearance	
Intake	0.0008 to 0.0021 inch
Exhaust	0.0016 to 0.0029 inch
Service limit	0.0039 inch maximum
Hydraulic valve lifters	
Lifter outside diameter	0.6278 to 0.6282 inch
Lifter guide inside diameter	0.6299 to 0.6304 inch
Lifter-to-guide clearance	0.0017 to 0.0026 inch

Camshaft

Journal to bearing clearance	
Standard	0.0018 to 0.0035 inch
Service limit	0.0059 inch maximum
Inner diameter of camshaft bearing	
Journal A	1.8504 to 1.8514 inches
Journal B	1.6732 to 1.6742 inches
Journal C	1.8898 to 1.8907 inches
Outer diameter of camshaft journal	
Journal A	1.8472 to 1.8480 inches
Journal B	1.6701 to 1.6709 inches
Journal C	1.8866 to 1.8874 inches
Camshaft bearing oil clearance	
Standard	0.0018 to 0.0035 inch
Service limit	0.006 inch maximum
Camshaft lobe height, intake and exhaust	
Standard	1.5332 to 1.5407 inches
Service limit	0.006 inch lobe lift loss
Camshaft endplay	0.0012 to 0.0024 inch
Camshaft runout limit	0.004 inch total indicator reading

Engine block

Deck warpage limit	0.0039 inch maximum
Cylinder bore diameter	
Standard	3.4252 to 3.4264 inches
Wear limit	0.0079 inch
Out-of-round limit	0.0006 inch maximum
Taper limit	0.0006 inch maximum
Main journal bore diameter	2.47884 to 2.4793 inches

Pistons and rings

Piston skirt diameter	3.4238 to 3.4250 inches
Piston-to-cylinder clearance	0.0010 to 0.0018 inch
Piston rings	
Side clearance	
Top compression ring	0.0016 to 0.0029 inch
Second compression ring	0.0012 to 0.0025 inch
Oil rail	0.0006 to 0.0075 inch
Service limit (all)	0.040 inch maximum
Ring end gap	
Top compression ring	0.0083 to 0.0173 inch
Second compression ring	0.0071 to 0.0173 inch
Oil rail	0.0079 to 0.0299 inch
Service limit (all)	0.039 inch maximum

Crankshaft

Main journal diameter .... 2.4784 to 2.4793 inches
Rod journal diameter .... 1.9667 to 1.9675 inches
Crankshaft journal out-of-round limit .... 0.0002 inch maximum
Endplay
    Standard.. 0.0020 to 0.0067 inch
    Service limit .... 0.0118 inch maximum
Main bearing oil clearance
    Standard.. 0.0011 to 0.0022 inch
    Service limit .... 0.0035 inch maximum
Rod bearing oil clearance
    Standard.. 0.0011 to 0.0022 inch
    Service limit .... 0.0035 inch maximum
Connecting rod side clearance (endplay)
    Standard.. 0.0079 to 0.0138 inch
    Service limit .... 0.0157 inch maximum

Torque specifications*

Ft-lbs (unless otherwise indicated)

Rear main oil seal retainer bolts .... 48 to 64 in-lbs
Connecting rod nuts
    Step one .... 10 to 12
    Step two .... 28 to 33
Main bearing cap bolts .... 67 to 74

Refer to Part A for additional torque specifications

1 General information - engine overhaul

Included in this portion of Chapter 2 are the general overhaul procedures for the cylinder head and internal engine components.

The information ranges from advice concerning preparation for an overhaul and the purchase of replacement parts to detailed, step-by-step procedures covering Removal and installation of internal engine components and the inspection of parts.

The following Sections have been written based on the assumption that the engine has been removed from the vehicle. For information concerning in-vehicle engine repair, as well as removal and installation of the external components necessary for the overhaul, see Chapter 2A.

The Specifications included in this Part are only those necessary for the inspection and overhaul procedures which follow. Refer to Chapter 2, Part A for additional Specifications.

It's not always easy to determine when, or if, an engine should be completely overhauled, as a number of factors must be considered.

High mileage is not necessarily an indication that an overhaul is needed, while low mileage doesn't preclude the need for an overhaul. Frequency of servicing is probably the most important consideration. An engine that's had regular and frequent oil and filter changes, as well as other required maintenance, will most likely give many thousands of miles of reliable service. Conversely, a neglected engine may require an overhaul very early in its life.

Excessive oil consumption is an indication that piston rings, valve seals and/or valve guides are in need of attention. Make sure that oil leaks aren't responsible before deciding that the rings and/or guides are bad. Perform a cylinder compression check to determine the extent of the work required (see Section 3). Also check the vacuum readings under various conditions (see Section 4).

Loss of power, rough running, knocking or metallic engine noises, excessive valve train noise and high fuel consumption rates may also point to the need for an overhaul, especially if they're all present at the same time. If a complete tune-up doesn't remedy the situation, major mechanical work is the only solution.

An engine overhaul involves restoring the internal parts to the specifications of a new engine. During an overhaul, the piston rings are replaced and the cylinder walls are reconditioned (re-bored and/or honed). If a re-bore is done by an automotive machine shop, new oversize pistons will also be installed. The main bearings, connecting rod bearings and camshaft bearings are generally replaced with new ones and, if necessary, the crankshaft may be reground to restore the journals. Generally, the valves are serviced as well, since they're usually in less-than-perfect condition at this point. While the engine is being overhauled, other components, such as the distributor, starter and alternator, can be rebuilt as well. The end result should be a like new engine that will give many trouble free miles. **Note:** *Critical cooling system components such as the hoses, drivebelts, thermostat and water pump should be replaced with new parts when an engine is overhauled. The radiator should be checked carefully to ensure that it isn't clogged or leaking (see Chapter 3). If you purchase a rebuilt engine or short block, some rebuilders will not warranty their engines unless the radiator has been professionally flushed. Also, we don't recommend overhauling the oil pump - always install a new one when an engine is rebuilt.*

Before beginning the engine overhaul, read through the entire procedure to familiarize yourself with the scope and requirements of the job. Overhauling an engine isn't difficult, but it is time-consuming. Plan on the vehicle being tied up for a minimum of two weeks, especially if parts must be taken to an automotive machine shop for repair or reconditioning. Check on availability of parts and make sure that any necessary special tools and equipment are obtained in advance. Most work can be done with typical hand tools, although a number of precision measuring tools are required for inspecting parts to determine if they must be replaced. Often an automotive machine shop will handle the inspection of parts and offer advice concerning reconditioning and replacement. **Note:** *Always wait until the engine has been completely disassembled and all components, especially the engine block, have been inspected before deciding what service and repair operations must be performed by an automotive machine shop. Since the block's condition will be the major factor to consider when determining whether to overhaul the original engine or buy a rebuilt one, never purchase parts or have machine work done on other components until the block has been thoroughly inspected.* As a general rule, time is the primary cost of an overhaul, so it doesn't pay to install worn or substandard parts.

As a final note, to ensure maximum life and minimum trouble from a rebuilt engine, everything must be assembled with care in a spotlessly-clean environment.

2B

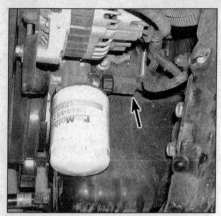

2.2 Remove the oil pressure sending unit (arrow) located on the oil filter adapter just below the alternator and connect an oil pressure gauge to obtain an accurate oil pressure reading

3.6 A compression gauge with a threaded fitting for the spark plug hole is preferred over the type that requires hand pressure to maintain the seal

4.4 A simple vacuum gauge can be very handy in diagnosing engine condition and performance

2   Oil pressure check

Refer to illustration 2.2

1   Low engine oil pressure can be a sign of an engine in need of rebuilding. A "low oil pressure" indicator (often called an "idiot light") is not a test of the oiling system. Such indicators only come on when the oil pressure is dangerously low. Even a factory oil pressure gauge in the instrument panel is only a relative indication, although much better for driver information than a warning light. A better test is with a mechanical (not electrical) oil pressure gauge. When used in conjunction with an accurate tachometer, an engine's oil pressure performance can be compared to factory Specifications for that year and model.

2   Locate the oil pressure indicator sending unit **(see illustration)**.

3   Remove the oil pressure sending unit and install a fitting which will allow you to directly connect your hand-held, mechanical oil pressure gauge. Use Teflon tape or sealant on the threads of the adapter and the fitting on the end of your gauge's hose.

4   Connect an accurate tachometer to the engine, according to the tachometer manufacturer's instructions.

5   Check the oil pressure with the engine running (full operating temperature) at the specified engine speed, and compare it to this Chapter's Specifications. If it's extremely low, the bearings and/or oil pump are probably worn out.

3   Cylinder compression check

Refer to illustration 3.6

1   A compression check will tell you what mechanical condition the upper end of your engine (pistons, rings, valves, cylinder head gaskets) is in. Specifically, it can tell you if the compression is down due to leakage caused by worn piston rings, defective valves and seats or a blown cylinder head gasket. **Note:** *The engine must be at normal operating temperature and the battery must be fully charged for this check.*

2   Begin by cleaning the area around the spark plugs before you remove them (compressed air should be used, if available). The idea is to prevent dirt from getting into the cylinders as the compression check is being done.

3   Remove all of the spark plugs from the engine (see Chapter 1).

4   Block the throttle wide open.

5   Detach the coil wire from the center of the distributor cap and ground it on the engine block. Use a jumper wire with alligator clips on each end to ensure a good ground. The fuel pump circuit should also be disabled and the engine fuel system pressure relieved (see Chapter 4).

6   Install the compression gauge in the spark plug hole **(see illustration)**.

7   Crank the engine over at least seven compression strokes and watch the gauge. The compression should build up quickly in a healthy engine. Low compression on the first stroke, followed by gradually increasing pressure on successive strokes, indicates worn piston rings. A low compression reading on the first stroke, which doesn't build up during successive strokes, indicates leaking valves or a blown cylinder head gasket (a cracked cylinder head could also be the cause). Deposits on the undersides of the valve heads can also cause low compression. Record the highest gauge reading obtained.

8   Repeat the procedure for the remaining cylinders and compare the results to this Chapter's Specifications.

9   Add some engine oil (about three squirts from a plunger-type oil can) to each cylinder, through the spark plug hole, and repeat the test.

10   If the compression increases after the oil is added, the piston rings are definitely worn. If the compression doesn't increase significantly, the leakage is occurring at the valves or cylinder head gasket. Leakage past the valves may be caused by burned valve seats and/or faces or warped, cracked or bent valves.

11   If two adjacent cylinders have equally low compression, there's a strong possibility that the cylinder head gasket between them is blown. The appearance of coolant in the combustion chambers or the crankcase would verify this condition.

12   If one cylinder is slightly lower than the others, and the engine has a slightly rough idle, a worn lobe on the camshaft could be the cause.

13   If the compression is unusually high, the combustion chambers are probably coated with carbon deposits. If that's the case, the cylinder head(s) should be removed and decarbonized.

14   If compression is way down or varies greatly between cylinders, it would be a good idea to have a leak-down test performed by an automotive repair shop. This test will pinpoint exactly where the leakage is occurring and how severe it is.

4   Vacuum gauge diagnostic checks

Refer to illustrations 4.4 and 4.6

A vacuum gauge provides valuable information about what is going on in the engine at a low-cost. You can check for worn rings or cylinder walls, leaking cylinder head or intake manifold gaskets, incorrect carburetor adjustments, restricted exhaust, stuck or burned valves, weak valve springs, improper ignition or valve timing and ignition problems.

Unfortunately, vacuum gauge readings are easy to misinterpret, so they should be used in conjunction with other tests to confirm the diagnosis.

Both the absolute readings and the rate of needle movement are important for accurate interpretation. Most gauges measure vacuum in inches of mercury (in-Hg). The following references to vacuum assume the

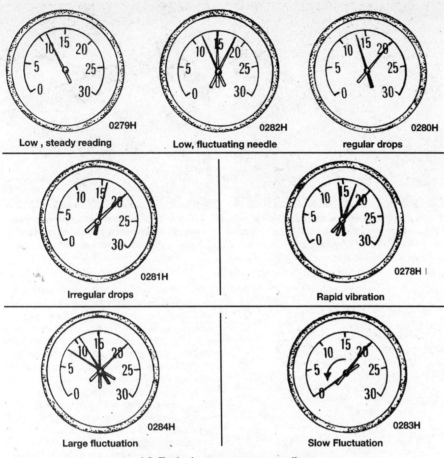

Low , steady reading | 0279H

Low, fluctuating needle | 0282H

regular drops | 0280H

Irregular drops | 0281H

Rapid vibration | 0278H

Large fluctuation | 0284H

Slow Fluctuation | 0283H

4.6 Typical vacuum gauge readings

diagnosis is being performed at sea level. As elevation increases (or atmospheric pressure decreases), the reading will decrease. For every 1,000 foot increase in elevation above approximately 2000 feet, the gauge readings will decrease about one inch of mercury.

Connect the vacuum gauge directly to intake manifold vacuum, not to ported (throttle body) vacuum **(see illustration)**. Be sure no hoses are left disconnected during the test or false readings will result.

Before you begin the test, allow the engine to warm up completely. Block the wheels and set the parking brake. With the transmission in Park, start the engine and allow it to run at normal idle speed. **Warning:** *Keep your hands and the vacuum gauge clear of the fans.*

Read the vacuum gauge; an average, healthy engine should normally produce about 17 to 22 in-Hg of vacuum with a fairly steady needle **(see illustration)**. Refer to the following vacuum gauge readings and what they indicate about the engine's condition:

1   A low steady reading usually indicates a leaking gasket between the intake manifold and cylinder head(s) or throttle body, a leaky vacuum hose, late ignition timing or incorrect camshaft timing. Check ignition timing with a timing light and eliminate all other possible causes, utilizing the tests provided in this Chapter before you remove the timing chain

cover to check the timing marks.
2   If the reading is three to eight inches below normal and it fluctuates at that low reading, suspect an intake manifold gasket leak at an intake port or a faulty fuel injector.
3   If the needle has regular drops of about two-to-four in-Hg at a steady rate, the valves are probably leaking. Perform a compression check or leak-down test to confirm this.
4   An irregular drop or down-flick of the needle can be caused by a sticking valve or an ignition misfire. Perform a compression check or leak-down test and read the spark plugs.
5   A rapid vibration of about four in-Hg vibration at idle combined with exhaust smoke indicates worn valve guides. Perform a leak-down test to confirm this. If the rapid vibration occurs with an increase in engine speed, check for a leaking intake manifold gasket or cylinder head gasket, weak valve springs, burned valves or ignition misfire.
6   A slight fluctuation, say one inch up and down, may mean ignition problems. Check all the usual tune-up items and, if necessary, run the engine on an ignition analyzer.
7   If there is a large fluctuation, perform a compression or leak-down test to look for a weak or dead cylinder or a blown cylinder head gasket.
8   If the needle moves slowly through a wide range, check for a clogged PCV system,

incorrect idle fuel mixture, carburetor/throttle body or intake manifold gasket leaks.
9   Check for a slow return after revving the engine by quickly snapping the throttle open until the engine reaches about 2,500 rpm and let it shut. Normally the reading should drop to near zero, rise above normal idle reading (about 5 in-Hg over) and then return to the previous idle reading. If the vacuum returns slowly and doesn't peak when the throttle is snapped shut, the rings may be worn. If there is a long delay, look for a restricted exhaust system (often the muffler or catalytic converter). An easy way to check this is to temporarily disconnect the exhaust ahead of the suspected part and redo the test.

5   Engine rebuilding alternatives

The do-it-yourselfer is faced with a number of options when performing an engine overhaul. The decision to replace the engine block, piston/connecting rod assemblies and crankshaft depends on a number of factors, with the number one consideration being the condition of the block. Other considerations are cost, access to machine shop facilities, parts availability, time required to complete the project and the extent of prior mechanical experience on the part of the do-it-yourselfer.

Some of the rebuilding alternatives include:

Individual parts - If the inspection procedures reveal that the engine block and most engine components are in reusable condition, purchasing individual parts may be the most economical alternative. The block, crankshaft and piston/connecting rod assemblies should all be inspected carefully. Even if the block shows little wear, the cylinder bores should be surface-honed.

Crankshaft kit - This rebuild package consists of a reground crankshaft and a matched set of pistons and connecting rods. The pistons will already be installed on the connecting rods. Piston rings and the necessary bearings will be included in the kit. These kits are commonly available for standard cylinder bores, as well as for engine blocks which have been bored to a regular oversize.

Short block - A short block consists of an engine block with renewed crankshaft and piston/connecting rod assemblies already installed. All new bearings are incorporated and all clearances will be correct. The existing cylinder head(s), camshaft, valve train components and external parts can be bolted to the short block with little or no machine shop work necessary.

Long block - A long block consists of a short block plus an oil pump, oil pan, cylinder heads, valve covers, camshaft and valve train components, timing sprockets, timing chain and timing cover. All components are installed with new bearings, seals and gaskets incorporated throughout. The installation of manifolds and external parts is all that is necessary.

2B

Used engine assembly - While overhaul provides the best assurance of a like-new engine, used engines available from wrecking yards and importers are often a very simple and economical solution. Many used engines come with warranties, but always give any engine a thorough diagnostic check-out before purchase. Check compression, vacuum and also for signs of oil leakage. If possible, have the seller run the engine, ether in the vehicle or on a test stand so you can be sure it runs smoothly with no knocking or other noises.

Give careful thought to which alternative is best for you and discuss the situation with local automotive machine shops, auto parts dealers or parts store countermen before ordering or purchasing replacement parts.

6   Engine removal - methods and precautions

If you've decided that an engine must be removed for overhaul or major repair work, several preliminary steps should be taken.

Locating a suitable place to work is extremely important. Adequate work space, along with storage space for the vehicle, will be needed. If a shop or garage isn't available, at the very least a flat, level, clean work surface made of concrete or asphalt is required.

Cleaning the engine compartment and engine before beginning the removal procedure will help keep tools clean and organized.

An engine hoist or A-frame will also be necessary. Make sure the equipment is rated in excess of the combined weight of the engine and transaxle. Safety is of primary importance, considering the potential hazards involved in lifting the engine out of the vehicle. The V6 engine and transaxle in the vehicles covered by this manual are intended to be removed from below, lowered out of the chassis. This is safest and easiest when there is access to a vehicle hoist, since the powertrain can be lowered to the floor with a hoist and the vehicle then raised high enough for powertrain removal.

If the engine is being removed by a novice, a helper should be available. Advice and aid from someone more experienced would also be helpful. There are many instances when one person cannot simultaneously perform all of the operations required when lifting the engine out of the vehicle.

Plan the operation ahead of time. Arrange for or obtain all of the tools and equipment you'll need prior to beginning the job. Some of the equipment necessary to perform engine removal and installation safely and with relative ease are (in addition to an engine hoist) a heavy duty floor jack, complete sets of wrenches and sockets as described in the front of this manual, wooden blocks and plenty of rags and cleaning solvent for mopping up spilled oil, coolant and gasoline. If the hoist must be rented, make sure that you arrange for it in advance and

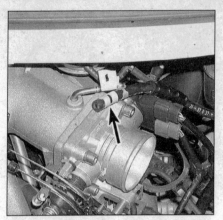

7.6   Label the hoses (arrow) and wires to ensure proper assembly

perform all of the operations possible without it beforehand. This will save you money and time.

Plan for the vehicle to be out of use for quite a while. A machine shop will be required to perform some of the work which the do-it-yourselfer can't accomplish without special equipment. These shops often have a busy schedule, so it would be a good idea to consult them before removing the engine in order to accurately estimate the amount of time required to rebuild or repair components that may need work.

Always be extremely careful when removing and installing the engine. Serious injury can result from careless actions. Plan ahead, take your time and a job of this nature, although major, can be accomplished successfully.

7   Engine - removal and installation

Warning: *The models covered by this manual are equipped with Supplemental Restraint Systems (SRS), more commonly known as airbags. Always disable the airbag system before working in the vicinity of any airbag system components to avoid the possibility of accidental deployment of the airbag(s), which could cause personal injury (see Chapter 12).*

Removal

Refer to illustrations 7.6, 7.15a, 7.15b, 7.17a, 7.17b and 7.19

Note: *Read through the entire Section before beginning this procedure. The engine and transaxle are removed as a unit from below and then separated outside the vehicle.*

1   Relieve the fuel system pressure (see Chapter 4).

2   Disconnect the negative battery cable (see Chapter 1). Remove the coolant overflow tank (see Chapter 3).

3   Place protective covers on the fenders and cowl and remove the hood (see Chapter 11).

4   Remove the air cleaner assembly (see Chapter 4).

5   Raise the vehicle and support it securely

7.15a   At the transaxle end of the engine, label and disconnect the electrical connectors (arrows indicate some), then pull the main harness away from the powertrain

on jackstands. Drain the cooling system, transaxle and engine oil and remove the drivebelts (see Chapter 1).

6   Clearly label, then disconnect all vacuum lines, coolant and emissions hoses, wiring harness connectors, ground straps and fuel lines. Masking tape and/or a touch up paint applicator work well for marking items **(see illustration)**. Take instant photos or sketch the locations of components and brackets.

7   Remove the cooling fans, and disconnect the radiator hoses and heater hoses (see Chapter 3).

8   Release the residual fuel pressure in the tank by removing the gas cap, then disconnect the fuel lines from the fuel rail (see Chapter 4). Plug or cap all open fittings.

9   Refer to Chapter 3 and unbolt and set aside the air-conditioning compressor, without disconnecting the refrigerant lines.

10   Disconnect the throttle linkage (and speed control cable, when equipped) from the engine (see Chapter 4).

11   Unbolt the power steering pump. Tie the pump aside without disconnecting the hoses (see Chapter 10).

12   Disconnect the exhaust pipe from the front manifold and at the converter, then remove the pipe (see Chapter 4).

13   Refer to Chapter 2, Part A and remove the upper intake manifold to make engine removal easier. Be sure to label and disconnect all hoses, connectors, and the two ground straps.

14   Refer to Chapter 5 and remove the ignition coil and distributor cap with spark plug wires.

15   Label and disconnect the main engine electrical harnesses at each end of the engine **(see illustrations)**.

16   Remove the driveaxles (see Chapter 8). Disconnect the electrical connectors, shift linkage and speed sensor from the transaxle (see Chapter 7).

17   Attach a lifting sling or chain to the brackets on the engine **(see illustration)**.

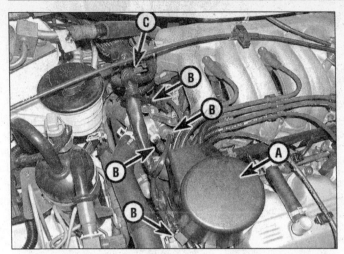

7.15b At the timing belt end of the engine, remove the distributor cap cover (A) and the distributor cap with the wires attached, disconnect all the electrical connectors (B indicate some) and pull the main electrical harness (C) away from the engine

7.17a Attach the chain or sling to a lifting eye (arrow indicates one at transaxle end)

Position a hoist and connect the sling to it. Take up the slack until there is slight tension on the hoist (see illustration).

18 Recheck to be sure nothing except the mounts are still connecting the engine/transaxle to the vehicle. Disconnect anything still remaining.

19 Support the transaxle with a floor jack. Place a block of wood on the jack head to prevent damage to the transaxle. Remove the throughbolts from the engine mounts (see Chapter 2, Part A). Move the refrigerant and coolant lines for the rear heater/air conditioning unit away from the crossmember (see illustration) and remove the crossmember (see Chapter 2, Part A). Warning: Do Not place any part of your body under the engine/transaxle when it's supported only by a hoist or other lifting device.

20 Slowly lower the engine/transaxle out of the vehicle.

21 Once the powertrain is on the floor, disconnect the engine lifting hoist and raise the

vehicle hoist until the powertrain can be slid out from under the vehicle. Note: A sheet of old hardboard or paneling between the engine and floor makes moving the powertrain easier. A helper will be needed to move the powertrain.

22 Separate the engine from the transaxle (see Chapter 7).

23 Place the engine on the floor or remove the driveplate and mount the engine on an engine stand.

Installation

24 Check the engine/transaxle mounts. If they're worn or damaged, replace them.

25 Inspect the converter seal and bushing, and apply a dab of grease to the nose of the converter and to the seal lips.

26 Carefully guide the transaxle into place, following the procedure outlined in Chapter 7. Caution: Do not use the bolts to force the engine and transaxle into alignment. It may crack or damage major components.

27 Install the engine-to-transaxle bolts and tighten them securely.

28 Slide the engine/transaxle over a sheet of hardboard or paneling until it is in the approximate position under the vehicle, then lower the vehicle on the vehicle hoist.

29 Roll the engine hoist into position, attach the sling or chain in a position that will allow a good balance, and slowly raise the powertrain until the mounts at the transaxle end can be attached.

30 Support the transaxle with a floorjack for extra security, then reinstall the crossmember and attach the right-side engine mounts. Follow the procedure in Chapter 2, Part A for the final tightening of all engine mount bolts.

31 Reinstall the remaining components and fasteners in the reverse order of removal.

32 Add coolant, oil, power steering and transmission fluids as needed (see Chapter 1).

33 Run the engine and check for proper operation and leaks. Shut off the engine and recheck the fluid levels.

2B

7.17b Attach a lifting sling to the lifting eyes or strong attachment points on the engine - raise the engine enough to remove the mounts and crossmember, then remove the jack and lower the engine/transaxle to the floor

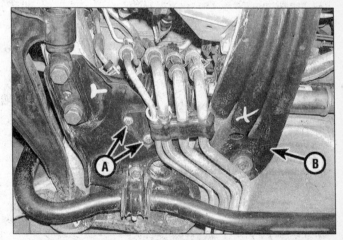

7.19 Remove the bracket bolts (A) for the rear heater/air conditioning lines and move the lines aside enough to access the bolts for the crossmember (B)

8   Engine overhaul - disassembly sequence

Refer to illustration 8.5

1   It's much easier to disassemble and work on the engine if it's mounted on a portable engine stand. A stand can often be rented quite cheaply from an equipment rental yard. Before the engine is mounted on a stand, the driveplate and engine rear plate should be removed from the engine.

2   If a stand isn't available, it's possible to disassemble the engine with it blocked up on the floor. Be extra careful not to tip or drop the engine when working without a stand.

3   If you're going to obtain a rebuilt engine, all external components must come off first, to be transferred to the replacement engine, just as they will if you're doing a complete engine overhaul yourself. These include:

*Alternator and brackets
Emissions control components
Distributor, spark plug wires and spark plugs
Thermostat and housing cover
Water pump
EFI components*

*Intake/exhaust manifolds
Oil filter
Engine mounts
Driveplate
Engine rear plate
Rear main seal plate*

Note: *When removing the external components from the engine, pay close attention to details that may be helpful or important during installation. Note the installed position of gaskets, seals, spacers, pins, brackets, washers, bolts and other small items.*

4   If you're obtaining a short block, which consists of the engine block, crankshaft, pistons and connecting rods all assembled, then the cylinder heads, oil pan and oil pump will have to be removed as well. See *Engine rebuilding alternatives* for additional information regarding the different possibilities to be considered.

5   If you're planning a complete overhaul, the engine must be disassembled and the internal components **(see illustration)** removed in the following general order:

*Valve covers
Rocker arm assemblies
Valve lifters and guides
Timing covers
Timing belt and sprockets*

*Cylinder heads
Camshafts
Oil pan and pick-up
Oil pump
Piston/connecting rod assemblies
Crankshaft and main bearings*

6   Before beginning the disassembly and overhaul procedures, make sure the following items are available. Also, refer to *Engine overhaul - reassembly sequence* for a list of tools and materials needed for engine reassembly.

*Common hand tools
Small cardboard boxes or plastic bags for storing parts
Gasket scraper
Ridge reamer
Vibration damper puller
Micrometers
Telescoping gauges
Dial indicator set
Valve spring compressor
Cylinder surfacing hone
Piston ring groove cleaning tool
Electric drill motor
Tap and die set
Wire brushes
Oil gallery brushes
Cleaning solvent*

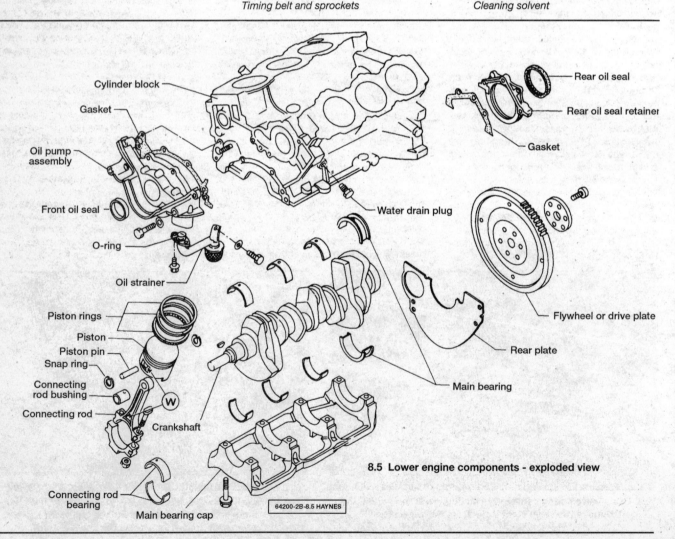

8.5 Lower engine components - exploded view

64200-2B-8.5 HAYNES

9   Cylinder head - disassembly

Refer to illustrations 9.2, 9.3 and 9.4
Note: *New and rebuilt cylinder heads are commonly available for most engines at dealerships and auto parts stores. Due to the fact that some specialized tools are necessary for the disassembly and inspection procedures, and replacement parts may not be readily available, it may be more practical and economical for the home mechanic to purchase replacement heads rather than taking the time to disassemble, inspect and recondition the originals.*

1   Cylinder head disassembly involves removal of the intake and exhaust valves and related components. If they're still in place, remove the rocker arms, lifters and camshafts (see Chapter 2, Part A) from the cylinder head. Label the parts or store them separately so they can be reinstalled in their original locations Refer to Section 21 for camshaft and lifter inspection procedures. **Caution:** *Do not lay the lifters on their side or upside down, or air can become trapped inside and the lifter will have to be bled (see Chapter 2, Part A). The lifters can be laid on their side only if they are submerged in a pan of clean engine oil until reassembly.*
2   Before the valves are removed, arrange to label and store them, along with their related components, so they can be kept separate and reinstalled in the same valve guides they are removed from **(see illustration)**.
3   Compress the springs on the first valve with a spring compressor and remove the valve stem locks **(see illustration)**. Carefully release the valve spring compressor and remove the retainer, the spring and the spring seat (if used).
4   Pull the valve out of the cylinder head, then remove the oil seal from the guide. If the valve binds in the guide (won't pull through), push it back into the cylinder head and deburr the area around the valve stem lock groove with a fine file or whetstone **(see illustration)**.

5   Repeat the procedure for the remaining valves. Remember to keep all the parts for each valve together so they can be reinstalled in the same locations.
6   Once the valves and related components have been removed and stored in an organized manner, the cylinder head should be thoroughly cleaned and inspected. If a complete engine overhaul is being done, finish the engine disassembly procedures before beginning the cylinder head cleaning and inspection process.

10   Cylinder head - cleaning and inspection

1   Thorough cleaning of the cylinder heads and related valve train components, followed by a detailed inspection, will enable you to decide how much valve service work must be done during the engine overhaul. **Note:** *If the engine was severely overheated, the cylinder heads are probably warped (see Step 12).*

Cleaning

2   Scrape all traces of old gasket material and sealing compound off the cylinder head gasket, intake manifold and exhaust manifold sealing surfaces. Be very careful not to gouge the cylinder head. Special gasket removal solvents that soften gaskets and make removal much easier are available at auto parts stores.
3   Remove all built up scale from the coolant passages.
4   Run a stiff wire brush through the various holes to remove deposits that may have formed in them.
5   Run an appropriate-size tap into each of the threaded holes to remove corrosion and thread sealant that may be present. If compressed air is available, use it to clear the holes of debris produced by this operation. **Warning:** *Wear eye protection when using compressed air!*
6   Clean the combustion chambers with a brass wire brush and solvent if carbon has

9.2 A small plastic bag, with an appropriate label, can be used to store the valve train components so they can be kept together and reinstalled in the original position

accumulated.
7   Clean the cylinder head with solvent and dry it thoroughly. Compressed air will speed the drying process and ensure that all holes and recessed areas are clean. **Note:** *Decarbonizing chemicals are available and may prove very useful when cleaning cylinder heads and valve train components. They are very caustic and should be used with caution. Be sure to follow the instructions on the container.*
8   Clean the rocker arms and shafts with solvent and dry them thoroughly (don't mix them up during the cleaning process). Compressed air will speed the drying process and can be used to clean out the oil passages.
9   Clean all the valve springs, spring seats, valve stem locks and retainers with solvent and dry them thoroughly. Do the components from one valve at a time to avoid mixing up the parts.
10   Scrape off any heavy deposits that may have formed on the valves, then use a motorized wire brush to remove deposits from the valve heads and stems. Again, make sure the valves don't get mixed up.

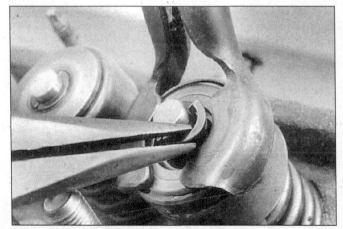

9.3 Use a valve spring compressor to compress the spring, then remove the valve stem locks from the valve stem

9.4 If the valve won't pull through the guide, deburr the edge of the stem end and the area around the top of the valve stem lock groove with a fine file or whetstone

2B

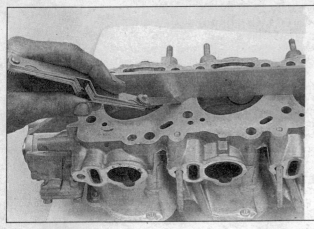

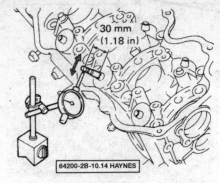

10.12 Check the cylinder head gasket surface for warpage by trying to slip a feeler gauge under the straightedge (see the Specifications for the maximum warpage allowed and use a feeler gauge of that thickness)

10.14 A dial indicator can be used to determine the valve stem-to-guide clearance (move the valve stem as indicated by the arrows)

Inspection

Note: *Be sure to perform all of the following inspection procedures before concluding that machine shop work is required. Make a list of the items that need attention.*

Cylinder head

Refer to illustrations 10.12 and 10.14

11   Inspect the heads very carefully for cracks, evidence of coolant leakage and other damage. If cracks are found, check with an automotive machine shop concerning repair. If repair isn't possible, a new cylinder head should be obtained.

12   Using a straightedge and feeler gauge, check the cylinder head gasket mating surface for warpage (see illustration). If the warpage exceeds the limit specified in this Chapter, it can be resurfaced at an automotive machine shop. **Note:** *The cylinder heads have a specific MINIMUM height, measured from the cylinder head gasket surface to the valve cover surface. If the cylinder head will fall below the minimum height (see Specifications) after it is machined, a new cylinder head will have to be purchased.*

13   Examine the valve seats in each of the combustion chambers. If they're pitted, cracked or burned, the cylinder head will require valve service that's beyond the scope of the home mechanic.

14   Check the valve stem-to-guide clearance by measuring the lateral movement of the valve stem with a dial indicator attached securely to the cylinder head (see illustration). The valve must be in the guide and approximately 1/16-inch off the seat. The total valve stem movement indicated by the gauge needle must be divided by two to obtain the actual clearance. After this is done, if there's still some doubt regarding the condition of the valve guides, they should be checked by an automotive machine shop (the cost should be minimal).

Valves

Refer to illustrations 10.15 and 10.16

15   Carefully inspect each valve face for uneven wear, deformation, cracks, pits and burned areas (see illustration). Check the valve stem for scuffing and galling and the neck for cracks. Rotate the valve and check for any obvious indication that it's bent. Look for pits and excessive wear on the end of the stem. The presence of any of these conditions indicates the need for valve service by an automotive machine shop.

16   Measure the margin width on each valve (see illustration). Any valve with a margin narrower than specified in this Chapter will have to be replaced with a new one.

Valve components

Refer to illustrations 10.17 and 10.18

17   Check each valve spring for wear (on the ends) and pits. Measure the free length and compare it to the Specifications in this Chapter (see illustration). Any springs that are shorter than specified have sagged and should not be reused. The tension of all springs should be checked with a special fixture before deciding that they're suitable for use in a rebuilt engine (take the springs to an automotive machine shop for this check).

18   Stand each spring on a flat surface and check it for squareness (see illustration). If any of the springs are distorted or sagged, replace all of them with new parts.

19   Check the spring retainers and valve stem locks for obvious wear and cracks. Any questionable parts should be replaced with new ones, as extensive damage will occur if they fail during engine operation.

Camshaft, lifters, rocker arms and shafts

20   Refer to Chapter 2, Part A for rocker arm and shaft inspection, and Section 21 of this Chapter for the camshaft, lifter and bearing inspection procedures.

21   Any damaged or excessively worn parts

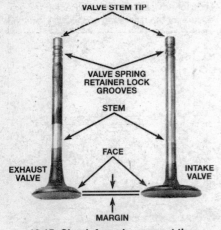

10.15   Check for valve wear at the points shown here

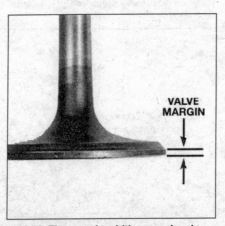

10.16   The margin width on each valve must be as specified (if no margin exists, the valve cannot be reused)

10.17   Measure the free length of each valve spring with a dial or vernier caliper

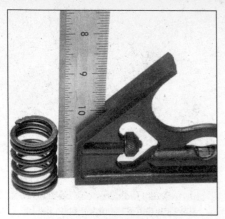

10.18 Check each valve spring for squareness

must be replaced with new ones.

22   If the inspection process indicates that the valve components are in generally poor condition and worn beyond the limits specified, which is usually the case in an engine that's being overhauled, reassemble the valves in the cylinder head and refer to Section 10 for valve servicing recommendations.

11   Valves - servicing

1   Because of the complex nature of the job and the special tools and equipment needed, servicing of the valves, the valve seats and the valve guides, commonly known as a valve job, should be done by a professional.

2   The home mechanic can remove and disassemble the heads, do the initial cleaning and inspection, then reassemble and deliver them to a dealer service department or an automotive machine shop for the actual service work. Doing the inspection will enable you to see what condition the cylinder head and valvetrain components are in and will ensure that you know what work and new parts are required when dealing with an automotive machine shop.

3   The dealer service department, or automotive machine shop, will remove the valves and springs, recondition or replace the valves and valve seats, recondition or replace the valve guides, check and replace the valve springs, spring retainers and valve stem locks (as necessary), replace the valve seals with new ones, reassemble the valve components and make sure the installed spring height is correct. The cylinder head gasket surface will also be resurfaced if it's warped.

4   After the valve job has been performed by a professional, the cylinder head will be in like-new condition. When the cylinder head is returned, be sure to clean it again before installation on the engine to remove any metal particles and abrasive grit that may still be present from the valve service or cylinder head resurfacing operations. Use compressed air, if available, to blow out all the oil holes and passages.

12   Cylinder head - reassembly

1   Regardless of whether or not the cylinder head was sent to an automotive repair shop for valve servicing, make sure it is clean before beginning reassembly.

2   If the cylinder head was sent out for valve servicing, the valves and related components will already be in place. Begin the reassembly procedure with Step 5.

3   Install the valves, with light oiling on the stems. Install new seals on each of the valve guides, carefully pushing the seals by hand over the top of the valves, then using the stem of the valves to align the seals into place on the guides. To install the intake oil seals, you will need a seal installation or an appropriate-size deep socket. Gently tap each seal into place until it is properly seated onto the guide (see Chapter 2, Part A). **Caution:** *Do not hammer on the guide seal once it is seated or you may damage the seal. Do not twist or cock the seals during installation or they will not seal properly on the valve stems.*

4   Slip the inner and outer valve spring seats in place on the cylinder head, then use a spring compressor to install the springs, retainers and valve stem locks (see Chapter 2, Part A).

5   Install the camshafts (see Chapter 2, Part A).

6   The hydraulic valve lifters, lifter guide assembly and rocker arms can now be installed on each cylinder head. **Note:** *Install the valve lifters in their original lifter bores. Hold them in place with rubber bands during lifter guide assembly installation (see Chapter 2A).*

7   Remove the rubber bands holding the lifters.

13   Pistons/connecting rods - removal

Refer to illustrations 13.1, 13.3 and 13.6
Note: *Prior to removing the piston/connecting rod assemblies, remove the cylinder heads, the oil pan and the oil pump pick-up by referring to the appropriate Sections in Chapter 2A, if not already removed.*

1   Use your fingernail to feel if a ridge has formed at the upper limit of ring travel (about 1/4-inch down from the top of each cylinder). If carbon deposits or cylinder wear have produced ridges, they must be completely removed with a special tool **(see illustration)**. Follow the manufacturer's instructions provided with the tool. Failure to remove the ridges before attempting to remove the piston/connecting rod assemblies may result in piston breakage.

2   After the cylinder ridges have been removed, turn the engine upside-down so the crankshaft is facing up.

3   Before the connecting rods are removed, check the side clearance (endplay) with feeler gauges. Slide them between the first connecting rod and the crankshaft throw until the play is removed **(see illustration)**. The side clearance is equal to the thickness of the feeler gauge(s). If the side clearance exceeds the service limit, new connecting rods will be required. If new rods (or a new crankshaft) are installed, the side clearance may fall under the specified minimum (if it does, the rods will have to be machined to restore it - consult an automotive machine shop for advice if necessary). Repeat the procedure for the remaining connecting rods.

2B

13.1 A ridge reamer is required to remove the ridge from the top of each cylinder - do this before removing the pistons!

13.3 Check the connecting rod side clearance with a feeler gauge as shown

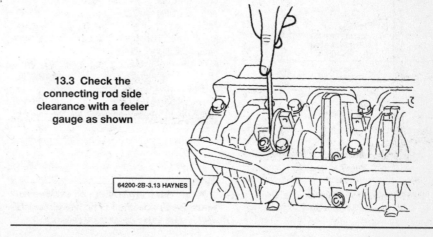

64200-2B-3.13 HAYNES

13.6 To prevent damage to the crankshaft journals and cylinder walls, slip sections of rubber or plastic hose over the connecting rod bolts before removing the pistons

14.1 Checking crankshaft endplay with a dial indicator

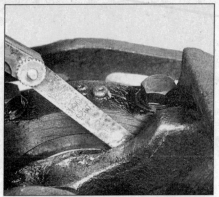

14.3 Crankshaft endplay can also be measured with a feeler gauge at the number four main bearing

4   Check the connecting rods and caps for identification marks. If they aren't plainly marked, use a small center punch to make the appropriate number of indentations on each rod and cap (1, 2, 3, etc.).

5   Loosen each of the connecting rod cap nuts 1/2-turn at a time until they can be removed by hand. Remove the number one connecting rod cap and bearing insert. Don't drop the bearing insert out of the cap.

6   Slip a short length of plastic or rubber hose over each connecting rod cap bolt to protect the crankshaft journal and cylinder wall as the piston is removed **(see illustration)**.

7   Remove the bearing insert and push the connecting rod/piston assembly out through the top of the engine. Use a wooden hammer handle to push on the upper bearing surface in the connecting rod. If resistance is felt, double-check to make sure that all of the ridge was removed from the cylinder.

8   Repeat the procedure for the remaining cylinders.

9   After removal, reassemble the connecting rod caps and bearing inserts in their respective connecting rods and install the cap nuts finger tight. Leaving the old bearing inserts in place until reassembly will help prevent the connecting rod bearing surfaces from being accidentally nicked or gouged.

10   Don't separate the pistons from the connecting rods (see Section 18 for additional information).

14   Crankshaft - removal

Refer to illustrations 14.1, 14.3 and 14.4
Note: *The crankshaft can be removed only after the engine has been removed from the vehicle. It's assumed that the driveplate, crankshaft pulley, timing belt, sprocket, oil pan, oil pump and piston/connecting rod assemblies have already been removed. The rear main oil seal retainer must be unbolted and separated from the block before proceeding with crankshaft removal.*

1   Before the crankshaft is removed, check the endplay. Mount a dial indicator with the

14.4 The main bearing cap assembly has a cast-in arrow which points toward the timing belt end of the engine

stem in line with the crankshaft and just touching one of the crank throws **(see illustration)**.

2   Push the crankshaft all the way to the rear and zero the dial indicator. Next, pry the crankshaft to the front as far as possible and check the reading on the dial indicator. The distance that it moves is the endplay. If it's greater than specified in this Chapter, check the crankshaft thrust surfaces for wear. If no wear is evident, new main bearings should correct the endplay.

3   If a dial indicator isn't available, feeler gauges can be used. Gently pry or push the crankshaft all the way to the front of the engine. Slip feeler gauges between the crankshaft and the front face of the rear (thrust) main bearing to determine the clearance **(see illustration)**.

4   The main bearing cap assembly has a cast-in arrow, which points to the timing belt end of the engine **(see illustration)**. Loosen the main bearing cap bolts 1/4-turn at a time each, until the assembly can be removed by hand. **Note:** *Loosen the bearing cap assembly bolts in the reverse of the tightening sequence (see Section 24).*

5   Gently tap the cap assembly with a soft-face hammer, then separate it from the engine block. If necessary, use the bolts as levers to remove the cap assembly. Try not to drop the bearing inserts if they come out with

the cap assembly.

6   Carefully lift the crankshaft out of the engine. It may be a good idea to have an assistant available, since the crankshaft is quite heavy. With the bearing inserts in place in the engine block and main bearing caps, return the cap assembly to it's location on the engine block and tighten the bolts finger tight.

15   Engine block - cleaning

Refer to illustrations 15.1a, 15.1b, 15.8 and 15.10
Caution: *The core plugs (also known as freeze or soft plugs) may be difficult or impossible to retrieve if they're driven completely into the block coolant passages.*

1   Using the blunt end of a punch, tap in on the outer edge of the core plug to turn the plug sideways in the bore. Then use pliers to pull the core plug from the engine block **(see illustrations)**.

2   Using a gasket scraper, remove all traces of gasket material from the engine block. Be very careful not to nick or gouge the gasket sealing surfaces.

3   Remove the main bearing cap assembly and separate the bearing inserts from the caps and the engine block. Label the bearings, indicating which cylinder they were

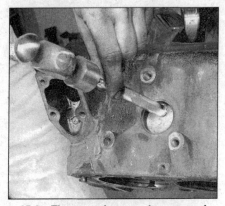

15.1a The core plugs can be removed by tapping in one edge until the plug turns sideways . . .

15.1b . . . then remove the core plug with pliers

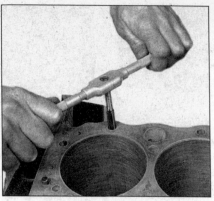

15.8 All bolt holes in the block - particularly the main bearing cap and cylinder head bolt holes - should be cleaned and restored with a tap (be sure to remove debris from the holes after this is done)

15.10 A large socket on an extension can be used to drive the new core plugs into the bores

removed from and whether they were in the cap or the block, then set them aside.

4   Remove all of the threaded oil gallery plugs from the block. The plugs are usually very tight - they may have to be drilled out and the holes retapped. Use new plugs when the engine is reassembled.

5   If the engine is extremely dirty, it should be taken to an automotive machine shop to be steam cleaned or hot tanked.

6   After the block is returned, clean all oil holes and oil galleries one more time. Brushes specifically designed for this purpose are available at most auto parts stores. Flush the passages with warm water until the water runs clear, dry the block thoroughly and wipe all machined surfaces with a light, rust-preventive oil. If you have access to compressed air, use it to speed the drying process and to blow out all the oil holes and galleries. **Warning:** *Wear eye protection when using compressed air!*

7   If the block isn't extremely dirty or sludged up, you can do an adequate cleaning job with hot soapy water and a stiff brush. Take plenty of time and do a thorough job. Regardless of the cleaning method used, be sure to clean all oil holes and galleries very thoroughly, dry the block completely and coat all machined surfaces with light oil.

8   The threaded holes in the block must be clean to ensure accurate torque readings during reassembly. Run the proper size tap into each of the holes to remove rust, corrosion, thread sealant or sludge and restore damaged threads **(see illustration).** If possible, use compressed air to clear the holes of debris produced by this operation. Now is a good time to clean the threads on the cylinder head bolts and the main bearing cap bolts as well.

9   Reinstall the main bearing caps and tighten the bolts finger tight.

10   After coating the sealing surfaces of the new core plugs with core plug sealant, install them in the engine block **(see illustration).** Make sure they're driven in straight and seated properly or leakage could result. Special tools are available for this purpose, but a large socket, with an outside diameter that will just slip into the core plug, a 1/2-inch

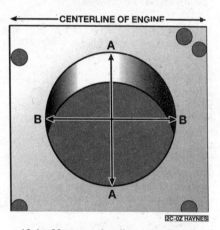

16.4a Measure the diameter of each cylinder at a right angle to the engine centerline (A), and parallel to engine centerline (B) - out-of-round is the distance between A and B; taper is the difference between A and B at the top of the cylinder and A and B at the bottom of the cylinder

drive extension and a hammer will work just as well. **Note:** *Make sure the socket only contacts the inside of the core plug, not the rim.*

11   Apply non-hardening thread sealant to the new oil gallery plugs and thread them into the holes in the block. Make sure they're tightened securely.

12   If the engine isn't going to be reassembled right away, cover it with a large plastic trash bag to keep it clean.

16 Engine block - inspection

Refer to illustrations 16.4a, 16.4b, 16.4c and 16.11

1   Before the block is inspected, it should be cleaned as described in Section 15.

2   Visually check the block for cracks, rust and corrosion. Look for stripped threads in the threaded holes. It's also a good idea to

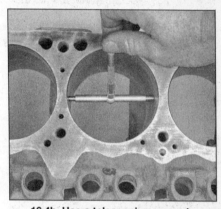

16.4b Use a telescoping gauge to measure the bore - the ability to "feel" when it is at the correct point will be developed over time, so work slowly and repeat the check until you're satisfied the bore measurement is accurate

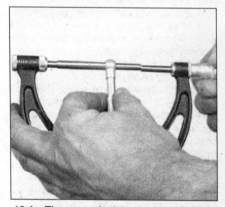

16.4c The gauge is then measured with a micrometer to determine the bore size

have the block checked for hidden cracks by an automotive machine shop that has the special equipment to do this type of work. If defects are found, have the block repaired, if possible, or replaced.

3   Check the cylinder bores for scuffing and scoring.

4   Check the cylinders for taper and out-of-round conditions as follows **(see illustrations):**

2B

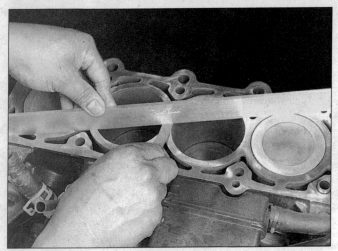

16.11 Check the flatness of the top of the block with a straightedge and feeler gauge - if distortion exceeds Specifications, the block deck will have to be machined

17.3a A "bottle brush" hone will produce better results if you've never honed cylinders before

5   Measure the diameter of each cylinder at the top (just under the ridge area), center and bottom of the cylinder bore, parallel to the crankshaft axis.

6   Next measure each cylinder's diameter at the same three locations perpendicular to the crankshaft axis.

7   The taper of the cylinder is the difference between the bore diameter at the top of the cylinder and the diameter at the bottom. The out-of-round specification of the cylinder bore is the difference between the parallel and perpendicular readings. Compare your results to those listed in this Chapter's Specifications.

8   Repeat the procedure for the remaining pistons and cylinders.

9   If the cylinder walls are badly scuffed or scored, or if they're out-of-round or tapered beyond the limits given in this Chapter's Specifications, have the engine block rebored and honed at an automotive machine shop. If a rebore is done, oversize pistons and rings will be required.

10   If the cylinders are in reasonably good condition and not worn to the outside of the limits, and if the piston-to-cylinder clearances can be maintained properly, then they don't have to be rebored. Honing is all that's necessary (see Section 17).

11   Using a precision straightedge and feeler gauge, check the block deck (the surface that mates with the cylinder head) for distortion **(see illustration)**.

17   Cylinder honing

Refer to illustrations 17.3a and 17.3b

1   Prior to engine reassembly, the cylinder bores must be honed so the new piston rings will seat correctly and provide the best possible combustion chamber seal. **Note:** *If you don't have the tools or don't want to tackle the honing operation, most automotive machine shops will do it for a reasonable fee.*

2   Before honing the cylinders, install the main bearing caps and tighten the bolts to the torque specified in this Chapter.

3   Two types of cylinder hones are commonly available - the flex hone or "bottle brush" type and the more traditional surfacing hone with spring-loaded stones. Both will do the job, but for the less experienced mechanic the "bottle brush" hone will probably be easier to use. You'll also need some kerosene or honing oil, rags and an electric drill motor. Proceed as follows:

a)   *Mount the hone in the drill motor, compress the stones and slip it into the first cylinder* **(see illustration)**. *Be sure to wear safety goggles or a face shield!*

b)   *Lubricate the cylinder with plenty of honing oil, turn on the drill and move the hone up-and-down in the cylinder at a pace that will produce a fine crosshatch pattern on the cylinder walls. Ideally, the crosshatch lines should intersect at approximately a 60-degree angle* **(see illustration)**. *Be sure to use plenty of lubricant and don't take off any more material than is absolutely necessary to produce the desired finish.* **Note:** *Piston ring manufacturers may specify a smaller crosshatch angle than the traditional 60-degrees - read and follow any instructions included with the new rings.*

c)   *Don't withdraw the hone from the cylinder while it's running. Instead, shut off the drill and continue moving the hone up-and-down in the cylinder until it comes to a complete stop, then compress the stones and withdraw the hone. If you're using a "bottle brush" type hone, stop the drill motor, then turn the chuck in the normal direction of rotation while withdrawing the hone from the cylinder.*

d)   *Wipe the oil out of the cylinder and repeat the procedure for the remaining cylinders.*

4   After the honing job is complete, cham-

fer the top edges of the cylinder bores with a small file so the rings won't catch when the pistons are installed. Be very careful not to nick the cylinder walls with the end of the file.

5   The entire engine block must be washed again very thoroughly with warm, soapy water to remove all traces of the abrasive grit produced during the honing operation. **Note:** *The bores can be considered clean when a lint-free white cloth - dampened with clean engine oil - used to wipe them out doesn't pick up any more honing residue, which will show up as gray areas on the cloth. Be sure to run a brush through all oil holes and galleries and flush them with running water.*

6   After rinsing, dry the block and apply a coat of light rust-preventive oil to all machined surfaces. Wrap the block in a plastic trash bag to keep it clean and set it aside until reassembly.

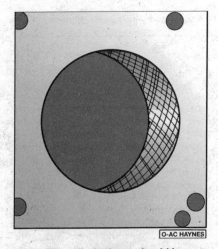

17.3b The cylinder hone should leave a smooth, crosshatch pattern with the lines intersecting at approximately a 60-degree angle

18 Pistons/connecting rods - inspection

Refer to illustrations 18.4a, 18.4b, 18.10 and 18.11

1   Before the inspection process can be carried out, the piston/connecting rod assemblies must be cleaned and the original piston rings removed from the pistons. **Note:** *Always use new piston rings when the engine is reassembled.*

2   Using a piston ring installation tool, carefully remove the rings from the pistons. Be careful not to nick or gouge the pistons in the process.

3   Scrape all traces of carbon from the top of the piston. A hand-held brass wire brush or a piece of fine emery cloth can be used (with solvent) once the majority of the deposits have been scraped away. Do not, under any circumstances, use a wire brush mounted in a drill motor to remove deposits from the pistons. The piston material is soft and may be eroded away by the wire brush.

4   Use a piston ring groove-cleaning tool to remove carbon deposits from the ring grooves. If a tool isn't available, a piece broken off the old ring will do the job. Be very careful to remove only the carbon deposits - don't remove any metal and do not nick or scratch the sides of the ring grooves **(see illustrations)**.

5   Once the deposits have been removed, clean the piston/rod assemblies with solvent and dry them with compressed air (if available). Make sure the oil return holes in the back sides of the ring grooves are clear.

6   If the pistons and cylinder walls aren't damaged or worn excessively, and if the engine block is not rebored, new pistons won't be necessary. Normal piston wear appears as even vertical wear on the piston thrust surfaces and slight looseness of the top ring in its groove. New piston rings, however, should always be used when an engine is rebuilt.

7   Carefully inspect each piston for cracks

18.4a The piston ring grooves can be cleaned with a special tool, as shown here . . .

18.4b . . . or a section of a broken ring

around the skirt, at the pin bosses and at the ring lands.

8   Look for scoring and scuffing on the thrust faces of the skirt, holes in the piston crown and burned areas at the edge of the crown. If the skirt is scored or scuffed, the engine may have been suffering from overheating and/or abnormal combustion, which caused excessively high operating temperatures. The cooling and lubrication systems should be checked thoroughly. A hole in the piston crown is an indication that abnormal combustion (preignition) was occurring. Burned areas at the edge of the piston crown are usually evidence of spark knock (detonation). If any of the above problems exist, the causes must be corrected or the damage will occur again. The causes may include intake air leaks, incorrect fuel/air mixture, incorrect ignition timing and EGR system malfunctions.

9   Corrosion of the piston, in the form of small pits, indicates that coolant is leaking into the combustion chamber and/or the crankcase. Again, the cause must be corrected or the problem may persist in the rebuilt engine.

10   Measure the piston ring side clearance

by laying a new piston ring in each ring groove and slipping a feeler gauge in beside it **(see illustration)**. Check the clearance at three or four locations around each groove. Be sure to use the correct ring for each groove - they are different. If the side clearance is greater than specified in this Chapter, new pistons will have to be used.

11   Check the piston-to-bore clearance by measuring the bore (see Section 16) and the piston diameter. Make sure the pistons and bores are correctly matched. Measure the piston across the skirt, at a 90-degree angle to the piston pin, 3/4-inch from the bottom of the skirt **(see illustration)**. Subtract the piston diameter from the bore diameter to obtain the clearance. If it's greater than specified in this Chapter, the block will have to be rebored and new pistons and rings installed.

12   Check the piston-to-rod clearance by twisting the piston and rod in opposite directions. Any noticeable play indicates excessive wear, which must be corrected. The piston/connecting rod assemblies should be taken to an automotive machine shop to have the pistons and rods resized and new pins installed.

2B

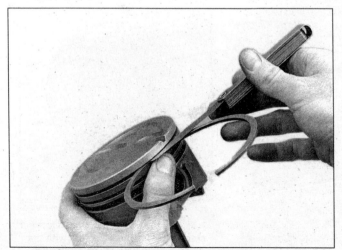

18.10 Check the ring side clearance with a feeler gauge at several points around the groove

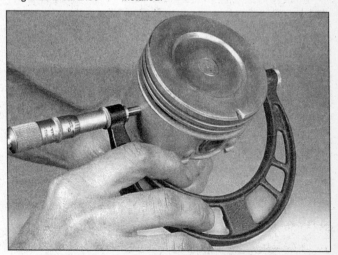

18.11 Measure the piston diameter at a 90-degree angle to the piston pin and in line with it

19.1 The oil holes should be chamfered so sharp edges don't gouge or scratch the new bearings

19.2 Use a wire or stiff plastic bristle brush to clean the oil passages in the crankshaft

19.5 Measure the diameter of each crankshaft journal at several points to detect taper and out-of-round conditions

13   If the pistons must be removed from the connecting rods for any reason, they should be taken to an automotive machine shop. While they are there have the connecting rods checked for bend and twist, since automotive machine shops have special equipment for this purpose. **Note:** *Unless new pistons and/or connecting rods must be installed, do not disassemble the pistons and connecting rods.*

14   Check the connecting rods for cracks and other damage. Temporarily remove the rod caps, lift out the old bearing inserts, wipe the rod and cap bearing surfaces clean and inspect them for nicks, gouges and scratches. After checking the rods, replace the old bearings, slip the caps into place and tighten the nuts finger tight. **Note:** *If the engine is being rebuilt because of a connecting rod knock, be sure to install new or rebuilt rods.*

19   Crankshaft - inspection

Refer to illustrations 19.1, 19.2, 19.5 and 19.7

1   Remove all burrs from the crankshaft oil holes with a stone, file or scraper **(see illustration)**.
2   Clean the crankshaft with solvent and dry it with compressed air (if available). Be sure to clean the oil holes with a stiff brush **(see illustration)** and flush them with solvent.
3   Check the main and connecting rod bearing journals for uneven wear, scoring, pits and cracks.
4   Check the rest of the crankshaft for cracks and other damage. It should be magnafluxed to reveal hidden cracks - an automotive machine shop will handle the procedure.
5   Using a micrometer, measure the diameter of the main and connecting rod journals **(see illustration)** and compare the results to the Specifications in this Chapter. By measuring the diameter at a number of points around each journal's circumference, you'll be able to determine whether or not the journal is out-of-round. Take the measurement at each end of the journal, near the crank

throws, to determine if the journal is tapered.
6   If the crankshaft journals are damaged, tapered, out-of-round or worn beyond the limits given in the Specifications in this Chapter, have the crankshaft reground by an automotive machine shop. Be sure to use the correct size bearing inserts if the crankshaft is reconditioned.
7   Check the oil seal journals at each end of the crankshaft for wear and damage. If the seal has worn a groove in the journal, or if it's nicked or scratched **(see illustration)**, the new seal may leak when the engine is reassembled. In some cases, an automotive machine shop may be able to repair the journal by pressing on a thin sleeve. If repair isn't feasible, a new or different crankshaft should be installed.
8   Refer to Section 20 and examine the main and rod bearing inserts.

20   Main and connecting rod bearings - inspection and main bearing selection

Inspection

Refer to illustration 20.1

1   Even though the main and connecting rod bearings should be replaced with new ones during the engine overhaul, the old bearings should be retained for close examination, as they may reveal valuable information about the condition of the engine **(see illustration)**.
2   Bearing failure occurs because of lack of lubrication, the presence of dirt or other foreign particles, overloading the engine and corrosion. Regardless of the cause of bearing failure, it must be corrected before the engine is reassembled to prevent it from happening again.
3   When examining the bearings, remove them from the engine block, the main bearing caps, the connecting rods and the rod caps and lay them out on a clean surface in the same general position as their location in the engine. This will enable you to match any

bearing problems with the corresponding crankshaft journal.
4   Dirt and other foreign particles get into the engine in a variety of ways. It may be left in the engine during assembly, or it may pass through filters or the PCV system. It may get into the oil, and from there into the bearings. Metal chips from machining operations and normal engine wear are often present. Abrasives are sometimes left in engine components after reconditioning, especially when parts are not thoroughly cleaned using the proper cleaning methods. Whatever the source, these foreign objects often end up embedded in the soft bearing material and are easily recognized. Large particles will not embed in the bearing and will score or gouge the bearing and journal. The best prevention for this cause of bearing failure is to clean all parts thoroughly and keep everything spotlessly clean during engine assembly. Frequent and regular engine oil and filter changes are also recommended.
5   Lack of lubrication (or lubrication breakdown) has a number of interrelated causes. Excessive heat (which thins the oil), overloading (which squeezes the oil from the bearing

19.7 If the seals have worn grooves in the crankshaft journals, or if the seal contact surfaces are nicked or scratched, the new seals will leak

CRATERS OR POCKETS
FATIGUE FAILURE

BRIGHT (POLISHED) SECTIONS
IMPROPER SEATING

SCRATCHES

OVERLAY WIPED OUT
...ACK OF OIL

...ADIUS RIDE
...RED JOURNAL

...s

...e bearing face (fatigue failure). ...he bearing material will loosen in ...ear away from the steel backing. ...iving leads to corrosion of bear- ...e insufficient engine heat is pro- ...ve off the condensed water and ...ases. These products collect in ...il, forming acid and sludge. As ...ried to the engine bearings, the ...and corrodes the bearing mate-

...ct bearing installation during ...mbly will lead to bearing failure ...t-fitting bearings leave insuffi- ...oil clearance and will result in oil ...irt or foreign particles trapped ...ring insert result in high spots on ...hich lead to failure.

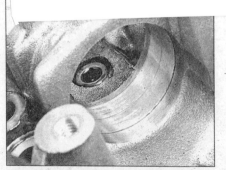

21.1 Inspect the cam bearing surfaces in each cylinder head for pits, score marks and abnormal wear - if wear or damage is noted, the cylinder head must be replaced

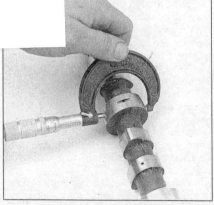

21.2a Measure the outside diameter of each camshaft journal and the inside diameter of each bearing to determine the clearance

Selection

8   If the original bearings are worn or damaged, or if the oil clearances are incorrect (see Sections 24 or 26), new bearings will have to be purchased. It is rare during a thorough rebuild of an engine with many miles on it that new replacement bearings would not be employed. However, if the crankshaft has been reground, new **undersize** bearings must be installed.

9   The automotive machine shop that reconditions the crankshaft will provide or help you select the correct size bearings. Depending on how much material has to be ground from the crankshaft to restore it, different undersize bearings are required. Crankshafts are normally ground in increments of 0.010-inch. Sometimes the amount of material machined on a crankshaft will differ between the mains and rod journals, especially if a rod journal was damaged. Markings on most reground crankshafts indicate how much was machined, such as "10-10", meaning that 0.010-inch was removed from both the rod and main journals. Such a crankshaft would require 0.010-inch undersize bearings, a common replacement bearing size.

10   Regardless of how the bearing sizes are determined, use the oil clearance, measured with Plastigage, as the final guide to ensure the bearings are the right size. If you have any questions or are unsure which bearings to use, get help from your machine shop or a dealer parts or service department.

21   Camshafts, lifters and bearings - inspection

Refer to illustrations 21.1, 21.2a, 21.2b, 21.3, 21.4, 21.5, 21.6, 21.7, 21.10 and 21.11

1   Visually check the camshaft bearing surfaces for pitting, score marks, galling and abnormal wear. If the bearing surfaces are damaged, the cylinder head will have to be replaced **(see illustration)**.

2   Measure the outside diameter of each camshaft bearing journal and record your measurements **(see illustrations)**. Compare them to the journal outside diameter specified in this Chapter, then measure the inside diameter of each corresponding camshaft bearing and record the measurements. Sub-

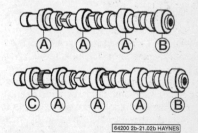

64200 2b-21.02b HAYNES

21.2b Camshaft journal designations - B are the rearmost journals, while C is the journal ahead of the distributor drive gear

2B

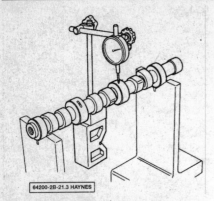

21.3 A dial indicator and V-blocks are needed to check camshaft runout; a machine shop can check this for you

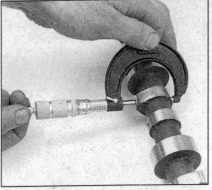

21.4 Measuring cam lobe height with a micrometer, make sure you move the micrometer to get the highest reading (top of cam lobe)

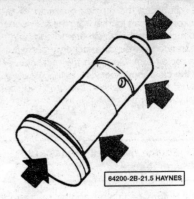

21.5 Check the contact and sliding surfaces of each lifter (arrows) for wear and damage

tract each cam journal outside diameter from its respective cam bearing bore inside diameter to determine the oil clearance for each bearing. Compare the results to the specified journal-to-bearing clearance. If any of the measurements fall outside the standard specified wear limits in this Chapter, either the camshaft or the cylinder head, or both, must be replaced.

3   Check camshaft runout by placing the camshaft between two V-blocks and set up a dial indicator on the center journal **(see illustration)**. Zero the dial indicator. Turn the camshaft slowly and note the dial indicator readings. Record your readings and compare them with the specified runout in this Chapter. If the measured runout exceeds the runout specified in this Chapter, replace the camshaft.

4   Check the camshaft lobe height by measuring each lobe with a micrometer **(see illustration)**. Compare the measurement to the cam lobe height specified in this Chapter. Then subtract the measured cam lobe height from the specified height to compute wear on the cam lobes. Compare it to the specified wear limit. If it's greater than the specified wear limit, replace the camshaft.

5   Inspect the contact and sliding surfaces of each lifter for wear and scratches **(see**

illustration)**. Note:** *If the lifter pad is worn, it's a good idea to check the corresponding camshaft lobe, because it will probably be worn too.* **Caution:** *Do not lay the lifters on their side or upside down, or air can become trapped inside and the lifter will have to be bled (see Chapter 2, Part A). The lifters can be laid on their side only if they are submerged in a pan of clean engine oil until reassembly.*

6   Measure the outside diameter of each lifter with a micrometer **(see illustration)** and compare it to the Specifications in this Chapter. If any lifter is worn beyond the specified limit, replace it.

7   Check each lifter bore diameter in the lifter guide assembly **(see illustration)** and compare the results to the Specifications in this Chapter. If any lifter bore is worn beyond the specified limit, the lifter guide assembly must be replaced.

8   Subtract the outside diameter of each lifter from the inside diameter of the lifter bore and compare the difference to the clearance specified in this Chapter. If both the lifter and the bore are within acceptable limits, this measurement should fall within tolerance as well. However, if you buy a new set of lifters alone, or a lifter guide assembly by itself, you may find that this clearance no longer falls

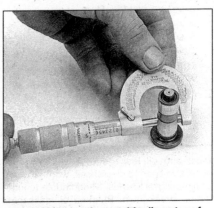

21.6 Measure the outside diameter of each lifter with a micrometer . . .

within the specified limit.

9   Check the rocker arms and shafts for abnormal wear, pits, galling, score marks and rough spots. Don't attempt to restore rocker arms by grinding the pad surfaces.

10   Measure the outside diameter of the rocker arm shaft at each rocker arm journal **(see illustration)**.

11   Measure the inside diameter of each rocker arm with either an inside micrometer or a dial caliper **(see illustration)**.

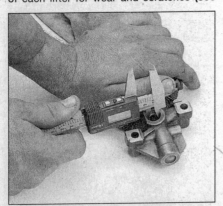

21.7 . . . and the inside diameter of each lifter bore, then subtract the lifter diameter to find the lifter-to-guide clearance (compare the results to the Specifications)

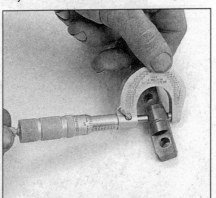

21.10 Measure the rocker shaft diameter at each journal where a rocker rides on the shaft

21.11 Measure the inside diameter of each rocker arm bore, subtract the corresponding rocker arm shaft diameter to obtain the clearance and compare the results to Specifications

12   Subtract the outside diameter of each rocker arm shaft journal from the corresponding rocker arm bore diameter to compute the clearance between the rocker arm shaft and the rocker arm. Compare the measurements to the clearance specified in this Chapter. If any of them fall outside the specified limits, replace either the rocker arms or the shaft, or both.

22 Engine overhaul - reassembly sequence

1   Before beginning engine reassembly, make sure you have all the necessary new parts (including new cylinder head bolts), gaskets and seals as well as the following items on hand:

   Common hand tools
   A 1/2-inch drive torque wrench
   Piston ring installation tool
   Piston ring compressor
   Short lengths of rubber or plastic hose to fit over connecting rod bolts
   Plastigage
   Feeler gauges
   A fine-tooth file
   New engine oil
   Engine assembly lube or moly-base grease
   Gasket sealant
   Thread locking compound

2   In order to save time and avoid problems, engine reassembly must be done in the following general order:

   Piston rings
   Crankshaft and main bearings
   Rear main oil seal and retainer
   Piston/connecting rod assemblies
   Oil pump
   Oil pan
   Cylinder heads, camshafts, lifters and rocker arms
   Timing belt and sprockets
   Timing belt covers
   Intake and exhaust manifolds
   Rocker arm covers
   Engine rear plate
   Driveplate

23 Piston rings - installation

Refer to illustrations 23.3, 23.4, 23.9a, 23.9b and 23.12

1   Before installing the new piston rings, the ring end gaps must be checked. It's assumed that the piston ring side clearance has been checked and verified correct (Section 18).
2   Lay out the piston/connecting rod assemblies and the new ring sets so the ring sets will be matched with the same piston and cylinder during the end gap measurement and engine assembly.
3   Insert the top (number one) ring into the first cylinder and square it up with the cylin-

23.3 When checking piston ring end gap, the ring must be square in the cylinder bore (this is done by pushing the ring down with the top of a piston as shown)

der walls by pushing it in with the top of the piston **(see illustration)**. The ring should be near the bottom of the cylinder, at the lower limit of ring travel.
4   To measure the end gap, slip feeler gauges between the ends of the ring until a gauge equal to the gap width is found **(see illustration)**. The feeler gauge should slide between the ring ends with a slight amount of drag. Compare the measurement to the Specifications in this Chapter. If the gap is larger or smaller than specified, double-check to make sure you have the correct rings before proceeding.
5   If the gap is too small, you may have to file the rings to fit or exchange the set. The type of ring set you buy, and the material the rings are faced with, determine whether they can be filed. Carefully read the instructions with the ring set.
6   Excess end gap isn't as critical as too little gap, unless the gap is greater than 0.040-inch. Compare your measurements to this Chapter's Specifications for maximum end gap. Again, double-check to make sure you have the correct rings for your engine. If you do file the ring gaps, mount a file in a vise, lubricate the tops of the jaws, and slide the

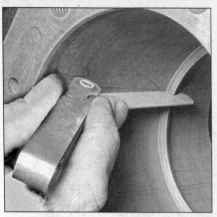

23.4 With the ring square in the cylinder, measure the end gap with a feeler gauge

ring back and forth across the file, resting the ring against the top of the jaws and with even pressure on both sides of the ring gap. File a little, then recheck that ring's end gap in the bore before filing any more. When the correct gap is achieved, use a whetstone or fine file to deburr the edges that have been filed.
7   Repeat the procedure for each ring that will be installed in the first cylinder and for each ring in the remaining cylinders. Remember to keep rings, pistons and cylinders matched up.
8   Once the ring end gaps have been checked/corrected, the rings can be installed on the pistons.
9   The oil control ring (lowest one on the piston) is usually installed first. It's composed of three separate components. Slip the spacer/expander into the groove **(see illustration)**. If an anti-rotation tang is used, make sure it's inserted into the drilled hole in the ring groove. Next, install the lower side rail. Don't use a piston ring installation tool on the oil ring side rails, as they may be damaged. Instead, place one end of the side rail into the groove between the spacer/expander and the ring land, hold it firmly in place and slide a finger around the piston while pushing the rail into the groove **(see illustration)**. Next, install the upper side rail in the same manner.

2B

23.9a Installing the spacer/expander in the oil control ring groove

23.9b DO NOT use a piston ring installation tool when installing the oil ring side rails

10   After the three oil ring components have been installed, check to make sure that both the upper and lower side rails can be turned smoothly in the ring groove.

11   The number two (middle) ring is installed next. It's usually stamped with a mark which must face up, toward the top of the piston. **Note:** *Always follow the instructions printed on the ring package or box - different manufacturers may require different approaches. Do not mix up the top and middle rings, as they have different cross sections.*

12   Use a piston ring installation tool and make sure the identification mark is facing the top of the piston, then slip the ring into the middle groove on the piston **(see illustration)**. Don't expand the ring any more than necessary to slide it over the piston.

13   Install the number one (top) ring in the same manner. Make sure the mark is facing up. Be careful not to confuse the number one and number two rings.

14   Repeat the procedure for the remaining pistons and rings.

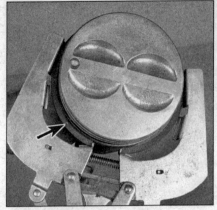

23.12 Installing the compression rings with a ring expander - the mark (arrow) must face up

24.5 Make sure the oil holes in the bearings are aligned with the oil holes in the block (arrows)

24   Crankshaft - installation and main bearing oil clearance check

Refer to illustrations 24.5, 24.6, 24.11, 24.13 and 24.15

1   Crankshaft installation is the first step in engine reassembly. It's assumed at this point that the engine block and crankshaft have been cleaned, inspected and repaired or reconditioned.

2   Position the engine on the stand with the crankcase facing up.

3   Remove the main bearing cap bolts and lift out the cap assembly.

4   If they're still in place, remove the original bearing inserts from the block and the main bearing caps. Wipe the bearing surfaces of the block and caps with a clean, lint-free cloth. They must be kept spotlessly clean.

Main bearing oil clearance check

5   Clean the back sides of the new main bearing inserts and lay one in each main bearing saddle in the block. If one of the bearing inserts from each set has a large groove in it, make sure the grooved insert is installed in the block. Lay the other bearing from each set in the corresponding main bearing cap. Make sure the tab on the bearing insert fits into the recess in the block or cap. **Caution:** *The oil holes in the block must line up with the oil holes in the bearing inserts* **(see illustration)**. *Do not hammer the bearing into place and don't nick or gouge the bearing faces. No lubrication should be used at this time.*

6   The flanged thrust bearing must be installed in the fourth (rear) cap and saddle **(see illustration)**.

7   Clean the faces of the bearings in the block and the crankshaft main bearing journals with a clean, lint-free cloth.

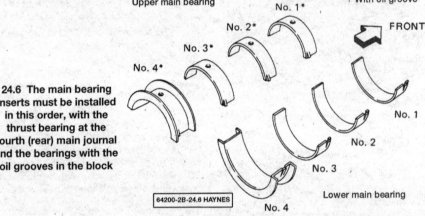

24.6 The main bearing inserts must be installed in this order, with the thrust bearing at the fourth (rear) main journal and the bearings with the oil grooves in the block

Upper main bearing

No. 1*

No. 2*

No. 3*

No. 4*

*: With oil groove

FRONT

No. 1

No. 2

No. 3

No. 4

Lower main bearing

64200-2B-24.6 HAYNES

8   Check or clean the oil holes in the crankshaft, as any dirt here can go only one way - straight through the new bearings.

9   Once you're certain the crankshaft is clean, carefully lay it in position in the main bearings.

10   Before the crankshaft can be permanently installed, the main bearing oil clearance must be checked.

11   Cut several pieces of the appropriate size Plastigage (they must be slightly shorter than the width of the main bearings) and place one piece on each crankshaft main bearing journal, parallel with the journal axis **(see illustration)**.

12   Clean the faces of the bearings in the cap assembly and install it with the arrow pointing toward the timing belt end of the engine. Don't disturb the Plastigage.

13   Starting with the center main and working out toward the ends, tighten the main bearing cap assembly bolts, in three steps, to the torque specified in this Chapter **(see illustration)**. Don't rotate the crankshaft at any time during this operation.

14   Remove the bolts and carefully lift off the main bearing cap assembly. Don't disturb the Plastigage or rotate the crankshaft.

15   Compare the width of the crushed Plastigage on each journal to the scale printed on

the Plastigage envelope to obtain the main bearing oil clearance **(see illustration)**. Check the Specifications in this Chapter to make sure it's correct.

16   If the clearance is not as specified, the bearing inserts may be the wrong size (which means different ones will be required). Before deciding that different inserts are needed, make sure that no dirt or oil was between the bearing inserts and the caps or block when the

24.11 Lay the Plastigage strips (arrow) on the main bearing journals, parallel to the crankshaft centerline

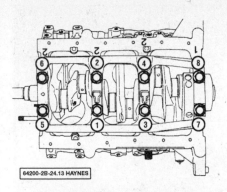

24.13 Tighten the main bearing cap retaining bolts in this sequence

24.15 Compare the width of the crushed Plastigage to the scale on the envelope to determine the main bearing oil clearance (always take the measurement at the widest point of the Plastigage); be sure to use the correct scale - standard and metric ones are included

clearance was measured. If the Plastigage was wider at one end than the other, the journal may be tapered (refer to Section 19).

17 Carefully scrape all traces of the Plastigage material off the main bearing journals and/or the bearing faces. Use your fingernail or the edge of a credit card - don't nick or scratch the bearing faces.

Final crankshaft installation

18 Carefully lift the crankshaft out of the engine.

19 Clean the bearing faces in the block, then apply a thin, uniform layer of moly-base grease or engine assembly lube to each of the bearing surfaces. Be sure to coat the thrust faces as well as the journal face of the thrust bearing.

20 Make sure the crankshaft journals are clean, then lay the crankshaft back in place in the block.

21 Clean the faces of the bearings in the cap assembly, then apply lubricant to them.

22 Install the cap assembly with the arrow pointing toward the timing belt end of the engine.

23 Tighten the bearing cap bolts to 10-to-12 ft-lbs.

24 Gently tap the ends of the crankshaft

forward and backward with a lead or brass hammer to line up the main bearing and crankshaft thrust surfaces.

25 Retighten all main bearing cap bolts to the specified torque, starting with the center main and working out toward the ends (see illustration 24.13).

26 Rotate the crankshaft a number of times by hand to check for any obvious binding.

27 The final step is to check the crankshaft endplay with a feeler gauge or a dial indicator as described in Section 14. The endplay should be correct if the crankshaft thrust faces aren't worn or damaged and new bearings have been installed.

28 Refer to Section 25 and install the new seal, then bolt the retainer to the block.

25 Rear main oil seal installation

Refer to illustrations 25.3 and 25.4

1 All models are equipped with a one-

25.3 Place the retainer between two blocks of wood and drive the seal out of the retainer from the rear

25.4 Drive the new seal into the retainer with a block of wood or a section of pipe - make sure that you don't cock the seal in the bore

piece seal that fits into a housing (retainer) attached to the transaxle end of the block. The crankshaft must be installed first and the main bearing caps bolted in place, then the new seal should be installed in the retainer and the retainer bolted to the block.

2 Check the seal contact surface very carefully for scratches and nicks that could damage the new seal lip and cause oil leaks. If the crankshaft is damaged, the only alternative is a new or different crankshaft.

3 The old seal can be removed from the retainer with a hammer and punch by driving it out from the back side (see illustration). Be sure to note how far it's recessed into the retainer bore before removing it; the new seal will have to be recessed an equal amount. Be very careful not to scratch or otherwise damage the bore in the retainer or oil leaks could develop.

4 Make sure the retainer is clean, then apply a thin coat of engine oil to the outer edge of the new seal. The seal must be pressed squarely into the retainer bore, so hammering it into place is not recommended. If you don't have access to a press, sandwich the retainer and seal between two smooth pieces of wood and press the seal into place with the jaws of a large vise. The pieces of wood must be thick enough to distribute the force evenly around the entire circumference of the seal. Work slowly and make sure the seal enters the bore squarely (see illustration).

5 The seal lips must be lubricated with moly-base grease or engine assembly lube before the seal/retainer is slipped over the crankshaft and bolted to the block. Use a new gasket - no sealant is required - and make sure the dowel pins are in place before installing the retainer.

6 Tighten the screws a little at a time until the torque specified in this Chapter is reached.

26 Pistons/connecting rods - installation and rod bearing oil clearance check

Refer to illustrations 26.5, 26.11, 26.13 and 26.17

1 Before installing the piston/connecting rod assemblies, the cylinder walls must be perfectly clean, the top edge of each cylinder must be chamfered, and the crankshaft must be in place.

2 Remove the cap from the end of the number one connecting rod (refer to the marks made during removal). Remove the original bearing inserts and wipe the bearing surfaces of the connecting rod and cap with a clean, lint-free cloth. They must be kept spotlessly clean.

Connecting rod bearing oil clearance check

3 Clean the back side of the new upper

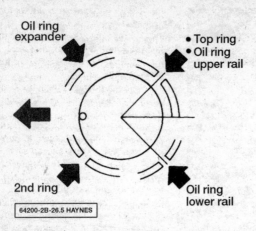

26.5 Stagger the ring end gaps as shown - the arrow at left
indicates the front of the engine

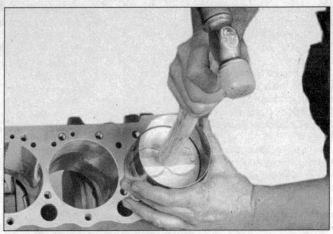

26.11 The piston can be driven (gently) into the cylinder bore with
the end of a wooden hammer handle

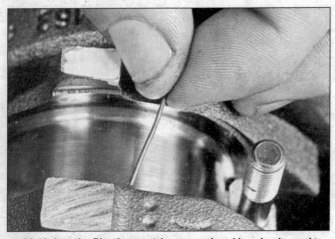

26.13 Lay the Plastigage strips on each rod bearing journal,
parallel to the crankshaft centerline

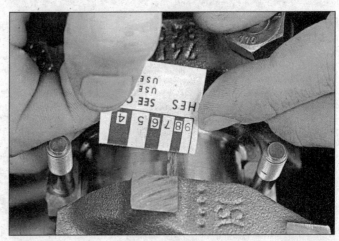

26.17 Measure the width of the crushed Plastigage to determine
the rod bearing oil clearance (be sure to use the correct scale -
standard and metric ones are included)

bearing insert, then lay it in place in the connecting rod. Make sure the tab on the bearing fits into the recess in the rod. Don't hammer the bearing insert into place and be very careful not to nick or gouge the bearing face. Don't lubricate the bearing at this time.

4   Clean the back side of the other bearing insert and install it in the rod cap. Again, make sure the tab on the bearing fits into the recess in the cap, and don't apply any lubricant. It's critically important that the mating surfaces of the bearing and connecting rod are perfectly clean and oil free when they're assembled for clearance checking.

5   Position the piston ring gaps at the specified intervals around the piston (see illustration).

6   Slip a section of plastic or rubber hose over each connecting rod cap bolt.

7   Lubricate the piston and rings with clean engine oil and attach a piston ring compressor to the piston. Leave the skirt protruding about 1/4-inch to guide the piston into the cylinder. The rings must be compressed until they're flush with the piston.

8   Rotate the crankshaft until the number one connecting rod journal is at BDC (bottom dead center) and apply a coat of engine oil to the cylinder walls.

9   With the notch on top of the piston facing the timing belt end of the engine, gently insert the piston/connecting rod assembly into the number one cylinder bore and rest the bottom edge of the ring compressor on the engine block. Note: *The front of each piston and connecting rod is also marked with a "W", which should face the front of the engine.*

10   Tap the top edge of the ring compressor to make sure it's contacting the block around its entire circumference.

11   Gently tap on the top of the piston with the end of a wooden hammer handle (see illustration) while guiding the end of the connecting rod into place on the crankshaft journal. The piston rings may try to pop out of the ring compressor just before entering the cylinder bore, so keep some downward pressure on the ring compressor. Work slowly, and if any resistance is felt as the piston enters the cylinder, stop immediately. Find out what's hanging up and fix it before proceeding. Do not, for any reason, force the piston into the cylinder - you might break a ring and/or the piston.

12   Once the piston/connecting rod assembly is installed, the connecting rod bearing oil clearance must be checked before the rod cap is permanently bolted in place.

13   Cut a piece of the appropriate size Plastigage slightly shorter than the width of the connecting rod bearing and lay it in place on the number one connecting rod journal, parallel with the journal axis (see illustration).

14   Clean the connecting rod cap bearing face, remove the protective hoses from the connecting rod bolts and install the rod cap. Make sure the mating mark on the cap is on the same side as the mark on the connecting rod.

15   Install the nuts and tighten them to the torque specified in this Chapter (work up to it in three steps). Note: *Use a thin-wall socket to avoid erroneous torque readings that can result if the socket is wedged between the rod cap and nut. If the socket tends to wedge itself between the nut and the cap, lift up on it slightly until it no longer contacts the cap. Do*

not rotate the crankshaft at any time during this operation.

16 Remove the nuts and detach the rod cap, being very careful not to disturb the Plastigage.

17 Compare the width of the crushed Plastigage to the scale printed on the Plastigage envelope to obtain the oil clearance **(see illustration)**. Compare it to the Specifications in this Chapter to make sure the clearance is correct.

18 If the clearance is not as specified, the bearing inserts may be the wrong size (which means different ones will be required). Before deciding that different inserts are needed, make sure that no dirt or oil was between the bearing inserts and the connecting rod or cap when the clearance was measured. Also, recheck the journal diameter. If the Plastigage was wider at one end than the other, the journal may be tapered (refer to Section 19).

Final connecting rod installation

19 Carefully scrape all traces of the Plastigage material off the rod journal and/or bearing face. Be very careful not to scratch the bearing - use your fingernail or the edge of a credit card.

20 Make sure the bearing faces are perfectly clean, then apply a uniform layer of clean moly-base grease or engine assembly lube to both of them. You'll have to push the piston into the cylinder to expose the face of the bearing insert in the connecting rod - be sure to slip the protective hoses over the rod bolts first.

21 Slide the connecting rod back into place on the journal, remove the protective hoses from the rod cap bolts, install the rod cap and tighten the nuts to the specified torque. Again, work up to the torque in three steps.

22 Repeat the entire procedure for the remaining pistons/connecting rods.

23 The important points to remember are . . .

a) *Keep the back sides of the bearing inserts and the insides of the connecting rods and caps perfectly clean when assembling them.*

b) *Make sure you have the correct piston/rod assembly for each cylinder.*

c) *The "W" mark on the piston and rod must face the timing belt end of the engine.*

d) *Lubricate the cylinder walls with clean oil.*

e) *Lubricate the bearing faces when installing the rod caps after the oil clearance has been checked.*

24 After all the piston/connecting rod assemblies have been properly installed, rotate the crankshaft a number of times by hand to check for any obvious binding.

25 As a final step, the connecting rod endplay must be checked. Refer to Section 13 for this procedure.

26 Compare the measured endplay to the Specifications to make sure it's correct. If it was correct before disassembly and the original crankshaft and rods were reinstalled, it should still be right. If new rods or a new crankshaft were installed, the endplay may be inadequate. If so, the rods will have to be removed and taken to an automotive machine shop for resizing. If the endplay is too great, new rods may be required.

27 Initial start-up and break-in after overhaul

Warning: *Have a fire extinguisher ready when starting the engine for the first time.*

1 Once the engine has been installed in the vehicle, double-check the engine oil and coolant levels.

2 With the spark plugs out of the engine and the ignition system disabled (see Section 3), crank the engine until oil pressure registers on the gauge.

3 Install the spark plugs, hook up the plug wires and restore the ignition system functions (see Section 3).

4 Start the engine. It may take a few moments for the fuel system to build up pressure, but the engine should start without a great deal of effort. **Note:** *If backfiring occurs through the throttle body, recheck the valve timing and ignition timing.*

5 After the engine starts, it should be allowed to warm up to normal operating temperature. While the engine is warming up, make a thorough check for fuel, oil and coolant leaks. Also check the automatic transaxle fluid level (if equipped).

6 Shut the engine off and recheck the engine oil and coolant levels.

7 Drive the vehicle to an area with no traffic, accelerate from 30 to 50 mph, then allow the vehicle to slow rapidly to 30 mph with the throttle closed. Repeat the procedure 10 or 12 times. This will load the piston rings and cause them to seat properly against the cylinder walls. Check again for oil and coolant leaks.

8 Drive the vehicle gently for the first 500 miles (no sustained high speeds) and keep a constant check on the oil level. It is not unusual for an engine to use oil during the break-in period.

9 At approximately 500 to 600 miles, change the oil and filter.

10 For the next few hundred miles, drive the vehicle normally. Do not pamper it or abuse it.

11 After 2000 miles, change the oil and filter again and consider the engine broken in.

2B

Notes

Chapter 3
Cooling, heating and air conditioning systems

Contents

3

Specifications

General

Coolant capacity	See Chapter 1
Drivebelt tension	See Chapter 1
Radiator pressure cap rating	11.8 to 15.8 psi
Thermostat rating	
Valve opens	180-degrees F
Fully open	194-degrees F
Refrigerant type	
1993	R-12
1994 and later	R-134a
Refrigerant capacity	
Without auxiliary system	2.25 pounds
With auxiliary system	3.50 pounds

Torque specifications

Thermostat housing cover bolts	144 to 180 in-lbs
Water pump retaining bolts	144 to 180 in-lbs

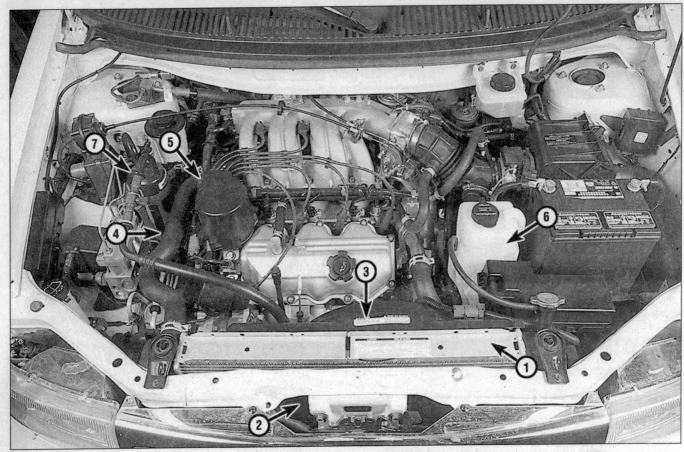

1.1 Cooling and air conditioning system components

1	Radiator	3	Engine cooling fan	5	Thermostat	7	Accumulator/drier
2	Condenser	4	Water pump	6	Coolant reservoir		

1   General information

Refer to illustrations 1.1 and 1.2

Engine cooling system

All vehicles covered by this manual employ a pressurized engine cooling system with thermostatically controlled coolant circulation **(see illustration)**. An impeller-type water pump mounted on the engine block pumps coolant through the engine. The coolant flows around each cylinder and toward the rear of the engine. Cast-in coolant passages direct coolant around the intake and exhaust ports, near the spark plug areas and in close proximity to the exhaust valve guides.

A wax-pellet type thermostat controls engine coolant temperature. During warm up, the closed thermostat prevents coolant from circulating through the radiator. As the engine nears normal operating temperature, the thermostat opens and allows hot coolant to travel through the radiator, where it's cooled before returning to the engine **(see illustration)**.

The cooling system is sealed by a pressure-type radiator cap, which raises the boil-ing point of the coolant and increases the cooling efficiency of the radiator. If the system pressure exceeds the cap pressure relief value, the excess pressure in the system forces the spring-loaded valve inside the cap off its seat and allows the coolant to escape through the overflow tube into a coolant reservoir. When the system cools the excess coolant is automatically drawn from the reservoir back into the radiator.

The coolant reservoir serves as both the point at which fresh coolant is added to the cooling system to maintain the proper fluid level and as a retaining tank for overheated coolant. This type of cooling system is known as a closed design because coolant that escapes past the pressure cap is saved and reused.

Heating system

The heating system consists of a blower fan and heater core located in the heater unit, the hoses connecting the heater core to the engine cooling system and the heater/air conditioning control panel on the dashboard. Hot engine coolant is circulated through the heater core. When the heater mode is activated, a flap door opens to expose the heater unit to the passenger compartment. A fan

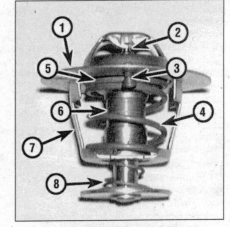

1.2 Typical thermostat

1	Flange	5	Valve seat
2	Piston	6	Valve
3	Jiggle valve	7	Frame
4	Main coil spring	8	Secondary coil spring

switch on the control head activates the blower motor, which forces air through the core, heating the air. A second heater core

2.4 The condition of your coolant can easily be checked with this type of hydrometer, available at auto parts stores

and fan assembly is mounted behind the left-rear interior panel on models equipped with an optional auxiliary heater/air conditioning system.

Air conditioning system

The air conditioning system consists of a condenser mounted in front of the radiator, an evaporator mounted adjacent to the heater core, a compressor mounted on the engine, a receiver-drier which contains a high pressure relief valve and the plumbing connecting all of the above components.

A blower fan forces the warmer air of the passenger compartment through the evaporator core (sort of a radiator-in-reverse), transferring the heat from the air to the refrigerant. The liquid refrigerant boils off into low pressure vapor, taking the heat with it when it leaves the evaporator. A second evaporator core assembly is mounted behind the left-rear interior panel on models equipped with an optional "auxiliary" heater/air conditioning system.

Warning: *The models covered by this manual are equipped with Supplemental Restraint Systems (SRS), more commonly known as airbags. Always disable the airbag system before working in the vicinity of any airbag system components to avoid the possibility of accidental deployment of the airbag(s), which could cause personal injury (see Chapter 12).*

2   Antifreeze - general information

Refer to illustration 2.4

Warning: *Do not allow antifreeze to come in contact with your skin or painted surfaces of the vehicle. Rinse off spills immediately with plenty of water. Antifreeze is highly toxic if ingested. Never leave antifreeze lying around in an open container or in puddles on the floor; children and pets are attracted by its sweet smell and may drink it. Check with local*

authorities about disposing of used antifreeze. Many communities have collection centers, which will see that antifreeze is disposed of safely. Never dump used anti-freeze on the ground or into drains.*

The cooling system should be filled with a water/ethylene glycol based antifreeze solution, which will prevent freezing down to at least -20-degrees F, or lower if local climate requires it. It also provides protection against corrosion and increases the coolant boiling point.

The cooling system should be drained, flushed and refilled at the specified intervals (see Chapter 1). Old or contaminated antifreeze solutions are likely to cause damage and encourage the formation of rust and scale in the system. Use distilled water with the antifreeze.

Before adding antifreeze, check all hose connections, because antifreeze tends to leak through very minute openings. Engines don't normally consume coolant, so if the level goes down, find the cause and correct it.

The exact mixture of antifreeze-to-water that you should use depends on the relative weather conditions. The mixture should contain at least 50-percent antifreeze, but should never contain more than 70-percent antifreeze. Consult the mixture ratio chart on the antifreeze container before adding coolant. Hydrometers are available at most auto parts stores to test the ratio of antifreeze to water **(see illustration)** or antifreeze test strips are available instead of the hydrometer gauge. Use antifreeze that meets the vehicle manufacturer's specifications.

3   Thermostat - check and replacement

Warning: *Do not attempt to remove the radiator cap, coolant or thermostat until the engine has cooled completely.*

Check

Refer to illustration 3.7

1   Before assuming the thermostat is responsible for a cooling system problem, check the coolant level (Chapter 1), drivebelt tension (Chapter 1) and temperature gauge (or light) operation.

2   If the engine takes a long time to warm up (as indicated by the temperature gauge or heater operation), the thermostat is probably stuck open. Replace the thermostat with a new one.

3   If the engine runs hot, use your hand to check the temperature of the upper radiator hose. If the hose is not hot, but the engine is, the thermostat is probably stuck in the closed position, preventing the coolant inside the engine from traveling through the radiator. Replace the thermostat. **Caution:** *Do not drive the vehicle without a thermostat. The computer may stay in open loop and emissions and fuel economy will suffer.*

H 12494

3.7 A thermostat can be accurately checked by heating it in a container of water with a thermometer and observing the opening and fully open temperature

4   If the lower radiator hose is hot, it means that the coolant is flowing and the thermostat is open. Consult the *Troubleshooting* Section at the front of this manual for further diagnosis.

5   A more thorough test of the thermostat can only be made when it is removed from the vehicle (see below). If the thermostat remains in the open position at room temperature, it is faulty and must be replaced.

6   To test it fully, suspend the (closed) thermostat on a length of string or wire in a container of cold water, with a thermometer (cooking type that reads beyond 212 degrees F).

7   Heat the water on a stove while observing the temperature and the thermostat. Neither should contact the sides of the container **(see illustration)**.

8   Note the temperature when the thermostat begins to open and when it is fully open. Compare the temperatures to the Specifications in this Chapter. The number stamped into the thermostat is generally the fully open temperature. Some manufacturers provide Specifications for the beginning-to-open temperature, the fully open temperature, and sometimes the amount the valve should open.

9   If the thermostat doesn't open and close as specified, or sticks in any position, replace it.

Replacement

Refer to illustrations 3.13 and 3.16

10   Disconnect the negative cable from the battery.

11   Drain the coolant from the radiator (see Chapter 1).

12   Detach the upper radiator hose from the coolant outlet at the intake manifold and the radiator, then unbolt the hose clamp at the timing belt cover and remove the radiator hose.

13   Detach the bypass hose from the thermostat cover, then remove the cover from

3

the engine (see illustration). Be prepared for some coolant to spill as the gasket seal is broken.

14   Remove the thermostat, noting the direction in which it was installed.

15   Scrape off any old gasket or sealant on the thermostat housing and the thermostat cover, then clean them with lacquer thinner.

16   Apply a bead of RTV sealant around the perimeter of the cover, install the new thermostat with the jiggle valve UP (see illustration) into the housing and bolt the cover in place within 5 minutes of applying the sealant.

17   Installation is the reverse of removal. Tighten the thermostat cover fasteners to the torque listed in this Chapter's Specifications, then reinstall the hoses.

18   Wait at least a half-hour for the sealant to cure. Refill and bleed the cooling system (see Chapter 1). Run the engine and check for leaks and proper operation.

4   Engine cooling fan and circuit - check and component replacement

Warning : *Do not work with your hands near the fans at any time that the engine is running or the key is ON. With the key ON, (even with the engine not running) the fan can start at any time, since it is controlled by coolant temperature.*

Check

Refer to illustrations 4.2 and 4.5

1   All models have a two-speed electric fan mounted in a plastic shroud attached to the back of the radiator.

2   Fan operation is controlled both by the PCM and the high and low-speed fan relays (see illustration). The coolant temperature sensor signals the PCM of engine temperature, and the PCM turns on the appropriate relay(s). At warm idle, the low-speed relay

3.13 Remove the thermostat cover bolts (arrows indicate three of the four bolts), pull off the cover and remove the thermostat from the housing

3.16 Install the thermostat as shown, with the jiggle valve (arrow) UP

turns the fan on at low speed. When coolant temperature reaches 221 degrees F, the PCM turns the high-speed relays 1 and 2 on, causing the fan to run at high speed. There are two high-speed relays to ensure proper cooling even if one relay fails, and they will also operate if the coolant temperature sensor fails.

3   If the fan operates continuously, the fault could be the coolant temperature sensor or the relays. Refer to Chapter 6 for diagnosis of the sensor, and Chapter 12 for diagnosis of the relays.

4   Warm the engine up until the gauge on the instrument panel indicates the high side of NORMAL. The fan should come on. If not, check the RAD FAN fuse in the center engine compartment fuse panel and the RLY COIL fuse in the interior fuse panel (see Chapter 12 for fuse locations).

5   If the fuses checked OK, disconnect the electrical connector from the electric fan motor (see illustration). Attach a fused jumper wire with battery voltage to either of the two power terminals on the fan, and a chassis-ground jumper to the black wire ter-

minal on the fan (see the wiring diagrams in Chapter 12). If the fan doesn't operate, it should be replaced.

6   If it does operate with jumper wires, but doesn't under normal driving conditions, connect a voltmeter to a chassis ground and probe the power terminals of the fan connector on the harness side. If the engine is hot and the temperature gauge shows above NORMAL, there should be battery voltage at one of these terminals.

7   Check the ground of the circuit by switching your meter to the ohms scale. Ground one side of the meter and probe the other side at the black wire terminal of the fan connector. Resistance should be no more than 5 ohms. If resistance is high, trace the ground wire circuit to the chassis.

8   If there had been no power at the terminals in Step 6, check that power is being supplied to the low-speed fan relay. One of its sockets on the relay panel should exhibit battery voltage at all times, and one only when the key is in the On or Start position.

9   If these sockets check OK, refer to Chapter 12 for checking continuity within the relays themselves.

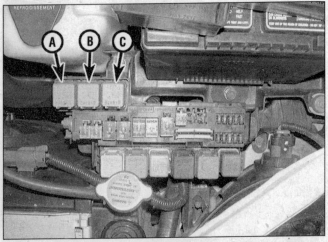

4.2 Typical engine cooling fan relay locations

A   Low-Speed
B   High speed no. 1
C   High speed no. 2

4.5 To test either fan motor, disconnect the electrical connector (arrow) and use jumper wires to connect the black wire terminal directly to ground; apply battery voltage to each of the other two terminals in turn - if the fan still doesn't work, or it works at one speed and not both, replace the motor

4.12 Remove the upper fan shroud mounting bolts/nuts (arrow indicates the right bolt)

5.2 Depress the clip (arrow) and lift the coolant reservoir straight up out of its bracket

5.9a Remove the upper transmission cooling line (arrow) from above

Replacement

Refer to illustration 4.12

10   Disconnect the electrical connector from the fan motor.

11   Disconnect the upper radiator hose and overflow hose at the radiator.

12   Remove the two fan shroud bolts and remove the fan/shroud assembly **(see illustration)**. Note: *The bottom of the fan shroud fits into tabs on the radiator.*

13   Remove the small clip retaining the fan to the motor shaft.

14   Remove the screws retaining the motor to the shroud.

15   With an assistant retaining the fan, hit the shaft of the motor with a hammer and blunt punch to separate the fan from the motor.

16   Installation is the reverse of removal.

5   Radiator and coolant reservoir - removal and installation

Warning: *Wait until the engine is completely cool before beginning this procedure.*

Coolant reservoir

Refer to illustration 5.2

1   The coolant reservoir is mounted adjacent to the battery in the left corner of the engine compartment.

2   Unscrew the cap with the hose still attached. Depress the clip and lift the reservoir straight up out of the bracket **(see illustration)**.

3   Pour the coolant into a container.

4   After washing the reservoir inside and out (use a household "bottle" brush to clean inside), inspect the reservoir for cracks and chafing. If it's damaged or so obscured by age as to make reading the water level difficult, replace it.

5   Installation is the reverse of removal.

Radiator

Refer to illustrations 5.9a. 5.9b, 5.10 and 5.12

6   Disconnect the negative battery cable

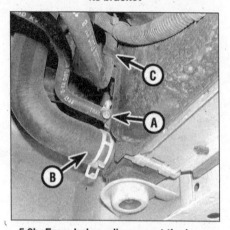

5.9b From below, disconnect the lower transmission cooling line (A), the lower radiator hose (B) and detach the electrical harness from the clip (C)

from the battery.

7   Set the parking brake and block the rear wheels. Raise the front of the vehicle and support it securely on jackstands.

8   Drain the cooling system (see Chapter 1). If the coolant is relatively new or in good condition, save it and reuse it. Read the Warning in Section 2.

9   Disconnect the transmission cooler lines from the radiator **(see illustrations)**. Use a drip pan to catch spilled fluid and plug the lines and fittings.

10   Loosen the hose clamps, then detach

5.10 Loosen the hose clamp and detach the upper radiator hose - marking one end of each hose connection with paint (arrows) makes reassembly easier

the radiator hoses from the fittings **(see illustration)**. If they're stuck, grasp each hose near the end with a pair of slip joint pliers and twist it to break the seal, then pull it off - be careful not to damage the radiator fittings! If the hoses are old or deteriorated, cut them off and install new ones. Also disconnect the small hose to the coolant reservoir.

11   Refer to Section 4 and remove the engine cooling fan assembly.

12   Unbolt the small brackets that attach the top of the radiator to the radiator support **(see illustration)**.

5.12 Remove the two bolts (arrows) that attach the upper radiator mounts to the radiator support

6.3 The water pump weep hole (arrow) is located on the underside of the water pump

6.9 Remove the water pump pulley bolts (arrows) while retaining the pulley with a strap wrench

13   Carefully lift out the radiator. Don't spill coolant on the vehicle or scratch the paint.

14   Inspect the radiator for leaks and damage. If it needs repair, have a radiator shop or dealer service department perform the work as special techniques are required.

15   Bugs and dirt can be removed from the radiator by spraying with a garden hose nozzle from the back side. The radiator should be flushed out with a garden hose before reinstallation.

16   Check the radiator mounts for deterioration and replace if necessary.

17   Installation is the reverse of the removal procedure. Guide the radiator into the mounts until they seat properly.

18   Refill and bleed the cooling system (see Chapter 1).

19   Start the engine and check for leaks. Allow the engine to reach normal operating temperature, indicated by the upper radiator hose becoming hot. Recheck the coolant level and add more if required.

20   Check and add transmission fluid as needed.

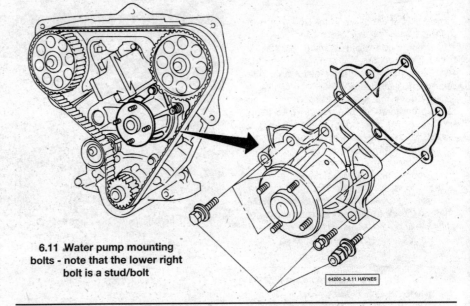

6.11 Water pump mounting bolts - note that the lower right bolt is a stud/bolt

6   Water pump - check and replacement

Warning: *Wait until the engine is completely cool before beginning this procedure.*

Check

Refer to illustration 6.3

1   A failure in the water pump can cause serious engine damage due to overheating.

2   There are two ways to check the operation of the water pump while it's installed on the engine. If the pump is defective, it should be replaced with a new or rebuilt unit.

3   Water pumps are equipped with weep (or vent) holes **(see illustration)**. If a failure occurs in the pump seal, coolant will leak from the hole. With the timing belt cover removed, you'll need a flashlight and small mirror to find the hole on the water pump from underneath to check for leaks.

4   If the water pump shaft bearings fail, there may be a howling sound at the pump while it's running. Shaft wear can be felt with the drivebelt belt removed if the water pump pulley is rocked up and down (with the engine off). Don't mistake drivebelt slippage, which causes a squealing sound, for water pump bearing failure.

5   Even a pump that exhibits no outward signs of a problem, such as noise or leakage, can still be due for replacement. Removal for close examination is the only sure way to tell. Sometimes the fins on the back of the impeller can corrode to the point that cooling efficiency is hampered.

Replacement

Refer to illustrations 6.9 and 6.11

6   Disconnect the negative battery cable from the battery.

7   Drain the cooling system (see Chapter 1). If the coolant is relatively new or in good condition, save it and reuse it.

8   Remove the drivebelts (see Chapter 1).

9   While retaining the water pump pulley with a strap wrench, remove the pulley bolts and pulley **(see illustration)**.

10   Remove the crankshaft pulley and timing belt covers (see Chapter 2, Part A).

11   Remove the bolts and detach the water pump from the engine **(see illustration)**. Check the impeller on the backside for evidence of corrosion or missing fins.

12   Clean the bolt threads and the threaded holes in the engine to remove corrosion and sealant.

13   Compare the new pump to the old one to make sure they're identical.

14   Remove all traces of old gasket sealant from the engine.

15   Clean the engine and new water pump mating surfaces with lacquer thinner or acetone.

16   Apply a thin layer of RTV sealant to the new pump, then carefully set a new gasket in place.

17   Carefully attach the pump to the engine and thread the bolts into the holes finger tight. Use a small amount of RTV sealant on the bolt threads, and make sure that the

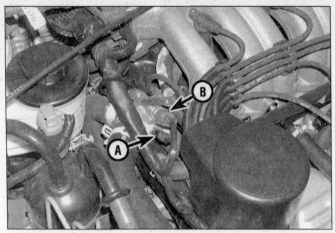

7.1 The temperature gauge sending unit (A) is the sensor with a single wire connector - (B) is the ECT sensor for the computer

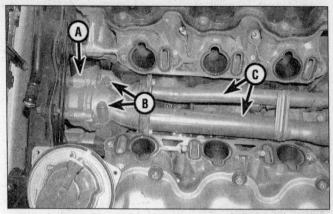

8.3 The thermostat cover (A) is bolted to the thermostat housing which is bolted down to the block with two bolts (B) - (C) is the coolant crossover tubes bolted to the thermostat housing with a flange

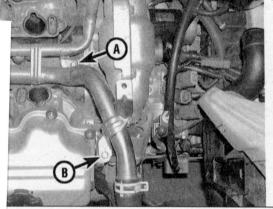

8.5 The crossover pipe assembly is bolted to the engine block (A) and the larger pipe (leading to the lower radiator hose) is bolted to the rear of the front cylinder head (B)

dowel pins, if used, are in their original loca-

...n on top of the sender to an engine ...th the engine warm (167 degrees ...ce should be 179 to 219 ohms. ...engine is hot (212 degrees F), the ...should drop to 60 to 72 ohms. If ...fails the test, replace it.

...ement

...sending unit must be replaced, ...from the engine and quickly install ...ement. Use a conductive sealant ...eads (not Teflon tape). Make sure ...e is cool before removing the defec- ...g unit. There will be some coolant ...e unit is removed, so be prepared to ...Check the coolant level after the ...nt part has been installed.

2 If an overheating indication occurs even when the engine is cold, check the wiring between the dash and the sending unit for a short circuit to ground.

3 If the gauge is inoperative, test the circuit by briefly grounding the wire to the sending unit while the ignition is On (engine not running for safety). If the gauge deflects full scale, replace the sending unit.

4 If the gauge doesn't respond in the test outlined in Step 3, check for an open circuit in the gauge wiring.

5 To test the sending unit, disconnect the electrical connector and attach an ohmmeter

8 Coolant crossover tubes - removal and installation

Refer to illustrations 8.3 and 8.5

1 Part of the system that carries coolant to and from the engine, thermostat housing and radiator is a pair of metal pipes located below the lower intake manifold. Because of the nearly inaccessible location, these pipes and connections are generally overlooked, yet a leak in this part of the cooling system could cause serious engine damage. Anytime the lower intake manifold is removed, or if coolant is observed at either end of the lower intake manifold, these pipes and connections should be inspected.

2 The lower intake manifold must be removed to inspect or replace the coolant crossover tubes (see Chapter 2, Part A for manifold removal).

3 To remove the crossover tubes, remove the hoses from the thermostat cover (see Section 3). The thermostat housing is bolted to the block at the timing belt end of the engine, and the coolant crossover tubes are bolted to a flange at the rear of the thermostat housing **(see illustration)**. Remove the thermostat housing mounting bolts.

4 Remove the coolant hoses attached to the driver-side ends of the two pipes.

5 Remove the bolts retaining the pipe assembly to the block and front cylinder head **(see illustration)**. Removing the pipe assembly while still attached to the thermostat housing is possible, but takes some maneuvering.

6 Installation is the reverse of removal. Use a new gasket and RTV sealant between the thermostat housing and the crossover tube flange, and use a bead of RTV sealant where the bottom water passage of the thermostat housing mates with the block. Bolt

3

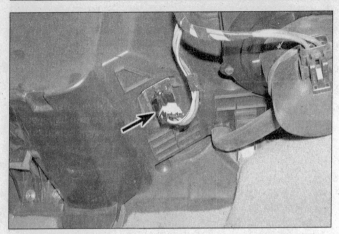

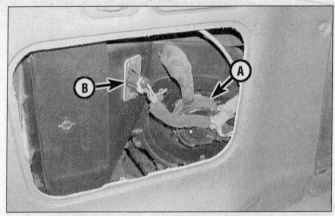

9.5a The resistor (arrow) for the front blower motor is located on the blower housing, under the right side of the dashboard

9.5b To service the optional rear heater/air conditioning blower motor (A) and resistor (B), remove the access panel in the rear driver's side interior panel

the thermostat housing down to the block within five minutes of applying the sealant. **Note:** *The pipes should be bolted to the thermostat housing before lowering the assembly in place to bolt it to the block.*

7   Refill and bleed the cooling system (see Chapter 1).

9   Blower motor circuit - check

Refer to illustrations 9.5a, 9.5b, 9.6 and 9.9
Warning: *The models covered by this manual are equipped with Supplemental Restraint Systems (SRS), more commonly known as airbags. Always disable the airbag system before working in the vicinity of any airbag system components to avoid the possibility of accidental deployment of the airbag(s), which could cause personal injury (see Chapter 12).*

1   When equipped with the optional auxiliary rear heater/air conditioning, there are two blower motors, two blower resistors and two blower switches, one each for the front and rear systems. The checks are virtually the same for front or rear, only the location of the components is different. Check the 65A FRT BLWR fuse in the engine compartment fuse/relay box, the 10A RELAYS and 7.5A A/C-CONT fuses in the interior fuse panel,

and all connections in the circuit for looseness and corrosion. For the rear heater/air conditioning unit, check the no. 24 and 25 fuses.

2   Make sure the battery is fully charged.

3   With the transmission in Park, the parking brake securely set, turn the ignition switch to the On position. It isn't necessary to start the vehicle.

4   Switch the heater controls to FLOOR and the blower speed to HI. Check for airflow at the ducts to verify if the blower is operating. If it is, then switch the blower speed to LO and check again. Try all the speeds.

5   The front blower motor resistor assembly is located on the evaporator housing under the right side of the dash, and the optional rear blower resistor is behind an access panel **(see illustrations)**. There are three resistor elements mounted on the resistor board to provide low and medium blower speeds (HI bypasses the resistor). The blower operates continuously, anytime the ignition switch is On and the mode switch is in any position other than Off. A thermal limiter resistor is integrated into the circuits to prevent heat damage to the components. If the thermal limiter circuit has been opened as a result of excessive heat, it should be replaced only with the identical replacement part. **Note:** *Do not replace your blower resistor with a resistor that does not incorporate the thermal limiter.*

6   With the resistor removed from the vehicle, visually check the limiter for damage, indicated by the material melting out between the

contacts of the limiter. Check the resistor block for continuity between terminals **(see illustration)**. There should be continuity between all terminals (with varying resistance at each set). If any of the resistor elements do not pass the tests, replace the blower resistor.

7   Locate the electrical connector at the blower motor. Backprobe the brown/white wire terminal (or the red/white wire on rear blower units); there should be at least 10 volts with the mode switch in any position other than Off and the ignition switch On. If not, there is a problem in the circuit from the fuse panel to the front blower motor relay to the blower motor.

8   If there is voltage at the feed wire, but the blower does not operate, backprobe the ground wire (not the wire you tested in Step 7) and connect it to a known good chassis ground with a jumper wire. If the blower now operates there is a problem in the ground circuit. If it still doesn't operate, replace the blower motor.

9   If the blower operates, but not at all speeds and you have already checked the blower resistor, refer to Section 11 and remove the heater/air conditioning control panel. Disconnect the electrical connector from the back of the blower speed switch and test the terminals for continuity **(see illustration)**. If the continuity is not as described, replace the blower speed switch.

10   Test the relays for the front or rear blowers (see Chapter 12). If the relay fails any of these tests, replace the relay.

9.6 Check that the thermal limiter (arrow) on the resistor for damage, then check that there is continuity between all terminals on the connector side

2	1
4	3

9.9 Blower speed switch terminal identification and continuity chart

SWITCH POSITION	CONTINUITY BETWEEN
Low	none
Med	3 and 2 only
Med High	3, 4 and 2 only
High	4, 1 and 2 only

64200-3-9.9 HAYNES

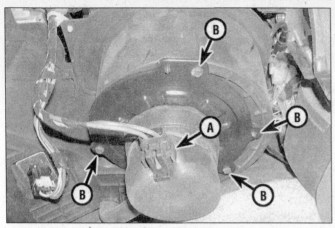

10.3 Disconnect the front blower's electrical connector (A), then remove the three mounting screws (B)

11.2 Remove the screws (arrows) retaining the control panel to the dashboard

10 Blower motor - removal and installation

Warning: *The models covered by this manual are equipped with Supplemental Restraint Systems (SRS), more commonly known as airbags. Always disable the airbag system before working in the vicinity of any airbag system components to avoid the possibility of accidental deployment of the airbag(s), which could cause personal injury (see Chapter 12).*

Front blower motor

Refer to illustration 10.3

1 Disconnect the negative battery cable.
2 Open the glove compartment and remove it (see Chapter 11).
3 Disconnect the blower motor electrical connector from the motor, remove the blower motor mounting screws, and pull the blower motor carefully out of the housing **(see illustration)**.
4 If the blower motor is being replaced, the fan wheel should be transferred to the new motor at this time. It is attached to the blower motor shaft with a push nut. Grasp the nut with pliers and pull it off or pry it off with a small screwdriver, being careful not to crack the push nut. To reinstall the nut, simply push it onto the shaft.
5 The remainder of the installation is the reverse of removal.

Optional rear heater/air conditioning blower motor

6 Some models have an auxiliary heater/air conditioning system located in the rear of the vehicle, behind the left-rear interior trim panel.
7 With the access panel pried out of the trim panel, there is access to remove/test the auxiliary blower motor **(see illustration 9.5b)**. The rear blower motor and resistor can be checked in the same manner as the front system (see Section 9). The standard front heater/air conditioning control panel has a separate control knob for the rear system.

11.3 Pull the control panel forward enough to disconnect the electrical connectors

11 Heater and air conditioning control assembly - removal and installation

Warning: *The models covered by this manual are equipped with Supplemental Restraint Systems (SRS), more commonly known as airbags. Always disable the airbag system before working in the vicinity of any airbag system components to avoid the possibility of accidental deployment of the airbag(s), which could cause personal injury (see Chapter 12).*

Removal

Front

Refer to illustrations 11.2 and 11.3

1 Refer to Chapter 11 for removal of the center dash bezel, around the control assembly and radio.
2 Remove the four screws retaining the control assembly to the instrument panel **(see illustration)** . **Note:** *The control assembly for the optional Electronic Automatic Temperature Control is a module that contains its own microprocessor (computer). The EATC system has its own self-diagnostic*

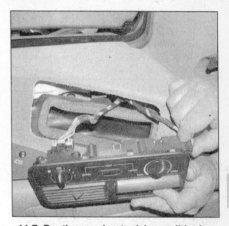

11.7 Pry the rear heater/air conditioning control panel out of the trim panel and disconnect the electrical connectors

capability (see Section 13).
3 Pull the control assembly out of the instrument panel and disconnect the electrical connectors **(see illustration)**.
4 Refer to Section 9 for electrical checks of the blower motor speed switch. The speed switch, function selector, and blend-control switch can all be removed from the control panel (manual air conditioning) by pulling the knob off from the front side, removing the four screws retaining the printed circuit housing, then depressing the plastic tabs on the back of the switch to release it from the control panel.
5 Installation is the reverse of the removal procedure.

Rear

Refer to illustration 11.7

6 The control panel for the auxiliary rear heater/air conditioning unit is located in the left rear quarter trim panel.
7 Use a trim panel removal tool to pry the control panel out of the quarter trim, then disconnect the electrical connectors **(see illustration)**.
8 Removal of the switches is as described in Step 4.

3

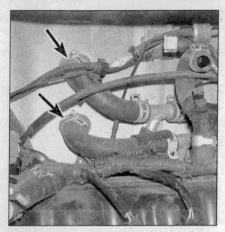

12.2 Loosen the two heater hose clamps and disconnect the heater hoses (arrows) from the heater core inlet and outlet pipes at the firewall

9   Installation is the reverse of the removal procedure.

12   Heater core - removal and installation

Warning 1: *The models covered by this manual are equipped with Supplemental Restraint Systems (SRS), more commonly known as airbags. Always disable the airbag system before working in the vicinity of any airbag system components to avoid the possibility of accidental deployment of the airbag(s), which could cause personal injury (see Chapter 12).*

Warning 2: *The air conditioning system is under high pressure. DO NOT loosen any fittings or remove any components until after the system has been discharged. Air conditioning refrigerant should be properly discharged into an EPA-approved container at a dealer service department or an automotive air conditioning repair facility. Always wear eye protection when disconnecting air conditioning system fittings.*

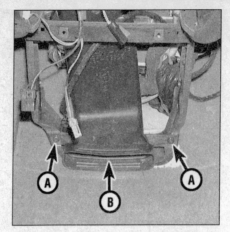

12.6 Remove the two screws (A) and pull out the center floor duct (B)

Front

Refer to illustrations 12.2, 12.6, 12.7, 12.8, 12.9, 12.10, 12.11, 12.12, 12.13, 12.14a, 12.14b, 12.14c and 12.15

1   Disconnect the cable from the negative battery terminal. Drain the cooling system (see Chapter 1).

2   Disconnect the heater hoses from the heater core inlet and outlet tubes at the firewall **(see illustration)**.

3   Refer to Chapter 11 and remove the center dash trim panel, the console cover and the two lower side panels, on either side of the console.

4   Refer to Chapter 12 and remove the radio and Section 11 for removal of the heater/air conditioning control panel.

5   Refer to Chapter 11 and remove the glove compartment and both the left and right below-dash covers.

6   Remove the two screws and the heater floor duct **(see illustration)**.

7   The upper duct is removed from above the heater unit **(see illustration)**.

8   A U-shaped steel framework supports the center area of the dashboard; it must be

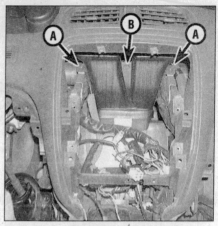

12.7 Remove the two screws (A) and the upper heater duct (B)

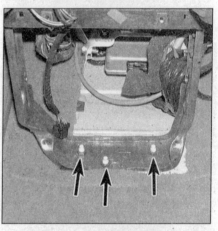

12.8 Remove the three nuts (arrows) securing the brace to the floor

removed to access the heater unit **(see illustration)**.

9   Remove the brace at the bottom of the glove box area **(see illustration)**.

10   Remove the bolts securing the upper ends of the center-dash support (the brace whose lower end was unbolted in Step 8) and

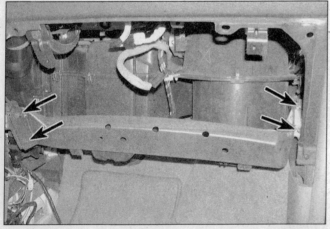

12.9 Remove the screws (arrows) and the brace for the glove box area

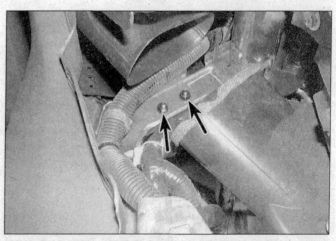

12.10 Remove the upper fasteners on the dash support - arrows indicate the two on the right side (there are two on the left side as well)

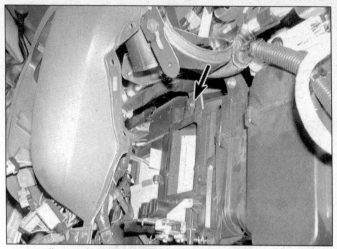

12.11 Remove the screws (arrow indicates one) retaining the duct outlet panel to the front of the heater unit

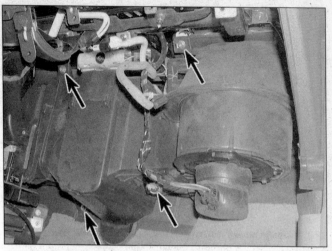

12.12 Loosen the four mounting screws (arrows) for the evaporator housing to aid in heater unit removal

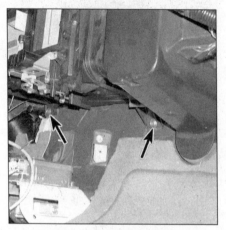

12.13 Remove the two lower screws (arrows) mounting the heater unit to the firewall

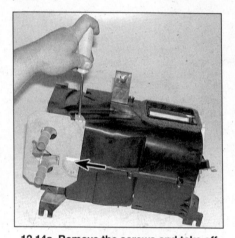

12.14a Remove the screws and take off the shield (arrow) . . .

remove the heater unit. However, the heater unit is removed by sliding it to the left and out from under the dash, which is made easier by loosening the mounting screws of the blower/evaporator housing **(see illustration)**.

13 At the center opening of the instrument panel, remove the top heater unit mounting screw that was revealed when the upper heater duct was removed **(see illustration 12.7)**. Remove the two lower heater unit screws **(see illustration)**. The heater unit must be pulled away from the firewall enough for the pipe to clear, then slide the unit to the left for removal. **Note:** *The accelerator pedal will have to be removed to allow enough room.* **Caution:** *Protect the carpeting with old towels in case any coolant spills during heater unit removal.*

14 Once the heater unit is out of the vehicle, remove the foam insulator, the sheet-metal shield and the plastic brace, then the heater core can be removed from the heater unit **(see illustrations)**.

15 Installation is the reverse of the removal

remove the support **(see illustration)**.
11 Remove the plastic heater duct outlet panel from the face of the heater unit, to

access mounting screws underneath **(see illustration)**.
12 The blower housing and evaporator housing do not need to be removed to

3

12.14b . . . then the plastic brace (arrow) . . .

12.14c . . . and the heater core can be slid out of the case

12.15 Make sure the foam seal is in place before replacing the heater unit back into the vehicle

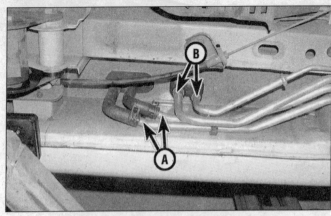

12.20 Under the left-rear of the chassis, detach the hoses from the two coolant tubes (A) and use a spring-lock coupling tool to separate the two refrigerant lines (B)

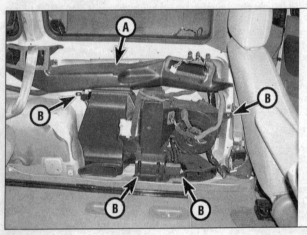

12.21 Remove the screws and the upper duct (A), then remove the four mounting screws (B) and pull the auxiliary heater/air conditioning unit out as an assembly

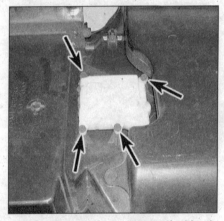

12.22a Remove the screws on the blend door actuator (arrows) . . .

procedure. When reinstalling the heater core in the housing, make sure the original foam sealing material is intact and in place **(see illustration)**.

16   Fill the cooling system (see Chapter 1). Run the engine and check for coolant leaks.

Rear

Refer to illustrations 12.20, 12.21, 12.22a, 12.22b and 12.23.

17   On some models, there is an optional

heater/air conditioning system located behind the left-rear interior trim panel. The assembly includes a blower, heater core and evaporator core.

18   Refer to Chapter 11 for removal of the left rear trim panel.

19   Have the air conditioning refrigerant discharged and recovered by a dealer or air conditioning shop.

20   Raise and suitably support the vehicle on a hoist or jackstands, to access the hose

connections under the mid-section of the vehicle chassis **(see illustration)**. Use a spring-lock coupling tool to disconnect the refrigerant lines underneath, then disconnect the coolant hoses for the heater unit.

21   Remove the screws retaining the upper duct to the auxiliary heater/air conditioning unit, then disconnect all electrical connectors at the blower motor, blower resistor, vent

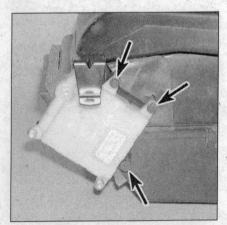

12.22b . . . and the vent door actuator (arrows)

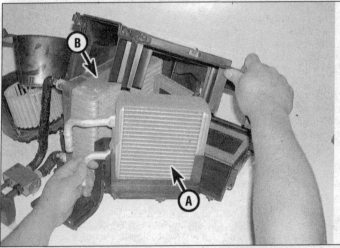

12.23 Remove the screws, then separate the case and remove the heater core (A) from the housing - the evaporator core (B) is also accessible

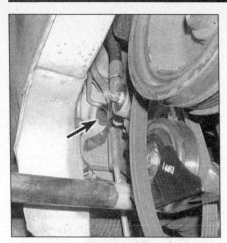

13.1 Check that the evaporator housing drain tube (arrow) at the firewall is clear of any blockage - view here is through the right fenderwell from below

13.9 Insert a thermometer in the center duct while operating the air conditioning system - the output air should be 35-40 degrees F less than the ambient temperature, depending on humidity (but not lower than 40-degrees F)

door actuator and blend door actuator. Remove the mounting screws and take the unit out as an assembly **(see illustration)**.

22   Remove the screws and both the blend door actuator and vent door actuators **(see illustrations)**.

23   Remove the screws retaining the heater core/evaporator core cover to the assembly, then remove the heater core or evaporator core **(see illustration)**.

24   Installation is the reverse of the removal procedure.

25   After the installation, refill the cooling system, have the refrigerant recharged and run the system to check for proper heating and cooling operation.

13   Air conditioning and heating system - check and maintenance

Air conditioning system

Refer to illustration 13.1

Warning: *The air conditioning system is under high pressure. Do not loosen any hose fittings or remove any components until after the system has been discharged. Air conditioning refrigerant should be properly discharged into an EPA-approved recovery/recycling unit at a dealer service department or an automotive air conditioning repair facility. Always wear eye protection when disconnecting air conditioning system fittings.*

Caution 1: *There are two types of refrigerants used on the models covered by this manual. 1993 models use R-12 refrigerant while 1994 and later models use environmentally friendly R-134a. The two refrigerants (and their appropriate refrigerants oils) are not compatible and must never be mixed or components will be damaged.*

Caution 2: *When replacing entire components, additional refrigerant oil should be added equal to the amount that is removed with the component being replaced. Be sure*

to read the can before adding any oil to the system, to make sure it is compatible with either the R-12 or R-134a system.

1   The following maintenance checks should be performed on a regular basis to ensure that the air conditioning continues to operate at peak efficiency.

a) *Inspect the condition of the compressor drivebelt. If it is worn or deteriorated, replace it (see Chapter 1).*

b) *Check the drivebelt tension and, if necessary, adjust it (see Chapter 1).*

c) *Inspect the system hoses. Look for cracks, bubbles, hardening and deterioration. Inspect the hoses and all fittings for oil bubbles or seepage. If there is any evidence of wear, damage or leakage, replace the hose(s).*

d) *Inspect the condenser fins for leaves, bugs and any other foreign material that may have embedded itself in the fins. Use a "fin comb" or compressed air to remove debris from the condenser.*

e) *Make sure the system has the correct refrigerant charge.*

f) *If you hear water sloshing around in the dash area or have water dripping on the carpet, check the evaporator housing drain tube* **(see illustration)** *and insert a piece of wire into the opening to check for blockage.*

2   It's a good idea to operate the system for about ten minutes at least once a month. This is particularly important during the winter months because long term non-use can cause hardening, and subsequent failure, of the seals. Note that using the Defrost function operates the compressor.

3   If the air conditioning system is not working properly, first make sure the compressor clutch is operating (see Section 14).

4   Because of the complexity of the air conditioning system and the special equipment necessary to service it, in-depth trou-

bleshooting and repairs are not included in this manual. However, simple checks and component replacement procedures are provided in this Chapter. For more complete information on the air conditioning system, refer to the *Haynes Automotive Heating and Air Conditioning Manual*. However, simple component replacement procedures are provided in this Chapter.

5   The most common cause of poor cooling is simply a low system refrigerant charge. If a noticeable drop in system cooling ability occurs, one of the following quick checks will help you determine whether the refrigerant level is low. Should the system lose its cooling ability, the following procedure will help you pinpoint the cause.

Check

Refer to illustration 13.9

6   Warm the engine up to normal operating temperature.

7   Place the air conditioning temperature selector at the coldest setting and put the blower at the highest setting. Open the doors (to make sure the air conditioning system doesn't cycle off as soon as it cools the passenger compartment).

8   After the system reaches operating temperature, feel the two pipes connected to the evaporator at the firewall.

9   The pipe (thinner tubing) leading from the condenser outlet to the evaporator should be cold, and the evaporator outlet line (the thicker tubing that leads back to the compressor) should be slightly colder (3 to 10 degrees F colder). If the evaporator outlet is considerably warmer than the inlet, the system needs a charge. Insert a thermometer in the center air distribution duct **(see illustration)** while operating the air conditioning system at its maximum setting - the temperature of the output air should be 35 to 40 degrees F below the ambient air temperature (down to approximately 40 degrees F). If the ambient (outside) air temperature is very high, say 110 degrees F, the duct air temperature may be as high as 60 degrees F, but generally the air conditioning is 35 to 40 degrees F cooler than the ambient air.

10   If the air isn't as cold as it used to be, the system probably needs a charge. Further inspection or testing of the system is beyond the scope of the home mechanic and should be left to a professional. Some on-board diagnostics capability on your vehicle can help point to areas for testing or repair.

Adding refrigerant (1994 and later models only)

Refer to illustrations 13.12, 13.14 and 13.15

Caution: *Make sure any refrigerant, refrigerant oil or replacement component your purchase is designated as compatible with environmentally friendly R-134a systems.*

11   1993 models use R-12 refrigerant. Because of federal restrictions on the sale of R-12 refrigerant, it isn't practical for refrigerant to be added by the home mechanic.

3

13.12 A basic charging kit for 134a systems is available at most auto parts stores - it must say 134a (not R-12) and so should the can of refrigerant

13.14 Attach the refrigerant kit to the low-side charging port (arrow) - it's near the right shock tower - the cap should be marked with an "L"

13.15 The air conditioning pressure switch (arrow) is located on top of the accumulator-drier - if the compressor will not stay engaged, disconnect the connector and bridge it with a jumper wire during the charging procedure

When the system needs recharging, take the vehicle to a dealer service department or professional air conditioning shop for evacuation, leak testing and recharging. On 1994 and later models using R-134a refrigerant, make sure any refrigerant, oil or replacement component is designated for environmentally-friendly R-134a systems.

12 Buy an R-134a automotive charging kit at an auto parts store **(see illustration)**. A charging kit includes a 12-ounce can of refrigerant, a tap valve and a short section of hose that can be attached between the tap valve and the system low side service valve. Because one can of refrigerant may not be sufficient to bring the system charge up to the proper level, it's a good idea to buy an additional can. **Warning:** *Never add more than two cans of refrigerant to the system.*

12 Hook up the charging kit by following the manufacturer's instructions. **Warning:** *DO NOT hook the charging kit hose to the system high side!* The fittings on the charging kit are designed to fit **only** on the low side of the system.

13 Back off the valve handle on the charging kit and screw the kit onto the refrigerant can, making sure first that the O-ring or rubber seal inside the threaded portion of the kit is in place. **Warning:** *Wear protective eyewear when dealing with pressurized refrigerant cans.*

14 Remove the dust cap from the low-side charging and attach the quick-connect fitting on the kit hose **(see illustration)**.

15 Warm up the engine and turn on the air conditioning. Keep the charging kit hose away from the fan and other moving parts. **Note:** *The charging process requires the compressor to be running. If the clutch cycles off, you can put the air conditioning switch on High and leave the car doors open to keep the clutch on and compressor working.* **Note:** *The compressor can be kept on during the charging by removing the connector from the low-pressure switch (combination high-limit and low-limit switch on some models) and*

bridging it with a paper clip or jumper wire during the procedure **(see illustration)**.

16 Turn the valve handle on the kit until the stem pierces the can, then back the handle out to release the refrigerant. You should be able to hear the rush of gas. Add refrigerant to the low side of the system, keeping the can upright at all times, but shaking it occasionally. Allow stabilization time between each addition. **Note:** *The charging process will go faster if you wrap the can with a hot-water-soaked shop rag to keep the can from freezing up.*

17 If you have an accurate thermometer, you can place it in the center air conditioning duct inside the vehicle and keep track of the output air temperature **(see illustration 13.9)**. A charged system that is working properly should cool down to approximately 40-degrees F. If the ambient (outside) air temperature is very high, say 110 degrees F, the duct air temperature may be as high as 60 degrees F, but generally the air conditioning is 30-40 degrees F cooler than the ambient air.

18 When the can is empty, turn the valve handle to the closed position and release the connection from the low-side port. Replace the dust cap.

19 Remove the charging kit from the can and store the kit for future use with the piercing valve in the UP position, to prevent inadvertently piercing the can on the next use.

Heating systems

20 If the carpet under the heater core is damp, or if antifreeze vapor or steam is coming through the vents, the heater core is leaking. Remove it (see Section 12) and install a new unit (most radiator shops will not repair a leaking heater core).

21 If the air coming out of the heater vents isn't hot, the problem could stem from any of the following causes:

a) *The thermostat is stuck open, preventing the engine coolant from warming up enough to carry heat to the heater core. Replace the thermostat (see Section 3).*

b) *There is a blockage in the system, preventing the flow of coolant through the heater core. Feel both heater hoses at the firewall. They should be hot. If one of them is cold, there is an obstruction in one of the hoses or in the heater core, or the heater control valve is shut. Detach the hoses and back flush the heater core with a water hose. If the heater core is clear but circulation is impeded, remove the two hoses and flush them out with a water hose.*

c) *If flushing fails to remove the blockage from the heater core, the core must be replaced (see Section 12).*

On-Board diagnostics

22 A system of self-diagnostics is used on models equipped with the optional Electronic Automatic Temperature Control (EATC), with the LED portion of the control panel allowing display of hard and intermittent fault codes.

23 To begin the self-test, turn the ignition key On, and set the temperature control between 65 and 85 degrees F. Press both the Floor and Off buttons at the same time and then the Auto button within two seconds. An LED light will circle around the temperature display for 30 seconds to a minute while the system is calibrating and checking.

24 If there are any malfunctions in the system, one or more codes will be displayed. If there are no codes stored, 88 will display. Look up the codes in the following chart to find the portion of the system that needs inspection or repair.

25 You must exit the self-diagnostics before turning the key to OFF. Exit by pushing the down side (blue) on the Temp button to keep the existing codes in memory, or push Defrost to exit with all codes cleared.

26 After any repair work, repeat the self-diagnostics procedure to check your work.

EATC TROUBLE CODE	FAULT DESCRIPTION	EATC TROUBLE CODE	FAULT DESCRIPTION
10	Rear blend door short (intermittent)	43	Ambient temperature sensor open (voltage high, intermittent)
12	Rear blend door short (hard fault)	50	Sunload sensor short (low voltage, hard fault)
16	Rear blend door out-of-limit on Hot side	52	Sunload sensor short (low voltage, intermittent)
17	Rear blend door out-of-limit on Cold side	60	EATC mode button stuck (intermittent)
18	Rear blend door timeout	61	Ignition voltage too high (16.5 volts or higher)
20	Front blend door short	80	Outside/recirc door short (intermittent)
22	Air mix door short	82	Outside/recirc door short (hard fault)
26	Front blend door out-of-limit on Hot side	86	Outside/recirc door out-of-limit (Recirc side)
27	Front blend door out-of-limit on Cold side	87	Outside/recirc door out-of-limit (Fresh side)
28	Front blend door timeout	88	Outside/recirc door timeout (hard fault)
30	Interior temperature sensor out of range (low)	90	Mode door short (intermittent)
31	Interior temperature sensor out of range (high)	92	Mode door short (hard fault)
40	Ambient temperature sensor short (voltage low, hard fault)	98	Mode door timeout (hard fault)
41	Ambient temperature sensor open (voltage high)		
42	Ambient temperature sensor short (low voltage, intermittent)		

Eliminating air conditioning odors

Refer to illustration 13.30

27   Unpleasant odors that often develop in air conditioning systems are caused by the growth of a fungus, usually on the surface of the evaporator core. The warm, humid environment there is a perfect breeding ground for mildew to develop.

28   The evaporator core on most vehicles is difficult to access, and factory dealerships have a lengthy, expensive process for eliminating the fungus by opening up the evaporator case and using a powerful disinfectant and rinse on the core until the fungus is gone. You can service your own system at home, but it takes something much stronger than basic household germ-killers or deodorizers.

29   Aerosol disinfectants for automotive air conditioning systems are available in most auto parts stores, but remember when shopping for them that the most effective treatments are also the most expensive. The basic procedure for using these sprays is to start by running the system in the RECIRC mode for ten minutes with the blower on its highest speed. Use the highest heat mode to dry out the system and keep the compressor from engaging by disconnecting the wiring connector at the compressor (see Section 15).

30   The disinfectant can usually comes with a long spray hose. Remove the blower motor resistor (see Section 9), point the nozzle inside the hole and to the left towards the evaporator core, and spray according to the manufacturer's recommendations **(see illus-**

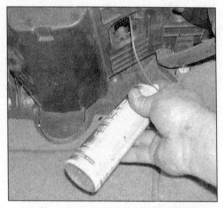

13.30 With the blower motor resistor removed, spray the disinfectant at the evaporator core

tration). Try to cover the whole surface of the evaporator core, by aiming the spray up, down and sideways. Follow the manufacturer's recommendations for the length of spray and waiting time between applications.

31   Once the evaporator has been cleaned, the best way to prevent the mildew from coming back again is to make sure your evaporator housing drain tube is clear **(see illustration 13.1)**.

14   Air conditioning compressor clutch circuit - check

1   Proper operation of the compressor clutch is essential to the function of the air con-

ditioning system. If your system doesn't seem to get cold, first check the clutch operation.

2   With the engine warmed up, set the air conditioning temperature selector on the coldest setting and the fan on high. Open the doors (to make sure the air conditioning system doesn't cycle off as soon as it cools the passenger compartment down).

3   Have an assistant switch the air conditioning On while you observe the front of the compressor. The clutch will make an audible click and the center of the clutch should rotate. If it doesn't, shut the engine off and disconnect the air conditioning system pressure switch **(see illustration 13.15)**. Bridge the terminals of the connector with a jumper wire and turn the air conditioning On again. If it works now, the system pressure is too high or too low. Have your system tested by a dealer service department or air conditioning shop.

4   If the clutch still didn't operate, check the appropriate fuses. Inspect the number 13 and 29 fuses in the interior fuse panel.

5   Remove the compressor clutch (AC) relay from the engine compartment relay panel and test it (see Chapter 12). With the relay out and the ignition On, check for battery power at two of the relay terminals (refer to the wiring diagrams for wire color designations to determine which terminals to check). There should be battery power with the key On, at the terminals for the relay control and power circuits.

6   Using a jumper wire, connect the terminals in the relay box from the relay power circuit to the terminal that leads to the compressor clutch (refer to the wiring diagrams for wire color designations to determine which

3

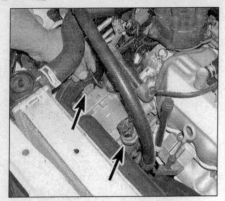

15.5 Disconnect the two electrical connectors (arrows) at the compressor

15.6 Remove the bolt (arrow) retaining the refrigerant manifold to the rear of the compressor

15.7 Loosen the upper compressor mounting bolts (A), then remove the lower bolts (B) and the compressor

terminals to connect). Listen for the clutch to click as you make the connection. If the clutch doesn't respond, disconnect the clutch connector at the compressor and check for battery voltage at the compressor clutch connector. Check for continuity to ground on the black wire terminal of the compressor clutch connector. If power and ground are available and the clutch doesn't operate when connected, the compressor clutch is defective.

7   If the compressor clutch, relay and related circuits are good and the system is fully charged with refrigerant and the compressor does not operate under normal conditions, have the PCM and related circuits checked by a dealer service department or other properly equipped repair facility.

15   Air conditioning compressor - removal and installation

Warning: *The air conditioning system is under high pressure. Do not loosen any hose fittings or remove any components until after the system has been discharged. Air conditioning refrigerant should be properly discharged into an EPA-approved recovery/recycling unit at a dealer service department or an automotive air conditioning repair facility. Always wear eye protection when disconnecting air conditioning system fittings.*
Note: *The accumulator/drier and evaporator orifice tube should be replaced whenever the compressor is replaced (see Sections 16 and 19).*

Removal

Refer to illustrations 15.5, 15.6 and 15.7
1   Have the air conditioning system refrigerant discharged and recycled by an air conditioning technician (see **Warning** above).
2   Disconnect the negative battery cable from the battery.
3   Set the parking brake, block the rear wheels and raise the front of the vehicle, supporting it securely on jackstands.
4   Remove the drivebelt (see Chapter 1).
5   Disconnect the compressor clutch wiring harness and the high pressure switch

electrical connector at the rear of the compressor **(see illustration)**.
6   Disconnect the refrigerant lines from the compressor. Plug the open fittings to prevent entry of dirt and moisture **(see illustration)**.
7   Unbolt the compressor from the mounting bracket and remove it from the vehicle **(see illustration)**. **Note:** *The upper mounting bolts will not come all the way out of the compressor - leave them in the compressor until it is removed from the vehicle.*

Installation

8   The clutch may have to be transferred from the old compressor to the new unit.
9   Add the proper amount of refrigerant oil to the new compressor using the following calculations:
   a) *Drain the refrigerant oil from the old compressor through the suction fitting and measure it in ounces.*
   b) *Drain any new oil from the new compressor.*
   c) *If the amount from the old compressor was 3 to 5 ounces, put that amount of clean, new oil in the new compressor.*
   d) *If the amount from the old compressor was less than 3 ounces, put 3 ounces of clean, new oil in the new compressor.*
   e) *If the amount from the old compressor was more than 5 ounces, put 5 ounces of clean, new oil in the new compressor.*
10   Installation is the reverse of removal, using new O-rings where the line manifold attaches to the compressor. **Note:** *Remember to slip the two upper mounting bolts into the compressor before installing the compressor in the vehicle.*
11   Have the system evacuated, recharged and leak tested by an air conditioning technician.

16   Air conditioning accumulator/drier - removal and installation

Warning: *The air conditioning system is under high pressure. DO NOT loosen any fit-*

tings or remove any components until after the system has been discharged. Air conditioning refrigerant should be properly discharged into an EPA-approved container at a dealer service department or an automotive air conditioning repair facility. Always wear eye protection when disconnecting air conditioning system fittings.

Removal

Refer to illustration 16.4
1   The accumulator/drier stores refrigerant and removes moisture from the system. When any major air conditioning component (compressor, condenser, evaporator) is replaced, or the system has been apart and exposed to air for any length of time, the accumulator/drier must be replaced.
2   Take the vehicle to a dealer service department or automotive air conditioning shop and have the air conditioning system discharged and the refrigerant recovered (see **Warning** above). Disconnect the cable at the negative battery terminal.
3   Disconnect the electrical connector at the compressor clutch cycling switch on top of the accumulator/drier. If the accumulator/drier is to be replaced with a new one, remove the cycling switch to transfer to the new drier.
4   Disconnect the refrigerant inlet and outlet lines **(see illustration)**. The outlet line is disconnected at the firewall **(see illustration 18.3)**. Use spring-lock coupling tools to disconnect the two lines. To disconnect a fitting, close the two halves of the tool over the connection and push the tool towards the garter spring. This expands the spring to release its hold. While the spring is expanded and tool is still in place, pull in opposite directions on the two lines to separate the connection. Cap or plug the open lines immediately. **Note:** *Special spring lock coupling tools are required to release the connectors used on the refrigerant lines throughout the air conditioning system, and are available at most auto parts stores in a set.*
5   Loosen the clamp-bolt on the mounting bracket and slide the accumulator/drier assembly up and out of the mounting bracket **(see illustration 16.4)**.

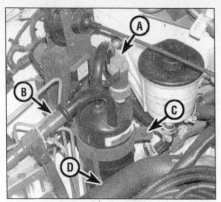

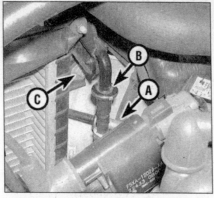

16.4 Disconnect the cycling switch (A), the inlet refrigerant line (B), the clamp bolt (C), and the rear line bracket (D, only if equipped with rear heat/AC), the outlet line is disconnected at the firewall

17.3 Use spring-lock coupling tools to disconnect the condenser-to-evaporator line connector (A), the condenser-to-compressor line connector (B), and remove the two condenser mounting bolts (C indicates the right-side bolt, radiator not yet removed in this photo)

18.3 Disconnect the suction line and the receiver line (arrows) from the evaporator at the engine side of the firewall - plug both lines to prevent contaminants and moisture from entering the system

Installation

6   If you are replacing the accumulator/drier, add two ounces of clean refrigerant oil to the new accumulator. This will maintain the correct oil level in the system after the repairs are completed.
7   Place the new accumulator/drier into position, tighten the mounting bracket bolt lightly, still allowing the accumulator drier to be turned to align the line connections.
8   Install the inlet and outlet lines. Lubricate the O-rings using clean refrigerant oil and reconnect the lines. Now tighten the clamp bolt securely and reconnect the electrical connector.
9   Connect the cable to the negative terminal of the battery.
10   Have the system evacuated, recharged and leak tested by a dealer service department or an air conditioning repair facility.

17   Air conditioning condenser - removal and installation

Warning: *The air conditioning system is under high pressure. Do not loosen any hose fittings or remove any components until after the system has been discharged. Air conditioning refrigerant should be properly discharged into an EPA-approved recovery/recycling unit at a dealer service department or an automotive air conditioning repair facility. Always wear eye protection when disconnecting air conditioning system fittings.*

Removal

Refer to illustration 17.3
1   Have the refrigerant discharged and recycled by an air conditioning technician (see **Warning** above).
2   Disconnect the negative cable from the battery and drain the cooling system (see Chapter 1).
3   Disconnect the condenser line and discharge line from the condenser **(see illustration)**. Cap the fittings on the condenser and

lines to prevent entry of dirt or moisture.
4   Refer to Section 5 and remove the radiator.
5   Remove the condenser retaining bolts **(see illustration 17.3)**.
6   Lean the condenser back toward the engine and remove it from the vehicle.

Installation

7   Installation is the reverse of removal. If a new condenser was installed, add 1 to 1.7 ounces of fresh refrigerant oil.
8   Have the system evacuated, charged and leak tested by an air conditioning technician.

18   Air conditioning evaporator core - removal and installation

Warning 1: *The models covered by this manual are equipped with Supplemental Restraint Systems (SRS), more commonly known as airbags. Always disable the airbag system before working in the vicinity of any airbag system components to avoid the possibility of accidental deployment of the airbag(s), which could cause personal injury (see Chapter 12).*
Warning 2: *The air conditioning system is under high pressure. DO NOT loosen any fittings or remove any components until after*

the system has been discharged. Air conditioning refrigerant should be properly discharged into an EPA-approved container at a dealer service department or an automotive air conditioning repair facility. Always eye wear protection when disconnecting air conditioning system fittings.

Front

Refer to illustrations 18.3, 18.5 and 18.7
1   The evaporator core is located inside the housing between the heater housing and blower housing. **Note:** *Before replacing an evaporator core, determine for certain that the core is leaking by having a leak test performed with special equipment at dealer service department or automotive air conditioning repair facility.*
2   Read all of the Steps before beginning this procedure. If you are going to replace the evaporator, have the refrigerant discharged and recovered at a dealer or air conditioning service shop (see **Warning** above).
3   Disconnect the refrigerant lines at the firewall **(see illustration)**.
4   Refer to Chapter 11 and remove the glove box assembly and the right-side under-dash panel.
5   Remove the four screws and the reinforcement bar in the glove box area **(see illustration)**.
6   Disconnect the electrical connectors at the evaporator and blower housings.
7   Remove the bolts retaining the

18.5 Remove the screws and the glove box reinforcement bar

3

18.7 Remove the five bolts (arrows) retaining the blower/evaporator case to the firewall

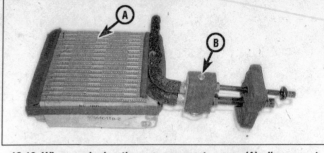

18.10 When replacing the rear evaporator core (A), disconnect the fittings at the expansion valve (B), then connect the new evaporator to the expansion valve

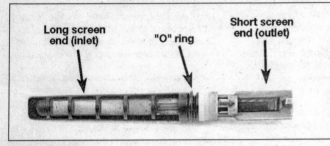

Long screen end (inlet)   "O" ring   Short screen end (outlet)

19.1 The expansion (orifice) tube contains a precision orifice and several screen filters - it should be replaced whenever a compressor is replaced

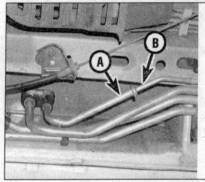

19.3 The orifice tube for the rear evaporator is located in this line (A) under the left-rear chassis - separate the connector (B) to replace the orifice tube

blower/evaporator case to the firewall **(see illustration)**.

8   Remove the screws and separate the two halves of the case to remove the evaporator core.

9   Installation is the reverse of the removal process. Add 1.5 to 2.5 ounces of new refrigerant oil to the new evaporator core's outlet tube. Also, before the lines are reconnected, it 's a good idea to replace the evaporator core orifice (see Section 19).

Rear

Refer to illustration 18.10

10   On some models, there is an optional, auxiliary rear heater/air conditioning system located behind the left-rear interior trim panel (behind the left-rear wheel housing). The assembly includes a blower, heater core and evaporator core. Removal and installation procedures for the rear evaporator core are the same as for the rear heater core (see Section 12). The rear evaporator core can be removed when the heater/evaporator housing is disassembled by taking out the screws retaining the two halves together **(see illustration)**.

11   If the rear evaporator core is being replaced, add 1.5 to 2.5 ounces of new refrigerant oil to the new evaporator. **Note:** *Whenever the rear evaporator core is replaced, it's a good idea to also replace the orifice tube as well (see Section 19). The orifice tube for the rear evaporator is located in the refrigerant line under the left-rear of the chassis.*

12   Have the system evacuated, recharged and leak tested by the dealer service department or an air conditioning repair facility.

19   Air conditioning expansion (orifice) tube - removal and replacement

Warning: *The air conditioning system is under high pressure. DO NOT loosen any fittings or remove any components until after the system has been discharged. Air conditioning refrigerant should be properly discharged into an EPA-approved container at a dealership service department or an automotive air conditioning repair facility. Always wear eye protection when disconnecting air conditioning system fittings.*

Front

Refer to illustration 19.1

1   The expansion tube is a tube with a fixed-diameter orifice and a mesh filter at each end **(see illustration)**. It's mounted in the refrigerant line from the condenser to the evaporator, and serves to both filter the refrigerant and cause the pressure to drop, cooling the evaporator.

2   On the models covered by this manual, the orifice tube for the front evaporator is permanently mounted inside the condenser-to-evaporator refrigerant line. A factory kit is available to install a new one, but installation involves precise cutting of the steel line and insertion of a new section (with the orifice tube), using compression fittings at each. Alignment of the two section of original pipe must be precise for the line to fit back in the vehicle. It is suggested that a dealer or air conditioning shop perform this job.

Rear

Refer to illustration 19.3

3   The orifice tube for the rear heater/air conditioning unit is located under the left-rear of the chassis, in the refrigerant pipe leading to the rear evaporator **(see illustration)**.

4   If you are going to replace the orifice tube, have the refrigerant discharged and recovered at a dealer or air conditioning service shop (see the **Warning** at the beginning of this Section).

5   Use a spring-lock coupling tool to disconnect the line fitting nearest the orifice tube **(see illustration 19.3)**. When you separate the pipe at the fitting you will see one end of the orifice tube inside the pipe leading to the evaporator. Use needle-nose pliers to remove the orifice tube. **Caution:** *Pull the core straight out, do not twist it.*

6   The orifice tube acts to meter the refrigerant, changing it from high-pressure liquid to low-pressure liquid. It is possible to reuse the orifice tube if:

a) *The screens aren't plugged with grit or foreign material*
b) *Neither screen is torn*
c) *The plastic housing over the screens is intact*
d) *The brass orifice inside the plastic housing is unrestricted*
e) *A new O-ring is used*

7   Installation is the reverse of removal. Be sure to insert the expansion tube with the shorter end in first, toward the evaporator, and lubricate the refrigerant line and the orifice tube with clean refrigerant oil to aid assembly.

8   Reconnnect the fitting and refrigerant line, then have the system evacuated, recharged and leak-tested by the shop that discharged it.

Chapter 4
Fuel and exhaust systems

Contents

4

Specifications

Fuel pressure

Key On, engine Off	40 to 43 psi
Fuel system pressure (at idle)	
Vacuum hose attached	34 to 38 psi
Vacuum hose detached	40 to 43 psi
Fuel pump pressure (maximum)	62 psi

Injector resistance (approximate) .... 10 to 14 ohms

Torque specifications
Ft-lbs (unless otherwise indicated)

Fuel injector cap screws	26 to 33 in-lbs
Fuel rail mounting bolts	17 to 20
Throttle body mounting bolts	
Step 1	80 to 97 in-lbs
Step 2	13 to 16

1   General information

Refer to illustration 1.1

The fuel system consists of a fuel tank, an electric fuel pump (located in the fuel tank), a fuel pressure regulator, a fuel pump relay, the fuel rail and fuel injectors, an air cleaner assembly and a throttle body unit. All models are equipped with a Sequential Electronic Fuel Injection (SEFI) system.

Sequential Electronic Fuel Injection (SEFI) system

Sequential Electronic Fuel Injection uses timed impulses to inject the fuel directly into the intake port of each cylinder according to its firing order. The injectors are controlled by the Powertrain Control Module (PCM). The PCM monitors various engine parameters and delivers the exact amount of fuel required into the intake ports **(see illustra-**

tion). The throttle body serves only to control the amount of air passing into the system. Because each cylinder is equipped with its own injector, much better control of the fuel/air mixture ratio is possible.

Fuel pump and lines

Fuel is circulated from the fuel tank to the fuel injection system, and back to the fuel tank, through a pair of metal lines running along the underside of the vehicle. An electric

1.1 Fuel injection system and related components (typical)

1	Idle Air Control (IAC) valve	4	Fuel filter
2	Throttle body	5	Air cleaner housing
3	Throttle Position Sensor (TPS)	6	Fuse/relay panel

7	Fuel pressure regulator
8	Fuel rail
9	Fuel injectors (front bank)

fuel pump and fuel level sending unit is located inside the fuel tank. A vapor return system routes all vapors back to the fuel tank through a separate return line.

The fuel pump relay is equipped with a primary and secondary voltage circuit. The primary circuit is controlled by the PCM and the secondary circuit is linked directly to battery voltage from the ignition switch. With the ignition switch On (engine not running), the PCM will energize the relay for five seconds. During cranking, the PCM supplies voltage to the fuel pump relay as long as the camshaft position sensor (CMP) sends its position signal (see Chapter 6). If there are no reference pulses, the fuel pump will shut off after five seconds.

The inertia switch will disable the fuel pump circuit in the event of a collision. The inertia switch is a cylindrical magnet with a steel ball that will release (breakaway) and trip a shutdown lever when the vehicle inertia reaches a certain peak value.

Exhaust system

The exhaust system includes a pair of exhaust manifolds, a diverter pipe fitted with an upstream (before catalytic converter) oxygen sensor, a catalytic converter, a muffler and a tail pipe. All 1994 and later vehicles are equipped with a warm-up (pre-cat) catalytic converter and all 1996 and later vehicles are

equipped with a downstream (after catalytic converter) oxygen sensor.

The catalytic converters are an emission control device added to the exhaust system to reduce pollutants. A single-bed converter is used in combination with a three-way (reduction) catalyst. Refer to Chapter 6 for more information regarding the catalytic converters.

2   Fuel pressure relief procedure

Refer to illustration 2.1
Warning: *Gasoline is extremely flammable, so take extra precautions when you work on any part of the fuel system. Don't smoke or allow open flames or bare light bulbs near the work area, and don't work in a garage where a natural gas-type appliance (such as a water heater or a clothes dryer) with a pilot light is present. Since gasoline is carcinogenic, wear latex gloves when there's a possibility of being exposed to fuel, and, if you spill any fuel on your skin, rinse it off immediately with soap and water. Mop up any spills immediately and do not store fuel-soaked rags where they could ignite. The fuel system is under constant pressure, so, if any fuel lines are to be disconnected, the fuel pressure in the system must be relieved first. When you perform any kind of work on the fuel system, wear*

safety glasses and have a Class B type fire extinguisher on hand.
Note: *After the fuel pressure has been relieved, it's a good idea to lay a shop towel over any fuel connection to be disassembled, to absorb the residual fuel that may leak out when servicing the fuel system.*
1   Remove the fuel pump relay from the engine compartment fuse/relay panel **(see illustration)**.
2   Start the engine and allow it to run until

2.1 Location of the fuel pump relay (1996 and later shown, 1995 and earlier similar)

3.3a Using a T-fitting, install the fuel pressure gauge between the fuel filter and the fuel rail

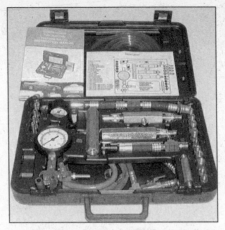

3.3b This aftermarket fuel pressure testing kit contains all the necessary fittings and adapters, along with the fuel pressure gauge, to test most automotive fuel systems

3.6 Connect a hand-held vacuum pump to the fuel pressure regulator and read fuel pressure with vacuum applied - pressure should decrease as vacuum is increased

it stops. This should take only a few seconds. Crank the engine several more times to ensure the fuel system has been completely relieved. Disconnect the cable from the negative terminal of the battery before working on the fuel system.

3   The fuel system pressure is now relieved. When you're finished working on the fuel system, simply install the fuel pump relay back into the fuse/relay panel and connect the negative cable to the battery.

4   It is a good idea to cover any fuel line that will be disconnected using a shop rag to catch fuel that might spill out.

3   Fuel pump/fuel pressure - check

Warning: *Gasoline is extremely flammable, so take extra precautions when you work on any part of the fuel system. See the* **Warning** *in Section 2.*

Note: *In order to perform the fuel pressure test, you will need to obtain a fuel pressure gauge capable of measuring high fuel pressure and an adapter set for the fuel injection system being tested.*

General checks

1   Check that there is adequate fuel in the fuel tank.

2   Verify the fuel pump actually runs. Remove the fuel filler cap. Have an assistant turn the ignition key to the On position (engine not running) while you listen at the fuel filler opening. You should hear a whirring sound that lasts for approximately five seconds as the pump comes on and pressurizes the system. If there is no response from the fuel pump (makes no sound) proceed to Step 9 and check the fuel pump electrical circuit.

Fuel pump output and pressure check

Refer to illustrations 3.3a, 3.3b, 3.6 and 3.7

3   Relieve the fuel system pressure (see Section 2). Install a fuel pressure gauge and

adapter in-line between the fuel filter and the rear fuel rail **(see illustrations)**.

4   Turn the ignition switch On (engine not running) with the air conditioning Off. The fuel pump should run for about five seconds - pressure should register on the gauge and should hold steady.

5   Start the engine and let it idle at normal operating temperature. Compare the pressure reading with the value listed in this Chapter's Specifications. Then disconnect the vacuum hose from the fuel pressure regulator - the pressure should increase immediately to the value listed in this Chapter's Specifications. If the pressure readings are correct, the system is operating properly.

6   If the pressure did not drop by 3 to 10 psi after starting the engine, apply 12 to 14 inches of vacuum to the pressure regulator, using a hand-held vacuum pump **(see illustration)**. If the pressure drops, repair the vacuum source to the regulator. If the pressure does not drop, replace the regulator.

7   If the fuel pressure is not within specifications, check the following:

a)   *If the pressure is higher than specified, check for vacuum to the fuel pressure*

regulator **(see illustration)**. *Vacuum must fluctuate with the increase or decrease in the engine rpm. If vacuum is present, check for a pinched or clogged fuel return hose or pipe. If the return line is OK, replace the regulator.*

b)   *If the pressure is lower than specified, change the fuel filter to rule out the possibility of a clogged filter (see Chapter 1). If the pressure is still low, start the engine (if possible) and slowly pinch the return hose shut. If the pressure rises above 43 psi, replace the regulator (see Section 14).* **Warning:** *Don't allow the fuel pressure to exceed 60 psi.*

c)   *Turn the engine Off and place the ignition switch in the On (engine not running) position. Monitor the pressure on the gauge for three minutes - pressure should decrease 8 psi in three minutes. If pressure decreases more than 8 psi, an injector (or injectors) may be leaking (see Section 15). If pressure does not decrease 8 psi the in-tank fuel pump leakdown valve may be faulty.*

8   After the testing is done, relieve the fuel pressure (see Section 2) and remove the fuel pressure gauge.

4

3.7 Detach the vacuum line from the fuel pressure regulator and verify vacuum is present when the engine is running

3.9 Remove the fuel pump fuse from the engine compartment fuse box (1996 and later models) - make sure it is not blown

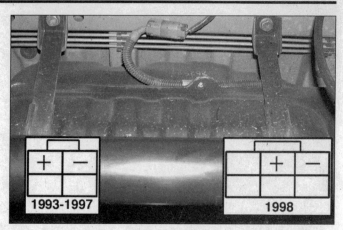

3.10a With the ignition key On (engine not running), check for battery voltage at the positive terminal and ground at the negative terminal on the harness side of the fuel pump connector – the harness connector is located under the vehicle at the rear of the fuel tank

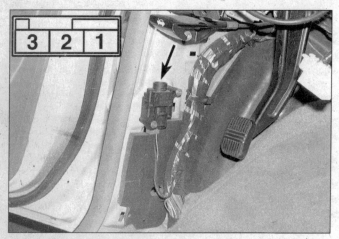

3.10b The inertia switch is located behind the driver's side kick panel – press the reset button (arrow) and check for continuity between terminals 2 and 3

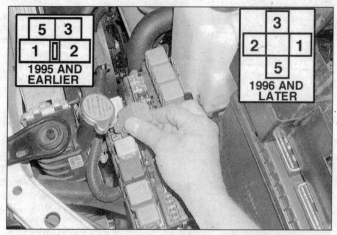

3.12 Remove the fuel pump relay from the engine compartment fuse/relay box - On 1995 and earlier models, check for battery voltage at terminals 1 and 3. On 1996 and later models, check for battery voltage at terminals 2 and 3

Fuel pump electrical circuit check

Refer to illustrations 3.9, 3.10a, 3.10b and 3.12

Note: *Refer to Chapter 12 for additional wiring schematics of the fuel pump circuit.*

9   If the pump does not turn on (makes no sound) with the ignition switch in the On position, check the fuel pump fuse **(see illustration)**. **Note:** *1995 and earlier models use a single fuse (labeled* FUEL) *located in the passenger compartment fuse panel to protect the power and control circuits of the fuel pump relay. 1996 and later models use a 10 amp fuse (labeled* RELAY) *in the passenger compartment fuse panel to protect the relay control circuit and a second 15 amp fuse (labeled* FUEL) *in the left-hand engine compartment fuse/relay panel to protect the power circuit of the fuel pump relay. Be sure to check both fuses on the 1996 and later models.* If the fuse(s) are blown, replace the fuse and see if the pump works. If the pump

now works, trace the fuel pump circuit for a short.

10   If the fuses are OK, check for battery voltage at the positive terminal of the fuel pump harness connector (located near the fuel tank) with the ignition key On engine not running **(see illustration)**. There should be battery voltage available. Next, check for continuity to ground at the ground terminal of the fuel pump harness connector. If a ground signal is present, replace the fuel pump. If a ground signal does not exist at the connector, check the inertia shut off switch **(see illustration)**. If the inertia switch is OK, check the wires from the switch to the fuel pump harness connector and the ground wire leading to the inertia switch for an open circuit.

11   If there is no voltage reaching the fuel pump connector check the fuel pump relay (see Chapter 12).

12   If the relay is OK, check the fuel pump relay circuit. With the help of an assistant turn the ignition key On (engine not running) and check for battery voltage at the relay connec-

tor **(see illustration)**. If battery voltage does not exist, check the wiring from the fuse panel to the relay connector for an open circuit.

13   If battery voltage exists at the relay connector, use a test light to probe terminals 2 and 3 on 1995 and earlier vehicles or terminals 1 and 2 on 1996 and later vehicles **(see illustration 3.12)**. The test light should light for approximately five seconds after the ignition key is turned On (engine not running). This will test if the ground circuit from the PCM is functioning correctly. **Note:** *The fuel pump relay is equipped with a primary and secondary circuit. The primary circuit is controlled by the PCM and the secondary circuit provides battery voltage to the fuel pump as the relay is energized. With the ignition switch ON (engine not running), the PCM will ground the relay for five seconds. During cranking, the PCM grounds the fuel pump relay as long as the camshaft position sensor (CMP) sends its position signal (see Chapter 6). If there are no reference pulses, the fuel pump will shut off after five seconds.*

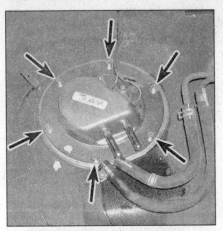

5.2 Disconnect the fuel feed and return lines, then remove the mounting bolts (arrows)

14 If the relay connector has battery voltage and a ground signal from the PCM as described above, check the circuit from the relay to the fuel pump harness connector for and open circuit.

---

4 Fuel lines and fittings - repair and replacement

Warning: *Gasoline is extremely flammable, so take extra precautions when you work on any part of the fuel system. See the* **Warning** *in Section 2.*

1 Always relieve the fuel pressure before servicing fuel lines or fittings (see Section 2).

2 The fuel feed, return and vapor lines extend from the fuel tank to the engine compartment. The lines are secured to the underbody with clip and screw assemblies. These lines must be occasionally inspected for leaks, kinks and dents.

3 If evidence of dirt is found in the system or fuel filter during disassembly, the line should be disconnected and blown out. Check the fuel strainer on the fuel pump pick-up unit (see Section 5) for damage and deterioration.

4 On later models, quick-disconnect fittings are used on the fuel pump and fuel tank lines. These fittings require a special tool to disconnect. The tool is available from auto parts stores and dealer service departments.

5.3 Carefully angle the fuel pump module out of the fuel tank without damaging the fuel level sending arm and float

Steel tubing

5 If replacement of a fuel line or emission line is called for, use welded steel tubing meeting the manufacturer's specifications.

6 Don't use copper or aluminum tubing to replace steel tubing. These materials cannot withstand normal vehicle vibration.

7 Because fuel lines used on fuel-injected vehicles are under high pressure, they require special consideration.

8 If the lines are replaced, always use original equipment parts, or parts that meet original equipment standards.

Flexible hose

Warning: *Use only original equipment replacement hoses or their equivalent. Others may fail from the high pressures generated by this system.*

9 Don't route fuel hose within four inches of any part of the exhaust system or within ten inches of the catalytic converter. Metal lines and rubber hoses must never be allowed to chafe against the frame. A minimum of 1/4-inch clearance must be maintained around a line or hose to prevent contact with the frame.

Removal and installation

10 Relieve the fuel pressure (see Section 2).

11 Remove all fasteners attaching the lines

to the vehicle body.

12 Loosen the hose clamp(s), slide the clamp down the hose away from the metal line and pull the hoses off the fitting.

13 Installation is the reverse of removal.

Repair

14 In the event of any fuel line damage (metal or flexible lines) it is necessary to replace the damaged lines with factory replacement parts. Others may fail from the high pressures of this system.

---

5 Fuel pump - removal and installation

Refer to illustrations 5.2, 5.3, 5.5, 5.6 and 5.7
Warning: *Gasoline is extremely flammable, so take extra precautions when you work on any part of the fuel system. See the* **Warning** *in Section 2.*

1 Relieve the fuel pressure (see Section 2) and remove the fuel tank from the vehicle (see Section 7).

2 Detach the fuel feed line and return lines and the mounting bolts from the fuel pump module **(see illustration)**. On later models, quick-disconnect fittings are used on the fuel pump and fuel tank lines. These fittings require a special tool to disconnect. The tool is available from auto parts stores and dealer service departments. Follow the instructions included with the tool.

3 Lift the fuel pump/sending unit assembly out of the tank **(see illustration)**. **Caution:** *The fuel level float and sending unit are delicate. Don't bump or bend them during removal or the accuracy of the sending unit may be affected.*

4 Inspect the condition of the O-ring around the opening of the tank. If it is dried, cracked or deteriorated, replace it.

5 Remove the strainer from the lower end of the fuel pump **(see illustration)**. If it's dirty, remove it and clean it with carburetor cleaner spray. If it's too dirty to be cleaned, replace it. **Note:** *Most new fuel pump assemblies come equipped with a new strainer.*

6 Loosen the fuel pump mounting clamp bolt **(see illustration)**.

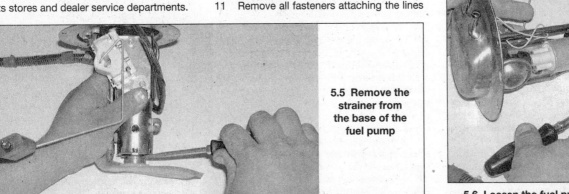

5.5 Remove the strainer from the base of the fuel pump

5.6 Loosen the fuel pump mounting clamp, then slide it down past the end of the mounting bracket

4

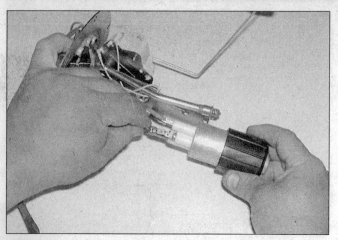

5.7 Disconnect the fuel pump electrical connector and the fuel line hose from the fuel pump

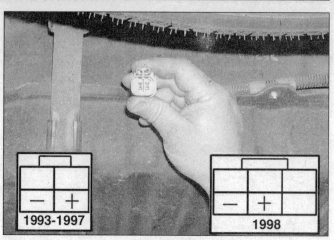

1993-1997   1998

6.3 Using an ohmmeter, probe the indicated terminals of the fuel level sending unit connector to check the resistance

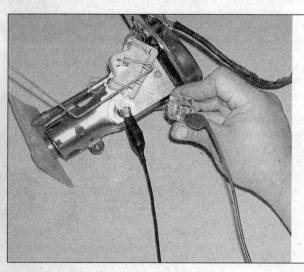

6.5 A more accurate check of the fuel level sending unit can be performed with the assembly on the bench. Connect the ohmmeter probes to the connector and check the resistance of the sending unit with the float positioned on "empty" and "full". Check for a smooth change in resistance as the float is moved

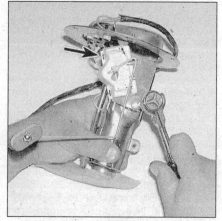

6.8 Detach the harness connectors (arrow), then remove the fuel level sending unit bolts from the fuel pump module

7   To separate the fuel pump from the assembly, remove the fuel hose lower clamp and disconnect the electrical connector from the fuel pump **(see illustration)**.

8   Installation of the fuel pump to the sending unit is the reverse of removal.

9   Clean the fuel pump mounting flange and the tank mounting surface and seal ring groove. Apply a thin coat of heavy grease to the new seal ring to hold it in place during assembly.

10   Position the O-ring around the opening in the fuel tank and guide the fuel pump/sending unit assembly into the tank.

11   Make sure the fuel lines are facing in there original position, then tighten the fuel pump module bolts securely.

12   Install the fuel tank (see Section 7).

6   Fuel level sending unit - check and replacement

Check

Refer to illustrations 6.3 and 6.5

1   Raise the vehicle and support it securely on jackstands.

2   Disconnect the electrical connector at the rear of the fuel tank for the fuel pump/fuel level sending unit.

3   Position the ohmmeter probes into the fuel pump/fuel level sending unit electrical connector and check the resistance **(see illustration)**. Use the 200-ohm scale on the ohmmeter.

4   With the fuel tank completely full, the resistance should be about 160.0 ohms. With the fuel tank nearly empty, the resistance of the sending unit should be about 15.0 ohms.

5   If the readings are incorrect, replace the sending unit. **Note:** *A more accurate check of the sending unit can be made by removing it from the fuel tank and checking its resistance while manually operating the float arm* **(see illustration)**.

Replacement

Refer to illustration 6.8

6   Remove the fuel tank (see Section 7).

7   Remove the fuel pump module from the fuel tank (see Section 5).

8   Remove the sending unit mounting bolt(s) **(see illustration)** and harness connectors from the fuel pump module.

9   Installation is the reverse of removal.

7   Fuel tank - removal and installation

Refer to illustrations 7.5, 7.6, 7.8, 7.9 and 7.11

Warning: *Gasoline is extremely flammable, so take extra precautions when you work on any part of the fuel system. See the* **Warning** *in Section 2.*

Note: *Don't begin this procedure until the gauge indicates that the tank is empty or nearly empty. If the tank must be removed when it's full (for example, if the fuel pump malfunctions), siphon any remaining fuel from the tank prior to removal.*

1   Unless the vehicle has been driven far enough to completely empty the tank, it's a good idea to siphon the residual fuel out before removing the tank from the vehicle. **Warning:** *DO NOT start the siphoning action by mouth! Use a siphoning kit (available at most auto parts stores).*

2   Relieve the fuel pressure (see Section 2).

3   Disconnect the cable from the negative terminal of the battery.

4   Raise the vehicle and support it securely

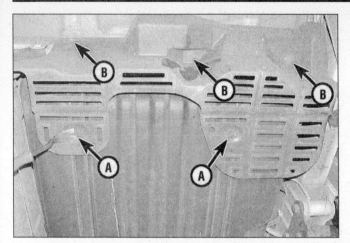

7.5 Pry out the plastic clips (A), detach the mounting bolts (B) and remove the splash shield from the front of the fuel tank

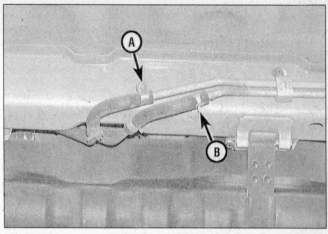

7.6 Disconnect the fuel feed line (A) and the fuel return line (B)

on jackstands.

5   Remove the splash shield from the front of the fuel tank **(see illustration)**.

6   Disconnect the fuel feed and return lines **(see illustration)**.

7   Disconnect the electrical connector attached at the rear of the fuel tank **(see illustration 7.11)**.

8   Loosen the hose clamps and detach the fuel tank filler hose and vapor hose from the fuel filler neck and the fuel tank **(see illustration)**. Remove the fuel tank skid plate (if equipped).

9   On 1998 and later California models remove the evaporative emissions canister splash shield. On all models disconnect the hose from the EVAP valve **(see illustration)**.

10   Place a floor jack under the tank and position a wood plank between the jack pad and the tank. Raise the jack until it's supporting the tank.

11   Remove the bolts that retain the fuel tank mounting straps **(see illustration)**. The straps are hinged at the other end so you can swing them out of the way.

12   Slowly lower the jack while guiding the

fuel tank past the muffler and tail pipe assembly. Remove the tank from the vehicle.

13   If you're replacing the tank, or having it cleaned or repaired, refer to Section 8.

14   Refer to Section 5 to remove and install the fuel pump or sending unit, if necessary.

15   Installation is the reverse of removal. Clean engine oil can be used as an assembly aid when pushing the fuel filler hose back onto the fuel tank. **Warning:** *All fuel tank protection shields must be reinstalled in their original positions to prevent damage to the fuel tank.*

8   Fuel tank - cleaning and repair

1   The fuel tank installed in the vehicles covered by this manual is not repairable.

2   If the fuel tank is removed from the vehicle, it should not be placed in an area where sparks or open flames could ignite the fumes coming out of the tank. Be especially careful inside a garage where a natural gas-type appliance is located, because the pilot light could cause an explosion.

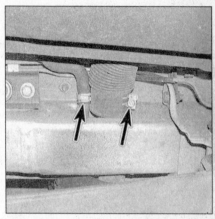

7.8 Disconnect the fuel filler hose and vent hose (arrows) from the fuel tank

4

9   Air cleaner housing - removal and installation

Refer to illustrations 9.2 and 9.5

1   Disconnect the cable from the negative terminal of the battery.

7.9 Disconnect the hose (arrow) from the EVAP valve

7.11 Remove the fuel tank strap bolts (arrows) and swing the straps out of the way

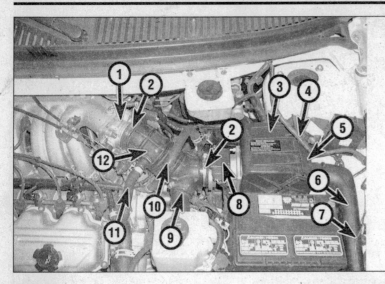

9.2 Air cleaner housing mounting details

1   Throttle body
2   Retaining clamp
3   Air cleaner housing (upper)
4   Spring clip
5   Air cleaner housing (lower)
6   Intake air resonator No.1
7   Intake Air Temperature (IAT) sensor
8   Mass airflow (MAF) sensor
9   Intake air resonator No.2
10   Bypass air inlet hose
11   Crankcase ventilation tube
12   Air cleaner outlet tube

9.5 The lower housing can be removed by detaching the bolts (arrow) and separating it from the No. 1 resonator tube (upper bolt shown, two lower bolts not visible)

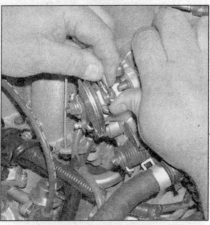

10.1 Rotate the throttle lever until the slot in the throttle lever aligns with the cable, then pass the cable through the slot

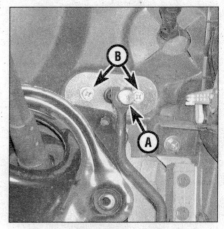

10.3 Working under the dash, pull the cable end (A) from the accelerator pedal recess and lift it through the slot, then remove the cable mounting bracket bolts (B)

2   Disconnect the MAF sensor wiring **(see illustration)**.
3   Disconnect the bypass air inlet hose, the crankcase ventilation tube and the No.2 intake air resonator from the air cleaner outlet tube.
4   Loosen the retaining clamp securing the air cleaner outlet tube to the throttle body. Detach the spring clip from the air cleaner upper housing. Separate the air cleaner outlet tube from the throttle body, disconnect the EGR regulator solenoid vacuum hose, then lift the upper air cleaner housing, MAF sensor and air cleaner outlet tube from the engine compartment as an assembly.
5   To remove the lower air cleaner housing simply detach the mounting bolts and separate it from the No.1
intake air resonator **(see illustration)**.
6   Installation Is the reverse of removal.

10   Accelerator cable - removal, installation and adjustment

Note: The adjustment procedure for the accelerator cable and the cruise control cable is similar except where noted below.

Removal

Refer to illustrations 10.1 and 10.3
1   Detach the accelerator cable and the cruise control cable (if equipped) from the throttle lever **(see illustration)**.
2   Loosen the cable locknut and adjusting nut, then separate the accelerator cable from the cable bracket.
3   Pull the cable end out from the accelerator pedal arm, then pass the cable through the slot in the arm. Remove the bolts securing the accelerator cable to the firewall **(see illustration)**.
4   Disconnect any remaining cable clips.
5   Remove the cable through the firewall from the engine compartment side.

Installation

6   Installation is the reverse of removal. Be sure the cable is routed correctly and to fasten all the cable retaining clips.
7   If necessary, at the engine compartment side of the firewall, apply sealant to the accel-
erator cable bracket where it mates to the firewall to prevent water from entering the passenger compartment.

Adjustment

Refer to illustration 10.8
8   To adjust the accelerator cable:
a)   Lift up on the cable to remove any slack.
b)   Turn the adjusting nut until the throttle lever just starts to move **(see illustration)**.
c)   Back off the adjusting nut two to three turns.
d)   Tighten the locknut and check cable deflection at the throttle linkage. Deflection should be approximately 3/8 to 1/2-inch.
e)   After you have adjusted the throttle cable, have an assistant help you verify that the throttle valve opens all the way when you depress the accelerator pedal to the floor and that it returns to the idle position when you release the accelerator. Verify the cable operates smoothly. It must not bind or stick.

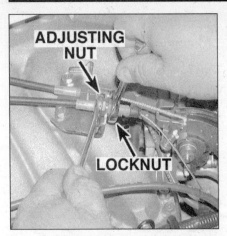

10.8 Accelerator cable and cruise control cable adjustment details

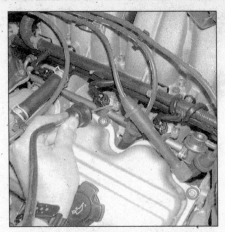

12.7 Use a stethoscope or screwdriver to determine if the injectors are working properly - they should make a steady clicking sound that rises and falls as engine speed changes

12.8 Install the fuel injector test light or "noid light" into the fuel injector electrical connector and confirm that it blinks when the engine is cranked or running

9   To adjust the cruise control cable:
 a) *Check the accelerator cable for proper adjustment.*
 b) *Turn the adjusting nut until the throttle lever starts to open.*
 c) *Back off the adjusting nut until the throttle lever just reaches the fully closed position.*
 d) *Back off the adjusting nut an additional one turn, tighten the locknut and check for proper operation of the cruise control system.*

11 Fuel injection system - general information

Sequential Electronic Fuel Injection (SEFI)

The Sequential Electronic Fuel Injection (SEFI) system is a multi-point fuel injection system. On the SEFI system, fuel is metered into each intake port in sequence with the engine firing order in accordance with engine demand through injectors (one per cylinder) mounted on an the intake manifold. The intake manifold incorporates an air intake plenum (upper manifold) to aid in air flow and distribution with a removable throttle body **(see illustration 1.1)**. The air intake plenum bolts to the lower intake manifold, which sits directly in the middle of the engine block.

The Sequential Electronic Fuel Injection system incorporates an on-board Electronic Engine Control (EEC) computer that accepts inputs from various engine sensors to compute the required fuel flow rate necessary to maintain a prescribed air/fuel ratio throughout the entire engine operational range. The computer then outputs a command to the fuel injectors to meter the approximate quantity of fuel. The system automatically senses and compensates for changes in altitude, load and speed. **Note:** *The computer terminology has changed from Electronic Control Module (ECM) to the Powertrain Control Module (PCM) due to standardization of the*

Self Diagnosis system within the automotive industry.

The fuel delivery systems include an electric in-tank fuel pump which forces pressurized fuel through a series of metal and rubber lines and an inline fuel filter to the fuel rail assembly. The SEFI system uses a single high-pressure pump mounted inside the tank.

The fuel rail assembly incorporates an electrically actuated fuel injector directly above each intake port. When energized, the injectors spray a metered quantity of fuel into the intake air stream.

A constant fuel pressure is supplied to the injectors by a pressure regulator. The regulator is positioned downstream from the fuel injectors. Excess fuel passes through the regulator and returns to the fuel tank through a fuel return line.

On the SEFI system, each injector is energized once every other crankshaft revolution in sequence with engine firing order. The period of time that the injectors are energized (known as "on time" or "pulse width") is controlled by the PCM. Air entering the engine is sensed by speed, pressure and temperature sensors. The outputs of these sensors are processed by the PCM. The computer determines the needed injector pulse width and outputs a command to the injector to meter the exact quantity of fuel.

12 Fuel injection system - check

Refer to illustrations 12.7, 12.8 and 12.9
Warning: *Gasoline is extremely flammable, so take extra precautions when you work on any part of the fuel system. See the* **Warning** *in Section 2.*
Note: *The following procedure is based on the assumption that the fuel pump is working and the fuel pressure is adequate (see Section 3).*

1   Check all electrical connectors that are related to the system. Loose electrical connectors and poor grounds can cause many problems that resemble more serious malfunctions.
2   Check to see that the battery is fully charged, as the control unit and sensors depend on an accurate supply voltage in order to properly meter the fuel.
3   Check the air filter element - a dirty or partially blocked filter will severely impede performance and economy (see Chapter 1).
4   Check the fuses. If a blown fuse is found, replace it and see if it blows again. If it does, search for a grounded wire in the harness to the fuel pump (see Chapter 12).
5   Check the condition of the vacuum hoses connected to the intake manifold.
6   Remove the air intake duct from the throttle body and check for dirt, carbon or other residue build-up in the throttle body, particularly around the throttle plate. **Caution:** *The throttle body on these models is coated with a sludge-resistant material designed to protect the bore and throttle plate. Do not attempt to clean the interior of the throttle body with carburetor or other spray cleaners. This throttle body is designed to resist sludge accumulation and cleaning may impair the performance of the engine.*
7   With the engine running, place an automotive stethoscope against each injector, one at a time, and listen for a clicking sound, indicating operation **(see illustration)**. If you don't have a stethoscope, you can place the tip of a long screwdriver against the injector and listen through the handle.
8   If an injector isn't functioning (not clicking), purchase a special injector test light (sometimes called a "noid" light) and install it into the injector electrical connector **(see illustration)**. Start the engine and check to see if the noid light flashes. If it does, the injector is receiving proper voltage. If it doesn't flash, further diagnosis should be performed by a dealer service department or other properly equipped repair facility.

4

12.9 Measure the resistance of each injector. It should be within Specifications

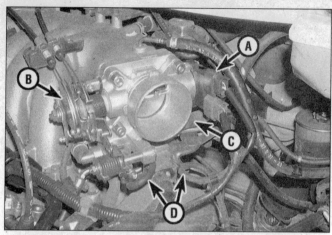

13.5 Disconnect the TPS connectors (A), the accelerator and cruise control cables (B), the coolant hoses (C) and the vacuum hoses (D)

13.6 Throttle body mounting fasteners (arrows) (upper intake manifold remove for clarity)

14.3 Disconnect the regulator vacuum hose (arrow), loosen the hose clamp and remove the fuel return line from the regulator

14.4 Remove the fuel pressure regulator bolts (arrows)(rear bolt not visible)

9   With the engine OFF and the fuel injector electrical connectors disconnected, measure the resistance of each injector **(see illustration)**. Check the Specifications listed in this Chapter for the correct injector resistance.

10   The remainder of the system checks can be found in Chapter 6.

13 Throttle body - removal and installation

Refer to illustrations 13.5 and 13.6

Warning: *Wait until the engine is completely cool before beginning this procedure.*

1   Disconnect the cable from the negative battery terminal.

2   Remove the air cleaner outlet tube from the throttle body (see Section 9).

3   Disconnect the Throttle Position Sensor (TPS) connectors from the throttle body (see Chapter 6). Also label and detach all vacuum hoses from the throttle body.

4   Detach the accelerator cable (see Section 10) and if equipped, the cruise control

cable.

5   Detach the coolant hoses from the throttle body **(see illustration)**. Plug the lines to prevent coolant loss.

6   Remove the four mounting bolts **(see illustration)** and remove the throttle body and gasket. Remove all traces of old gasket material from the throttle body and air intake plenum.

7   Installation is the reverse of removal. Be sure to use a new gasket. Adjust the accelerator cable and the cruise control actuator cable (see Section 10). Check the coolant level and add some, if necessary (see Chapter 1).

14 Fuel pressure regulator - removal and installation

Refer to illustrations 14.3 and 14.4

Warning: *Gasoline is extremely flammable, so take extra precautions when you work on any part of the fuel system. See the* **Warning** *in Section 2.*

1   Relieve the fuel pressure (see Section 2). Disconnect the cable from the negative terminal of the battery.

2   Clean any dirt from around the fuel pressure regulator.

3   Detach the vacuum hose and the fuel return hose from the fuel pressure regulator **(see illustration)**.

4   Remove the two bolts retaining the fuel pressure regulator **(see illustration)** and detach the regulator from the fuel rail.

5   Install new O-rings on the pressure regulator and lubricate them with a light coat of oil.

6   Installation is the reverse of removal. Tighten the pressure regulator mounting bolts securely.

15 Fuel rail and injectors - removal and installation

Refer to illustrations 15.4, 15.5a, 15.5b, 15.6 and 15.8

Warning: *Gasoline is extremely flammable, so take extra precautions when you work on*

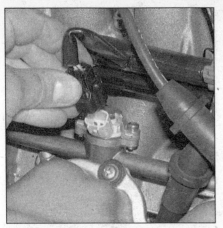

15.4 Detach the connectors from the fuel injectors

15.5a If fuel injector service is necessary, remove the cap screws (arrows) and pull the injector(s) from the fuel rail

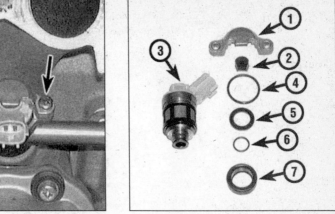

15.5b Fuel injector components

1 Cap	6 Bottom O-
2 Insulator	ring
3 Fuel injector	7 Fuel rail
4 Top O-ring	insulator
5 Center O-ring	

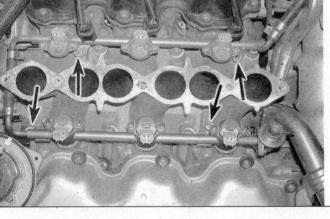

15.6 Fuel rail mounting bolt locations (arrows)

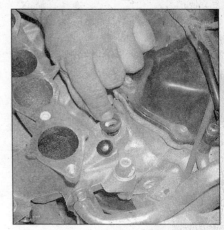

15.8 Install the fuel rail insulators into the lower intake manifold and lubricate them with a light coat of oil before installing the fuel rail assembly

any part of the fuel system. See the **Warning** in Section 2.

Note: *The fuel injectors on the front bank can be serviced without removing of the upper intake manifold. However servicing the fuel injectors on the rear bank requires removal of the upper intake manifold. It is not necessary to remove the fuel rail if you're only servicing a fuel injector. Fuel injectors can be removed without detaching the fuel rail.*

1   Relieve the fuel pressure (see Section 2).
2   Disconnect the cable from the negative terminal of the battery.
3   Remove the air intake plenum (upper intake manifold) from the lower intake manifold (see Chapter 2A).
4   Disconnect the fuel injector connectors **(see illustration)**.
5   If servicing of the fuel injector(s) is necessary, remove the injector cap screws and cap, then pull the injector(s) from the fuel rail cup **(see illustration)**. Inspect the injector O-rings (three per injector) for signs of deterioration **(see illustration)**. Replace as required. Lubricate the new O-rings with light grade oil. **Caution:** *Do not use silicone grease. It will clog the injectors.* Using a light twisting motion, install the injector(s) into the fuel rail cup. Ensure that the injector caps are clean and free of contamination and tighten the cap

screws to the torque listed in this Chapter's Specifications.
6   If removal of the fuel rail assembly is necessary, disconnect the fuel feed and return lines then remove the fuel rail retaining bolts (two on each side) **(see illustration)**.
7   Using a rocking, side to side motion, carefully lift the fuel rail and the fuel injectors as an assembly from the lower intake manifold.
8   Installation is the reverse of removal with the following exceptions: Inspect the fuel rail insulators (one per injector) for signs of deterioration and replace as required. Install the fuel rail insulators into the lower intake manifold and lubricate them with a light coat of oil before installing the fuel rail assembly onto the lower intake manifold **(see illustration)**.

16 Exhaust system servicing - general information

Refer to illustrations 16.4a, 16.4b, 16.4c and 16.4d
Warning 1: *Inspection and repair of exhaust system components should be done only after enough time has elapsed after driving the vehicle to allow the system components*

to cool completely. Also, when working under the vehicle, make sure it is securely supported on jackstands.
Warning 2: *All models covered by this manual are equipped with an exhaust system flex tube which is extremely sensitive to sharp bends. Do not allow the flex tube to hang downward during servicing or damage will occur.*

1   The exhaust system consists of the exhaust manifold(s), the catalytic converter(s), the muffler, the tailpipe and all connecting pipes, brackets, hangers and clamps. The exhaust system is attached to the body with mounting brackets and rubber hangers. If any of the parts are improperly installed, excessive noise and vibration will be transmitted to the body.
2   Conduct regular inspections of the exhaust system to keep it safe and quiet. Look for any damaged or bent parts, open seams, holes, loose connections, excessive

4

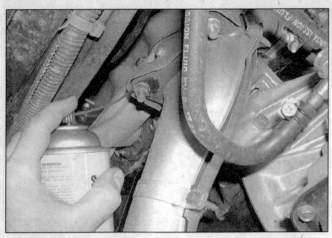

16.4a Be sure to apply penetrating lubricant to the exhaust system fasteners before attempting to remove them

16.4b Do not allow the flex tube (arrow) to bend during servicing or damage will occur

16.4c Remove the center support bracket bolts (arrows)

16.4d Check the condition of the rubber hangers (arrows) that support the exhaust system

corrosion or other defects which could allow exhaust fumes to enter the vehicle. Deteriorated exhaust system components should not be repaired; they should be replaced with new parts.

3   If the exhaust system components are extremely corroded or rusted together, welding equipment will probably be required to remove them. The convenient way to accomplish this is to have a muffler repair shop remove the corroded sections with a cutting torch. If, however, you want to save money by doing it yourself (and you don't have a welding outfit with a cutting torch), simply cut off the old components with a hacksaw. If

you have compressed air, special pneumatic cutting chisels can also be used. If you do decide to tackle the job at home, be sure to wear safety goggles to protect your eyes from metal chips and work gloves to protect your hands.

4   Here are some simple guidelines to follow when repairing the exhaust system **(see illustrations)**:

a) *Work from the back to the front when removing exhaust system components.*
b) *Apply penetrating oil to the exhaust system component fasteners to make them easier to remove.*
c) *Use new gaskets, hangers and clamps*

when installing exhaust systems components.
d) *Apply anti-seize compound to the threads of all exhaust system fasteners during reassembly.*
e) *Be sure to allow sufficient clearance between newly installed parts and all points on the underbody to avoid overheating the floor pan and possibly damaging the interior carpet and insulation. Pay particularly close attention to the catalytic converter and heat shield.*
f) *Always remove oxygen sensors and connectors before servicing exhaust system components (see Chapter 6).*

Chapter 5
Engine electrical systems

Contents

5

Specifications

Battery voltage
Engine off .... 12 volts
Engine running .... 14-to-15 volts

Firing order (all models) 1-2-3-4-5-6

Spark plug wire resistance (approximate) .... 5,000 to 9,000 ohms per foot

Ignition coil resistance
Primary resistance .... 1.0 ohm
Secondary resistance .... 10 k-ohms

Ignition timing (base setting)
All models .... See Chapter 1

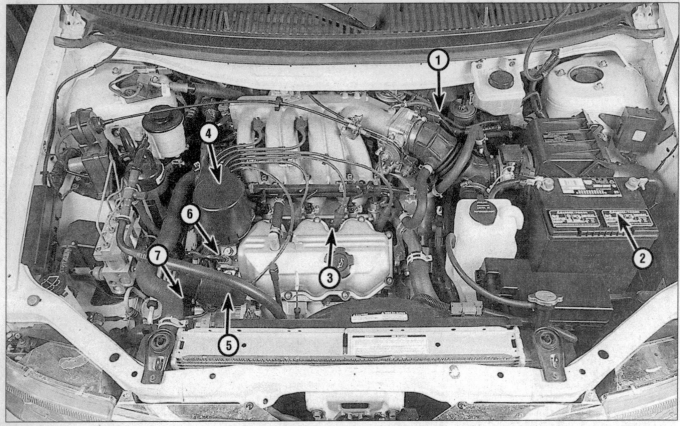

1.1 Starting, charging and ignition system components

1	Starter motor (not visible)	4	Distributor	6	Power transistor
2	Battery	5	Ignition coil	7	Alternator (not visible)
3	Spark plugs and wires (front bank)				

1   General information

Refer to illustration 1.1

The engine electrical systems include all ignition, charging and starting components **(see illustration)**. Because of their engine-related functions, these components are considered separately from chassis electrical devices like the lights, instruments, etc.

Be very careful when working on the engine electrical components. They are easily damaged if checked, connected or handled improperly. The alternator is driven by an engine drivebelt which could cause serious injury if your hands, hair or clothes become entangled in it with the engine running. Both the starter and alternator are connected directly to the battery and could arc or even cause a fire if mishandled, overloaded or shorted out.

Never leave the ignition switch on for long periods of time with the engine off. Don't disconnect the battery cables while the engine is running. Correct polarity must be maintained when connecting battery cables from another source, such as another vehicle, during jump starting. Always disconnect the negative cable first and hook it up last or the battery may be shorted by the tool being

used to loosen the cable clamps.

Additional safety related information on the engine electrical systems can be found in *Safety first* near the front of this manual. It should be referred to before beginning any operation included in this Chapter.

2   Battery - emergency jump starting

Refer to the *Booster battery (jump) start-ing* procedure at the front of this manual.

3   Battery - check and replacement

Caution : *Always disconnect the negative cable first and hook it up last or the battery may be shorted by the tool being used to loosen the cable clamps.*

Check

Refer to illustrations 3.1a, 3.1b, 3.1c and 3.1d

1   A battery cannot be accurately tested until it is at or near a fully charged state. Disconnect the negative battery cable, then the positive cable from the battery and perform the following tests:

a) ***Battery state of charge test*** - *Visually inspect the indicator eye (if equipped) on the top of the battery, if the indicator eye is black in color, charge the battery as described in Chapter 1. On batteries with removable caps (Nissan models)*

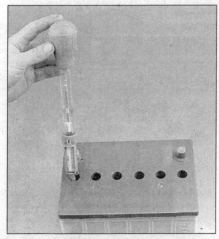

3.1a On Nissan models, use a battery hydrometer to draw electrolyte from the battery cell – this hydrometer is equipped with a thermometer to make temperature corrections

3.1b To test the open circuit voltage of the battery, simply touch the black probe of the voltmeter to the negative terminal and the red probe to the positive terminal of the battery – a fully charged battery should read between 11.5 to 12.5 volts depending on the outside air temperature

3.1c Some battery load testers are equipped with an ammeter which enables the battery load to be precisely dialed in, as shown – less expensive testers have a load switch and a voltmeter only

check the battery electrolyte. The electrolyte level should be above the upper edge of the plates. If the level is low, add distilled water. DO NOT OVERFILL. The excess electrolyte may spill over during periods of heavy charging. Test the specific gravity of the electrolyte using a hydrometer **(see illustration)**. *Remove the caps and extract a sample of the electrolyte and observe the float inside the barrel of the hydrometer. Follow the instructions from the tool manufacturer and determine the exact condition of the solution for each cell. A normal battery will indicate approximately 1.270 (green zone). If the electrolyte content is too low (red zone), charge the battery as described in Chapter 1.*

b) **Open voltage circuit test** - *Using a digital voltmeter, perform an open voltage circuit test* **(see illustration)**. **Note:** *The battery's surface charge must be removed before accurate voltage measurements can be made. Turn On the high beams for ten seconds, then turn them Off, let the vehicle stand for two minutes. With the engine and all accessories Off, touch the negative probe of the voltmeter to the negative terminal of the battery and the positive probe to the positive terminal of the battery. The battery voltage should be 11.5 to 12.5 volts or slightly above. If the battery is less than the specified voltage, charge the battery before proceeding to the next test. Do not proceed with the battery load test unless the battery charge is correct.*

c) **Battery load test** - *An accurate check of the battery condition can only be performed with a load tester (available at most auto parts stores). This test evaluates the ability of the battery to operate the starter and other accessories during periods of heavy amperage draw (load). Install a special battery load testing tool onto the terminals* **(see illustration)**.

3.1d To find out whether there's a drain on the battery, simply detach the negative cable and hook up a test light between the battery post and the cable clamp

Load test the battery according to the manufacturer's instructions for the particular tool. This tool utilizes a carbon pile to increase the load demand (amperage draw) on the battery. Maintain the load on the battery for 15 seconds or less and observe that the battery voltage does not drop below 9.6 volts. If the battery condition is weak or defective, the tool will indicate this condition immediately. **Note:** *Cold temperatures will cause the minimum voltage requirements to drop slightly. Follow the chart given in the manufacturer's instructions to compensate for cold climates. Minimum load voltage for freezing temperatures (32 degrees F) should be approximately 9.1 volts.*

d) **Battery drain test** – *This test will indicate whether there's a constant drain on the vehicle's electrical system that can cause the battery to discharge. Make sure all accessories are turned Off. If the vehicle has an underhood light, verify it's working properly, then disconnect it.*

3.3a Remove the nuts (arrows) from the battery hold-down clamp (1995 and earlier)

Disconnect the cable from the negative terminal of the battery and attach one lead of a test light to the negative battery cable and the other end to the negative battery terminal **(see illustration)**. *The test light should not glow. If the test light glows, it indicates a constant drain on the battery which could cause the battery to discharge.* **Note:** *On vehicles equipped with On-Board computers, digital clocks, digital radios, power seats with memory and/or other components which normally cause a key-Off battery drain, it's normal for the test light to glow dimly. If you suspect the drain is excessive, hook up an ammeter in place of the test light. The reading should not exceed 0.05 amps (50 milliamps).*

Replacement

Refer to illustrations 3.3a, 3.3b and 3.6

2   Disconnect the negative battery cable, then the positive cable from the battery.

3   Remove the battery hold-down clamp **(see illustrations)**. Remove the battery cover (if equipped).

5

**3.3b Battery hold down clamp bolt (arrow)
(1996 and later)**

**3.6 Battery tray mounting bolts
(1996 and later)**

Terminal end corrosion or damage.

Insulation cracks.

Chafed insulation
or exposed wires.

Burned or melted insulation.

4.2 Typical battery cable problems

4   Lift out the battery. Be careful - it's heavy. **Note:** *Battery straps and handlers are available at most auto parts stores for a reasonable price. They make it easier to remove and carry the battery.*

5   While the battery is out, inspect the battery tray for corrosion.

6   If corrosion exists on the battery tray, detach the bolts and remove the tray from the engine compartment **(see illustration)**. Clean the deposits from the metal underneath the tray to prevent further corrosion. **Note:** *On 1995 and earlier models it will be necessary to loosen and set aside the LH fuse panel, the center fuse panel and the coolant reservoir tank to allow access to the battery tray.*

7   If you are replacing the battery, make sure you get one that's identical, with the same dimensions, amperage rating, cold cranking rating, etc.

8   Installation is the reverse of removal.

4   Battery cables - check and replacement

Refer to illustrations 4.2, 4.4a, 4.4b, 4.4c and 4.4d

1   Periodically inspect the entire length of each battery cable for damage, cracked or burned insulation and corrosion. Poor battery cable connections can cause starting problems and decreased engine performance.

2   Check the cable-to-terminal connections at the ends of the cables for cracks, loose wire strands and corrosion **(see illustration)**. The presence of white, fluffy deposits under the insulation at the cable terminal connection is a sign that the cable is corroded and should be replaced. Check the terminals for distortion, missing mounting bolts and corrosion.

3   When replacing the cables, always disconnect the negative cable first and hook it up last or the battery may be shorted by the tool used to loosen the cable clamps. Even if only the positive cable is being replaced, be sure to disconnect the negative cable from the battery first.

4   Disconnect and remove the cable **(see illustrations)**. Make sure the replacement cable is the same length and diameter.

5   Clean the threads of the relay or ground connection with a wire brush to remove rust and corrosion. Apply a light coat of petroleum jelly to the threads to prevent future corrosion.

6   Attach the cable to the relay or ground connection and tighten the mounting nut/bolt securely.

7   Before connecting the new cable to the battery, make sure that it reaches the battery post without having to be stretched. Clean the battery posts thoroughly and apply a light coat of petroleum jelly to prevent corrosion (see Chapter 1).

**4.4a Detach any battery cable ties (arrow)
or retaining clips**

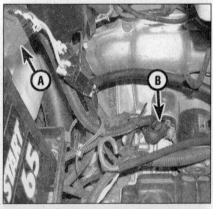

**4.4b The positive cable is fastened at the
battery to a fusible link connector (A) and
at the starter solenoid (B)**

**4.4c The negative cable is fastened to the
frame (arrow) . . .**

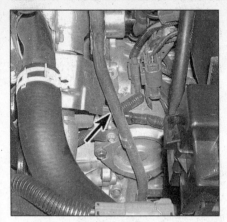

4.4d . . . and to the transaxle housing (arrow)

6.2 To use a calibrated ignition tester, simply disconnect a spark plug wire, clip the tester to a convenient ground (like a valve cover bolt) and operate the starter - if there is enough power to fire the plug, sparks will be visible between the electrode tip and the tester body

8   Connect the positive cable first, followed by the negative cable.

5   Ignition system - general information

Warning: *Because of the high voltage generated by the ignition system, extreme care should be taken whenever an operation is performed involving ignition components. This not only includes the power transistor, coil, distributor and spark plug wires, but related components such as plug connectors, tachometer and other test equipment.*

1   The ignition system is designed to ignite the fuel/air charge entering each cylinder at just the right moment. It does this by producing a high voltage spark between the electrodes of each spark plug.

2   The vehicles covered by this manual are equipped with an electronic ignition system which consists of the distributor, camshaft position sensor (located in the distributor), the power transistor, the ignition coil, an ignition circuit resistor/condenser and the primary and secondary wiring.

3   The camshaft position sensor is the basis of this computer controlled ignition system. It monitors engine speed and piston position and relays this data to the PCM which in turn controls the fuel injection duration (fuel injector on/off time) and ignition timing. The camshaft position sensor consists of a rotor plate, Light Emitting Diodes (LED) and photo diodes, which produce a wave forming circuit (see Chapter 6 for more information). This signal is then sent to the PCM, which produces an ignition signal. The power transistor amplifies the ignition signal from the PCM and intermittently grounds the primary circuit to the ignition coil which generates high voltage in the secondary circuit, thus sending spark from the ignition coil to the distributor, through the spark plug wires and to the spark plugs.

4   The Powertrain Control Module (PCM) receives input signals from various sensors

and switches and controls all spark timing advance and retard functions through the power transistor and ignition coil.

5   The Electronic Ignition system is also integrated with the Knock Sensor (KS) system which uses a knock sensor in connection with the Powertrain Control Module (PCM) to retard spark timing. The KS system allows the engine to have maximum spark advance without spark knock which also improves driveability and fuel economy.

Secondary (spark plug) wiring

6   The secondary (spark plug) wires are a carbon-impregnated cord conductor encased in a rubber jacket with an outer silicone jacket. This type of wire will withstand very high temperatures and provides an excellent insulator for the high secondary ignition voltage. Silicone spark plug boots form a tight seal on the plug. The boot should be twisted 1/2-turn before removing (for more information on spark plug wiring refer to Chapter 1).

6   Ignition system - check

Refer to illustrations 6.2, 6.7 and 6.9
Warning: *Because of the high voltage generated by the ignition system, extreme care should be taken whenever an operation is performed involving ignition components. This not only includes the power transistor, coil, distributor and spark plug wires, but related components such as plug connectors, tachometer and other test equipment.*

1   If a malfunction occurs and the vehicle won't start, do not immediately assume that the ignition system is causing the problem. First, check the following items:

a) *Make sure the battery cable clamps, where they connect to the battery, are clean and tight.*
b) *Test the condition of the battery (see Section 3). If it does not pass all the tests, replace it with a new battery.*

c) *Check the external distributor and ignition coil wiring and connections.*
d) *Check the fusible links (if equipped) inside the engine compartment fuse box (see Chapter 12). If they're burned, determine the cause and repair the circuit*

2   Check the ignition spark at the plug. If the engine turns over but won't start, disconnect the spark plug wire from any spark plug and attach it to a calibrated tester (available at most auto parts stores) **(see illustration)**. Connect the clip on the tester to a bolt or metal bracket on the engine. Crank the engine and watch the end of the tester or spark plug wire to see if bright blue, well-defined sparks occur.

3   If sparks occur, sufficient voltage is reaching the plug to fire it (repeat the check at the remaining plug wires to verify that the distributor cap and rotor are OK). However, the plugs themselves may be fouled, so remove and check them as described in Chapter 1.

4   If no sparks or intermittent sparks occur, check the cap, rotor and spark plug wires for damage and corrosion as described in Chapter 1. If moisture is present, dry out the cap and rotor, then reinstall the cap and repeat the spark test.

5   If there's still no spark, detach the coil secondary wire from the distributor cap and hook it up to the tester (reattach the plug wire to the spark plug), then repeat the spark check.

6   If sparks now occur, the distributor cap, rotor or plug wire(s) may be defective.

7   If no sparks occur, check for battery voltage to the ignition coil from the ignition switch with the ignition key On (engine not running). Attach a 12 volt test light to the battery negative (-) terminal or other good ground. Disconnect the coil electrical connector and check for power at the one of the terminals **(see illustration)**. Battery voltage should be available. If there is no battery voltage, check the wiring and/or circuit between the coil and ignition switch (see Chapter 12

5

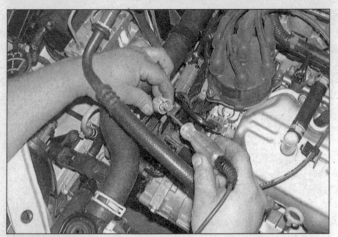

6.7 Disconnect the electrical connector from the ignition coil and check for battery voltage to the coil at one of the terminals with the ignition key On, then connect an LED test light to the positive battery terminal and the coil negative (-) terminal on the harness connector and watch for a blinking light when the engine is cranked

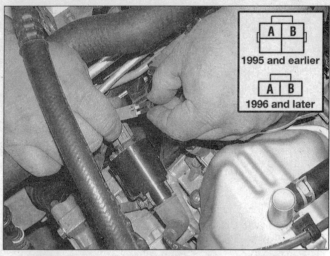

6.9 Remove the resistor from its square case and check the resistance between terminals A and B. There should be approximately 2.2 k-ohms

for additional information on the wiring schematics).

8   If battery voltage is available to the ignition coil, attach an LED test light to the battery positive (+) terminal and to the negative (-) terminal of the coil harness connector (vehicle harness side) **(see illustration 6.7)**, then crank the engine. Confirm that the test light flashes. This test checks for the trigger signal (ground) from the computer and the power transistor. If a trigger signal is present at the coil, the computer, camshaft position sensor and or the power transistor are functioning properly. **Caution:** *Use only an LED test light to avoid damaging the PCM.*

9   If a trigger signal is not present at the ignition coil, check the ignition circuit resistor/condenser **(see illustration)** and the power transistor (see section 8). **Note:** *The*

resistor/condenser and connector is taped to the wiring harness just to the left of the distributor. If the power transistor and the resistor are OK, refer to Chapter 6 and check the camshaft position sensor.

10   If battery voltage and a trigger signal exist at the ignition coil and there still are no sparks, check the primary and secondary resistance of the ignition coil (see Section 7). If an open is found (verified by an infinite reading), replace the coil.

11   All additional checks on the ignition system should be performed by a dealer service department or other qualified repair shop.

7   Ignition coil - check and replacement

Check

Refer to illustrations 7.1 and 7.2

1   With the ignition off, disconnect the electrical connector(s) from the coil **(see illustration 1.1)**. Connect an ohmmeter across the coil positive (+) terminal and the

negative (-) terminal **(see illustration)**. The resistance should be as listed in this Chapter's Specifications. If not, replace the coil.

2   Connect an ohmmeter between the secondary terminal **(see illustration)** (the one that the spark plug wires connect to) and to the positive primary terminal. The resistance should be as listed in this Chapter's Specifications. If not, replace the coil.

Replacement

Refer to illustration 7.6

3   Disconnect the cable from the negative terminal of the battery.

4   Disconnect the ignition coil electrical connector.

5   Disconnect the secondary high tension (coil to cap) wire from the coil.

6   Remove the coil mounting bolts and detach it from the engine **(see illustration)**.

7   Installation is the reverse of the removal procedure with the following additions: Before installing the spark plug wire connector into the ignition coil, coat the entire interior of the rubber boot with silicone dielectric compound.

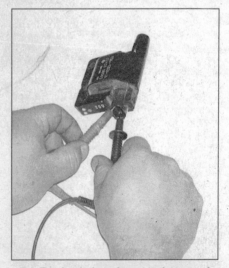

7.1 To check the primary resistance of the ignition coil, connect the probes on the meter to the positive (+) terminal and the negative (-) terminal of the coil

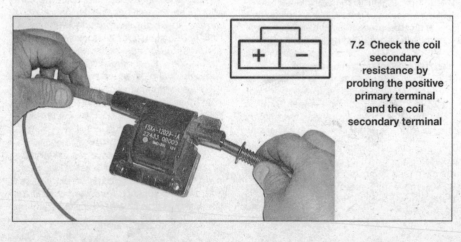

7.2 Check the coil secondary resistance by probing the positive primary terminal and the coil secondary terminal

7.6 Detach the electrical connector (A), the secondary high tension lead (B), the coil mounting bolts (C) and lift the ignition coil from the engine

8.3 Power transistor terminal guide

8 Power transistor - check and replacement

Caution: *The power transistor is a delicate and relatively expensive electrical component. Failure to follow the step-by-step procedures could result in damage to the module and/or other electronic devices, including the PCM. Additionally, all PCM controlled devices are protected by a Federally mandated emissions warranty. Check with the dealer concerning this warranty before attempting to diagnose and replace this unit yourself.*

Check

Refer to illustration 8.3

1   Disconnect the cable from the negative terminal of the battery.
2   Disconnect the electrical connector from the power transistor **(see illustration 1.1)**.
3   Using an ohmmeter, connect the positive probe of the ohmmeter to terminal A and the negative probe of the ohmmeter to terminal B **(see illustration)**. The meter should indicate continuity. Connect the negative probe of the ohmmeter to terminal A and the positive probe of the ohmmeter to terminal C. The meter should indicate NO continuity (infinity).
4   If the test results are incorrect, replace the power transistor with a new part.

Replacement

Refer to illustration 8.7

5   Disconnect the cable from the negative terminal of the battery.
6   Disconnect the electrical connector from the power transistor.
7   Remove the bolt that secures the power transistor and retaining bracket to the cylinder head **(see illustration)**.
8   Remove two retaining bracket bolts. Install a new power transistor onto the retaining bracket.

8.7 Remove the power transistor mounting bolt (arrow) and lift the unit from the cylinder head

9   The remainder of the installation is the reverse of removal.

9 Distributor - removal and installation

Removal

Refer to illustrations 9.5a and 9.5b

1   Disconnect the cable from the negative terminal of the battery.
2   Remove the distributor cap cover (if equipped) and note the position of the raised "1" on the distributor cap. This marks the location for the number one cylinder spark plug wire terminal. **Note:** *Some distributor caps may not be marked with the number 1 terminal position.*
3   Disconnect the main electrical connector and ground connector from the distributor. Follow the wires as they exit the distributor to find the connector if necessary.
4   Remove the distributor cap (see Chapter 1). Using a socket and breaker bar on the crankshaft pulley bolt, rotate the engine until the rotor is pointing toward the number one spark plug terminal (see the TDC locating

procedure in Chapter 2A).
5   Make a mark on the edge of the distributor base directly below the rotor tip and inline with it **(see illustration)**. Also, mark the distributor base and the engine block to ensure that the distributor can be reinstalled

9.5a Apply an alignment mark on the perimeter of the distributor body in line with the rotor tip (arrows)

5

9.5b Mark the base of the distributor body and the engine block to clearly define the position of the distributor

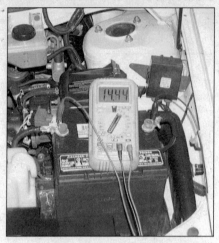

11.3 To measure charging voltage, attach the voltmeter leads to the battery terminals, start the engine and record the voltage reading

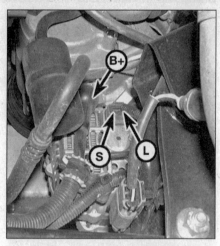

11.7 Alternator terminal identification

correctly **(see illustration)**.

6   Remove the distributor hold-down bolt, then pull the distributor straight out to remove it. **Caution:** *DO NOT turn the engine while the distributor is removed, or the alignment marks will be useless.*

Installation

7   Insert the distributor into the engine in exactly the same relationship to the block that it was in when removed.

8   To mesh the helical gears on the camshaft and the distributor, it may be necessary to turn the rotor slightly. Make sure the distributor is seated completely and the alignment marks made previously are aligned. If not, remove the distributor and reposition it. **Note:** *If the crankshaft has been moved while the distributor is out, locate Top Dead Center (TDC) for the number one piston (see Chapter 2A) and position the distributor and rotor accordingly.*

9   Loosely install the hold-down bolt.

10   Install the distributor cap and tighten the screws securely.

11   Plug in the electrical connectors.

12   Reattach the spark plug wires to the plugs (if removed).

13   Connect the cable to the negative terminal of the battery.

14   Check and, if necessary, adjust the ignition timing (see Chapter 1) and tighten the distributor hold-down bolt securely. Reinstall the distributor cap cover (if equipped).

10   Charging system - general information and precautions

The charging system includes the alternator, a voltage regulator (mounted on the backside of the alternator), a charge indicator or warning light, the battery, a large fusible link and the wiring between all the components. The charging system supplies electrical power for the ignition system, the lights,

the radio, etc. The alternator is driven by a drivebelt at the front of the engine.

The purpose of the voltage regulator is to limit the alternator's voltage to a preset value. This prevents power surges, circuit overloads, etc., during peak voltage output. All models are equipped with integral type voltage regulator, If a voltage regulator malfunctions, it will be necessary to replace the entire alternator.

The charging system is protected by a large fusible link which is located in the engine compartment fuse box. In the event of charging system problems, check the fusible link for damage or broken contacts.

The charging system doesn't ordinarily require periodic maintenance. However, the drivebelt, battery and wires and connections should be inspected at the intervals outlined in Chapter 1.

Be very careful when making electrical circuit connections to a vehicle equipped with an alternator and note the following:

a) *When reconnecting wires to the alternator from the battery, be sure to note the polarity.*

b) *Before using arc welding equipment to repair any part of the vehicle, disconnect the wires from the alternator and the battery terminals.*

c) *Never start the engine with a battery charger connected.*

d) *Always disconnect both battery cables before using a battery charger (always disconnect negative cable first, positive cable last).*

11   Charging system - check

Refer to illustrations 11.3 and 11.7

1   If a malfunction occurs in the charging circuit, do not immediately assume that the alternator is causing the problem. First, check the following items:

a) *The battery cables where they connect to the battery. Make sure the connections are clean and tight.*

b) *Check the battery state of charge (see Section 3).*

c) *Check the external alternator wiring and connections.*

d) *Check the drivebelt condition and tension (see Chapter 1).*

e) *Check the alternator mounting bolts for tightness.*

f) *Run the engine and check the alternator for abnormal noise.*

g) *Check the fusible links in the engine compartment fuse box (see Chapter 12). If they're burned, determine the cause and repair the circuit.*

h) *Refer to wiring diagrams in Chapter 12 and check all the fuses in series with the charging system. The location of the fuses may vary from year to year but the designations are the same.*

2   Using a voltmeter, check the battery voltage with the engine off. It should be approximately 12-volts.

3   Start the engine and check the battery voltage again. It should now be approximately 14 to 15-volts **(see illustration)**.

4   Turn ON the headlights. The voltage should drop and then come back up if the charging system is working properly.

5   If the voltage reading is more than the specified charging voltage, the voltage regulator is defective. Replace the alternator (see Section 12).

6   If the voltage reading is less than the specified charging voltage, check the alternator as follows:

7   Using a voltmeter and working on the backside of the alternator, backprobe the "B+" terminal. There should be 12 volts present with the ignition key Off **(see illustration)**.

8   With the ignition key On (engine not running), backprobe each terminal. There should be 12 volts at the "S" terminal, 1.5 to 2.0 volts at the "L" terminal and 12 volts at the "B+" terminal.

9   Start the engine, then raise the engine speed to 2000 rpm and backprobe each ter-

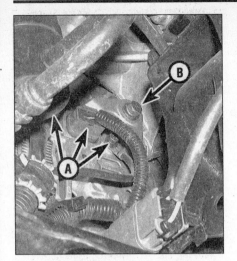

12.5a Working at the rear of the alternator, disconnect the wiring (A) and the rear retaining bolt (B)

minal again. There should be 14.0 to 14.7 volts at the "S" terminal and "B+" terminal and 13.0 to 14.0 volts at the "L" terminal.

10 If the voltages are not as specified, check the wiring harness. If the wiring harness is not defective, replace the alternator.

11 If you suspect that there is a voltage drain on the battery while the vehicle is sitting in the driveway, see Section 3 and perform a battery drain test.

12 If a drain is indicated, carefully remove the fuses one-by-one that govern accessories such as radio, blower motor, trunk lights, etc. until the test light goes out. Track down the short circuit in the particular fused circuit and repair the problem. Recheck the electrical system as described.

13 If all the fuses are pulled out and the test light remains lit, remove the output cable at the rear of the alternator then unplug all the connectors from the backside of the alternator. If the test light goes out, then there is an internal drain in the alternator or voltage regulator. Replace the alternator.

12 Alternator - removal and installation

Refer to illustrations 12.5a and 12.5b

1 Disconnect the cable from the negative terminal of the battery.

2 Raise the vehicle and support it securely on jackstands. Remove the lower splash shield (if equipped) from beneath the alternator.

3 Unplug the electrical connectors from the rear of the alternator and remove the wire harness retaining bracket.

4 Remove the drivebelt (see Chapter 1).

5 Remove the bolts and separate the alternator from the engine **(see illustrations)**.

6 Installation is the reverse of removal.

7 After the alternator is installed, install the drivebelt and reconnect the cable to the negative terminal of the battery. Adjust the drivebelt following the procedure in Chapter 1.

13 Starting system - general information and precautions

The starting system is composed of the starter motor, starter/inhibit relay, battery, ignition switch and connecting wires.

Turning the ignition key to the Start position actuates the starter relay through the starter control circuit. The starter relay then connects the battery to the starter solenoid.

These models are equipped with a starter/solenoid assembly that is mounted to the transmission bellhousing.

All vehicles are equipped with a Transmission Range sensor in the starter control circuit, which prevents operation of the starter unless the shift lever is in Neutral or Park.

The starter circuit is equipped with a starter/inhibit relay. This relay is located in the engine compartment LH fuse/relay box (see Chapter 12).

Never operate the starter motor for more than 15 seconds at a time without pausing to allow it to cool for at least two minutes. Excessive cranking can cause overheating, which can seriously damage the starter.

14 Starter motor and circuit - in-vehicle check

Refer to illustrations 14.3 and 14.7

1 If a malfunction occurs in the starting circuit, do not immediately assume that the starter is causing the problem. First, check the following items:

  a) *Make sure the battery cable clamps, where they connect to the battery, are clean and tight.*

  b) *Check the condition of the battery cables (see Section 4). Replace any defective battery cables with new parts.*

  c) *Test the condition of the battery (see Section 3). If it does not pass all the tests, replace it with a new battery.*

  d) *Check the starter solenoid wiring and connections.*

  e) *Check the starter mounting bolts for tightness.*

2 If the starter does not activate when the ignition switch is turned to the start position, check for battery voltage to the solenoid with the ignition switch Off. There should be battery voltage at the positive battery cable on the solenoid if the battery and/or cables are in good working order.

3 Backprobe the S terminal on the starter solenoid and check for voltage as the ignition switch is turned to the start position. This will determine if the solenoid is receiving the correct voltage signal from the ignition switch. If voltage is not available, check the fusible links in the engine compartment fuse box (see Chapter 12). If they're burned, determine the cause and repair the circuit. Also, check the ignition switch fuse (30 amp) in the engine compartment fuse box **(see illustration)** and the electronic transaxle fuse (10 amp) in the passenger compartment fuse panel (see

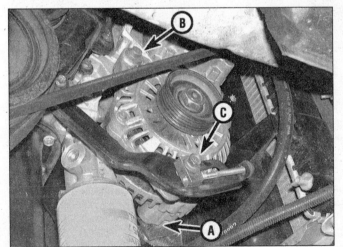

12.5b Working at the front of the alternator, detach the wiring harness retaining bracket (A) the upper bolt (B) and the adjuster lock bolt (C)

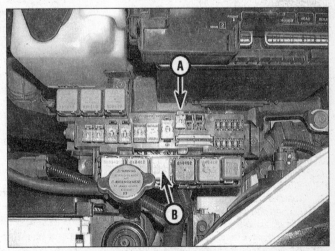

14.3 Location of the ignition switch fuse (A) and starter/inhibit relay (B) (1996 and later)

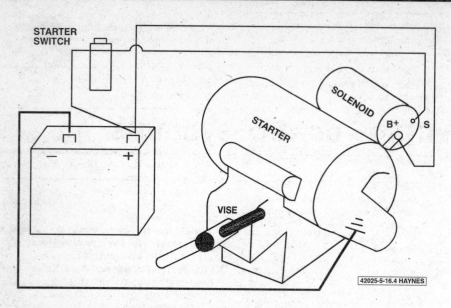

14.7 Starter motor bench testing details

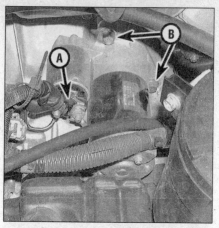

15.4 Remove the electrical connectors (A) and the starter mounting bolts (B) and separate the assembly from the transaxle bellhousing

Chapter 12). If the fuses and fusible links are OK, check the starter/inhibit relay and circuit for proper operation. Refer to Chapter 12 for the relay locations, wiring diagrams and the relay checking procedure.

4   If the starter/inhibit relay circuit is not functioning, check the operation of the transaxle range sensor (see Chapter 7) Make sure the shift lever is in PARK or NEUTRAL.

5   If the vehicle is equipped with an anti-theft alarm, check the circuit and the control module for shorts or damaged components.

6   If voltage is available and there is no movement from the starter motor, remove the starter from the engine (see Section 15) and bench test the starter.

7   If the starter is receiving voltage but does not activate, remove and check the starter/solenoid assembly on the bench. Most likely the solenoid is defective. In some rare cases, the engine may be seized so be sure to try and rotate the crankshaft pulley (see Chapter 2A) before proceeding. With the starter/solenoid assembly mounted in a vise on the bench, install one jumper cable from the negative terminal (-) to the body of the starter **(see illustration)**. Install another jumper cable from the positive terminal (+) on the battery to the B+ terminal on the starter. Install a starter switch and apply battery voltage to the solenoid S terminal (for 10 seconds or less) and observe the solenoid plunger, shift lever and overrunning clutch extend and rotate the pinion drive. If the pinion drive extends but does not rotate, the solenoid is operating but the starter motor is defective. If there is no movement but the

solenoid clicks, the solenoid and/or the starter motor is defective. If the solenoid plunger extends and rotates the pinion drive, the starter/solenoid assembly is working properly.

---

15   Starter motor - removal and installation

Refer to illustration 15.4

1   Disconnect the cable from the negative terminal of the battery.

2   Remove the air intake duct and the air cleaner housing assembly from the engine compartment (see Chapter 4).

16.3a Remove the solenoid mounting screws (arrows)

3   Disconnect the battery cable and the solenoid terminal connection from the starter solenoid.

4   Remove the starter motor mounting bolts **(see illustration)** and detach the starter from the engine.

5   Installation is the reverse of removal.

---

16   Starter solenoid - replacement

Refer to illustrations 16.3a and 16.3b

1   Remove the starter assembly from the engine compartment (see Section 15).

2   Remove the electrical connector from the solenoid lower terminal.

3   Remove the solenoid mounting screws and separate the solenoid from the starter body **(see illustrations)**.

4   Installation is the reverse of removal.

16.3b Separate the solenoid from the starter

Chapter 6
Emissions and engine control systems

Contents

1   General information

Refer to illustrations 1.1 and 1.7

To prevent pollution of the atmosphere from incompletely burned and evaporating gases, and to maintain good driveability and fuel economy, a number of emission control systems are incorporated **(see illustration)**.

They include the:

Electronic Engine Control system (EEC) OBD-I (1995 and earlier)
Electronic Engine Control system (EEC) OBD-II (1996 and later)
Evaporative Emission Controls System (EVAP)
Positive Crankcase Ventilation (PCV) system
Exhaust Gas Recirculation (EGR) system
Catalytic converter

All of these systems are linked, directly or indirectly, to the emission control system.

The Sections in this Chapter include general descriptions, checking procedures within the scope of the home mechanic and component replacement procedures (when possible) for each of the systems listed above.

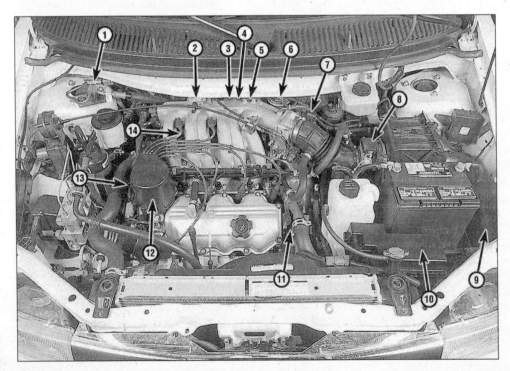

1.1 Typical emission and engine control system components

1   Power steering pressure switch
2   Idle Air Control (IAC) valve and Fast Idle Control (FIC) solenoid housing
3   Bypass Air (BPA) valve (1995 and earlier models)
4   PCV valve (on rear of intake plenum)
5   EGR modulator valve
6   Exhaust Gas Recirculation (EGR) valve
7   Throttle Position Sensor (TPS)
8   Mass Airflow (MAF) sensor
9   Intake Air Temperature (IAT) sensor
10 Power distribution box
11 Crankshaft position (CKP) sensor
12 Camshaft position (CMP) sensor
13 Engine Coolant Temperature (ECT) sensor (behind distributor)
14 Knock sensor (beneath intake manifold)

6

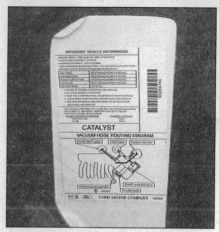

1.7 The Vehicle Emission Control Information (VECI) label is located in the engine compartment and contains information on the emission devices on your vehicle, vacuum line routing, etc.

Before assuming that an emissions control system is malfunctioning, check the fuel and ignition systems carefully. The diagnosis of some emission control devices requires specialized tools, equipment and training. If checking and servicing become too difficult or if a procedure is beyond your ability, consult a dealer service department. Remember, the most frequent cause of emissions problems is simply a loose or broken vacuum hose or wire, so always check the hose and wiring connections first.

This doesn't mean, however, that emission control systems are particularly difficult to maintain and repair. You can quickly and easily perform many checks and do most of the regular maintenance at home with common tune-up and hand tools. **Note:** *Because of a Federally mandated extended warranty which covers the emission control system*

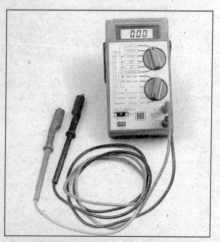

2.1 Digital multimeters can be used for testing all types of circuits; because of their high impedance, they are much more accurate than analog meters for measuring low-voltage computer circuits

components, check with your dealer about warranty coverage before working on any emissions-related systems. Once the warranty has expired, you may wish to perform some of the component checks and/or replacement procedures in this Chapter to save money.

Pay close attention to any special precautions outlined in this Chapter. It should be noted that the illustrations of the various systems may not exactly match the system installed on the vehicle you're working on because of changes made by the manufacturer during production or from year-to-year.

A Vehicle Emissions Control Information (VECI) label is located in the engine compartment **(see illustration)**. This label contains important emissions specifications and adjustment information, as well as a vacuum hose schematic with emissions components identified. When servicing the engine or emissions systems, the VECI label in your particular vehicle should always be checked for up-to-date information.

2   On Board Diagnosis (OBD) system and trouble codes

Note: *1995 and earlier vehicles are equipped with OBD-I self diagnosis system, while 1996 and later vehicles are equipped with OBD-II self diagnosis system. The diagnostic trouble codes on both systems can be extracted from the Powertrain Control Module (PCM) using a specialized SCAN tool or by placing the PCM in the diagnostic mode and flashing codes on the Malfunction Indicator Lamp (MIL) (see Step 31). The information sensor checks and replacement procedures apply to both systems.*

Diagnostic tool information

Refer to illustrations 2.1, 2.2 and 2.4

1   A digital multimeter is necessary for checking fuel injection and emission related components **(see illustration)**. A digital volt-ohmmeter is preferred over the older style analog multimeter for several reasons. The analog multimeter cannot display the volts-ohms or amps measurement in hundredths and thousandths increments. When working with electronic circuits which are often very low voltage, this accurate reading is most important. Another good reason for the digital multimeter is the high impedance circuit. The digital multimeter is equipped with a high resistance internal circuitry (10 million ohms). Because a voltmeter is hooked up in parallel with the circuit when testing, it is vital that none of the voltage being measured should be allowed to travel the parallel path set up by the meter itself. This dilemma does not show itself when measuring larger amounts of voltage (9 to 12 volt circuits) but if you are measuring a low voltage circuit such as the oxygen sensor signal voltage, a fraction of a volt may be a significant amount when diag-

nosing a problem. Obtaining the diagnostic trouble codes is one exception where using an analog voltmeter is necessary.

2   Hand-held scanners are the most powerful and versatile tools for analyzing engine management systems used on later model vehicles **(see illustration)**. Early model scanners handle codes and some diagnostics for many OBD-I systems. Each brand scan tool must be examined carefully to match the year, make and model of the vehicle you are working on. Often interchangeable cartridges are available to access the particular manufacturer (Ford, GM, Chrysler, etc.). Some manufacturers will specify by continent (Asia, Europe, USA, etc.).

3   With the arrival of the Federally mandated emission control system (OBD-II), a specially designed scanner has also been developed. Several tool manufacturers have released OBD-II scan tools for the home mechanic. Ask the parts salesman at a local auto parts store for additional information concerning dates and costs.

4   Another type of code reader is available at parts stores **(see illustration)**. These tools simplify the procedure for extracting codes from the engine management computer on OBD-I systems by simply "plugging in" to the diagnostic connector on the vehicle wiring harness.

OBD system general description

5   All 1995 and earlier vehicles are equipped with the Electronic Engine Control (EEC) (OBD-I) system. All 1996 and later engines and powertrain combinations described in this manual are equipped with the EEC (OBD-II) system. Both systems consist of an onboard computer, known as the Powertrain Control Module (PCM), and information sensors, which monitor various functions of the engine and send data to the PCM. Based on the data and the information programmed into the computer's memory, the PCM generates output signals to control various engine functions via control relays, solenoids and other output actuators.

6   The PCM is the "brain" of the Electronic Engine Control (EEC) system. It receives data from a number of sensors and other electronic components (switches, relays, etc.). Based on the information it receives, the PCM generates output signals to control various relays, solenoids and other actuators. The PCM is specifically calibrated to optimize the emissions, fuel economy and driveability of the vehicle.

7   Because of a Federally mandated extended warranty which covers the EEC system components and because any owner-induced damage to the PCM, the sensors and/or the control devices may void the warranty, it isn't a good idea to attempt diagnosis or replacement of the PCM at home while the vehicle is under warranty. Take the vehicle to a dealer service department if the PCM or a system component malfunctions.

2.2 Scanners like the Actron Scantool and the AutoXray XP240 are powerful diagnostic aids - programmed with comprehensive diagnostic information, they can tell you just about anything you want to know about your engine management system

2.4 Trouble code tools simplify the task of extracting the trouble codes on OBD-I systems

Information sensors

8   Heated Oxygen sensors (HO2S) - The HO2S generates a voltage signal that varies with the difference between the oxygen content of the exhaust and the oxygen in the surrounding air.

9   Crankshaft position (CKP) sensor – The CKP is used to detect crankshaft fluctuation during each engine revolution. Its main function is to detect engine misfires and is used on OBD-II systems only.

10   Camshaft position (CMP) sensor - The CMP sensor provides information on camshaft position and the engine speed signal to the PCM.

11   Engine coolant temperature (ECT) sensor - The ECT monitors engine coolant temperature and sends the PCM a voltage signal that affects PCM control of the fuel mixture, ignition timing, and EGR operation.

12   Intake Air Temperature (IAT) sensor - The IAT provides the PCM with intake air temperature information. The PCM uses this information to control fuel flow, ignition timing, and EGR system operation.

13   Throttle Position Sensor (TPS) - The TPS senses throttle movement and position, then transmits a voltage signal to the PCM. This signal enables the PCM to determine when the throttle is closed, in a cruise position, or wide open.

14   Mass airflow (MAF) sensor - The MAF sensor measures the molecular mass of the intake airflow entering the engine. The MAF sensor, along with the IAT sensor, provide mass airflow and air temperature information for the most precise fuel metering.

15   Manifold Absolute Pressure (MAP) sensor - This sensor is used on 1998 California models only, in conjunction with a MAP sensor solenoid valve to monitor intake manifold pressure and ambient barometric pressure. The PCM uses this input signal to control the EVAP system.

16   Vehicle speed sensor (VSS) - The vehicle speed sensor provides information to the PCM to indicate vehicle speed.

17   Knock sensor (KS) - The knock sensor is a piezoresistive microphone that detects the sound of engine detonation, or "pinging". The PCM uses the input signal from the knock sensor to recognize detonation and retard spark advance to avoid engine damage.

18   Exhaust Gas Recirculation Temperature (EGRT) sensor - The EGR temperature sensor is used to monitor the rate and flow of exhaust gas recirculation into the intake system.

19   Power steering pressure (PSP) switch - The PSP sensor is used to detect excessive line pressure in the power steering system. The PCM uses this input signal to adjust the idle speed under increased engine loads during low-speed vehicle maneuvers.

20   A/C clutch control switch When battery voltage is applied to the air conditioning compressor solenoid, a signal is sent to the PCM, which interprets the signal as an added load created by the compressor and increases engine idle speed accordingly to compensate.

Output actuators

21   PCM power relay - The main PCM power relay is activated by the ignition switch and supplies battery power to the PCM and the EEC system when the switch is in the Start or Run position. On 1995 and earlier models the PCM power relay is located in the engine compartment left-hand fuse panel. On 1996 and later models, the power relay is mounted on top of the PCM behind the instrument panel glove box. Refer to Chapter 12 or your owner's manual for more information on relay location.

22   Fuel pump relay - The fuel pump relay is activated by the PCM with the ignition

switch in the Start or Run position. When the ignition switch is turned on, the relay is activated to supply initial line pressure to the system. On 1995 and earlier models the fuel pump relay is located in the engine compartment left-hand relay panel. On 1996 and later models, the fuel pump relay is located in the engine compartment left-hand fuse/relay panel. Refer to Chapter 12 or your owner's manual for more information on relay location. For more information on fuel pump check and replacement, refer to Chapter 4.

23   Fuel injectors - The PCM opens the fuel injectors individually in firing order sequence. The PCM also controls the time the injector is open, called the "pulse width." The pulse width of the injector (measured in milliseconds) determines the amount of fuel delivered. For more information on the fuel delivery system and the fuel injectors, including injector replacement, refer to Chapter 4.

24   Power transistor – the power transistor amplifies the ignition signal from the PCM and intermittently grounds the primary circuit to the ignition coils which generates high voltage in the secondary circuit, thus sending spark from the ignition coil to the distributor. Refer to Chapter 5 for more information on the power transistor.

25   Idle Air Control (IAC) valve - The IAC valve controls the amount of air to bypass the throttle plate when the throttle valve is closed or at idle position. The IAC valve opening and the resulting airflow is controlled by the PCM.

26   Fast Idle Control (FIC) solenoid – The FIC solenoid helps maintain a constant idle speed due to increased engine loads when the air conditioning is operating by allowing additional air to enter the intake manifold.

27   Bypass Air (BPA) valve – The bypass air valve is used on 1995 and earlier models to increase idle speed during cold weather conditions. It functions similar to a choke on a carbureted vehicle.

6

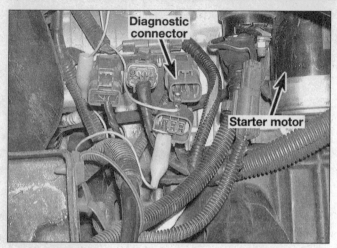

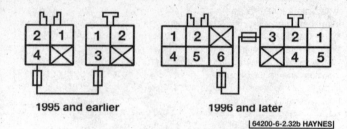

1995 and earlier   1996 and later

64200-6-2.32b HAYNES

2.32a Engine compartment diagnostic connector location

2.32b Engine compartment diagnostic connector terminal identification - use jumper wires to bridge the indicated terminals

28 **EGR and EVAP vacuum control solenoids -** The EGR vacuum solenoid is controlled by the PCM to regulate the opening of the vacuum-operated EGR valve. 1998 models are equipped with a EVAP vacuum control solenoid to help control the purging of the EVAP system.

29 **EVAP canister purge valve -** The evaporative emission canister purge valve is a solenoid valve, operated by the PCM to purge the fuel vapor canister and route fuel vapor to the intake manifold for combustion.

30 **Transmission Control Module (TCM) -** The TCM receives input signals from various sensors and switches such as the vehicle speed sensor, transaxle range sensor, turbine shaft speed sensor, throttle position sensor and the camshaft position sensor to determine shifting points, required line pressure and torque converter lock-up operations of the transaxle. The TCM is a separate control module from the PCM although both control modules are used to determine operational characteristics of the transaxle.

Obtaining OBD-I and OBD-II system codes

Refer to illustrations 2.32a, 2.32b and 2.33

31 The PCM will illuminate the CHECK

2.33 Typical Data Link Connector (DLC) on an OBD-II vehicle

ENGINE light (also known as the Malfunction Indicator Lamp) on the dash if it recognizes a component fault for two consecutive drive cycles. It will continue to set the light until the codes are cleared or the PCM does not detect any malfunction for three or more consecutive drive cycles.

32 The diagnostic codes for OBD-I and OBD-II systems can be extracted from the PCM using two methods. The first method requires a jumper wire to bridge the terminals of the engine compartment diagnostic connector to flash the trouble codes on the CHECK ENGINE light/MIL lamp. To extract the diagnostic trouble codes using this method proceed as follows:

a) *Turn the ignition key ON (engine not running). The CHECK ENGINE light on the dash should remain ON. This indicates that the PCM is receiving power and the CHECK ENGINE light bulb is not defective.*

b) *Turn the ignition key OFF, locate and disconnect the diagnostic connector in the engine compartment (see illustration). Turn the ignition key ON (engine not running). Using a suitable jumper wire bridge the appropriate terminals (see illustration). Wait two seconds and remove the jumper wire, then reconnect the engine compartment diagnostic connector.* **Note:** *Failure to follow this procedure exactly as described may erase stored trouble codes from the PCM memory.*

c) *Carefully observe the CHECK ENGINE light/MIL lamp flashes on the instrument cluster. If everything in the self diagnosis system is functioning properly, the computer will flash a code 55 (OBD-I) or a code 0505 (OBD-II). Both codes will be represented by five long flashes on the CHECK ENGINE light/MIL lamp followed by five short flashes. If the computer has actual trouble codes stored, carefully observe the flashes and record the exact number onto paper. For example, code 43 or code 0403 (throttle position sensor*

or TPS circuit) is indicated by four long flashes followed by three short flashes. Refer to the trouble code charts below for the exact codes and component failures.

d) *If the ignition key is turned OFF during the code extraction process and possibly turned back ON, the self diagnostic system will automatically invalidate the procedure. Restart the procedure to extract the codes.* **Note:** *The self diagnostic system cannot be accessed if the engine is running.*

33 The second method is used on OBD-II equipped vehicles only. It uses a special SCAN tool that is programmed to interface with the new OBD-II system by plugging into the DLC **(see illustration)**. When used, the SCAN tool has the ability to diagnose in-depth driveability problems and it allows freeze frame data to be retrieved from the PCM stored memory. Freeze frame data is an OBD-II PCM feature that records all related sensor and actuator activity on the PCM data stream whenever an engine control or emissions fault is detected and a DTC is set. This ability to look at the circuit conditions and values when the malfunction occurs provides a valuable tool when trying to diagnose intermittent driveability problems. **Note:** *OBD-II SCAN tools use different trouble code number designations (referred to as P0 or P1 codes) than the CHECK ENGINE light/ MIL lamp codes described above. Refer to the SCAN tool column of the OBD-II trouble code chart below for the exact codes and component failures. If the tool is not available and intermittent driveability problems exist, have the vehicle checked at a dealer service department or other qualified repair shop.*

Clearing codes

34 After the system has been repaired, the codes can be cleared from the PCM memory. To clear the codes, turn the ignition key OFF for at least three seconds. Turn the ignition key back ON and disconnect the engine compart-

ment diagnostic connector **(see illustration 2.32a)**. Using a suitable jumper wire bridge the appropriate terminals **(see illustration 2.32b)**. Wait two seconds and remove the jumper wire, then reconnect the engine compartment diagnostic connector and turn the ignition key OFF. **Caution:** *Do not disconnect the battery from the vehicle to clear the codes. This will erase stored operating parameters from the memory and cause the engine to run rough for a period of time while the computer relearns*

the information. If necessary, have the codes cleared by a dealer service department or other qualified repair facility. **Note:** *If using a OBD-II SCAN tool, scroll the menu for the function that describes "CLEARING CODES" and follow the prescribed method for that particular SCAN tool.*

35 Always clear the codes from the PCM before a new electronic emission control component is installed onto the engine. The PCM will often store trouble codes during

sensor malfunctions. The PCM will also record new trouble codes if a new sensor is allowed to operate before the parameters from the old sensor have been erased. Clearing the codes will allow the computer to relearn the new operating parameters relayed by the new component. During the computer relearning process, the engine may experience a rough idle or slight driveability changes. This period of time, however, should last no longer than 15 to 20 minutes.

OBD-I Trouble codes – 1995 and earlier models

Trouble code	Code identification
Code 11*	Camshaft position (CMP) sensor and or circuit fault
Code 12	Mass airflow (MAF) sensor and or circuit fault
Code 13	Engine Coolant temperature (ECT) sensor and or circuit fault
Code 14	Vehicle speed sensor (VSS) and or circuit fault
Code 21*	Ignition signal circuit fault
Code 31	Powertrain Control Module (PCM) unit fault
Code 32	EGR Control solenoid and or circuit fault
Code 33*	Oxygen (O2) sensor and or circuit fault
Code 34*	Knock sensor (KS) and or circuit fault
Code 35	Exhaust gas Recirculation Temperature (EGRT) sensor and or circuit fault
Code 43	Throttle position sensor (TPS) and or circuit fault
Code 45	Fuel injector leak
Code 51	Fuel injector signal circuit fault
Code 55*	EFI system normal operation

These codes do not illuminate the CHECK ENGINE light on the dash if a malfunction occurs, but it is possible to access the OBD-I system and read the stored codes.

OBD-II Trouble codes - 1996 and later models

Scan tool trouble code	CHECK ENGINE light flash code	Code identification
P000	0505	No failures
P0100	0102	Mass Airflow (MAF) sensor and or circuit fault
P0105	0803	Absolute pressure sensor (California) and or circuit fault
P0110	0401	Intake Air Temperature (IAT) sensor and or circuit fault
P0115	0103	Electronic Coolant Temperature (ECT) sensor and or circuit fault
P0120	0403	Throttle Position Sensor (TPS) and or circuit fault
P0125	0908	Insufficient coolant temperature for closed loop operation
P0130	0503	Upstream heated O2 sensor and or circuit fault
P0131	0411	Upstream heated O2 sensor lean shift monitor fault
P0132	0410	Upstream heated O2 sensor rich shift monitor fault

Scan tool trouble code	CHECK ENGINE light flash code	Code identification
P0133	0409	Upstream heated O2 sensor circuit slow response fault
P0134	0412	Upstream heated O2 sensor high voltage fault
P0135	0901	Upstream heated O2 sensor heater fault
P0136	0707	Downstream heated O2 sensor or circuit fault
P0137	0511	Downstream heated O2 sensor minimum voltage monitor fault
P0138	0510	Downstream heated O2 sensor maximum voltage monitor fault
P0139	0707	Downstream heated O2 sensor circuit slow response fault
P0140	0512	Downstream heated O2 sensor high voltage fault
P0141	0902	Downstream heated O2 sensor heater fault
P0150	0303	Upstream heated O2 sensor or circuit fault
P0155	0101	Upstream heated O2 sensor heater fault
P0171	0115	System Adaptive fuel too lean
P0172	0114	System Adaptive fuel too rich
P0180	0402	Fuel tank temperature sensor (California) and or circuit fault
P0300	0701	Multiple cylinder misfire detected
P0301	0608	Cylinder no. 1 misfire detected
P0302	0607	Cylinder no. 2 misfire detected
P0303	0606	Cylinder no. 3 misfire detected
P0304	0605	Cylinder no. 4 misfire detected
P0305	0604	Cylinder no. 5 misfire detected
P0306	0603	Cylinder no. 6 misfire detected
P0325	0304	Knock sensor (KS) and or circuit fault
P0335	0802	Crankshaft position (CKP) sensor and or circuit fault
P0340	0101	Camshaft position (CMP) sensor and or circuit fault
P0400	0302	EGR insufficient flow detected
P0402	0306	EGR excessive flow detected
P0420	0702	Catalyst system efficiency below threshold
P0440	0705	EVAP system leak (California)
P0443	1008	EVAP canister purge volume control valve circuit fault (California)
P0446	0903	EVAP canister vent control valve circuit fault (California)
P0450	0704	EVAP system pressure sensor fault (California)
P0500	0104	Vehicle Speed Sensor (VSS) and or circuit fault
P0505	0205	Idle Air Control (IAC) valve and or circuit fault
P0510	0203	Closed throttle position switch and or circuit fault
P0600	No code	A/T control unit fault

Scan tool trouble code	CHECK ENGINE light flash code	Code identification
P0605	0301	PCM Read Only Memory test error
P0705	1101	Transaxle range (TR) sensor and or circuit fault
P0710	1208	Transaxle temperature sensor and or circuit fault
P0720	1102	Vehicle speed sensor (VSS) and or circuit fault
P0725	1207	Camshaft position (CMP) sensor and or circuit fault
P0731	1103	A/T first gear signal fault
P0732	1104	A/T second gear signal fault
P0733	1105	A/T third gear signal fault
P0734	1106	A/T fourth gear signal fault
P0740	1204	TCC solenoid and or circuit fault
P0744	1107	A/T TCC solenoid valve fault
P0745	1205	Line pressure solenoid and or circuit fault
P0750	1108	Shift solenoid A fault
P0750	1201	Shift solenoid B fault
P1105	1302	Manifold Absolute Pressure (MAP) sensor switch and or circuit fault
P1148	0307	Closed loop control fault
P1320	0201	Ignition signal primary circuit fault
P1336	0905	Crankshaft Position (CKP) sensor fault and or flywheel damage
P1400	1005	EGR solenoid valve fault
P1401	0305	EGR temperature (EGRT) sensor and or circuit fault
P1402	0514	EGR high flow detected
P1440	0213	EVAP system small leak (California)
P1444	0214	EVAP canister purge volume control valve fault (California)
P1446	0215	EVAP canister vent control valve closed (California)
P1447	0111	EVAP purge flow monitor fault (California)
P1448	0309	EVAP canister vent control valve open (California)
P1490	0801	Vacuum Cut Valve Bypass Valve fault (California)
P1491	0311	Vacuum Cut Valve Bypass Valve fault (California)
P1492	0807	EVAP canister purge control valve solenoid valve fault (California)
P1493	0312	EVAP canister purge control valve solenoid valve fault (California)
P1605	0804	A/T control unit fault
P1705	1206	Throttle Position sensor (TPS) to A/T signal fault
P1706	1003	Transaxle range (TR) sensor and or circuit fault
P1760	1203	Overrun clutch solenoid and or circuit fault

6

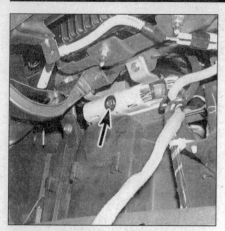

3.5 Remove the bolt (arrow) and detach the connector from the PCM

3.6 Remove the PCM bracket mounting bolts (arrows)

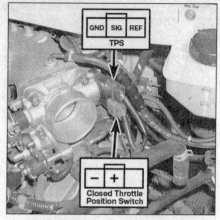

4.2 The TPS is mounted to the side of the throttle body

3   Powertrain Control Module (PCM) - removal and installation

Refer to illustrations 3.5 and 3.6
Warning: *The models covered by this manual are equipped with Supplemental Restraint systems (SRS), more commonly known as airbags. Always disable the airbag system before working in the vicinity of the impact sensors, steering column or instrument panel to avoid the possibility of accidental deployment of the airbag, which could cause personal injury (see Chapter 12).*

1   The Powertrain Control Module (PCM) is located behind the instrument panel glove box.
2   Disconnect the cable from the negative terminal of the battery.
3   Remove the lower console or CD changer cover and the glove compartment from the instrument panel (see Chapter 11).
4   Remove the passenger side airbag (see Chapter 12).
5   Disconnect the harness connector from the PCM **(see illustration)**.
6   Remove the retaining bolts from the

4.7 TPS upper mounting screw (arrow) (lower screw not visible)

PCM mounting bracket **(see illustration)**.
7   On 1996 and later models disconnect the PCM power relay connector. Carefully slide the PCM out the instrument panel and disconnect any remaining electrical connectors. **Note:** *Avoid any static electricity damage to the computer by using gloves and a special anti-static pad to store the ECM on once it is removed.*
8   Installation is the reverse of removal. Tighten the PCM electrical connector bolt until the red indicator appears in the connector window.

4   Throttle Position Sensor (TPS) – check, replacement and adjustment

Check
Refer to illustration 4.2
Note: *If the following tests indicate that a sensor is good, and not the cause of a driveability problem or DTC, check the wiring harness and connectors between the sensor and the PCM for an open or short circuit. If no problems are found, have the vehicle checked by a dealer service department or other qualified repair shop.*
1   The Throttle Position Sensor (TPS) is a variable-resistance potentiometer, mounted on the side of the throttle body and connected to the throttle shaft **(see illustration 1.1)**. By monitoring the output voltage from the TPS, the PCM can determine fuel delivery based on throttle valve angle (driver demand). A broken or loose TPS can cause intermittent bursts of fuel from the injector and an unstable idle because the PCM thinks the throttle is moving. A problem with the TPS and or circuit will set a diagnostic trouble code. **Note:** *All vehicles use a closed throttle position switch as part of the throttle angle detection system. The switch shuts on/off only at particular points in the throttle angle range. The switch is wired directly to the automatic transaxle control module.*

2   Check the reference voltage from the PCM to the TPS. Disconnect the TPS harness connector and install the probes of a voltmeter on the REF terminal (+) and the GND terminal (-). With the ignition key ON (engine not running), it should read approximately 5.0 volts **(see illustration)**. If reference voltage is not available, there is an open circuit to the PCM or a defective PCM.
3   Next, probe the SIG terminal (+) and the GND terminals on the TPS and check the resistance of TPS with the throttle fully closed, then gradually open the throttle to full throttle. There should be 1 K-ohms of resistance with the throttle closed and 9 K-ohms at full throttle. The resistance should increase smoothly as the throttle is opened.
4   Disconnect the closed throttle position switch connector and probe the positive terminal (+) and the negative terminals (-) of the switch **(see illustration 4.2)**. Check for continuity at the switch with the throttle fully closed. There should be NO continuity at the switch when it is at part or full throttle. If the readings are incorrect, replace the TPS.

Replacement
Refer to illustration 4.7
5   Disconnect the cable from the negative terminal of the battery.
6   Remove the air intake duct (see Chapter 4) and disconnect the TPS and closed throttle position switch electrical connectors.
7   Remove the two retaining screws **(see illustration)** and separate the TPS from the throttle body.
8   Install the new TPS leaving the mounting screws loose.
9   Adjust the TPS as described below (see Step 12) and tighten the screws securely.

Adjustment
10   Remove the air intake duct (see Chapter 4).
11   Loosen the TPS mounting screws **(see illustration 4.7)**.
12   Using a digital voltmeter, backprobe the electrical connector SIG terminal (+) and the GND terminal (-). Be very careful not to dam-

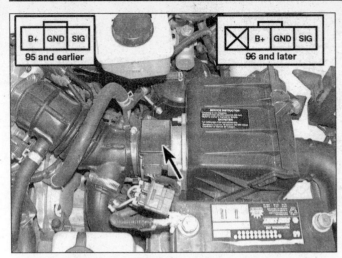

5.3 The MAF sensor (arrow) is located in the air intake duct - check for battery voltage to the B+ terminal of the MAF sensor connector (key ON engine not running)

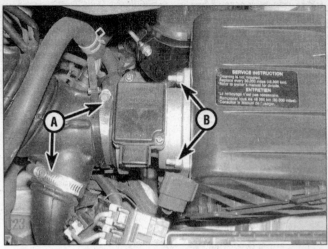

5.10 Loosen the retaining clamps (A) and disconnect the air inlet duct. Remove the upper (B) and lower retaining nuts and separate the MAF sensor from the air cleaner housing

age the wiring harness **(see illustration 4.2)**. With the ignition key ON (engine not running) and the throttle fully closed, the voltage should read approximately 0.4 to 0.5 volts.

13 If the readings are incorrect, rotate the TPS body until the correct voltage is attained and tighten the mounting screws.

5 Mass Airflow (MAF) sensor - check and replacement

Check

Refer to illustration 5.3

Note: *If the following tests indicate that a sensor is good, and not the cause of a driveability problem or DTC, check the wiring harness and connectors between the sensor and the PCM for an open or short circuit. If no problems are found, have the vehicle checked by a dealer service department or other qualified repair shop.*

1 The Mass Airflow (MAF) sensor is installed in the air intake duct **(see illustration 1.1)**. This sensor uses a hot-wire sensing element to measure the molecular mass (or weight) of air entering the engine. The air passing over the hot wire causes it to cool, and the sensor converts this temperature change into an analog voltage signal to the PCM. The PCM in turn calculates the required fuel injector pulse width to obtain the necessary air/fuel ratio. A defective MAF sensor can cause surging, stalling, rough idle and other driveability problems. The Electronic Engine Control (EEC) system can detect several different MAF sensor problems and set trouble codes to indicate the specific fault.

2 To check for power to the MAF sensor, disconnect the MAF sensor electrical connector.

3 Connect the positive (+) lead of your voltmeter to the B+ terminal of the harness

connector; connect the meter negative (-) lead to the sensor connector GND terminal **(see illustration)**.

4 Turn the ignition On but do not start the engine. The meter should read more than 10 volts or close to battery voltage.

5 Reconnect the electrical connector and use straight pins or other suitable probes to backprobe the MAF SIG (+) and GND (-) terminals with the voltmeter. Start the engine and check the voltage, it should be 1.0 to 1.7 volts at idle.

6 Increase the engine rpm. The MAF signal voltage should increase from 1.7 to 3.0 volts. It is impossible to simulate driving conditions in the driveway, but it is necessary to watch the voltmeter for an increase in signal voltage as the engine speed is raised. The engine is not under load, but signal voltage should vary slightly.

7 If you suspect a defective MAF sensor, stop the engine and disconnect the MAF harness connector. Using an ohmmeter, probe the MAF SIG (+) and GND (-) terminals. If the hot-wire element inside the sensor has been damaged, the ohmmeter will show an open circuit (infinite resistance).

8 If the voltage readings are correct, refer to the wiring diagrams and check the wiring harness for open circuits or a damaged harness. **Note:** *If MAF related driveability problems continue but these general tests don't indicate a MAF fault, have the sensor tested by a dealer service department or other qualified repair shop. A MAF sensor can develop voltage signal problems that can't be seen on a voltmeter. The PCM can see such signal faults and a driveability problem will result.*

Replacement

Refer to illustration 5.10

Note: *The plastic MAF sensor body and the metal air duct on which it is mounted are an assembly that must be replaced as a unit. Do not try to separate the sensor body from the metal duct.*

9 Disconnect the electrical connector from the MAF sensor.

10 Remove the clamp that secures the sensor to the intake air duct. Remove the four nuts that secure the sensor to the air cleaner housing **(see illustration)**.

11 Install and connect the new sensor.

6 Manifold Absolute Pressure (MAP) sensor and solenoid valve (1998 California models) - check and replacement

Check

Refer to illustrations 6.2 and 6.5

1 The Manifold Absolute Pressure (MAP) sensor in conjunction with a MAP sensor solenoid valve is used to monitor the intake manifold pressure and ambient barometric pressure changes resulting from changes in engine load and speed. The PCM uses the MAP sensor signal to control Evaporative emissions system. When the PCM applies voltage to the solenoid valve (ON) it switches the vacuum signal and allows the MAP sensor to monitor ambient barometric pressure. When voltage is not supplied to the solenoid valve (OFF) it switches the vacuum signal again and allows the MAP sensor to monitor intake manifold pressure. As the vacuum signal changes the MAP sensor converts this information into a voltage output signal and sends it to the PCM. The voltage will vary from 0.5 volts at closed throttle (high vacuum) and approximately 5.0 volts at wide open throttle (low vacuum). The voltage range values will vary slightly according to changes in altitude. The MAP sensor and the solenoid valve are mounted to the cowl in the engine compartment. The Electronic Engine Control (EEC) system can detect several different MAP sensor problems and set trouble codes to indicate the specific fault.

6

6.2 The MAP sensor (arrow) is mounted next to the brake fluid reservoir (1998 California models)

6.5 The MAP sensor solenoid valve is located next to throttle body

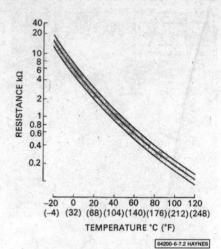

7.2 Intake Air Temperature (IAT) and Engine Coolant Temperature (ECT) sensors approximate temperature vs. resistance values

2   Check the reference voltage from the PCM to the MAP. Disconnect the MAP harness connector and install the probes of a voltmeter on the REF terminal (+) and the GND terminal (-). With the ignition key ON (engine not running), it should read approximately 5.0 volts (see illustration). If reference voltage is not available, there is a short or open circuit to the PCM or a defective PCM.

3   Next, check the MAP signal voltage with the engine not running. Disconnect the vacuum hose from the sensor. Connect the MAP sensor connector and backprobe the connector using pins. Check for voltage on the SIG terminal (+) and GND terminal (–) with the ignition key ON (engine not running). There should be approximately 3.2 to 4.8 volts. This checks signal voltage from the MAP sensor.

4   Reconnect the vacuum hose and check the MAP signal voltage as vacuum is applied to the sensor. Start the engine and observe that the voltage from the signal wire increases as the rpm are raised. Voltage should increase as vacuum decreases. At idle, engine vacuum is high and the MAP sensor signal should decrease to below 2.0 volts. After the engine rpm is raised, manifold vacuum drops and the voltage signal from the MAP sensor should increase.

5   If the signal voltage does not fluctuate as indicated in Step 4, disconnect the hose from the MAP sensor and check for vacuum from the solenoid valve. If vacuum is present five seconds after the engine has been started and the MAP sensor is receiving a REF signal as described in Step 2, replace the MAP sensor. If vacuum is not present, check the hoses to and from the solenoid valve for cracks and clogging. If the hoses are OK, disconnect the solenoid valve harness connector and check for battery voltage between the terminals with the ignition key ON (engine not running) (see illustration). If voltage is not present at the solenoid valve refer to the wiring diagrams and check the wiring harness for open circuits or a damaged harness. If battery voltage is present replace the solenoid valve and retest the system.

Replacement

6   Disconnect the cable from the negative terminal of the battery.

7   Disconnect the electrical connector from the MAP sensor and or solenoid valve.

8   Remove the nut or bolt that retains the MAP sensor and or solenoid valve to the cowl. Detach the vacuum hose(s) and remove the MAP sensor and or solenoid valve (see illustrations 6.2 and 6.5).

9   Installation is the reverse of removal.

7   Intake Air Temperature (IAT) sensor - check and replacement

Check

Refer to illustration 7.2

Note: *If the following tests indicate that a sensor is good, and not the cause of a driveability problem or DTC, check the wiring harness and connectors between the sensor and the PCM for an open or short circuit. If no problems are found, have the vehicle checked by a dealer service department or other qualified repair shop.*

1   The IAT sensor is a thermistor that changes resistance as temperature changes. The sensor is installed in the intake air duct to sense air temperature (see illustrations 1.1). As temperature increases, sensor resistance decreases and vice versa. The PCM uses this information to compute the intake temperature and fine tune fuel metering. A problem in the IAT sensor circuit will set a trouble code. The fault may be in the circuit wiring or connections or in the sensor itself.

2   With the engine cool, disconnect the IAT sensor and use an ohmmeter to measure resistance across the two terminals of the sensor. For example, at 68-degrees F the resistance should be approximately 2,100 to 2,900 ohms (see illustration).

3   Next, start the engine and warm it up until it reaches operating temperature. Turn the engine off, disconnect the sensor and measure the resistance again. It should be lower. If the sensor resistance doesn't

change as described, replace it.

4   If the resistance values of the sensor are correct, check for reference voltage from the PCM to the sensor connector. The open-circuit voltage at the sensor connector should be approximately 5 volts.

Replacement

Refer to illustration 7.5

5   Disconnect the electrical connector, then carefully remove the IAT sensor from the air intake duct (see illustration). Be careful not to damage any of the plastic parts.

6   Install and connect the new sensor.

8   Engine Coolant Temperature (ECT) sensor - check and replacement

Check

Refer to illustration 8.2

Note 1: *If the following tests indicate that a sensor is good, and not the cause of a driveability problem or DTC, check the wiring har-*

7.5 Disconnect the electrical connector, then carefully pull the IAT sensor (arrow) from the air intake duct

8.2 The ECT sensor (arrow) has a two-wire connector, and the plastic shell is usually gray

8.6 Wrap the threads of the ECT sensor with Teflon tape before installing it

magnetic field near the sensor to change this in turn varies the voltage signal to the PCM. This sensor is used only as the on-board diagnostic device for detecting engine misfire.

2   Disconnect the CKP sensor electrical connector and check the resistance between the crankshaft sensor terminals. It should be 432 to 528 ohms. If the resistance values are correct, refer to the wiring diagrams and check the wiring harness for open circuits or a damaged harness. **Note:** *The sensor terminals may be difficult to access due to the position of the exhaust manifold crossover tube. It may be easier to remove the sensor first (see Step 3) then perform the test indicated above.*

Replacement

Refer to illustration 9.3

3   Remove the CKP sensor heat shield retaining nut and the heat shield **(see illustration)**.
4   Disconnect the electrical connector from the CKP sensor.
5   Remove the crankshaft sensor retaining bolt and pull the sensor from the bellhousing.
6   Installation is the reverse of removal.

---

10 Camshaft position (CMP) sensor - check and replacement

Check

Refer to illustration 10.2

Note: *If the following tests indicate that a sensor is good, and not the cause of a driveability problem or DTC, check the wiring harness and connectors between the sensor and the PCM for an open or short circuit. If no problems are found, have the vehicle checked by a dealer service department or other qualified repair shop.*

1   The camshaft position (CMP) sensor monitors engine speed and piston position and relays this data to the computer which in turn controls the fuel injection duration (fuel injector on/off time) and ignition timing. The camshaft position sensor consists of a rotor plate and a wave forming circuit. The rotor plate has 360 slits for each degree, or one percent signal (engine speed signal) and six slits for the 120-degree camshaft position signal. Light Emitting Diodes (LED) and photo diodes are built into the wave forming circuit. When the rotor plate passes the space between the LED and the photo diode, the slits on the rotor plate continually cut the beam of light sent to the photo diode from the LED. They are then converted into on-off pulses by the wave forming circuit and then sent to the ECM.

2   Disconnect the distributor/CMP sensor connector and connect the positive (+) lead of your voltmeter to the B+ terminal of the harness connector; connect the meter negative (-) lead to the sensor connector ground terminal **(see illustration)**.

ness and connectors between the sensor and the PCM for an open or short circuit. If no problems are found, have the vehicle checked by a dealer service department or other qualified repair shop.

Note 2: *Before condemning an ECT sensor, check the coolant level in the system.*

1   Like the IAT sensor, the ECT sensor is a thermistor, which is a variable resistor that changes its resistance as temperature changes. The sensor is installed in the engine cooling system by the thermostat housing **(see illustrations 1.1)** to sense coolant temperature. As coolant temperature increases, sensor resistance decreases and vice versa. The PCM uses this information to compute the engine operating temperature. A problem in the ECT sensor circuit will set a trouble code. The fault may be in the circuit wiring or connections or in the sensor itself.

2   Some engines have two almost identical coolant temperature sensor units **(see illustration)** mounted next to each other. One is the sender for the instrument panel temperature gauge, the other is the ECT sensor for the Electronic Engine Control (EEC) system. The temperature sender connector for the instrument panel gauge has a tan or brown plastic body, the ECT sensor connector has a gray plastic body.

9.3 The CKP sensor (arrow) is located on the left side of the engine compartment on the transaxle bellhousing

3   Disconnect the ECT sensor and use an ohmmeter to measure resistance across the two terminals of the sensor. At 68 degrees F, resistance should be approximately 2,100 to 2,900 ohms **(see illustration 7.2)**.
4   Next, start the engine and warm it up until it reaches operating temperature. The resistance should be lower. For example, at 176-degrees F resistance should be 300 to 330 ohms.
5   If the resistance values of the sensor are correct, check for reference voltage from the PCM to the sensor connector. The open-circuit voltage at the sensor connector should be approximately 5 volts.

Replacement

Refer to illustration 8.6

Warning: *Wait until the engine is completely cool before performing this procedure.*

6   Before installing the new sensor, wrap the threads with Teflon sealing tape to prevent leakage and thread corrosion **(see illustration)**.
7   Disconnect the electrical connector, then unscrew the ECT sensor from the engine. Install the new sensor as quickly as possible to minimize coolant loss. Tighten the sensor securely and reconnect the electrical connector.
8   Check the coolant level as described in Chapter 1, adding some, if necessary. Start the engine and allow it to reach normal operating temperature, then check for coolant leaks. Check the coolant level in the expansion tank after the engine has warmed up and then cooled down again.

---

9 Crankshaft position (CKP) sensor - check and replacement

Check

1   The crankshaft position sensor is mounted on the transaxle bellhousing **(see illustration 1.1)**. It detects changes in crankshaft speed using a permanent magnet, core and coil. The changing gap causes the

6

10.2 The CMP sensor (arrow) is an integral part of the distributor

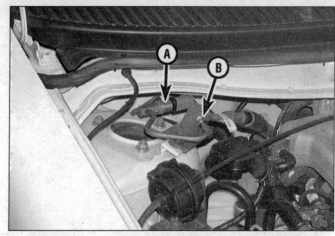

11.4 The Power Steering Pressure (PSP) switch (A) and the high pressure line junction block (B) are located in the right rear corner of the engine compartment

3   With the ignition ON (engine not running). The meter should read more than 10 volts or close to battery voltage.

4   Turn the ignition OFF and remove the distributor from the engine (see Chapter 5). Reconnect the distributor connector then use straight pins or other suitable probes to backprobe the CMP sensor signal (SIG) and ground (GND) terminals with the voltmeter. With the ignition ON (engine not running), slowly rotate the distributor shaft and check the voltage, the meter should fluctuate between 0 volts and 5 volts six times per revolution of the distributor shaft. This will test camshaft position 120 degree signal.

5   Turn the ignition OFF and backprobe the CMP sensor reference (REF) and ground (GND) terminals with the voltmeter. With the ignition ON (engine not running), slowly rotate the distributor shaft and check the voltage, the meter should fluctuate between 0 volts and 5 volts 360 times per revolution of the distributor shaft. This will test camshaft position 1 degree signal.

6   If the CMP sensor doesn't produce a pulsating voltage signal and battery voltage is present as indicated in Step 3, the sensor is defective. The camshaft position sensor is an integral part of the distributor, therefore if the CMP sensor is defective the distributor must be replaced (see Chapter 5).

11   Power Steering Pressure (PSP) switch - check and replacement

Check

Refer to illustration 11.4

1   The power steering pressure (PSP) switch is a normally open switch, mounted in the pressure line between the steering gear and the power steering pump. When steering system pressure reaches a high-pressure setpoint, the PSP switch closes and sends a signal to the PCM that the PCM uses to maintain engine idle speed during parking maneuvers. The Electronic Engine Control (EEC) system

can detect switch problems and set trouble codes to indicate specific faults.

2   Check the operation of the PSP switch if the engine stalls during parking or if the engine idles continuously at high rpm.

3   Refer to the wiring diagrams at the end of this manual to identify the functions of connector terminals.

4   Disconnect the PSP switch connector and connect an ohmmeter to the terminals on the switch body **(see illustration)**.

5   Start the engine and let it idle.

6   Turn the steering wheel to point the front wheels straight ahead and read the ohmmeter. It should indicate an open circuit (infinite resistance).

7   Turn the steering wheel to either side and watch the ohmmeter. The PSP switch should close as the wheel nears the steering stop on either side, and the meter should indicate continuity of close to zero ohms.

8   If the switch fails either test, replace it. If the switch is OK, troubleshoot the engine idle control operation if high idle speed or stalling problems continue.

Replacement

9   Disconnect the electrical connector from the switch. Using a suitable drain pan, unscrew the high pressure line from the junction block and drain the fluid from the line.

10   Using a back-up wrench on the high pressure line hex fitting, unscrew the switch from the high pressure line.

11   Install and connect the new switch. Refer to Chapter 10 and bleed air from the power steering system. Add fluid as required (see Chapter 1).

12   Oxygen sensor (O2S) - check and replacement

Check

Refer to illustrations 12.1 and 12.2
Note: *If the following tests indicate that a*

sensor is good, and not the cause of a driveability problem or DTC, check the wiring harness and connectors between the sensor and the PCM for an open or short circuit. If no problems are found, have the vehicle checked by a dealer service department or other qualified repair shop.

1   The oxygen in the exhaust reacts with the O2S to produce a voltage output that varies from 0.1 volt (high oxygen, lean mixture) to 0.9 volt (low oxygen, rich mixture). The upstream O2S in the exhaust system provides a feedback signal to the PCM that indicates the amount of leftover oxygen in the exhaust **(see illustration)**. The PCM monitors this variable voltage continuously to determine the required fuel injector pulse width and to control the engine air/fuel ratio. A mixture ratio of 14.7 parts air to 1 part fuel is the ideal ratio for minimum exhaust emissions, as well as the best combination of fuel economy and engine performance. Based on O2S signals, the PCM tries to maintain this air/fuel ratio of 14.7:1 at all times.

2   The downstream O2S in the exhaust system has no effect on PCM control of the air/fuel ratio. This sensor is identical to the upstream sensor and operates in the same way **(see illustration)**. The PCM uses the downstream signal, however, for the catalyst monitor system. A downstream O2S will produce a slower fluctuating voltage signal that reflects the lower oxygen content in the post-catalyst exhaust. **Note:** *1995 earlier models are only equipped with one (upstream) O2S while 1996 and later models are equipped with one upstream and one downstream O2S.*

3   An O2S produces no voltage when it is below its normal operating temperature of about 600-degrees F. During this warm-up period, the PCM operates in an open-loop fuel control mode. It does not use the O2S signal as a feedback indication of residual oxygen in the exhaust. Instead, the PCM controls fuel metering based on the inputs of other sensors and its own programs.

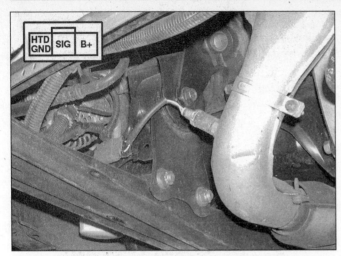

12.1 Location of the upstream oxygen sensor

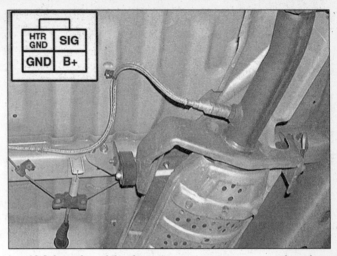

12.2 Location of the downstream oxygen sensor equipped on 1996 and later vehicles

4   Proper operation of an O2S depends on four conditions:

a) **Electrical** - *The low voltages generated by the sensor require good, clean connections which should be checked whenever a sensor problem is suspected or indicated.*

b) **Outside air supply** - *The sensor needs air circulation to the internal portion of the sensor. Whenever the sensor is installed, make sure the air passages are not restricted.*

c) **Proper operating temperature** - *The PCM will not react to the sensor signal until the sensor reaches approximately 600-degrees F. This factor must be considered when evaluating the performance of the sensor.*

d) **Unleaded fuel** - *Unleaded fuel is essential for proper operation of the sensor.*

5   The Electronic Engine Control (EEC) system can detect several different O2S problems and set DTC's to indicate the specific fault. When an O2S fault occurs that sets a DTC, the PCM will disregard the O2S signal voltage and revert to open-loop fuel control as described previously. **Note:** *Refer to the wiring diagrams in Chapter 12 to identify circuit functions by wire color coding for the following tests.* **Caution:** *The O2S is very sensitive to excessive circuit loads and circuit damage of any kind. For safest testing, install jumper wires in the O2S connector to connect your voltmeter. If jumper wires aren't available, carefully backprobe the wires in the connector shell with straight pins or similar devices. Do not puncture the O2S wires or try to backprobe the sensor itself. Use only a digital voltmeter to test an O2S.*

6   Turn the ignition ON but do not start the engine. Connect your voltmeter negative (-) lead to a good ground and the positive (+) lead to the SIG wire at the O2S connector **(see illustrations 12.1 and 12.2)**. The meter should read approximately 400 to 450 millivolts (0.40 to 0.45 volt). If it doesn't, trace and

repair the circuit from the sensor to the PCM.

7   Start the engine and let it warm up to normal operating temperature; again check the O2S signal voltage.

a) *Voltage from an upstream sensor should range from 100 to 900 millivolts (0.1 to 0.9 volt) and switch actively between high and low readings.*

b *Voltage from a downstream sensor should also read between 100 to 900 millivolts (0.1 to 0.9 volt) but it should not switch actively. The downstream O2S voltage may stay toward the center of its range (about 400 millivolts) or stay for relatively longer periods of time at the upper or lower limits of the range.*

8   Also check the battery voltage supply to the O2S heating circuits. Move the voltmeter negative (-) lead to the HTR GND terminal and the positive (+) lead to the B+ terminal of the sensor connector **(see illustrations 12.1 and 12.2)**. With the ignition ON, the meter should read more than 10 volts. Battery voltage is supplied to the sensors

through a relay for only about three seconds when the engine is not running. Have an assistant turn the ignition ON while you read the voltmeter. Refer to the wiring diagrams in Chapter 12 for more information on the circuits and relays.

Replacement

Refer to illustration 12.12

9   The exhaust pipe contracts when cool, and the O2S may be hard to loosen when the engine is cold. To make sensor removal easier, start and run the engine for a minute or two; then shut it off. Be careful not to burn yourself during the following procedure. Also observe these guidelines when replacing an O2S.

a) *The sensor has a permanently attached pigtail and electrical connector which should not be removed from the sensor. Damage or removal of the pigtail or electrical connector can harm operation of the sensor.*

b) *Keep grease, dirt and other contaminants away from the electrical connector and the louvered end of the sensor.*

c) *Do not use cleaning solvents of any kind on the oxygen sensor.*

d) *Do not drop or roughly handle the sensor.*

10   Raise the vehicle and place it securely on jackstands.

11   Disconnect the electrical connector from the sensor.

12   Using a suitable wrench or specialized O2 sensor socket, unscrew the sensor from the exhaust manifold **(see illustration)**.

13   Anti-seize compound must be used on the threads of the sensor to aid future removal. The threads of most new sensors will be coated with this compound. If not, be sure to apply anti-seize compound before installing the sensor.

14   Install the sensor and tighten it securely.

15   Lower the vehicle and reconnect the electrical connector for the sensor.

12.12 A special socket (available at many auto parts stores) that allows clearance for the wiring harness is required for oxygen sensor removal

6

13.2a The knock sensor sub-harness connector is located on the passenger side of the engine compartment next to the intake manifold (connector not visible in this photo)

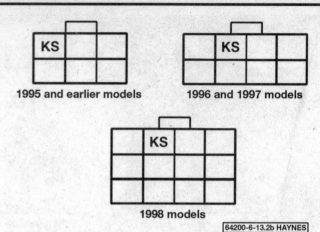

13.2b Knock Sensor (KS) sub-harness connector terminal identification - the knock sensor signal wire is typically white in color

13   Knock sensor - general information

Check

Refer to illustrations 13.2a and 13.2b

1   Knock sensors detect abnormal vibration in the engine. The knock control system is designed to reduce spark knock during periods of heavy detonation. This allows the engine to use maximum spark advance to improve driveability. Knock sensors produce AC output voltage which increases with the severity of the knock. The signal is fed into the PCM and the timing is retarded to compensate for the severe detonation.

2   To check a knock sensor, disconnect the KS sub-harness electrical connector **(see illustration)**. These type of sensors must be checked by observing voltage fluctuations with a voltmeter. Simply switch the voltmeter to the lowest AC voltage scale and connect the negative probe (-) to ground and the positive probe to the sensor terminal on the sub-harness connector **(see illustration)**. With the voltmeter connected to the sub-harness connector, tap sharply on the intake manifold with a hammer or similar device (this simulates the knock from the engine) and observe voltage fluctuations on the meter. If no voltage fluctuations can be detected, the sensor is bad and should be replaced with a new part.

Replacement

Refer to illustration 13.5

Warning: *Wait for the engine to cool completely before performing this procedure.*

3   Remove the upper and lower intake manifold (see Chapter 2A).

4   Remove the coolant crossover tube (see Chapter 3).

5   Unplug the electrical connector, then remove the sensor retaining bolt and the sensor from the engine block **(see illustration)**.

6   Install the new sensor, tighten the sensor retaining bolt to 18 to 25 ft-lbs. and connect the electrical connector.

7   Install the intake manifold (see Chapter 2A). Refill the cooling system as necessary (see Chapter 1).

14   Vehicle Speed Sensor (VSS) - check and replacement

Check

Refer to illustrations 14.1 and 14.5

Note: *If the following tests indicate that a sensor is good, and not the cause of a driveability problem or DTC, check the wiring harness and connectors between the sensor and the PCM for an open or short circuit. If no problems are found, have the vehicle checked by a dealer service department or other qualified repair shop.*

1   The vehicle speed sensor (VSS) is a pickup coil (variable-reluctance) sensor mounted on the transaxle case **(see illustration)**. It produces an AC voltage sine wave, the frequency of which is proportional to vehicle speed. The PCM uses the sensor input signal for several different engine and transmission control functions. The VSS signal also drives the speedometer on the instrument panel. A defective VSS can cause

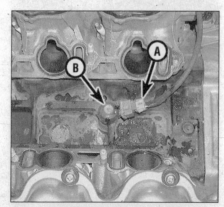

13.5 Unplug the electrical connector (A), then remove the knock sensor retaining bolt (B)

various driveability and transmission problems. The Electronic Engine Control (EEC) system can detect sensor problems and set trouble codes to indicate specific faults.

2   Refer to the wiring diagrams in Chapter 12 to identify the functions of connector terminals.

3   Disconnect the VSS connector and turn the ignition ON but do not start the engine. Use a voltmeter to check for voltage between the sensor connector and ground as shown on the wiring diagrams. Approximately 1 to 5 volts should be present on one of the sensor wires with the key ON and the engine OFF.

4   Remove the VSS from the vehicle as described below.

5   Connect a voltmeter to the VSS, set the meter on the AC scale, and check for voltage pulses as you spin the sensor drive gear **(see illustration)**.

6   If no pulsing voltage signal is produced, replace the sensor.

Replacement

Refer to illustration 14.10

7   Raise the vehicle and support it securely on jackstands.

8   Disconnect the electrical connector from the VSS.

9   Remove the hold-down bolt and clamp and remove the VSS from the transaxle **(see illustration 13.1)**.

10   Inspect the O-ring on the sensor **(see illustration)** and replace it if damaged. If you are installing a new sensor, use a new O-ring.

11   Installation is the reverse of removal.

15   Idle Air Control (IAC) valve – check and replacement

Check

Refer to illustration 15.2

1   The Idle Air Control (IAC) valve controls the amount of air that bypasses the throttle valve, which controls the engine idle speed.

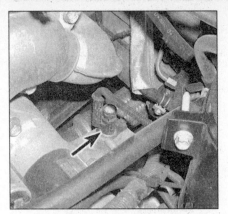

14.1 Location of the Vehicle Speed Sensor (VSS) (arrow)

14.5 Remove the VSS and check for a pulsing AC voltage signal as the VSS gear is turned

14.10 Inspect the sensor O-ring – install a new one if damaged or if your installing a new sensor

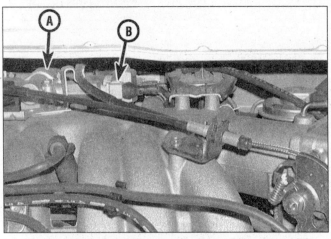

15.2 Location of the IAC valve (A) and the FIC solenoid (B) connectors – It will be necessary to reach under the cowl to access either connector

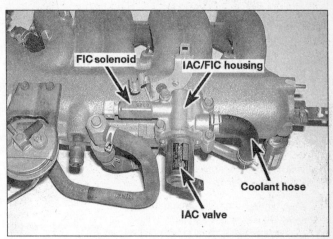

15.6 IAC/FIC housing component identification (manifold removed for clarity)

FIC solenoid
IAC/FIC housing
Coolant hose
IAC valve

This output actuator is mounted on the upper intake plenum (manifold) and is controlled by voltage pulses sent from the PCM (computer). The IAC valve within the body moves in or out, allowing more or less intake air into the system. To increase idle speed, the PCM extends the IAC valve from the seat and allows more air to bypass the throttle bore. To decrease idle speed, the PCM retracts the IAC valve towards the seat, reducing the air flow.

2   To check the system, first check for the voltage signal from the PCM. Turn the ignition key On (engine not running) and with a voltmeter, probe the wires of the IAC valve electrical connector (harness side). It should be approximately 10.5 to 12.5 volts **(see illustration)**. This indicates that the IAC valve is receiving the proper signal from the PCM.

3   If the IAC valve is receiving proper voltage, check the condition of the valve itself. Measure the resistance across the terminals on the IAC valve. There should be approximately 10 ohms. If the resistance is incorrect, replace the IAC valve.

4   Check the IAC valve for an internal short circuit. Measure resistance from either terminal to the IAC body. There should be 10,000 ohms or greater. If less, the internal circuitry

is grounding against the case; replace the IAC valve.

5   Next, remove the valve (proceed to Step 6) and check the pintle for excessive carbon deposits. If necessary, clean it with a soft rag. Also clean the valve housing to remove any deposits.

Replacement

Refer to illustrations 15.6 and 15.8

6   Unplug the electrical connector from the IAC valve and the FIC solenoid **(see illustration)**.

7   Remove the coolant hose from the IAC/FIC housing.

8   Remove the IAC/FIC housing mounting bolts, then detach the housing and the gasket from the upper intake manifold **(see illustration)**.

9   Remove the two IAC valve attaching screws and withdraw the valve from the IAC/FIC housing.

10   Check the condition of the O-ring. If it's hardened or deteriorated, replace it.

11   Clean the sealing surface and the bore of the IAC/FIC housing with a shop rag or soft cloth to ensure a good seal. **Caution:** *The IAC valve itself is an electrical component and*

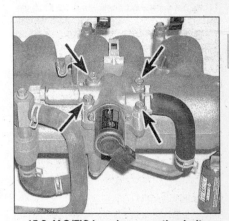

15.8 IAC/FIC housing mounting bolts (manifold removed for clarity)

must not be soaked in any liquid cleaner, as damage may result.

12   Position the new O-ring on the housing. Lubricate the O-ring with a light film of engine oil.

13   Install the IAC valve and tighten the screws securely.

14   The remainder of the installation is the reverse of the removal.

6

16   Fast Idle Control (FIC) solenoid – check and replacement

Check

1   The Fast Idle Control (FIC) solenoid helps maintain a constant idle speed due to increased engine loads when the air conditioning is operating. When the A/C is turned ON the PCM sends a ground signal to FIC solenoid relay which then completes the circuit to the solenoid. When the FIC solenoid is opened it allows additional air to enter the intake manifold thus raising the idle speed. A fault in this system will not be detected by the OBD system.

2   To check the system, first check for the voltage signal from the PCM. Start the engine, place the A/C and the blower fan switch in the ON position. Using a voltmeter, probe the wires of the FIC solenoid electrical connector (harness side). It should be approximately 10.5 to 12.5 volts **(see illustration 15.2)**. This indicates that the FIC solenoid is receiving the proper signal from the PCM.

3   If the FIC solenoid is receiving proper voltage, check the condition of the solenoid itself. Turn the engine OFF, then using a pair of fused jumper wires apply battery voltage to the solenoid terminals. The solenoid should make a distinct clicking sound. If the solenoid does not click, replace the FIC solenoid.

4   Next, remove the solenoid (proceed to Step 5) and check the plunger for free movement. If the plunger is seized or the detent spring is broken replace the solenoid.

Replacement

5   Unplug the electrical connector from the FIC solenoid.

6   Using a wrench remove the solenoid from the IAC/FIC housing **(see illustration 15.6)**.

7   Install a new copper washer onto the solenoid and tighten the solenoid securely.

8   The remainder of the installation is the reverse of removal.

17   Bypass Air (BPA) valve (1995 and earlier) – check and replacement

Check

1   The Bypass Air (BPA) valve is used on 1995 and earlier models to increase idle speed during cold weather conditions. It functions similar to a choke on a carbureted vehicle. The BPA consists of a heater, rotary shutter and a bimetal spring. When the outside temperature is cold the bimetal spring is in its normal retracted position. This allows air to bypass into the intake manifold thus raising the idle speed during warm-up. As the engine is started, current from the fuel pump relay is applied to the heater section of the

valve this causes the bimetal spring to expand, and slowly turn the rotary shutter which closes the bypass port. After warm up the valve remains closed until the engine is shut Off and the bimetal spring retracts.

2   To check the valve, first check for a voltage signal from the fuel pump relay. Start the engine, using a voltmeter, probe the wires of the BPA valve electrical connector (harness side). It should be approximately 10.5 to 12.5 volts. This indicates that the BPA valve is receiving the proper signal from the fuel pump relay.

3   If the BPA valve is receiving proper voltage, check the condition of the valve itself. Turn the engine OFF, measure the resistance across the terminals on the BPA valve. There should be approximately 70 to 80 ohms. If the resistance is incorrect, replace the BPA valve.

4   Next, remove the valve (proceed to Step 5) and check the valve for clogging or excessive carbon deposits. If necessary, clean it. Also clean the valve housing to remove any deposits.

Replacement

5   Remove the upper intake manifold (see Chapter 2A).

6   Detach the coolant hose from the BPA valve. Remove the mounting bolts and the BPA valve from the upper intake manifold.

7   Install a O-ring onto the valve and tighten the solenoid securely.

8   The remainder of the installation is the reverse of removal.

18   Positive Crankcase Ventilation (PCV) system

Refer to illustration 18.2

1   The Positive Crankcase Ventilation (PCV) system reduces hydrocarbon emissions by scavenging crankcase vapors. It does this by circulating fresh air from the air cleaner through the crankcase, where it

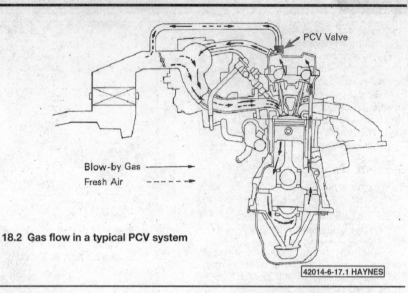

Blow-by Gas ⟶
Fresh Air ⤏

18.2   Gas flow in a typical PCV system

42014-6-17.1 HAYNES

mixes with blow-by gases and is then rerouted through a PCV valve to the intake manifold.

2   The PCV system consists of a replaceable PCV valve and the crankcase ventilation hoses **(see illustration)**.

3   To maintain idle quality, the PCV valve restricts the flow when the intake manifold vacuum is high. If abnormal operating conditions arise, the system is designed to allow excessive amounts of blow-by gases to flow back through the crankcase vent tube into the air cleaner to be consumed by normal combustion.

4   Checking and replacement of the PCV valve and filter is covered in Chapter 1.

19   Exhaust Gas Recirculation (EGR) system

General description

Refer to illustration 19.1

1   The EGR system is used to lower NOx (oxides of nitrogen) emission levels caused by high combustion temperatures. The EGR recirculates a small amount of exhaust gases into the intake manifold **(see illustration)**. The additional mixture lowers the temperature of combustion thereby reducing the formation of NOx compounds.

2   The EGR system is equipped with an EGR valve, an EGR Control (EGRC) solenoid valve which receives ported and manifold vacuum, an EGR Temperature (EGRT) sensor and a EGR Control Backpressure Transducer (EGRC-BPT) valve. The operation of the system is controlled by the PCM which operates the EGR control solenoid. The manifold vacuum system utilizes a vacuum tap in the air intake system positioned after the throttle valve. The ported vacuum control system uses a vacuum tap in the throttle body which is exposed to an increasing percentage of manifold vacuum as the throttle valve is

opened during acceleration.

3   The backpressure transducer (EGRC-BPT) valve monitors the exhaust backpressure as the engine rpm increases or decreases to aid in controlling the amount of the EGR vacuum signal. The EGR Temperature (EGRT) sensor is used to inform the PCM of temperature changes in the EGR passageways. This helps the PCM determine the EGR On/Off time.

System check

Refer to illustration 19.5

4   Check all hoses for cracks, kinks, broken sections and proper connection. Inspect all system connections for damage, cracks and leaks.

5   To check the EGR system operation, bring the engine up to operating temperature and, with the transmission in Neutral (parking brake set and tires blocked to prevent movement), allow it to idle for 70 seconds. Open the throttle so the engine speed is between 2,000 and 4,000 rpm and then allow it to close. The EGR valve stem should move if the control system is working properly. The test should be repeated several times. Movement of the stem indicates the control system is functioning correctly **(see illustration)**. If the EGR valve stem does not move, Check the vacuum signal to the EGR valve. Remove the hose from the valve, place your finger over the end of the hose and perform the procedure again. If no vacuum is present at the end of the hose check the hose connections to make sure they are not leaking or clogged, then check the EGRC solenoid (see Step 11).

Component checks

EGR Valve

6   With the engine Off, disconnect the vacuum hose and apply ten inches of vacuum with a hand-held vacuum pump to the EGR valve. If the valve opens, measure the valve travel to make sure it is approximately 1/8-inch. If the stem does not move, replace the EGR valve with a new one.

7   Next apply vacuum with the pump and then clamp the hose shut. The valve should stay open for 30 seconds or longer. If it does not, the diaphragm is leaking and the valve should be replaced with a new one.

8   Start the engine and apply vacuum to the valve. The engine should idle roughly when the valve is open. If it doesn't, the passages in the manifold are probably clogged. If there's no difference in idle quality with the valve open or closed the EGR valve is probably not closing all the way. Remove the EGR valve and inspect the poppet and seat area for deposits.

9   If the deposits are more than a thin film of carbon, the valve should be cleaned. To clean the valve, apply solvent and allow it to penetrate and soften the deposits, making sure that none gets on the valve diaphragm, as it could be damaged.

10   Use a vacuum pump to hold the valve open and carefully scrape the deposits from

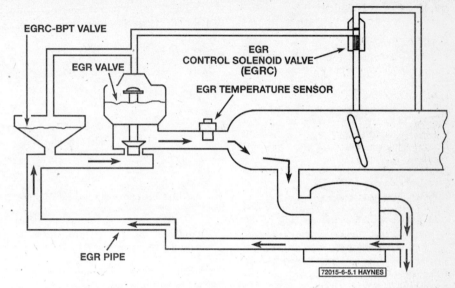

19.1 Schematic of the EGR system

the seat and poppet area with a tool. Inspect the poppet and stem for wear and replace the valve with a new one if wear is found.

EGR Control (EGRC) solenoid

Refer to illustration 19.11

11   First check for a vacuum signal to the solenoid with the engine running. If no vacuum is present check the hose to and from the solenoid for cracks and clogging. If the hose is OK, check the throttle body port for clogging. If vacuum is present at the solenoid, disconnect the solenoid valve harness connector and check for battery voltage between the terminals with the ignition key ON (engine not running) **(see illustration)**. Battery voltage should be present. If voltage is not present at the solenoid valve refer to the wiring diagrams and check the wiring har-

ness for open circuits or a damaged harness.

12   To check the operation of this EGR solenoid, disconnect the wiring from it and connect a ground wire to one of its terminals and fused battery voltage to the other terminal.

13   It should be possible to blow air through the two vacuum ports that are adjacent to one another when there is battery power applied, but impossible to do so when it is not energized with battery voltage.

EGR Control Backpressure Transducer (EGRC-BPT) valve

Refer to illustration 19.14

14   Locate the EGRC-BPT valve and plug one of the ports with a finger **(see illustration)**. Use a hand-held vacuum pump and apply vacuum to the valve. The valve should

19.5 The EGR valve (A) and EGRC-BPT valve (B) are located on the rear of the upper intake manifold - Be careful not to burn your hand when checking for EGR valve diaphragm movement - The diaphragm and rod beneath it should move when the engine is revved

19.11 The EGRC solenoid (arrow) is mounted below the throttle body (except 1998 California models)

6

19.14 Connect the vacuum pump hose to one port of the EGRC-BPT valve and apply vacuum. There should be a moderate amount of leakage

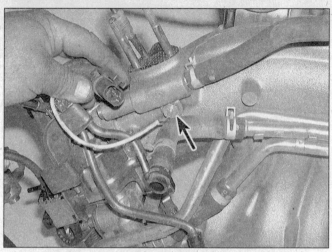

19.15 The EGRT sensor (arrow) is located below the EGR valve (manifold remove for clarity)

leak. **Note:** *It should stop leaking when pressure greater than 4 in-Hg is applied to the port under the valve (the valve must be removed from the engine to apply pressure at this point).* If the valve is defective replace it.

EGR Temperature (EGRT) sensor

Refer to illustration 19.15

15   Disconnect the harness connector for the EGR gas temperature sensor **(see illustration)** and measure the resistance of the sensor. Resistance should decrease as temperature increases and at 212-degrees F the sensor resistance should measure 77 to 94 K-ohms.

Component replacement

EGR valve

Refer to illustrations 19.17 and 19.18

16   Remove the air intake duct from the throttle body and air cleaner housing (see Chapter 4).

17   Detach the vacuum line from the EGR valve. Disconnect the EGR pipe nut **(see illustration)**.

18   Remove the EGR valve mounting fasteners **(see illustration)**.

19   Remove the EGR valve and gasket from the manifold. Discard the gasket.

20   With a wire wheel, buff the exhaust deposits from the EGR valve mounting surface on the manifold and, if you plan to use the same valve, the mounting surface of the valve itself. Look for exhaust deposits in the valve outlet. Remove deposit build-up with a screwdriver. **Caution:** *Never wash the valve in solvents or degreaser - both agents will permanently damage the diaphragm. Sandblasting is also not recommended because it will affect the operation of the valve.*

21   If the EGR passage contains an excessive build-up of deposits, clean it out with a wire wheel. Make sure that all loose particles are completely removed to prevent them from clogging the EGR valve or from being ingested into the engine.

22   If there are large amounts of deposits within the EGR valve, remove the EGR pipe from the exhaust manifold and clean out the deposits inside the tube. **Note:** *Remove the EGRC-BPT valve and pipe and clean any deposits from the passages.*

23   Installation is the reverse of removal.

EGR Control (EGRC) solenoid

24   Unplug the electrical connector from the solenoid.

25   Clearly label and detach the vacuum hoses.

26   Remove the solenoid mounting nut and remove the solenoid .

27   Installation is the reverse of removal.

EGR Temperature (EGRT) sensor

28   Remove the upper intake manifold (see Chapter 2A).

29   Unscrew the sensor from the manifold **(see illustration 19.15)**.

30   Apply anti-seize to the threads of the sensor before installing it.

31   Installation is the reverse of removal.

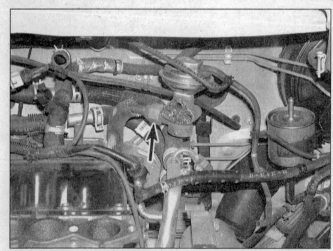

19.17 Remove the EGR flange nut (arrow) from the EGR valve using a large open end wrench (manifold remove for clarity)

19.18 The EGR valve is attached to the manifold by two studs (arrows) - remove the mounting nuts and detach the valve (manifold remove for clarity)

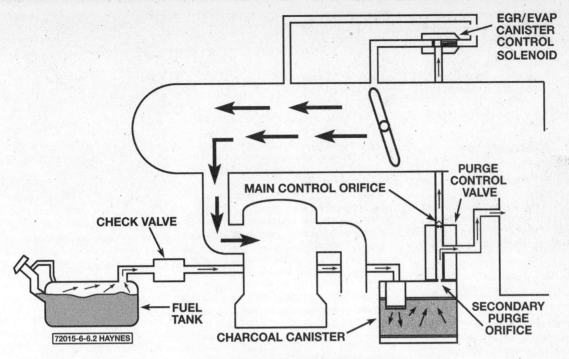

20.2a Schematic of the EVAP system

20   Evaporative Emissions Control System (EVAP)

General description

Refer to illustrations 20.2a and 20.2b

1   The fuel evaporative emissions control (EVAP) system absorbs fuel vapors and, during engine operation, releases them into the engine intake where they mix with the incoming air-fuel mixture.

2   The Evaporative Emission Control System (EVAP) consists of a charcoal-filled canister and the lines connecting the canister to the fuel tank, ported vacuum and intake manifold vacuum **(see illustration)**. The canister has a purge control valve mounted on it. On 1996 and later models, the purge control valve is operated by a (dual function) EGR and EVAP canister control solenoid. **Note: *1998 and later California models use a separate EVAP control solenoid not associated with the EGR system which is located on top of the throttle body (see illustration). They are also equipped with a canister purge volume control valve which is mounted under the cowl by the IAC/FIC housing.***

3   Fuel vapors are transferred from the fuel tank, throttle body and intake manifold to a canister where they are stored when the engine is not operating. When the engine is running, the fuel vapors are purged from the canister by the purge control valve (on top of charcoal canister). The gasses are consumed in the normal combustion process. Small amounts of fuel vapors flow into the intake manifold through the secondary purge orifice. When engine speed and vacuum increases on 1996 and later models, the PCM activates the EGR/EVAP canister control solenoid thereby routing fuel vapors into the intake manifold through the main and secondary purge orifices.

Check

Refer to illustration 20.10

4   Poor idle, stalling and poor driveability can be caused by a defective EGR/EVAP canister control solenoid valve, a damaged canister, split or cracked hoses or hoses connected to the wrong tubes.

5   Evidence of fuel loss or fuel odor can be caused by the following items: fuel leaking from fuel lines or a cracked or damaged canister, an inoperative fuel tank check valve, an inoperative purge valve, disconnected, misrouted, kinked, deteriorated or damaged vapor or control hoses or an improperly seated air cleaner or air cleaner gasket.

6   Inspect each hose attached to the canister for kinks, leaks and breaks along its entire length. Repair or replace as necessary.

7   Inspect the canister. If it is cracked or damaged, replace it.

8   Look for fuel leaking from the bottom of the canister. If fuel is leaking, replace the canister and check the hoses and hose routing.

9   Apply a short length of hose to the lower tube of the purge control valve and attempt to blow through it. Little or no air should pass into the canister (a small amount of air will pass because the canister has a constant purge hole).

10   With a hand-held vacuum pump, apply vacuum to the purge control valve signal tube (upper tube) **(see illustration)**.

6

20.2b 1998 and later California models use a separate EVAP control solenoid (arrow) located on the upper intake manifold under the cowl

20.10 Apply vacuum to the purge control valve (arrow) and make sure that it holds vacuum for at least 20 seconds

11   If the purge control valve does not hold vacuum for at least 20 seconds, the purge control valve is leaking and must be replaced.

12   If the diaphragm holds vacuum, apply battery voltage to the EGR and canister control solenoid valve and see if vacuum (vapors) are allowed to pass through to the intake system. **Note:** *Follow the testing procedure in Section 19 to test the EGR Control (EGRC) solenoid.*

Canister replacement

Refer to illustration 20.14

13   Clearly label, then detach, all vacuum lines from the canister.

14   Remove the canister mounting bolts and pull the canister assembly out **(see illustration)**.

15   Installation is the reverse of removal.

---

21   Catalytic converter

Note: *Because of a Federally mandated extended warranty which covers emissions-related components such as the catalytic converter, check with a dealer service department before replacing the converter at your own expense.*

General description

1   The catalytic converter is an emission control device added to the exhaust system to reduce pollutants from the exhaust gas stream. A single-bed converter design is used in combination with a three-way (reduction) catalyst. The catalytic coating on the three-way catalyst contains platinum and rhodium, which lowers the levels of oxides of nitrogen (NOx) as well as hydrocarbons (HC) and carbon monoxide (CO).

Check

2   The test equipment for a catalytic converter is expensive and highly sophisticated. If you suspect that the converter on your vehicle is malfunctioning, take it to a dealer or authorized emissions inspection facility for diagnosis and repair.

3   Whenever the vehicle is raised for servicing of underbody components, check the converter for leaks, corrosion, dents and other damage. Check the welds/flange bolts that attach the front and rear ends of the converter to the exhaust system. If damage is discovered, the converter should be replaced.

4   Although catalytic converters don't break too often, they can become plugged. The easiest way to check for a restricted converter is to use a vacuum gauge to diagnose the effect of a blocked exhaust on intake vacuum.

   a) Connect a vacuum gauge to an intake manifold vacuum source.
   b) Warm the engine to operating temperature, place the transaxle in park and apply the parking brake.
   c) Note and record the vacuum reading at idle.

20.14 EVAP canister mounting bolt (arrow)

   d) Open the throttle until the engine speed is about 2000 rpm.
   e) Release the throttle quickly and record the vacuum reading.
   f) Perform the test three more times, recording the reading after each test.
   g) If the reading after the fourth test is more than one in-Hg lower than the reading recorded at idle, the catalytic converter, muffler or exhaust pipes may be plugged or restricted.

Component replacement

5   Refer to the exhaust system servicing section in Chapter 4.

Chapter 7
Automatic transaxle

Contents

Specifications

General

Fluid type and capacity	See Chapter 1

Torque specifications

	Ft-lbs (unless otherwise indicated)
Transaxle range sensor mounting bolts	27 in-lbs
Parking brake pedal mounting bolts and nuts	71 to 97 in-lbs
Shift cable grommet nuts	77 to 88 in-lbs
Shift cable lock nut	96 to 132 in-lbs
Shift lock solenoid mounting screws	62 to 97 in-lbs
Transaxle-to-engine bolts	
Upper bolts	29 to 36
Side bolts	29 to 36
Lower bolts	22 to 30
Transaxle ground strap mounting bolt	20 to 22
Torque converter-to-driveplate bolts	33 to 43

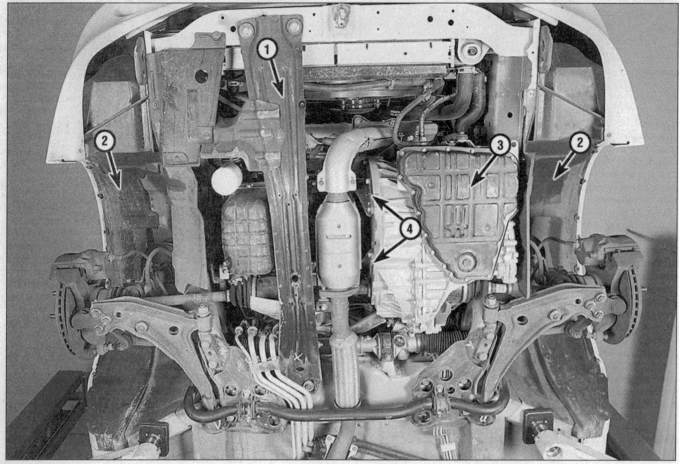

1.2 An underside view of the automatic transaxle and related components (1996 Villager shown)

1	Center member	3	Transaxle oil pan
2	Inner fender splash shield	4	Transaxle-to-engine braces

1 General information

Refer to illustration 1.2

All models covered by this manual are equipped with an automatic transaxle.

The automatic transaxle is an electronically controlled, 4-speed unit **(see illustration)**. The automatic transaxles are designated 4F20E. The transaxle model number is stamped onto a plate on the transaxle. Refer to *Vehicle identification numbers* at the front of this manual for the location of the plate. **Note:** *These transaxle designations are Ford factory letters and numbers. Mazda uses their own equivalent designations; the Ford 4F20E is the Mazda RE4FO4A. Be sure to consult with a dealer parts department or other qualified auto parts counterperson when ordering replacement transaxle parts.*

The 4F20E automatic transaxle is an electronically controlled transaxle featuring a combination of electronic and mechanical systems. The transaxle includes a lock-up torque converter system controlled by the PCM (computer) for economy and quietness, a self-diagnosis system, an overdrive ON/OFF button for fourth gear operation and

sensors and output actuators that transmit and receive data from the PCM.

These models also are equipped with two different driving modes to accommodate different driving conditions; the Economy Mode and the Power Mode. With the Power E-AT switch OFF, the transaxle shifts early, providing better fuel economy. In Power Mode, the transaxle delays the upshifts to allow the engine to develop higher rpm levels and consequently more power and torque. The shifting is controlled by transaxle control solenoids actuated in response to the PCM (computer) commands.

Due to the complexity of the clutches and the hydraulic control system, and because of the special tools and expertise required to perform an automatic transaxle overhaul, it should not be undertaken by the home mechanic. Therefore, the procedures in this Chapter are limited to general diagnosis, routine maintenance, adjustment and transaxle removal and installation.

If the transaxle requires major repair work, it should be left to a dealer service department or an automotive or transmission repair shop. You can, however, remove and install the transaxle yourself and save the

expense, even if the repair work is done by a transmission shop (but be sure a proper diagnosis has been made before removing the transaxle).

2 Diagnosis - general

Note: *Automatic transaxle malfunctions may be caused by five general conditions: poor engine performance, improper adjustments, hydraulic malfunctions, mechanical malfunctions or malfunctions in the computer or its signal network. Diagnosis of these problems should always begin with a check of the easily repaired items: fluid level and condition (see Chapter 1), shift control cable adjustment and transaxle range sensor adjustment. Next, perform a road test to determine if the problem has been corrected or if more diagnosis is necessary. If the problem persists after the preliminary tests and corrections are completed, additional diagnosis should be done by a dealer service department or transmission repair shop. Refer to the Troubleshooting section at the front of this manual for information on symptoms of transaxle problems.*

Transaxle self-diagnosis system

1   The automatic transaxle is equipped with a self-diagnosis system that operates completely independent of the Powertrain Control Module (PCM). This system consists of various sensors and output actuators mounted on the engine and transaxle that respond to driving conditions during vehicle operation. Sensors include the transaxle fluid temperature sensor, range sensor, Brake On/Off (BOO) switch, throttle position sensor, vehicle speed sensor, pulse signal generator and idle switch. Output actuators include the shift solenoid assembly, which is mounted in the transaxle valve body, and the OverDrive (OD) control switch. This self-diagnostic system is also equipped with a separate computer called the Transaxle Control Module (TCM). The TCM is mounted next to the PCM (see Chapter 6).

2   The self-diagnosis system on early models flash vehicle specific codes using the O/D OFF light on the dash while on later models, it is necessary to install a special SCAN tool that will display codes similar to the OBD-II codes for the powertrain self-diagnosis system. Refer to Chapter 6 for additional information on the On Board Diagnostic system. In the event the self-diagnosis system for the transaxle must be accessed for troubleshooting purposes, have a dealer service department or other qualified automotive repair facility extract the codes.

Preliminary checks

3   Drive the vehicle to warm the transaxle to normal operating temperature.

4   Check the fluid level as described in Chapter 1:

 a) *If the fluid level is unusually low, add enough fluid to bring the level within the designated area of the dipstick, then check for external leaks (see below).*

 b) *If the fluid level is abnormally high, drain off the excess, then check the drained fluid for contamination by coolant. The presence of engine coolant in the automatic transmission fluid indicates that a failure has occurred in the internal radiator walls that separate the coolant from the transmission fluid (see Chapter 3).*

 c) *If the fluid is foaming, drain it and refill the transaxle, then check for coolant in the fluid, or a high fluid level.*

5   Check the engine idle speed. **Note:** *If the engine is malfunctioning, do not proceed with the preliminary checks until it has been repaired and runs normally.*

6   Check the throttle control cable for freedom of movement (see Section 4).

7   Inspect the shift control linkage (see Section 4). Make sure that it's properly adjusted and that the linkage operates smoothly.

Fluid leak diagnosis

8   Most fluid leaks are easy to locate visually. Repair usually consists of replacing a seal or gasket. If a leak is difficult to find, the following procedure may help.

9   Identify the fluid. Make sure it's transmission fluid and not engine oil or brake fluid (automatic transmission fluid is a deep red color).

10   Try to pinpoint the source of the leak. Drive the vehicle several miles, then park it over a large sheet of cardboard. After a minute or two, you should be able to locate the leak by determining the source of the fluid dripping onto the cardboard.

11   Make a careful visual inspection of the suspected component and the area immediately around it. Pay particular attention to gasket mating surfaces. A mirror is often helpful for finding leaks in areas that are hard to see.

12   If the leak still cannot be found, clean the suspected area thoroughly with a degreaser or solvent, then dry the area.

13   Drive the vehicle for several miles at normal operating temperature and varying speeds. After driving the vehicle, visually inspect the suspected component again.

14   Once the leak has been located, the cause must be determined before it can be properly repaired. If a gasket is replaced but the sealing flange is bent, the new gasket will not stop the leak. The bent flange must be straightened.

15   Before attempting to repair a leak, check to make sure that the following conditions are corrected or they may cause another leak. **Note:** *Some of the following conditions cannot be fixed without highly specialized tools and expertise. Such problems must be referred to a transmission shop or a dealer service department.*

Gasket leaks

16   Check the right side cover periodically. Make sure the bolts are tight, no bolts are missing, the gasket is in good condition and the cover is not damaged.

17   If the leak is from the right side cover area, the bolts may be too tight, the sealing surface of the transaxle housing may be damaged, the gasket may be damaged or the transaxle casting may be cracked or porous. If sealant instead of gasket material has been used to form a seal between the cover and the transaxle housing, it may be the wrong sealant.

Seal leaks

18   If a transaxle seal is leaking, the fluid level or pressure may be too high, the vent may be plugged, the seal bore may be damaged, the seal itself may be damaged or improperly installed, the surface of the shaft protruding through the seal may be damaged or a loose bearing may be causing excessive shaft movement.

19   Make sure the dipstick tube seal is in good condition and the tube is properly seated. Periodically check the area around the speedometer gear or sensor for leakage. If transmission fluid is evident, check the O-ring for damage.

Case leaks

20   If the case itself appears to be leaking, the casting is porous and will have to be repaired or replaced.

21   Make sure the oil cooler hose fittings are tight and in good condition.

Fluid comes out vent pipe or fill tube

22   If this condition occurs, the transaxle is overfilled, there is coolant in the fluid, the case is porous, the dipstick is incorrect, the vent is plugged or the drain-back holes are plugged.

3   Shift indicator cable - adjustment

Warning: *The models covered by this manual are equipped with Supplemental Restraint systems (SRS), more commonly known as airbags. Always disable the airbag system before working in the vicinity of any airbag system components to avoid the possibility of accidental deployment of the airbag, which could cause personal injury (see Chapter 12).*

1   If equipped with a tilt steering column, unscrew the handle and shaft from the column.

2   Remove the steering column cover from the lower section of the steering column (see Chapter 11).

3   Position the selector lever into Neutral.

4   Turn the indicator adjustment wheel until the indicator lines up with the N on the instrument cluster. The adjustment wheel is located just forward of the ignition switch.

5   Select each gear position and check that the shift indicator is centered on each gear position; P, R, N, D, 1, 2.

6   Install the shift column cover.

7   Install the tilt lever back into the steering column.

4   Shift cable - removal, installation and adjustment

Warning: *The models covered by this manual are equipped with Supplemental Restraint systems (SRS), more commonly known as airbags. Always disable the airbag system before working in the vicinity of any airbag system components to avoid the possibility of accidental deployment of the airbag, which could cause personal injury (see Chapter 12).*

Removal

Refer to illustrations 4.5, 4.7 and 4.8

1   Remove the coolant reservoir (see Chapter 3).

2   Working under the dash in the driver's compartment, remove the mounting nuts and bolts from the parking brake pedal assembly and position the brake assembly off to the side. Refer to Chapter 9 for additional details.

3   Remove the shift cable grommet bolts directly at the firewall and separate the cable

7

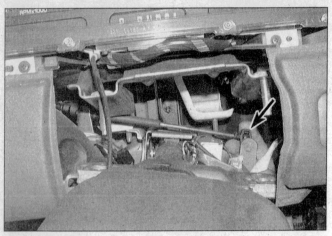

4.5 Carefully pry the shift cable end from the selector lever (arrow)

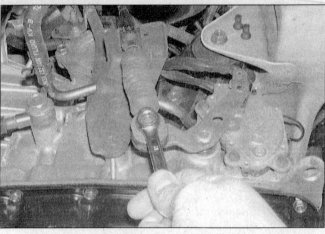

4.7 Remove the shift cable lock nut from the range sensor linkage

and bracket from the firewall.

4   Remove the steering column covers (see Chapter 11), remove the steering column mounting bolts and lower the steering column (see Chapter 10).

5   Working in the dash area above the steering column, pry the shift cable end from the selector shaft **(see illustration)**.

6   Squeeze the lock tabs on the shift cable and remove the cable from the bracket.

7   Raise the vehicle and support it securely on jackstands. Remove the undervehicle splash shield **(see illustration 10.11)**, then remove the nut from the shift cable end **(see illustration)** and separate the shift cable from the transaxle shift lever.

8   Use a small screwdriver to disengage the shift cable locking pin from the shift cable bracket **(see illustration)**.

9   Remove the shift cable from the bracket.

10   Remove the shift cable from the vehicle.

Installation

11   Insert the shift cable through the opening in the firewall.

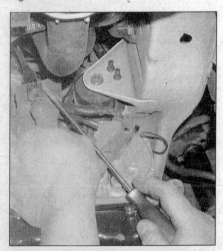

4.8 Use a punch or screwdriver tip to disengage the shift cable locking pin

12   Working in the dash area of the driver's compartment, pull the cable and insert the cable end onto the selector lever.

13   Working in the transaxle area, install the shift cable onto the transaxle shift lever. Make sure the shift cable locks into the bracket.

14   Install the coolant reservoir (see Chapter 3).

15   Working on the firewall, position the shift cable grommet onto the two studs and tighten the nuts to the torque listed in this Chapter's Specifications.

16   Move the shift lever to each gear to verify the correct shifting position.

Adjustment

17   Raise the vehicle and support it securely on jackstands.

18   Remove the splash shield from under the engine **(see illustration 10.11)**. Remove the left side inner splash shield.

19   Shift the selector lever into the PARK position. **Note:** *Be sure the shift indicator cable is properly adjusted (see Section 3).*

20   Loosen the shift cable lock nut on the range sensor linkage arm.

21   Pull down on the shift cable to remove the slack. Tighten the shift cable lock nut to the torque listed in this Chapter's Specifications.

22   Start the engine and check the shift lever in all gears.

**5   Shift Interlock system -
    description, check and
    component replacement**

Warning: *The models covered by this manual are equipped with Supplemental Restraint systems (SRS), more commonly known as airbags. Always disable the airbag system before working in the vicinity of any airbag system components to avoid the possibility of accidental deployment of the airbag, which could cause personal injury (see Chapter 12).*

Description

1   Vehicles equipped with an automatic transaxle have an interlock system to prevent unintentional shifting. The key interlock system simultaneously activates the shift lock solenoid with a shift lock rod.

2   The key interlock system prevents the ignition key from being removed from the ignition switch unless the shift lever is in the PARK position. If you insert the key when the shift lever is in any position other than PARK, a solenoid is activated, making it impossible for you to remove the key until the shift lever is moved to the PARK position.

3   The shift lock system prevents the shift lever from moving from the PARK position into the REVERSE or DRIVE positions unless the brake pedal is depressed. Nor can the shift lever be shifted when the brake pedal and the accelerator pedal are depressed at the same time.

4   The shift interlock system varies slightly between years. 1993 through 1995 shift interlock systems consists of the transaxle range sensor, the shift lock solenoid, the shift lock relay, the Brake On/Off (BOO) switch and the circuit fuses. 1996 and later shift interlock systems consists of the transaxle range sensor, the shift lock solenoid and the Brake On/Off (BOO) switch. The transaxle range sensor is located on the side of the transaxle. The check and replacement procedures for the range sensor are in Section 6. The shift lock solenoid is mounted on the top section of the steering column. The shift lock relay is located behind the left side instrument panel to the right of the steering column. Refer to Chapter 12 for relay locations and testing procedures. Follow the tests for the shift lock solenoid in this section. The Brake On/Off switch is located near the brake pedal. The check and replacement procedure for the BOO switch is in Chapter 9. **Note:** *1996 and later Quest models are equipped with a shift lock rod that actuates the shift lock solenoid when the key is turned. Other models incorporate a modular steering column that houses the ignition lock and the shift lock solenoid.*

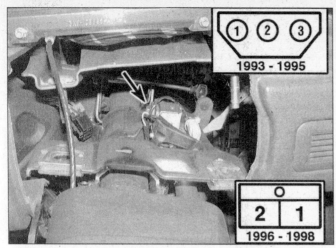

5.11 Disconnect the shift lock solenoid connector (arrow) and check for battery voltage to the shift lock solenoid with the ignition key ON (engine not running)

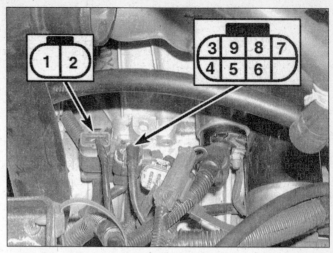

6.2 Disconnect the electrical connectors (arrows) to test the transaxle range sensor

Check

5   The following checks are simple tests of the shift lock solenoid. This component check assumes that the other components of the Shift Interlock System (the transaxle range sensor, the shift lock relay and the BOO switch) have all been tested. If all the component checks are in order, further testing of the interlock system should be left to a dealer service department or other qualified repair shop.

Shift lock solenoid

Refer to illustration 5.11
6   Check the condition of the 10A ELECTRON IGN and the 15A STOP LAMP fuses (1993 through 1995) or the 10A RELAYS fuse (1996 and later). Refer to Chapter 12 for the exact location. Replace the fuses if necessary, If the fuse(s) are blown, check the circuit from the shift lock solenoid to the fuse panel. Refer to the wiring diagrams at the end of Chapter 12. Repair the wiring harness if necessary. If the fuses are OK, check the shift lock solenoid.
7   Remove the trim covers from the lower section of the instrument panel (see Chapter 11).
8   Remove the steering column covers (see Chapter 11).
9   Remove the steering column mounting bolts and lower the steering column (see Chapter 10).
10   Disconnect the electrical connector from the OverDrive ON/OFF switch.
11   Check for power to the shift lock solenoid **(see illustration)**.
  a) On 1993 through 1995 models, with the ignition key ON (engine not running), check for battery voltage on terminal number 3. Battery voltage should be present. If not, check the circuit to the ignition switch for damage. Refer to the wiring schematics at the end of Chapter 12 for additional information.
  b) On 1996 and later models, with the ignition key ON (engine not running) and the brake pedal released, check for battery voltage on terminal number 2. Battery voltage should be present. Depress the brake pedal and voltage should be approximately 1 volt.
12   On 1993 through 1995 models, with the ignition key OFF, check for battery voltage to the shift lock relay. Battery voltage should be present at all times. If there is no voltage, check the circuit to the 15A ELECTRON IGN fuse.
13   If battery voltage is available on both tests, and the shift lock solenoid does not actuate the lock position, replace the shift lock solenoid.

Component replacement

Shift lock solenoid

14   Remove the steering column covers (see Chapter 11).
15   Remove the lower dashboard trim panels on the driver's side (see Chapter 11).
16   Remove the heater duct (see Chapter 3).
17   Remove the steering column bolts and lower the steering column to access the shift lock solenoid.
18   On 1996 and later Quest models, disconnect the shift lock rod (see Steps 26 through 35) from the ignition key.
19   Disconnect the ignition switch electrical connector (see Chapter 12).
20   On 1996 and later Quest models, disconnect the shift control tube mounting bolts and remove the shift control tube from the steering column.
21   Disconnect the shift lock solenoid electrical connector **(see illustration 5.11)**.
22   Remove the shift lock solenoid bolts.
23   On 1996 and later Quest models, remove the park position switch mounting bolts and separate the switch from the steering column.
24   Remove the shift lock solenoid from the steering column assembly.
25   Installation is the reverse of removal.

Shift lock rod (1996 through 1998 Nissan Quest models)

26   Remove the steering column covers (see Chapter 11).
27   Turn the ignition switch to ACC position.
28   The shift lock rod is a two piece assembly that is joined together by a slider. Squeeze the tabs and unlock the slider.
29   Remove the shift lock rod from the key interlock rod which is attached to the key lock cylinder.
30   Remove the retaining clip from the shift lock rod and the shift lock solenoid linkage.
31   Installation is the reverse of removal.
32   Place the selector into Park. Turn the ignition key to ACC.
33   Insert shift lock rod into slider.
34   Hold the key interlock rod and push toward the shift lock rod to join components. Do not hold the shift lock rod while installing the assembly.
35   Test the operation of the shift lock rod by switching the ignition key and observing the shift lock rod activate the shift lock solenoid.

6   Transaxle range sensor - check, adjustment and replacement

Check

Refer to illustrations 6.2 and 6.3
1   The range sensor prevents accidental movement caused by engine cranking with the shift selector in reverse or forward gears. The range sensor is wired in series with the starter relay and only allows the starter motor to crank when the transaxle is in Park or Neutral. Refer to Chapter 5 for the starter relay check and replacement procedure.
2   Disconnect the electrical connectors for the transaxle range sensor **(see illustration)**. There are two connectors associated with the range sensor; the 8-pin connector and the 2-pin connector. The 2-pin connector governs

7

SWITCH POSITION	CONTINUITY BETWEEN
Park	1 and 2; 3 and 4
Reverse	3 and 5
Neutral	1 and 2; 3 and 6
Drive	3 and 7
2	3 and 8
1	3 and 9

64200-7-6.3 HAYNES

6.3 Continuity chart for the transaxle range sensor

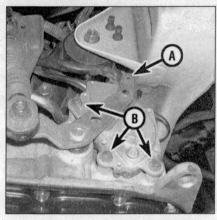

6.9 Insert an appropriately sized drill bit through the hole in the linkage (A), into the range sensor alignment hole, then tighten the range sensor mounting bolts (B) to the correct torque

the starter circuit.

3   Move the shift lever into each position and check for continuity between the indicated terminals in accordance with the accompanying table **(see illustration)**.

4   If the continuity isn't as designated in the table, attempt to adjust the switch. If the switch can't be adjusted to obtain the proper continuity, replace the switch.

Adjustment

Refer to illustration 6.9

5   Raise the vehicle and support it securely on jackstands.

6   Remove the splash shield from under the engine. Remove the left side inner splash shield.

7   Shift the selector lever into the Neutral position.

8   Remove the shift cable lock nut on the range sensor linkage arm.

9   Loosen the switch mounting bolts slightly. Install a drill bit through the hole in the lever and into the alignment hole in the range sensor **(see illustration)**.

10   Tighten the mounting bolts to the torque listed in this Chapter's Specifications. Install the connector and shift cable.

11   Follow the continuity chart and make sure that continuity exists on the designated terminals **(see illustration 6.3)**.

12   Install the shift cable. The remaining installation is the reverse of removal.

Replacement

13   Raise the vehicle and support it securely on jackstands.

14   Disconnect the range sensor electrical connectors **(see illustration 6.2)**.

15   Place the shift lever in the Neutral position.

16   Remove the transaxle range sensor mounting bolts.

17   Install the new switch onto the control shaft. Make sure the switch remains in the Neutral position when you tighten the bolts.

18   Adjust the range sensor (see Steps 5 through 12).

19   Make sure the engine starts only when the shift lever is in the Neutral or Park position.

7   Transaxle Control Switch (TCS) - check and replacement

1   The Transaxle Control Switch (TCS) located on the shift lever allows the driver to turn the Overdrive capability On or Off.

Check

Refer to illustrations 7.2 and 7.6

2   Pull the cover, located on the end of the shift lever, from the TCS **(see illustration)**.

3   Use a voltmeter to check for battery voltage at one of the pin sockets in the end of

the shift lever, with the ignition key in the On position (engine not running). Battery voltage should be present. If battery voltage is not present, check the transaxle control switch circuit and the fuses. Refer to the wiring diagrams at the end of Chapter 12.

4   With an ohmmeter, check the continuity across the pins of the TCS. There should be no continuity only when the switch is ON.

5   Switch the TCS to the OFF position and confirm that continuity does exist.

6   The TCS simply pulls out of the end of the shift lever. To replace it, push the new switch into the lever, making sure the pins are aligned with the sockets. Press the cover back on **(see illustration)**.

8   Transaxle oil cooler - general information

A transaxle oil cooler is incorporated into the left side radiator tank. If it develops a leak, which would be indicated by coolant in the transaxle fluid or transaxle fluid in the engine coolant, remove the radiator and take it to a radiator repair shop for service (see Chapter 3). Also, be sure to change the transaxle fluid and filter, and the engine coolant if necessary, if a leak was present.

9   Driveaxle oil seals - replacement

Refer to illustration 9.4

1   Oil leaks frequently occur due to wear of the driveaxle oil seals. Replacement of these seals is relatively easy, since the repair can be performed without removing the transaxle from the vehicle.

2   The driveaxle oil seals are located at the sides of the transaxle, where the driveaxles are attached. If leakage at the seal is suspected, raise the vehicle and support it securely on jackstands. If the seal is leaking,

7.2 Remove the cap from the end of the Transaxle Control Switch

7.6 Remove the TCS and check for continuity

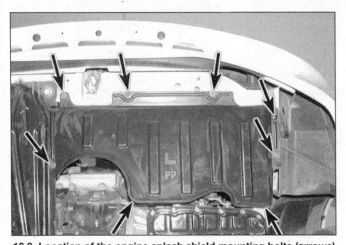

9.4 Removing a driveaxle oil seal with a seal removal tool and a hammer

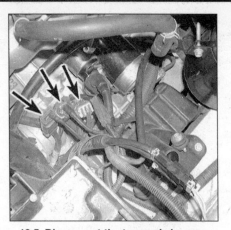

10.5 Disconnect the transaxle harness connectors (arrows) from the top section of the transaxle

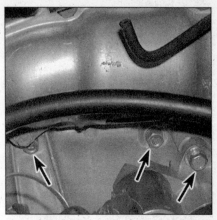

10.7 Location of the upper transaxle mounting bolts (arrows)

10.9 Location of the engine splash shield mounting bolts (arrows) - the two lower bolts are not visible

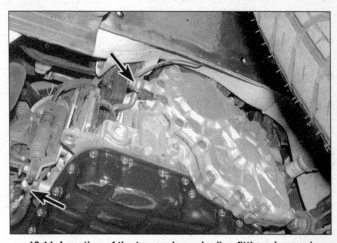

10.11 Location of the transaxle cooler line fittings (arrows)

lubricant will be found on the sides of the transaxle, below the seals.

3   Refer to Chapter 8 and remove the driveaxle(s).

4   Using a screwdriver, prybar or seal removal tool, carefully pry the oil seal out of the transaxle bore **(see illustration)**.

5   Using a seal driver, a large section of pipe or a large deep socket (slightly smaller than the outside diameter of the seal) as a drift, install the new oil seal. Drive it into the bore squarely and make sure it's completely seated. Coat the seal lip with transaxle lubricant.

6   Install the driveaxle(s). Be careful not to damage the lip of the new seal.

10   Automatic transaxle - removal and installation

Removal

Refer to illustrations 10.5, 10.7, 10.9, 10.11, 10.15, 10.19, 10.20a, 10.20b and 10.23

1   Disconnect the negative cable and then the positive cable from the battery. Remove the battery and the battery tray (see Chap-

ter 5). **Caution:** *If the stereo in your vehicle is equipped with an anti-theft system, make sure you have the correct activation code before disconnecting the battery.*

2   Remove the air intake duct and the air cleaner housing (see Chapter 4).

3   Remove the starter motor (see Chapter 5).

4   Disconnect the transaxle ground cable.

5   Disconnect the transaxle harness connectors from the top of the transaxle **(see illustration)**.

6   Disconnect the electrical connector for the vehicle speed sensor (VSS) (see Chapter 6).

7   Remove the upper transaxle-to-engine mounting bolts **(see illustration)**.

8   Raise the vehicle and support it securely on jackstands. Remove the front wheels.

9   Remove the splash shield from below the engine compartment **(see illustration)**.

10   Disconnect the shift cable from the transaxle (see Section 4).

11   Disconnect the transaxle fluid cooler lines from the transaxle **(see illustration)**. Plug the lines and fittings to prevent spillage and contamination.

12   Support the engine from above using an

10.15 **Remove the exhaust pipe bracket bolts (arrows)**

engine support fixture or an engine hoist and chain (see Chapter 2B).

13   Drain the transaxle fluid (see Chapter 1).

14   Remove the catalytic converter (see Chapter 6).

15   Unbolt the exhaust pipe bracket from the engine and the center member **(see illustration)**.

7

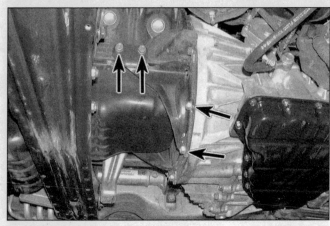

10.19 Location of the transaxle brace bolts (arrows)

10.20a Location of the engine-to-transaxle side bolt (arrow) as viewed from the rear

16   Disconnect the control arms from the steering knuckles (see Chapter 10).

17   Remove the bolts from the intermediate shaft bearing support (see Chapter 8). Pry the right driveaxle and the intermediate shaft from the transaxle as a complete unit (see Chapter 8). Support the intermediate shaft out of the way with a piece of wire.

18   Pry the left driveaxle out of the transaxle (see Chapter 8). Support the driveaxle out of the way with a piece of wire.

19   Remove the transaxle-to-engine brace mounting bolts **(see illustration)**.

20   Remove the transaxle-to-engine lower bolts **(see illustrations)**.

21   Disconnect the valve body wiring harness from the side of the transaxle.

22   Remove the exhaust bracket assembly from the lower section of the transaxle. Remove the torque converter access plate.

23   Remove the torque converter bolts **(see illustration)**.

24   Place a transaxle jack under the transaxle and secure it with safety chains. Raise the transaxle just enough to take the weight off the engine mounts.

25   Remove the left front and left rear transaxle mount and mount bracket (center member). Refer to Chapter 2A for additional information on the mounts.

26   Disconnect the transaxle breather tube from the transaxle breather.

27   Make a final check that all wires and hoses have been disconnected from the transaxle, then carefully pull the transaxle and jack away from the engine. Lower the transaxle and remove it from under the vehicle.

28   With the transaxle removed, inspect the torque converter and torque converter seal and other transaxle seals (side cover seal, VSS seal, etc.) for damage and wear. Replace the torque converter seal and torque converter if necessary.

Installation

29   If removed, install the torque converter into the transaxle. Make sure it is fully seated by pushing in and turning it until it drops into place.

30   With the transaxle secured to the jack

by a chain, raise it into position behind the engine, then carefully slide it forward, engaging the dowel pins on the transaxle with the corresponding holes in the block, and the bolt holes in the driveplate with the torque converter. Do not use excessive force to install the transaxle - if the torque converter does not slide into place, readjust the angle of the transaxle so it is level. **Caution:** *Don't use the transaxle-to-engine bolts to draw the components together.*

31   Install the engine-to-transaxle mounting bolts. Tighten the bolts in the correct order and to the torque listed in this Chapter's Specifications:

a)   *Step 1 - tighten the upper and side engine-to-transaxle bolts to the torque listed in this Chapter's Specifications* **(see illustrations 10.7, 10.20a and 10.20b)**.

b)   *Step 2 - tighten the lower transaxle-to-engine bolts to the torque listed in this Chapter's Specifications* **(see illustration 10.19)**.

32   Install the left front and left rear transaxle mounts and the center member.

33   Tighten the transaxle mount bolts. Refer to Chapter 2A for the installation procedure and the torque specifications for the mounts.

34   Install the shift cable onto the transaxle

bracket and range sensor linkage (see Section 4).

35   Align the marks on the driveplate and torque converter, then install the torque converter bolts and tighten them to the torque listed in this Chapter's Specifications **(see illustration 10.24)**. **Note:** *Install all of the bolts before tightening any of them.*

36   Install the remaining engine-to-transaxle mounting bolts.

37   Install the transaxle ground strap and tighten the bolt to the torque listed in this Chapter's Specifications.

38   Install the intermediate shaft and the left driveaxle (see Chapter 8). Be sure to use a new retaining clip on the left driveaxle.

39   Connect the control arms to the steering knuckles (see Chapter 10).

40   Install the splash shield and front wheels and lower the vehicle.

41   The remainder of installation is the reverse of removal.

42   Refill the transaxle with the specified amount of lubricant (see Chapter 1).

43   Road test the vehicle for proper operation and check for leaks.

44   Loosen and retighten the engine mounts in sequence (see Chapter 2A) if vibration is evident.

10.20b Location of the transaxle-to-engine side bolt (arrow) as viewed from the front

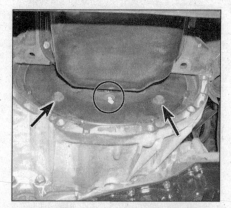

10.23 Make an alignment mark on the driveplate and the torque converter (circled), then remove the torque converter bolts (arrows)

Chapter 8   Driveaxles

Contents

Specifications

CV joint boot length
Outer boot	3-13/32 to 3-31/64 inches
Inner boot	3-63/64 to 4-5/64 inches

Torque specifications
	Ft-lbs
Axle bearing retainer bolts	8 to 14
Driveaxle hub nut	174 to 231
Wheel lug nuts	See Chapter 1

1   Driveaxles - general information and inspection

Power is transmitted from the transaxle to the wheels through a pair of driveaxles. The inner end of each driveaxle is splined into the differential side gear. The outer ends of the driveaxles are splined to the axle hubs and locked in place by a large locknut.

The inner ends of the driveaxles are equipped with sliding Constant Velocity (CV) joints, which are capable of both angular and axial motion. The inner CV joint assembly consists of the "ball-and-cage" type, which consist of an inner hub/race, ball bearings, an outer cage, and a outer race/housing. The inner joints can be disassembled and cleaned in the event of a boot failure (see Section 3), but if any parts are damaged, the joints must be replaced as a unit.

The outer CV joints are the "ball-and-cage" type, which have ball bearings running between an inner race and an outer cage, allowing angular but not axial movement. The outer joints should be cleaned, inspected and

repacked when replacing the boot, but they cannot be disassembled. If an outer joint is damaged, it must be replaced along with the axleshaft (the outer joint and axleshaft are a matched set and sold as a single component).

The CV joints are protected by rubber boots, which are retained by clamps so the joints are protected from water and dirt. The boots should be inspected periodically (see Chapter 1). The inner boots have very small breather holes which may leak a small amount of lubricant under some circumstances, such as when the joint is compressed during removal. Damaged CV joint boots must be replaced immediately or the joints can be damaged. Boot replacement involves removing the driveaxles (Section 2). It's a good idea to disassemble, clean, inspect and repack the CV joint whenever replacing a CV joint boot to make sure the joint isn't contaminated with moisture or dirt, which would cause premature failure of the CV joint (see Section 3).

The most common symptom of worn or damaged CV joints, besides lubricant leaks, are a clicking noise in turns, a clunk when

accelerating from a coasting condition or vibration at highway speeds.

Some specialized tools and procedures are required to disassemble and overhaul the CV joints in a driveaxle. The outer joint is not rebuildable, and is sold only as an assembly, with the shaft, outer joint, ABS sensor ring and front wheel dust shield. The inner joint on all models can be rebuilt using a repair kit.

Warning 1: *Since many of the procedures covered in this Chapter involve working under the vehicle, make sure it's securely supported on sturdy jackstands or on a hoist where the vehicle can easily be raised and lowered.*

Warning 2: *Whenever the driveaxle hub is loosened or removed it must be replaced with a new hub nut. Whenever the driveaxle is removed, the driveaxle circlips must be replaced with new circlips. Whenever any of the suspension fasteners are loosened or removed they must be inspected and if necessary replaced with new fasteners. All fasteners must be replaced with new fasteners of the same part number or of the original equipment quality and design. Torque specifications must be followed for proper assembly and component retention.*

8

2.2 Before raising the vehicle, remove the wheel center cap and loosen the hub/driveaxle nut using a socket and breaker bar

2.8 Use a two or three jaw puller to separate the driveaxle stub shaft from the wheel hub

2.9 Using a large prybar, pry sharply against the inner CV joint housing to free the left driveaxle from the transaxle

2.10a Mark the relationship of the bearing retainer to the support bracket

2   Driveaxles - removal and installation

Removal

Refer to illustrations 2.2, 2.8, 2.9, 2.10a and 2.10b

1   Remove the wheel cover or hub cap. Remove the cotter pin, retainer and insulator from the driveaxle stub shaft.

2   Break the hub nut loose with a socket and large breaker bar **(see illustration)**.

3   Loosen the wheel lug nuts, raise the vehicle and support it securely on jackstands. Remove the wheel. Drain the transaxle lubricant (see Chapter 1).

4   Detach the lower balljoint from the steering knuckle (see Chapter 10).

5   Disconnect the stabilizer bar link from the lower control arm (see Chapter 10).

6   Using a large prybar, pry the lower control arm down and separate the balljoint from the steering knuckle.

7   Remove the brake caliper and suspend it aside with wire. **Caution:** *Do not allow the brake caliper to hang by the brake hose.*

Remove the brake disc.

8   Remove the driveaxle hub nut and washer. Using a two-jaw puller, press the stub shaft until it breaks free of the hub **(see illustration)**.

9   To remove the left-side driveaxle, position a prybar behind the flange of the inner CV joint and pry sharply to free the circlip on the inner CV joint stub shaft from the transaxle side gears **(see illustration)**. **Caution:** *Be careful not to damage the transaxle case, CV joint housing, driveaxle oil seal or the CV joint boot with the prybar.*

10   To remove the right-side driveaxle, Mark the relationship between the axle bearing retainer and bracket and remove the front axle bearing retainer bolts **(see illustrations)**.

11   Pull the strut assembly out away from the vehicle and separate the driveaxle stub shaft from the hub.

12   Support the CV joints and carefully remove the driveaxle from the vehicle. **Caution:** *Do not tear the inner or outer boots on any sharp components as you withdraw the driveaxle. Do not nick the ABS exciter ring on the outer joint of each driveaxle.*

2.10b Remove the three axle bearing retainer bolts (arrows)

Installation

Refer to illustrations 2.13 and 2.16

13   On the left-side driveaxle assembly, install a new circlip on the stub shaft of the inner CV joint **(see illustration)**. Lubricate the driveaxle oil seals with multi-purpose grease.

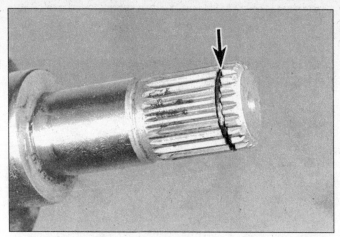

2.13 Always replace the circlip (arrow) on the inner CV joint stub shaft

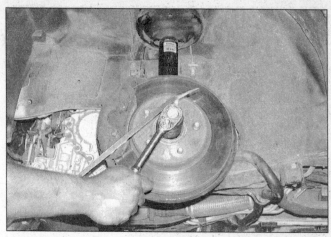

2.16 Install the washer and new driveaxle hub nut and tighten the nut securely

3.3 Cut the old boot clamps off and discard them

3.4 Slide the boot back and wipe off as much of the old CV joint grease as possible

3.5 Use pliers or a screwdriver to remove the inner retaining ring

14 To install the left-side driveaxle, insert the splined end of the inner CV joint into the differential side gear. While supporting the CV joints, seat the shaft in the side gear by pushing the shaft into the transaxle sharply until you feel the circlip engage. Grasp the inner joint housing and pull outward (away from the transaxle) to ensure that the circlip is engaged.

15 Install the right-side driveaxle through the axle bearing retainer bracket and engage the splines on the inner shaft with the differential side gear. **Note:** *No circlip is used on the right-side driveaxle.* Align the marks made during removal and install the axle bearing retainer bolts. Tighten the axle bearing retainer bolts to the torque listed in this Chapter's Specifications.

16 Pull the strut assembly out away from the vehicle and insert the outer stub shaft through the hub, making sure the splines are aligned. Install the washer and new driveaxle hub nut. **Warning:** *The axle hub nut must be NEW, do not reuse the old nut.* While holding the rotor, and tighten the hub nut securely **(see illustration).**

17 The remainder of installation is the reverse of removal. Tighten the driveaxle hub nut to the torque listed in this Chapter's Specifications with the wheel/tire installed and the vehicle on the ground.

3   Driveaxle boot - replacement

Note: *If the CV joints exhibit wear indicating the need for an overhaul (usually due to torn boots), explore all options before beginning the job. Complete rebuilt driveaxles are available on an exchange basis, which eliminates a lot of time and work. Whatever is decided, check on the cost and availability of parts before beginning this procedure.*

1   Remove the driveaxle (see Section 2).
2   Place the driveaxle in a vise lined with soft jaws to avoid damage to the shaft.

Inner CV joint

Refer to illustrations 3.3, 3.4, 3.5, 3.6, 3.7 ,3.9, 3.10, 3.11, 3.12a, 3.12b, 3.14, 3.15, 3.16, 3.17, 3.18, 3.20, 3.21, 3.22a, 3.22b, 3.22c, 3.22d and 3.22e

3   Cut off the boot seal retaining clamps **(see illustration).**
4   Slide the boot towards the center of the

3.6 With the retainer removed, the housing can be pulled off the ball-and-cage assembly

driveaxle. Wipe off as much of the old grease as possible **(see illustration)** using a rag or shop towel.
5   Remove the front retaining ring, if equipped **(see illustration).**
6   Withdraw the ball-and-cage assembly from the housing **(see illustration).**

8

3.7 Push the inner race back to expose and remove the circlip with pliers or a screwdriver

3.9 Apply index marks on the inner race and cage so they can be assembled in the same relative position

3.10 Pry the balls from the cage with a screwdriver (be careful not to nick or scratch them)

3.11 Tilt the inner race 90 degrees and rotate it out of the cage

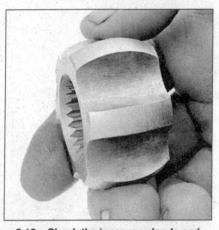

3.12a Check the inner race lands and grooves for pitting and score marks

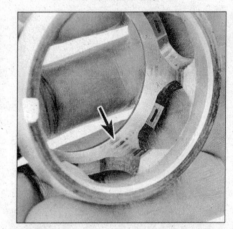

3.12b Check the cage for cracks, pitting and score marks (shiny spots are normal and don't affect operation)

7   Push the inner race back enough to remove the circlip **(see illustration)**. Pull the inner bearing assembly off the axleshaft.

8   Before installing a new boot, disassemble, clean and inspect the bearing assembly as follows.

9   Mark the inner race and cage to ensure that they are reassembled in the same relative position **(see illustration)**.

10   Using a screwdriver or piece of wood, pry the balls from the cage **(see illustration)**. Be careful not to scratch the inner race, the balls or the cage.

11   Rotate the inner race 90-degrees, align the inner race lands with the cage windows and rotate the race out of the cage **(see illustration)**.

12   Clean all of the old grease out of the housing and the bearing assembly. Inspect the balls, cage, inner race and housing for scoring, pitting and other signs of abnormal wear. Apply a coat of CV joint grease to the inner bearing surfaces to hold the balls in place when reassembling the bearing assembly. Shiny, polished spots are normal and will not adversely affect CV joint performance

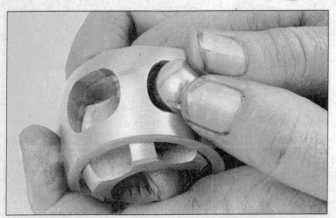

3.14 Press the balls into the cage through the windows

3.15 Before installing the CV joint boot, wrap the axle splines with electrical tape to prevent damage to the boot

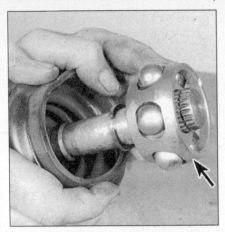

3.16 Install the inner race and cage assembly with the ''bulge'' (arrow) facing the axleshaft end

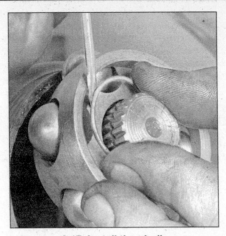

3.17 Install the circlip

3.18 Pack grease into the bearing until it's completely full

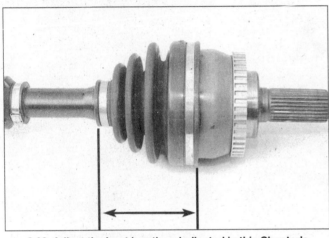

3.20 Adjust the boot length as indicated in this Chapter's Specifications and tighten the clamps

3.21 Equalize the pressure inside the boot by inserting a small, dull screwdriver between the boot and the housing

(see illustrations).

13   Begin reassembly by inserting the inner race into the cage. Verify that the match-marks are on the same side. However, it's not necessary for them to be in direct alignment with each other.

14   Press the balls into the cage windows with your thumbs (see illustration).

15   Wrap the axleshaft splines with tape to avoid damaging the boot. Slide the small boot clamp and boot onto the axleshaft, then remove the tape (see illustration).

16   Install the inner race and cage assembly on the axleshaft with the larger diameter side or "bulge" of the cage facing the axleshaft end (see illustration).

17   Install the new circlip (see illustration).

18   Fill the outer race and boot with CV joint grease (normally included with the new boot kit). Pack the inner race and cage assembly with grease, by hand, until grease is worked completely into the assembly (see illustration). Note: *The inner joint requires 8.0 ounces of hi-temp CV joint grease.*

19   Slide the outer race down onto the inner race and install the wire ring retainer, if equipped. Wipe any excess grease from the

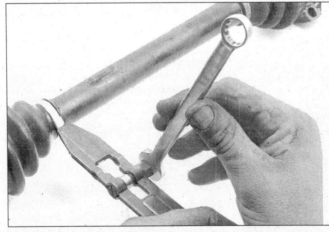

axle boot groove on the outer race. Seat the small diameter of the boot in the recessed area on the axleshaft and install the clamp. Push the other end of the boot onto the outer race.

20   Adjust the length of the driveaxle boot to the dimension listed in this Chapter's Specifications (see illustration).

3.22a You'll need a special installation tool to install "band" type boot clamps: install the band with its end pointing in the direction of axle rotation and tighten it securely

8

21   With the axle set to the proper length, equalize the pressure in the boot by inserting a dull screwdriver between the boot and the outer race (see illustration). Don't damage the boot with the tool.

22   Install the boot clamp. There are three types of clamps you are likely to encounter; the band type, which requires a special tight-

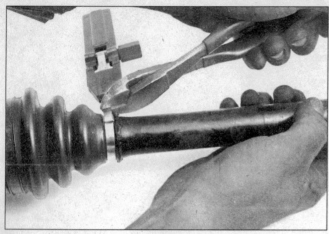

3.22b Bend down the end of the clamp back and cut off the excess

3.22c If you are installing crimp-type boot clamps, you'll need a pair of special crimping pliers (available at most auto parts stores)

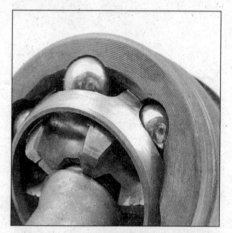

3.22d To install fold-over type boot clamps, bend the tang down . . .

3.22e . . . and tap the tabs over to hold it in place

3.27 After the assembly has been cleaned and dried thoroughly, rotate the joint through its full range of motion, inspecting the components for wear or damage

ening tool; the crimp type, which also requires a special tool and the fold-over type **(see illustrations)**.

23   Install the driveaxle as described in Section 2.

Outer CV joint

Refer to illustration 3.27

24   The outer boot can only be replaced after removing the inner joint and boot. Follow the procedure above and remove the inner joint and boot. On the left side driveaxle, it will be necessary to remove the dynamic damper as well. Be sure to paint reference marks on the dynamic damper and the driveshaft to insure correct positioning when it is reinstalled.

25   Cut the clamps off and slide the outer boot off the driveaxle.

26   Using an approved solvent, wash away all the grease from inside the housing and around the bearing assembly. Use compressed air, if available, to remove the solvent and dry the assembly. **Caution:** *Always wear eye protection when using compressed air!* It may be difficult to completely clean and dry

the bearing assembly, but it is imperative that the job be done thoroughly, so take your time and do it right.

27   Bend the outer CV joint at an angle to the driveaxle to expose the bearings, inner race and cage **(see illustration)**. If any of the components show excessive wear or damage, the joint must be replaced. New outer joints are available only with the axleshaft.

28   Pack the inner race and cage assembly with CV joint grease (normally included with the new boot kit), by hand, until grease is worked completely into the assembly. **Note:** *The outer CV joint requires 6.8 ounces of hi-temp CV joint grease.*

29   Tape the axle splines to protect the boot **(see illustration 3.15)**, and slide the new boot into place. When the small end of the boot is in position, place the remaining grease into the boot and position the large end of the boot over the housing until it seats into the groove. Install a new clamp on the outboard side and tighten both boot clamps (see Step 22).

30   Adjust the length of the driveaxle boot to the dimension listed in this Chapter's Specifications **(see illustration 3.20)**.

31   Assemble the inner CV joint and boot onto the axleshaft.

32   Install the driveaxle as described in Section 2.

---

4   Axle bearing (right-side) - inspection and replacement

1   Remove the right-side driveaxle assembly (see Section 2).

2   Hold the extension shaft and rotate the bearing. It should operate smoothly and quietly.

3   If the bearing is rough or noisy, take the assembly to an automotive machine shop. Have the old bearing pressed off the shaft and install a new bearing. Be sure to install three new dust shields (two inner and one outer shield) along with the new bearing.

4   Install the driveaxle assembly (see Section 2). Be sure to tighten the axle bearing retainer bolts to the torque listed in this Chapter's Specifications.

Chapter 9   Brakes

Contents

Specifications

General
Brake fluid type .... See Chapter 1

Disc brakes
Minimum pad thickness	See Chapter 1
Brake disc minimum thickness	0.945 inch*
Maximum disc runout	0.003 inch
Maximum disc thickness variation	0.0004 inch

Rear drum brakes
Shoe friction lining minimum thickness	See Chapter 1
Maximum inside diameter	9.9 inch*
Maximum drum runout	0.002 inch
Maximum out-of-round	0.0006 inch
Dual load sensing valve spring length	
1993 through 1996	5-15/16 to 6-1/16 inches
1997 and later	6-1/4 to 6-3/8 inches

If different specifications are cast into the disc or drum, they supersede information printed here

Power brake booster
Output rod length	13/32 inch
Booster-to-clevis hole dimension	4-3/4 inches

Brake pedal adjustments

Free height..	7-11/16 to 8-5/64 inches
Freeplay	3/64 to 7/64 inch
Depressed height..	4-17/32 to 5-1/8 inches

Brake light switch

Plunger-to-pedal stopper clearance...............................	1/64 to 1/32 inch

Torque specifications

	Ft-lbs (unless otherwise indicated)
Brake booster-to-body mounting nuts.............................	108 to 144 in-lbs
Brake caliper mounting bolts...	18 to 25
Brake hose-to-caliper banjo bolt.....................................	144 to 168 in-lbs
Caliper and wheel cylinder bleeder screws.....................	61 to 78 in-lbs
Dual load sensing valve bolts..	15 to 20
Dual load sensing valve spring bracket bolts	
Villager models	
1993 through 1995..	12 to 15
1996 and later..	15 to 20
Quest models..	15 to 20
Master cylinder-to-brake booster retaining nuts...............	132 in-lbs
Wheel cylinder retaining bolts	52 to 95 in-lbs

1   General information

The vehicles covered by this manual are equipped with hydraulically operated front and rear brake systems. The front brakes are disc type and the rear brakes are drum type. Both the front and rear brakes are self adjusting. The disc brakes automatically compensate for pad wear, while the drum brakes incorporate an adjustment mechanism which is activated as the parking brake is applied.

Hydraulic system

The hydraulic system consists of two separate circuits. The master cylinder has separate reservoirs for the two circuits, and, in the event of a leak or failure in one hydraulic circuit, the other circuit will remain operative. On non-ABS models, the left front and right rear brakes are on one circuit while the right front and the left rear are on another circuit. Models with ABS are equipped with a different hydraulic circuit than non-ABS models.

These models are equipped with a dual load sensing valve above the rear axle. When the vehicle is unloaded, the valve closes partially, thereby reducing hydraulic pressure to the rear brakes. After the vehicle is loaded, the weight pushes down on the back end, activating the valve which opens and supplies more hydraulic pressure to the rear brakes. When the vehicle is completely loaded, the system provides full hydraulic pressure to the rear brakes.

Power brake booster

The power brake booster, utilizing engine manifold vacuum and atmospheric pressure to provide assistance to the hydraulically operated brakes, is mounted on the firewall in the engine compartment.

Parking brake

The parking brake operates the rear brakes only, through cable actuation.

Service

After completing any operation involving disassembly of any part of the brake system, always test drive the vehicle to check for proper braking performance before resuming normal driving. When testing the brakes, perform the tests on a clean, dry, flat surface. Conditions other than these can lead to inaccurate test results.

Test the brakes at various speeds with both light and heavy pedal pressure. The vehicle should stop evenly without pulling to one side or the other. Avoid locking the brakes, because this slides the tires and diminishes braking efficiency and control of the vehicle.

Tires, vehicle load and wheel alignment are factors which also affect braking performance.

2   Anti-lock Brake System (ABS) - general information

1   The Anti-lock Brake System (ABS) is designed to maintain vehicle steerability, directional stability and optimum deceleration under severe braking conditions and on most road surfaces. It does so by monitoring the rotational speed of each wheel and controlling the brake line pressure to each wheel during braking. This prevents the wheels from locking up. The ABS consists of the hydraulic actuator, the front and rear wheel speed sensors, the ABS control module, the motor relay and the solenoid relay.

Components

Actuator assembly

Refer to illustration 2.2

2   The actuator assembly (**see illustration**) consists of an electric hydraulic pump and three solenoid valves: front left, front right and rear. The electric pump provides hydraulic pressure to charge the reservoirs in the actuator, which supplies pressure to the braking system. The solenoid valves modulate brake line pressure during ABS operation. The body contains four valves - one for each wheel. The pump, the reservoirs and the solenoid valves are all housed in the actuator assembly.

2.2 The ABS hydraulic actuator (A) houses an electric hydraulic pump, a reservoir and three solenoid valves. The ABS relays are located under the cover (B)

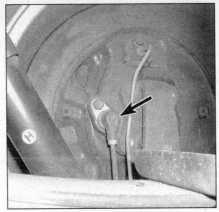

2.3a Location of the front wheel speed sensor (arrow)

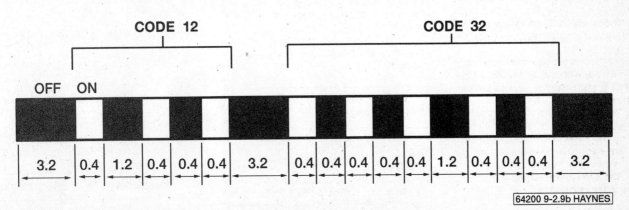

2.9a To put the control unit into output mode, ground the L terminal (arrow) on the Data Link Connector

Speed sensors

Refer to illustrations 2.3a and 2.3b

3 The speed sensors, which are located at each wheel **(see illustrations)**, generate a small sine wave current when the toothed sensor rotors are turning. This analog voltage signal is monitored by the ABS control unit, which converts it to a digital signal from which it can determine wheel rotational speed.

4 The front speed sensors are mounted on the steering knuckles in close relationship to the toothed sensor rotors, which are integral with the outer constant velocity (CV) joints.

5 The rear wheel sensors are bolted to the axle carriers (rear knuckles). The toothed sensor rotors are integral with the rear wheel hub/bearing assemblies.

ABS computer

6 The ABS control unit, which is mounted behind the center console under the dash, is the "brain" of the ABS system. The function of the control unit is to monitor and process information received from the wheel speed sensors to control the hydraulic line pressure, avoiding wheel lock up. The control unit also

monitors the system for malfunctions, even when the ABS system is inactive during normal driving conditions.

7 Each time you start the engine, the system turns on the ABS warning light for about one second. As soon as the engine is running, the light should go off. The system then performs a self-test the first time the vehicle speed exceeds four mph. You may hear a mechanical noise during the test; this is normal. If the system detects a problem, the ABS light will come on and remain on. A diagnostic code will also be stored in the control unit, which indicates the problem area or component.

Diagnosis and repair

Refer to illustrations 2.9a and 2.9b

8 If the ABS warning light on the dash comes on and stays on while the vehicle is in operation, the ABS system requires attention. Diagnosis is quite complex, involving a number of lengthy diagnostic procedures, so we don't recommend attempting to fix the ABS system at home. However, if you're willing to do a little work, you can obtain a diagnostic trouble code - which will indicate the general area of the problem - as follows:

9 To access the ABS self diagnosis system, drive the vehicle above 20 mph for at least one minute. Stop the vehicle and turn OFF the engine. Ground terminal L on the Data Link Connector **(see illustration)**. With terminal L grounded, turn the ignition switch to On (engine not running). After 3.2 seconds, the ABS warning light will begin by flashing a code 12. The code is determined by counting the number of ON and OFF flashes **(see illustration)**. The sequence always begins with a 3.2-second "off" period, followed by a flash, then a 1.2-second off period, then two flashes. This "Code 12" (the "start" code, not a trouble code) is followed by another 3.2-second off period, then the trouble codes are displayed, in the order in which they were stored, starting with the latest stored code. All codes are two-digit codes, so the first flash(es) indicate the tens place, followed by a longer delay, followed by the single-digit flash(es). For example, a sequence of four flashes, then a pause, followed by a sequence of five flashes, would indicate a Code 45 (front left actuator solenoid valve). Count the number of flashes of the ABS light, then refer to the accompanying table.

9

CODE 12 **CODE 32**

OFF	ON															
3.2	0.4	1.2	0.4	0.4	0.4	3.2	0.4	0.4	0.4	0.4	0.4	1.2	0.4	0.4	0.4	3.2

64200 9-2.9b HAYNES

2.9b The LED on the ABS control unit indicates a problem in a particular circuit by the number of flashes. For example, three 0.4-second flashes, followed by a 1.2-second interval, followed by two more 0.4-second flashes indicates a code 32, which means there's a short circuit in the rear right sensor circuit

Code	Malfunctioning part
12	Start code
18	Sensor rotor
21	Front right sensor (open circuit)
22	Front right sensor (short circuit)
25	Front left sensor (open circuit)
26	Front left sensor (short circuit)
31	Rear right sensor (open circuit)
32	Rear right sensor (short circuit)
35	Rear left sensor (open circuit)
36	Rear left sensor (short circuit)
41	Front right actuator solenoid valve
42	Front right actuator inlet solenoid valve
45	Front left actuator solenoid valve
46	Front left actuator inlet solenoid valve
51	Rear right actuator outlet solenoid valve
52	Rear right actuator inlet solenoid valve
55	Rear left actuator outlet solenoid valve
56	Rear left actuator inlet solenoid valve
57	Power supply low voltage
61	Actuator motor or motor relay
63	Solenoid valve relay circuit
71	Control module

Symptom	Malfunctioning part or circuit
ABS warning light stays on when ignition switch is turned on	Control module power supply circuit ABS warning light bulb circuit Control module or control module connector Solenoid valve relay stuck Power supply for solenoid valve relay coil Blown fuse (10A ELECTRON IGN, 15A STOP LAMP 10A METER, 20A ANTI SKID, 30A ANTI SKID)
ABS warning light stays on during self-diagnosis	Control module
ABS warning light does not come on when ignition switch is turned on	Fuse, warning light bulb or warning light circuit Control module
ABS warning light does not come on during self-diagnosis	Control module

9   A trouble code can be set by a simple malfunction. Although you can't troubleshoot the types of malfunctions listed in the accompanying trouble code table, you *can* check the following things:

a) *Check the brake fluid level in the reservoir.*
b) *Verify that all electrical connectors are securely connected.*
c) *Check the fuses.*
d) *Check the brake system (see Chapter 1).*
e) *Check the brake pads (see Section 3).*
f) *Check the brake pedal (see Section 15).*

10   After verifying that all of the above are okay, try to erase the stored trouble code(s) as follows: Unground terminal L; the ABS warning light should remain on. Within 10 seconds, ground the L terminal three successive times; each ground must last more than one second. The ABS light should now go out.

a) *If the light stays on, take the vehicle to a dealer service department or other qualified repair shop and have the ABS system repaired.*
b) *If the light doesn't stay on, drive the vehicle above 20 mph for at least one*

minute and verify that the warning light on the dash doesn't come on again. If it does, take the vehicle to a dealer service department or other qualified repair shop and have the ABS system repaired.

3   Disc brake pads - replacement

Refer to illustrations 3.5 and 3.6a through 3.6g
Warning: *Disc brake pads must be replaced on both front wheels at the same time - never replace the pads on only one wheel. Also, the*

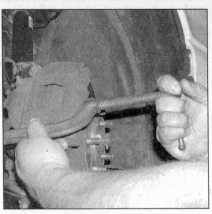

3.5 Use a C-clamp to depress the piston into the caliper before removing the caliper and pads

dust created by the brake system may contain asbestos, which is harmful to your health. Never blow it out with compressed air and don't inhale any of it. An approved filtering mask should be worn when working on the brakes. Do not, under any circumstances, use petroleum-based solvents to clean brake parts. Use brake system cleaner only!

1　Remove the cap from the brake fluid reservoir.

2　Loosen the front or rear wheel lug nuts, raise the front or rear of the vehicle and support it securely on jackstands. Block the wheels at the opposite end.

3　Remove the wheels. Work on one brake assembly at a time, using the assembled brake for reference if necessary.

4　Inspect the brake disc carefully as outlined in Section 5. If machining is necessary, follow the information in that Section to remove the disc, at which time the pads can be removed as well.

5　Push the piston back into its bore to provide room for the new brake pads. A C-clamp can be used to accomplish this **(see illustration)**. As the piston is depressed to the bottom of the caliper bore, the fluid in the master cylinder will rise. Make sure that it doesn't overflow. If necessary, siphon off

3.6a Before disassembling the brake, wash it thoroughly with brake system cleaner and allow it to dry - position a drain pan under the brake to catch the residue - DO NOT use compressed air to blow off brake dust!

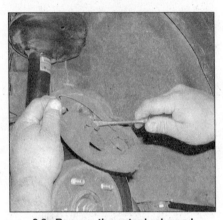

3.6c Remove the outer brake pad

some of the fluid.

6　Follow the accompanying photos **(see illustrations 3.6a through 3.6g)**, for the actual pad replacement procedure. Be sure to stay in order and read the caption under each illustration.

7　When reinstalling the caliper, be sure to tighten the mounting bolts to the torque listed

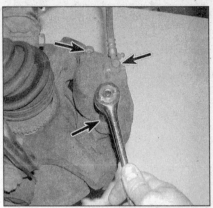

3.6b Remove these two bolts (upper and lower arrows) to detach the caliper from the steering knuckle; the middle arrow points to the brake hose banjo bolt (which shouldn't be removed unless the caliper requires service)

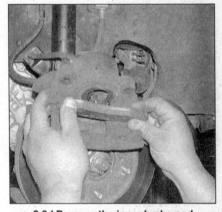

3.6d Remove the inner brake pad

in this Chapter's Specifications.

8　After the job has been completed, firmly depress the brake pedal a few times to bring the pads into contact with the disc. Check the level of the brake fluid, adding some if necessary. Check the operation of the brakes carefully before placing the vehicle into normal service.

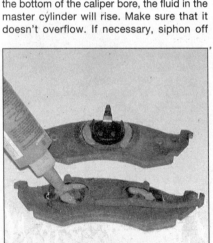

3.6e Apply anti-squeal compound to the back of both pads (let the compound "set up" a few minutes before installing them)

3.6f Install the inner brake pad

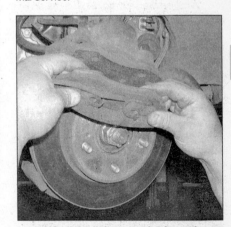

3.6g Install the outer brake pad

9

4   Brake caliper - removal and installation

Warning: *The dust created by the brake system may contain asbestos, which is harmful to your health. Never blow it out with compressed air and don't inhale any of it. An approved filtering mask should be worn when working on the brakes. Do not, under any circumstances, use petroleum-based solvents to clean brake parts. Use brake system cleaner only!*

Removal

Refer to illustration 4.2

1   Loosen - but don't remove - the lug nuts on the front wheels. Raise the front of the vehicle and place it securely on jackstands. Remove the front wheels.

2   Disconnect the brake line from the caliper **(see illustration 3.6b)** and plug it to keep contaminants out of the brake system and to prevent losing any more brake fluid than is necessary **(see illustration).**

3   Remove the caliper mounting bolts **(see illustration 3.6b).**

4   Detach the caliper from the steering knuckle.

Installation

5   Install the caliper by reversing the removal procedure. Remember to replace the sealing washers on either side of the brake line fitting with new ones. Tighten the caliper mounting bolts and the banjo bolt to the torque listed in this Chapter's Specifications.

6   Bleed the brake system (see Section 10).

7   Install the wheels and lug nuts and lower the vehicle. Tighten the wheel lug nuts to the torque listed in the Chapter 1 Specifications.

5   Brake disc - inspection, removal and installation

Inspection

Refer to illustrations 5.2, 5.3, 5.4a, 5.4b, 5.5a and 5.5b

1   Loosen the wheel lug nuts, raise the vehicle and support it securely on jackstands. Remove the wheel and install the lug nuts with 3 mm thick washers under them to hold the disc in place.

2   Remove the brake caliper (see Section 4), but don't disconnect the brake hose. After removing the caliper bolts, suspend the caliper out of the way with a piece of wire **(see illustration).**

3   Visually inspect the disc surface for scoring or damage **(see illustration).** Light scratches and shallow grooves are normal after use and may not always be detrimental to brake operation, but deep scoring (over 0.015 inch) requires refinishing by an automotive machine shop. Be sure to check both sides of the disc.

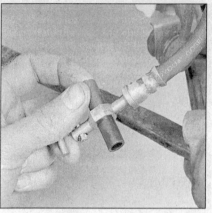

4.2 Using a short piece of rubber hose of the appropriate diameter, plug the brake line banjo fitting

4   If you've noted pulsation during braking, suspect disc runout. To check disc runout, place a dial indicator at a point about 1/2-inch from the outer edge of the disc **(see illustration).** Set the indicator to zero and turn the disc. The indicator reading should not exceed the specified allowable runout limit. If it does, have the disc refinished by an automotive machine shop. **Note:** *Professionals recommend that the discs be resurfaced regardless of the dial indicator reading, as this will impart a smooth finish and ensure a perfectly flat surface, eliminating any brake pedal pulsation or other undesirable symptoms related to questionable discs. At the very least, if you elect not to have the discs resurfaced, remove the glazing from the surface with emery cloth or sandpaper using a swirling motion* **(see illustration).**

5   It is absolutely critical that the disc not be machined to a thickness less than the minimum allowable thickness. The minimum wear (or discard) thickness is stamped on the disc **(see illustration).** The disc thickness can be checked with a micrometer **(see illustration).** Check the thickness at several points.

5.4a Make sure the disc lug nuts are tight, then rotate the disc and check the runout with a dial indicator – if the reading exceeds the maximum allowable runout limit, the disc will have to be machined or replaced

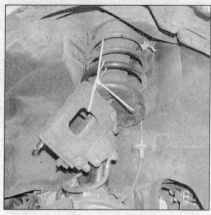

5.2 Support the caliper from the strut/coil spring assembly while the brake disc is being removed

5.3 The brake pads on this vehicle were obviously neglected, as they wore down to the rivets and cut deep grooves into the disc, and now the disc must be replaced

Removal

Refer to illustration 5.7

6   If not already done, remove the two caliper-to-steering knuckle bolts **(see illus-**

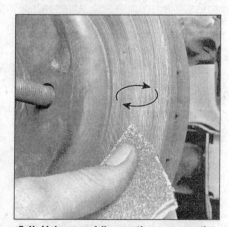

5.4b Using a swirling motion, remove the glaze from the disc surface with sandpaper or emery cloth

5.5a The minimum allowable thickness is stamped onto the disc (typical)

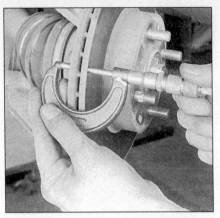

5.5b A micrometer is used to measure disc thickness

5.7 If the disc is stuck, thread two bolts into the disc and tighten them to force the disc off the hub

tration 3.6b) and remove the brake caliper (see Section 4).

7   Remove the lug nuts which were put on to hold the disc in place and remove the disc from the hub. If the disc is stuck to the hub and won't come off, thread two bolts into the holes provided **(see illustration)** and tighten them. Alternate between the bolts, turning them a little at a time, until the disc is free.

Installation

8   Place the disc in position over the threaded studs.

9   Install the caliper and brake pads over the disc. Tighten the caliper mounting bolts to the torque listed in this Chapter's Specifications.

10   Install the wheel, then lower the vehicle to the ground. Depress the brake pedal a few times to bring the brake pads into contact with the disc. Bleeding of the system will not be necessary unless the fluid hose was disconnected from the caliper. Check the operation of the brakes carefully before placing the vehicle into normal service.

6   Drum brake shoes - replacement

Warning: *Drum brake shoes must be replaced on both wheels at the same time - never replace the shoes on only one wheel. Also, the dust created by the brake system may contain asbestos, which is harmful to your health. Never blow it out with compressed air and don't inhale any of it. An approved filtering mask should be worn when working on the brakes. Do not, under any circumstances, use petroleum-based solvents to clean brake parts. Use brake system cleaner only!*

Caution: *Whenever the brake shoes are replaced, the return and hold-down springs should also be replaced. Due to the continuous heating/cooling cycle the springs are subjected to, they lose tension over a period of time and may allow the shoes to drag on the drum and wear at a much faster rate than normal.*

6.4 If a brake drum is "frozen" to the hub flange, insert two bolts in the holes provided and tighten them until they push against the hub flange, which will force the drum off

Drum removal

Refer to illustration 6.4

1   Loosen the wheel lug nuts, raise the rear of the vehicle and support it on jackstands. Make sure the parking brake is released.

2   Block the front wheels and remove the rear wheels from the vehicle.

3   Grasp the brake drum and pull it off. If the drum is stuck, remove the rubber plug from the backing plate and loosen the brake adjuster star wheel **(see illustration 7.4)**. **Note:** *The rubber plug for the brake adjustment access hole is located directly below the wheel cylinder on the backing plate.*

4   If the rear brake drum remains attached to the hub, thread two bolts into the drum in the holes provided and turn them clockwise until the drum breaks loose from the hub **(see illustration)**. Be sure to turn the bolts evenly to keep the drum parallel to the hub.

Inspection

Refer to illustration 6.5

5   Check the drum for cracks, score marks, deep grooves and signs of overheating of the shoe contact surface. If the drums have blue spots, indicating overheated areas,

6.5 Notice the maximum allowable diameter cast into the drum surface (typical)

they should be replaced. Also, look for grease or brake fluid on the shoe contact surface. Grease and brake fluid can be removed from the drum with rubbing alcohol or brake system cleaner, but the brake shoes must be replaced if they are contaminated. Surface glazing, which is a glossy, highly polished finish, can be removed from the drum with sandpaper or emery cloth. **Note:** *Professionals recommend resurfacing the drums whenever a brake job is done. Resurfacing will eliminate the possibility of out-of-round drums. If the drums are worn so much that they can't be surfaced without exceeding the maximum allowable diameter (see illustration), then new ones will be required.*

6   Inspect the wheel cylinder for fluid leakage as described in Chapter 1.

7   Inspect the surface of the brake shoes for cracks, contamination from grease, and wear and compare their thickness to the Chapter 1 Specifications.

Shoe replacement

Refer to illustrations 6.8a through 6.8q

8   Follow the accompanying photos **(see illustrations 6.8a through 6.8q)** for the actual shoe replacement procedure. Be sure to stay in order and read the information in

9

6.8a Before disassembling the brake, wash it thoroughly with brake system cleaner and allow it to dry - position a drain pan under the brake to catch the residue - DO NOT use compressed air to blow the brake dust off!

6.8b Use a pair of pliers to remove the upper spring (arrow)

6.8c Remove the brake shoe adjusting lever (arrow)

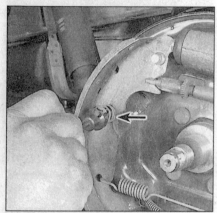

6.8d Using a hold-down spring tool, remove the leading shoe's hold-down spring (arrow)

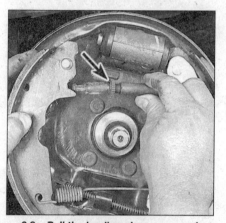

6.8e Pull the leading shoe away and remove the adjuster assembly (arrow)

6.8f Release the lower spring (arrow) and remove the leading shoe

6.8g Remove the hold-down spring on the trailing shoe

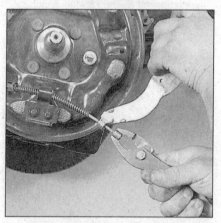

6.8h Pull the parking brake cable end out of the end of the lever with pliers

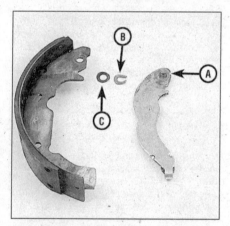

6.8i Pry the old horseshoe clip (B) from the old shoe - grease the pin (A) of the lever and assemble it to the new trailing shoe with the wave-washer (C) and a new horseshoe clip

the caption under each illustration.

9   Once the new shoes are in place, turn the adjuster until the diameter of the shoe assembly is just smaller than the inner diameter of the brake drum. **Note:** *Work on only one side of the vehicle at a time. The left and right adjusters are different, with a right-hand*

thread for the right side and left-hand thread for the left side. The socket ends are marked R and L, and the right-side nut has two machined grooves, while the left side nut has only one.

10   Install the brake drum. Insert a narrow screwdriver or brake adjusting tool through the adjustment hole and turn the star wheel until the brakes drag slightly as the drum is turned.

11   Turn the star wheel in the opposite

direction until the drum turns freely. Keep the adjuster lever from contacting the star wheel or it won't turn.

12   Repeat the shoe replacement procedure on the opposite wheel, then adjust the shoes.

13   Install the plug in the backing plate access hole.

14   Install the wheels and lower the vehicle.

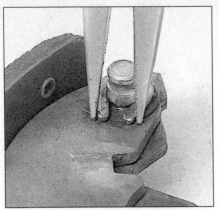

6.8j Squeeze the new clip over the lever's pin

6.8k Clean the backing plate and apply high-temperature brake grease at the points indicated

6.8l Connect the parking brake cable to the lever, then install the trailing shoe and hold-down spring

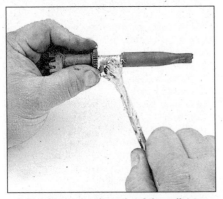

6.8m Clean the threads of the adjuster and lubricate it with high-temperature brake grease

6.8n Install the adjuster and the new leading shoe

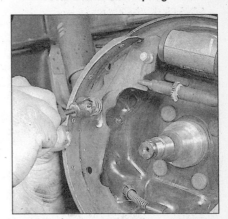

6.8o Secure the leading shoe with its hold-down spring

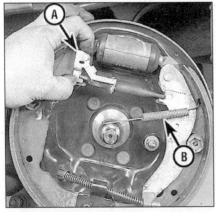

6.8p Install the adjuster lever (A) and hook the upper spring (B) into the hole in the top of the adjuster lever

6.8q Hook the lower spring into the hole in the trailing shoe from the back side (arrow), then into the hole in the leading shoe

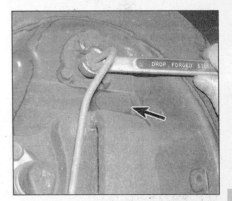

7.4 To remove the wheel cylinder, disconnect the brake line fitting, then remove the wheel cylinder bolts - the arrow points to the access plug for the adjuster star wheel

Tighten the lug nuts to the torque listed in the Chapter 1 Specifications.

15   Pump the brake pedal several times and top off the master cylinder with brake fluid, if necessary (see Chapter 1). Drive the vehicle backwards and forwards a few times, applying the brakes sharply at each stop (this will adjust the brake shoes). Recheck the fluid level. Check brake operation carefully before driving the vehicle in traffic.

7   Wheel cylinder - removal and installation

Refer to illustration 7.4

Removal

1   Raise the rear of the vehicle and support it securely on jackstands. Block the front

wheels to keep the vehicle from rolling.
2   Remove the brake shoe assembly (see Section 6).
3   Remove all dirt and foreign material from around the wheel cylinder.
4   Unscrew the brake line fitting **(see illustration)**. **Note:** *If available, use a flare-nut wrench to avoid rounding off the corners of the fittings*. Don't pull the brake line away from the wheel cylinder.

9

8.5 Disconnect the brake hydraulic lines (arrows) from the master cylinder

8.11 Have an assistant depress the brake pedal and hold it down, then loosen the fitting nut, allowing the air and fluid to escape; repeat this procedure on both fittings until the fluid is clear of air bubbles

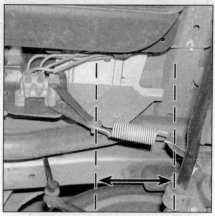

9.1 Check the length of the dual load sensing valve spring with the vehicle unloaded

5   Remove the wheel cylinder mounting bolts.

6   Detach the wheel cylinder from the brake backing plate. Immediately plug the brake line to prevent fluid loss and contamination. Golf tees or rubber vacuum caps work well for plugging or capping flared metal lines. **Note:** *If the brake shoe linings are contaminated with brake fluid, install new brake shoes and clean the drums with brake system cleaner.*

Installation

7   Apply RTV sealant to the mating surface of the wheel cylinder and the brake backing plate, place the cylinder in position and connect the brake line. Don't tighten the fitting completely yet.

8   Install the mounting bolts, tightening them to the torque listed in this Chapter's Specifications. Tighten the brake line fitting. Install the brake shoe assembly.

9   Bleed the brakes (see Section 11).

10   Check brake operation before driving the vehicle in traffic. **Warning:** *Do not operate the vehicle if you are in doubt about the effectiveness of the brake system.*

8   Master cylinder - removal and installation

Removal

Refer to illustration 8.5

1   The master cylinder is located in the engine compartment, mounted to the power brake booster.

2   Remove as much fluid as you can from the reservoir with a syringe, such as an old turkey baster. **Warning:** *If a baster is used, never again use it for the preparation of food.*

3   Remove the two reservoir hoses from the master cylinder. Place a shop rag under the hoses to prevent excess brake fluid from dripping onto the surrounding components.

4   Place rags under the fluid fittings and prepare caps or plastic bags to cover the ends of the lines once they are disconnected. **Caution:** *Brake fluid will damage paint. Cover*

all body parts and be careful not to spill fluid during this procedure.

5   Loosen the fittings at the ends of the brake lines where they enter the master cylinder **(see illustration)**. To prevent rounding off the corners on these nuts, the use of a flare-nut wrench, which wraps around the nut, is preferred. Pull the brake lines slightly away from the master cylinder and plug the ends to prevent contamination.

6   Remove the nuts attaching the master cylinder to the power booster. Pull the master cylinder off the studs and out of the engine compartment. Again, be careful not to spill the fluid as this is done. **Note:** *Some models are equipped with a fuel filter bracket that attaches to the master cylinder mounting studs. Be sure to install the bracket onto the new master cylinder.*

Installation

Refer to illustration 8.11

7   Because the master cylinder is equipped with an external reservoir, bleed the master cylinder after it is mounted in the engine compartment.

8   Install the master cylinder over the studs on the power brake booster and tighten the attaching nuts only finger tight at this time.

9   Thread the brake line fittings into the master cylinder. Since the master cylinder is still a bit loose, it can be moved slightly in order for the fittings to thread in easily.

10   Fully tighten the mounting nuts to the torque listed in this Chapter's Specifications, then the brake line fittings.

11   Fill the master cylinder reservoir with fluid of the recommended type (see Chapter 1), then bleed the master cylinder. Have an assistant depress the brake pedal and hold the pedal to the floor. Loosen the hydraulic line fitting to allow air and fluid to escape **(see illustration)**. Repeat this procedure on both fittings until the fluid is clear of air bubbles. **Caution:** *Have plenty of rags on hand to catch the fluid - brake fluid will ruin*

painted surfaces. After the bleeding procedure is completed, rinse the area under the master cylinder with clean water.

12   Bleed the entire brake system as described in Section 11.

13   Fill the master cylinder reservoir with brake fluid of the recommended type (see Chapter 1).

14   Test the operation of the brake system carefully before placing the vehicle into normal service. **Warning:** *Do not operate the vehicle if you are in doubt about the effectiveness of the brake system.*

9   Dual load sensing valve - check and replacement

Check

Refer to illustration 9.1

1   With the vehicle unloaded and parked on a level driveway, measure the length of the load sensing valve spring **(see illustration)**. Refer to the Specifications listed in this Chapter for the correct length.

2   Have an assistant sit on the rear seat then slowly step out of the vehicle to stabilize the suspension. Recheck the spring length. If it is still incorrect, adjust the spring length.

3   Working on the eye bracket opposite the load sensing valve, loosen the bracket and adjust the spring length. Tighten the bracket bolts to the torque listed in this Chapter's Specifications.

Replacement

4   The dual load sensing valve is mounted on the frame above the axle. The valve is not serviceable; if you suspect it's malfunctioning, have it checked by a dealer service department or other repair shop equipped with the necessary pressure gauges.

5   If the valve is leaking or has been determined to be defective, replace it by unscrewing the four brake lines with a flare-nut wrench and unbolting the valve from its mounting bracket. After the new valve is

10.3 Loosen the threaded fitting on the brake line (arrow); use a flare-nut wrench to protect the corners of the nut and then pull off the U-clip with a pair of pliers

installed, tighten the bolts to the torque listed in this Chapter's Specifications and bleed the brake system (see Section 11).

10   Brake hoses and lines - inspection and replacement

Inspection

1   About every six months, with the vehicle raised and supported securely on jackstands, the rubber hoses which connect the steel brake lines with the front and rear brake assemblies should be inspected for cracks, chafing of the outer cover, leaks, blisters and other damage. These are important and vulnerable parts of the brake system and inspection should be complete. A light and mirror will be helpful for a thorough check. If a hose exhibits any of the above conditions, replace it with a new one.

Replacement

Front brake hose

Refer to illustration 10.3

2   Loosen the wheel lug nuts, raise the vehicle and support it securely on jackstands. Remove the wheel.
3   At the bracket, unscrew the brake line fitting from the hose **(see illustration)**. Use a flare-nut wrench to prevent rounding off the corners.
4   Remove the U-clip from the female fitting at the bracket with a pair of pliers then pass the hose through the bracket.
5   At the caliper end of the hose, remove the banjo bolt, then separate the hose from the caliper. Note that there are two copper sealing washers on either side of the banjo fitting - they should be replaced with new ones during installation.
6   Remove the U-clip from the strut bracket, then detach the hose from the bracket.
7   To install the hose, pass the caliper fitting end through the strut bracket, then con-

nect the fitting to the caliper with the banjo bolt and new copper washers.
8   Make sure the hose isn't twisted between the caliper and the strut bracket.
9   Route the hose into the frame bracket, again making sure it isn't twisted, then connect the brake line fitting, starting the threads by hand. Install the U-clip, then tighten the fitting securely.
10   Bleed the caliper (see Section 11).
11   Install the wheel and lug nuts, lower the vehicle and tighten the lug nuts to the torque listed in the Chapter 1 Specifications.

Rear brake hose

12   The rear brake hoses serve as the flexible connection between the rigid metal lines on the body and the others on the axle. Both ends of the hoses are attached to these metal lines with threaded fittings and U-clips. Refer to Steps 2, 3 and 4. Be sure to bleed the wheel cylinders when you're done (see Section 11).

Metal brake lines

13   When replacing brake lines, be sure to use the correct parts. Don't use copper tubing for any brake system components. Purchase steel brake lines from a dealer or auto parts store.
14   Prefabricated brake line, with the tube ends already flared and fittings installed, is available at auto parts stores and dealer parts departments.
15   When installing the new line, make sure it's securely supported in the brackets and has plenty of clearance between moving or hot components.
16   After installation, check the master cylinder fluid level and add fluid as necessary. Bleed the brake system (see Section 11) and test the brakes carefully before driving the vehicle in traffic.

11   Brake hydraulic system - bleeding

Refer to illustration 11.8

Warning: *Wear eye protection when bleeding the brake system. If the fluid comes in contact with your eyes, immediately rinse them with water and seek medical attention.*
Note: *Bleeding the hydraulic system is necessary to remove any air that manages to find its way into the system when it's been opened during removal and installation of a hose, line, caliper or master cylinder.*
1   You'll probably have to bleed the system at all four brakes if air has entered it due to low fluid level, or if the brake lines have been disconnected at the master cylinder.
2   If a brake line was disconnected only at a wheel, then only that caliper or wheel cylinder must be bled.
3   If a brake line is disconnected at a fitting located between the master cylinder and any of the brakes, that part of the system served by the disconnected line must be bled.

11.8 When bleeding the brakes, a hose is connected to the bleed screw at the caliper or wheel cylinder and then submerged in brake fluid - air will be seen as bubbles in the tube and container (all air must be expelled before moving to the next wheel)

4   Remove any residual vacuum from the brake power booster by applying the brake several times with the engine off.
5   Remove the master cylinder reservoir cap and fill the reservoir with brake fluid. Reinstall the cover. **Note 1:** *Check the fluid level often during the bleeding operation and add fluid as necessary to prevent the fluid level from falling low enough to allow air bubbles into the master cylinder.* **Note 2:** *If you're working on a model equipped with ABS, turn the ignition switch off and disconnect the electrical connectors for the ABS actuator or detach the battery ground cable.*
6   Have an assistant on hand, as well as a supply of new brake fluid, a clear plastic container partially filled with clean brake fluid, a length of 3/16-inch plastic, rubber or vinyl tubing to fit over the bleeder valve and a wrench to open and close the bleeder valve.
7   Beginning at the right rear wheel (non-ABS) or left front wheel (ABS), loosen the bleeder valve slightly, then tighten it to a point where it's snug but can still be loosened quickly and easily.
8   Place one end of the tubing over the bleeder valve and submerge the other end in brake fluid in the container **(see illustration)**.
9   Have the assistant depress the brake pedal slowly and hold the pedal down firmly.
10   While the pedal is held down, open the bleeder valve just enough to allow a flow of fluid to leave the valve. Watch for air bubbles to exit the submerged end of the tube. When the fluid flow slows after a couple of seconds, close the valve and have your assistant release the pedal.
11   Repeat Steps 9 and 10 until no more air is seen leaving the tube, then tighten the bleeder valve and proceed to remaining wheels:
     Non ABS models - The left front wheel, the left rear wheel and the right front wheel, in that order, and perform the same procedure.
     ABS models - The right front wheel, the

9

left rear wheel and the right rear wheel and perform the same procedure. Be sure to check the fluid in the master cylinder reservoir frequently.

12   Never use old brake fluid. It contains moisture which will deteriorate the brake system components and could cause the fluid to boil, which could render the brake system inoperative.

13   Refill the master cylinder with fluid at the end of the operation. If you're working on a model with ABS, be sure to reconnect the electrical connectors to the ABS actuator or reconnect the battery.

14   Check the operation of the brakes. The pedal should feel solid when depressed, with no sponginess. If necessary, repeat the entire process. **Warning:** *Do not operate the vehicle if you're in doubt about the effectiveness of the brake system.*

12   Power brake booster - check, replacement and adjustment

Check

Operating check

1   Depress the brake pedal several times with the engine off and make sure there's no change in the pedal reserve distance.

2   Depress the pedal and start the engine. If the pedal goes down slightly, operation is normal.

Airtightness check

3   Start the engine and turn it off after one or two minutes. Depress the brake pedal slowly several times. If the pedal depresses less each time, the booster is airtight.

4   Depress the brake pedal while the engine is running, then stop the engine with the pedal depressed. If there's no change in the pedal reserve travel after holding the pedal for 30 seconds, the booster is airtight.

Replacement and adjustment

Refer to illustrations 12.7, 12.9, 12.11 and 12.12

Note: *Power brake booster units shouldn't be disassembled. They require special tools not normally found in most automotive repair stations or shops. They're fairly complex and, because of their critical relationship to brake performance, should be replaced with a new or rebuilt one.*

5   Remove the brake master cylinder (see Section 8).

6   Disconnect the vacuum hose leading from the engine to the booster. Be careful not to damage the hose when removing it from the booster fitting.

7   Remove the trim panel below the steering column. Locate the pushrod clevis connecting the booster to the brake pedal **(see illustration)**.

8   Remove the clevis pin retaining clip with pliers and pull out the clevis pin.

12.7 Remove this retaining clip (arrow), pull out the clevis pin and detach the pushrod from the brake pedal

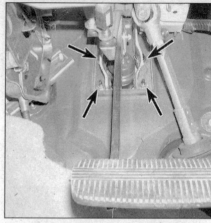

12.9 Remove the four power brake booster mounting nuts (arrows)

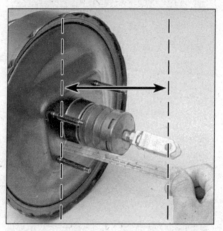

12.11 Measure the distance between the power brake booster and the hole in the clevis and compare your measurement to the dimension listed in this Chapter's Specifications; if they're not the same, adjust the clevis before installing the power brake booster

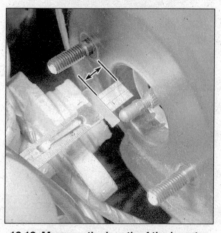

12.12 Measure the length of the booster output rod from the top of the rod to the master cylinder mounting surface and compare your measurement to the specified length listed in this Chapter's Specifications

9   Remove the four nuts and washers holding the brake booster to the firewall **(see illustration)**.

10   Slide the booster straight out from the firewall until the studs clear the holes.

11   Before installing the new booster, measure the distance between the power brake booster and the hole in the clevis **(see illustration)** and compare it to the booster-to-clevis dimension listed in this Chapter's Specifications. If it isn't the same, loosen the adjusting nut and turn the clevis in or out to the specified length, then tighten the nut.

12   Apply about 20 in-Hg of vacuum to the brake booster with a hand-operated vacuum pump, measure the length of the output rod **(see illustration)** and compare your measurement to the dimensions listed in this Chapter's Specifications. If the rod length is outside specifications, turn the adjusting nut (on the end of the output rod) in or out, as necessary.

13   Installation is the reverse of removal.

If you detached the brake lines from the master cylinder, be sure to bleed the brake system (including the master cylinder) (see Section 11).

13   Parking brake - check and adjustment

Check

1   The parking brake pedal, when properly adjusted, should travel 11 to 12 clicks when a moderate pressing force is applied with the foot.

2   If the parking brake pedal travels less than the specified minimum number of clicks, it might not be releasing completely and the shoes or pads could even be dragging against the drum or disc. If the pedal travels more than the specified maximum number of clicks, the parking brake may not hold adequately on an incline, allowing the car to roll.

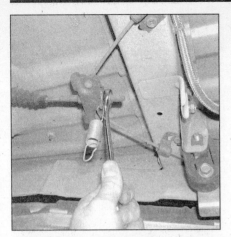

13.4 To adjust parking brake travel, turn this adjusting nut until the specified number of clicks is obtained on the parking brake pedal

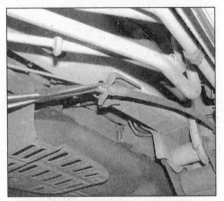

14.6 Squeeze the tangs on the retainers to separate the cable housing from the bracket

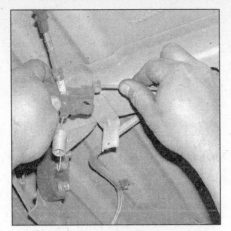

14.4 Disengage the rear parking brake cables from the equalizer

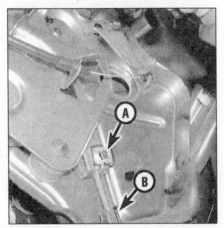

14.14 First, remove the clip (A) from the cable bracket on the parking brake control assembly and then lift the parking brake cable through the slot. Next, squeeze the tangs (B) on the retainer and push the cable housing through the parking brake pedal bracket

14.5 Disconnect the parking brake cable bracket (arrow) and cable from the frame

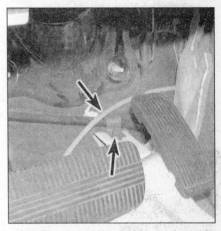

14.16 Disconnect the parking brake cable bracket bolts (arrows) from the floor behind the accelerator pedal

Adjustment

Refer to illustration 13.4

3   Raise the vehicle and support it securely on jackstands. The parking brake adjustment nut is located under the center of the vehicle, slightly toward the rear of the vehicle.

4   Loosen or tighten the adjusting nut **(see illustration)** until the desired travel is attained. Turn the nut clockwise to tighten the cable and decrease the number of clicks at the parking brake pedal, or turn it counter-clockwise to loosen the cable and increase the number of clicks at the pedal.

14 Parking brake cables - replacement

Rear cables

Refer to illustrations 14.4, 14.5 and 14.6

1   Make sure the parking brake is completely released.

2   Loosen the rear wheel lug nuts, raise the rear of the vehicle and support it securely on jackstands. Block the front wheels. Remove the wheel.

3   Remove the brake drum and brake shoes, and disconnect the cable from the parking brake lever on the rear shoe **(see illustration 6.8h)**. Disconnect the cable retainer from the backing plate and pull the cable through the backing plate.

4   Disengage the rear cables from the equalizer **(see illustration)**.

5   Remove the cable bracket bolts **(see illustration)**.

6   Squeeze the tangs on the retainers and pass the cable housing through the brackets **(see illustration)**.

7   Installation is the reverse of removal. Apply a light coat of grease to the portion of the cable end that engages with the equalizer.

8   Adjust the parking brake when you're done (see Section 13).

Front cable

Refer to illustrations 14.14 and 14.16

9   Disconnect the negative battery cable.

10   Remove the left side kick panel near the parking brake pedal (see Chapter 11).

11   Remove the accelerator pedal stop screw and remove the accelerator pedal stop.

12   Pull the carpet back all the way to the front seat for additional clearance.

13   Remove the mounting bolts from the parking brake opening cover and separate the cover from the floor.

14   Disconnect the front parking brake cable and housing from the parking brake pedal assembly **(see illustration)**. First, disengage the front parking brake cable from the control assembly by removing the clip and lifting the cable through the slot in the bracket.

15   Next, squeeze the tangs on the cable retainer and pull the cable and the housing through the control assembly.

16   Remove the cable bracket from the floor, near the accelerator pedal **(see illustration)**.

17   Remove the cable end from the parking brake control lever and lift the parking brake cable from the passenger compartment.

18   Installation is the reverse of removal. Apply a light coat of grease to the portion of the cable end that engages with the control lever.

9

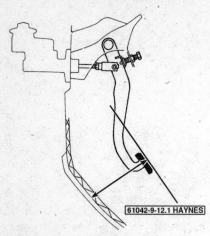

61042-9-12.1 HAYNES

15.1 With the brake pedal fully released, measure the distance from the top of the pad to the floor

19   Adjust the parking brake assembly when you're done (see Section 13).

15   Brake pedal - adjustment

Brake pedal released height

Refer to illustrations 15.1 and 15.3

1   With the brake pedal fully released, measure the distance from the top of the pad to the floor **(see illustration)**. It will be necessary to pull back the carpet to position the ruler against the floor.

2   If the height is not as listed in the Specifications Section at the beginning of this Chapter, it must be adjusted.

3   Loosen the locknut just in front of the power brake booster clevis **(see illustration)**.

4   Turn the booster input rod until the pedal height is correct.

5   Tighten the locknut.

6   After adjusting the pedal height, check the freeplay.

Brake pedal freeplay

Refer to illustration 15.7

7   Press down lightly on the brake pedal and, with a ruler, measure the distance that it moves freely before resistance is felt **(see illustration)**. The freeplay should be within the specified limits. If it isn't, it must be adjusted.

8   Loosen the locknut for the brake booster clevis **(see illustration 15.3)**.

9   Turn the booster input rod until the pedal freeplay is correct.

10   Tighten the locknut.

Brake pedal depressed height

11   After checking and, if necessary, adjusting the pedal released height and freeplay,

15.3 To adjust brake pedal released height, loosen the locknut (arrow) in front of the brake booster clevis and turn the input rod until free height is correct (this procedure is also used to adjust brake pedal freeplay)

the pedal depressed height must be checked.

12   With the engine running, press the brake pedal fully and measure the pedal pad-to-floor distance. It will be necessary to pull back the carpet to position the ruler against the floor.

13   If the minimum depressed height is below that listed in the Specifications Section listed at the beginning of this Chapter, check the brake system for leaks or other damage.

16   Brake light switch - check and replacement

Check

Refer to illustration 16.1

1   The brake light switch **(see illustration)** is located on a bracket at the top of the brake pedal. The switch activates the brake lights at the rear of the vehicle when the pedal is depressed.

2   To check the brake light switch, simply note whether the brake lights come on when the pedal is depressed and go off when the pedal is released.

3   If the brake lights don't come on when the brake pedal is depressed, make sure the brake pedal is correctly adjusted (see Section 15). Then try adjusting the switch as follows.

4   A locknut secures the switch to the bracket. Loosen the locknut, then screw the switch in or out to provide a 1/64 to 1/32-inch clearance between the switch plunger and the pedal stopper, with no pressure on the plunger, and tighten the locknut. Recheck the clearance to verify that it didn't change when you tightened the locknut. The switch should

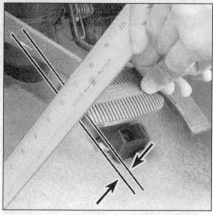

15.7 To measure brake pedal freeplay, press down lightly on the brake pedal and, with a ruler, measure the distance that it moves freely before resistance is felt

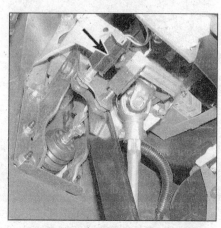

16.1 The brake light switch (arrow) is located at the top of the brake pedal; to remove the switch, unplug the electrical connector, loosen the locknut and unscrew the switch from the bracket

now function properly.

5   If the switch still doesn't work properly, either it isn't getting voltage, or the switch itself is defective. Use a voltmeter or test light to verify that there's voltage at the switch connector. With the pedal at rest, voltage should be present at one of the terminals of the switch. With the pedal depressed, voltage should be present at both terminals. If voltage isn't present at both terminals when the pedal is depressed, replace the switch.

Replacement

6   Unplug the electrical connector from the brake light switch.

7   Remove the locknut, unscrew the switch and remove it.

8   Installation is the reverse of removal.

9   Adjust the brake pedal (see Section 15), then adjust the switch (see above).

Chapter 10
Suspension and steering systems

Contents

Specifications

Torque specifications

Ft-lbs (unless otherwise indicated)

Front suspension

Balljoint-to-steering knuckle nut	52 to 63
Balljoint-to-control arm bolts	56 to 80
Control arm	
Front nut	94 to 115
Rear bolts	87 to 108
Gusset bolts	87 to 108
Stabilizer bar	
Link-to-stabilizer nut	34 to 38
Link-to-control arm bolt	12 to 16
Stabilizer clamp bolts and nuts	31 to 37
Strut/coil spring assembly	
Strut-to-steering knuckle bolts/nuts	94 to 108
Strut-to-body upper mounting nuts	29 to 40
Piston rod nut	43 to 58
Steering stop bolt jam nut	58 to 72

10

Rear suspension

Axle bumper-to-frame rail.. 12 to 16
Axle nut... 145 to 210
Brake backing plate-to-axle bolts .... 28 to 38
Leaf spring assembly
    Front mount nuts.. 40 to 55
    U-bolt nuts .... 53 to 72
    Shackle nuts (rear)... 37 to 50
Shock absorber nuts .... 22 to 30
Stabilizer bar
    Stabilizer bar bushing clamp nuts... 23 to 31
    Stabilizer bar-to-link rod nuts.. 29 to 33
    Stabilizer bar link-to-bushing bracket bolts .... 12 to 16

Steering

Airbag module Torx bolts .... 11 to 18
Intermediate shaft cover nuts .... 17 to 22
Power steering pump bolts .... 22 to 27
Power steering pump pulley bolt.. 40 to 50
Power steering pump-to-high pressure line banjo bolt .... 36 to 51
Power steering pump return line bolts .... 10 to 13
Steering column lower yoke pinch bolt .... 30 to 42
Steering column mounting nuts.. 9 to 13
Steering gear mounting bracket bolts .... 54 to 72
Steering gear-to-intermediate shaft pinch bolt .... 17 to 22
Steering wheel nut .... 22 to 29
Tie-rod end-to-steering knuckle nut.. 22 to 29

1.1 Typical front suspension components

1	Control arm gusset	4	Steering knuckle
2	Control arm	5	Strut/coil spring assembly
3	Balljoint	6	Steering gear
		7	Stabilizer bar

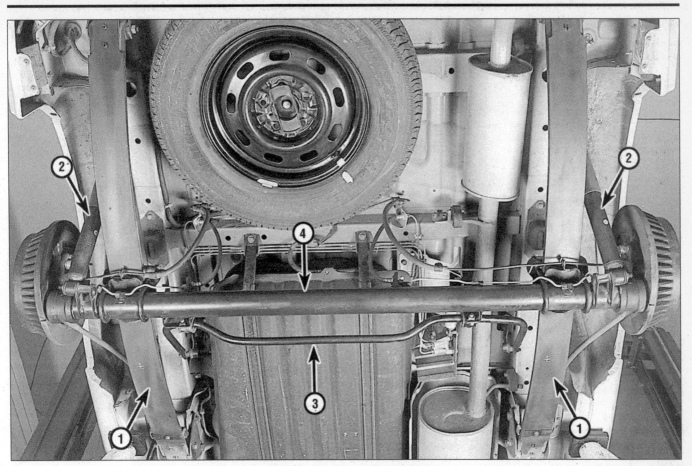

1.2 Typical rear suspension components

| 1 | Leaf spring | 2 | Shock absorber | 3 | Stabilizer bar | 4 | Axle assembly |

1   General information

Refer to illustrations 1.1 and 1.2

The front suspension system is a strut/coil spring design **(see illustration)**. The upper end of each strut is attached to the vehicle body. The lower end of the strut is connected to the upper end of the steering knuckle. The steering knuckle is attached to a balljoint mounted on the outer end of the control arm. The control arms are attached to the lower arm gussets. Both the control arms and the gussets must be checked after curb damage, improper hoisting or alignment problems. A stabilizer bar is used on all models. The stabilizer bar is attached to the lower arm gussets with a pair of clamps and to the control arms with link rods.

The rear suspension is composed of leaf springs and a tube axle housing mounted on the axle pad by U-bolts, spring plates and nuts **(see illustration)**. The leaf springs vary according to the package. The optional handling package requires a heavy duty leaf spring. This system can be identified by the rear stabilizer bar. Light duty versions are not equipped with the stabilizer bar. The rear stabilizer bar which is attached to the rear axle tube and the frame brackets through link

rods, provides increased stability for handling and load control. A pair of shock absorbers control vehicle "bounce".

The rack-and-pinion steering gear is located behind the engine/transaxle assembly at the bottom of the firewall. The steering gear actuates the tie-rods, which are attached to the steering knuckles. The inner ends of the tie-rods are protected by rubber boots which should be inspected periodically for secure attachment, tears and leaking lubricant.

The power assist system consists of a belt-driven pump and associated lines and hoses. The fluid level in the power steering pump reservoir should be checked periodically (see Chapter 1).

The steering wheel operates the steering shaft, which actuates the steering gear through universal joints. Looseness in the steering can be caused by wear in the steering shaft universal joints, the steering gear, the tie-rod ends and loose retaining bolts.

These models are equipped with either a passive seat belt restraint system (automatic seat belts) or regular seat belts and a supplemental restraint system (airbag). Any work in the vicinity of the steering column, instrument panel or near the airbag sensors will require the airbag to be disarmed. When the airbag

system is functioning normally, the AIRBAG warning light on the dash will illuminate for about seven seconds when the ignition switch is placed in the ON or START positions. Refer to Chapter 12 for the airbag disabling procedure.

Frequently, when working on the suspension or steering system components, you may come across fasteners, which seem impossible to loosen. These fasteners on the underside of the vehicle are continually subjected to water, road grime, mud, etc., and can become rusted or "frozen," making them extremely difficult to remove. In order to unscrew these stubborn fasteners without damaging them (or other components), be sure to use lots of penetrating oil and allow it to soak in for a while. Using a wire brush to clean exposed threads will also ease removal of the nut or bolt and prevent damage to the threads. Sometimes a sharp blow with a hammer and punch will break the bond between a nut and bolt threads, but care must be taken to prevent the punch from slipping off the fastener and ruining the threads. Heating the stuck fastener and surrounding area with a torch sometimes helps too, but isn't recommended because of the obvious dangers associated with fire. Long breaker bars and extension, or "cheater,"

10

pipes will increase leverage, but never use an extension pipe on a ratchet - the ratcheting mechanism could be damaged. Sometimes tightening the nut or bolt first will help to break it loose. Fasteners that require drastic measures to remove should always be replaced with new ones.

Since most of the procedures dealt with in this Chapter involve jacking up the vehicle and working underneath it, a good pair of jackstands will be needed. A hydraulic floor jack is the preferred type of jack to lift the vehicle, and it can also be used to support certain components during various operations. **Warning:** *Never, under any circumstances, rely on a jack to support the vehicle while working on it. Whenever any of the suspension or steering fasteners are loosened or removed they must be inspected and, if necessary, replaced with new ones of the same part number or of original equipment quality and design. Torque specifications must be followed for proper reassembly and component retention. Never attempt to heat or straighten any suspension or steering components. Instead, replace any bent or damaged part with a new one.*

2 Strut/coil spring assembly (front) - removal, inspection and installation

Removal

Refer to illustrations 2.2, 2.3 and 2.6

1   Loosen the front wheel lug nuts, raise the front of the vehicle and support it securely on jackstands. Remove the wheels.

2   Unclip the brake hose from the strut bracket **(see illustration)** and detach it from the bracket.

3   If the vehicle is equipped with ABS, detach the speed sensor wiring harness from the strut by removing the clamp bracket bolt **(see illustration)**.

4   Remove the strut-to-knuckle nuts and knock the bolts out with a hammer and punch.

5   Separate the strut from the steering knuckle. Be careful not to overextend the inner CV joint and don't let the knuckle fall outward, as this could damage the brake hose.

6   Make a reference mark on one of the strut mounting studs and the strut tower. Support the strut and spring assembly with one hand and remove the three strut upper mounting nuts **(see illustration)**. Remove the assembly out from the fenderwell.

Inspection

7   Check the strut body for leaking fluid, dents, cracks and other obvious damage, which would warrant repair or replacement.

8   Check the coil spring for chips or cracks in the spring coating (this will cause premature spring failure due to corrosion). Inspect the spring seat for cuts, hardness and general deterioration.

9   If any undesirable conditions exist, pro-

2.2 Remove the retaining clip with a pair of pliers and detach the brake hose from the strut

ceed to the strut disassembly procedure (see Section 3).

Installation

10   Guide the strut assembly up into the fenderwell and insert the upper mounting studs through the holes in the shock tower. Be sure to install the stud with the mark made in Step 6 into the designated hole in the strut tower. Once the studs protrude from the strut tower, install the nuts so the strut won't fall back through. This is most easily accomplished with the help of an assistant, as the strut is quite heavy and awkward.

11   Slide the steering knuckle into the strut flange and insert the bolts. Install <u>new</u> nuts and tighten them to the torque listed in this Chapter's Specifications.

12   Guide the brake hose through its bracket in the strut and install the retaining clip.

13   Install the wheel and lug nuts, then lower the vehicle and tighten the lug nuts to the torque listed in the Chapter 1 Specifications.

14   Tighten the upper mounting nuts to the torque listed in this Chapter's Specifications.

3 Strut/coil spring assembly - replacement

1   If the struts or coil springs exhibit the telltale signs of wear (leaking fluid, loss of damping capability, chipped, sagging or cracked coil springs) explore all options before beginning any work. The strut/shock absorber assemblies are not serviceable and must be replaced if a problem develops. However, strut assemblies complete with springs may be available on an exchange basis, which eliminates much time and work. Whichever route you choose to take, check on the cost and availability of parts before disassembling your vehicle. **Warning:** *Disassembling a strut is potentially dangerous and utmost attention must be directed to the job, or serious injury may result. Use only a high-*

2.3 To detach the strut assembly from the steering knuckle, remove the wheel speed sensor harness bracket bolt (right arrow), remove the two nuts (left arrows), then drive out the strut-to-knuckle bolts with a hammer and punch

quality spring compressor and carefully follow the manufacturer's instructions furnished with the tool. After removing the coil spring from the strut assembly, set it aside in a safe, isolated area.

Disassembly

Refer to illustrations 3.3, 3.4, 3.5, 3.7 and 3.8

2   Remove the strut and spring assembly following the procedure described in the previous Section. Mount the strut assembly in a vise. Line the vise jaws with wood or rags to prevent damage to the unit and don't tighten the vise excessively.

3   Following the tool manufacturer's instructions, install the spring compressor (which can be obtained at most auto parts stores or equipment yards on a daily rental basis) on the spring and compress it sufficiently to relieve all pressure from the upper spring seat **(see illustration)**. This can be verified by wiggling the spring.

4   Remove the damper shaft nut **(see illustration)**.

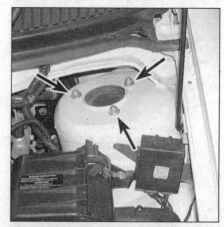

2.6 To detach the upper end of the strut assembly from the body, remove the upper mounting nuts (arrows)

3.3 Install the spring compressor according to the tool manufacturer's instructions and compress the spring until all pressure is relieved from the upper spring seat

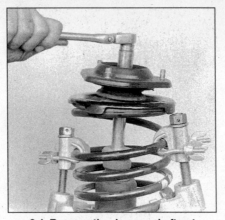

3.4 Remove the damper shaft nut

3.5 Lift the suspension support off the damper shaft

5   Remove the upper suspension support **(see illustration)**. Check the rubber portion of the suspension support for cracking and general deterioration. If there is any separation of the rubber, replace it.

6   Remove the bearing from the spring seat. Inspect the bearing for smooth operation. If it does not turn smoothly, replace it.

7   Lift the spring seat and upper insulator from the damper shaft **(see illustration)**. Check the rubber spring seat for cracking and hardness, replacing it if necessary.

8   Carefully lift the compressed spring from the assembly **(see illustration)** and set it in a safe place. **Warning:** *Carry the spring carefully and never place any part of your body near the end of the spring!*

9   Slide the dust boot off the damper shaft.

10   Check the lower insulator (if equipped) for wear, cracking and hardness and replace it if necessary.

Reassembly

Refer to illustrations 3.12, 3.13a and 3.13b

11   If the lower insulator is being replaced, set it into position with the dropped portion seated in the lowest part of the seat. Extend

3.7 Remove the spring seat from the damper shaft

the damper rod to its full length and install the dust boot.

12   Carefully place the compressed coil spring onto the lower insulator, with the end of the spring resting in the lowest part of the insulator **(see illustration)**.

13   Install the upper insulator and the spring seat. Make sure the cutout on the spring seat is facing out (away from the vehicle), in line with the strut-to-knuckle flange opening **(see illustrations)**.

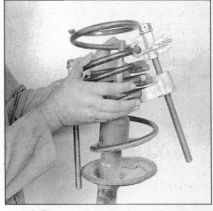

3.8 Remove the compressed spring assembly - keep the ends of the spring pointed away from your body

14   Install the bearing onto the spring seat.

15   Install the dust seal and suspension support to the damper shaft.

16   Install the nut and tighten it to the torque listed in this Chapter's Specifications.

17   Carefully release the tension on the spring and remove the spring compressor.

18   Install the strut/coil spring assembly (see Section 2).

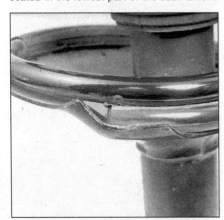

3.12 When installing the spring, make sure the end fits into the recessed portion of the lower seat (arrow)

3.13a Make sure this cutout in the upper seat . . .

3.13b . . . is facing out (toward the strut-to-knuckle flange)

10

4.1 Unstake the driveaxle hub nut using a chisel and hammer – install the spare tire onto the hub if the nut is not accessible through the wheel

4.2 Use a breaker bar and socket to loosen the driveaxle hub nut

4   Steering knuckle - removal and installation

Warning: *Dust created by the brake system may contain asbestos, which is harmful to your health. Never blow it out with compressed air and don't inhale any of it. Do not, under any circumstances, use petroleum-based solvents to clean brake parts. Use brake system cleaner only.*

Removal

Refer to illustrations 4.1, 4.2, 4.8a, 4.8b, 4.8c and 4.8d

1   Remove the center cap and unstake the driveaxle/hub nut **(see illustration)**. **Note:** *If the driveaxle/hub nut cannot be accessed through the opening in the wheel, install the spare tire and wheel.*

2   Use a breaker bar and socket and loosen the driveaxle/hub nut **(see illustration)**.

3   Loosen the wheel lug nuts slightly, raise the front of the vehicle and support it securely on jackstands. Remove the wheel and the driveaxle/hub nut.

4   Remove the brake caliper and the brake disc, and disconnect the brake hose from the strut (see Chapter 9).

5   If the vehicle is equipped with ABS, disconnect and remove the wheel speed sensor (see Chapter 9).

6   Remove the strut-to-steering knuckle nuts, but don't remove the bolts yet (see Section 2).

7   Separate the tie-rod end from the steering knuckle arm (see Section 15).

8   Remove the cotter pin and loosen the balljoint stud nut **(see illustrations)**. Separate the balljoint stud from the steering knuckle with a "picklefork" type balljoint separator **(see illustration)**. Be sure to grease the picklefork to protect the balljoint dust boot. Separate the arm from the steering knuckle **(see illustration)**.

9   Press the driveaxle from the hub (see Chapter 8). Pull the steering knuckle out away from the vehicle and withdraw the driveaxle stubshaft from the hub splines. Support the end of the driveaxle with a sec-

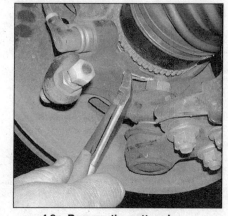

4.8a Remove the cotter pin . . .

tion of wire.

10   Remove the strut-to-knuckle bolts and separate the knuckle from the strut.

11   If necessary, remove the steering stop bolt from the knuckle. Paint an alignment mark on the threads to insure correct installation.

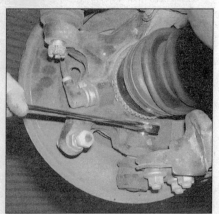

4.8b . . . loosen the balljoint stud nut and back it off as far as it will go (without actually removing it) . . .

4.8c . . . then separate the balljoint stud from the steering knuckle with a "picklefork" (be sure to grease the pickle fork to protect the balljoint dust boot)

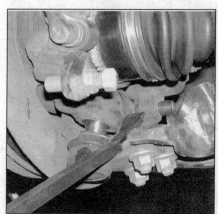

4.8d Separate the control arm from the steering knuckle by prying it down with a prybar or large screwdriver

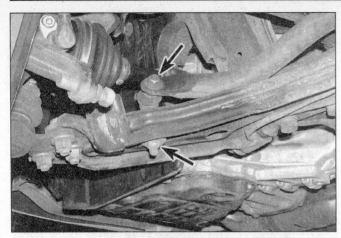

6.2 To disconnect the stabilizer link from the control arm, remove the nut that attaches the link to the control arm (lower arrow); to disconnect the link from the stabilizer bar, remove the upper nut (upper arrow)

6.3 To disconnect the stabilizer bar from the body, remove the bushing clamp nuts and bolts (arrows) from both sides of the control arm gussets

Installation

12 Guide the knuckle and hub assembly into position, inserting the driveaxle into the hub.
13 Push the knuckle into the strut flange and install the bolts and nuts, but don't tighten them yet.
14 Attach the control arm to the steering knuckle. Tighten the balljoint stud nut to the torque listed in this Chapter's Specifications and insert a new cotter pin.
15 Attach the tie-rod end to the steering knuckle arm (see Section 15).
16 Tighten the strut-to-knuckle nuts to the torque listed in this Chapter's Specifications.
17 Place the brake disc on the hub and install the caliper (see Chapter 9). Install the wheel speed sensor (if equipped) and connect the brake hose to the strut.
18 Install the driveaxle/hub nut and tighten it securely (but not completely yet).
19 Install the steering stop bolt, if removed. Tighten the jam nut to the torque listed in this Chapter's Specifications.
20 Install the wheel and tighten the lug nuts but don't torque them yet.
21 Lower the vehicle and tighten the wheel

lug nuts to the torque listed in the Chapter 1 Specifications. Tighten the driveaxle/hub nut to the torque listed in the Chapter 8 Specifications.

5 Hub and wheel bearing assembly (front) - removal and installation

Due to the special tools and expertise required to press the hub and bearing from the steering knuckle, this job should be left to a professional mechanic. However, the steering knuckle and hub may be removed and the assembly taken to a dealer service department or other repair shop. See Section 4 for the steering knuckle and hub removal procedure.

6 Stabilizer bar (front) - removal and installation

Refer to illustrations 6.2 and 6.3
1 Loosen the wheel lug nuts, raise the front of the vehicle, support it securely on jackstands and remove the wheels.

2 Disconnect the stabilizer bar-to-link nuts from both control arms **(see illustration)**.
3 Remove both stabilizer bar clamps **(see illustration)** from the control arm gussets.
4 Remove the stabilizer bar and link assembly.
5 Inspect the clamp bushings and the link bushings. If they're cracked or torn, replace them.
6 Installation is the reverse of removal. Be sure to tighten all fasteners to the torque listed in this Chapter's Specifications.

7 Control arm - removal, inspection and installation

Removal

Refer to illustrations 7.4 and 7.5
1 Loosen the wheel lug nuts on the side to be dismantled, raise the front of the vehicle, support it securely on jackstands and remove the wheel.
2 Disconnect the stabilizer bar link from the control arm (see Section 6).
3 Separate the balljoint from the control arm **(see illustration 8.3)**.
4 Remove the front pivot bolt nut and/or bolt **(see illustration)** from the control arm gusset.
5 Remove the rear bushing clamp bolts **(see illustration)**. Remove the control arm.
6 If necessary, remove the lower arm gussets. Each lower arm gusset is attached to the frame by five bolts. Remove the bolts and separate the gusset from the vehicle.

Inspection

7 Inspect the front and rear bushings for cracks and tears. If either bushing is damaged or worn, replace the damaged bushing. The front and rear bushings must be installed into the control arm using a press. Have the bushing(s) installed by a dealer service department or other automotive repair facility.

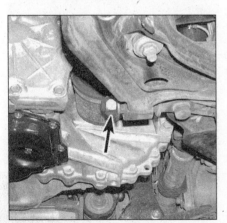

7.4 Remove the front pivot stud nut (arrow)

7.5 Remove the rear bushing clamp bolts (arrows)

10

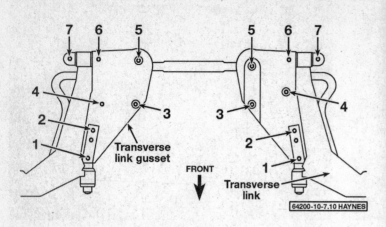

7.10 Gusset bolt tightening sequence

8.3 Remove the nuts (arrows) to separate the balljoint from the control arm

8   Inspect the control arm for straightness. If it's bent, replace it. Do not attempt to straighten a bent control arm.
9   Inspect the control arm gusset for straightness. If it is bent or damaged, replace it with a new control arm gusset.

Installation

Refer to illustration 7.10
10   If the control arm gussets were removed, install the gussets and bolts and tighten the bolts to the torque listed in this Chapter's Specifications. Follow the recommended tightening sequence **(see illustration)**.
11   Installation is the reverse of removal. Tighten all of the fasteners to the torque listed in this Chapter's Specifications. Be sure to install a new cotter pin through the balljoint stud.
12   Install the wheel and lug nuts, lower the vehicle and tighten the lug nuts to the torque listed in the Chapter 1 Specifications.

8   Balljoints - replacement

Refer to illustration 8.3
1   Loosen the wheel lug nuts, raise the vehicle and support it securely on jackstands. Remove the wheel.
2   Separate the balljoint from the steering knuckle (see Section 4).
3   Remove the three control arm-to-balljoint nuts **(see illustration)**.
4   Remove the balljoint from the control arm.
5   Installation is the reverse of removal.
6   Be sure to tighten all fasteners to the torque listed in this Chapter's Specifications. Install a new cotter pin through the balljoint stud.
7   Install the wheel and lug nuts. Lower the vehicle and tighten the lug nuts to the torque listed in the Chapter 1 Specifications.

9   Shock absorbers (rear) - removal and installation

Removal

Refer to illustrations 9.3 and 9.4
1   Raise the rear of the vehicle and support it securely on jackstands. Block the front wheels to keep the vehicle from moving.
2   Support the axle with a floor jack. Raise the jack just enough to support the weight of the axle.
3   Remove the upper shock absorber nut **(see illustration)**.
4   Remove the lower mounting nut **(see illustration)** and pull the shock absorber off its mounts.

Installation

5   Position the shock absorber onto its mounts. Install the upper mounting nut finger tight.
6   Install the lower mounting nut bolt finger tight.
7   Tighten the nuts to the torque listed in this Chapter's Specifications.

9.3 Remove the upper shock absorber nut (arrow) at the frame rail

10   Hub and wheel bearing assembly (rear) - removal and installation

Refer to illustrations 10.3, 10.4, 10.5 and 10.7
Note: *Due to the special tools and expertise required to press the hub and bearing from the knuckle, this job should be left to a professional mechanic. However, the hub and bearing assembly may be removed and the assembly taken to a dealer service department or other repair shop.*
1   Loosen the wheel lug nuts slightly, raise the rear of the vehicle and support it securely on jackstands. Remove the wheel.
2   Remove the brake drum (see Chapter 9).
3   Remove the center cap **(see illustration)**.
4   Remove the cotter pin from the spindle **(see illustration)**.
5   Use a breaker bar and socket and loosen the hub nut **(see illustration)**.
6   Remove the hub nut.
7   Remove the hub and bearing assembly **(see illustration)**.
8   Installation is the reverse of removal. Be sure to tighten all fasteners to the torque listed in this Chapter's Specifications. Install a new cotter pin.

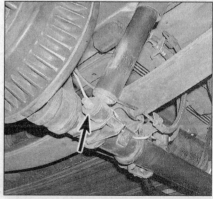

9.4 Remove the lower shock absorber nut (arrow) at the axle

10.3 Use a chisel and hammer to remove the grease cap from the hub

10.4 Use a pair of pliers to remove the cotter pin from the spindle

10.5 Unscrew the axle nut from the spindle

10.7 Slide the hub and wheel bearing assembly off the spindle

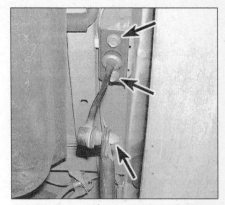

11.2 To disconnect the stabilizer link from the frame, remove the upper bolts (upper arrows) - to disconnect the stabilizer link from the stabilizer bar, remove the nut (lower arrow)

11 Stabilizer bar (rear) - removal, inspection, and installation

Removal

Refer to illustrations 11.2 and 11.3

1   Raise the vehicle and support it securely on jackstands.
2   Remove the two stabilizer bar-to-link arm bolts on each side of the vehicle (see illustration).

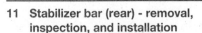

3   Remove the stabilizer bar bracket bolts on each side of the vehicle (see illustration).
4   Remove the stabilizer bar from the vehicle.
5   If the link arms need to be replaced, remove the link arm-to-bracket bolt and remove the link arm from the frame rail bracket.

Inspection

6   Inspect for broken or distorted clamps and bushings. Replace parts as necessary.

Installation

7   Connect the link arms to the frame rail brackets. Do not tighten them yet.
8   Place the stabilizer bar bushing on the stabilizer bar.
9   Place the bar on the rear axle and install the brackets and bolts. Do not tighten them yet.
10   Install the link arm bolts on the stabilizer bar. Do not tighten them yet.
11   Tighten all bolts to the torque listed in this Chapter's Specifications.

12 Leaf spring - removal and installation

10

Removal

Refer to illustrations 12.3, 12.5, 12.6 and 12.7

1   Raise the vehicle and support it securely on jackstands. Block the front tires to keep the vehicle from moving.
2   Place a floor jack under the axle and raise the axle until the weight is off the leaf spring.
3   Remove the U-bolt nuts from the top of the spring plate (see illustration).

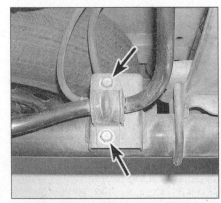

11.3 To disconnect the rear stabilizer bushing clamps, remove these bolts (arrows)

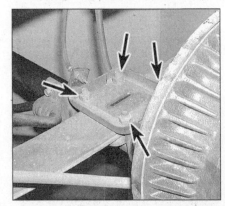

12.3 Remove the U-bolt nuts (arrows) from the spring plate

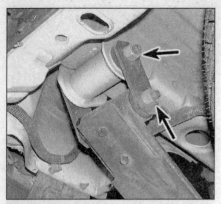

12.5 Remove the shackle nuts (arrows) from the rear of the leaf spring

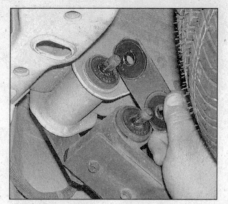

12.6 Remove the shackle end plate from the leaf spring and the frame mount

12.7 Remove the pivot bolt (arrow) from the front mount of the leaf spring

4   Remove the U-bolts and the spring plate from the leaf spring.

5   Remove the rear shackle bracket nuts **(see illustration)**.

6   Remove the shackle from the leaf spring bushing **(see illustration)**.

7   Loosen the leaf spring front pivot bolt **(see illustration)**.

8   Remove the leaf spring front pivot bolt and remove the leaf spring.

9   If necessary, remove the front mount-to-body bolts and remove the mount. **Note:** *To remove the front mounting plate from the right side of the vehicle, it will be necessary to remove the muffler resonator assembly (see Chapter 4). To remove the front mounting plate on the left side of the vehicle, it will be necessary to remove the fuel tank (see Chapter 4).*

Installation

10   Installation is the reverse of removal. If removed, tighten the front mount-to-body bolts to the torque listed in this Chapter's Specifications. **Note:** *On the left side leaf spring, mount the front pivot bolt and the front leaf spring mount bolts with the head of the bolts on the mounting plate marked INNER. On the right side leaf spring, mount the front pivot bolt and the front leaf spring mount bolts with the head of the bolts on the mounting plate marked OUTER.*

11   Do not tighten the rear spring shackle nuts and the front pivot bolt until the vehicle is lowered and the full weight of the vehicle is

on the rear wheels.

12   Tighten the nuts and bolts to the torque listed in this Chapter's Specifications.

---

13   Axle assembly (rear) - removal and installation

Removal

Refer to illustration 13.3

1   Loosen the rear wheel lug nuts, raise the vehicle and support it securely on jackstands.

2   Remove the rear wheels and the brake drums. Disconnect the parking brake cables from the actuating lever and the backing plate (see Chapter 9). Secure the parking brake cables aside.

3   Disconnect the brake hoses from the brake lines at the brackets on the rear axle assembly (one on each side) **(see illustration)**. Cap the open brake lines to prevent the loss of brake fluid.

4   If equipped, remove the ABS wheel speed sensors. Remove the bolt from the speed sensor harness bracket and secure the harness aside.

5   Disconnect the brake load sensing proportioning valve from the rear axle assembly (see Chapter 9).

6   Disconnect the rear stabilizer bar from the rear axle assembly (see Section 11).

7   Support the axle with a floor jack.

8   Remove the shock absorber lower bolts

(see Section 9).

9   Remove the spring plate and U-bolts from the axles **(see illustration 12.3)**.

10   Lower the axle assembly and remove it from under the vehicle.

Installation

11   If necessary, transfer the brake backing plate, brake components and spindle to the replacement axle assembly. **Note:** *The spindle and backing plate are retained to the axle flange by the same four bolts.*

12   Place the axle assembly under the vehicle with the axle pad in the correct position in relation to the leaf spring on each side of the vehicle. Raise the axle assembly and align the pilot hole in the axle pad with the alignment bolt.

13   Install the U-bolts and spring plates and raise the axle into position against the leaf springs. Tighten the spring plate nuts to the torque listed in this Chapter's Specifications.

14   Install the lower shock absorber mounting nuts. Tighten the nuts to the torque listed this Chapter's Specifications.

15   Install the stabilizer bar (see Section 11). Tighten the bolts to the torque listed in this Chapter's Specifications.

16   Connect the brake hoses to the brake lines and install the retaining clips.

17   Install the parking brake cables and the ABS wheel speed sensors.

18   Connect the brake load sensing proportioning valve (see Chapter 9).

19   Install the rear brake drums and the rear wheels.

20   Bleed the rear brakes before placing the vehicle back in service (see Chapter 9).

---

14   Steering wheel - removal and installation

Warning: *Some models are equipped with Supplemental Restraint Systems (SRS), more commonly known as airbags. Always disable the airbag system before working in the vicinity of any airbag system components to avoid the possibility of accidental deployment of the airbag(s) which could cause personal injury (see Chapter 12).*

13.3 At each side, disconnect the brake line from the brake hose and remove the clip (right arrow) retaining the hose to the bracket - immediately cap the open brake lines to prevent the loss of brake fluid (left arrow indicates the wheel speed sensor harness bracket bolt)

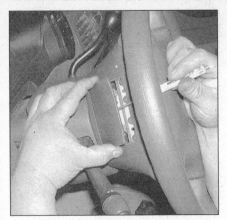

14.3 Pry off the access cover from the underside of the steering wheel and unplug the airbag module connector (steering wheel rotated for easy access)

14.4 Unplug the airbag harness connector

14.5 Pry off the two small covers from each side of the steering wheel

14.6a Remove the Torx bolt (arrow) (right side shown); the Torx bolts are coated with a special bonding agent, so they must be discarded - be sure to replace them during reassembly

14.6b Location of the airbag module bolt (arrow) under the left side access cover

14.7 Carefully remove the airbag module

Airbag models

Warning: *The airbag module bolts are coated with a special thread-locking compound. Once removed, they cannot be reused. Discard the bolts and obtain new airbag module bolts for installation.*

14.8 Disconnect the electrical connector for the cruise control switches; after the steering wheel retaining nut has been removed, mark the relationship of the steering wheel to the steering shaft (arrows)

14.10 Use a steering wheel puller to separate the steering wheel from the steering shaft

Removal

Refer to illustrations 14.3, 14.4, 14.5, 14.6a, 14.6b, 14.7, 14.8, 14.10 and 14.11

1   Disconnect the cable from the negative battery terminal, then the positive battery terminal and wait at least ten minutes before removing the steering wheel.

2   Turn the steering wheel so that the front wheels are pointing straight ahead.

3   Remove the access cover from the bottom of the steering wheel **(see illustration).**

4   Unplug the airbag module connector **(see illustration).**

5   Remove the right and the left side covers from each side of the steering wheel **(see illustration)** to access the airbag module bolts.

6   Remove and discard the airbag module bolts **(see illustrations).**

7   Disconnect the airbag module harness connector from the clockspring mechanism and lift the airbag module off the steering wheel **(see illustration). Warning:** *Handle the airbag module with care, carry the module with the trim cover side facing away from your body and store it in a safe location with the trim side facing up. See the precautions in Chapter 12.*

8   Remove the steering wheel retaining nut, then mark the relationship of the steering wheel to the steering shaft **(see illustration).**

9   Disconnect the electrical connector for the cruise control wiring harness, if equipped.

10   Remove the steering wheel from the steering shaft **(see illustration).** When removing the wheel, make sure the electrical leads for the airbag module and the cruise control system don't snag on the wheel. **Warning:** *Do not turn the steering shaft while the steering wheel is removed.*

10

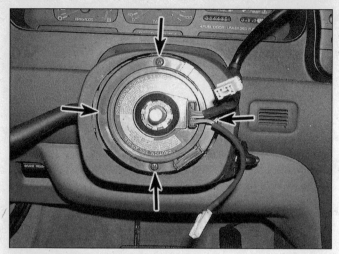

14.11 If the clockspring must be removed from the steering column, tape the center hub to the outer ring so the center hub cannot rotate and remove the mounting screws (arrows)

15.2 Loosen the jam nut, then mark the position of the tie-rod end in relation to the inner tie-rod threads

11   Remove the clockspring only if the steering column will be removed or if the steering column switches must be checked or replaced. **Caution:** *Regardless if the clockspring will be removed or not, tape the center hub of the clockspring to the outer ring so the center hub cannot rotate. This will retain the clockspring in the centered position* **(see illustration).**

12   If necessary, remove the screws, disconnect the clockspring connector and separate the clockspring from the steering column.

Installation

13   Install the clockspring onto the steering column if it was removed. Be sure the connector wire has been attached before installing the clockspring.

14   Verify that the front wheels are pointing straight ahead.

15   Make absolutely sure you have not turned the steering shaft while the wheel was removed or allowed the center hub of the clockspring assembly to become uncentered. If necessary, center the clockspring as follows:

a) *Rotate the clockspring hub clockwise until it stops. Apply alignment marks at the 12 o'clock position on the clockspring hub and clockspring outer ring as a reference point.*

b) *Rotate the clockspring hub counterclockwise counting the number of turns until the clockspring hub stops.*

c) *Rotate the clockspring hub clockwise 1/2 the total number of turns recorded in paragraph b) to center the clockspring. For example: if the total number of turns between stops was 6 turns, rotate the hub back 3 turns; if the total number of turns was 5, rotate the hub back 2-1/2 turns. Use the alignment marks on the clockspring hub and the outer ring as reference.*

16   Install the clockspring mounting screws and tighten them securely.

17   Pull the electrical leads for the airbag module and the cruise control system through the steering wheel and install the steering wheel.

18   Install the steering wheel retaining nut and tighten it to the torque listed in this Chapter's Specifications.

19   Install the airbag module and secure it with new Torx bolts. Do not reuse the old bolts. Tighten the bolts to the torque listed in this Chapter's Specifications. Install the side covers.

20   Verify that the airbag circuit is operational by turning the ignition key to the On or Start position. The "AIR BAG" warning light should illuminate for about seven seconds, then turn off.

Non-airbag models

Removal

21   Disconnect the cable from the negative terminal of the battery.

22   To remove the horn pad, insert a Phillips screwdriver into the hole on the lower side of the steering wheel and remove the screw, then lift off the horn pad by hand.

15.3a Remove the cotter pin . . .

23   Disconnect the horn electrical connector and the cruise control connector, if equipped.

24   Remove the steering wheel bolt.

25   Remove the mass damper screws and the mass damper.

26   The remainder of removal is similar to that for an airbag-equipped model (see Steps 8 through 10).

Installation

27   Position the mark on the steering wheel directly in line with the mark on the steering column shaft.

28   Install the mass damper and the mass damper screws and tighten them securely.

29   Install the steering wheel bolt and tighten it to the torque listed in this Chapter's Specifications.

30   Connect the horn wire and install the horn pad.

31   Connect the negative battery cable.

---

15 Tie-rod ends - removal and installation

Removal

Refer to illustrations 15.2, 15.3a, 15.3b and 15.4

1   Loosen the front wheel lug nuts. Raise the vehicle and support it securely on jackstands. Remove the front wheels.

2   Loosen the tie-rod jam nut and back it off several turns. Mark the position of the tie-rod end in relation to the inner tie-rod threads **(see illustration).**

3   Remove the cotter pin and loosen, but don't remove, the nut on the tie-rod end stud **(see illustrations).**

4   Disconnect the tie-rod end from the steering knuckle arm with a puller **(see illustration).** Remove the nut and separate the tie-rod end.

5   Unscrew the tie-rod end from the tie-rod.

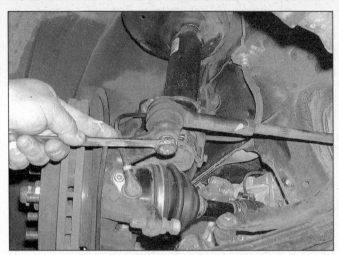

15.3b . . . then loosen - but don't remove - the tie-rod end ballstud nut

15.4 Disconnect the tie-rod end from the steering knuckle arm with a puller

Installation

6   Thread the tie-rod end on to the marked position and insert the stud into the steering knuckle arm. Tighten the jam nut securely.
7   Install the castle nut on the stud and tighten it to the torque listed in this Chapter's Specifications. Install a new cotter pin.
8   Install the wheel and lug nuts. Lower the vehicle and tighten the lug nuts to the torque listed in the Chapter 1 Specifications.
9   Have the front end alignment checked and, if necessary, adjusted.

16 Steering gear boots - replacement

Refer to illustrations 16.3a and 16.3b

1   Loosen the lug nuts, raise the vehicle and support it securely on jackstands. Remove the wheel.
2   Remove the tie-rod end and jam nut (see Section 15).
3   Remove the outer steering gear boot clamp **(see illustration)** with a pair of pliers.

Cut off the inner boot clamp **(see illustration)** with a pair of diagonal cutters. Slide the boot off.
4   Before installing the new boot, wrap the threads on the end of the inner tie-rod rod with tape so the small end of the new boot isn't cut by the threads.
5   Slide the new boot into position on the steering gear until it seats in the groove in the inner tie-rod and install new clamps.
6   Remove the tape and install the tie-rod end (see Section 15).
7   Install the wheel and lug nuts. Lower the vehicle and tighten the lug nuts to the torque listed in the Chapter 1 Specifications.

17 Steering gear - removal and installation

Warning: The models covered by this manual are equipped with Supplemental Restraint Systems (SRS), more commonly known as airbags. Always disable the airbag system before working in the vicinity of any airbag

system components to avoid the possibility of accidental deployment of the airbag(s) which could cause personal injury (see Chapter 12).

Removal

Refer to illustrations 17.2, 17.6 and 17.7

1   Loosen the front wheel lug nuts, raise the vehicle and support it securely on jackstands. Apply the parking brake and remove the front wheels. Remove the engine splash shields.
2   Place a drain pan under the steering gear. Detach the power steering pressure and return lines and cap the ends to prevent excessive fluid loss and contamination **(see illustration)**.
3   Remove the master cylinder reservoir mounting screws and position the reservoir off to the side (see Chapter 9). Do not disconnect the brake hoses. Use wire to support the reservoir.
4   Remove the front stabilizer bar (see Section 6).
5   Separate the tie-rod ends from the steering knuckle arms (see Section 15).

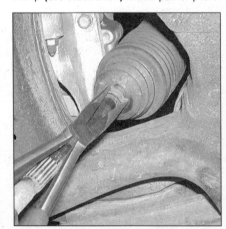

16.3a The outer end of each steering gear boot is secured by a spring-type clamp which can be slid off simply by pinching the ends together

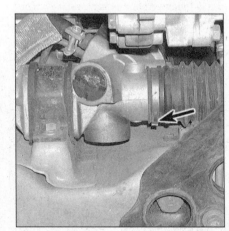

16.3b The inner end of each steering gear boot is retained by a clamp (arrow) which must be cut off and discarded

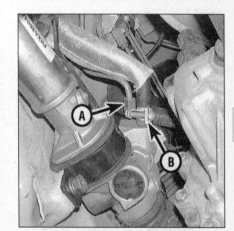

17.2 Disconnect the power steering pressure (A) and return line (B) fittings from the steering gear

10

6   From inside the vehicle, remove the universal joint cover **(see illustration)**. Slide the boot up to gain clearance. Remove the pinch bolt from the upper section of the steering shaft **(see illustration 20.15)**.

7   Support the steering gear and remove the steering gear mounting bolts **(see illustration)**. Lower the steering gear slightly and remove the intermediate shaft-to-steering gear pinch bolt. Separate the intermediate shaft from the steering gear input shaft and remove the steering gear assembly pulling it out towards the driver's side of the vehicle. **Warning:** *Do not turn the steering wheel while the steering gear is removed on a model equipped with an airbag. If the steering wheel is inadvertently turned, remove the steering wheel and center the clockspring (see Section 14). To prevent the steering wheel from turning, loop the seat belt through the steering wheel and fasten it into its latch.*

8   Check the steering gear rubber mounts for excessive wear or deterioration, replacing them if necessary.

Installation

Refer to illustration 17.10

Note: *Make sure the steering gear is centered from side-to-side before installing it.*

9   Slide the steering gear into position from the driver's side of the vehicle. Connect the intermediate shaft to the steering gear, install and tighten the pinch bolt. Raise the steering gear into position and connect the upper section of the intermediate shaft onto the steering column (see Section 20).

10   Install the mounting brackets and bolts. Make sure the UP mark on the brackets are correctly positioned. Tighten all the bolts snugly at first, then following the recommended tightening sequence, tighten them to the torque listed in this Chapter's Specifications. **(see illustration)**.

11   Connect the tie-rod ends to the steering knuckle arms (see Section 15).

12   Install the intermediate shaft-to-steering column pinch bolt and tighten it to the torque listed in this Chapter's Specifications.

13   Connect the power steering pressure and return hoses to the steering gear and fill

17.6 Remove the U-joint cover nuts (arrows)

the power steering pump reservoir with the recommended fluid (see Chapter 1).

14   Install the wheels and lug nuts, then lower the vehicle and tighten the lug nuts to the torque listed in the Chapter 1 Specifications. Bleed the steering system (see Section 19).

18   Power steering pump - removal and installation

Removal

Refer to illustrations 18.4 and 18.7

1   Disconnect the cable from the negative battery terminal.

2   Using a large syringe or suction gun, withdraw much fluid from the power steering fluid reservoir as possible. Place a drain pan under the vehicle to catch any fluid that spills out when the hoses are disconnected.

3   Raise the vehicle and support it securely with jackstands.

4   Working below the engine compartment, remove the pressure line-to-pump fitting or banjo bolt **(see illustration)**, then detach the line from the pump. Remove and discard the copper sealing washers. They

must be replaced when installing the pump.

5   Loosen the bolt and disconnect the fluid return hose from the pump **(see illustration 18.4)**.

6   Remove the drivebelt (see Chapter 1). Using a strap wrench to hold the pulley, remove the pulley bolt with a socket and breaker bar. Remove the power steering pump pulley.

7   Remove the pump mounting bolts **(see illustration)**, then remove the pump from the vehicle. There are three bolts mounting the front of the power steering pump and one bolt at the rear of the pump.

Installation

8   Installation is the reverse of removal. Be sure to tighten the pressure line fitting or banjo bolt to the torque listed in this Chapter's Specifications. Adjust the drivebelt tension following the procedure described in Chapter 1.

9   Top up the fluid level in the reservoir (see Chapter 1) and bleed the system (see Section 19).

19   Power steering system - bleeding

1   Following any operation in which the power steering fluid lines have been disconnected, the power steering system must be bled to remove all air and obtain proper steering performance.

2   With the front wheels in the straight ahead position, check the power steering fluid level and, if low, add fluid until it reaches the Cold mark on the dipstick.

3   Start the engine and allow it to run at fast idle. Recheck the fluid level and add more if necessary to reach the Cold mark on the dipstick.

4   Bleed the system by turning the wheels from side to side, without hitting the stops. This will work the air out of the system. Keep the reservoir full of fluid as this is done.

5   When the air is worked out of the system, return the wheels to the straight ahead position and leave the vehicle running for several more minutes before shutting it off.

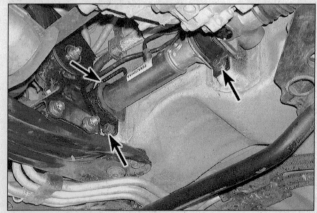

17.7 To remove the steering gear assembly, remove the five bolts (arrows) (two of the upper bolts are hidden from view)

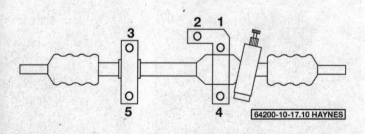

64200-10-17.10 HAYNES

17.10 Steering gear mounting bolt TIGHTENING sequence

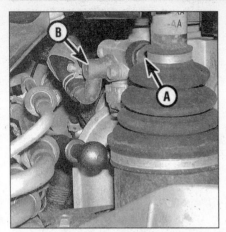

18.4 Disconnect the high pressure hose (A) from the power steering pump and then disconnect the return hose (B) mounting bolt

18.7 Remove the three power steering pump bolts (arrows) from the front, then the single bolt from the rear of the power steering pump

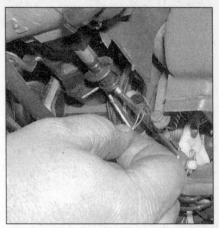

20.8 Remove the cable loop from the pin on the shift indicator lever

6   Road test the vehicle to be sure the steering system is functioning normally and noise free.

7   Recheck the fluid level to be sure it is up to the Hot mark on the dipstick while the engine is at normal operating temperature. Add fluid if necessary (see Chapter 1).

20   Steering column - removal and installation

Warning 1: *The models covered by this manual are equipped with Supplemental Restraint Systems (SRS), more commonly known as airbags. Always disable the airbag system before working in the vicinity of any airbag system components to avoid the possibility of accidental deployment of the airbag(s) which could cause personal injury (see Chapter 12).*
Warning 2: *On models equipped with airbags, make sure the steering shaft is not turned while the steering wheel is removed or you could damage the airbag system. To prevent the shaft from turning, position the*

wheels straight ahead, turn the ignition key to the lock position and remove the key before beginning work. Due to the possible damage to the airbag system, we recommend only experienced mechanics attempt this procedure.

Removal

Refer to illustrations 20.8, 20.9, 20.15 and 20.16

1   Disconnect the cable from the negative battery terminal.
2   Position the front wheels in the straight ahead position, lock the steering column and remove the ignition key.
3   Remove the steering wheel and the clockspring assembly from the steering column (see Section 14). **Caution:** *Be sure to tape the clockspring in the centered position before removal.*
4   Remove the instrument panel steering column cover (see Chapter 11).
5   Remove the lower steering column knee bolster (see Chapter 11).
6   Remove the heater outlet duct from

below the steering column.
7   Remove the steering column covers (see Chapter 11).
8   Disconnect the shift indicator cable loop from the pin on the shift indicator lever **(see illustration)**.
9   Remove the mounting bolt and separate the shift indicator cable adjustment assembly from the steering column **(see illustration)**.
10   Disconnect the shift cable from the selector lever arm (see Chapter 7).
11   Disconnect the shift lock actuator connector (see Chapter 7).
12   Remove the multi-function switch (see Chapter 12) and position it off to the side. It is not necessary to disconnect the harness connector from the switch.
13   Disconnect the Transaxle Control Switch (TCS) (see Chapter 7).
14   Disconnect the ignition switch harness from the ignition switch (see Chapter 12).
15   Remove the pinch bolt from the lower steering column shaft yoke **(see illustration)**.
16   While supporting the steering column, remove the steering column mounting nuts **(see illustration)** and remove the steering column from the vehicle.

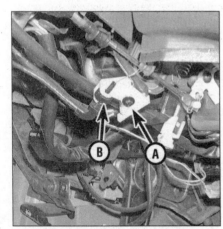

20.9 Remove Bolt A and separate the indicator cable and the thumbwheel adjustment mechanism (B) from the steering column

20.15 Remove the pinch bolt and nut (arrow) from the lower universal joint yoke clamp

20.16 Location of the steering column mounting nuts (arrows)

10

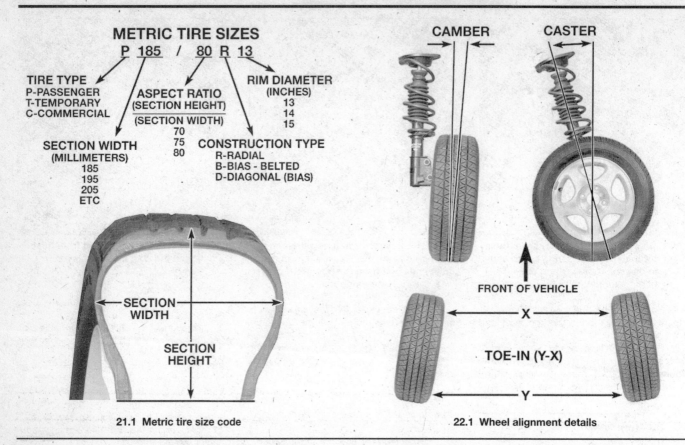

21.1 Metric tire size code

22.1 Wheel alignment details

Installation

17   Place the steering column in position, engaging the lower yoke with the splines of the intermediate steering shaft. Install the mounting bolts and tighten them to the torque listed in this Chapter's Specifications. Install the lower yoke pinch bolt and tighten it to the torque listed in this Chapter's Specifications.

18   The remainder of installation is the reverse of removal. Be sure the clockspring is centered before installing the steering wheel (see Section 14).

21   Wheels and tires - general information

Refer to illustration 21.1

1   All vehicles covered by this manual are equipped with metric-sized steel belted radial tires **(see illustration)**. Use of other size or type of tires may affect the ride and handling of the vehicle. Don't mix different types of tires, such as radials and bias belted, on the same vehicle as handling may be seriously affected. It's recommended that tires be replaced in pairs on the same axle, but if only one tire is being replaced, be sure it's the same size, structure and tread design as the other.

2   Because tire pressure has a substantial effect on handling and wear, the pressure on all tires should be checked at least once a month or before any extended trips (see Chapter 1).

3   Wheels must be replaced if they are bent, dented, leak air, have elongated bolt holes, are heavily rusted, out of vertical symmetry or if the lug nuts won't stay tight. Wheel repairs that use welding or peening are not recommended.

4   Tire and wheel balance is important in the overall handling, braking and performance of the vehicle. Unbalanced wheels can adversely affect handling and ride characteristics as well as tire life. Whenever a tire is installed on a wheel, the tire and wheel should be balanced by a shop with the proper equipment.

22   Wheel alignment - general information

Refer to illustration 22.1

A wheel alignment refers to the adjustments made to the wheels so they are in proper angular relationship to the suspension and the ground. Wheels that are out of proper alignment not only affect vehicle control, but also increase tire wear. The front end angles normally measured are camber, caster and toe-in **(see illustration)**. Camber and caster are preset at the factory on the vehicle covered by this manual; toe-in is the only adjustable angle on this vehicle.

Getting the proper wheel alignment is a very exacting process, one in which complicated and expensive machines are necessary to perform the job properly. Because of this, you should have a technician with the proper equipment perform these tasks. We will, however, use this space to give you a basic idea of what is involved with a wheel alignment so you can better understand the process and deal intelligently with the shop that does the work.

Toe-in is the turning in of the wheels. The purpose of a toe specification is to ensure parallel rolling of the wheels. In a vehicle with zero toe-in, the distance between the front edges of the wheels will be the same as the distance between the rear edges of the wheels. The actual amount of toe-in is normally only a fraction of an inch. On the front end, toe-in is controlled by the tie-rod end position on the tie-rod. There is no adjustment on the rear suspension.

Camber is the tilting of the wheels from vertical when viewed from one end of the vehicle. When the wheels tilt out at the top, the camber is said to be positive (+). When the wheels tilt in at the top the camber is negative (-). The amount of tilt is measured in degrees from vertical and this measurement is called the camber angle. This angle affects the amount of tire tread which contacts the road and compensates for changes in the suspension geometry when the vehicle is cornering or traveling over an undulating surface.

Caster is the tilting of the front steering axis from the vertical. A tilt toward the rear is positive caster and a tilt toward the front is negative caster.

Chapter 11 Body

Contents

1 General information

These models feature a "unibody" construction, using a floor pan with left and right frame side rails which support the body components, front and rear suspension systems and other mechanical components. Certain components are particularly vulnerable to accident damage and can be unbolted and repaired or replaced. Among these parts are the body moldings, bumpers, hood and trunk lids and all glass.

Only general body maintenance practices and body panel repair procedures within the scope of the do-it-yourselfer are included in this Chapter.

2 Body - maintenance

1 The condition of your vehicle's body is very important, because the resale value depends a great deal on it. It's much more difficult to repair a neglected or damaged body than it is to repair mechanical components. The hidden areas of the body, such as the wheel wells, the frame and the engine compartment, are equally important, although they don't require as frequent attention as the rest of the body.

2 Once a year, or every 12,000 miles, it's a good idea to have the underside of the body steam cleaned. All traces of dirt and oil will be removed and the area can then be inspected carefully for rust, damaged brake lines, frayed electrical wires, damaged cables and other problems. The front suspension components should be greased after completion of this job.

3 At the same time, clean the engine and the engine compartment with a steam cleaner or water soluble degreaser.

4 The wheel wells should be given close attention, since undercoating can peel away and stones and dirt thrown up by the tires can cause the paint to chip and flake, allowing rust to set in. If rust is found, clean down to the bare metal and apply an anti-rust paint.

5 The body should be washed about once a week. Wet the vehicle thoroughly to soften the dirt, then wash it down with a soft sponge

11

and plenty of clean soapy water. If the surplus dirt is not washed off very carefully, it can wear down the paint.

6   Spots of tar or asphalt thrown up from the road should be removed with a cloth soaked in solvent.

7   Once every six months, wax the body and chrome trim. If a chrome cleaner is used to remove rust from any of the vehicle's plated parts, remember that the cleaner also removes part of the chrome, so use it sparingly.

3   Vinyl trim - maintenance

Don't clean vinyl trim with detergents, caustic soap or petroleum-based cleaners. Plain soap and water works just fine, with a soft brush to clean dirt that may be ingrained. Wash the vinyl as frequently as the rest of the vehicle.

After cleaning, application of a high quality rubber and vinyl protectant will help prevent oxidation and cracks. The protectant can also be applied to weatherstripping, vacuum lines and rubber hoses (which often fail as a result of chemical degradation) and to the tires.

4   Upholstery and carpets - maintenance

1   Every three months remove the carpets or mats and clean the interior of the vehicle (more frequently if necessary). Vacuum the upholstery and carpets to remove loose dirt and dust.

2   Leather upholstery requires special care. Stains should be removed with warm water and a very mild soap solution. Use a clean, damp cloth to remove the soap, then wipe again with a dry cloth. Never use alcohol, gasoline, nail polish remover or thinner to clean leather upholstery.

3   After cleaning, regularly treat leather upholstery with a leather wax. Never use car wax on leather upholstery.

4   In areas where the interior of the vehicle is subject to bright sunlight, cover leather seats with a sheet if the vehicle is to be left out for any length of time.

5   Body repair - minor damage

Plastic body panels

The following repair procedures are for minor scratches and gouges. Repair of more serious damage should be left to a dealer service department or qualified auto body shop. Below is a list of the equipment and materials necessary to perform the following repair procedures on plastic body panels. Although a specific brand of material may be mentioned, it should be noted that equivalent products from other manufacturers may be

used instead.

   *Wax, grease and silicone removing
      solvent*
   Cloth-backed body tape
   Sanding discs
   Drill motor with three-inch disc holder
   Hand sanding block
   Rubber squeegees
   Sandpaper
   Non-porous mixing palette
   Wood paddle or putty knife
   Curved tooth body file
   Flexible parts repair material

Flexible panels (front and rear bumper fascia)

1   Remove the damaged panel, if necessary or desirable. In most cases, repairs can be carried out with the panel installed.

2   Clean the area(s) to be repaired with a wax, grease and silicone removing solvent applied with a water-dampened cloth.

3   If the damage is structural, that is, if it extends through the panel, clean the backside of the panel area to be repaired as well. Wipe dry.

4   Sand the rear surface about 1-1/2 inches beyond the break.

5   Cut two pieces of fiberglass cloth large enough to overlap the break by about 1-1/2 inches. Cut only to the required length.

6   Mix the adhesive from the repair kit according to the instructions included with the kit, and apply a layer of the mixture approximately 1/8-inch thick on the backside of the panel. Overlap the break by at least 1-1/2 inches.

7   Apply one piece of fiberglass cloth to the adhesive and cover the cloth with additional adhesive. Apply a second piece of fiberglass cloth to the adhesive and immediately cover the cloth with additional adhesive insufficient quantity to fill the weave.

8   Allow the repair to cure for 20 to 30 minutes at 60-degrees to 80-degrees F.

9   If necessary, trim the excess repair material at the edge.

10   Remove all of the paint film over and around the area(s) to be repaired. The repair material should not overlap the painted surface.

11   With a drill motor and a sanding disc (or a rotary file), cut a "V" along the break line approximately 1/2-inch wide. Remove all dust and loose particles from the repair area.

12   Mix and apply the repair material. Apply a light coat first over the damaged area; then continue applying material until it reaches a level slightly higher than the surrounding finish.

13   Cure the mixture for 20 to 30 minutes at 60-degrees to 80-degrees F.

14   Roughly establish the contour of the area being repaired with a body file. If low areas or pits remain, mix and apply additional adhesive.

15   Block sand the damaged area with sandpaper to establish the actual contour of the surrounding surface.

16   If desired, the repaired area can be temporarily protected with several light coats of primer. Because of the special paints and techniques required for flexible body panels, it is recommended that the vehicle be taken to a paint shop for completion of the body repair.

Steel body panels

See photo sequence

Repair of minor scratches

17   If the scratch is superficial and does not penetrate to the metal of the body, repair is very simple. Lightly rub the scratched area with a fine rubbing compound to remove loose paint and built-up wax. Rinse the area with clean water.

18   Apply touch-up paint to the scratch, using a small brush. Continue to apply thin layers of paint until the surface of the paint in the scratch is level with the surrounding paint. Allow the new paint at least two weeks to harden, then blend it into the surrounding paint by rubbing with a very fine rubbing compound. Finally, apply a coat of wax to the scratch area.

19   If the scratch has penetrated the paint and exposed the metal of the body, causing the metal to rust, a different repair technique is required. Remove all loose rust from the bottom of the scratch with a pocket knife, then apply rust inhibiting paint to prevent the formation of rust in the future. Using a rubber or nylon applicator, coat the scratched area with glaze-type filler. If required, the filler can be mixed with thinner to provide a very thin paste, which is ideal for filling narrow scratches. Before the glaze filler in the scratch hardens, wrap a piece of smooth cotton cloth around the tip of a finger. Dip the cloth in thinner and then quickly wipe it along the surface of the scratch. This will ensure that the surface of the filler is slightly hollow. The scratch can now be painted over as described earlier in this section.

Repair of dents

20   When repairing dents, the first job is to pull the dent out until the affected area is as close as possible to its original shape. There is no point in trying to restore the original shape completely as the metal in the damaged area will have stretched on impact and cannot be restored to its original contours. It is better to bring the level of the dent up to a point which is about 1/8-inch below the level of the surrounding metal. In cases where the dent is very shallow, it is not worth trying to pull it out at all.

21   If the back side of the dent is accessible, it can be hammered out gently from behind using a soft-face hammer. While doing this, hold a block of wood firmly against the opposite side of the metal to absorb the hammer blows and prevent the metal from being stretched.

22   If the dent is in a section of the body which has double layers, or some other factor makes it inaccessible from behind, a different

technique is required. Drill several small holes through the metal inside the damaged area, particularly in the deeper sections. Screw long, self-tapping screws into the holes just enough for them to get a good grip in the metal. Now the dent can be pulled out by pulling on the protruding heads of the screws with locking pliers.

23 The next stage of repair is the removal of paint from the damaged area and from an inch or so of the surrounding metal. This is done with a wire brush or sanding disk in a drill motor, although it can be done just as effectively by hand with sandpaper. To complete the preparation for filling, score the surface of the bare metal with a screwdriver or the tang of a file, or drill small holes in the affected area. This will provide a good grip for the filler material. To complete the repair, see the subsection on filling and painting later in this Section.

Repair of rust holes or gashes

24 Remove all paint from the affected area and from an inch or so of the surrounding metal using a sanding disk or wire brush mounted in a drill motor. If these are not available, a few sheets of sandpaper will do the job just as effectively.

25 With the paint removed, you will be able to determine the severity of the corrosion and decide whether to replace the whole panel, if possible, or repair the affected area. New body panels are not as expensive as most people think and it is often quicker to install a new panel than to repair large areas of rust.

26 Remove all trim pieces from the affected area except those which will act as a guide to the original shape of the damaged body, such as headlight shells, etc. Using metal snips or a hacksaw blade, remove all loose metal and any other metal that is badly affected by rust. Hammer the edges of the hole in to create a slight depression for the filler material.

27 Wire brush the affected area to remove the powdery rust from the surface of the metal. If the back of the rusted area is accessible, treat it with rust inhibiting paint.

28 Before filling is done, block the hole in some way. This can be done with sheet metal riveted or screwed into place, or by stuffing the hole with wire mesh.

29 Once the hole is blocked off, the affected area can be filled and painted. See the following subsection on filling and painting.

Filling and painting

30 Many types of body fillers are available, but generally speaking, body repair kits which contain filler paste and a tube of resin hardener are best for this type of repair work. A wide, flexible plastic or nylon applicator will be necessary for imparting a smooth and contoured finish to the surface of the filler material. Mix up a small amount of filler on a clean piece of wood or cardboard (use the hardener sparingly). Follow the manufacturer's instructions on the package, other-

wise the filler will set incorrectly.

31 Using the applicator, apply the filler paste to the prepared area. Draw the applicator across the surface of the filler to achieve the desired contour and to level the filler surface. As soon as a contour that approximates the original one is achieved, stop working the paste. If you continue, the paste will begin to stick to the applicator. Continue to add thin layers of paste at 20-minute intervals until the level of the filler is just above the surrounding metal.

32 Once the filler has hardened, the excess can be removed with a body file. From then on, progressively finer grades of sandpaper should be used, starting with a 180-grit paper and finishing with 600-grit wet-or-dry paper. Always wrap the sandpaper around a flat rubber or wooden block, otherwise the surface of the filler will not be completely flat. During the sanding of the filler surface, the wet-or-dry paper should be periodically rinsed in water. This will ensure that a very smooth finish is produced in the final stage.

33 At this point, the repair area should be surrounded by a ring of bare metal, which in turn should be encircled by the finely feathered edge of good paint. Rinse the repair area with clean water until all of the dust produced by the sanding operation is gone.

34 Spray the entire area with a light coat of primer. This will reveal any imperfections in the surface of the filler. Repair the imperfections with fresh filler paste or glaze filler and once more smooth the surface with sandpaper. Repeat this spray-and-repair procedure until you are satisfied that the surface of the filler and the feathered edge of the paint are perfect. Rinse the area with clean water and allow it to dry completely.

35 The repair area is now ready for painting. Spray painting must be carried out in a warm, dry, windless and dust free atmosphere. These conditions can be created if you have access to a large indoor work area, but if you are forced to work in the open, you will have to pick the day very carefully. If you are working indoors, dousing the floor in the work area with water will help settle the dust which would otherwise be in the air. If the repair area is confined to one body panel, mask off the surrounding panels. This will help minimize the effects of a slight mismatch in paint color. Trim pieces such as chrome strips, door handles, etc., will also need to be masked off or removed. Use masking tape and several thickness of newspaper for the masking operations.

36 Before spraying, shake the paint can thoroughly, then spray a test area until the spray painting technique is mastered. Cover the repair area with a thick coat of primer. The thickness should be built up using several thin layers of primer rather than one thick one. Using 600-grit wet-or-dry sandpaper, rub down the surface of the primer until it is very smooth. While doing this, the work area should be thoroughly rinsed with water and the wet-or-dry sandpaper periodically rinsed as well. Allow the primer to dry before spray-

ing additional coats.

37 Spray on the top coat, again building up the thickness by using several thin layers of paint. Begin spraying in the center of the repair area and then, using a circular motion, work out until the whole repair area and about two inches of the surrounding original paint is covered. Remove all masking material 10 to 15 minutes after spraying on the final coat of paint. Allow the new paint at least two weeks to harden, then use a very fine rubbing compound to blend the edges of the new paint into the existing paint. Finally, apply a coat of wax.

6   Body repair - major damage

1   Major damage must be repaired by an auto body shop specifically equipped to perform unibody repairs. These shops have the specialized equipment required to do the job properly.

2   If the damage is extensive, the body must be checked for proper alignment or the vehicle's handling characteristics may be adversely affected and other components may wear at an accelerated rate.

3   Due to the fact that all of the major body components (hood, fenders, etc.) are separate and replaceable units, any seriously damaged components should be replaced rather than repaired. Sometimes the components can be found in a wrecking yard that specializes in used vehicle components, often at considerable savings over the cost of new parts.

7   Hinges and locks - maintenance

Once every 3000 miles, or every three months, the hinges and latch assemblies on the doors, hood and trunk should be given a few drops of light oil or lock lubricant. The door latch strikers should also be lubricated with a thin coat of grease to reduce wear and ensure free movement. Lubricate the door and trunk locks with spray-on graphite lubricant.

8   Windshield and fixed glass - replacement

Replacement of the windshield and fixed glass requires the use of special fast-setting adhesive/caulk materials and some specialized tools. It is recommended that these operations be left to a dealer or a shop specializing in glass work.

9   Radiator grille - removal and installation

Refer to illustrations 9.1 and 9.3

1   Open the hood and remove the retaining

11

These photos illustrate a method of repairing simple dents. They are intended to supplement *Body repair - minor damage* in this Chapter and should not be used as the sole instructions for body repair on these vehicles.

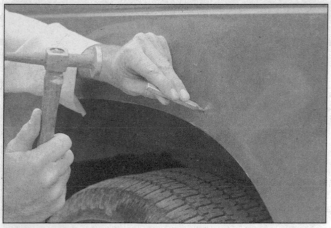

1   If you can't access the backside of the body panel to hammer out the dent, pull it out with a slide-hammer-type dent puller. In the deepest portion of the dent or along the crease line, drill or punch hole(s) at least one inch apart . . .

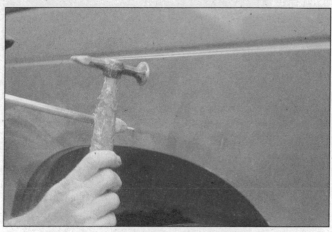

2   . . . then screw the slide-hammer into the hole and operate it. Tap with a hammer near the edge of the dent to help 'pop' the metal back to its original shape. When you're finished, the dent area should be close to its original contour and about 1/8-inch below the surface of the surrounding metal

3   Using coarse-grit sandpaper, remove the paint down to the bare metal. Hand sanding works fine, but the disc sander shown here makes the job faster. Use finer (about 320-grit) sandpaper to feather-edge the paint at least one inch around the dent area

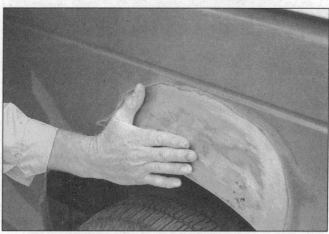

4   When the paint is removed, touch will probably be more helpful than sight for telling if the metal is straight. Hammer down the high spots or raise the low spots as necessary. Clean the repair area with wax/silicone remover

5   Following label instructions, mix up a batch of plastic filler and hardener. The ratio of filler to hardener is critical, and, if you mix it incorrectly, it will either not cure properly or cure too quickly (you won't have time to file and sand it into shape)

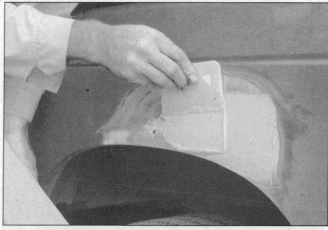

6   Working quickly so the filler doesn't harden, use a plastic applicator to press the body filler firmly into the metal, assuring it bonds completely. Work the filler until it matches the original contour and is slightly above the surrounding metal

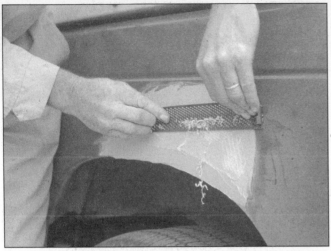

7   Let the filler harden until you can just dent it with your fingernail. Use a body file or Surform tool (shown here) to rough-shape the filler

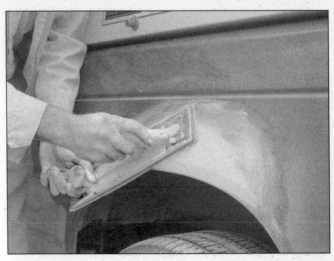

8   Use coarse-grit sandpaper and a sanding board or block to work the filler down until it's smooth and even. Work down to finer grits of sandpaper - always using a board or block - ending up with 360 or 400 grit

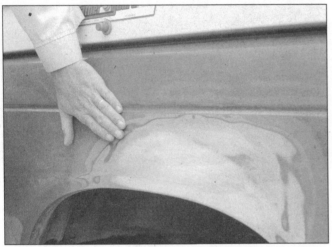

9   You shouldn't be able to feel any ridge at the transition from the filler to the bare metal or from the bare metal to the old paint. As soon as the repair is flat and uniform, remove the dust and mask off the adjacent panels or trim pieces

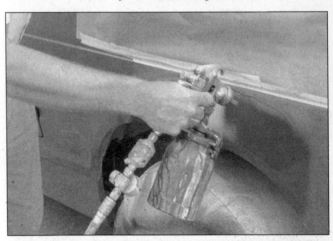

10   Apply several layers of primer to the area. Don't spray the primer on too heavy, so it sags or runs, and make sure each coat is dry before you spray on the next one. A professional-type spray gun is being used here, but aerosol spray primer is available inexpensively from auto parts stores

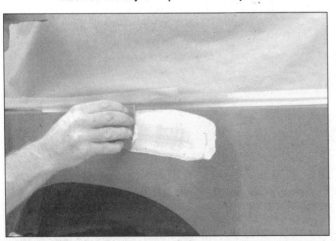

11   The primer will help reveal imperfections or scratches. Fill these with glazing compound. Follow the label instructions and sand it with 360 or 400-grit sandpaper until it's smooth. Repeat the glazing, sanding and respraying until the primer reveals a perfectly smooth surface

12   Finish sand the primer with very fine sandpaper (400 or 600-grit) to remove the primer overspray. Clean the area with water and allow it to dry. Use a tack rag to remove any dust, then apply the finish coat. Don't attempt to rub out or wax the repair area until the paint has dried completely (at least two weeks)

9.1   Remove the grille retaining screws and retainers (arrows) (1996 Villager shown)

9.3   Remove the retaining clips from the radiator support and body and insert them back into the grille

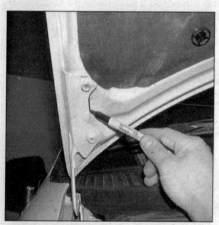

10.2   Before removing the hood, draw a mark around the hinge plate

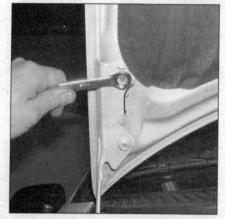

10.4   Remove the hinge-to-hood retaining bolts and lift off the hood with the help of an assistant

10.10   Make a line around the latch to use as a reference point - to adjust the hood latch, loosen the retaining bolts, move the latch and retighten bolts, then close the hood to check the fit

screws securing the grille **(see illustration)**. Some models use square-headed plastic grille retainers. On these models, detach the retainers by turning the retainer heads 45 degrees with a screwdriver.

2   Grasp the grille securely and detach it from the vehicle.

3   Installation is the reverse of removal. On models so equipped, remove the grille retainers from the body and install them in the grille before installation **(see illustration)**.

10   Hood - removal, installation and adjustment

Note: *The hood is heavy and somewhat awkward to remove and install - at least two people should perform this procedure.*

Removal and installation

Refer to illustrations 10.2 and 10.4

1   Use blankets or pads to cover the cowl area of the body and fenders. This will protect the body and paint as the hood is lifted off.

2   Make marks or scribe a line around the hood hinge to ensure proper alignment during installation **(see illustration)**.

3   Disconnect any cables or wires that will interfere with removal.

4   Have an assistant support one side of the hood. Take turns removing the hinge-to-hood retaining bolts **(see illustration)**.

5   Lift off the hood.

6   Installation is the reverse of removal.

Adjustment

Refer to illustrations 10.10 and 10.11

7   Fore-and-aft and side-to-side adjustment of the hood is done by moving the hinge plate slot after loosening the bolts or nuts.

8   Scribe a line around the entire hinge plate so you can determine the amount of movement **(see illustration 10.2)**.

9   Loosen the bolts or nuts and move the hood into correct alignment. Move it only a little at a time. Tighten the hinge bolts and carefully lower the hood to check the position.

10   If necessary after installation, the entire hood latch assembly can be adjusted up-and-down as well as from side-to-side on the radiator support so the hood closes securely and flush with the fenders. To make the adjustment, scribe a line or mark around the hood latch mounting bolts to provide a reference point, then loosen them and reposition

the latch assembly, as necessary **(see illustration)**. Following adjustment, retighten the mounting bolts.

11   Finally, adjust the hood bumpers on the radiator support so the hood, when closed, is flush with the fenders **(see illustration)**.

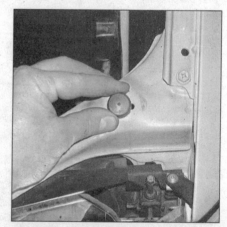

10.11   Adjust the hood closing height by turning the hood bumpers in or out

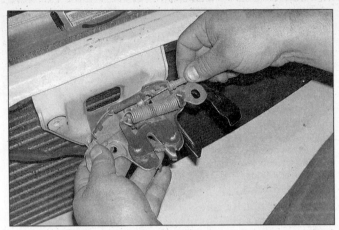

11.2 Unscrew the hood latch assembly cable assembly retaining bolts (arrows), then disengage the cable

11.5 Remove the hood release lever and cable retaining screws (arrows) and pull the cable into the passenger compartment

12.3 Remove the plastic retainers on the lower edge of the bumper cover

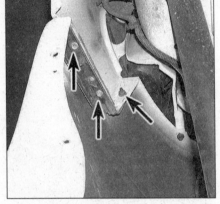

12.5 Remove the bumper cover-to-body bolts and nuts (arrows)

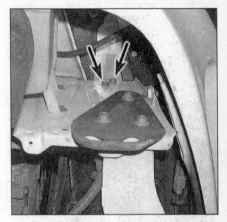

12.6 Remove the upper bumper cover bracket retaining bolts (arrows)

12   The hood latch assembly, as well as the hinges, should be periodically lubricated with white, lithium-base grease to prevent binding and wear.

11   Hood release latch and cable - removal and installation

Latch

Refer to illustration 11.2

1   Raise the hood, and on 1995 and earlier Villager models, remove the grille illumination bar. Remove the radiator grille then scribe a line around the latch to aid alignment when installing, detach the latch retaining bolts from the radiator support **(see illustration 10.10)** and remove the latch.

2   Disconnect the hood release cable by disengaging the cable from the latch assembly **(see illustration)**.

3   Installation is reverse of the removal. **Note:** *Adjust the latch so the hood engages securely when closed and the hood bumpers are slightly compressed.*

Cable

Refer to illustration 11.5

4   Disconnect the hood release cable from

the latch assembly as described above.

5   Working in the passenger's compartment, remove the driver side kick panel. Then remove the two release lever mounting bolts and detach the hood release lever and cable assembly **(see illustration)**.

6   Attach a piece of stiff wire to the latch end of the cable, then detach the cable retaining clips.

7   Detach the grommet and pull the cable through the firewall into the passenger compartment compartment. Ensure that the new cable has a grommet attached, then remove the old cable from the wire and replace it with the new cable.

8   Pull the wire back through the firewall and connect the cable to the latch assembly.

9   Installation is the reverse of the removal. **Note:** *Push on the grommet to seat it in the firewall completely.*

12   Bumpers - removal and installation

Warning: *The models covered by this manual are equipped with Supplemental Restraint systems (SRS), more commonly known as airbags. Always disconnect the negative battery cable, then the positive battery cable and*

wait ten minutes before working in the vicinity of the impact sensors, steering column or instrument panel to avoid the possibility of accidental deployment of the airbag, which could cause personal injury (see Chapter 12). Do not use electrical test equipment on any of the airbag system wiring or tamper with them in any way.

Front bumper

1993 through 1998

Refer to illustrations 12.3, 12.5, 12.6 and 12.8

1   Apply the parking brake, raise the vehicle and support it securely on jackstands.

2   Disconnect the negative battery cable, then the positive battery cable and wait ten minutes before proceeding any further.

3   Working under the vehicle, detach the plastic clips securing the front lower edge of the bumper cover **(see illustration)**.

4   Working in the front wheel opening, detach the retaining screws securing the bumper cover to inner fenderwell splash shields.

5   Remove the bumper cover-to-body attaching screws and nuts **(see illustration)**.

6   Remove the turn signal lights (see Chapter 12) and the upper bumper cover bracket bolts **(see illustration)**.

11

7   Remove the bumper cover.

8   To remove the bumper, remove the bumper retaining bolts and pull the bumper assembly out and away from the vehicle **(see illustration)**.

9   Installation is the reverse of removal.

1999 and later models

10   Apply the parking brake.

11   Disconnect the negative battery cable, then the positive battery cable and wait ten minutes before proceeding any further.

12   On 1999 and 2000 models, remove the radiator grille (see Section 9).

13   Remove both front combination lights and both headlight assemblies (see Chapter 12).

14   If so equipped, remove the screw and clips securing both fog lamp assemblies and remove the housings.

15   Detach the clips securing the front bumper to the radiator support.

16   Raise the vehicle and support is securely on jackstands.

17   Detach the clips securing the left and right splash shields to the front bumper.

18   Detach the clips securing the front bumper to the bumper reinforcement.

19   Remove the nuts securing the front bumper to both front fenders and pull the front bumper assembly away from the vehicle.

20   Installation is the reverse of removal.

Rear bumper

Refer to illustrations 12.11a, 12.11b, 12.12, 12.13, 12.14a and 12.14b

21   Apply the parking brake, raise the vehicle and support it securely on jackstands.

22   Working under the vehicle, detach the plastic clips and screws securing the upper and lower edges of the bumper cover **(see illustrations)**.

23   Remove the screws securing the bumper cover in the rear wheel openings **(see illustration)**.

24   Remove the screws securing the front lower edges of the bumper cover **(see illustration)**.

25   Open the rear liftgate, open the storage compartment doors for access, then remove the bumper cover retaining nuts **(see illustrations)**. Pull the bumper cover assembly out and away from the vehicle.

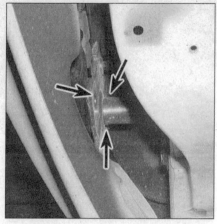

12.8 Remove the bumper retaining bolts (arrows)

26   To remove the bumper, remove the bumper retaining bolts.

27   Remove the side marker lights and pull the bumper assembly out and away from the vehicle.

28   Installation is the reverse of removal.

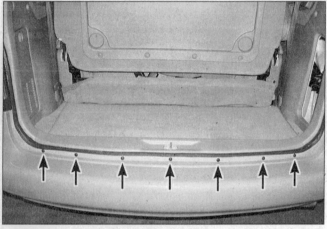

12.22a Use a Phillips screwdriver to remove the screws (arrows) securing the upper . . .

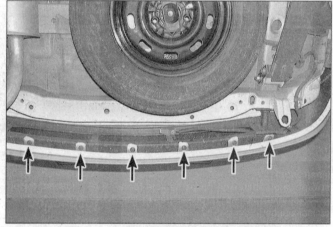

12.22b . . . and lower edge of the bumper cover

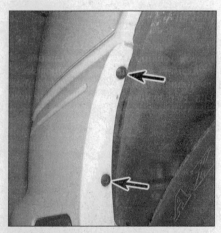

12.23 Remove the screws (arrows) securing the bumper cover to the wheel opening

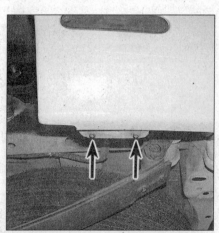

12.24 Remove the screws (arrows) securing the lower edges of the bumper cover

12.25a Open the storage compartment doors on each side, then . . .

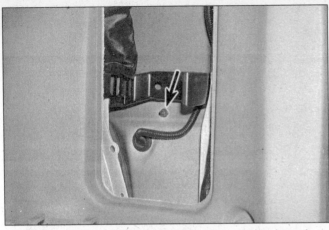

12.25b . . . remove the bumper cover retaining nuts (arrow) - there are six on each side

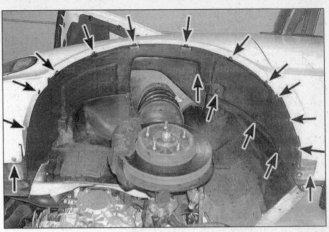

13.3 Detach inner fenderwell screws and clips (arrows) and remove it from the vehicle

13.4 Detach the bolts (arrows) securing the front edge of the fender to the radiator support

13.5a Remove the fender-to-rocker panel retaining bolt (arrow)

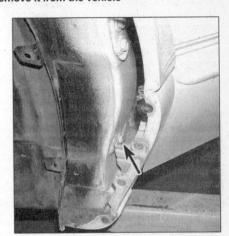

13.5b Remove the fender-to-door pillar lower bolt (arrow)

13 Front fender - removal and installation

Refer to illustrations 13.3, 13.4, 13.5a, 13.5b, 13.5c and 13.5d

1   Raise the vehicle, support it securely on jackstands and remove the front wheel, and if necessary, the radio antenna (see Chapter 12).

2   Remove the cowl cover (see Section 14) and fender-to-front bumper cover screws **(see illustration 12.5)**.

3   Detach the inner fenderwell screws and clips, then remove the inner fenderwell **(see illustration)**.

4   Detach the retaining bolts securing the headlight housing panel and the front edge of the fender to the radiator support **(see illustration)**.

5   Remove the remaining fender mounting bolts **(see illustrations)**.

6   Detach the fender. It's a good idea to

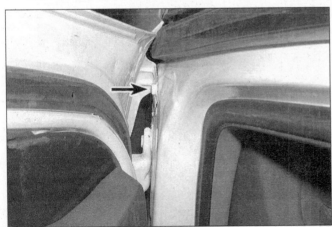

13.5c Open the door to access and remove the fender-to-door pillar upper bolt (arrow)

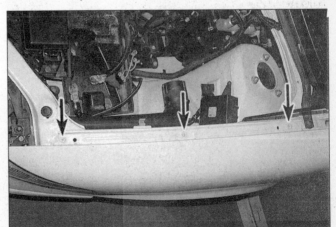

13.5d Detach the remaining bolts located in the hood opening (arrows)

11

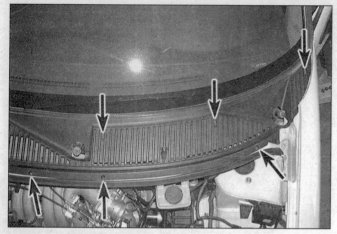

14.2 Remove the cowl cover retaining screws and fasteners (arrows)

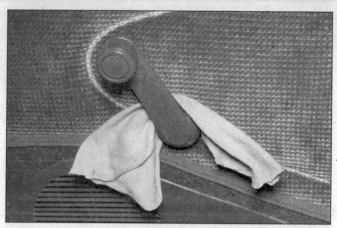

15.2 Work a cloth up behind the inside window crank, then move it back-and-forth until the handle retaining clip releases from the shaft

15.3 Pry out the cover and remove the armrest switch plate screw

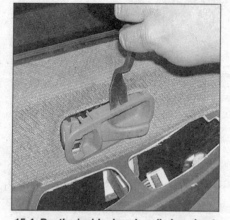

15.4 Pry the inside door handle bezel out

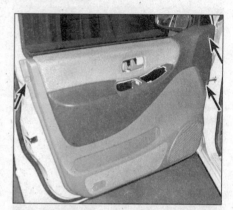

15.5 Detach the screws (arrows) securing the outer edge of the door trim panel

have an assistant support the fender while it's being moved away from the vehicle to prevent damage to the surrounding body panels.

7   Installation is the reverse of removal.

14   Cowl cover - removal and installation

Refer to illustration 14.2

1   Remove the windshield wiper arms (see Chapter 1).

2   Remove the cowl top panel seal from the front edge of the cowl cover by carefully prying it out with a large screwdriver.

3   Remove the retaining screws securing the cowl cover **(see illustration)**.

4   Detach the cowl cover and remove it from the vehicle.

5   Installation is the reverse of removal.

15   Door trim panel - removal and installation

1   Disconnect the cable from the negative terminal of the battery.

Front door

Refer to illustrations 15.2, 15.3, 15.4 and 15.5

2   On manual window equipped models, remove the window crank by working a cloth back-and-forth behind the handle to dislodge the retaining clip **(see illustration)**. A special tool is available for this purpose, but it is not essential. With the retaining clip removed, pull off the handle.

3   On power window equipped models, remove the retaining screw, detach the armrest switch control plate and disconnect the electrical connections **(see illustration)**.

4   Pry out the door handle bezel **(see illustration)**.

5   Remove the screws securing the outer edge of the door trim panel **(see illustration)**.

6   Insert a wide putty knife, a thin screwdriver or a special removal tool behind the trim panel and detach the retaining clips. Pull the lower edge of the trim panel away from the door, disconnect any electrical connectors and remove the trim panel from the vehicle by gently pulling it up and out.

7   For access to the inner door, peel back the watershield, taking care not to tear it. To install the trim panel, first press the watershield back into place. If necessary, add more sealant to hold it in place.

8   The remainder of the installation is the reverse of removal.

Sliding door

Refer to illustrations 15.9, 15.10 and 15.13

9   Carefully pry the door handle bezel off **(see illustration)**.

10   Insert a wide putty knife or a special trim panel removal tool between the door trim panel and the head of the retaining clip to

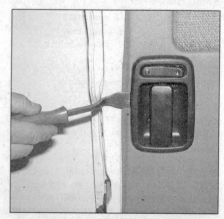

15.9 Pry the door handle bezel off

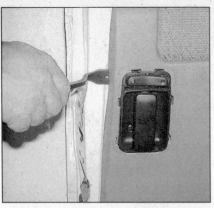

15.10 Use a trim panel removal tool to detach the trim panel retaining clips, then pull the sliding door trim panel up and out of the door

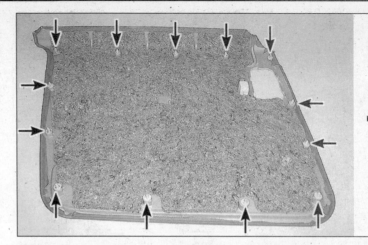

15.13 Reinstall any clips that remained in the door back into the trim panel

disengage the door panel retaining clips **(see illustration)**. **Note:** *Door trim panel retaining clips are approximately six to ten inches apart. Pry at the clip location only. Prying in between clips will result in a distorted or damaged door trim panel.*

11   Once all of the clips are disengaged, detach the trim panel and remove the trim panel from the vehicle by gently pulling it up and out.

12   For access to the inner door, peel back the watershield, taking care not to tear it. To install the trim panel, first press the watershield back into place. If necessary, add more sealant to hold it in place.

13   Prior to installation, reinstall any clips that have remained the door and in the door trim panel **(see illustration)**. The remainder of installation is the reverse of removal.

16   Door - removal, installation and adjustment

Note: *The doors are heavy and somewhat awkward to remove and install - at least two people should perform this procedure.*

Removal and installation

Front door

Refer to illustrations 16.8 and 16.9

1   Raise the window completely in the door and then disconnect the cable from negative terminal of the battery.

2   Open the door all the way and support it on jacks or blocks covered with rags to prevent damaging the paint.

3   Remove the door trim panel and water deflector (see Section 15).

4   Remove the door speaker (see Chapter 12).

5   Unplug all electrical connections, ground wires and harness retaining clips from the door. **Note:** *It is a good idea to label all connections to aid the reassembly process.*

6   Working through the door speaker hole and the door opening, detach the rubber conduit between the body and the door.

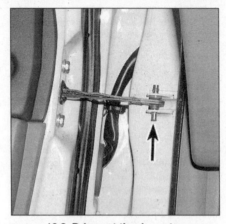

16.8 Drive out the door stop link pin (arrow)

Then pull wiring harness through conduit hole and remove it from door.

7   Mark around the door hinges with a pen or a scribe to facilitate realignment during reassembly.

8   Remove the door stop lock pin and detach the link **(see illustration)**.

9   Have an assistant hold the door, remove the hinge-to-door bolts **(see illustration)** from the upper and lower hinge and lift the door off.

10   Installation is the reverse of the removal.

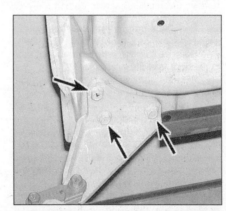

16.13a Remove the three lower sliding door hinge retaining bolts (arrows) . . .

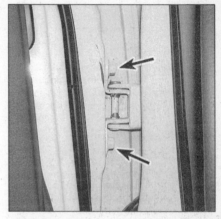

16.9 Remove the upper and lower door retaining bolts (arrows)

Sliding door

Refer to illustrations 16.13a and 16.13b

11   Open the sliding door several inches and support it on jacks or blocks covered with rags to prevent damaging the paint.

12   Remove the door trim panel and water deflector as described in (Section 15).

13   Mark around the sliding door guide roller brackets with a pen or a scribe to facilitate realignment during reassembly. Remove the bolts securing the sliding door to the upper and lower guide rollers brackets **(see illustrations)**.

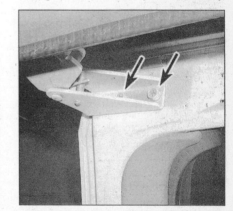

16.13b . . . followed by the two upper hinge retaining bolts (arrows)

11

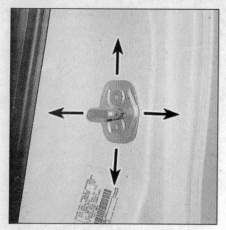

16.19 After loosening the mounting screws, tap the front door lock striker gently in the desired direction to adjust its position

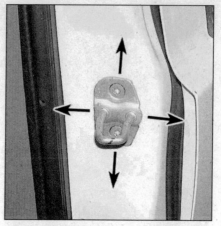

16.22 Adjust the sliding door lock striker by loosening the mounting screws and gently tapping the striker in the desired direction

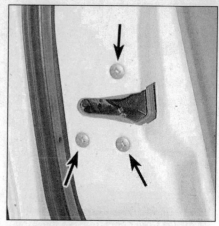

17.2 Remove the latch retaining screws (arrows) from the end of the door, then detach the locking rods and pull the latch assembly through the access hole (front door shown, sliding door similar)

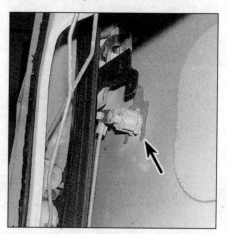

17.8 To remove the lock cylinder, detach the plastic clip securing the lock rod, then pry off the lock cylinder retaining clip (arrow)

14   With the help of an assistant, lift the sliding door upward three to four inches and remove it from the vehicle.

15   Installation is the reverse of the removal.

Adjustment

Front door

Refer to illustration 16.19

16   Having proper door-to-body alignment is a critical part of a well-functioning door assembly. First check the door hinge pins for excessive play. Fully open the door and lift up and down on the door without lifting the body. If a door has 1/16-inch or more excessive play, the hinges should be replaced.

17   Door to body alignment adjustments are made by loosening the hinge-to-body or hinge to door bolts and moving the door. Proper body alignment is achieved when the top of door is aligned parallel with the roof panel and the bottom of the door is aligned parallel with the lower rocker panel. If these goals can't be reached by adjusting the hinge-to-body or hinge-to-door bolts, body alignment shims may have to be purchased and inserted behind the hinges to achieve correct alignment.

18   To adjust the door closed position, first check that the door latch is contacting the center of the latch striker. If not, remove the striker and add or subtract shims to achieve correct alignment.

19   Finally, adjust the latch striker as necessary (up and down or sideways) to provide positive engagement with the latch mechanism **(see illustration)** and so the door panel is flush with the center pillar.

Sliding door

Refer to illustration 16.22

20   Adjust the up-and-down position by loosening the door hinge bracket retaining bolts and moving the door as necessary **(see illustrations 16.13a and 16.13b)**. Proper door alignment is achieved when the top of

door is aligned parallel with the roof panel and the bottom of the door is aligned parallel with the lower rocker panel. **Note:** *The door trim panel must first be removed for this step (see Section 15).*

21   To adjust the door closed position, first check that the door latch is contacting the center of the rear latch striker. If not, remove striker and add or subtract shims to achieve correct alignment.

22   Finally adjust latch striker as necessary (sideways) to provide positive engagement with the latch mechanism **(see illustration)** and the door panel is flush with the rear quarter panel.

17 Door latch, lock cylinder and handles - removal and installation

Note: *The procedures described below apply to both front doors and the sliding door except where noted.*

Door latch

Refer to illustration 17.2

1   Remove the door trim panel and watershield as described in Section 15.

2   Remove the screws securing the latch to the door **(see illustration)**.

3   Working through the large access hole, position the latch as necessary to disengage the outside door handle and outside lock cylinder from the latch rods.

4   All door locking rods are attached by plastic clips. The plastic clips can be removed by unsnapping the portion engaging the connecting rod and then by pulling the rod out of its locating hole.

5   Position the latch as necessary to disengage it from the door lock solenoid (if equipped). Then remove the latch assembly from the door.

Door lock cylinder and outside handle

Refer to illustrations 17.8, 17.9 and 17.10

6   To remove the lock cylinder, raise the window and remove the door trim panel and watershield as described in Section 15.

7   Working through the large access hole, disengage the plastic clip that secures the lock cylinder to the latch rod.

8   Using a screwdriver, slide the lock cylinder retaining clip out of engagement and remove the lock cylinder from the door **(see illustration)**.

9   To remove the outside handle on front doors, remove door glass run retaining screw **(see illustration)**. Working through the access hole, disengage the outside handle-to-latch rod.

10   Working through the two access holes, remove the two handle retaining nuts and remove the handle from the door **(see illus-**

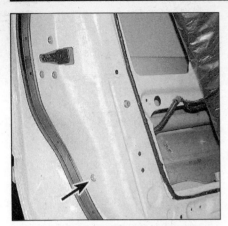

17.9   On front doors, remove the door glass run retainer screw (arrow)

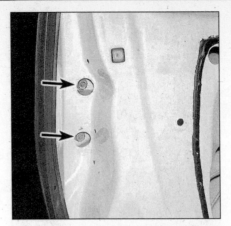

17.10   Remove two retaining nuts (arrows) and detach the front outside door handle

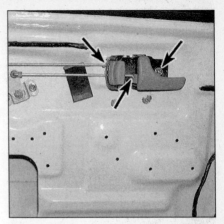

17.13   Remove the bolt and detach the links (arrows) and lift the door handle off

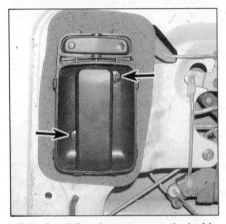

17.14   On sliding doors, remove the inside handle retaining screws and detach the link

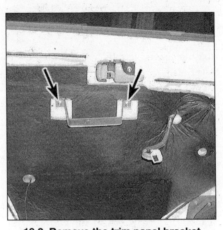

18.2   Remove the trim panel bracket bolts (arrows)

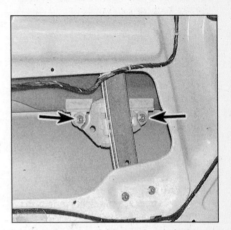

18.3   Remove the front door window glass-to-run channel retaining nuts (arrows)

tration). On sliding doors, remove the out-side handle retaining nuts, detach the link and pull the handle from the door.

11   Installation is the reverse of removal.

Inside handle

Refer to illustrations 17.13 and 17.14

12   Remove the door trim panel as described in Section 15 and peel away the watershield.

13   On front doors, remove the bolt securing the inside handle, rotate the handle out, then detach the two links and remove it from the vehicle **(see illustration)**.

14   On sliding doors, remove the screws and link securing the inside handle control mechanism to the door **(see illustration)**.

15   Installation is the reverse of removal.

18   Door window glass - removal and installation

Refer to illustrations 18.2 and 18.3
Note: *The procedure described below applies to front doors only.*

1   Remove the door trim panel and the plastic watershield (see Section 15).

2   Remove the bolts and detach the trim panel bracket **(see illustration)**.

3   Lower the window glass all the way down in the door frame. Remove the window glass-to-run channel retaining nuts **(see illustration)**.

4   Place a rag over the glass to help prevent scratching the glass, then remove the glass by pulling it up and out.

5   Installation is the reverse of removal.

19   Door window glass regulator - removal and installation

Refer to illustrations 19.5a and 19.5b
Note: *The procedure described below applies to the front doors only.*

1   Remove the door trim panel and the plastic watershield (see Section 15).

2   Remove the window glass assembly (see Section 18).

3   On power operated windows, disconnect the electrical connector from the window regulator motor.

4   Remove the bolts and detach the door brace (if equipped).

5   Remove the window track assembly and regulator mounting bolts and rivets **(see illustrations)**.

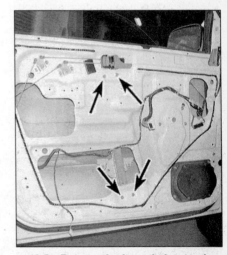

19.5a   Remove the four window track bolts (arrows) . . .

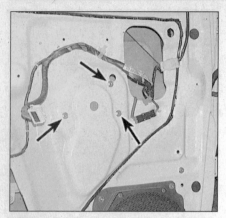

19.5b . . . then drill out the regulator rivets (arrows) (power window equipped model shown)

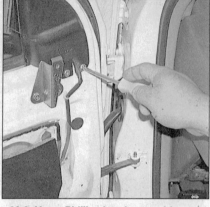

20.2 Use a Phillips head screwdriver to remove the mirror trim cover screws

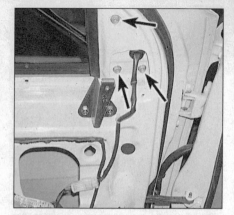

20.4 Remove the mirror retaining screws (arrows) and detach the mirror from the vehicle

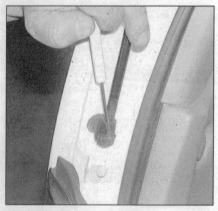

21.2 Use a small screwdriver to pry the clips out of its locking groove, then detach both ends of the strut from the locating studs

6   Pull the track and regulator/motor assembly through the service hole in the door frame to remove it.

7   Installation is the reverse of removal.

---

20 Mirrors - removal and installation

Outside mirrors

Refer to illustrations 20.2 and 20.4

1   Remove the door trim panel (see Section 15).

2   Remove the screws and detach the mirror trim cover **(see illustration).**

3   Disconnect the electrical connector from the mirror (if equipped).

4   Remove the three mirror retaining screws and detach the mirror from the vehicle **(see illustration).**

5   Installation is the reverse of removal.

Inside mirror

6   Insert a small screwdriver into the slot located at the base of the mirror and gently pry rearward until the mirror snaps off its retaining bracket.

7   To install the mirror, simply snap it back into place on the mirror retaining bracket.

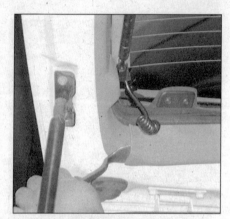

22.2a Detach the liftgate trim piece

---

21 Liftgate support struts - removal and installation

Refer to illustration 21.2
Note: *The rear liftgate is heavy and somewhat awkward to hold - at least two people should perform this procedure.*

1   Open the liftgate and support it securely.

2   Use a small screwdriver to detach the retaining clips at both ends of the support strut **(see illustration).** Then pry or pull sharply to detach it from the vehicle.

3   Installation is the reverse of removal.

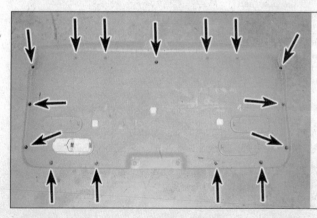

22.2c Liftgate trim panel retainer locations (arrows)

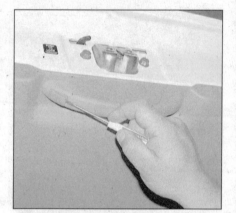

22.2b Use a small screwdriver to pry out the covers and remove the screws retaining the liftgate inside handle

---

22 Liftgate - removal, installation and adjustment

Note: *The liftgate is heavy and somewhat awkward to hold - at least two people should perform this procedure.*

Removal and installation

Refer to illustrations 22.2a, 22.2b, 22.2c, 22.3, 22.5 and 22.8

1   Open the liftgate and support it securely.

2   Remove the liftgate glass trim piece

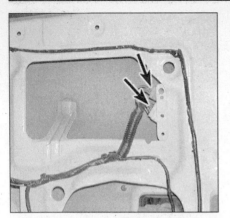

22.3 Disconnect any electrical connectors (arrows) that would interfere with liftgate removal

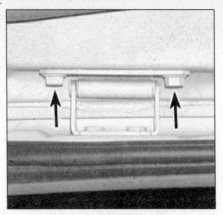

22.5 Remove the liftgate retaining bolts (arrows)

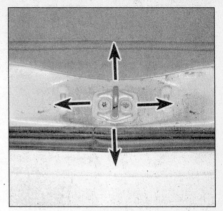

22.8 Loosen the screws and move the liftgate latch striker as necessary to adjust the closed position

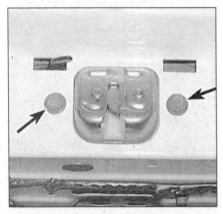

23.2 Remove the liftgate latch retaining screws (arrows), then detach the actuating cables and rods

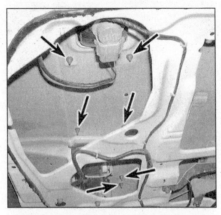

23.6 Remove the liftgate handle/license plate mount cover retaining nuts (arrows) - there are 20 in all

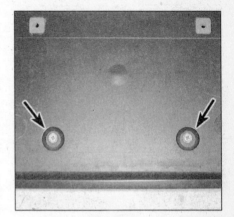

23.7 Remove the license plate mount bolts (arrows)

(see illustration). Remove the liftgate handle, then pry around the trim panel perimeter to detach the retainer clips and remove the liftgate trim panel (see illustrations).

3   Disconnect the wiring connectors, wiper washer hose and any other connectors that would interfere with removal (see illustration).

4   While an assistant supports the liftgate, detach both ends of the support struts (see Section 21).

5   Remove the hinge-to-liftgate bolts and detach the liftgate from the vehicle (see illustration).

6   Installation is the reverse of removal. Prior to installing the liftgate trim panel, reinstall any retainers that may have remained in the body.

Adjustment

Refer to illustration 22.8

7   Adjustments are made by loosening the hinge-to-liftgate bolts and moving the liftgate. Proper alignment is achieved when the edges of the liftgate are parallel with the rear quarter panels and the roof panel.

8   Finally, adjust the latch striker assembly as necessary to provide positive engagement with the latch mechanism (see illustration).

23   Liftgate latch, handle and lock cylinder - removal and installation

Refer to illustrations 23.2, 23.6, 23.7 and 23.10

1   Open the liftgate and remove the liftgate trim panel retaining screws and clips (see Section 22).

Latch

2   Remove the latch mounting screws (see illustration) from the liftgate.

3   Disconnect the actuating rods and cables from the latch and any electrical connections, then remove the latch from the liftgate.

4   Installation is the reverse of removal.

Handle

5   Working through the access hole in the liftgate, disconnect the actuating rod from the back of the handle.

6   The liftgate handle is incorporated into the license plate/backup light housing assembly. Remove the 20 retaining nuts (see illustration).

7   Close the liftgate, remove the two

23.10 Detach the actuating rod, then pry off the retaining clip (arrow) and remove the lock cylinder

retaining bolts in the license plate housing on the outside of the liftgate, then detach the handle assembly (see illustration).

8   Installation is the reverse of removal.

Lock cylinder

9   Detach the plastic clip securing the lock actuating rod.

10   Remove the retaining clip securing the lock cylinder to the liftgate (see illustration).

11

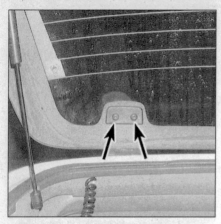

24.3 Remove the Torx head screws (arrows) at the top of the liftgate glass

24.4 Remove the window latch-to-glass nuts (arrows)

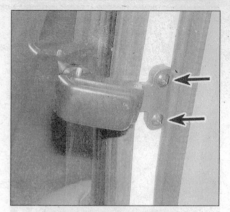

25.1 While an assistant holds the window glass remove the hinge retaining screws (arrows)

25.2 Pry the trim piece free of the door and detach it for access to the front edge of the window

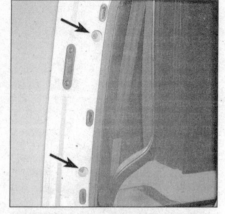

25.3 Remove the window glass retaining nuts (arrows)

26.1 Remove the rear quarter latch-to-window glass retaining screw (arrow)

11   Pull the lock cylinder out and remove it from the door.
12   Installation is the reverse of removal.

24   Liftgate glass replacement

Refer to illustrations 24.3 and 24.4
1   Disconnect the rear window defogger electrical connector.
2   Remove the liftgate struts (see Section 21).
3   Use a Torx head tool to remove the four upper glass retaining screws **(see illustration)**.
4   Remove the window latch-to-glass screws and remove the glass from the vehicle **(see illustration)**.
5   Installation is the reverse of removal.

25   Sliding door window glass - replacement

Refer to illustrations 25.1, 25.2 and 25.3
Note: *The sliding door window glass is fragile and somewhat awkward to remove and install - at least two people should perform this procedure.*

1   Open the window latch assembly and remove the screws that secure the latch to the body **(see illustration)**.
2   Pry off the trim piece and detach the rubber moulding from the front edge of the glass for access **(see illustration)**.
3   Remove the two nuts securing the glass to the door **(see illustration)**.
4   With an assistant supporting the window glass, remove the window glass from the vehicle.
5   Installation is the reverse of removal.

26   Rear quarter window glass - replacement

Refer to illustration 26.1
Note: *The rear quarter window glass is fragile and somewhat awkward to remove and install - at least two people should perform this procedure.*
1   Remove the retaining screw securing the latch to the glass **(see illustration)**.
2   Remove the upper rear quarter trim panel located in front of the rear quarter window (see Section 27).
3   With an assistant holding the window glass, remove the retaining nuts securing the

hinges to the body.
4   Remove the rear quarter window glass from the vehicle.
5   To remove the rear quarter window latch, first remove the upper rear quarter trim panel located between the rear quarter window and the liftgate, disconnect the electrical connector (if equipped) and remove the latch retaining bolts **(see illustration 26.1)**.
6   Installation is the reverse of removal.

27   Rear quarter trim panels - removal and installation

Refer to illustrations 27.2a, 27.2b, 27.2c, 27.3, 27.5, 27.6a and 27.6b
1   Remove the rear seat (see Section 30).
2   Remove the upper rear quarter trim panels surrounding the rear quarter window glass **(see illustrations)**.
3   When removing trim panels on vehicles equipped with rear air conditioning, detach the air conditioning service cover and disconnect the blower switch electrical connector **(see illustration)**.
4   Remove the air conditioning and radio control panel (see Chapter 12).
5   Remove the rear cargo net retainers, if equipped **(see illustration)**.

27.2a Pry open the trim cover and remove the seat belt anchor bolt . . .

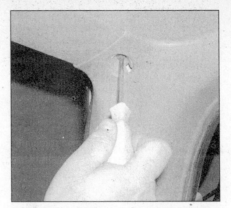

27.2b . . . then pry out the upper rear quarter trim panel screw covers and remove the screws at the top . . .

27.2c . . . and bottom (arrow)

27.3 Remove the rear air conditioning service cover

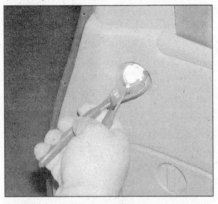

27.5 Remove the cargo net retainers

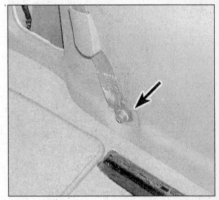

27.6a Remove the seat belt bolt (arrow)

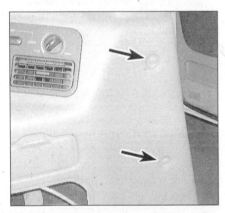

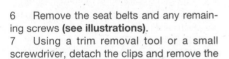

27.6b Detach the covers and remove the retaining screws (arrows)

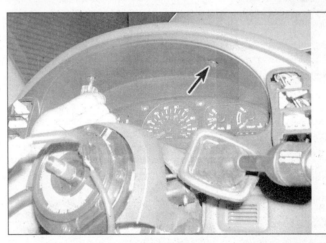

28.4 Remove the two cluster bezel retaining screws

6   Remove the seat belts and any remaining screws **(see illustrations)**.

7   Using a trim removal tool or a small screwdriver, detach the clips and remove the rear quarter trim panel.

8   Installation is the reverse of removal.

---

28 Dashboard trim panels - removal and installation

Warning: *The models covered by this manual are equipped with Supplemental Restraint systems (SRS), more commonly known as airbags. Always disconnect the negative battery cable, then the positive battery cable and wait ten minutes before working in the vicinity of the impact sensors, steering column or instrument panel to avoid the possibility of accidental deployment of the airbag, which could cause personal injury (see Chapter 12). Do not use electrical test equipment on any of the airbag system wiring or tamper with them in any way.*

1   Disconnect the negative battery cable, then the positive battery cable and wait ten minutes before proceeding any further (see **Warning** above).

Instrument cluster bezel

Refer to illustration 28.4

2   Place the shift lever in the Low position, turn the ignition key to the Accessory position and tilt the steering wheel down to the lowest position.

3   Remove the bezel-mounted electrical switches (see Chapter 12).

4   Remove the two retaining screws at the top of bezel **(see illustration)**.

5   Grasp the bezel securely and pull back

11

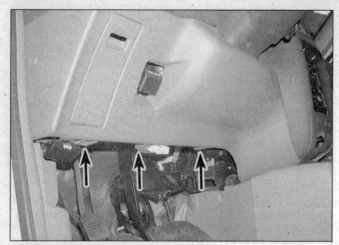

28.7 Remove the knee bolster retaining screws (arrows) then detach the bolster from the dash

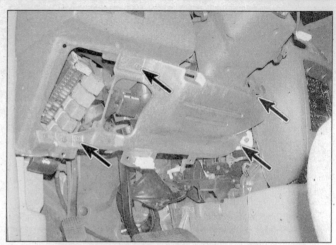

28.8 The knee bolster reinforcement panel can be removed after the retaining bolts (arrows) are unscrewed

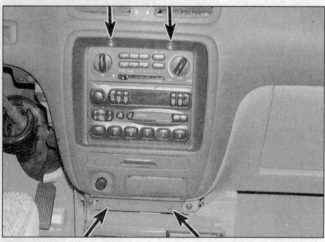

28.11 Remove the retaining screws (arrows) and detach the lower center trim panel and radio/CD player bezel assembly

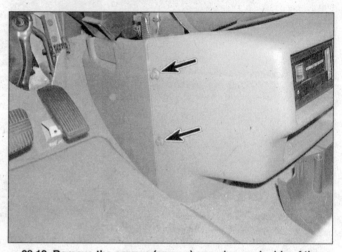

28.13 Remove the screws (arrows) securing each side of the storage compartment

sharply to detach it from the dash.

6　　Installation is the reverse of removal.

Knee bolster and reinforcement panel

Refer to illustrations 28.7 and 28.8

7　　Remove the screws and lower the knee bolster from the dash **(see illustration)**.

8　　Remove the bolts and lower the reinforcement panel from the dash **see illustration)**. Disconnect the diagnostic connector and remove the reinforcement panel.

9　　Installation is the reverse of removal.

Lower center trim panel and radio/CD player bezel

Refer to illustration 28.13

10　　Remove the knee bolster and reinforcement panel.

11　　Remove the ash tray and the lower center trim panel and radio/CD player bezel retaining screws, then detach the assembly

from the dash **(see illustration)**.

12　　Installation is the reverse of removal.

Storage compartment

Refer to illustration 28.13

13　　Remove the retaining screws located on each side of the storage compartment, then pull the compartment straight out to remove it from the instrument panel **(see illustration)**.

14　　Installation is the reverse of removal.

Lower center trim panels

Refer to illustration 28.15

15　　Detach the three retaining screws on each side and remove the lower center trim panels **(see illustration)**.

16　　Installation is the reverse of removal.

Glove box

Refer to illustration 28.19

17　　Remove the lower center trim panels and storage compartment.

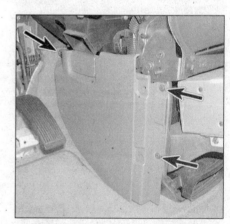

28.15 Remove the screws (arrows) securing the each lower center trim panel

18　　Open the glove box door.

19　　Detach the retaining screws and remove the glove box from the dash **(see illustration)**.

20　　Installation is the reverse of removal.

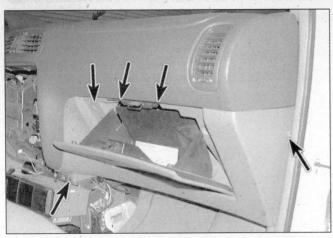

28.19 Remove the retaining screws (arrows) and detach the glove box

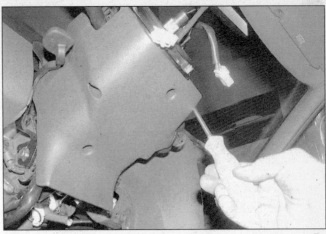

29.2 Remove the steering column cover screws

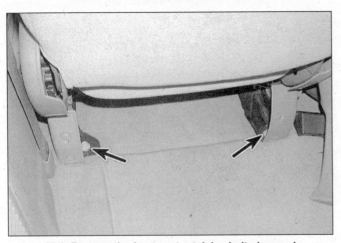

30.2 Remove the front seat retaining bolts (arrows)

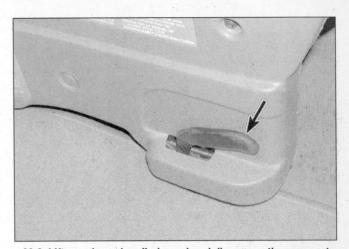

30.6 Lift up release handle (arrow) and disengage the rear seat from the hooks in the floor

29   Steering column cover - removal and installation

Refer to illustration 29.2

1   Remove the knee bolster (see Section 28).
2   Remove the screws from the lower steering column cover **(see illustration)**.
3   Separate the cover halves then detach them from the steering column. On 1995 and earlier models it may be necessary to remove the lock cylinder (see Chapter 12).
4   Installation is the reverse of removal.

30   Seats - removal and installation

Front seat

Refer to illustration 30.2

1   Position the seat all the way forward or all the way to the rear to access the front seat retaining bolts.
2   Detach any bolt trim covers and remove the retaining bolts **(see illustration)**.
3   Tilt the seat upward to access the underneath, then disconnect any electrical connectors and lift the seat from the vehicle.
4   Installation is the reverse of removal.

Rear seats

Refer to illustration 30.6

5   Fold the rear seat back to the down position.
6   Lift up the rear seat latch handle **(see illustration)**, then disengage the rear seat from the hooks in the floor and remove it from the vehicle.
7   Installation is the reverse of removal.

11

Notes

Chapter 12
Chassis electrical system

Contents

1 General information

The electrical system is a 12-volt, negative ground type. Power for the lights and all electrical accessories is supplied by a lead/acid-type battery which is charged by the alternator.

This Chapter covers repair and service procedures for the various electrical components not associated with the engine. Information on the battery, alternator, distributor and starter motor can be found in Chapter 5. It should be noted that when portions of the electrical system are serviced, the negative battery cable should be disconnected from the battery to prevent electrical shorts and/or fires.

Warning: *The models covered by this manual are equipped with Supplemental Restraint Systems (SRS), more commonly known as airbags. Always disable the airbag system before working in the vicinity of any airbag system components to avoid the possibility of accidental deployment of the airbag(s), which could cause personal injury (see Section 26).*

2 Electrical troubleshooting

Refer to illustrations 2.5a, 2.5b, 2.6, 2.9 and 2.15

A typical electrical circuit consists of an electrical component, any switches, relays, motors, fuses, fusible links or circuit breakers related to that component and the wiring and connectors that link the component to both the battery and the chassis. To help you pinpoint an electrical circuit problem, wiring diagrams are included at the end of this Chapter.

Before tackling any troublesome electrical circuit, first study the appropriate wiring diagrams to get a complete understanding of what makes up that individual circuit. Trouble spots, for instance, can often be narrowed down by noting if other components related to the circuit are operating properly. If several components or circuits fail at one time, chances are the problem is in a fuse or ground connection, because several circuits are often routed through the same fuse and ground connections.

Electrical problems usually stem from simple causes, such as loose or corroded connections, a blown fuse, a melted fusible link or a failed relay. Visually inspect the condition of all fuses, wires and connections in a problem circuit before troubleshooting the circuit.

If test equipment and instruments are going to be utilized, use the diagrams to plan ahead of time where you will make the necessary connections in order to accurately pinpoint the trouble spot.

The basic tools needed for electrical troubleshooting include a circuit tester or voltmeter (a 12-volt bulb with a set of test leads can also be used), a continuity tester, which includes a bulb, battery and set of test leads, and a jumper wire, preferably with a circuit breaker incorporated, which can be used to bypass

12

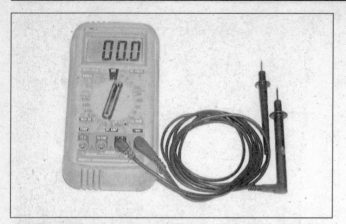

2.5a The most useful tool for electrical troubleshooting is a digital multimeter, that can check volts, amps, and test continuity

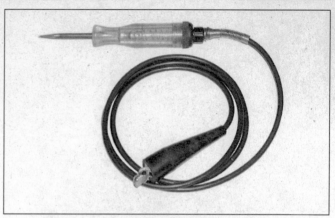

2.5b A simple test light is very handy, especially when testing for voltage

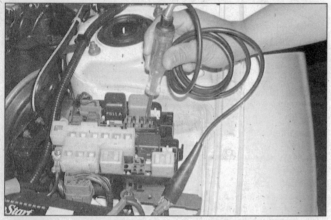

2.6 In use, a basic test light's lead is clipped to a known good ground, then the pointed probe can test connectors, wires or electrical sockets - if the bulb lights, the part being tested has battery voltage

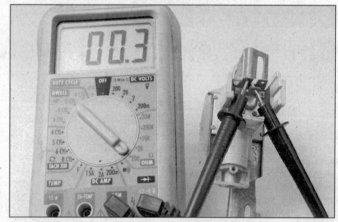

2.9 With a multimeter set to the ohms scale, resistance can be checked across two terminals - when checking for continuity, a low reading indicates continuity, a high reading indicates lack of continuity

electrical components **(see illustrations)**. Before attempting to locate a problem with test instruments, use the wiring diagram(s) to decide where to make the connections.

Voltage checks

Voltage checks should be performed if a circuit is not functioning properly. Connect one lead of a circuit tester to either the negative battery terminal or a known good ground. Connect the other lead to a connector in the circuit being tested, preferably nearest to the battery or fuse **(see illustration)**. If the bulb of the tester lights, voltage is present, which means that the part of the circuit between the connector and the battery is problem free. Continue checking the rest of the circuit in the same fashion. When you reach a point at which no voltage is present, the problem lies between that point and the last test point with voltage. Most of the time the problem can be traced to a loose connection. **Note:** *Keep in mind that some circuits receive voltage only when the ignition key is in the Accessory or Run position.*

Finding a short

One method of finding shorts in a circuit

is to remove the fuse and connect a test light or voltmeter in place of the fuse terminals. There should be no voltage present in the circuit. Move the wiring harness from side-to-side while watching the test light. If the bulb goes on, there is a short to ground somewhere in that area, probably where the insulation has rubbed through. The same test can be performed on each component in the circuit, even a switch.

Ground check

Perform a ground test to check whether a component is properly grounded. Disconnect the battery and connect one lead of a continuity tester or multimeter (set to the ohms scale), to a known good ground. Connect the other lead to the wire or ground connection being tested. If the resistance is low (less than 5 ohms), the ground is good. If the bulb on a self-powered test light does not go on, the ground is not good.

Continuity check

A continuity check is done to determine if there are any breaks in a circuit - if it is passing electricity properly. With the circuit off (no power in the circuit), a self-powered

continuity tester or multimeter can be used to check the circuit. Connect the test leads to both ends of the circuit (or to the "power" end and a good ground), and if the test light comes on the circuit is passing current properly **(see illustration)**. If the resistance is low (less than 5 ohms), there is continuity; if the reading is 10,000 ohms or higher, there is a break somewhere in the circuit. The same procedure can be used to test a switch, by connecting the continuity tester to the switch terminals. With the switch turned On, the test light should come on (or low resistance should be indicated on a meter).

Finding an open circuit

When diagnosing for possible open circuits, it is often difficult to locate them by sight because oxidation or terminal misalignment is hidden by the connectors. Merely wiggling a connector on a sensor or in the wiring harness may correct the open circuit condition. Remember this when an open circuit is indicated when troubleshooting a circuit. Intermittent problems may also be caused by oxidized or loose connections.

Electrical troubleshooting is simple if you keep in mind that all electrical circuits are

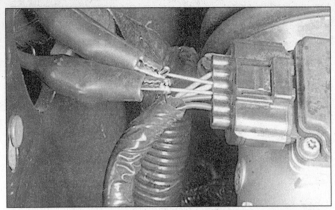

2.15 To backprobe a connector, insert a small, sharp probe (such as a straight-pin) into the back of the connector alongside the desired wire until it contacts the metal terminal inside; connect your meter leads to the probes - this allows you to test a functioning circuit

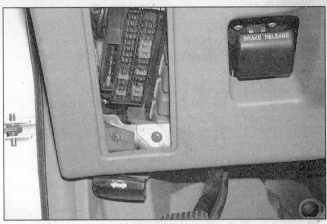

3.1a The interior fuse/relay block is located at the end of the driver's side of the instrument panel (access panel removed in photo)

3.1b On 1996 and later models, the main engine compartment fuse/relay box is located just in front of the battery - 1995 and earlier models are equipped with a center fuse panel located just to the right of the battery and a left-hand fuse panel mounted to the driver's side inner fenderwell

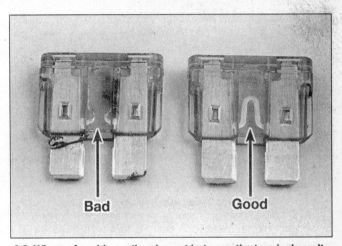

3.3 When a fuse blows, the element between the terminals melts – the fuse on left is blown, the fuse on right is good

basically electricity running from the battery, through the wires, switches, relays, fuses and fusible links to each electrical component (light bulb, motor, etc.) and to ground, from which it is passed back to the battery. Any electrical problem is an interruption in the flow of electricity to and from the battery.

Connectors

Most electrical connections on these vehicles are made with multiwire plastic connectors. The mating halves of many connectors are secured with locking clips molded into the plastic connector shells. The mating halves of large connectors, such as some of those under the instrument panel, are held together by a bolt through the center of the connector.

To separate a connector with locking clips, use a small screwdriver to pry the clips apart carefully, then separate the connector halves. Pull only on the shell, never pull on the wiring harness as you may damage the individual wires and terminals inside the connectors. Look at the connector closely before trying to separate the halves. Often the locking clips are engaged in a way that is not

immediately clear. Additionally, many connectors have more than one set of clips.

Each pair of connector terminals has a male half and a female half. When you look at the end view of a connector in a diagram, be sure to understand whether the view shows the harness side or the component side of the connector. Connector halves are mirror images of each other, and a terminal shown on the right side end view of one half will be on the left side end view of the other half.

It is often necessary to take circuit voltage measurements with a connector connected. Whenever possible, carefully insert a small straight pin (not your meter probe) into the rear of the connector shell to contact the terminal inside, then clip your meter lead to the pin. This kind of connection is called "backprobing" **(see illustration)**. When inserting a test probe into a male terminal, be careful not to distort the terminal opening. Doing so can lead to a poor connection and corrosion at that terminal later. Using the small straight pin instead of a meter probe results in less chance of deforming the terminal connector.

3 Fuses - general information

Refer to illustrations 3.1a, 3.1b and 3.3

The electrical circuits of the vehicle are protected by a combination of fuses and circuit breakers. Fuse blocks are located under the instrument panel and in the engine compartment **(see accompanying illustrations and illustration 5.1b)**.

Each of the fuses is designed to protect a specific circuit (or circuits), and the various circuits are identified on the fuse panel itself.

Miniaturized fuses are employed in the fuse block. These compact fuses, with blade terminal design, allow fingertip removal and replacement. If an electrical component fails, always check the fuse first. The easiest way to check fuses is with a test light. Check for power at the exposed terminal tips of each fuse. If power is available on one side of the fuse but not the other, the fuse is blown. A blown fuse can also be confirmed by visually inspecting it **(see illustration)**.

Be sure to replace blown fuses with the correct type. Fuses of different ratings are

12

4.1 In addition to the circuit breakers contained in the engine compartment fuse/relay panels, there are two circuit breakers (arrow) under the left end of the dashboard used to protect several accessory control modules and the power window relay circuit

5.1a There is an additional relay panel (arrow) on the right side of the engine compartment

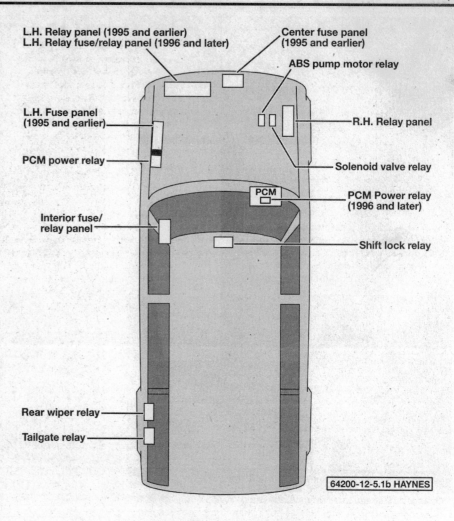

L.H. Relay panel (1995 and earlier)
L.H. Relay fuse/relay panel (1996 and later)

Center fuse panel (1995 and earlier)

ABS pump motor relay

L.H. Fuse panel (1995 and earlier)

R.H. Relay panel

PCM power relay

Solenoid valve relay

PCM Power relay (1996 and later)

Interior fuse/ relay panel

Shift lock relay

Rear wiper relay

Tailgate relay

64200-12-5.1b HAYNES

5.1b Relay location diagram

physically interchangeable, but only fuses of the proper rating should be used. Replacing a fuse with one of a higher or lower value than specified is not recommended. Each electrical circuit needs a specific amount of protection. The amperage value of each fuse is molded into the fuse body.

If the replacement fuse immediately fails, don't replace it again until the cause of the problem is isolated and corrected. In most cases, the cause will be a short circuit in the wiring caused by a broken or deteriorated wire.

All models are equipped with a main fuse which protects all the circuits coming from the battery. If these circuits are overloaded, the main fuse blows, preventing damage to the main wiring harness. The main fuse consists of a metal strip which will be visibly melted when overloaded. Always disconnect the battery before replacing a main fuse (available from your dealer). The main

fuse is located in the engine compartment fuse box. It's very similar in appearance to standard fuses/relays and is replaced in the same way. If you have to replace a main fuse, make sure you install a replacement unit that's equivalent to the old fuse. In other words, if the old main fuse is an 80A unit, replace it with an 80A fuse; if it's a 100A unit, replace it with a 100A fuse. Don't switch amperage ratings on the main fuse!

4   Circuit breakers - general information

Refer to illustration 4.1

Circuit breakers protect components such as sunroof motors and power window motors **(see illustration)**.

On some models the circuit breaker resets itself automatically, so an electrical overload in a circuit-breaker-protected system will cause the circuit to fail momentarily, then come back on. If the circuit does not come back on, check it immediately. Once the condition is corrected, the circuit breaker

will resume its normal function. Some circuit breakers must be reset manually.

5   Relays - general information and testing

General information

Refer to illustrations 5.1a and 5.1b

1   Several electrical accessories in the vehicle, such as the fuel injection system, horns, starter, and fog lamps use relays to transmit the electrical signal to the component. Relays use a low-current circuit (the control circuit) to open and close a high-current circuit (the power circuit). If the relay is defective, that component will not operate properly. Most relays are mounted in the engine compartment and interior fuse/relay boxes **(see illustrations 3.1a and 3.1b)**. Additional relay are located around the vehicle **(see illustrations)**. If a faulty relay is suspected, it can be removed and tested using the procedure below or by a dealer service department or a repair shop. Defective relays must be replaced as a unit.

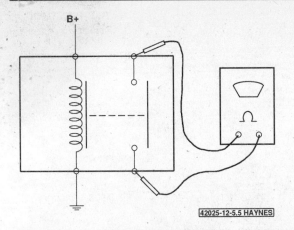

5.5 To test a typical four-terminal, normally-open relay, connect an ohmmeter to the two terminals of the power circuit - the meter will indicate no continuity until battery power and ground are applied to the two terminals of the control circuit, then the relay will click and continuity will be indicated

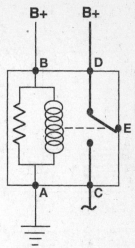

Relay with internal resistor

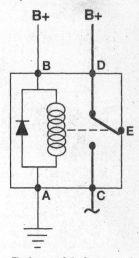

Relay with internal clamping diode

5.6 Testing typical five-terminal relays

Testing

Refer to illustrations 5.5, 5.6 and 5.7

2   It's best to refer to the wiring diagram for the circuit to determine the proper hook-ups for the relay you're testing. However, if you're not able to determine the correct hook-up from the wiring diagrams, you may be able to determine the test hook-ups from the information that follows.

3   On most relays, two of the terminals are the relay's control circuit (they connect to the relay coil which, when energized, closes the large contacts to complete the circuit). The other terminals are the power circuit (they are connected together within the relay when the control-circuit coil is energized).

4   Some relays are marked as an aid to help you determine which terminals are the control circuit and which are the power circuit. Otherwise, refer to the wiring diagrams for reference.

5   To test a standard four-terminal relay, connect a fused jumper wire between one of the two control circuit terminals and the positive battery terminal. Connect another jumper wire between the other control circuit terminal and ground. When the connections are made,

the relay should click (**see illustration**).

6   Standard five-terminal relays with diodes are tested in much the same way (**see illustration**). There should be continuity between terminals D and E with the relay not energized. With the relay energized, there should be continuity between D and C. Relays with internal diodes must be tested with battery polarity at terminals A and B connected as shown, while relays with internal resistors can be tested with the polarity at A and B connected in either direction with respect to B+ and ground.

7   Some circuits such as the blower motor circuit use six terminal relays On these relays there is one control circuit and two power circuits (**see illustration**).

8   If the relay fails any of the above tests, replace it.

6   Turn signal/hazard flasher - check and replacement

Refer to illustration 6.1

Warning: *The models covered by this manual are equipped with Supplemental Restraint Systems (SRS), more commonly known as airbags. Always disable the airbag system before working in the vicinity of any airbag system components to avoid the possibility of accidental deployment of the airbag(s), which could cause personal injury (see Section 26).*

1   The turn signal and hazard flashers are controlled from a single electronic flasher unit which is mounted below the interior fuse block (**see illustration**). **Note:** *The flasher module on 1993 models is mounted between the steering column and the heater control panel.*

2   When the flasher unit is functioning properly, an audible click can be heard during its operation. If the turn signals fail on one side or the other and the flasher unit does not make its characteristic clicking sound, a faulty turn signal bulb is indicated.

3   If both turn signals fail to blink, the problem may be due to a blown fuse, a faulty flasher unit, a broken switch or a loose or open connection. If a quick check of the fuse box indicates that the turn signal fuse has

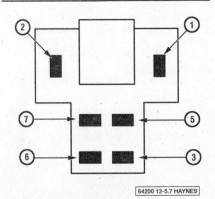

5.7 The front blower motor relay terminal identification - with terminal 1 connected to battery power and terminal 2 connected to ground, there should be continuity between terminals 3 and 5 and continuity between terminals 6 and 7

6.1 The turn signal/hazard flasher (arrow) on 1994 and later vehicles is accessed from below the left end of the dashboard with the knee bolster removed

12

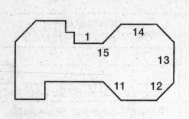

10	4
9	3
8	X
7	X
6	2
5	1

SWITCH POSITION	CONTINUITY BETWEEN
High beam (lever forward)	9 and 10
Flash-to-pass (lever rearward)	5 and 6 / 7 and 8
Left turn	14 and 15
Right turn	13 and 15
Left turn (cornering lamps)	4 and 13
Right turn (cornering lamps)	4 and 12

TURN SIGNAL/DIMMER SWITCH

SWITCH POSITION	CONTINUITY OR RESISTANCE BETWEEN
Off	2 and 3, 47.6 K-ohm
Intermittent	2 and 3, 11.33 K-ohm
Low	2 and 3, 4.08 K-ohm
High	2 and 3, continuity
Interval timer, rotate	1 and 2 3.3 to 103.3 K-ohm
Washer switch On (wiper Off)	1 and 2, continuity
Washer switch Off (wiper Off)	1 and 2, 103.3 K-ohm

WIPER/WASHER SWITCH

64200-12-7.13 HAYNES

7.3 Multi-function switch terminal identification guide and continuity charts

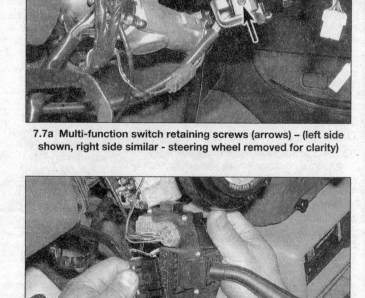

7.7a Multi-function switch retaining screws (arrows) – (left side shown, right side similar - steering wheel removed for clarity)

7.7b Pull the multi-function switches out for access, then unplug the connectors (steering wheel removed for clarity)

blown, check the wiring for a short before installing a new fuse.

4   To replace the flasher, remove the driver's side knee bolster (see Chapter 11), then simply unplug it from the bracket under the dash **(see illustration 6.1)**.

5   Make sure that the replacement unit is identical to the original. Compare the old one to the new one before installing it.

6   Installation is the reverse of removal.

7   Multi-function switch- check and replacement

Warning: *The models covered by this manual are equipped with Supplemental Restraint Systems (SRS), more commonly known as airbags. Always disable the airbag system before working in the vicinity of any airbag system components to avoid the possibility of accidental deployment of the airbag(s), which could cause personal injury (see Section 26).*

Check

Refer to illustration 7.3

1   The multi-function switch is located on the left and right side of the steering column. It incorporates the turn signal, hazard and headlight dimmer functions into one switch on the left side of the column and a wiper/washer switch on the right side of the column.

2   Remove the multi-function switch (see Step 4).

3   Using an ohmmeter or self-powered test light and the accompanying diagrams, check for continuity between the indicated switch terminals, with the switch in each of the indicated positions **(see illustration)**. If the continuity isn't as specified, replace the switch.

Replacement

Refer to illustrations 7.7a and 7.7b

4   Refer to Section 26 and disable the airbag system.

5   Remove driver's knee bolster and the

steering column covers (see Chapter 11).

6   Refer to Section 8 and remove the ignition key lock cylinder.

7   Remove the switch retaining screws, disconnect the electrical connectors, then detach the switch from the steering column **(see illustrations)**.

8   Installation is the reverse of removal.

8   Ignition switch and key lock cylinder - check and replacement

Warning: *The models covered by this manual are equipped with Supplemental Restraint Systems (SRS), more commonly known as airbags. Always disable the airbag system before working in the vicinity of any airbag system components to avoid the possibility of accidental deployment of the airbag(s), which could cause personal injury (see Section 26).*

1   Remove the steering column covers and driver's side knee bolster (see Chapter 11).

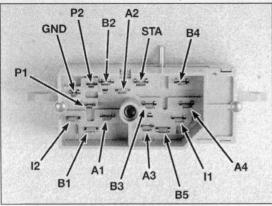

8.4a Ignition switch terminal identification (1995 and earlier)

IGNITION SWITCH POSITION	CONTINUITY BETWEEN TERMINALS
Lock or Off	None
Accessory	B5 and A1
On	B1 and A1, B3 and A3, B4 and A4
Start	B5 and I1, B1 and I2, B4 and STA

8.4b Ignition switch continuity tests (1995 and earlier)

3	2	1
6	5	4

8.4c Ignition switch terminal identification and continuity tests (1996 and later) - test at the switch side of the connector at the bottom of the steering column

SWITCH POSITION	CONTINUITY BETWEEN
Lock	None
Accessory	1 and 6
On	1 and 6, 1 and 5, 1 and 3
Start	1 and 2, 1 and 5, 1 and 4

64200-12-8.4c HAYNES

Check

Refer to illustrations 8.4a, 8.4b and 8.4c

2   Check the IGN SW maxi-fuse in the main engine compartment fuse/relay panel.

3   On 1996 and later models, follow the ignition switch harness down to the connector at the bottom of the steering column and disconnect the connector. On 1995 and earlier models, disconnect the connector from the ignition switch. Check the white/purple wire at the harness side of the connector for battery voltage. If there is no voltage on the harness side of the connector, check the circuit from the connector to the fuse-relay panel.

4   If there was voltage present, and the ignition switch is not functioning correctly, check the ignition switch for continuity. On 1996 and later models, test at the switch side of the connector **(see illustrations)**.

5   If the continuity is not as specified, replace the switch.

6   Check the lock cylinder in each position to make sure it isn't worn or loose and that the key position corresponds to the markings on the housing.

Replacement

Ignition switch

7   Refer to Section 26 and disable the airbag system.

8   On 1996 and later models, remove the steering wheel (see Chapter 10).

9   Remove the upper and lower steering column shrouds (see Chapter 11).

1995 and earlier models

Refer to illustration 8.13

10   Turn the ignition key lock cylinder to the Run position.

11   Unplug the connector at the ignition switch and remove the two switch-mounting screws.

12   Disengage the ignition switch from the actuator pin and remove the switch.

13   Make sure the actuator pin is in the Run position for installation **(see illustration)**.

Note: *A new switch will be set in this position.*

14   Place the new switch in position on the actuator pin and install the screws. It may be necessary to move the switch back and forth to line up the screw holes.

1996 and later models

Refer to illustration 8.17

15   Remove the lock cylinder as described below.

16   Refer to Chapter 10 and lower the steering column.

17   Use a drill to remove the two shear-head bolts securing the ignition switch/lock housing to the steering column **(see illustration)**.

18   Remove the switch/housing with its

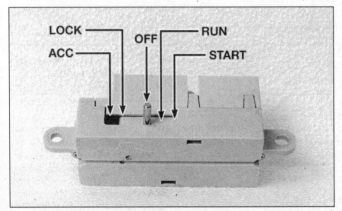

8.13 Ignition switch position details (1995 and earlier)

8.17 With the steering column lowered, drill out the heads of the bolts (arrows) securing the switch/housing to the column (1996 and later)

12

wiring harness. If the switch is faulty, the switch and housing must be replaced as a unit.

19 Installation is the reverse of the removal procedure. When installing the new housing, tighten the new bolts in place until the breakaway heads break off, ensuring the proper torque.

Lock Cylinder

Refer to illustration 8.22

20 Refer to Section 26 and disable the airbag system.

21 On 1995 and earlier models, remove the lower steering column cover. On 1996 and later models, remove the upper and lower steering column covers (see Chapter 11).

22 Turn the ignition key to the On position, then depress the retaining pin and pull the cylinder out **(see illustration)**. **Note:** *Be sure to catch the small spring that will pop out as the lock cylinder is withdrawn from the housing.*

23 When reinstalling the lock cylinder, position the small spring under the rod on the cylinder and slide the cylinder into the housing until the retaining pin pops back into the hole in the lower part of the housing.

24 Insert the key and check the lock cylinder for proper operation.

25 The remainder of installation is the reverse of removal.

9 Instrument panel switches - check and replacement

Warning: *The models covered by this manual are equipped with Supplemental Restraint Systems (SRS), more commonly known as airbags. Always disable the airbag system*

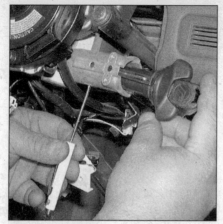

8.22 Use a drill bit or small screwdriver to push up on the retaining pin while you withdraw the lock cylinder

before working in the vicinity of any airbag system components to avoid the possibility of accidental deployment of the airbag(s), which could cause personal injury (see Section 26).

1 There are two switch "pods", one on either side of the instrument cluster. In the left pod are the cruise control switch, headlight switch, dashboard light rheostat, and the Autolamp switch. The right pod contains the rear wiper/washer switch, rear defogger, and hazard switch.

Check

Cruise control On/Off switch

Refer to illustration 9.2

2 To check the switch it must first be removed (see below).

3 Using an ohmmeter or self-powered test light and the accompanying diagram, check

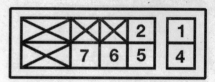

9.2 Cruise control On/Off switch terminals - there should be continuity between 5 and 7; 5 and 4; 7 and 4; only when the switch is ON

for continuity between the indicated switch terminals with the switch in each of the indicated positions **(see illustration)**. If the continuity isn't as specified, replace the switch.

Headlight switch, dash light dimmer and Autolamp switch

Refer to illustrations 9.5a and 9.5b

4 To check the switches they must first be removed (see below).

5 Using an ohmmeter or self-powered test light and the accompanying diagram, check for continuity between the indicated switch terminals with the switch in each of the indicated positions **(see illustrations)**. If the continuity isn't as specified, replace the switch.

Rear wiper/washer switch

Refer to illustration 9.7

6 To check the switches they must first be removed (see below).

7 Using an ohmmeter or self-powered test light and the accompanying diagram, check for continuity between the indicated switch

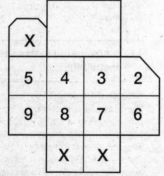

SWITCH POSITION	CONTINUITY BETWEEN
Headlight position (On)	7 and 8, 3 and 4 (only at On)
Park position	2 and 6 (in Park or Head only)
Park or head (bulb circuit)	5 and 9 (moving switch to Park or Head)

9.5a Headlight switch terminal identification and continuity tests

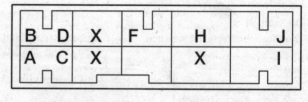

SWITCH POSITION	CONTINUITY BETWEEN
Instrument panel Bright	H and J
Instrument panel Dark	F and J
Switch bulb circuit	D and B (in all positions)
Autolamp switch any position except Off (left detent)	I and C
Delayed exit rheostat (rotate to the right)	A and C, resistance 3.3 to 103.3 K-ohms

9.5b Instrument panel light dimmer/Autolamp control switch terminal identification and continuity tests

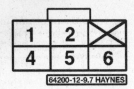

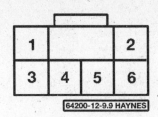

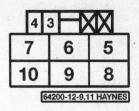

9.7 Rear wiper/washer switch terminal identification - there should be continuity between 5 and 6 only with the wiper On, and continuity between 4 and 5 only with the washer On

9.9 Rear defogger switch terminal guide

9.11 Hazard switch terminal identification - there should be continuity between 7 and 9; 5 and 6; 5 and 8, when the switch is On

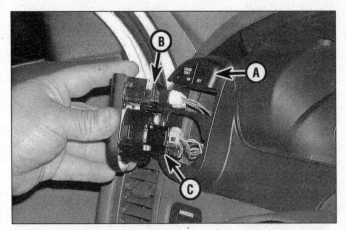

9.12 Left switch pod - (A) is the cruise control On/Off switch, (B) the instrument panel dimmer control, and (C) is the headlight switch

11.3 Remove the instrument cluster screws (arrows)

terminals with the switch in each of the indicated positions **(see illustration)**. If the continuity isn't as specified, replace the switches.

Rear window defogger

Refer to illustration 9.9

8   To check the switch it must first be removed from the right switch pod (see below).

9   Using an ohmmeter or self-powered test light, check for continuity between terminals 4 and 6 on the switch **(see illustration)**. There should be continuity only when the defogger switch is depressed. If the continuity isn't as specified, replace the switch.

Hazard warning switch

Refer to illustration 9.11

10   To check the switch it must first be removed from the right switch pod (see below).

11   Test for continuity between the terminals of the switch **(see illustration)**. If the switch fails, replace it.

Replacement

Refer to illustration 9.12

12   To remove the switches from either left or right switch pods, pry it from the instrument panel with a screwdriver, pull it out and disconnect the electrical connector **(see illustration)**. **Note:** *Tape the tip of the screwdriver to avoid damaging the instrument panel covering.*

13   Installation is the reverse of removal.

10   Instrument panel gauges - check

Warning: *The models covered by this manual are equipped with Supplemental Restraint Systems (SRS), more commonly known as airbags. Always disable the airbag system before working in the vicinity of any airbag system components to avoid the possibility of accidental deployment of the airbag(s), which could cause personal injury (see Section 26).* **Note:** *This procedure applies to conventional analog type gauges (NON-digital) only.*

Fuel and temperature gauges

Note: *The following tests relate to the conventional instrument cluster. If equipped with the electronic instrument cluster, refer testing to a dealership service department or other qualified shop.*

1   All tests below require the ignition switch to be turned to Off position before testing.

2   If the gauge pointer does not move from the empty or cold positions, check the fuse. If the fuse is OK, locate the particular sending unit for the circuit you're working on (see Chapter 4 for fuel sending unit location or Chapter 3 for the temperature gauge sending unit location). Connect the sending unit connector to ground with a jumper wire.

3   Turn the ignition key to On momentarily. If the pointer goes to the full or hot position replace the sending unit. **Note:** *Turn the key Off right away, grounding the sending unit for too long could damage the gauge.* If the

pointer stays in same position, use a jumper wire to ground the sending unit terminal on the back of the gauge. If necessary, refer to the wiring diagrams at the end of this Chapter. If the pointer moves, the problem lies in the wiring between the gauge and the sending unit. If the pointer does not move with the sending unit terminal on the back of the gauge grounded, check for voltage at the other terminal of the gauge. There should not be voltage.

11   Instrument cluster - removal and installation

Refer to illustration 11.3

Warning: *The models covered by this manual are equipped with Supplemental Restraint Systems (SRS), more commonly known as airbags. Always disable the airbag system before working in the vicinity of any airbag system components to avoid the possibility of accidental deployment of the airbag(s), which could cause personal injury (see Section 26).*

1   Refer to Section 26 and disable the airbag system.

2   Remove the instrument cluster bezel (see Chapter 11).

3   Remove the instrument cluster screws, pull out the cluster and unplug the electrical connectors **(see illustration)**.

4   Installation is the reverse of removal. Be sure to connect the positive cable to the battery first, then the negative cable.

12

12.3a Remove the screws (arrows) securing the radio to the instrument panel

12.3b Pull the radio out and disconnect the antenna lead and the electrical connector

12.6 With the cover off, remove the four CD changer mounting screws (arrows indicate two on the left side)

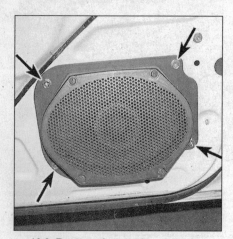

12.8 Remove the speaker mounting screws (arrows), pull the speaker away from the door and disconnect the electrical connector

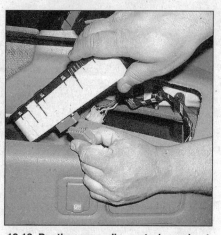

12.13 Pry the rear radio control panel out of the quarter trim panel and disconnect the electrical connectors

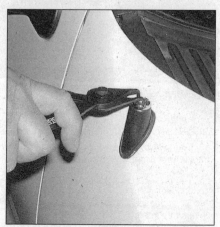

13.3 To remove the antenna nut/bezel, use snap-ring pliers or an antenna tool - be careful not to scratch the paint

---

12 Radio and speakers - removal and installation

Radio

Refer to illustrations 12.3a and 12.3b

1   Remove the center instrument panel trim bezel (see Chapter 11).
2   Remove the heating/air conditioning control panel (see Chapter 3).
3   Remove the retaining screws and pull the radio outward to access the backside, then disconnect the electrical connectors and the antenna lead and lift the radio out of the vehicle **(see illustrations)**.
4   Installation is the reverse of removal.

Compact Disc changer

Refer to illustration 12.6

5   Remove the CD changer cover at the bottom of the console area (see Chapter 11).
6   Remove the retaining screws and pull the CD changer outward to access the backside, then disconnect the electrical connector **(see illustration)**.

Front speakers

Refer to illustration 12.8

7   Remove the front door trim panel (see Chapter 11).
8   Remove the speaker retaining screws **(see illustration)**. Disconnect the electrical connector and remove the speaker from the vehicle.
9   Installation is the reverse of removal.

Rear speakers

10   Remove the rear quarter trim panel (left or right) for access to the speaker retaining screws (see Chapter 11). Disconnect the electrical connector and remove the speaker from the vehicle.
11   Installation is the reverse of removal.

Rear air conditioning and radio control panel

Refer to illustration 12.13

12   Some models have air conditioning and radio controls mounted in the left rear quarter interior trim panel.
13   Pry the control from the left rear quarter trim panel, disconnect the electrical connec-

tor and remove the controls from the vehicle **(see illustration)**.
14   Installation is the reverse of removal.

13 Antenna – removal and installation

Refer to illustrations 13.3 and 13.5

1   The vehicles covered by this manual are equipped with a fixed-mast antenna or a power antenna.
2   Use a wrench (on the hex portion of the antenna mast) to remove the exterior antenna on fixed-mast models.
3   Remove the antenna nut/bezel with snap-ring pliers or a similar tool **(see illustration)**.
4   The antenna base is accessed by removing the passenger-side front fender inner splash shield (see Chapter 11).
5   Disconnect the antenna lead-in cable and electrical connector from the base of the antenna and remove the bracket retaining bolt **(see illustration)**.
6   Installation is the reverse of removal.

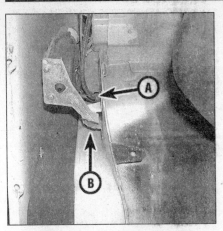

13.5 With the inner wheel housing removed, disconnect the antenna lead and electrical connector (A), then remove the bracket retaining bolt (B)

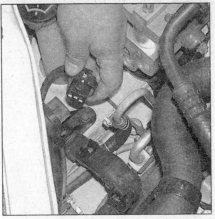

14.2 Disconnect the electrical connector from the rear of the headlight housing

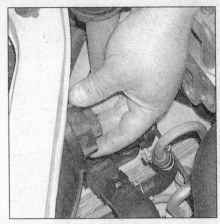

14.3 Twist the headlight bulb holder counterclockwise and remove it from the headlight housing

15.1 Headlight adjustment is made with the horizontal adjuster (A) and the vertical adjuster (B)

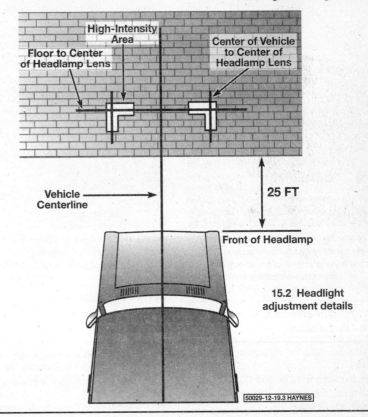

15.2 Headlight adjustment details

14 Headlight bulb - replacement

Refer to illustrations 14.2 and 14.3

Warning: *Halogen gas filled bulbs are under pressure and may shatter if the surface is scratched or the bulb is dropped. Wear eye protection and handle the bulbs carefully, grasping only the base whenever possible. Do not touch the surface of the bulb with your fingers because the oil from your skin could cause it to overheat and fail prematurely. If you do touch the bulb surface, clean it with rubbing alcohol.*

1   Open the hood.

2   Disconnect the electrical connector at the rear of the headlight housing **(see illustration)**.

3   Rotate the headlight bulb holder counterclockwise as viewed from the rear and remove it **(see illustration)**.

4   Withdraw the bulb assembly from the headlight housing.

5   Remove the bulb from the bulb holder by pulling it straight out.

6   Without touching the glass with your bare fingers, insert the new bulb into the socket assembly and then lock the bulb holder into the place by aligning the tabs with the headlight housing and rotating the bulb holder clockwise until it stops.

7   Reinstall the retaining ring and the electrical connector and test the headlight operation.

15 Headlights - adjustment

Refer to illustrations 15.1 and 15.2

Note: *The headlights must be aimed correctly. If adjusted incorrectly they could blind the driver of an oncoming vehicle and cause a serious accident or seriously reduce your ability to see the road. The headlights should be checked for proper aim every 12 months and any time a new headlight is installed or front end body work is performed. It should be emphasized that the following procedure is only an interim step which will provide temporary adjustment until the headlights can be adjusted by a properly equipped shop.*

1   The headlights have two adjusting screws each, one inboard and one outboard. Both adjusters are accessible from the top of the headlight assembly and are turned using a Phillips screwdriver or a small socket and extension **(see illustration)**.

2   Position masking tape vertically on the wall in reference to the vehicle centerline and the centerlines of both headlights **(see illustration)**.

12

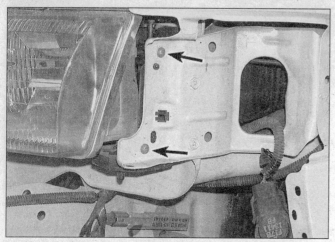

16.4a   Remove the two outside headlight housing mounting screws (arrows)

16.4b   Remove the two inner headlight housing mounting screws (arrow)

3   Position a horizontal tape line in reference to the centerline of all the headlights. **Note:** *It may be easier to position the tape on the wall with the vehicle parked only a few inches away.*

4   Adjustment should be made with the vehicle parked 25 feet from the wall, sitting level, the gas tank half-full and no unusually heavy load in the vehicle.

5   Starting with the low beam adjustment, position the high intensity zone so it is two inches below the horizontal line and two inches to the right of the headlight vertical line. Adjustment is made by turning the top adjusting screw clockwise to raise the beam and counterclockwise to lower the beam. The adjusting screw on the side should be used in the same manner to move the beam left or right.

6   With the high beams on, the high intensity zone should be vertically centered with the exact center just below the horizontal line. **Note:** *It may not be possible to position the headlight aim exactly for both high and low beams. If a compromise must be made, keep in mind that the low beams are the most used and have the greatest effect on safety.*

7   Have the headlights adjusted by a dealer service department or service station at the earliest opportunity.

16   Headlight housing - replacement

Refer to illustrations 16.4a and 16.4b
Warning: *The models covered by this manual are equipped with Supplemental Restraint Systems (SRS), more commonly known as airbags. Always disable the airbag system before working in the vicinity of any airbag system components to avoid the possibility of accidental deployment of the airbag(s), which could cause personal injury (see Section 26).*

1   Unplug the electrical connectors, and remove the halogen bulbs (see Section 14).
2   Remove the combination lights (see Section 17).

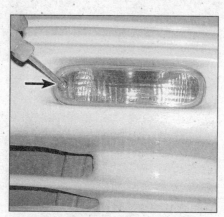

17.1   Remove the screw(s) to take out the front turn signal lens

3   Remove the radiator grille (see Chapter 11).
4   Remove the headlight housing mounting bolts and remove the housing **(see illustrations)**.
5   On the back of the headlight housing are three spring clips. Remove the clips to replace the glass portion of the lamp housing.
6   Installation is the reverse of removal. After you're done, adjust the headlights (see Section 15).

17   Bulb replacement

Warning: *Bulbs remain hot for up to twenty minutes after they're turned off. Be sure bulbs are off and cool before you touch them.*

Front turn signal lights

Refer to illustration 17.1
1   Remove the screw(s) from the front turn signal light lens and pull the lens out **(see illustration)**.
2   Turn the bulb holder counterclockwise and pull it out of the housing.
3   Pull the bulb out of the holder.
4   Installation is the reverse of removal.

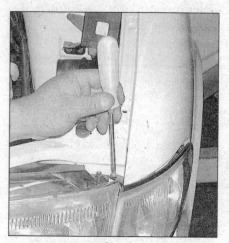

17.5   Remove the screw and pull the combination light forward, away from the body

Front combination lights

Refer to illustrations 17.5 and 17.6
5   Open the hood and remove the screw at the front of the combination light, just behind the headlight housing **(see illustration)**. Pull the combination light housing straight forward, until the front clip and rear tab clear the body.
6   Twist the bulb holder one-quarter turn counterclockwise and pull them out from the lens **(see illustration)**.
7   Pull the bulbs straight out of the socket.
8   Installation is the reverse of removal.

Rear turn signal, brake and tail lights (body mounted)

Refer to illustration 17.9
9   Open the liftgate. Pull out the access panel in the rear quarter interior panel to access the bulb holders **(see illustration)**.
10   Rotate either bulb holder 1/8-turn counterclockwise and pull it out of the housing, then pull the bulb out.

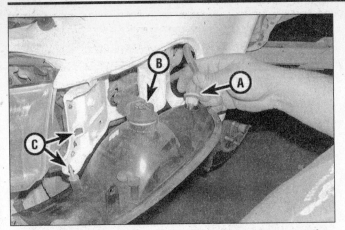

17.6 With the combination light housing pulled out, remove the side marker bulb holder (A) and the cornering/park bulb holder (B) - when reinstalling, align the pin with the hole in the body (C)

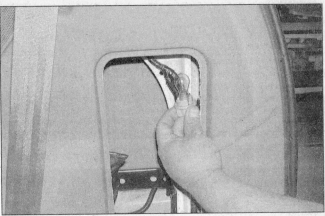

17.9 With the rear quarter trim access panel removed, you can reach both the turn signal bulb and the stoplight/taillight bulb

Tail light and backup lights (liftgate-mounted)

Refer to illustration 17.11

11 Open the liftgate. Remove the access panel and turn the bulb holder 1/8-turn counterclockwise and pull it out of the housing **(see illustration)**.

12 Pull the bulb straight out of the holder.

13 Installation is the reverse of removal.

High-mounted brake light

Refer to illustration 17.14

14 The high-mounted brake light is on the top exterior of the liftgate **(see illustration)**. Remove the four screws and lift the housing up enough to access the bulb holder.

15 Twist the bulb holder counterclockwise to remove it, then pull the bulb straight out of the holder.

16 Installation is the reverse of removal.

License plate lights

Refer to illustration 17.17

17 Remove the screws and pull the license plate light assembly out from the body **(see illustration)**.

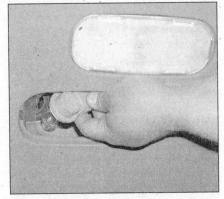

17.11 Behind the liftgate access panels, there are bulb holders on either side for the taillight and the backup light

18 Remove the bulb holder by releasing the clips on the lens housing.

19 Pull the bulb straight out of the holder.

20 Installation is the reverse of removal.

Instrument panel lights

Refer to illustration 17.22

Note: *On electronic instrument panels, only the indicator bulbs are replaceable. The*

17.14 Remove the screws holding the high-mounted brake light to the top of the liftgate

remainder of the display is self-illuminating.

21 To gain access to the instrument panel lights, the instrument cluster will have to be removed first (see Section 11).

22 To remove the conventional instrument cluster illumination bulbs, rotate the bulb counterclockwise and remove it from the instrument cluster **(see illustration)**. Pull the bulb straight out of the holder.

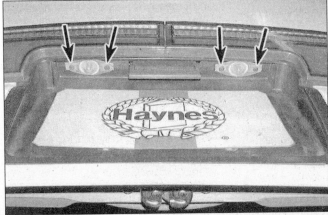

17.17 Remove the screws (arrows), lower the license plate lights and remove the bulbs

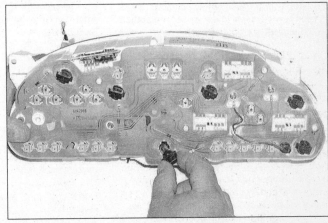

17.22 To remove a conventional instrument cluster bulb, depress it and turn it counterclockwise

23 To remove the indicator bulbs on both types of instrument clusters, rotate the bulb counterclockwise and remove it from the instrument cluster.

24 Installation is the reverse of removal. **Note:** *Make sure you replace the bulb with the same wattage as the original bulb. On the conventional instrument cluster, the illumination bulbs have a higher wattage than the indicator bulbs.*

Dome, door, vanity and cargo lights

Refer to illustrations 17.25a and 17.25b

25 All of the dome light, door light, trunk light and vanity (right sunvisor) lights are replaced in the same manner. Carefully pry the lens off **(see illustrations)**.

26 Remove the bulb from the terminals. It may be necessary to pry the bulb out - if this is the case, pry on the ends of the glass (otherwise the glass may shatter).

27 Installation is the reverse of removal.

18 Wiper motor - check and replacement

Wiper motor circuit check

Refer to illustration 18.2

Note: *Refer to the wiring diagrams for wire colors and locations in the following checks. When checking for voltage, probe a grounded 12-volt test light to each terminal at a connector until it lights; this verifies voltage (power) at the terminal. If the following checks fail to locate the problem, have the system diagnosed by a dealer service department or other properly equipped repair facility.*

1 If the wipers work slowly, make sure the battery is in good condition and has a strong charge (see Chapter 1). If the battery is in good condition, remove the wiper motor (see below) and operate the wiper arms by hand. Check for binding linkage and pivots. Lubricate or repair the linkage or pivots as necessary. Reinstall the wiper motor. If the wipers still operate slowly, check for loose or corroded connections, especially the ground

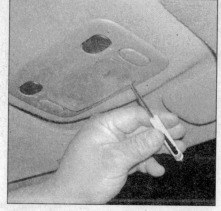

17.25a Pry the lens gently downward with a tape-wrapped screwdriver, then remove it (dome light shown, others similar)

connection. If all connections look OK, replace the motor.

2 If the wipers fail to operate when activated, check the fuse. If the fuse is OK, connect a jumper wire between the wiper motor and ground, then retest. If the motor works now, repair the ground connection. If the motor still doesn't work, turn the wiper switch to the HI position and check for voltage at the motor with the ignition key On. **Note:** *The cowl cover will have to be removed (see Chapter 11).* If there's voltage at the connector, remove the motor and check it off the vehicle with fused jumper wires from the battery **(see illustration)**. If the motor now works, check for binding linkage (see Step 1 above). If the motor still doesn't work, replace it. If there's no voltage to the motor, check for voltage at the accessory relay (located in the interior fuse/relay panel). If there's voltage at the wiper motor, check the switch for continuity (see Section 7).

3 If the interval (delay) function is inoperative, check the continuity of all the wiring between the switch and wiper control module. If the wiring is OK, check the resistance of the delay control knob of the multi-function switch (see Section 7).

4 If the wipers stop at the position they're in when the switch is turned off (fail to park),

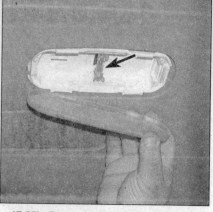

17.25b Remove the bulb from its clips (cargo light shown, others also pull straight out of their sockets)

check for a good ground at terminal 4 on the connector side at the motor. With an ohmmeter connected between 4 and a known ground, resistance should be less than 5 ohms.

5 If the wipers won't shut off unless the ignition is OFF, disconnect the wiring from the wiper control switch. If the wipers stop, replace the switch. If the wipers keep running, there's a defective limit switch in the motor; replace the motor.

6 If the wipers won't retract below the hood line, check for mechanical obstructions in the wiper linkage or on the vehicle's body which would prevent the wipers from parking. If there are no obstructions, check the wiring between the switch and motor for continuity. If the wiring is OK, replace the wiper motor.

Wiper motor replacement

Front

Refer to illustrations 18.7, 18.10 and 18.11

7 Remove the windshield wiper arms **(see illustration)**.

8 Remove the cowl cover (see Chapter 11).

9 Disconnect the electrical connector from the wiper motor **(see illustration 18.2)**.

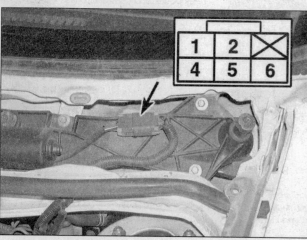

18.2 Wiper motor connector (arrow) terminal identification - with voltage applied at 6 and ground applied at 2, the motor should operate at Low speed; with the ground jumper switched to 1, the motor should operate at High speed

18.7 Tilt the wiper arm to upright position, pry out locking tab, then pull the arm off carefully

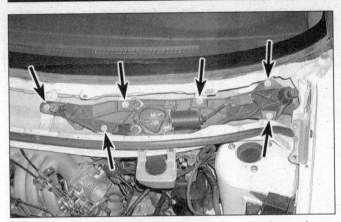

18.10 Remove the wiper linkage-to-body bolts (arrows)

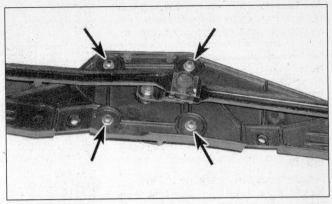

18.11 Mark the position of the wiper link to the linkage assembly, then remove the motor-to-linkage assembly bolts (arrows)

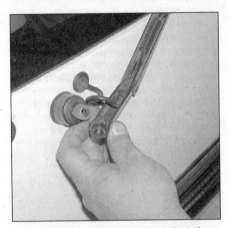

18.14 Depress the retaining tab at the base of the wiper arm and pull the rear wiper arm straight out from the splined shaft

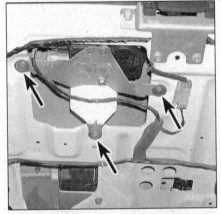

18.16 Disconnect the electrical connector and remove the three mounting bolts (arrows) at the rear wiper motor

10   Detach the wiper motor/linkage assembly from the cowl **(see illustration)**.

11   Remove the wiper motor retaining bolts **(see illustration)**.

12   Remove the wiper motor from the wiper linkage assembly.

13   Installation is the reverse of removal.

Rear

Refer to illustrations 18.14 and 18.16

14   Depress the retaining tab at the base of the wiper arm and pry the rear wiper arm straight up from the splined shaft **(see illustration)**. **Caution:** *Take care not to scratch the paint on the liftgate. You may want to apply masking tape around the wiper shaft before*

removal. Remove the wiper shaft trim bezel and remove the wiper shaft retaining nut.

15   Refer to Chapter 11 and remove the liftgate's interior trim panel.

16   Disconnect the electrical connector at the wiper motor and remove the motor mounting screws **(see illustration)**.

17   Installation is the reverse of removal.

19 Horn - check and replacement

Check

Refer to illustration 19.3

Note: *Check the fuses before beginning electrical diagnosis. To access the horns, the left front inner fenderwell must first be removed (see Chapter 11).*

1   Disconnect the electrical connector from the horns.

2   To test the horns, connect battery voltage to the horn terminal with a pair of jumper wires. If either horn doesn't sound, replace it.

3   If the horn does sound, check for voltage at the horn connector when the horn switch is depressed **(see illustration)**. If there's voltage at the connector, check for a bad ground at the horn.

4   If there's no voltage at the horn, check the relay (see Section 5).

5   If the relay is OK, check for voltage to the relay power and control circuits. If either of the circuits is not receiving voltage, inspect the wiring between the relay and the fuse panel.

6   If both relay circuits are receiving voltage, depress the horn switch and check the circuit from the relay to the horn switch for continuity to ground. If there's no continuity, check the circuit for an open. If there's no open circuit, replace the horn switch.

7   If there's continuity to ground through the horn switch, check for an open or short in the circuit from the relay to the switch.

Replacement

Refer to illustration 19.9

8   To access the horns, the left front inner splash shield must first be removed from the fenderwell (see Chapter 11).

9   Disconnect the electrical connectors

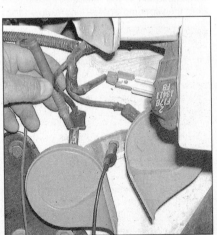

19.3 Connect a voltmeter to the horn terminal and ground - test for voltage while the switch is depressed

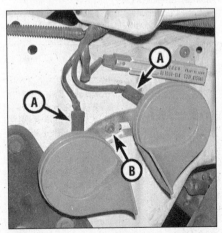

19.9 Disconnect the electrical connectors (A), remove the bolt (B) and detach the horns

12

and remove the bracket bolt **(see illustration)**.

10   Installation is the reverse of removal.

20   Daytime Running Lights (DRL) - general information

The Daytime Running Lights (DRL) system used on Canadian models illuminates the headlights whenever the engine is running. The only exception is with the engine running and the parking brake engaged. Once the parking brake is released, the lights will remain on as long as the ignition switch is on, even if the parking brake is later applied.

The DRL system supplies reduced power to the headlights so they won't be too bright for daytime use, while prolonging headlight life.

21   Rear window defogger - check and repair

1   The rear window defogger consists of a number of horizontal heating elements baked onto the inside surface of the glass. Power is supplied through a large fuse from the power distribution box in the engine compartment. The heater is controlled by the instrument panel switch.

2   Small breaks in the element can be repaired without removing the rear window.

Check

Refer to illustrations 21.5, 21.6 and 21.8

3   Turn the ignition switch and defogger switches to the ON position.

4   Using a voltmeter, place the positive probe against the defogger grid positive terminal and the negative probe against the ground terminal. If battery voltage is not indicated, check the fuse, defogger switch and related wiring. If voltage is indicated, but all or part of the defogger doesn't heat, proceed with the following tests.

5   When measuring voltage during the next two tests, wrap a piece of aluminum foil around the tip of the voltmeter positive probe and press the foil against the heating element with your finger **(see illustration)**. Place the negative probe on the defogger grid ground terminal.

6   Check the voltage at the center of each heating element **(see illustration)**. If the voltage is 5 to 6 volts, the element is okay (there is no break). If the voltage is 0 volts, the element is broken between the center of the element and the positive end. If the voltage is 10 to 12 volts the element is broken between the center of the element and the ground side. Check each heating element.

7   If none of the elements are broken, connect the negative probe to a good chassis ground. The voltage reading should stay the same, if it doesn't the ground connection is bad.

21.5 When measuring the voltage at the rear window defogger grid, wrap a piece of aluminum foil around the positive probe of the voltmeter and press the foil against the wire with your finger

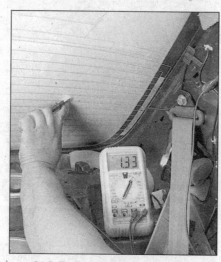

21.8 To find the break, place the voltmeter negative lead against the defogger ground terminal, place the voltmeter positive lead with the foil strip against the heat wire at the positive terminal end and slide it toward the negative terminal end - the point at which the voltmeter deflects from several volts to zero volts is the point at which the wire is broken

8   To find the break, place the voltmeter negative probe against the defogger ground terminal. Place the voltmeter positive probe with the foil strip against the heating element at the positive side and slide it toward the negative side. The point at which the voltmeter deflects from several volts to zero is the point where the heating element is broken **(see illustration)**.

Repair

Refer to illustration 21.14

9   Repair the break in the element using a repair kit specifically for this purpose, such as Dupont paste No. 4817 (or equivalent). The

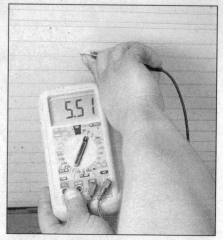

21.6 To determine if a wire has broken, check the voltage at the center of each wire. If the voltage is 5 to 6 volts, the wire is unbroken; if the voltage is 10 to 12 volts, the wire is broken between the center of the wire and the ground side; if the voltage is 0 volts, the wire is broken between the center of the wire and the power side

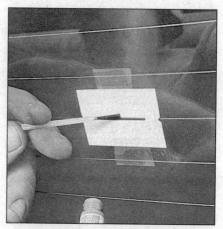

21.14 To use a defogger repair kit, apply masking tape to the inside of the window at the damaged area, then brush on the special conductive coating

kit includes conductive plastic epoxy.

10   Before repairing a break, turn off the system and allow it to cool for a few minutes.

11   Lightly buff the element area with fine steel wool; then clean it thoroughly with rubbing alcohol.

12   Use masking tape to mask off the area being repaired.

13   Thoroughly mix the epoxy, following the kit instructions.

14   Apply the epoxy material to the slit in the masking tape, overlapping the undamaged area about 3/4-inch on either end **(see illustration)**.

15   Allow the repair to cure for 24 hours before removing the tape and using the system.

22.5a The cruise control servo assembly (arrow) is mounted next to the right shock tower in the engine compartment

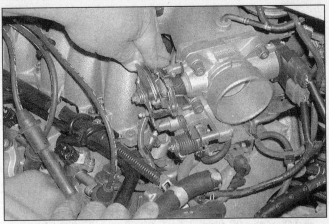

22.5b Make sure the cruise control and accelerator linkage mounted on the throttle body are not damaged and that they operate smoothly together when the throttle is opened

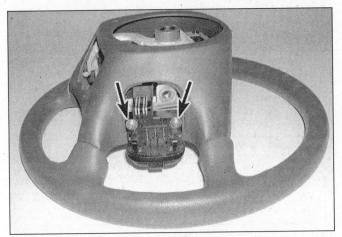

22.9 With the access cover removed, remove the screws (arrows) and the cruise control switch (steering wheel removed for clarity)

X	●		X
1	2	3	4

SWITCH POSITION	CONTINUITY BETWEEN
Set/Coast	1 and 3
Resume/Accel	1 and 2
Cancel	1 and 3 (diode), 1 and 2 (diode)

64200-12-22.10 HAYNES

22.10 Cruise control switch connector terminals and continuity tests - on tests marked as having a diode in the circuit, reverse the meter leads if the continuity isn't displayed, these connections are polarity sensitive

22 Cruise control system – description and check

Refer to illustrations 22.5a, 22.5b, 22.9 and 22.10

1   The cruise control system maintains vehicle speed with a servo motor located in the engine compartment (on the passenger-side fenderwell), which is connected to the throttle linkage by a cable. The system consists of the servo motor, brake switch, control switches, speed sensors and relays. Some features of the system require special testers and diagnostic procedures which are beyond the scope of this manual. Listed below are some general procedures that may be used to locate common problems.

2   Locate and check the fuse (see Section 3).

3   The brake pedal position (BPP) switch (or stop lamp switch) deactivates the cruise control system. Have an assistant press the brake pedal while you check the stop lamp operation.

4   If the brake lights do not operate properly, correct the problem and retest the cruise control.

5   Check the control cable between the cruise control servo/amplifier and the throttle linkage and adjust/replace as necessary **(see illustrations)**. See Chapter 4 for cable adjustment procedure, which is the same for accelerator cable and cruise control cable.

6   The cruise control system uses a speed sensing device. The speed sensor is located in the transmission. To test the speed sensor, see Chapter 6.

7   The testing of the cruise control On/Off switch is covered in Section 9.

8   The cruise control actuator switch is mounted in the steering wheel.

9   To test the actuator switch, refer to Section 26 and disable the airbag system, then remove the airbag module screw cover to access the two screws and the switch **(see illustration)**. **Note:** *On 1993 models, the switch is in the center of the horn pad (see Chapter 10 for removal), on 1994 and 1995 models the switch is on the right side of the steering wheel, and on 1996 and later models, the switch is on the left side of the wheel.*

10   Use an ohmmeter to test for continuity of the switch **(see illustration)**. If the switch fails the tests, replace it. **Note:** *Make sure the horn works before testing the cruise control system, as the cruise control switch gets power from the horn relay.*

11   Test drive the vehicle to determine if the cruise control is now working. If it isn't, take it to a dealer service department or an automotive electrical specialist for further diagnosis.

23 Power window system - description and check

Refer to illustrations 23.12a, 23.12b, 23.12c, 23.12d, 23.12e and 23.14

1   The power window system operates electric motors, mounted in the doors, which lower and raise the windows. The system consists of the control switches, the motors, regulators, glass mechanisms and associated wiring.

2   The power windows can be lowered and raised from the master control switch by the driver or by remote switches located at the

12

23.12a Check for voltage at the switch with the ignition key in the On position

7	X	1	2
X	6	5	4	3

SWITCH POSITION	CONTINUITY BETWEEN
Normal (nothing pressed)	7 and 3, 3 and 5
Left switch, Up	7 and 4
Left switch, Down	1 and 7, 1 and 3, 7 and 3
Left switch, One-touch	2 and 1, 2 and 7, 2 and 3, 1 and 7, 1 and 3, 7 and 3
Right switch, Up	3 and 5, 4 and 6
Right switch, Down	3 and 6, 4 and 5
Lock, Off position	3 and 5

64200-12-23.12b HAYNES

23.12b Power window master switch terminal identification and continuity tests (1995 and earlier)

5	4	X	X	3	2	1
12	11	10	9	8	7	6

SWITCH POSITION	CONTINUITY BETWEEN
Left switch, Up	9 and 5,
Left switch, Down	9 and 6, 5 and 3
Left switch, One-touch	3 and 6, (Up) 9 and 6 (Down)
Right switch, Up	10 and 3, 9 and 7
Right switch, Down	7 and 3, 9 and 10
Window lock, Unlock position	7 and 3
Door lock, Unlock position	4 and 3
Door lock, Lock position	1 and 3

64200-12-23.12c HAYNES

23.12c Power window master switch terminal identification and continuity tests (1996 and later)

1	X	X	2
X	4	5	6

SWITCH POSITION	VOLTAGE AT
Up	Less than 1V @ 1 more than 10V @ 4
Normal	Less than 1V @ 1 and 4
Down	Less than 1V @ 4 more than 10V @ 1

64200-12-23.12d HAYNES

23.12d Passenger-side power window switch terminal identification and voltage tests – backprobe the switch connector and measure voltage at the indicated terminals with the switch in the indicated positions

individual windows. Each window has a separate motor which is reversible. The position of the control switch determines the polarity and therefore the direction of operation.

3   The circuit is protected by a fuse and a circuit breaker. Each motor is also equipped with an internal circuit breaker; this prevents one stuck window from disabling the whole system.

4   The power window system will only operate when the ignition switch is ON. In addition, many models have a window lockout switch at the master control switch which, when activated, disables the switches at the rear windows and, sometimes, the switch at the passenger's window also. Always check these items before troubleshooting a window problem.

5   These procedures are general in nature, so if you can't find the problem using them, take the vehicle to a dealer service department or other properly equipped repair facility.

6   If the power windows won't operate, always check the fuse and circuit breaker first.

7   If only the rear windows are inoperative, or if the windows only operate from the master control switch, check the rear window lockout switch for continuity in the unlocked position. Replace it if it doesn't have continuity.

8   Check the wiring between the switches and fuse panel for continuity. Repair the wiring, if necessary.

9   If only one window is inoperative from the master control switch, try the other control switch at the window. **Note:** *This doesn't apply to the drivers door window.*

10   If the same window works from one switch, but not the other, check the switch for continuity.

11   If the switch tests OK, check for a short or open in the circuit between the affected switch and the window motor.

12   If one window is inoperative from both

switches, remove the trim panel from the affected door and check for voltage at the switch and at the motor while the switch is operated. If a defective switch is suspected, remove the switch and check it for continuity as indicated **(see illustrations)**.

13   If voltage is reaching the motor, disconnect the glass from the regulator (see Chapter 11). Move the window up and down by hand while checking for binding and damage. Also check for binding and damage to the regulator. If the regulator is not damaged and the window moves up and down smoothly, replace the motor. If there's binding or damage, lubricate, repair or replace parts, as necessary.

14   If voltage isn't reaching the motor, check the wiring in the circuit for continuity between the switches and motors. You'll need to consult the wiring diagram for the vehicle. If the circuit is equipped with a relay, check that the relay is grounded properly and receiving voltage **(see illustration)**.

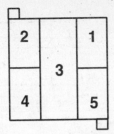

23.12e Rear quarter power window switch terminal identification and continuity tests

SWITCH POSITION	CONTINUITY BETWEEN
Both switches, all positions	No continuity between 3 and 2
Left switch, Open	3 and 5, 1 and 2
Left switch, Close	3 and 1, 5 and 2
Right switch, Open	3 and 1, 5 and 2
Right switch, Close	3 and 5, 1 and 2

64200-12-23.12e HAYNES

23.14 The power window relay (arrow) located under the left side of the instrument panel

15   Test the windows after you are done to confirm proper repairs.

24   Power door lock and keyless entry system - description and check

Power door lock system

Refer to illustrations 24.7 and 24.9

1   The power door lock system operates the door lock actuators mounted in each door. The system consists of the switches, actuators, and associated wiring. Diagnosis can usually be limited to simple checks of the wiring connections and actuators for minor faults which can be easily repaired.

X		2
	3	
1		X

1995 and earlier

1	2	3	X
X	X	7	8

1996 and later (passenger side)

64200-12-24.7 HAYNES

24.7 Power door lock switch terminal identification

2   Power door lock systems are operated by bi-directional solenoids or motors located in the doors. The lock switches have two operating positions: Lock and Unlock. On later models with keyless entry the switches activate a module which in turn connects voltage to the door lock solenoids or motors. Depending on which way the switch is activated, it reverses polarity, allowing the two sides of the circuit to be used alternately as the feed (positive) and ground side. On earlier models without keyless entry, the switches directly activate the door lock solenoids or motors.

3   If you are unable to locate the trouble using the following general steps, consult a dealer service department or other qualified repair facility.

4   Always check the circuit protection first. On these models the battery voltage passes through the power window fuse (in the engine compartment fuse panel) and circuit breaker no. 1, located under the driver-side of the instrument panel **(see Section 4)**.

5   Operate the door lock switches in both directions (Lock and Unlock) with the engine off. Listen for the faint click of the door lock relay operating.

6   If there's no click, check for voltage at the switches. If no voltage is present, check the wiring between the fuse block and the switches for shorts and opens.

7   If voltage is present but no click is heard, test the switch for continuity **(see illustration)**. On 1996 and later models, the driver-side power door lock switch is part of the master power window switch (see Section 23 for tests). On 1995 and earlier models there should be continuity between 2 and 3 when pushing Unlock, and continuity between 1 and 3 when pushing Lock. On 1996 and later models there should be continuity between 1 and 3 when pushing Unlock, and continuity between 3 and 8 when pushing Lock. Replace any switch if there's no continuity in both switch positions.

8   If the switch has continuity but the solenoid or motor doesn't click, check the wiring between the switch and solenoid for continuity. Repair the wiring if there's not continuity.

9   If all but one lock solenoids operate, remove the trim panel from the affected door (see Chapter 11) and check for voltage at the solenoid while the lock switch is operated **(see illustration)**. One of the wires should have voltage in the Lock position; the other should have voltage in the unlock position.

10   If the inoperative solenoid is receiving voltage, replace the solenoid. **Note:** *It's common for wires to break in the portion of the harness between the body and door (opening and closing the door fatigues and eventually breaks the wires).*

Keyless entry system

Refer to illustrations 24.13 and 24.14

11   The keyless entry system on 1996 and later vehicles consists of a remote control transmitter that sends a coded infrared signal to a receiver which then operates the door lock system.

12   Replace the transmitter batteries when

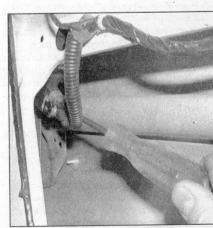

24.9 Check for power at the door lock actuator with the switch depressed - check the door lock actuator operation by using jumper wires to apply battery voltage and ground to the terminals

12

the red LED light on the side of the case doesn't light when the button is pushed.

13   Use a small screwdriver to carefully separate the case halves **(see illustration)**.

14   Replace the CR 2016 lithium batteries **(see illustration)**.

15   Snap the case halves together.

25   Electric side view mirrors - description and check

Refer to illustrations 25.7a and 25.7b

1   Most electric rear view mirrors use two motors to move the glass; one for up-and-down adjustments and one for left-to-right adjustments. In addition, some mirrors have electrically heated glass defroster circuits, which are usually powered through the rear window defogger relay.

2   The control switch usually has a selector portion which sends voltage to the left or right side mirror. With the ignition ON but the engine OFF, roll down the windows and operate the mirror control switch through all functions (left-right and up-down) for both the left and right side mirrors.

3   Listen carefully for the sound of the electric motors running in the mirrors.

4   If the motors can be heard but the mirror glass doesn't move, there's probably a problem with the drive mechanism inside the mirror. Remove and disassemble the mirror to locate the problem.

5   If the mirrors don't operate and no sound comes from the mirrors, check the fuse (see Chapter 1).

6   If the fuse is OK, remove the mirror control switch from its mounting without disconnecting the wires attached to it. Turn the ignition ON and check for voltage at the switch. There should be voltage at one terminal (see the wiring diagrams at the end of this Chapter). If there's no voltage at the switch, check for an open or short in the wiring between the fuse panel and the switch.

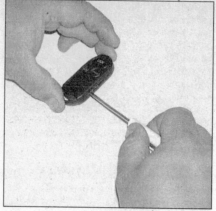

24.13 Use a small screwdriver to separate the transmitter halves

7   If there's voltage at the switch, disconnect it. Check the switch for continuity in all its operating positions **(see illustrations)**. If the switch does not have the designated continuity, replace it.

8   Re-connect the switch. Locate the wire going from the switch to ground. Leaving the switch connected, connect a jumper wire between this wire and ground. If the mirror works normally with this wire in place, repair the faulty ground connection.

9   If the mirror still doesn't work, remove the cover and check the wires at the mirror for voltage with a test light. Check with ignition ON and the mirror selector switch on the appropriate side. Operate the mirror switch in all its positions. There should be voltage at one of the switch-to-mirror wires in each switch position (except the neutral "off" position).

10   If there's no voltage in any switch position, check the wiring between the mirror and control switch for opens and shorts.

11   If there's voltage, remove the mirror and test it off the vehicle with jumper wires. Replace the mirror if it fails this test (see Chapter 11).

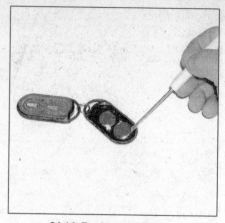

24.14 Replace the lithium batteries (arrows)

26   Airbag system - general information

Description

Refer to illustration 26.2

1   All models except 1993 are equipped with a Supplemental Restraint System (SRS), more commonly known as an airbag. 1994 and 1995 models have only a driver's airbag, while on 1996 and later models there are two airbags, one for the driver and one for the front seat passenger. The SRS system is designed to protect the driver (and on later models, the passenger as well) from serious injury in the event of a head-on or frontal collision.

2   The SRS system consists of an SRS unit which contains a safing sensor, self-diagnosis circuit and a back-up power circuit, a front impact sensor (on 1994 and 1995 models), an airbag assembly in the center of the steering wheel and a second airbag assembly (on 1996 and later models) for the front seat passenger, located in the top of the dashboard right above the glove box. The SRS

4		2	1
9	8	7	6

SWITCH POSITION	CONTINUITY BETWEEN
Left mirror, Down movement	1 and 4, 7 and 2
Left mirror, Up movement	1 and 7, 4 and 2
Left mirror, Left movement	1 and 9, 4 and 2
Left mirror, Right movement	1 and 4, 9 and 2
Right mirror, Down movement	1 and 4, 6 and 2
Right mirror, Up movement	1 and 6, 4 and 2
Right mirror, Left movement	1 and 8, 4 and 2
Right mirror, Right movement	1 and 4, 8 and 2

64200-12-25.7a HAYNES

25.7a Power mirror switch connector identification and continuity tests (1995 and earlier)

4	3	2	1
8	7	6	5

SWITCH POSITION	CONTINUITY BETWEEN
Left mirror, Down movement	5 and 3, 7 and 2
Left mirror, Up movement	5 and 7, 3 and 2
Left mirror, Left movement	5 and 8, 3 and 2
Left mirror, Right movement	5 and 3, 8 and 2
Right mirror, Down movement	5 and 3, 4 and 2
Right mirror, Up movement	5 and 4, 3 and 2
Right mirror, Left movement	5 and 6, 3 and 2
Right mirror, Right movement	5 and 3, 6 and 2

64200-12-25.7b HAYNES

25.7b Power mirror switch connector identification and continuity tests (1996 and later)

26.2 The airbag diagnostic module (arrow) is mounted on top of the transmission tunnel ahead of the console front cover

unit is located under the dash, directly in front of the floor console **(see illustration),**

Operation

3   For the airbag(s) to deploy, an impact sensor or the safing sensor must be activated. When this condition occurs, the circuit to the airbag inflator is closed and the airbag inflates. If the battery is destroyed by the impact, or is too low to power the inflator, a back-up power unit inside the SRS unit provides power.

Self-diagnosis system

4   A self-diagnosis circuit in the SRS unit displays a light when the ignition switch is turned to the On position. If the system is operating normally, the light should go out after about six seconds. If the light doesn't come on, or doesn't go out after six seconds, or if it comes on while you're driving the vehicle, there's a malfunction in the SRS system. Have it inspected and repaired as soon as possible. Do not attempt to troubleshoot or service the SRS system yourself. Even a small mistake could cause the SRS system to malfunction when you need it.

Servicing components near the SRS system

5   Nevertheless, there are times when you need to remove the steering wheel, radio or service other components on or near the dashboard. At these times, you'll be working around components and wire harnesses for the SRS system. The SRS wiring harnesses are easy to identify: They're all bright yellow. Do not unplug the connectors for these wires. And do not use electrical test equipment on yellow wires; it could cause the airbag(s) to deploy. *ALWAYS DISABLE THE SRS SYSTEM BEFORE WORKING NEAR THE SRS SYSTEM COMPONENTS OR RELATED WIRING.*

Disabling the SRS system

Warning: *Any time you are working in the vicinity of airbag wiring or components, DISABLE THE SRS SYSTEM.*
6   Disconnect the battery negative cable and wait ten minutes before proceeding.

Driver's side airbag

7   Remove the access panel in the steering wheel below the airbag and unplug the two-pin connector between the airbag and the clockspring (see Chapter 10).

Passenger's side airbag

8   Remove the panel below the glove box (see Chapter 11).
9   Unplug the two-pin electrical connector between the passenger side airbag and the SRS main wiring harness.

Enabling the system

10   After you've disabled the airbag and performed the necessary service, reconnect the two-pin airbag connector into the two-pin clockspring connector (driver's side) or the SRS main harness (passenger's side). Reinstall the lid to the underside of the steering wheel or reinstall the glove box.
11   Turn the ignition switch to the Off position.
12   Reattach the negative battery cable.

Removal and installation

Driver's side airbag

13   Refer to Chapter 10 for removal and installation of the driver's side airbag.

Passenger side airbag

14   Disconnect the battery cable and wait ten minutes before proceeding.
15   Refer to Chapter 11 and remove the console CD changer cover or front storage compartment, the left and right console lower side panels, the passenger-side lower dash panel and the glove box. Remove the instrument panel to air bag module bracket.
16   Disconnect the two-pin connector. Remove the four nuts and gently remove the airbag unit from the dashboard.
17   Installation is the reverse of the removal procedure.

27   Windshield/rear washer fluid reservoir and pump - removal and installation

1   Loosen the right front wheel lug nuts. Raise the front of the vehicle and support it securely on jackstands. Remove the wheel.
2   Remove the inner fender splash shield (see Chapter 11, Section 13).
3   Unplug the electrical connectors from the washer fluid pumps and fluid level sensor.
4   Position a drain pan under the reservoir, then detach the hoses from the pumps. **Note:** *The hose for the rear washer fluid pump is color coded to match its pump.*
5   Remove the reservoir mounting bolts and slide the reservoir out of the slots.
6   To remove a pump from the reservoir, pull it out of its grommet. Make sure the grommet is in good condition; if not, replace it.
7   Installation is the reverse of removal.

28   Wiring diagrams - general information

Since it isn't possible to include all wiring diagrams for every year and model covered by this manual, the following diagrams are those that are typical and most commonly needed.

Prior to troubleshooting any circuits, check the fuse and circuit breakers (if equipped) to make sure they're in good condition. Make sure the battery is properly charged and check the cable connections (see Chapter 1).

When checking a circuit, make sure that all connectors are clean, with no broken or loose terminals. When unplugging a connector, do not pull on the wires. Pull only on the connector housings themselves.

12

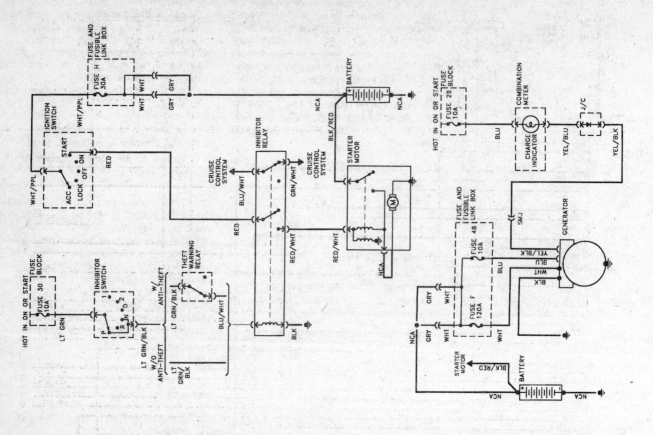

Starting and charging systems - 1996 and later models

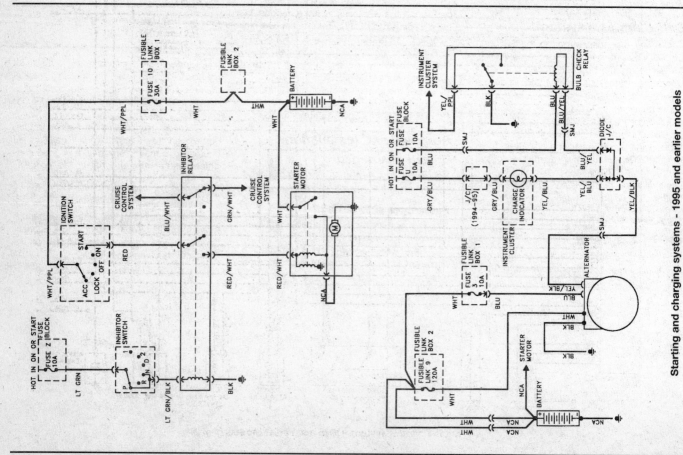

Starting and charging systems - 1995 and earlier models

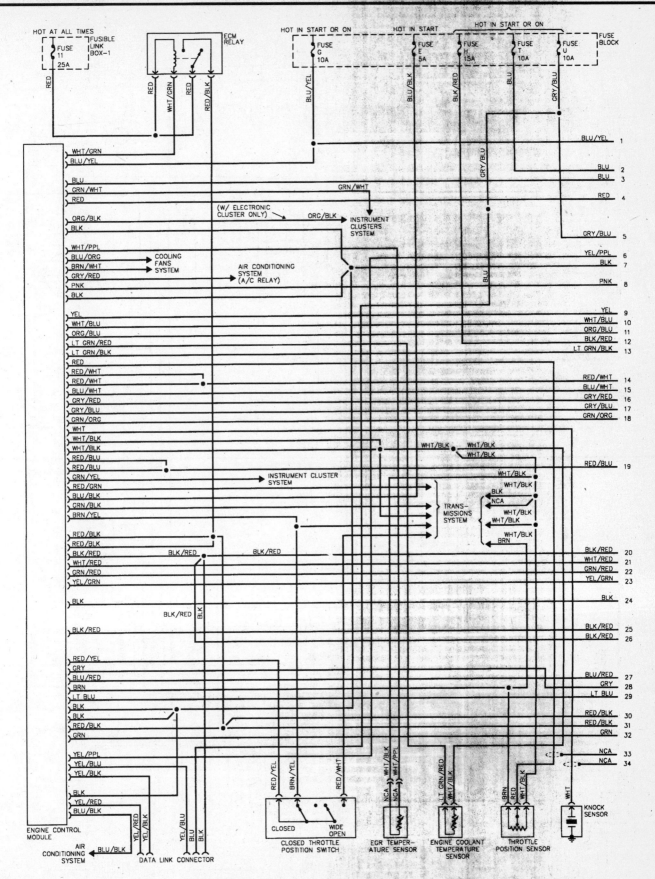

Engine control system - 1995 and earlier models (1 of 2)

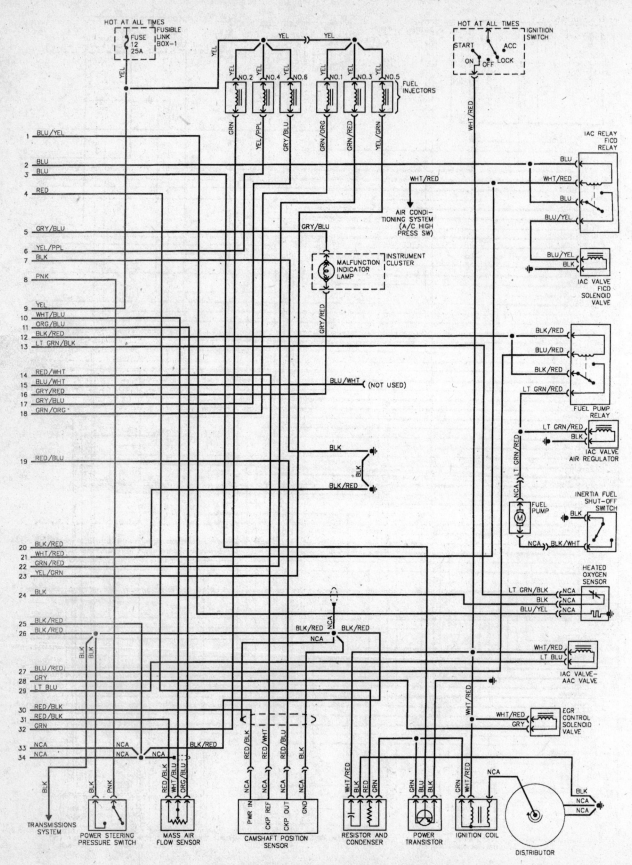

Engine control system - 1995 and earlier models (2 of 2)

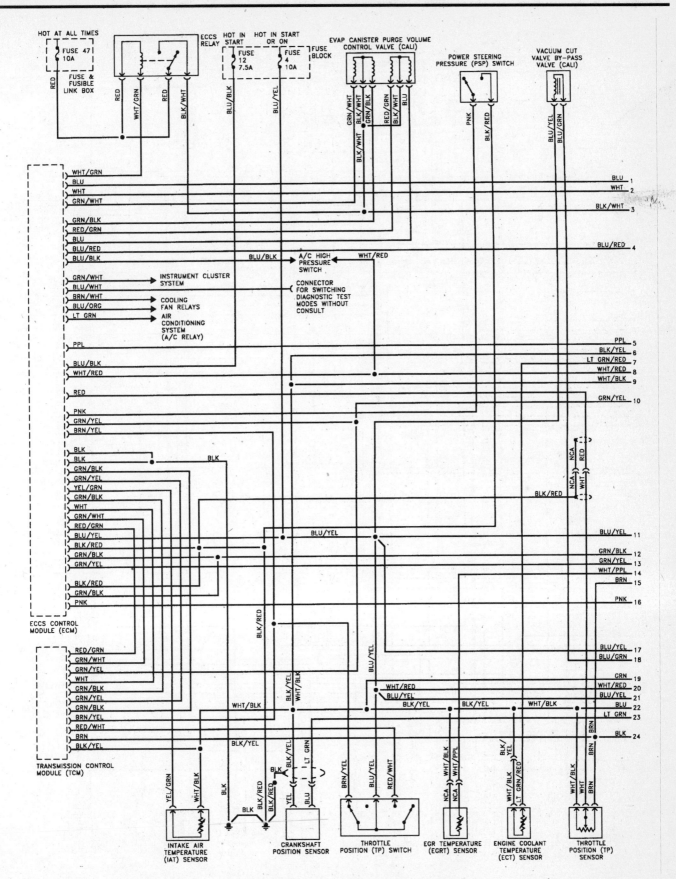

Engine control system - 1996 and later models (1 of 3)

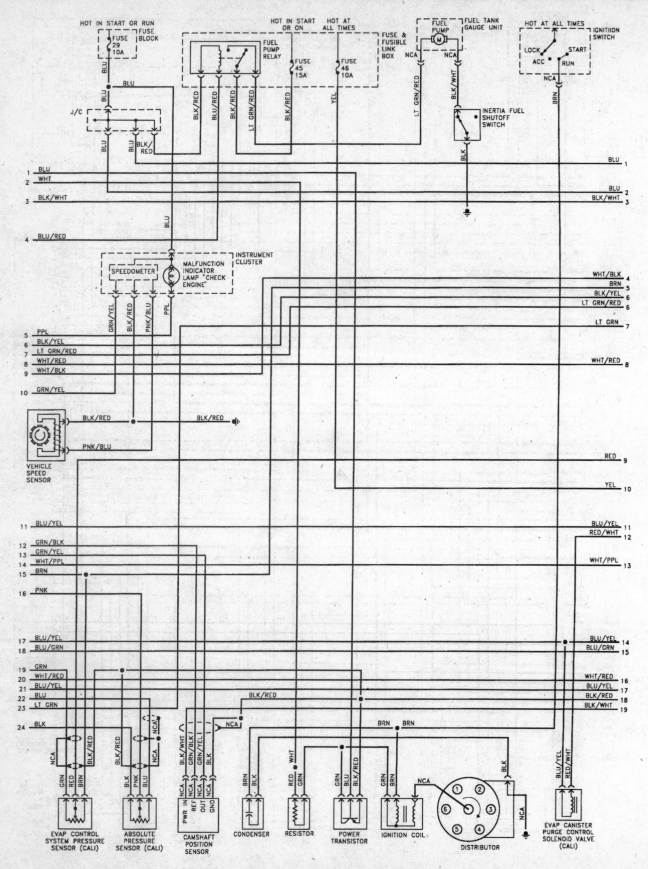

Engine control system - 1996 and later models (2 of 3)

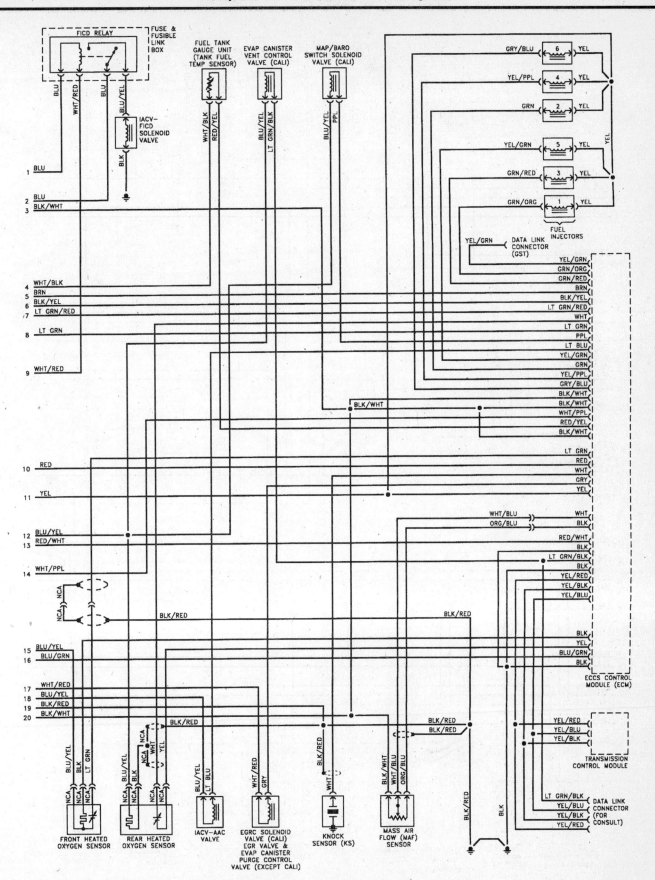

Engine control system - 1996 and later models (3 of 3)

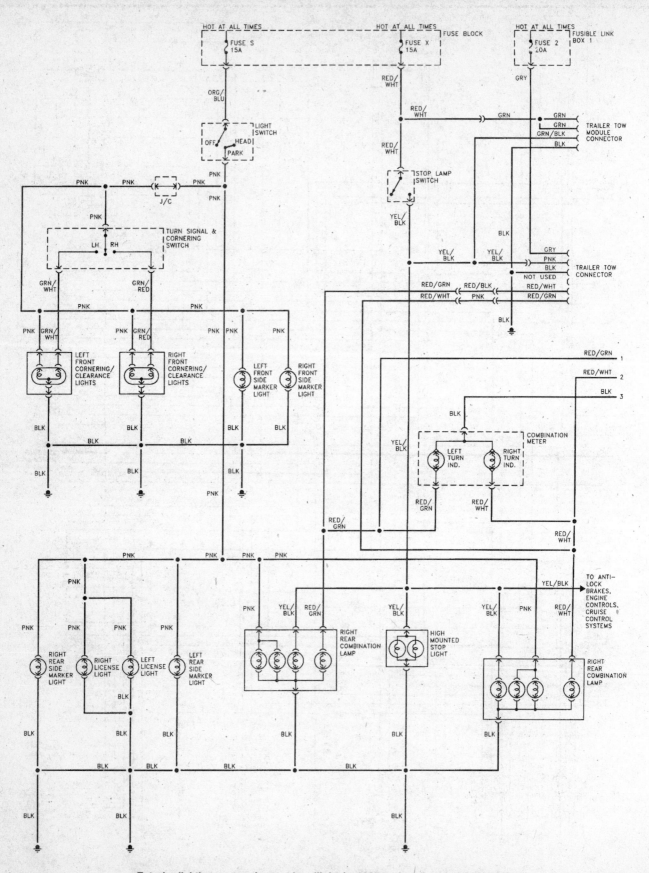

Exterior lighting system (except headlights) - 1995 and earlier models (1 of 2)

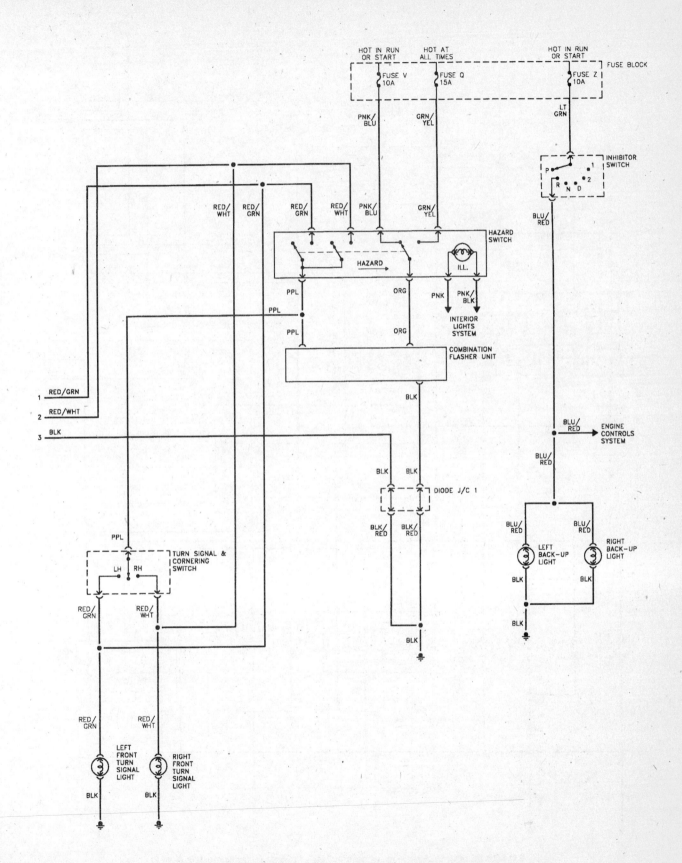

Exterior lighting system (except headlights) - 1995 and earlier models (2 of 2)

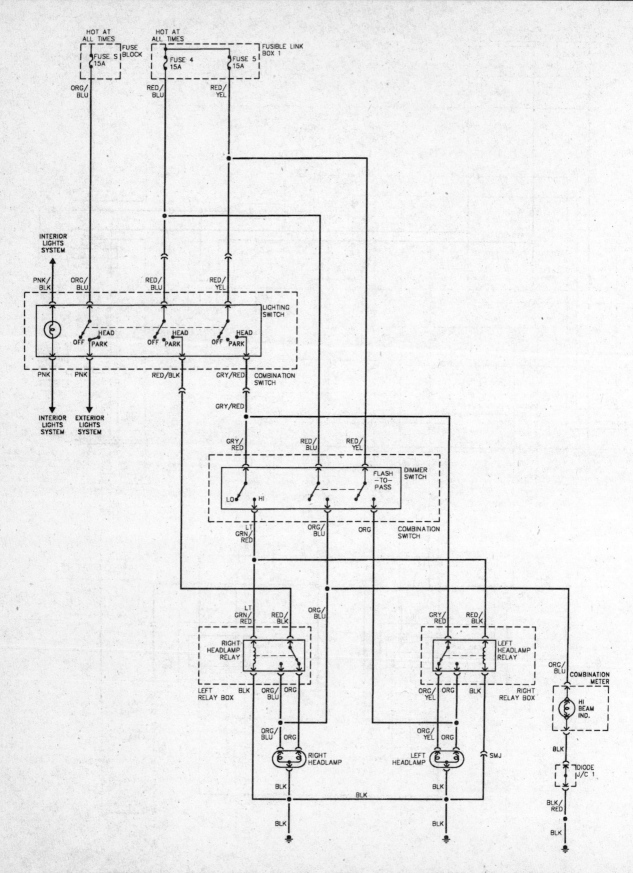

Headlight system - 1995 and earlier models (without Daytime Running Lights - without Autolamp system)

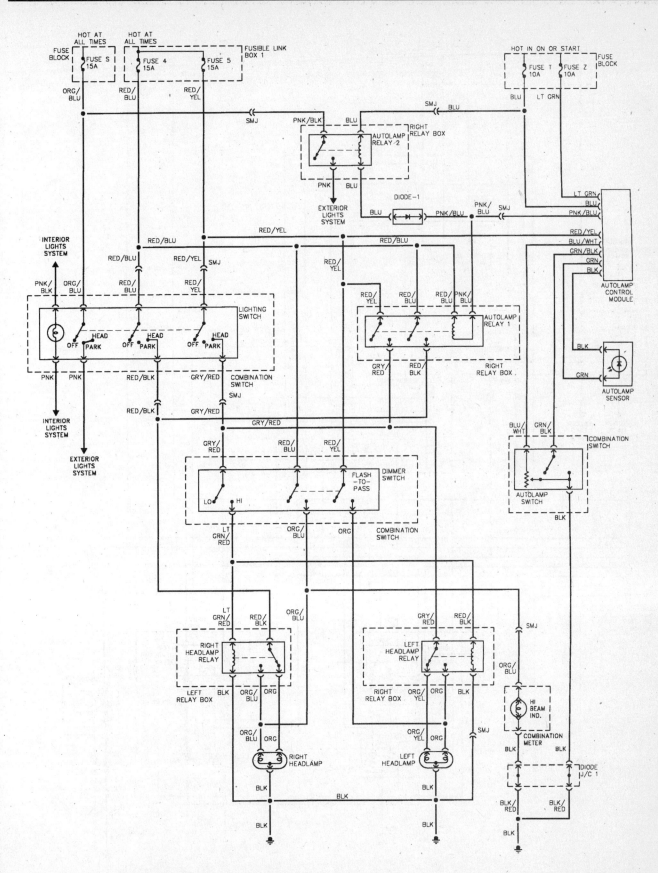

Headlight system - 1995 and earlier models (without Daytime Running Lights - with Autolamp system)

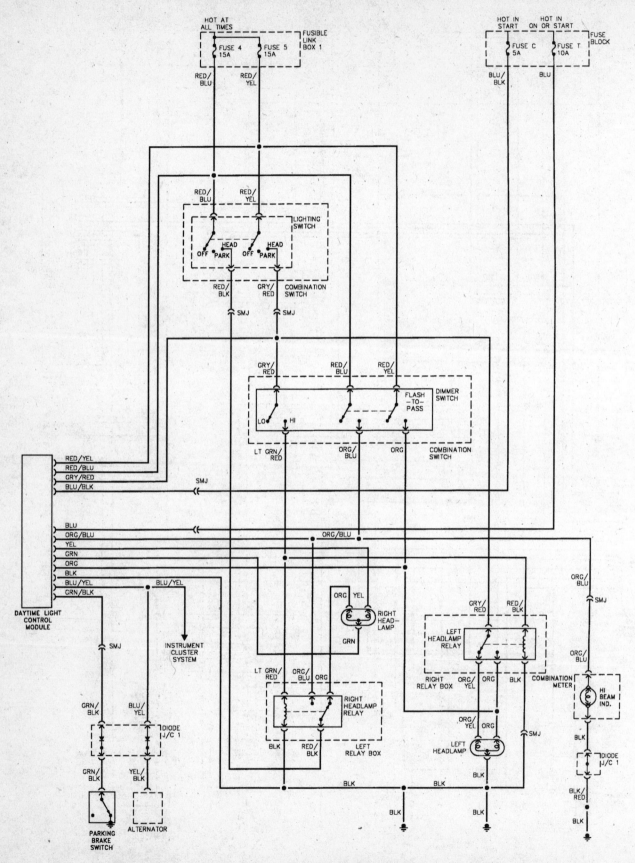

Headlight system - 1995 and earlier models (with Daytime Running Lights - without Autolamp system)

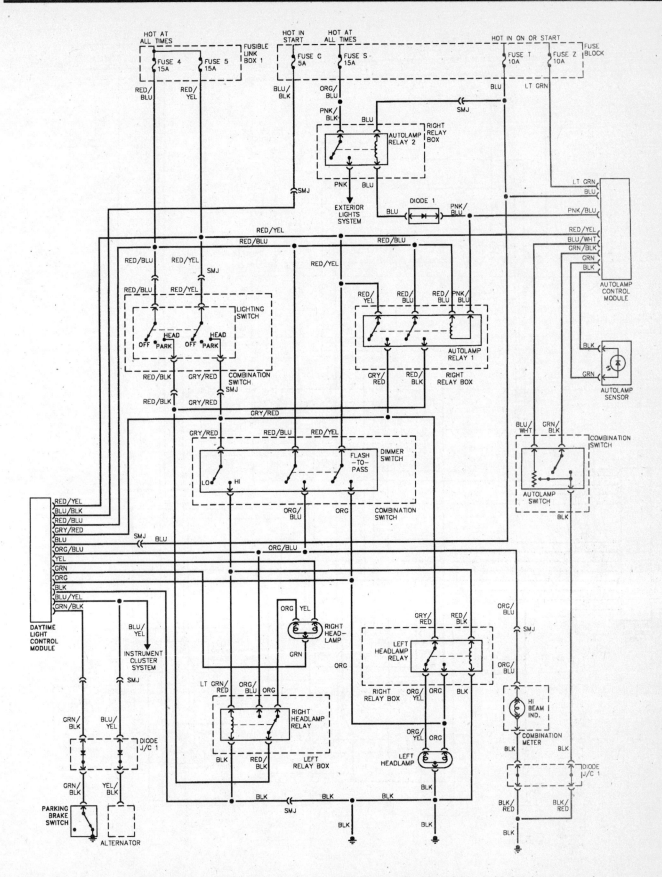

Headlight system - 1995 and earlier models (with Daytime Running Lights - with Autolamp system)

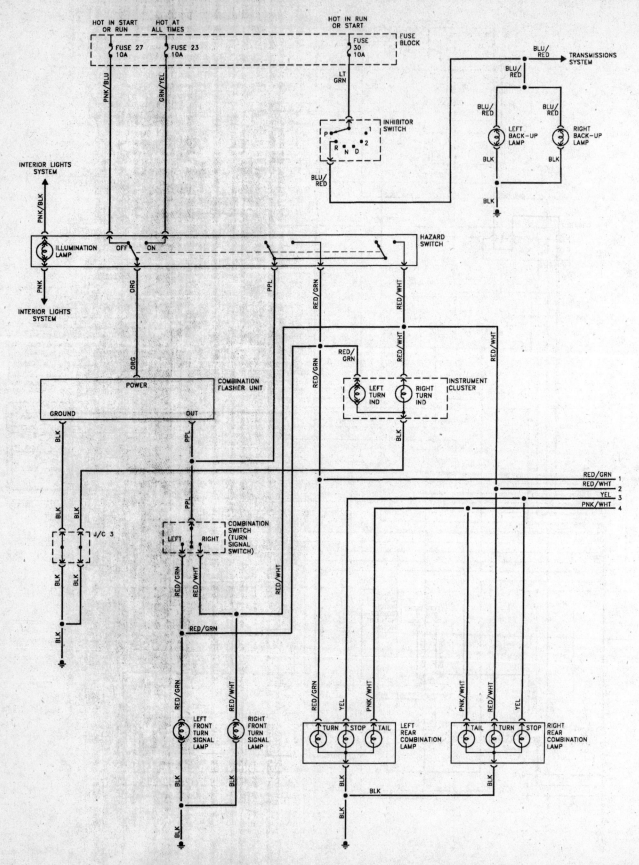

Exterior lighting system (except headlights) - 1996 and later models (1 of 2)

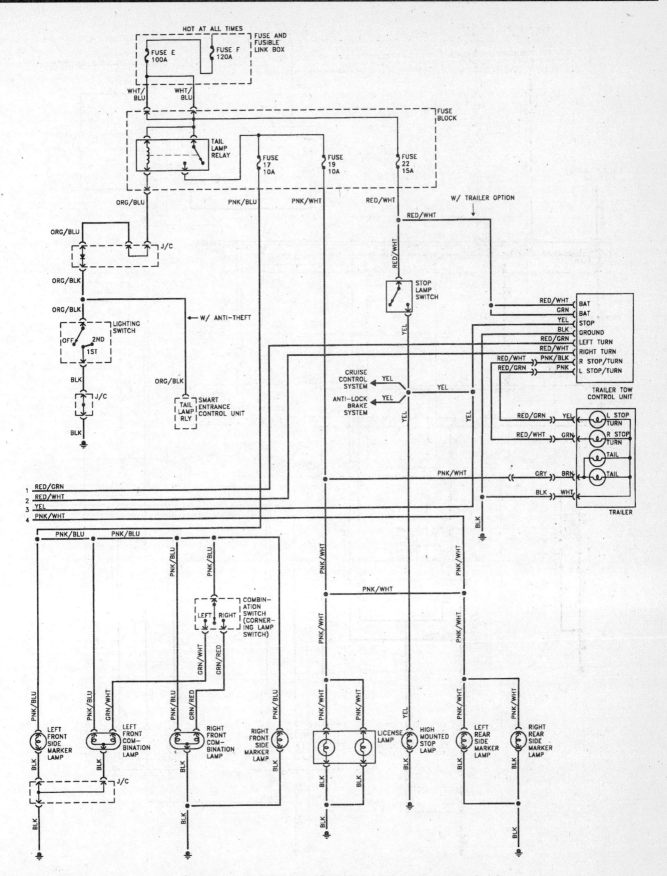

Exterior lighting system (except headlights) - 1996 and later models (2 of 2)

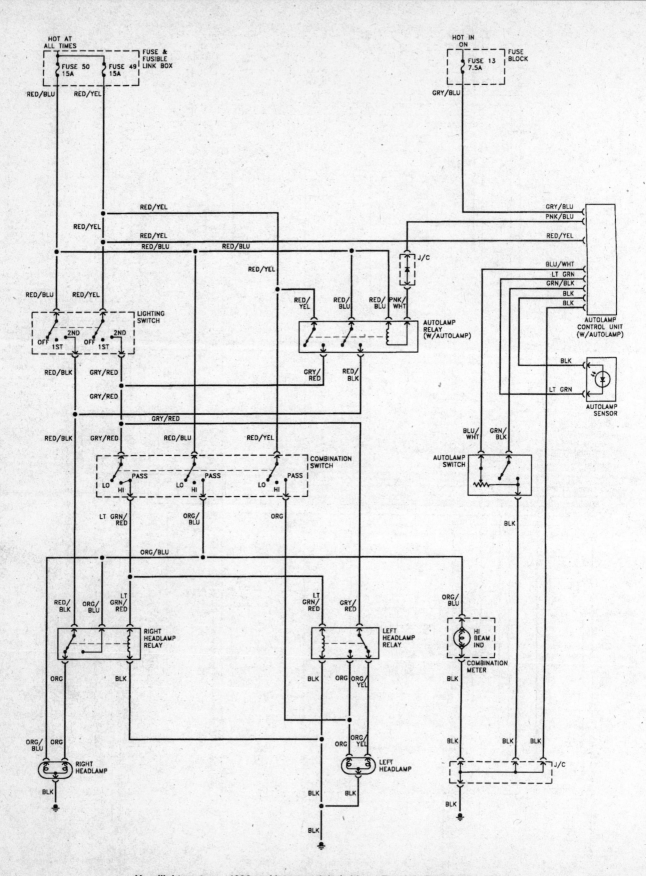

Headlight system - 1996 and later models (without Daytime Running Lights)

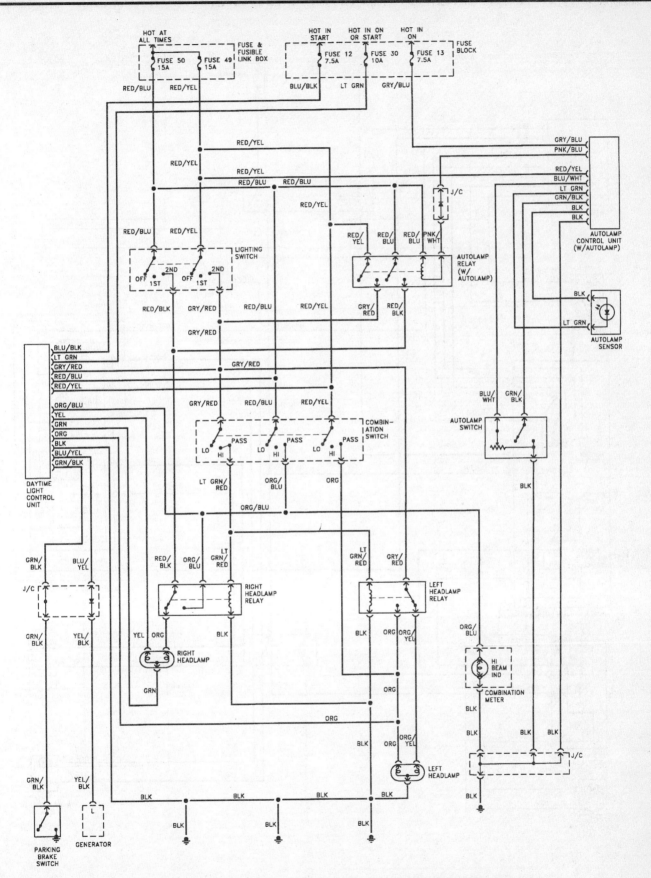

Headlight system - 1996 and later models (with Daytime Running Lights)

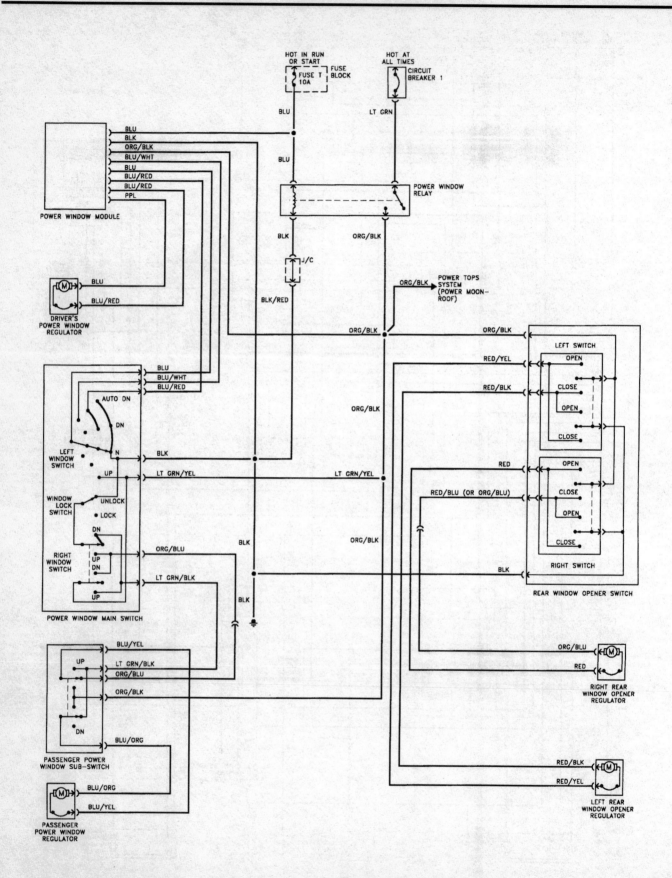

Power window system - 1995 and earlier models

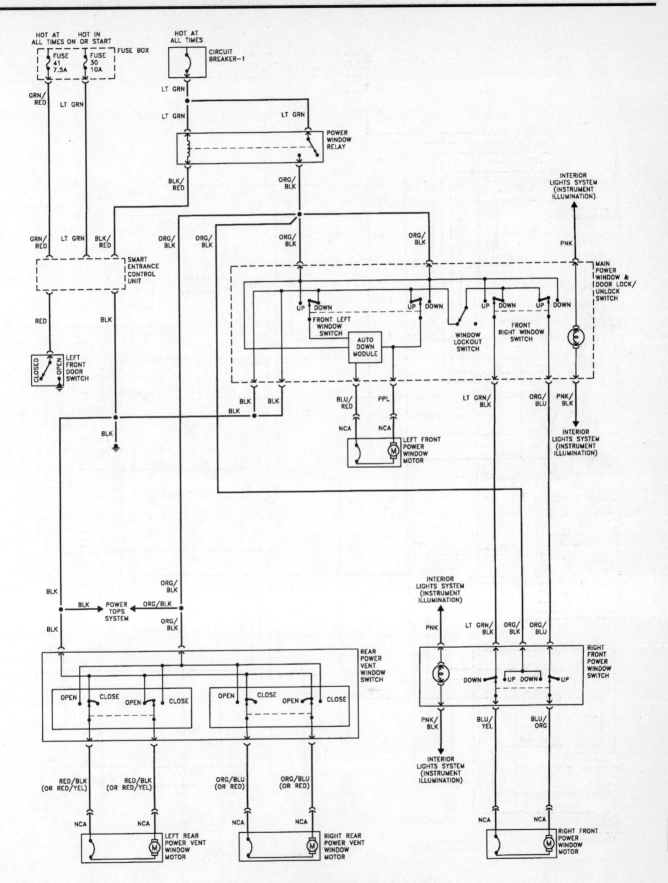

Power window system - 1996 and later models

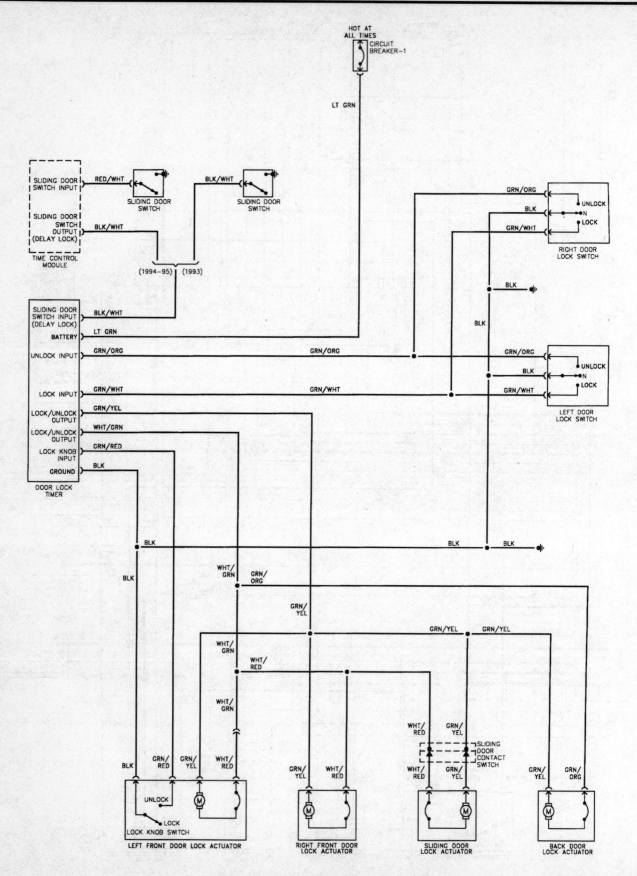

Power door lock system - 1995 and earlier models

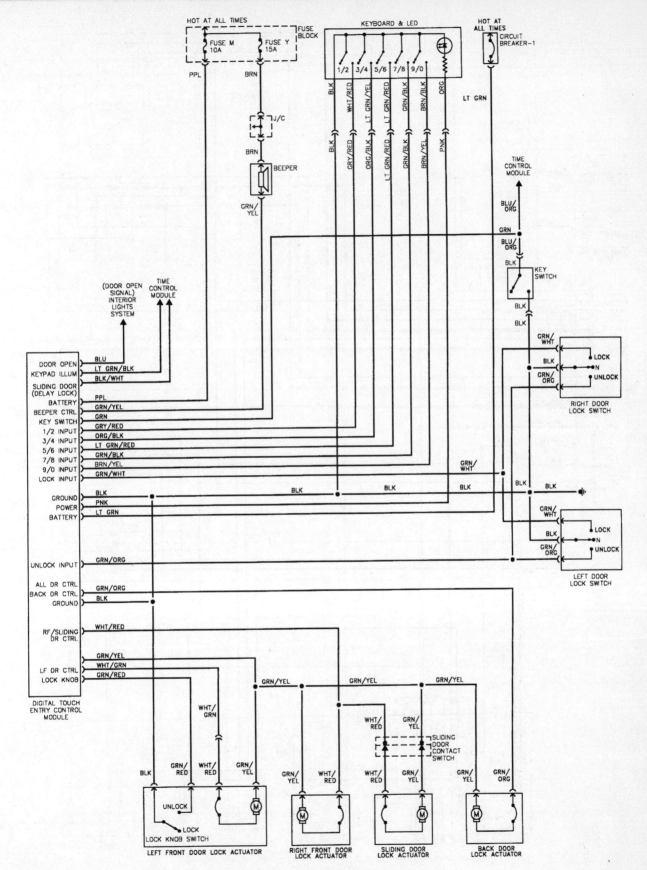

Keyless entry system - 1995 and earlier models

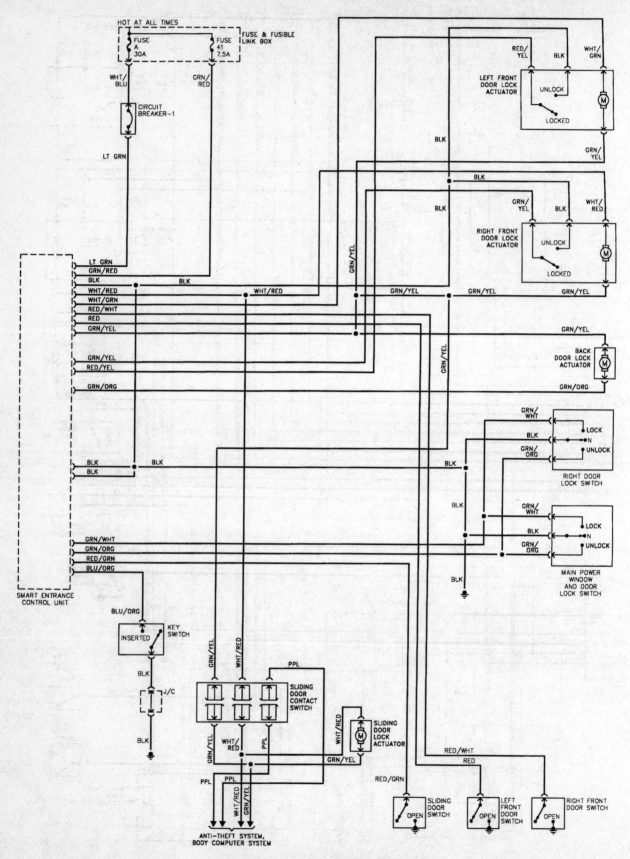

Power door lock system - 1996 and 1997 models

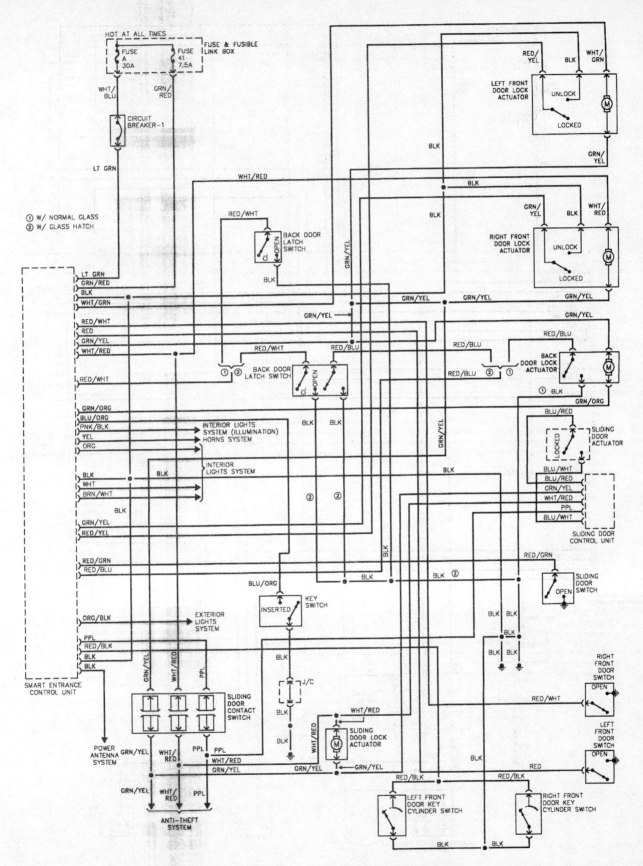

Keyless entry system - 1996 and 1997 models

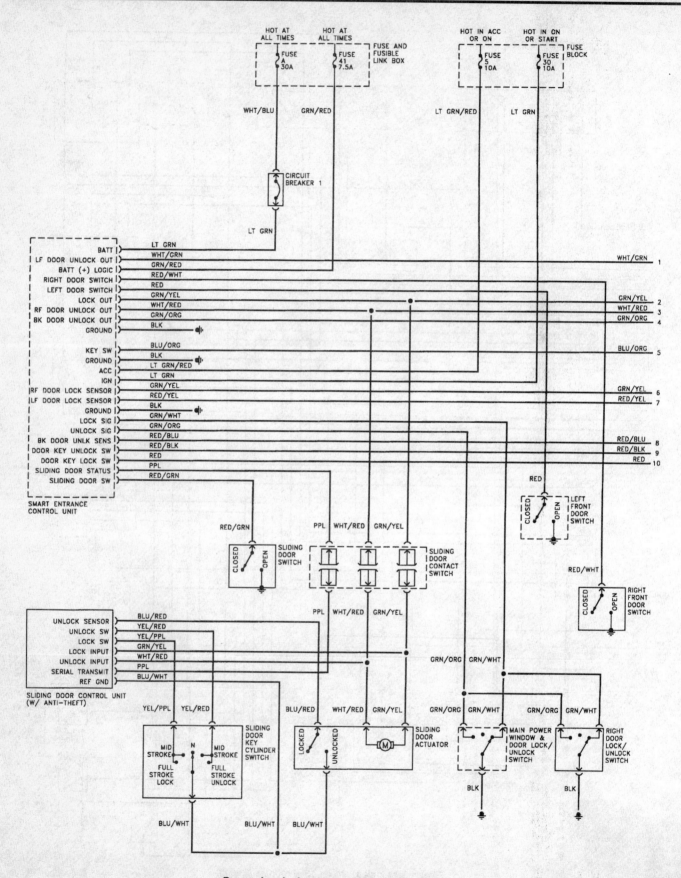

Power door lock system - 1998 models (1 of 2)

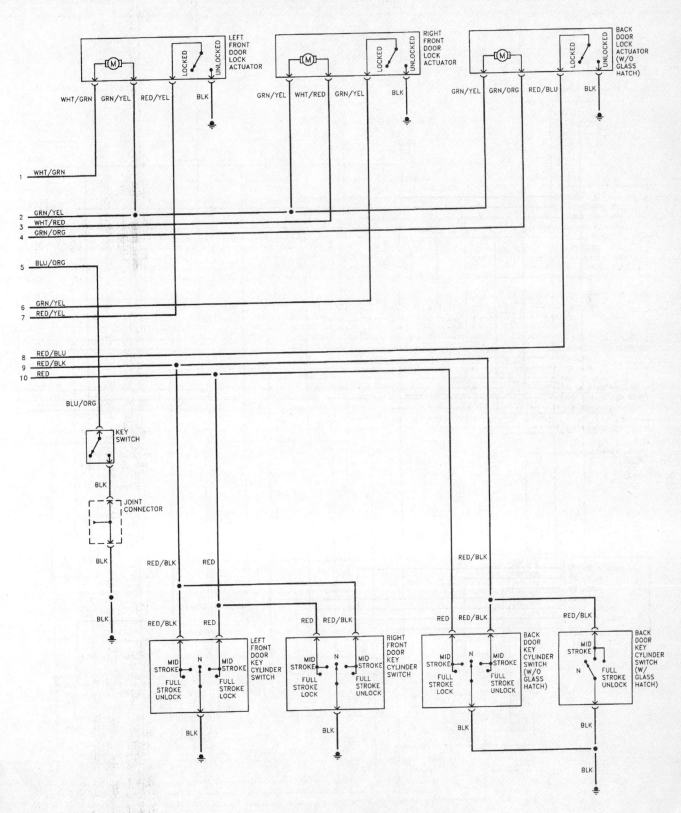

Power door lock system - 1998 models (2 of 2)

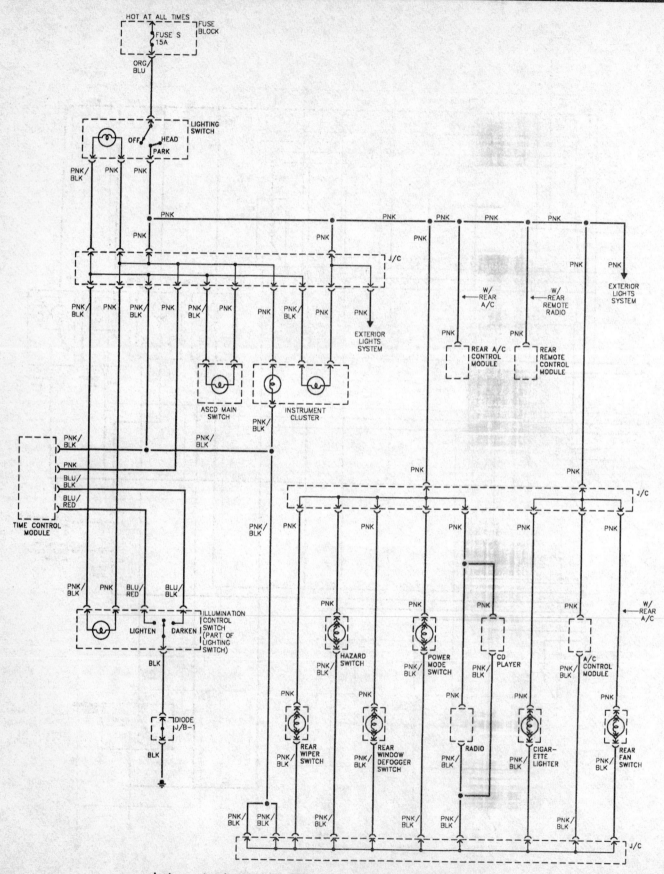

Instrument and control panel lighting system - 1995 and earlier models

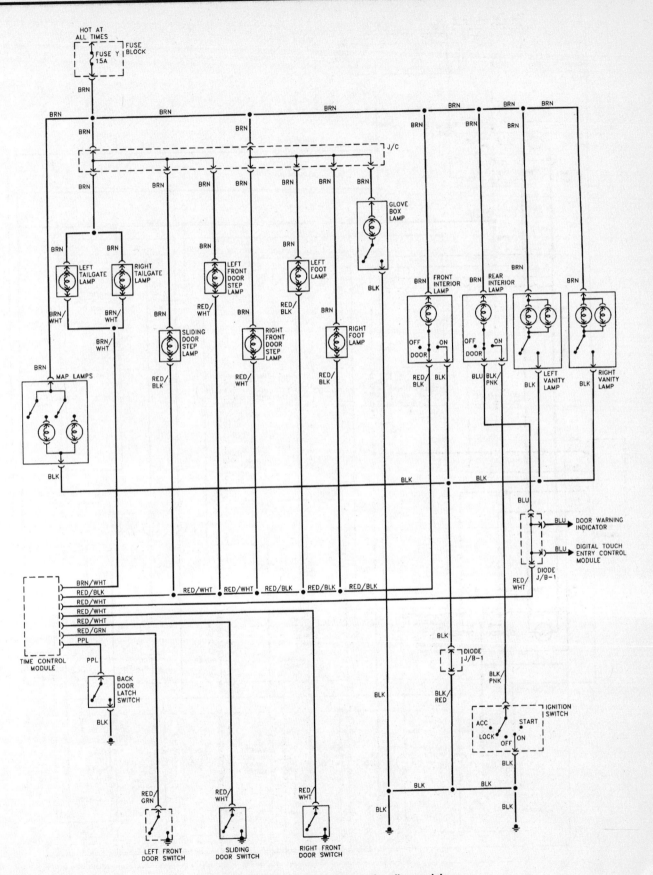

Courtesy lighting system - 1995 and earlier models

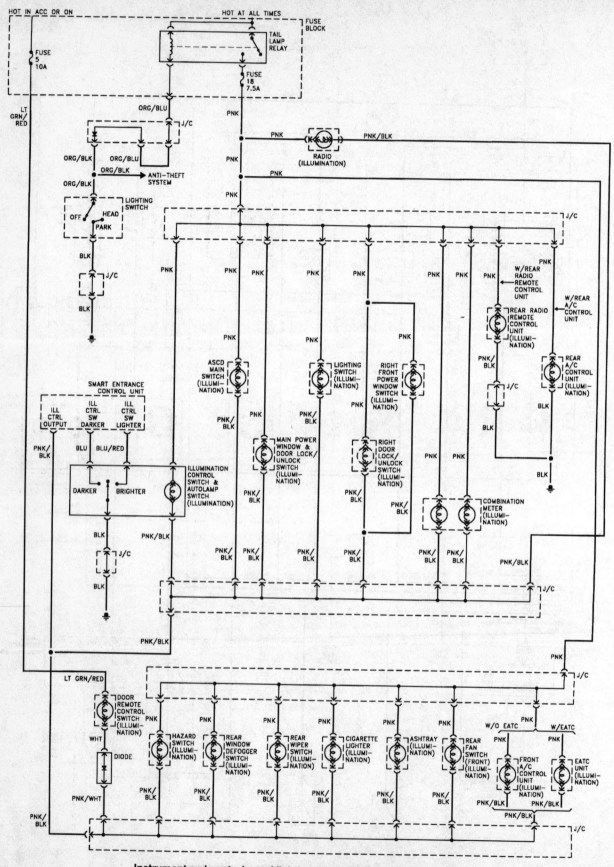

Instrument and control panel lighting system - 1996 and later models

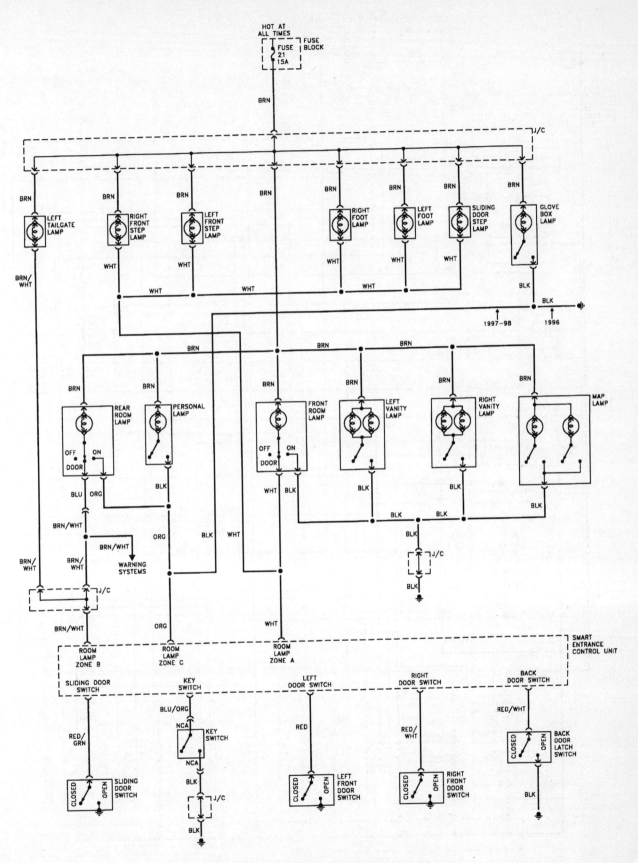

Courtesy lighting system - 1996 and later models

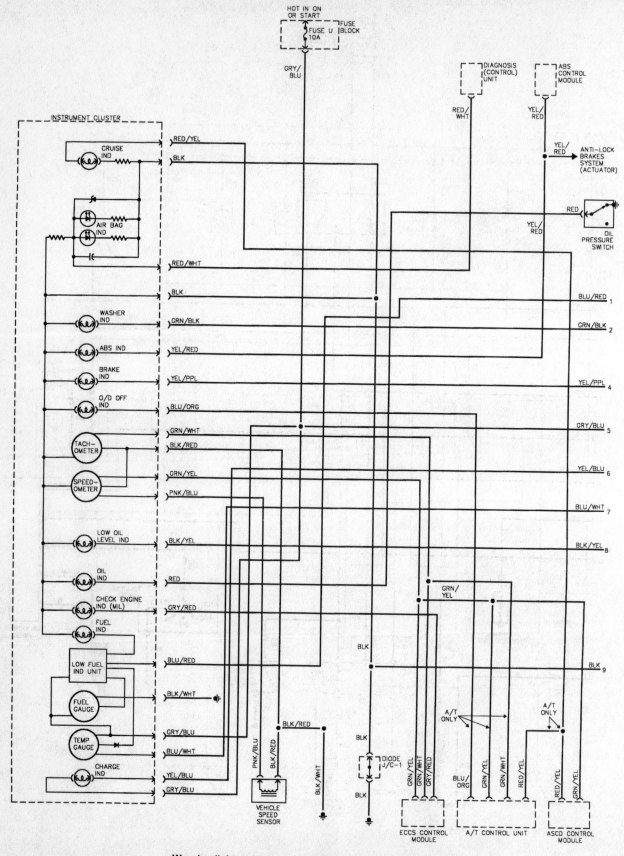

Warning lights and gauges - 1995 and earlier models (1 of 2)

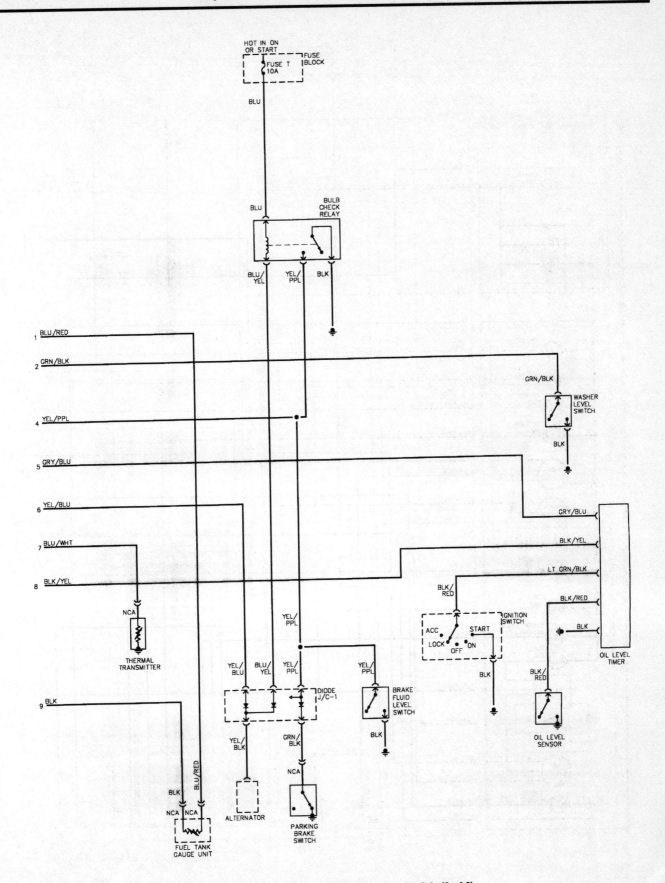

Warning lights and gauges - 1995 and earlier models (2 of 2)

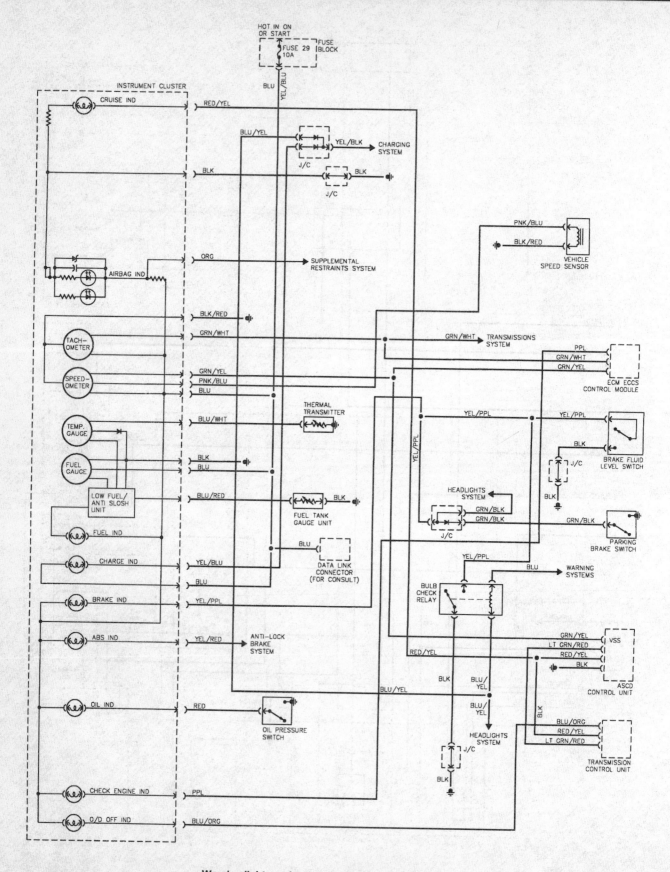

Warning lights and gauges - 1996 and later models

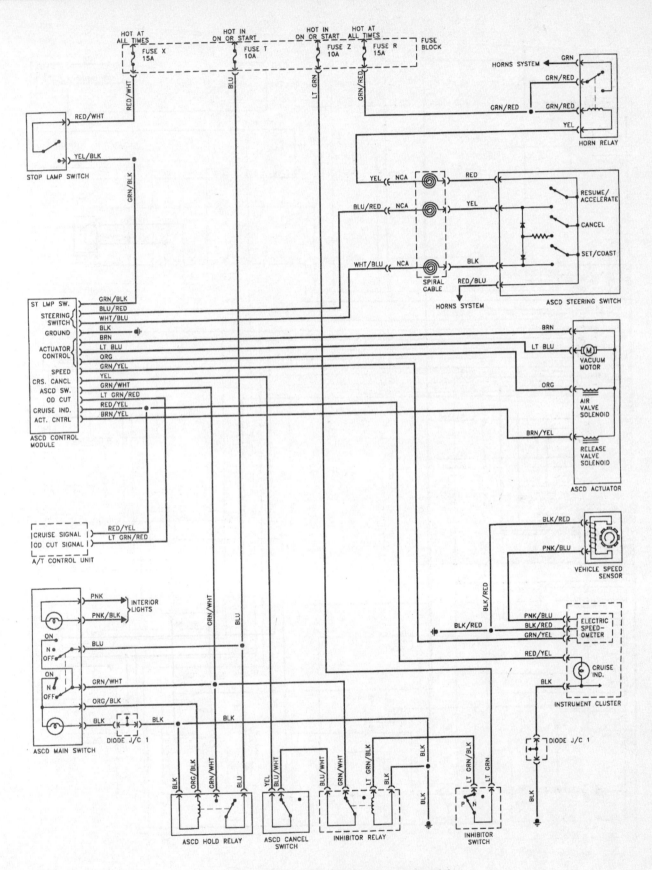

Cruise control system - 1995 and earlier models

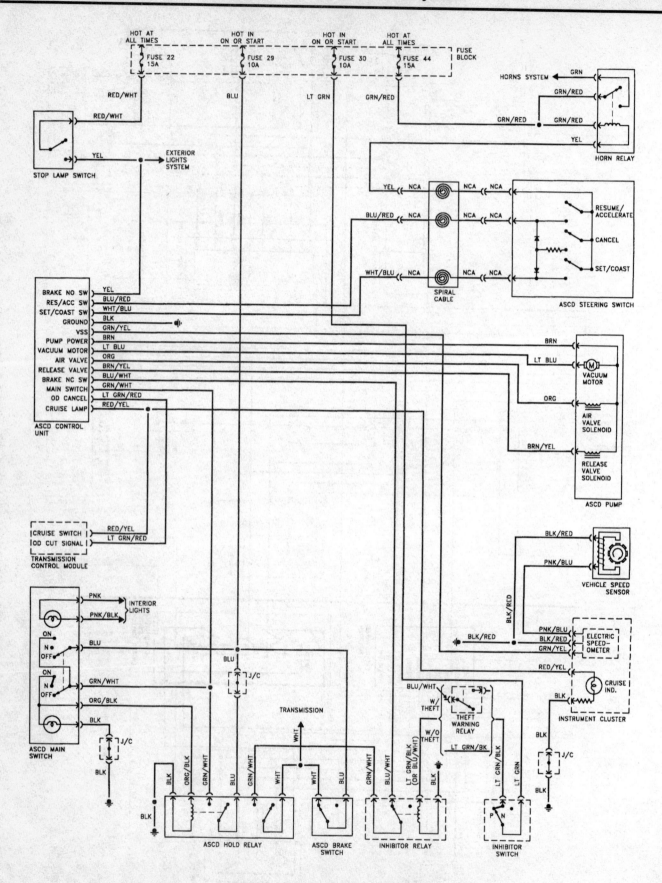

Cruise control system - 1996 and later models

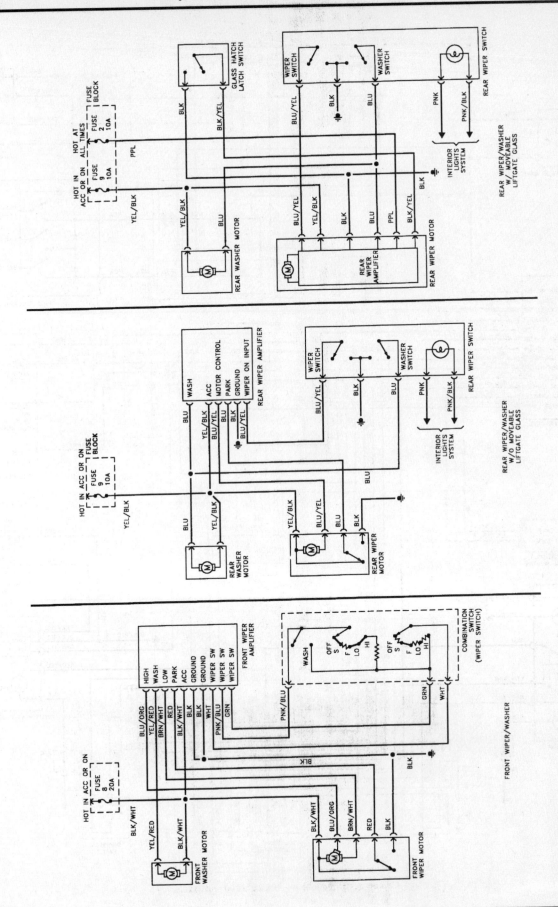

Windshield wiper and washer system – 1995 and earlier models

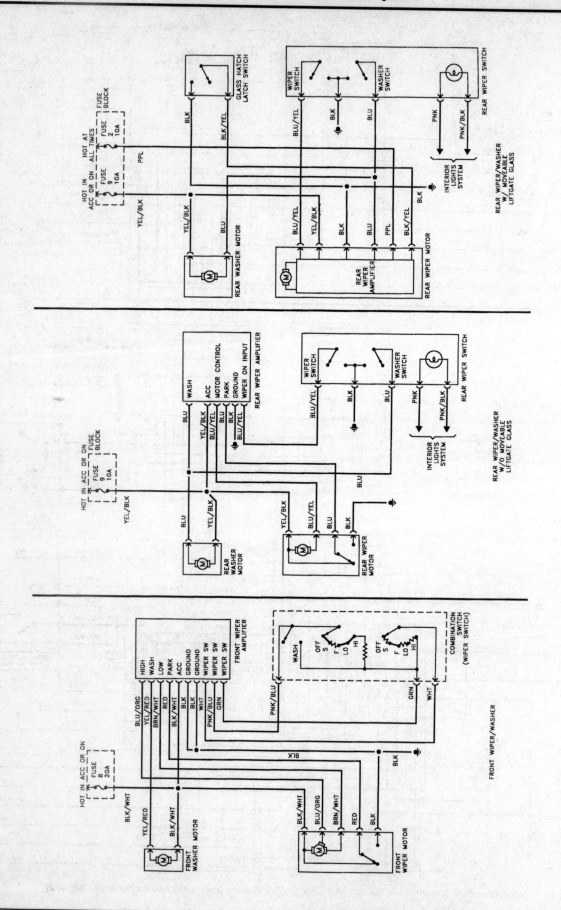

Windshield wiper and washer system - 1996 and later models

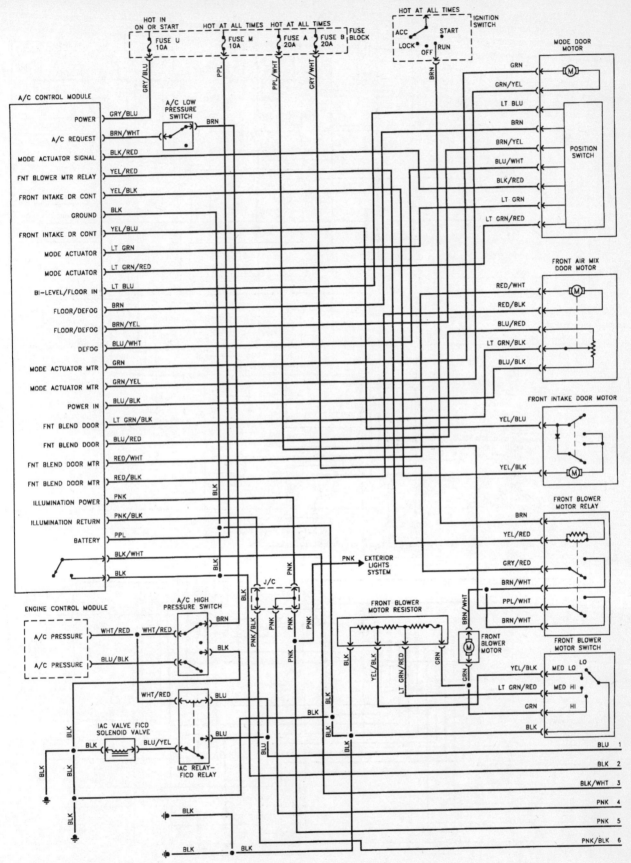

Heating and air conditioning system (including engine cooling fan) - 1995 and earlier models (1 of 2)

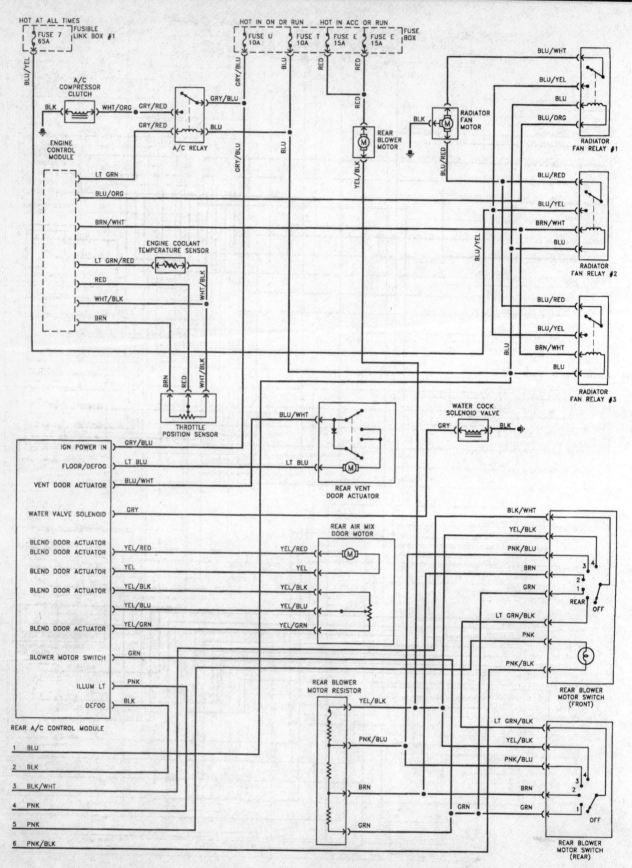

Heating and air conditioning system (including engine cooling fan) - 1995 and earlier models (2 of 2)

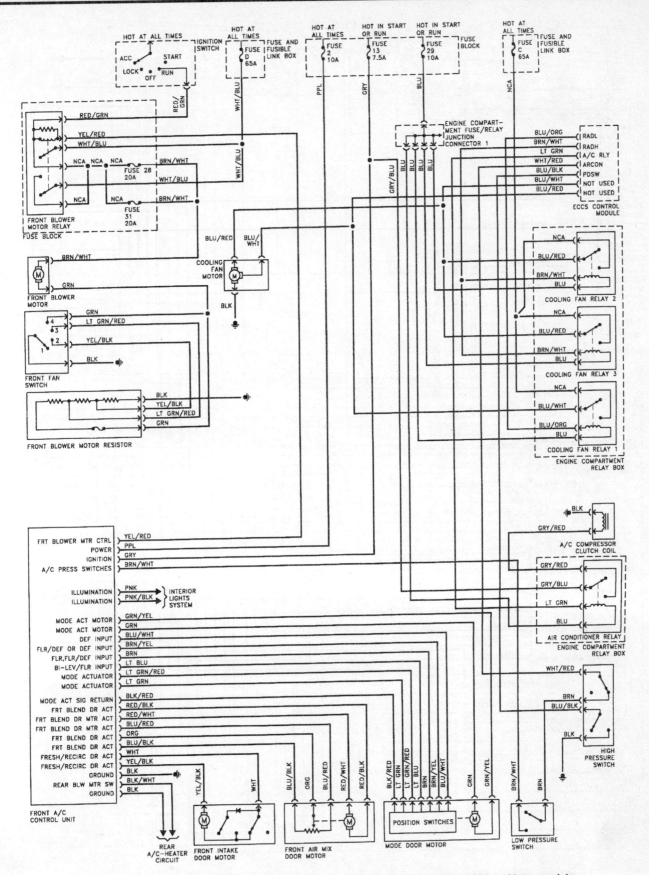

Manual heating and air conditioning system (including engine cooling fan) - 1996 and later models

12

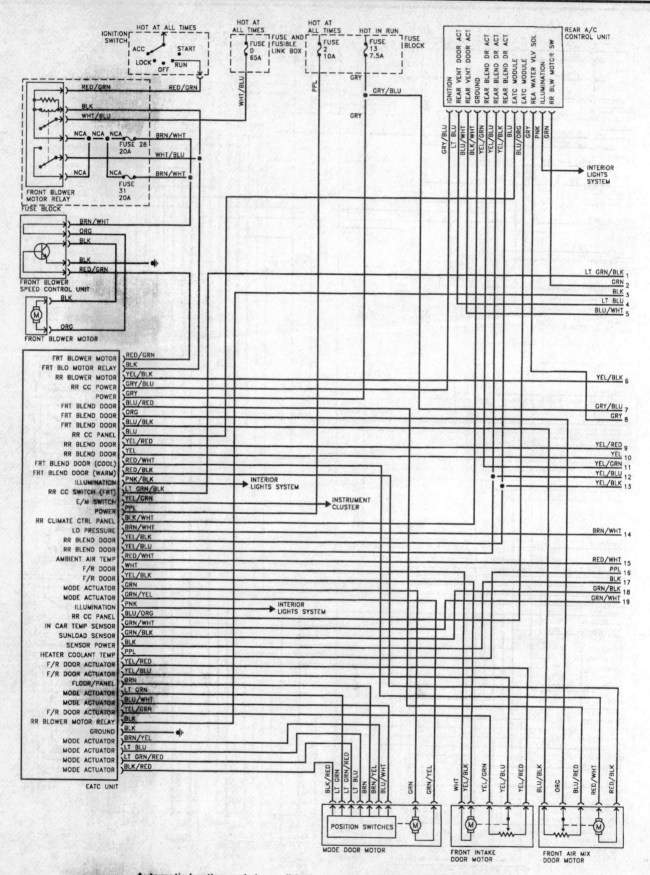

Automatic heating and air conditioning system - 1996 and later models (1 of 2)

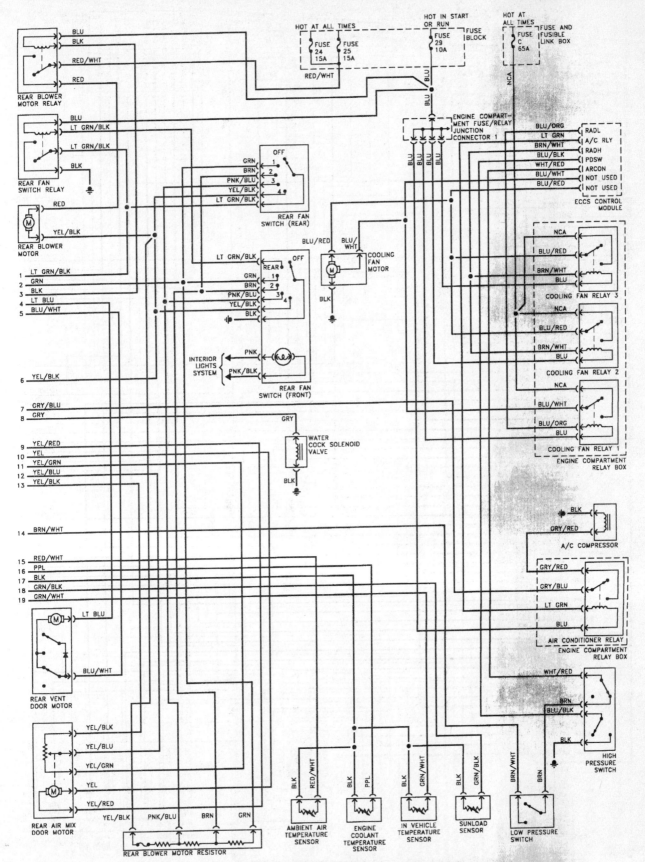

Automatic heating and air conditioning system - 1996 and later models (2 of 2)

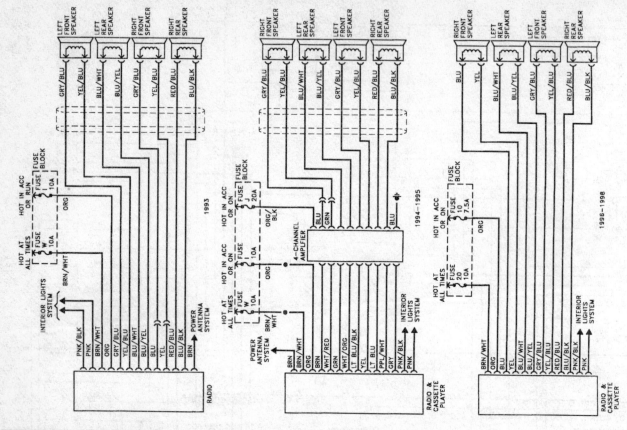

Typical stereo system

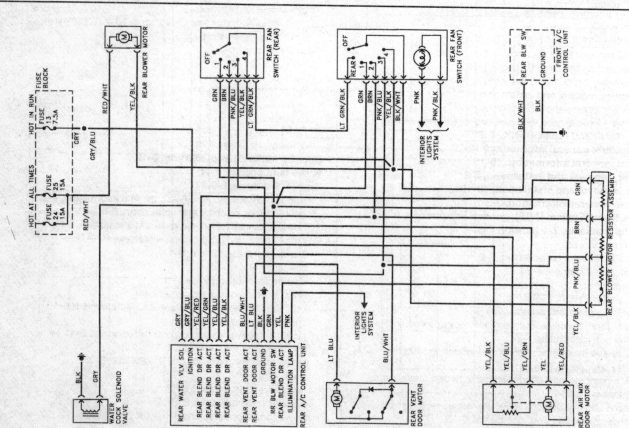

Auxiliary rear heating and air conditioning system - 1996 and later models

Index

Haynes Automotive Manuals

NOTE: New manuals are added to this list on a periodic basis. If you do not see a listing for your vehicle, consult your local Haynes dealer for the latest product information.

ACURA
*12020 Integra '86 thru '89 & Legend '86 thru '90

AMC
        Jeep CJ - see JEEP (50020)
14020   Concord/Hornet/Gremlin/Spirit '70 thru '83
14025   (Renault) Alliance & Encore '83 thru '87

AUDI
15020   4000 all models '80 thru '87
15025   5000 all models '77 thru '83
15026   5000 all models '84 thru '88

AUSTIN
        Healey Sprite - see MG Midget (66015)

BMW
*18020 3/5 Series '82 thru '92
*18021 3 Series except 325iX models '92 thru '97
18025   320i all 4 cyl models '75 thru '83
18035   528i & 530i all models '75 thru '80
18050   1500 thru 2002 except Turbo '59 thru '77

BUICK
        Century (FWD) - see GM (38005)
*19020 Buick, Oldsmobile & Pontiac Full-size
        (Front wheel drive) '85 thru '98
        Buick Electra, LeSabre and Park Avenue;
        Oldsmobile Delta 88 Royale, Ninety Eight
        and Regency; Pontiac Bonneville
19025   Buick Oldsmobile & Pontiac Full-size
        (Rear wheel drive)
        Buick Estate '70 thru '90, Electra '70 thru '84,
        LeSabre '70 thru '85, Limited '74 thru '79;
        Oldsmobile Custom Cruiser '70 thru '90,
        Delta 88 '70 thru '85,Ninety-eight '70 thru '84
        Pontiac Bonneville '70 thru '81,
        Catalina '70 thru '81, Grandville '70 thru '75,
        Parisienne '83 thru '86
19030   Mid-size Regal & Century '74 thru '87
        Regal - see GENERAL MOTORS (38010)
        Skyhawk - see GM (38030)
        Skylark - see GM (38020, 38025)
        Somerset - see GENERAL MOTORS (38025)

CADILLAC
*21030 Cadillac Rear Wheel Drive '70 thru '93
        Cimarron, Eldorado & Seville - see
        GM (38015, 38030)

CHEVROLET
10305   Chevrolet Engine Overhaul Manual
*24010 Astro & GMC Safari Mini-vans '85 thru '93
24015   Camaro V8 all models '70 thru '81
24016   Camaro all models '82 thru '92
        Cavalier - see GM (38015)
        Celebrity - see GM (38005)
24017   Camaro & Firebird '93 thru '97
24020   Chevelle, Malibu, El Camino '69 thru '87
24024   Chevette & Pontiac T1000 '76 thru '87
        Citation - see GENERAL MOTORS (38020)
*24032 Corsica/Beretta all models '87 thru '96
24040   Corvette all V8 models '68 thru '82
24041   Corvette all models '84 thru '96
24045   Full-size Sedans Caprice, Impala,
        Biscayne, Bel Air & Wagons '69 thru '90
24046   Impala SS & Caprice and
        Buick Roadmaster '91 thru '96
        Lumina '90 thru '94 - see GM (38010)
24048   Lumina & Monte Carlo '95 thru '98
        Lumina APV - see GM (38035)
24050   Luv Pick-up all 2WD & 4WD '72 thru '82
24055   Monte Carlo all models '70 thru '88
        Monte Carlo '95 thru '98 - see LUMINA
24059   Nova all V8 models '69 thru '79
*24060 Nova/Geo Prizm '85 thru '92
24064   Pick-ups '67 thru '87 - Chevrolet & GMC,
        all V8 & in-line 6 cyl, 2WD & 4WD '67 thru '87;
        Suburbans, Blazers & Jimmys '67 thru '91
*24065 Pick-ups '88 thru '98 - Chevrolet & GMC,
        all full-size models '88 thru '98; Blazer &
        Jimmy '92 thru '94; Suburban '92 thru '98;
        Tahoe & Yukon '95 thru '98
*24070 S-10 & GMC S-15 Pick-ups '82 thru '93
*24071 S-10, Gmc S-15 & Jimmy '94 thru '96
*24075 Sprint & Geo Metro '85 thru '94
*24080 Vans - Chevrolet & GMC '68 thru '96

CHRYSLER
10310   Chrysler Engine Overhaul Manual
*25015 Chrysler Cirrus, Dodge Stratus,
        Plymouth Breeze, '95 thru '98
*25020 Full-size Front-Wheel Drive '88 thru '93
        K-Cars - see DODGE Aries (30008)
        Laser - see DODGE Daytona (30030)
25025   Chrysler LHS, Concorde & New Yorker,
        Dodge Intrepid, Eagle Vision, '93 thru '97
*25030 Chrysler/Plym. Mid-size '82 thru '95
        Rear-wheel Drive - see DODGE (30050)

DATSUN
28005   200SX all models '80 thru '83
28007   B-210 all models '73 thru '78
28009   210 all models '78 thru '82
28012   240Z, 260Z & 280Z Coupe '70 thru '78
28014   280ZX Coupe & 2+2 '79 thru '83
        300ZX - see NISSAN (72010)
28016   310 all models '78 thru '82
28018   510 & PL521 Pick-up '68 thru '73
28020   510 all models '78 thru '81
28022   620 Series Pick-up all models '73 thru '79
        720 Series Pick-up - NISSAN (72030)
28025   810/Maxima all gas models, '77 thru '84

DODGE
        400 & 600 - see CHRYSLER (25030)
*30008 Aries & Plymouth Reliant '81 thru '89
30010   Caravan & Ply. Voyager '84 thru '95
*30011 Caravan & Ply. Voyager '96 thru '98
30012   Challenger/Plymouth Saporro '78 thru '83
        Challenger '67-'76 - see DART (30025)
30016   Colt/Plymouth Champ '78 thru '87
*30020 Dakota Pick-ups all models '87 thru '96
30025   Dart, Challenger/Plymouth Barracuda
        & Valiant 6 cyl models '67 thru '76
*30030 Daytona & Chrysler Laser '84 thru '89
        Intrepid - see Chrysler (25025)
*30034 Dodge & Plymouth Neon '95 thru '97
*30035 Omni & Plymouth Horizon '78 thru '90
30040   Pick-ups all full-size models '74 thru '93
30041   Pick-ups all full-size models '94 thru '96
*30045 Ram 50/D50 Pick-ups & Raider and
        Plymouth Arrow Pick-ups '79 thru '93
30050   Dodge/Ply./Chrysler RWD '71 thru '89
*30055 Shadow/Plymouth Sundance '87 thru '94
*30060 Spirit & Plymouth Acclaim '89 thru '95
*30065 Vans - Dodge & Plymouth '71 thru '96

EAGLE
        Talon - see MITSUBISHI Eclipse (68030)
        Vision - see CHRYSLER (25025)

FIAT
34010   124 Sport Coupe & Spider '68 thru '78
34025   X1/9 all models '74 thru '80

FORD
10355   Ford Automatic Transmission Overhaul
10320   Ford Engine Overhaul Manual
*36004 Aerostar Mini-vans '86 thru '96
        Aspire - see FORD Festiva (36030)
*36006 Contour/Mercury Mystique '95 thru '98
36008   Courier Pick-up all models '72 thru '82
36012   Crown Victoria & Mercury
        Grand Marquis '88 thru '96
36016   Escort/Mercury Lynx '81 thru '90
*36020 Escort/Mercury Tracer '91 thru '96
        Expedition - see FORD Pick-up (36059)
*36024 Explorer & Mazda Navajo '91 thru '95
36028   Fairmont & Mercury Zephyr '78 thru '83
36030   Festiva & Aspire '88 thru '97
36032   Fiesta all models '77 thru '80
36036   Ford & Mercury Full-size,
        Ford LTD & Mercury Marquis ('75 thru '82);
        Ford Custom 500,Country Squire, Crown
        Victoria & Mercury Colony Park ('75 thru '87);
        Ford LTD Crown Victoria &
        Mercury Gran Marquis ('83 thru '87)
36040   Granada & Mercury Monarch '75 thru '80
36044   Ford & Mercury Mid-size,
        Ford Thunderbird & Mercury
        Cougar ('75 thru '82);
        Ford LTD & Mercury Marquis ('83 thru '86);
        Ford Torino,Gran Torino, Elite, Ranchero
        pick-up, LTD II, Mercury Montego, Comet,
        XR-7 & Lincoln Versailles ('75 thru '86)
36048   Mustang V8 all models '64-1/2 thru '73
36049   Mustang II 4 cyl, V6 & V8 '74 thru '78
36050   Mustang & Mercury Capri incl. Turbo
        Mustang, '79 thru '93; Capri, '79 thru '86
*36051 Mustang all models '94 thru '97
36054   Pick-ups and Bronco '73 thru '79
36058   Pick-ups and Bronco '80 thru '96
*36059 Pick-ups, Expedition &
        Lincoln Navigator '97 thru '98
36062   Pinto & Mercury Bobcat '75 thru '80
36066   Probe all models '89 thru '92
*36070 Ranger/Bronco II gas models '83 thru '92
*36071 Ford Ranger '93 thru '97 &
        Mazda Pick-ups '94 thru '97
36074   Taurus & Mercury Sable '86 thru '95
*36075 Taurus & Mercury Sable '96 thru '98
36078   Tempo & Mercury Topaz '84 thru '94
36082   Thunderbird/Mercury Cougar '83 thru '88
36086   Thunderbird/Mercury Cougar '89 and '97
36090   Vans all V8 Econoline models '69 thru '91
*36094 Vans full size '92 thru '95
*36097 Windstar Mini-van '95 thru '98

GENERAL MOTORS
*10360 GM Automatic Transmission Overhaul
*38005 Buick Century, Chevrolet Celebrity,
        Olds Cutlass Ciera & Pontiac 6000
        all models '82 thru '96
*38010 Buick Regal, Chevrolet Lumina,
        Oldsmobile Cutlass Supreme & Pontiac
        Grand Prix front wheel drive '88 thru '95
*38015 Buick Skyhawk, Cadillac Cimarron,
        Chevrolet Cavalier, Oldsmobile Firenza
        Pontiac J-2000 & Sunbird '82 thru '94
*38016 Chevrolet Cavalier &
        Pontiac Sunfire '95 thru '98
38020   Buick Skylark, Chevrolet Citation,
        Olds Omega, Pontiac Phoenix '80 thru '85
38025   Buick Skylark & Somerset, Olds Achieva,
        Calais & Pontiac Grand Am '85 thru '95
38030   Cadillac Eldorado & Oldsmobile
        Toronado '71 thru '85, Seville '80 thru '85,
        Buick Riviera '79 thru '85
*38035 Chevrolet Lumina APV, Oldsmobile
        Silhouette & Pontiac Trans Sport '90 thru '95
        General Motors Full-size
        Rear-wheel Drive - see BUICK (19025)

GEO
        Metro - see CHEVROLET Sprint (24075)
        Prizm - see CHEVROLET (24060) or
        TOYOTA (92036)
*40030 Storm all models '90 thru '93
        Tracker - see SUZUKI Samurai (90010)

GMC
        Safari - see CHEVROLET ASTRO (24010)
        Vans & Pick-ups - see CHEVROLET

HONDA
42010   Accord CVCC all models '76 thru '83
42011   Accord all models '84 thru '89
42012   Accord all models '90 thru '93
*42013 Accord all models '94 thru '95
42020   Civic 1200 all models '73 thru '79
42021   Civic 1300 & 1500 CVCC '80 thru '83
42022   Civic 1500 CVCC all models '75 thru '79
42023   Civic all models '84 thru '91
42024   Civic & del Sol '92 thru '95
        Passport - see ISUZU Rodeo (47017)
*42040 Prelude CVCC all models '79 thru '89

HYUNDAI
*43015 Excel all models '86 thru '94

ISUZU
        Hombre - see CHEVROLET S-10 (24071)
*47017 Rodeo '91 thru '97, Amigo '89 thru '94,
        Honda Passport '95 thru '97
*47020 Trooper '84 thru '91, Pick-up '81 thru '93

JAGUAR
*49010 XJ6 all 6 cyl models '68 thru '86
*49011 XJ6 all models '88 thru '94
*49015 XJ12 & XJS all 12 cyl models '72 thru '85

JEEP
*50010 Cherokee, Comanche & Wagoneer
        Limited all models '84 thru '96
50020   CJ all models '49 thru '86
*50025 Grand Cherokee all models '93 thru '98
*50029 Grand Wagoneer & Pick-up '72 thru '91
*50030 Wrangler all models '87 thru '95

LINCOLN
        Navigator - see FORD Pick-up (36059)
59010   Rear Wheel Drive all models '70 thru '96

MAZDA
61010   GLC (rear wheel drive) '77 thru '83
61011   GLC (front wheel drive) '81 thru '85
*61015 323 & Protegé '90 thru '97
*61016 MX-5 Miata '90 thru '97
*61020 MPV all models '89 thru '94
        Navajo - see FORD Explorer (36024)
61030   Pick-ups '72 thru '93
        Pick-ups '94 on - see Ford (36071)
61035   RX-7 all models '79 thru '85
*61036 RX-7 all models '86 thru '91
*61040 626 (rear wheel drive) '79 thru '82
*61041 626 & MX-6 (front wheel drive) '83 thru '91

MERCEDES-BENZ
63012   123 Series Diesel '76 thru '85
*63015 190 Series 4-cyl gas models, '84 thru '88
63020   230, 250 & 280 6 cyl sohc '68 thru '72
63025   280 123 Series gas models '77 thru '81
63030   350 & 450 all models '71 thru '80

MERCURY
        See FORD Listing

MG
66010   MGB Roadster & GT Coupe '62 thru '80
66015   MG Midget & Austin Healey Sprite
        Roadster '58 thru '80

MITSUBISHI
*68020 Cordia, Tredia, Galant, Precis &
        Mirage '83 thru '93
*68030 Eclipse, Eagle Talon &
        Plymouth Laser '90 thru '94
*68040 Pick-up '83 thru '96, Montero '83 thru '93

NISSAN
72010   300ZX all models incl. Turbo '84 thru '89
*72015 Altima all models '93 thru '97
*72020 Maxima all models '85 thru '91
72030   Pick-ups '80 thru '96, Pathfinder '87 thru '95
72040   Pulsar all models '83 thru '86
72050   Sentra all models '82 thru '94
*72051 Sentra & 200SX all models '95 thru '98
*72060 Stanza all models '82 thru '90

OLDSMOBILE
*73015 Cutlass '74 thru '88
        For other OLDSMOBILE titles, see
        BUICK, CHEVROLET or
        GENERAL MOTORS titles

PLYMOUTH
        For PLYMOUTH titles, see DODGE.

PONTIAC
79008   Fiero all models '84 thru '88
79018   Firebird V8 models except Turbo '70 thru '81
79019   Firebird all models '82 thru '92
        For other PONTIAC titles, see
        BUICK, CHEVROLET or
        GENERAL MOTORS listing.

PORSCHE
*80020 911 Coupe & Targa models '65 thru '89
80025   914 all 4 cyl models '69 thru '76
80030   924 all models incl. Turbo '76 thru '82
*80035 944 all models incl. Turbo '83 thru '89

RENAULT
        Alliance, Encore - see AMC (14020)

SAAB
*84010 900 including Turbo '79 thru '88

SATURN
*87010 Saturn all models '91 thru '96

SUBARU
89002   1100, 1300, 1400 & 1600 '71 thru '79
*89003 1600 & 1800 2WD & 4WD '80 thru '94

SUZUKI
*90010 Samurai/Sidekick/Geo Tracker '86 thru '96

TOYOTA
*92005 Camry all models '83 thru '91
92006   Camry all models '92 thru '96
92015   Celica Rear Wheel Drive '71 thru '85
*92020 Celica Front Wheel Drive '86 thru '93
92025   Celica Supra all models '79 thru '92
92030   Corolla all models '75 thru '79
92032   Corolla rear wheel drive models '80 thru '87
*92035 Corolla front wheel drive models '84 thru '92
92036   Corolla & Geo Prizm '93 thru '97
92040   Corolla Tercel all models '80 thru '82
92045   Corona all models '74 thru '82
92050   Cressida all models '78 thru '82
92055   Land Cruiser Series FJ40, 43, 45 & 55
        '68 thru '82
*92056 Land Cruiser Series FJ60, 62, 80 &
        FZJ80 '68 thru '82
*92065 MR2 all models '85 thru '87
92070   Pick-up all models '69 thru '78
*92075 Pick-up all models '79 thru '95
*92076 Tacoma '95 thru '98,
        4Runner '96 thru '98, T100 '93 thru '98
*92080 Previa all models '91 thru '95
*92085 Tercel all models '87 thru '94

TRIUMPH
94007   Spitfire all models '62 thru '81
94010   TR7 all models '75 thru '81

VW
96008   Beetle & Karmann Ghia '54 thru '79
96012   Dasher all gasoline models '74 thru '81
*96016 Rabbit, Jetta, Scirocco, & Pick-up gas
        models '74 thru '91 & Convertible '80 thru '92
*96017 Golf & Jetta '93 thru '97
96020   Rabbit, Jetta, Pick-up diesel '77 thru '84
96030   Transporter 1600 all models '68 thru '79
96035   Transporter 1700, 1800, 2000 '72 thru '79
96040   Type 3 1500 & 1600 '63 thru '73
96045   Vanagon air-cooled models '80 thru '83

VOLVO
97010   120, 130 Series & 1800 Sports '61 thru '73
97015   140 Series all models '66 thru '74
*97020 240 Series all models '76 thru '93
*97025 260 Series all models '75 thru '82
*97040 740 & 760 Series all models '82 thru '88

TECHBOOK MANUALS
10205   Automotive Computer Codes
10210   Automotive Emissions Control Manual
10215   Fuel Injection Manual, 1978 thru 1985
10220   Fuel Injection Manual, 1986 thru 1996
10225   Holley Carburetor Manual
10230   Rochester Carburetor Manual
10240   Weber/Zenith/Stromberg/SU Carburetor
10305   Chevrolet Engine Overhaul Manual
10310   Chrysler Engine Overhaul Manual
10320   Ford Engine Overhaul Manual
10330   GM and Ford Diesel Engine Repair
10340   Small Engine Repair Manual
10345   Suspension, Steering & Driveline
10355   Ford Automatic Transmission Overhaul
10360   GM Automatic Transmission Overhaul
10405   Automotive Body Repair & Painting
10410   Automotive Brake Manual
10415   Automotive Detailing Manual
10420   Automotive Eelectrical Manual
10425   Automotive Heating & Air Conditioning
10430   Automotive Reference Dictionary
10435   Automotive Tools Manual
10440   Used Car Buying Guide
10445   Welding Manual
10450   ATV Basics

SPANISH MANUALS
98903   Reparación de Carrocería & Pintura
98905   Códigos Automotrices de la Computadora
98910   Frenos Automotriz
98915   Inyección de Combustible 1986 al 1994
99040   Chevrolet & GMC Camionetas '67 al '87
99041   Chevrolet & GMC Camionetas '88 al '95
99042   Chevrolet Camionetas Cerradas '68 al '95
99055   Dodge Caravan/Ply. Voyager '84 al '95
99075   Ford Camionetas y Bronco '80 al '94
99077   Ford Camionetas Cerradas '69 al '91
99083   Ford Modelos de Tamaño Grande '75 al '87
99088   Ford Modelos de Tamaño Mediano '75 al '86
99091   Ford Taurus & Mercury Sable '86 al '95
99095   GM Modelos de Tamaño Grande '70 al '90
99100   GM Modelos de Tamaño Mediano '70 al '88
99110   Nissan Camionetas '80 al '96,
        Pathfinder '87 al '95
99118   Nissan Sentra '82 al '94
99125   Toyota Camionetas y 4-Runner '79 al '95

---

* Listings shown with an asterisk (*) indicate model coverage as of this printing. These titles will be periodically updated to include later model years - consult your Haynes dealer for more information.

Nearly 100 Haynes
motorcycle manuals
also available

5-98